PERU

1ST EDITION

Where to Stay and Eat
for All Budgets

Must-See Sights
and Local Secrets

Ratings You Can Trust

Fodor's Travel Publications   New York, Toronto, London, Sydney, Auckland
www.fodors.com

FODOR'S PERU
Editor: Paul Eisenberg

Editorial Production: Tom Holton
Editorial Contributors: Gregory Benchwick, Joan Gonzalez, Satu Hummasti, Deborah Kaufman, Holly S. Smith, Mark Sullivan, Jeffrey Van Fleet
Maps: David Lindroth, *cartographer;* Bob Blake and Rebecca Baer, *map editors*
Design: Fabrizio La Rocca, *creative director;* Guido Caroti, *art director;* Melanie Marin, *senior picture editor*
Production/Manufacturing: Colleen Ziemba
Cover Photo (woman pulling a llama past Sacsayhuamán): Victor Englebert

First Edition

ISBN 1–4000–1283–X

ISSN 1542–3433

SPECIAL SALES
Fodor's Travel Publications are available at special discounts for bulk purchases for sales promotions or premiums. Special editions, including personalized covers, excerpts of existing guides, and corporate imprints, can be created in large quantities for special needs. For more information, contact your local bookseller or write to Special Markets, Fodor's Travel Publications, 1745 Broadway, New York, NY 10019. Inquiries from Canada should be directed to your local Canadian bookseller or sent to Random House of Canada, Ltd., Marketing Department, 2775 Matheson Boulevard East, Mississauga, Ontario L4W 4P7. Inquiries from the United Kingdom should be sent to Fodor's Travel Publications, 20 Vauxhall Bridge Road, London SW1V 2SA, England.

AN IMPORTANT TIP & AN INVITATION
Although all prices, opening times, and other details in this book are based on information supplied to us at press time, changes occur all the time in the travel world, and Fodor's cannot accept responsibility for facts that become outdated or for inadvertent errors or omissions. So **always confirm information when it matters,** especially if you're making a detour to visit a specific place. Your experiences—positive and negative—matter to us. If we have missed or misstated something, **please write to us.** We follow up on all suggestions. Contact the Peru editor at editors@fodors.com or c/o Fodor's at 1745 Broadway, New York, New York 10019.

PRINTED IN THE UNITED STATES OF AMERICA

10 9 8 7 6 5 4 3 2 1

DESTINATION PERU

The day begins in Puerto Maldonado, as it does in many parts of the southern Amazon, with the call of two monkeys: the dominant male and female, screeching as one, broadcast the position of their pack to the other monkeys in the forest. Meanwhile, 300 miles west, in Cusco, the early train embarks on its lurching three-hour ride to Machu Picchu. Fifty miles northwest of Cusco in Maras, multi-colored hot air balloons commence their slow drift over the Sacred Valley of the Incas, where the Pisac market is setting up its stands of vegetables, ceramics, and woolens. At the same time, 750 miles south-west of the market, work days of another kind uncoil in Lima, where the streets are already clogged with commuter traffic. Business is slower but transit more rapid in Huanchaco, 350 miles northwest of Lima, where fishermen, some since dawn, have been riding tiny reed boats over the waves. There are hundreds of ways to wake up in this country, and you'll want to try more than one, so don't sleep in. This is Peru. Good morning.

Karen Cure, Editorial Director

CONTENTS

ABOUT THIS BOOK

There's no doubt that the best source for travel advice is a like-minded friend who's just been where you're headed. But with or without that friend, you'll have a better trip with a Fodor's guide in hand. Once you've learned to find your way around its pages, you'll be in great shape to find your way around your destination.

SELECTION Our goal is to cover the best properties, sights, and activities in their category, as well as the most interesting communities to visit. We make a point of including local food-lovers' hot spots as well as neighborhood options, and we avoid all that's touristy unless it's really worth your time. You can go on the assumption that everything you read about in this book is recommended wholeheartedly by our writers and editors. Flip to On the Road with Fodor's to learn more about who they are. It goes without saying that no property mentioned in the book has paid to be included.

RATINGS Orange stars ★ denote sights and properties that our editors and writers consider the very best in the area covered by the entire book. These, the best of the best, are listed in the Fodor's Choice section in the front of the book. Black stars ★ highlight the sights and properties we deem Highly Recommended, the don't-miss sights within any region. Fodor's Choice and Highly Recommended options in each region are usually listed on the title page of the chapter covering that region. Use the index to find complete descriptions. In cities, sights pinpointed with numbered map bullets ❶ in the margins tend to be more important than those without bullets.

SPECIAL SPOTS Pleasures & Pastimes focuses on types of experiences that reveal the spirit of the destination. Watch for Off the Beaten Path sights. Some are out of the way, some are quirky, and all are worth your while. If the munchies hit while you're exploring, look for Need a Break? suggestions.

TIME IT RIGHT Wondering when to go? Check On the Calendar up front and the chapters' Timing sections for weather and crowd overviews and best days and times to visit.

SEE IT ALL Use Fodor's exclusive Great Itineraries as a model for your trip. (For a good overview of the entire destination, follow those that begin the book, or mix regional itineraries from several chapters.) In cities, Good Walks guide you to important sights in each neighborhood; ⚐ indicates the starting points of walks and itineraries in the text and on the map.

BUDGET WELL Hotel and restaurant price categories from ¢ to $$$$ are defined in the opening pages of each chapter—expect to find a balanced selection for every budget. For attractions, we always give standard adult admission fees; reductions are usually available for children, students, and senior citizens. Look in Discounts & Deals in Smart Travel Tips for information on destination-wide ticket schemes.

BASIC INFO Smart Travel Tips lists travel essentials for the entire area covered by the book; city- and region-specific basics end each chapter. To find the best way to get around, see the transportation section; see individual modes of travel ("By Car," "By Train") for details. We assume you'll check Web sites or call for particulars.

ON THE MAPS	Maps throughout the book show you what's where and help you find your way around. Black and orange numbered bullets ❶ ➊ in the text correlate to bullets on maps.
BACKGROUND	In general, we give background information within the chapters in the course of explaining sights as well as in **CloseUp** boxes and in **Understanding Peru** at the end of the book. The **Glossary** can be invaluable help.
FIND IT FAST	Within the book, chapters are arranged regionally. Chapters are divided into smaller regions, within which towns are covered in logical geographical order; attractive routes and interesting places between towns are flagged as **En Route**. Heads at the top of each page help you find what you need within a chapter.
DON'T FORGET	**Restaurants** are open for lunch and dinner daily unless we state otherwise; we mention dress only when there's a specific requirement, and reservations only when they're essential or not accepted—it's always best to book ahead. **Hotels** have private baths, phones, TVs, and air-conditioning and operate on the European Plan (EP, meaning without meals). We always list facilities but not whether you'll be charged extra to use them, so when pricing accommodations, find out what's included.

SYMBOLS

Many Listings
- ★ Fodor's Choice
- ★ Highly recommended
- ⊠ Physical address
- ✛ Directions
- ⌖ Mailing address
- ☎ Telephone
- 🖷 Fax
- ⊕ On the Web
- ✉ E-mail
- 💵 Admission fee
- ☉ Open/closed times
- ▶ Start of walk/itinerary
- Ⓜ Metro stations
- ⊟ Credit cards

Outdoors
- 🏌 Golf
- ⛺ Camping

Hotels & Restaurants
- 🏨 Hotel
- 🛏 Number of rooms
- ⚭ Facilities
- 🍽 Meal plans
- ✕ Restaurant
- ⚮ Reservations
- 👔 Dress code
- 🚭 Smoking
- 🍷 BYOB
- ✕🏨 Hotel with restaurant that warrants a visit

Other
- ☺ Family-friendly
- 🛈 Contact information
- ⇨ See also
- ✉ Branch address
- ☞ Take note

ON THE ROAD WITH FODOR'S

A trip takes you out of yourself. Concerns of life at home completely disappear, driven away by more immediate thoughts—about, say, what marvels will beguile the next day, or where you'll have dinner. That's where Fodor's comes in. We make sure that you know all your options, so that you don't miss something that's around the next bend just because you didn't know it was there. Because the best memories of your trip might well have nothing to do with what you came to Peru to see, we guide you to sights large and small all over the region. You might set out to explore Machu Picchu and the country's other archaeological treasures, but back at home you find yourself unable to forget harvesting the Pisac market for bargains or sampling tangy *ceviche* in as many restaurants as you could manage. With Fodor's at your side, serendipitous discoveries are never far away.

Our success in showing you every corner of Peru is a credit to our extraordinary writers. Although there's no substitute for travel advice from a good friend who knows your style, our contributors are the next best thing—the kind of people you would poll for travel advice if you knew them.

Colorado-based Gregory Benchwick first visited South America in 1999 when he spent a year as the editor of *The Bolivian Times*. While researching the North Coast and Amazon Basin chapters Gregory swam with pink dolphins, visited with local tribesman, and sampled the Peruvian delicacy *suri* (palm-tree grubs). He continues to travel extensively throughout Latin America and has contributed to several Fodor's titles covering Central and South America.

Joan Gonzalez began her writing career as a reporter and sports editor for newspapers in her home state of Ohio. Her involvement with South America began with a brief stint as a flight attendant for Pan Am, flying to Mexico and Central and South America. As a freelance writer, she authored the first edition of *Selling to South America* for the U.S. Travel Industry Association of America, co-authored the first edition of *Fodor's Los Cabos* pocket guide, and has covered Ecuador, Bolivia, and the northeast cities of Brazil as a Fodor's updater. She also writes for travel-industry publications and in-flight magazines.

Costa Rica–based freelance writer and pharmacist Jeffrey Van Fleet divides his time between Central America and Wisconsin, but always looks for opportunities to enjoy South America. He is a regular writer for Costa Rica's English-language *Tico Times*. Jeff, who updated the Cusco–Machu Picchu and southern Amazon basin sections for this book, has also contributed to Fodor's guides to Costa Rica, Chile, Argentina, and Central and South America.

A travel and outdoor adventure writer for more than a decade, Holly S. Smith has covered much of the world for Fodor's. As a regular series updater, she has explored Australia, Indonesia, and her hometown of Seattle, and she has edited many Fodor's titles as well. Her own books include *Adventuring in Indonesia, Aceh: Art & Culture,* and *How to Bounce Back Quickly After Losing Your Job.* She now travels the world with her three children (age five and under), proving that life can be an adventure wherever you go.

Former Fodor's editor Mark Sullivan has traveled extensively in South America, seeing everything from the towering glaciers of Tierra del Fuego to the mysterious monoliths of Easter Island. Lima, though, is his home away from home. He edited editions of *Fodor's South America, Fodor's Central America,* and *UpClose Central America.*

You can rest assured that you're in good hands—and that no property mentioned in the book has paid to be included. Each has been selected strictly on its merits, as the best of its type in its price range.

Our thanks to the Peru tourism organization PromPerú for their assistance.

Time Zones

Numbers below vertical bands relate each zone
to Greenwich Mean Time (0 hrs.).
Local times frequently differ from these general indications,
as indicated by light-face numbers on map.

Anchorage	2	Honolulu	1	New York City	18
Atlanta	20	Juneau	3	Ottawa	15
Bogotá	23	Lima	25	Rio de Janeiro	30
Buenos Aires	27	Los Angeles	7	San Francisco	5
Caracas	24	Mexico City	13	San José (CR)	22
Chicago	10	Miami	21	Santiago	26
Dallas	11	Minneapolis	9	São Paolo	29
Denver	8	Montevideo	28	Toronto	14
Edmonton	4	Montréal	16	Vancouver	5
Halifax	17	New Orleans	12	Washington, D.C.	19

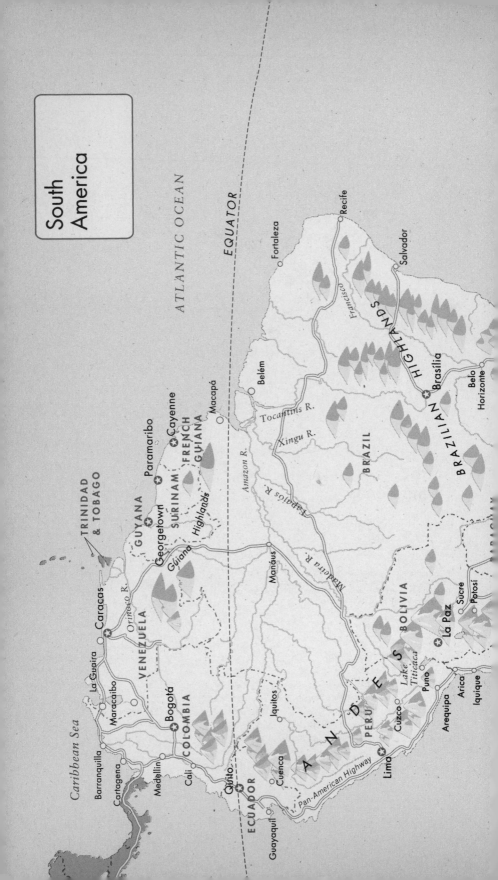

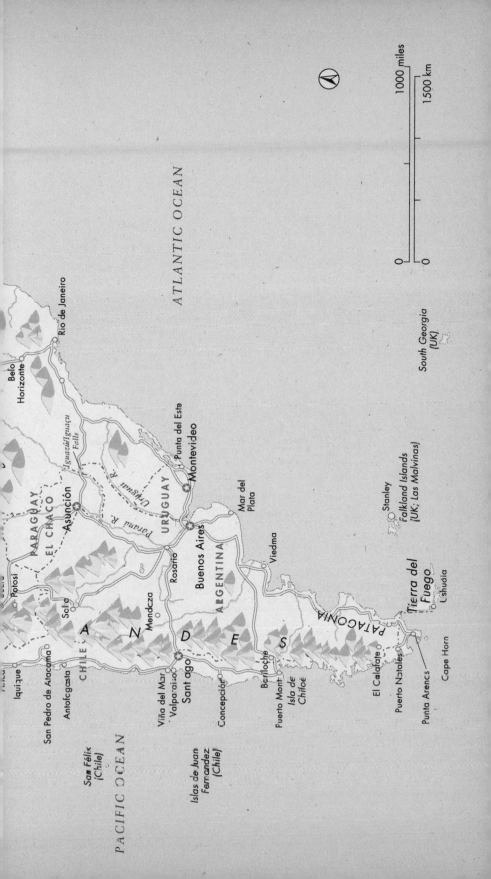

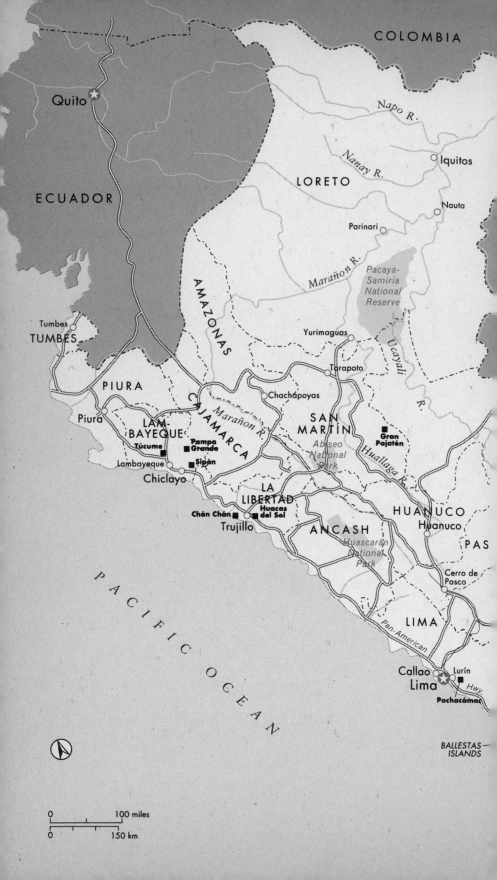

① Lima

Lima remains the political and cultural center of Peru. On the coast about halfway between Trujillo and Ica, it is where all journeys to the country typically begin. Founded along the banks of the Rimac River by Francisco Pizarro in 1535, the city served as the capital of Spain's South American empire for 300 years. The "City of Kings" has a regal history that lingers on in its sophistication, the decaying beauty of its boulevards, and the liveliness of its intellectual life. The majority of Lima's most splendid buildings and museums are in the Centro, around the Plaza Mayor. From here the main roads lead like spokes of a wheel to the city's most important districts, through working-class neighborhoods like Breña, Rimac, and La Victoria to upscale seafront residential neighborhoods like Miraflores and San Isidro. There are also posh neighborhoods like La Molina in the foothills of the Andes, where Lima's wealthiest live surrounded by watered lawns behind high walls. West of the Centro, the city is flat, but the Peruvian coast is so narrow that spiky hills jut into the sky just 10 minutes to the east.

② The South

Between the Andes mountains to the east and the Pacific Ocean to the west, the vast section of desert between Lima and the Chilean border belongs to southern Peru. Moving down the coastline, Pisco is the first major stop, where golden tropical beaches are interspersed with rocky shores that define such natural areas as Paracas National Reserve and the Ballestas Islands. The Pan-American Highway then moves inland through the desert, passing through the oases of Ica and Nazca. This section of desert is also the site of one of the country's most famous ancient and mysterious ruins, the Nazca Lines. From Nazca you have a choice: head east to the Andes, where Cusco and Machu Picchu await, or continue down the coast. Take the latter route and you'll pass through quiet fishing villages and near Colca and Cotahuasi canyons, two of the world's deepest gorges. Arequipa, an old Spanish colonial town built of bone-white *sillar* stone from the surrounding volcanoes, is the last major town before Tacna and the Chilean border.

③ Cusco, Machu Picchu & the Sacred Valley

A repository of history, archaeology, and culture, Cusco, chock-full of colonial structures built atop Inca ruins, sits high in the Andes of south-central Peru, overlooking the southern Amazon Basin. The Río Urubamba passes through a lower-elevation valley not far from Cusco and defines the evocatively named "Sacred Valley of the Inca," a land of rural farms and charms. In the northeast sector of the region lie the fabled ruins of Machu Picchu, the famed "lost city of the Inca," rediscovered and reintroduced to the world in 1911.

④ Amazon Basin

The indentation of Brazil into Peru's eastern territory splits the Amazon Basin into two distinct sectors separated by 600 km (360 mi). The pulsing city of Iquitos anchors Peru's northern Amazon region, largely contained in the department of Loreto, the portion of the country where the Amazon River itself actually flows. Many jungle lodges and wildlife areas, most notably the Pacaya-Samira National Reserve, are upriver from Iquitos. The smaller southern city of Puerto Maldonado lies 1,200 km (720 mi) from Iquitos as the macaw flies—you, however, would need to fly back to Lima to connect between the two—and is the metropolis of the southern Amazon and capital of the Madre de Dios department. The Madre de Dios, Tambopata, and Heath rivers, tributaries of the Amazon that connect with the big river via Brazil and Bolivia, pass through the south, site of the Tambopata National Reserve and the world-famous Manu Biosphere Reserve.

⑤ Central Highlands

Forming a crescent of snow-covered mountains bordered by jungle to the east and ocean to the west, the Central Highlands are carved right into the heart of Peru. The road east from Lima provides spectacular views as it stretches through the Andes toward La Oroya, where it splits into a northern route through highland plains and plateaus toward Tingo María, and a narrow road south through the peaks toward Ayacucho and the stark deserts beyond. Major settlements along the northern route are Junín, on the shore of Lago Junín, the mining town of Cerro de Pasco, and the market settlement of Huánuco. Once the domain of the Shining Path terrorists, this area is now safe for travelers, although monitored by many military checkpoints to prevent the guerrilla activity and drug-running that plagued the region until the mid-1990s. The journey south has stops in the compact mountain towns of Jauja, Huancayo, Huancavelica, and Ayacucho. You can also take the train through Huancavelica.

⑥ The North Coast & Northern Highlands

A vast coastal desert runs the entire length of Peru's North Coast, which begins north of Lima and stretches all the way to the Ecuadorian border. The land here is dry and stark. There is very little flora and fauna, just occasional desert brush. Thanks to the marvels of hydraulic engineering, the lands around the rivers have been cultivated since pre-Inca times and offer welcome swaths of green cut in hard juxtaposition to the endless brown of the desert. The Northern Highlands and Cordillera Blanca lie directly inland from the North Coast and are a mountainous region. The soaring Andean peaks, deep green valleys, and steep hills of this area are truly breathtaking. The highest parts of the Highlands are found around Huaraz. From Cajamarca and Chachapoyas, the land slowly drops into the Amazon Basin, the earth becoming greener and damper.

GREAT ITINERARIES

Hitting the Highlights
9 days

LIMA 1 day. On your first full morning in Peru's capital, take a three-hour tour to see the downtown historic center, the Museo de Oro, and (by car or other vehicle) the modern suburbs of San Isidro and Miraflores. In the afternoon visit the Museo Nacional de Antropología y Arqueología and the Museo Rafael Larco Herrera—both are in the Pueblo Libre district. Since you're in the neighborhood, finish the day by browsing through the Feria Artesanal, an artisans' market. ⇨ Lima *in* Chapter 1.

NAZCA 1 day. In the morning, fly out of Lima and along the coast for a survey of the huge candelabra etched on the cliffs before landing at the Nazca site. Take off in a different plane to circle over the Nazca lines. It's best to have lunch after the flight (both planes are rather small). Return to Lima in the afternoon. ⇨ The South *in* Chapter 2.

AREQUIPA 1 day. Fly from Lima, and if you haven't already arranged for a two-day trip to the Colca Canyon from Arequipa, do so upon arrival, then spend the day wandering the Plaza de Armas, stopping in at the La Compañia church and the Cathedral, the Museo Santuarios Andinos, and the 400-year-old Convento de la Santa Catalina. In the evening, take a taxi to Calle San Francisco, a street lined with restaurants and bars. ⇨ The South *in* Chapter 2.

COLCA CANYON 1 day. Leave Arequipa early in the morning, stopping at the town of Chiva near the Misti Volcano and the vicuña reserve. Continue to the Condor's Cross to watch the birds fly and see the Colca Canyon. Rafting or trekking trips can be arranged. Overnight and return to Arequipa the next day. ⇨ The South *in* Chapter 2.

CUSCO 1 day. From Arequipa it's a short flight to Cusco; check into your hotel as soon as you arrive. The adjustment to Cusco's altitude of 3,500 m (11,500 ft) will be easier since you are coming from Arequipa, with an altitude of 2,335 m (7,661 ft). Tour Cusco in the afternoon. ⇨ Cusco, Machu Picchu, and the Sacred Valley *in* Chapter 3.

MACHU PICCHU 2 days. From Cusco, catch the train to this ancient sanctuary, overnighting either at the Citidel or in a hotel at Aguas Calientes. Return to Cusco late afternoon the following day. ⇨ Cusco, Machu Picchu, and the Sacred Valley *in* Chapter 3.

PUNO 2 days. From Cusco, take the PeruRail train to Puno, spending the night there, also taking time to tour Lake Titicaca. From Juliaca, a commercial center 50 km (31 mi) north of Puno, fly back to Lima to catch your flight home. ⇨ The South *in* Chapter 2.

The Low Altitude Tour
14 days

If high altitudes are not your thing, try this "low level" tour.

LIMA 1 day. On your first morning, tour the historical Plaza de Armas. In the Pueblo Libre, take the afternoon to see the Museo Nacional de Antropología y Arqueología and the Museo Rafael Larco Herrera and do some handicraft shopping at the outdoor Feria Artesanal. ⇨ Lima *in* Chapter 1.

CHICLAYO 2 days. From Lima, fly to Chiclayo and check in at your hotel. Visit the Cathedral and the witches market, where shamans and folk healers sell their herbs. It might be possible to arrange a special audience with a shaman in the evening. The next morning, tour the burial platform of Huaca Rajada to see the tomb of the Lord of Sipán and the on-site museum. Continue to Pampa Grande, site of the largest pyramid in South America. In the afternoon, explore the nearby mud-brick pyramids at Tucume and the Bruning museum at Lambayeque. Overnight again in Chiclayo. ⇨ The North Coast and Northern Highlands *in* Chapter 6.

TRUJILLO 2 days. Take a bus to Trujillo (208 km/129 miles) from Chiclayo and check into your hotel. If you're around the Plaza de Armas, explore it at your own pace. The Libertador hotel on the Plaza is a good spot for lunch or dinner. The next morning, continue touring the city, visiting the beach resort of Huanchaco for lunch. Local fishermen set out from here in their *caballitos de totora,* or reed boats. In the afternoon, travel to the adobe-brick city of Chán Chán and the Pyramids of the Sun and the Moon, and catch a late afternoon flight back to Lima. ⇨ The North Coast and Northern Highlands *in* Chapter 6.

LIMA 1 day. See more museums and shop in San Isidro or Miraflores. Arrange for a bus tour to Paracas, Ica, and the Nazca lines, which will fill the next few days on this itinerary. ⇨ Lima *in* Chapter 1.

ICA 1 day. Leave Lima early by bus or car, heading south on the Pan-American highway to Ica, Peru's wine-growing area. Check into the Las Dunas Resort and arrange for an afternoon tour of one of the wineries and Ica's Museo Histórico Regional. This small museum has displays of fine Paracas weavings and a study comparing ancient diseases with those of today. Overnight in Ica. ⇨ The South *in* Chapter 2.

NAZCA 1 day. In the morning, survey the lines and drawings of Nazca before leaving by bus or car for Paracas. Take an afternoon boat trip to the Balestas Islands to see sea lions, birds, and tiny penguins, passing by the large candelabra etched on a cliff. Catch an afternoon bus back to Lima. ⇨ The South *in* Chapter 2.

IQUITOS AND THE AMAZON JUNGLE 6 days. A one-hour flight takes you to Iquitos, on the Amazon River. From here, base yourself in rain-forest lodge. Consider taking a cruise on a small ship downriver to Leticia on the Brazilian border, visiting small Indian villages. Also stop in the town of Pevas to see the paintings of Francisco Grippa. Consider a cruise upriver to the Pacaya–Samiria National Reserve. From Iquitos, return to Lima for your flight home. ⇨ The Amazon Basin *in* Chapter 4.

Biking with the Inca
14 days

The hearty ought to consider this unusual adventure through Cusco, Machu Picchu, Puno, and Lake Titicaca, mixing transport by plane, train, motor vehicle, boat, foot, and bicycle.

CUSCO 2 days. Arrive here two days before the trek itself to allow yourself time to adjust to the altitude. ⇨ Cusco, Machu Picchu, and the Sacred Valley *in* Chapter 3.

SACSAYHUAMAN 1 day. Stow your bike in a taxi and visit this Inca fortress. Later, bike to the market in Pisac—mostly downhill pedaling. Return to Cusco by taxi or van. ⇨ Cusco, Machu Picchu, and the Sacred Valley *in* Chapter 3.

PUNO 1 day. From Cusco, fly to Puno's airport at Juliaca and overnight. ⇨ The South *in* Chapter 2.

LAKE TITICACA 1 day. Visit the floating Uros islands in Lake Titicaca and continue by boat to the island of Taquile for an overnight. ⇨ The South *in* Chapter 2.

PUNO 1 day. Return to Puno to begin your bike ride through the Altiplano to Lake Umayo, and visit the pre-Inca burial towers of Sillustani; set up camp for an overnight. ⇨ The South *in* Chapter 2.

LA RAYA PASS 1 day. Continue on a paved road for a steady climb from Puno's 3,812 m (12,500 ft) to La Raya Pass at 4,361 m (14,300 ft.), before the downhill ride to camp alongside hot springs. ⇨ The South *in* Chapter 2.

VILCANOTA RIVER 1 day. From La Raya it's mostly a downhill ride along the Vilcanota River to your next campsite. ⇨ Cusco, Machu Picchu, and the Sacred Valley *in* Chapter 3.

YUCAY VALLEY 1 day. Following a paved country road, continue to the Yucay Valley for overnight in a hotel. ⇨ Cusco, Machu Picchu, and the Sacred Valley *in* Chapter 3.

CHINCHERO 1 day. The ride today takes you to the market at Chinchero, then along the Urubamba River to Ollantaytambo, where you'll overnight. ⇨ Cusco, Machu Picchu, and the Sacred Valley *in* Chapter 3.

MACHU PICCHU 1 day. Plan a combination train and hiking trip to Machu Picchu. ⇨ Cusco, Machu Picchu, and the Sacred Valley *in* Chapter 3.

OLLANTAYTAMBO 3 days. From Aguas Calientes, return to Ollantaytambo by train and explore the site further. The following day, return to Cusco by van, taking some time to decompress before flying back to Lima the following day. ⇨ Cusco, Machu Picchu, and the Sacred Valley *in* Chapter 3.

°C | °F
100 | 212
40 | 105
37 | 98.6
30 | 90
25 | 80
20 | 70
15 | 60
10 | 50
5 | 40
0 | 32
−5 | 20
−10 | 10
−15 |
−20 | 0

Seasons below the equator are the reverse of those in the north—summer in the lower part of South America runs from December to March and winter from June to September. The tourist season in Peru runs from May through September, which corresponds to the dry season in the Sierra and Selva. The best time to visit is May through July, when the cool, misty weather is just beginning on the Costa, and the highlands are dressed in bright green under crystalline blue skies. June brings major festivals to Cusco, such as Inti Raymi (the Inca festival of the sun) and Corpus Christi. Other important festival months are February, which means Carnaval throughout Peru and Virgen de la Candelaria (Candlemas) celebrations in Puno, and October, when chanting, purple-clad devotees of El Señor de los Milagros (the Lord of the Miracles) fill the streets of Lima.

Climate

When it's dry in the Sierra and the Selva, it's wet on the Costa, and vice versa. The Selva is hot and humid year-round, with endless rain between January and April. Friajes from Patagonia occasionally sweep through the southern rain forests of Madre de Dios, but the average daily minimum and maximum temperatures in the Selva are 20°C (69°F) and 32°C (90°F).

In the Sierra expect rain between October and April, and especially January through March. The rest of the year the weather is dry and the temperatures fickle. The sun can be hot, but in the shade it's refreshingly cool. Nights are chilly, and the temperature may drop to freezing. Temperatures during Cusco's dry months average 0°C (32°F)–22°C (71°F).

It never rains in the coastal desert, but a dank, heavy fog called the garua coats Lima from June through December. Outside Lima, coastal weather is clearer and warm.

The following are average daily maximum and minimum temperatures for Lima.

Jan.	27C	81F	May	25C	77F	Sept.	19C	66F
	21	70		19	66		15	59
Feb.	28C	82F	June	23C	73F	Oct.	21C	70F
	21	70		17	63		16	61
Mar.	29C	84F	July	18C	64F	Nov.	23C	73F
	23	73		15	59		17	63
Apr.	27C	81F	Aug.	18C	64F	Dec.	24C	75F
	22	72		15	59		18	64

Forecasts Weather Channel Connection ☎ 900/932–8437, 95¢ per minute from a Touch-Tone phone ⊕ www.weather.com.

ON THE CALENDAR

As rich as Peru's history are the events that celebrate it. Festivals and processions observing faith, victories past, or the dawn of a new season fill the country's timetable. If you want your visit to coincide with one of these occasions, be sure to plan well in advance.

Dec.

Virgen de Guadalupe is honored December 3 through 13 in the Central Highlands. Around Ayacucho, December 4 through 10 is Semana de la Libertad Americana, which celebrates the victory of the battle of Ayacucho.

Craftsmen selling traditional artwork of leather, wood, wool, clay, and silver gather at Cusco's main plaza December 24 to sell saints, a custom that originated in Colonial times and is called Santuranticuy.

Inmaculada Concepción, Navidad, Los Galos, and The Fiesta de los Negritos are among the events celebrated in Huancayo, Huánuco, and other towns on Christmas day.

Jan.

January 1 is not just the new year in rural Cusco department, but also a time for handing over power to new community leaders in the Entrega de Varas, the elaborate ritual passing of the *varayoc*, the ceremonial staff wielded by town mayors, in a ceremony dating from Inca times.

The Aniversario de Lima, (Founding of Lima) January 18, 1535, is celebrated with open-air concerts of criolla music around the city several days (see local newspapers for time and place) prior to the eve of the anniversary, which is marked by a concert in the Plaza de Armas.

In early January, dancing and parades for the Festival of the Magi take place in Puno, Cusco, and nearby Ollantaytambo.

The last week of January is party time in Trujillo, when couples from all over Peru compete for the title of the best typical Creole dance team during the Concurso Nacional de Mariner (Marinera National Dance Contest). Dances are performed to the accompaniment of guitars and the *cajón*, a boxlike, wood percussion instrument.

Feb.

Ceremonies and fireworks begin the end of January in Puno, but February 2 heralds one of the most impressive celebrations in Peru, the Fiesta de la Virgen de la Candelaria. Hundreds of folkloric dancers participate in colorful processions. The feast is related to pre-Hispanic agrarian rites of sowing and harvesting, and mining activity. Huancayo is one of several towns that celebrates this day with grand festivities.

The religious Cruz de Chalpón (or Cruz de Motupe) festival takes place in Motupe, 80 km (48 mi) northwest of Chiclayo on the Pan-American Highway.

Carnaval is observed throughout Peru. In many cities, especially Iquitos, the party has degenerated into a water fight—people throw buckets of water and water balloons—but Carnaval in Arequipa, Cajamarca, and Puno remains a colorful affair, with parades and dancing in the streets. Carnaval Huanchaquero in Trujillo takes place on Huanchaco Beach February 25–27.

Mar.	In Ica, the Festival de la Vendimia (Grape Harvest Festival) during the first two weeks of March celebrates the region's vineyards. Among the events are wine tastings, dances, Peruvian Paso horse exhibitions, cockfights, parades, and the election of the Queen of the Festival: the best *festejo* (most popular African Peruvian dance) dancer. Pisco, Lunahuaná, Condoroy, and Chincha also hold wine festivals in early March.
	The highlight of Ica's El Señor de Luren, when thousands of pilgrims honor the town patron, is an all-night parade on the third Monday of the month. The ceremony also takes place in June and October.
	Holy Week, or Semana Santa, brings colorful religious processions through the streets of Cusco, with reenactments of the events of the Passion. Ayacucho's celebrations are particularly festive, with nightly processions by candlelight, horse races, and daily parties through Easter Sunday. Easter Monday sees the parading of Nuestro Señor de los Temblores (The Lord of the Earthquakes) through the streets. According to tradition, this gold crucifix protected Cusco from extensive damage in a 1650 earthquake.
Apr.	The third week in April is the Concurso Nacional de Caballos de Paso (Peruvian Paso Horse National Competition) at Mamacona, a former ranch 30 km (19 mi) south of Lima. Activities include exhibitions, folk dances, music, and a handicraft fair. If you need a new saddle, this is a good time to buy one.
	April 25 honors the founding of Huamanga province.
May	Labor Day, on the 1st, commemorates the country's working adults. San José, or Saint Joseph's Day, also falls on this day.
	The feast of the Huancané Cross takes place on Taquile, a small island in Lake Titicaca near Puno, in early May, with folkloric dances as the main attraction. Trujillo's Festival of the Sea, which includes a surfboard competition, is on nearby Huanchaco Beach in mid-May.
	La Cruz de Mayo in Huánuco is on May 3. Fiesta de las Cruces occurs throughout the month in Huancayo.
	Sixty days after Resurrection Monday (Holy Week) is the celebration of Corpus Christi, one of the most beautiful religious celebrations in Cusco. Statues of saints from Cusco's churches are taken in procession to the Cathedral, a rite imposed by the Spanish conquerors during colonial times to replace the processions of mummies by the Inca. After residing in the Cathedral for a week, the statues are returned to their respective churches, accompanied by musicians, dancers, and the faithful. This celebration sometimes falls in June.
June	Ica Week celebrates the city's founding, and occurs mid-month. During the mid-month festival of El Señor de Lurén, which also takes place in March and October, all night parades march around the city with an image of the crucified Christ.
	Fiesta de Torre-Torre is on varying dates in Huancavelica. Huancayo has celebrations on the 15th for the Virgen de las Mercedes.

Cusco's most spectacular event is Inti Raymi, the Festival of the Sun, held in the Sacsayhuaman fortress on the outskirts of Cusco on June 24. The celebration of the Inca winter solstice is commemorated with music, dancing, parades, and performances at the fortress by a cast of thousands. To thoroughly enjoy this spectacle, you should book the event through a tour operator who will arrange for transportation, a ticket for a bleacher seat, and a box lunch.

As befits a region so dependent on water, Madre de Dios does up the June 24 Fiesta de San Juan Bautista (St. John the Baptist) in style, with parades and music. Several days of merrymaking lead into the June 29 feast day of San Pedro y San Pablo (Sts. Peter and Paul), patron saints of the town of Cochuela, who are also honored in the coastal fishing villages of the south.

July — Fiesta Perricholi takes place mid-month in Huanuco. Throughout the Central Highlands, the Fiesta de la Virgen del Carmen is on July 16. Huancayo celebrates Santiago on the 24th and 25th. Peru's Fiestas Patrias, or Independence Day, festivities fall on July 28 and 29.

Aug. — The 4th is San Juan de Dios in Huancayo. Tourist Week in Huánuco takes place August 12–18.

Arequipa, Peru's second-largest city, was founded August 15, 1540, and the Fiesta Jubilar de Arequipa is the most important non-religious celebration in the region. In addition to fireworks and a concert the night before, the day is celebrated with bullfights, a horse exhibition, and parades with dance groups and beauty queens; *tunas* (musical choral groups) walk the streets serenading the city.

Every August 30 during the Festival de Santa Rosa, thousands of the faithful leave notes at Lima's Santuario de Santa Rosa de Lima requesting that the saint hear their prayers.

Sept. — The Fiesta of the Virgen de Cocharcas on the 8th is a major celebration throughout the Central Highlands. Also on the 8th, the Paracas region celebrates the moment when General San Martín first entered Peru after liberating Argentina in 1820. Huancayo honors the Virgen de la Natividad on the 15th, the Virgen de las Mercedes on the 24th and 25th, and San Miguel Arcángel on the 29th. Tourist Week in Huancavelica also takes place this month, with a huge crafts market, music, dancing, and various festivals.

Trujillo, called the "City of the Eternal Spring" because of its mild weather, celebrates the arrival of spring the last week of September with a Festival Internacional de la Primavera (International Spring Festival). Handicraft and art exhibits, classical and folk music concerts, sports contests, gastronomy contests, a beauty pageant, and a closing parade mark this special event.

Oct. — Ica celebrates El Señor de Luren in March and June and also the weeks of October 7 through 20. The event culminates in an all-night parade, which takes place the third Monday of the month.

The Battle of Angamos is commemorated on October 8.

Procesion del Señor de los Milagros (Lord of the Miracles) is celebrated between October 18 and 28 in Lima and throughout the Central Highlands. In the colonial era, an Angolan slave painted the image of the crucified Christ on the wall of a long-gone church in the Pachacamilla neighborhood. It became an object of worship when it survived an earthquake that destroyed much of Lima. Thousands of devout people dressed in purple carry a heavy statue of Christ through Lima's streets. A cake called *turron de Doña Pepa* is prepared and eaten throughout the month.

On October 28 and 29, Huánuco celebrates its patron saint during Fiesta del Rey y del Señor de Burgos. The 20th through the 29th is Tantamayo Touristic Week.

Nov.

All the saints are honored during Día de Todos los Santos on the 1st. On Día de los Muertos (All Souls' Day), November 2, families carry edibles and flowers to their ancestors' graves.

Escenifacion de la Leyenda de Manco Capac Y Mama Ocllo. A reenactment of the emergence from Lake Titicaca of a mythical couple, Manco Capac and Mama Ocllo, explaining the creation of the Inca Empire, is dramatized on the lake Nov. 5 at Puno. A thanksgiving ritual is then performed and dancers and musicians from the nearby communities entertain.

Ancient Cities

From every mountaintop, valley, or coastal plain in Peru you can almost hear the echoes of past civilizations. And just as each new archaeological discovery is thought, surely, to be the last, another ancient city reveals itself. The temples, palaces, shrines, and steep stone staircases of Machu Picchu are Peru's most famous, but there are extensive ruins throughout the country. North of Lima, 5 km (3 miles) from Trujillo is Chán Chán, the largest adobe city in the world and 1,759 km (1,092 mi) northwest of Trujillo, near Chachapoyas is Kuelap, called "The City of the Cloud People" because of the white skin of its former inhabitants. Kuelap was built on a mountaintop overlooking the Utcabamba River.

Caral, in the Supe Valley, is reportedly the oldest city in the Americas. It is 193 km (120 mi) north of Lima and 23 km (14 mi) inland from the Pacific Coast. It was settled around 2600 BC and is older than the pyramids of Egypt. The public area has a huge plaza surrounded by six mounds; the largest, Piramide Mayor, is 18 m (60 ft) tall. An unusual find were 32 flutes made of condor and pelican wing bones. In 2002, Caral was put on the World Monuments Watch List due to heavy damage from wind erosion and looting.

Machu Picchu, Chán Chán, and areas of Kuelap and Caral are offered on tours, but other impressive sites, like Gran Pajaten in the Río Abiseo National Park on the eastern slope of the Andes, 402 km (250 mi) east of Trujillo, or Cota Coca, 40 km (25 mi) east of Machu Picchu, are difficult to reach and not quite ready for tourism. The Ríp Abiseo area was declared a National Park in 1983, not only to protect the overall area and the exceptionally preserved buildings, terraces, and roads of a pre-Hispanic civilization.

It isn't only ancient cities that are constantly being discovered or uncovered in Peru—in July 2002, Peruvian geologists found the perfectly preserved skeleton of a horse in the department of Arequipa 1,000 km (600 mi) south of Lima, proving that the horse existed in South America long before it was introduced by the Spaniards. The skeleton, on display in Peru's Natural History Museum in Lima, reveals that this early equine had a large head, thick neck, and short legs.

Arts & Crafts

When the subject of art comes up in Peru, the talk is usually either about art from the Cusco School of painting or handicrafts, but one of Peru's most famous artists is Francisco Grippa, who lives in the jungle town of Pevas (population 2,000) on the Amazon River, about halfway between Iquitos and Leticia, Colombia. Yagua, Huitoto, and Bora Indian villages are nearby. If he isn't off somewhere in Europe or the United States, Grippa welcomes visitors from passing tourist boats into his home, La Casa de Arte, to have refreshments and see his art, which is also for sale.

Some of Peru's most valuable artworks are in the Cathedral, churches and convents in Cusco, which developed a distinctive style of painting that infused religious scenes based on the art of Europe with Indian elements. Peruvian artists are probably best known for their high-quality crafts and folk art, from the geometric designs in their textiles, silver, and tin work; distinct pottery from various areas of Peru; and the colorful, detailed scenes in wooden boxes called *retablos*.

Dancing
Clubs in modern Peru are playing much the same music and dancing the same dances as in most other parts of the world, so it is usually necessary to go to a special performance or festival or to a remote village to enjoy the typical music and dance of yesteryear. The best and most beautiful dance is the *marinera* and it's in Trujillo, north of Lima, where it is best known. The dance differs slightly from region to region, but it's basically performed with much vigor by a courting couple executing a series of elegant and complex movements while holding a handkerchief in their hands, but never physically touching. The *cajón*, an instrument of Afro-Peruvian origin, provides the music. It is crafted from a wooden box with a sound-hole in the back. The player sits on top and raps out a rhythm with his palms.

Other musical instruments include the *quena*, a wind instrument dating to pre-Hispanic times, and the harp; although the harp is not a native instrument it has become popular in Peru, especially in the Andes, where you will hear the Latin version of the blues, called *huayno*.

The most challenging dance, performed in the Andes, is the *tijeras* (scissors), a display of dexterity and strength involving gymnastic leaps to the strains of the harp and violin. In colonial times, priests claimed the dancers had a magical halo, the result of a pact with the Devil that enabled them to perform their feats that included sword-swallowing, sticking pins into their faces, and eating insects, frogs and sometimes snakes. The dance has been tamed a bit since colonial times.

Hiking & Climbing
The most popular hiking expedition is the Inca Trail from Cusco to Machu Picchu, but many other areas are conducive to treks and climbs. The Cordillera Blanca and Huauhuash ranges in the department of Ancash, between Lima and Trujillo, are the best known of Peru's large concentration of snow peaks. The highest in the Peruvian Andes is Mt. Huascarán at 6,768 m (21, 910 ft), and in the Amazon Basin the highest is Yerupajá, at 6,634 m (21,766ft). Alpamayo, at 5,947 m (19,512 ft) is ranked as one of the most beautiful mountains in the world. A much easier climb is El Misti, the snow-capped volcano near Arequipa. At 5,825 m (19,113 ft), it can be conquered in two days and does not require mountaineering experience, just an experienced guide to lead you. The best time for mountain climbing is in the dry season between May and October.

Peppers, Paiche & Potatoes
From the Amazon to the Andes, the food is as varied as the landscapes, though all regions have one thing in common: the use of a small, thin *ají* pepper. Hot peppers are common ingredients throughout Latin America, especially Mexico, but Peruvian chefs strip the pepper of its veins and seeds and soak it or boil it in water to cool it down, all the while retaining its flavor.

Peruvian cuisine is hard to define, as it has evolved from pre-Inca and Spanish colonial times and has been influenced by African, European, and Asian cooking. Fresh fish is everywhere, including shrimp, lobster, piranha, *corvina* (a variety of sea bass), and *paiche* (the world's largest freshwater fish, found in jungle lakes). Some of Peru's best dishes include *ceviche* (marinated fish with onions and peppers), *ají de gallina* (hen in a cream sauce), *lomo saltado* (sautéed beef with onions and peppers, served with fried potatoes and rice), *pachamanca* (a meat and vegetable stew), *anticuchos* (a shish kebab of marinated beef hearts), and *choclo* (Peru's version of corn on the cob). *Chupe de camarones* (shrimp soup) is made with vegetables, milk, cheese, and shrimp. For dessert, try *suspiro a la limeña,* a rich, sweet pudding, and *mazamorra morada,* a fruity purple pudding.

Both Peru and Ecuador claim to have given the world the potato, and hundreds of varieties are grown here. Among the tastier recipes are *papas a la huancaina* (potatoes in spicy cheese sauce), *papas ocopa* (potatoes in spicy peanut sauce), and *carapulcra* (a stew of dried potatoes served over rice). Peru has wonderful fruit, such as *chirimoya* (custard apple) and *tuna* (cactus fruit).

Preserves

Peru has 50 natural areas under state protection, designated as national parks, reserves, sanctuaries, or protected forests. Most of these preserves are available to tourists, with a few open only to researchers. Two popular natural areas for tourists are the Manu National Park, reached from Cusco, and the Pacaya-Samiria National Reserve on the Amazon, upriver from Iquitos. Manu goes from the cloud forests of the Andean highlands to the Amazon lowlands and has a tapir lick, macaw lick, and a trail through the rain forest watched over by monkeys, leading to a lake populated by giant otters. Pacaya-Samiria is protected as a National Reserve and is reached by boat. More than 330 bird species, 130 types of mammals, amphibians, and reptiles make their home here along with giant otters, black caymans, and paiche.

FODOR'S CHOICE

The sights, restaurants, hotels, and other travel experiences on these pages are our editors' top picks—our Fodor's Choices. They're the best of their type in the area covered by the book—not to be missed and always worth your time and sure to yield a very special travel experience. In the destination chapters that follow, you'll find all the details.

LODGING

$$$$ **Country Club Lima Hotel, Lima.** With hand-painted tiles and a stained-glass ceiling in the lobby, this hacienda-style hotel dating from 1927 is a work of art.

$$$$ **ExplorNapo.** On the Napo River, deep in the heart of the Amazon Basin, you find this explorer's camp, complete with a giant canopy walkway, comfortable rooms, and easy access to the sights and sounds of the rain forest.

$$$$ **Machu Picchu Pueblo Hotel, Aguas Calientes.** In this semitropical oasis, stone bungalows have cathedral ceilings, exposed beams, and flagstone floors, which add up to a rustic elegance.

$$$ **Sandoval Lake Lodge, Madre de Dios.** Think about it; you can already be at this scenic jungle lodge by noon of your first day while other travelers are still in transit to their lodgings.

$$–$$$ **Hotel Laguna Seca.** Relax in the thermal baths at this country spa and resort next to the historic Baños del Inca. Every room comes with its own bath, so you can enjoy the restorative waters privately.

$$ **Gran Hotel Bolívar, Lima.** A magnificent stained-glass dome greets you as you enter this grand hotel dating from 1924. The rooms retain a taste of the sumptuousness that once welcomed heads of state.

$$ **Hotel Antigua Miraflores, Lima.** Dating back more than a century, this salmon-colored mansion is perhaps the city's loveliest lodging. A hand-carved staircase leads you up to the elegantly appointed rooms.

$$ **Hotel Caballito de Mar.** In the sunny coastal hamlet of Punta Sal you'll find this seaside resort, complete with a seahorse-shaped infinity pool and stunning beach views from every room.

$$ **Posada Amazonas, Madre de Dios.** River otters, parrots, and a 30-m (100-ft) canopy tower to survey them and other fauna from mark this lodge largely run by and for the benefit of the indigenous Ese'eja community.

$–$$ **Hotel Nazca Lines, Nazca.** This historic hacienda, the former home of Maria Reiche, is where many international travelers and archaeologists stay while investigating the Nazca Lines.

BUDGET LODGING

$ **La Castellana, Lima.** A towering turret dominates the courtyard of this castlelike lodging. It's rare to find such comfortable accommodations at a price that won't break your budget.

Colca Lodge, Arequipa. The hotel's adobe and clay walls and thatched roof complement the surrounding wilderness, while its proximity to Colca Canyon enables hikes, horseback rides, bike trips, trout fishing, and dips in the hot springs.

La Florida, Tarma. A Spanish hacienda turned attractive bed-and-breakfast has camping, hiking, and highland tours.

Grand Hotel Huánuco A swanky exterior hides reasonably priced, comfortable, and welcoming accommodations with modern facilities.

Hostal El Marqués de Valdelirios, Ayacucho. This 1940s casona in a quiet neighborhood brings the colonial era to life with an elegant courtyard and pretty rooms.

Hostal Santa Catalina, Arequipa. Pleasant, homey surroundings, cheap rooms, and wash facilities make this a popular choice.

Hotel de la Borda, Nazca. Set in fragrant gardens and surrounded by cotton fields, this quiet, 80-year-old hacienda outside Nazca offers a taste of life on a coastal farm.

Hotel Mossone, Huacachina. Relaxation and recreation delicately converge at this property with a lakeside situation, blossoming Spanish courtyard, and free bicycles and sandboards.

El Patio de Monterrey, Huaraz area This country hacienda has its own chapel, large rooms with wood-beamed ceilings, and a charm not found in many other Northern Peru lodgings.

La Posada del Puente, Arequipa. Set beside the Río Chili and overlooking Volcán Misti, this hotel pampers with comfortable rooms and remarkable local fare.

RESTAURANTS

$$–$$$$	**Astrid y Gaston, Lima.** If you think the restaurant itself is a work of art, it's just a warm-up for the imaginative entrées. The eye-catching *pato asado con mil especies* (roast duck with 1,000 spices) is accompanied by a pepper bubbling over with basil risotto.
$$–$$$	**Huaca Pucllana, Lima.** Facing the ruins of a 1,500-year-old pyramid, this restaurant makes you feel like a part of history. Watch archaeologists at work as you enjoy the *novo andino* cuisine.
$$	**La Taberna, Ica.** Bodega El Catador outside Ica opened this romantic restaurant serving exquisite local specialties at candlelit tables and with live Peruvian music.
$–$$	**El Cartujo, Lima.** Monks who took a vow of silence gave this place its name, but you won't be able to say enough about the sole stuffed with lobster or the sea bass topped with crab. There's a top-notch wine list, too.
$–$$	**L'eau Vive, Lima.** A group of singing nuns performs "Ave Maria" every evening at this beautifully restored mansion in the historic center. Trout in cognac is a winner.
$–$$	**Siam de Los Andes, Huaraz.** Quite possibly the only Thai restaurant in northern Peru, Siam de los Andes has authentic, delicate-yet-powerful cuisine and is a welcome break from *pollo a la brasa*.

¢–$$ **La Santitos, Piura.** Rare is the European-style bistro that serves everything from Parmesan lobster to homemade ice cream.

BUDGET RESTAURANTS

Le Bistrot, Arequipa. This streetside café is straight out of Paris, with an ever-changing menu specializing in crêpes, high-grade espresso drinks, and desserts.

La Cabaña, Huancayo. While live music plays, enjoy Peruvian and Continental specialties in the garden or around the fireplace.

Club Colonial, Huanchaco. Watch Humboldt penguins play in their private pond as you enjoy a light seafood lunch or dinner. The Huanchaco beach is just a few blocks away for a casual after-meal stroll.

Fitzcarraldo, Iquitos. Originally a private home during Iquitos's rubber boom of the late 19th century, the Fitzcarraldo has a sumptuous menu of exotic jungle game dishes and great views of the Amazon River.

Granja Heidi, Cusco. Farm-fresh ingredients and top-notch service with a German touch at this cozy, artsy restaurant epitomize the equally cozy, artsy San Blas neighborhood.

El Griego Restaurant, Nazca. Huge portions of Peruvian specialties are served up to the backpacking crowd.

Mixto's Cebichería, Arequipa. Romantically situated above the glowing white Catedral, this spot is ideal for trying some of Arequipa's best seafood dishes.

Restaurant Urpicha, Ayacucho. Listen to local folk music play as you sample Andean specialties in this quaint Spanish home.

CITIES, TOWNS & VILLAGES

Belén. The houses and stores of Iquitos's Belén District—the "Venice of the Amazon"—literally float on water. Paddling through the floating houses in a dugout canoe is an other-wordly experience.

Chán Chán. The world's largest mud city, Chán Chán was built around AD 1300 by the great Chimú culture. The ruins are easily visited from the close-by colonial town of Trujillo.

Huari, Ayacucho. Part of the Santuario Histórico Pampas de Ayacucho, this ancient city is scattered with relics and huge, crumbled walls built by the Huari culture, which evolved 500 years before the Inca.

Machu Picchu. The most important archaeological site in South America, the "lost city of the Inca" is rediscovered every day by adventurous travelers.

Nazca. Surrounded by fruit orchards and snow-covered peaks, this desert town is a fascinating focal point from which to explore the Nazca Lines and other regional archaeological sites.

HISTORY

Convento de la Santa Catalina. Arequipa's five-acre, mud-brick, Iberian-style convent, founded in 1579 and still operating, is one of Peru's most famed cultural treasures.

Convento de Santa Rosa de Ocopa, Huancayo. This Franciscan monastery originally housed missionaries to the Amazon tribes; tour the massive library and natural-history museum.

El Cuarto del Rescate. The site of one of history's most treacherous double-crosses, the large El Cuarto del Rescate, in present-day Cajamarca, was filled twice with silver and once with gold as a ransom for the life of the Inca Atahualpa.

Iglesia de San Francisco, Lima. The vast catacombs beneath this church are filled with the bones of 75,000 people, making a tour of this maze of underground tunnels spooky fun.

Inca Trail. Hike where Inca travelers once did on the 50 km (31 mi) of rugged mountain trails leading through the Sacred Valley of the Incas.

Pampas de Quinua, Huánuco. The site where Peru's battle for independence was won in 1824 is a classic highlands panorama of mountains and pampas.

Qorikancha, Cusco. When a 1953 earthquake crumbled the walls of the Church of Santo Domingo, the foundations of the ancient Inca Temple of the Sun were revealed underneath.

Sacsayhuamán. The massive fortress of Sacsayhuamán, perhaps the most important Inca monument after Machu Picchu, is built of blocks of stone weighing up to 361 tons.

MUSEUMS

Museo Arqueológico Rafael Larco Herrera, Lima. This museum's famous *sala erótica* reveals that Peru's ancient artists were surprisingly uninhibited. Everyday objects are adorned with images that are frankly sexual and frequently humorous.

Museo Histórico Regional. Ica's vast, well-preserved collection of Inca, Nazca, and Paracas history is on display, including textiles, Inca counting strings, and a scale model of the Nazca Lines.

Museo Inka, Cusco. If you know Spanish, the museum in Cusco's former Admiral's Palace, newly revamped, refurbished, and retooled, is a good introduction to Inca and pre-Inca culture.

Museo Hilario Mendívil, Cusco. The friendly, enthusiastic staff will acquaint you with one of Peru's most well-known religious artists and his quirky, long-necked figures of the Virgin Mary.

Museo Pedro de Osma, Lima. The colonial-era art is remarkable, but this museum in a century-old mansion would still be worth a trip to see its inlaid wood floors, delicately painted ceilings, and intricate stained-glass windows.

Museo Tumbas Reales de Sipán, Lambayeque. Often called South America's most important discovery, the treasures excavated from the Tomb of Sipán are on exhibit here. Among the gold and ceramics are informative displays, highlighting the history of the area's pre-Inca civilizations.

NATURE

Cotahuasi Canyon. As the world's deepest gorge, Cotahuasi is an off-the-beaten path site with challenging hiking and kayaking.

Laguna Llanganuco. Bristling Andean peaks are reflected in the clear emerald waters of this glorious alpine lake. The surrounding towers of snow-capped peaks are truly awesome.

Manu Biosphere Reserve, Madre de Dios. More than 4½ million acres of pristine wilderness, including cloud forest and tropical rain forest, make up this sprawling natural reserve.

SMART TRAVEL TIPS

Finding out about your destination before you leave home means you won't squander time organizing everyday minutiae once you've arrived. You'll be more streetwise when you hit the ground as well, better prepared to explore the aspects of Peru that drew you here in the first place. The organizations in this section can provide information to supplement this guide; contact them for up-to-the-minute details, and consult the A to Z sections that end each chapter for facts on the various topics as they relate to Peru's many regions. Happy landings!

ADDRESSES

Avenida (Av.) is the most common street designation, except in older or historic districts, where *Jirón* (Jr.) is still used. The term *Calle* (street) is seen only occasionally, and in many cases, only the name is given, since there is no pattern of avenues running east and west and streets north and south, or vice versa. When an address doesn't have a number, sometimes you will see "s/n" *sin número,* meaning "no street number," and when there is a number, it often follows the street name, as in *San Martin 208.*

AIR TRAVEL

Airlines flying non-stop from the United States into Jorge Chavez International Airport, 11 km (7 mi) west of Lima, include AeroContinente from Miami; American Airlines from Dallas and Miami; Continental from Houston and Newark; and LanChile/LanPeru from Miami, New York and Los Angeles. AeroContinente also has a Sunday nonstop flight from Miami to Iquitos and continuing on to Lima. From Canada, code-share agreements determine connections through U.S. gateways.

From London, connections can be made to nonstop flights out of New York, Miami, Dallas, or Houston, or via Madrid on Iberia. Connections from Australia and New Zealand are usually through Los Angeles; however, if you are interested in also visiting Chile, LanChile has code-share agreements with carriers from Auckland and Sydney to connect in Papeete with their flights to Santiago via Easter Island. LanChile has daily nonstops between Santiago and Lima.

With four mountain ranges running through Peru plus a large swath of the

Amazon jungle, flying is the best way to travel between most cities and towns. Three excellent airlines, AeroContinente, LanPeru and Taca Peru provide air service to 12 airports between Tumbes on the border of Ecuador and Tacna on the Chilean border. Aero Cóndor operates a daily small plane service between Lima, Cajamarca and Trujillo, as well as daily touristic flights from Lima over the Plains of Nazca, and charter services.

BOOKING

When you book, **look for nonstop flights** and **remember that "direct" flights stop at least once.** Try to avoid connecting flights, which require a change of plane. Two airlines may operate a connecting flight jointly, so ask whether your airline operates every segment of the trip; you may find that the carrier you prefer flies you only part of the way. To find more booking tips and to check prices and make on-line flight reservations, log on to www.fodors.com.

CARRIERS

🔲 North American Airlines American. In North America, ☎ 800/433-7300. In Lima 01/211-7000. ⊕ www.aa.com. Continental. In North America, ☎ 800/525-0280, in Lima, 01/222-7080. ⊕ www.continental.com.

🔲 South American Airlines Aero Cóndor ☎ 01/442-5215 in Lima ⊕ www.aerocondor.com.pe. Aero Continente 888/586-9400 in North America; ☎ 01/242-4242, in Lima. ⊕ www.aerocontinente.com. LanChile ☎ 800/735-5526 in North America, 01/241-5522 in Lima ⊕ www.lanchile.com. LanPeru ☎ 800-735-5590 in North America; 01/221-3764 in Lima. 🖨 01/421-8914 ⊕ www.lanperu.com. Taca Peru 🖨 01/446-0033 or 01/446-0033 🖨 01/241-7077, in Lima.

🔲 From the U.K. Connections can be made in Madrid with Iberia's nonstop flights to Lima. Iberia ⊕ www.iberia.com.

🔲 From Australia & New Zealand with connections through Los Angeles or Papeete Air New Zealand ☎ 0800/737-000 in New Zealand ⊕ www.airnz.co.nz. Qantas ☎ 13-13-13 in Australia ⊕ www.qantas.com.au.

CHECK-IN & BOARDING

Always **ask your carrier about its check-in policy.** Plan to arrive at the airport about two hours before your scheduled departure time for domestic flights and 2½ to 3 hours before international flights. You may need to arrive earlier if you're flying

from one of the busier airports or during peak air-traffic times. To avoid delays at airport-security checkpoints, try not to wear any metal. Jewelry, belt and other buckles, steel-toe shoes, barrettes, and underwire bras are among the items that can set off detectors.

Assuming that not everyone with a ticket will show up, airlines routinely overbook planes. When everyone does, airlines ask for volunteers to give up their seats. In return, these volunteers usually get a several-hundred-dollar flight voucher, which can be used toward the purchase of another ticket, and are rebooked on the next flight out. If there are not enough volunteers, the airline must choose who will be denied boarding. The first to get bumped are passengers who checked in late and those flying on discounted tickets, so **get to the gate and check in as early as possible,** especially during peak periods.

Always **bring a government-issued photo I.D. to the airport;** even when it's not required, a passport is best.

Be prepared to show your passport when leaving any South American country and to pay hefty airport taxes. Upon arrival, find out how much airport departure taxes are and whether you can pay in your local currency. Fees on international flights from Peru should be around US$28 and domestic flights US$5. In Peru, taxes must be paid in cash and you can, of course, pay with the local currency, the Nueva Sole, but U.S. dollars are preferred.

CUTTING COSTS

The least expensive airfares to Peru are priced for round-trip travel and must usually be purchased in advance. Airlines generally allow you to change your return date for a fee; most low-fare tickets, however, are nonrefundable. It's smart to **call a number of airlines and check the Internet;** when you are quoted a good price, **book it on the spot**—the same fare may not be available the next day, or even the next hour. Always **check different routings** and look into using alternate airports. Also, price off-peak flights, which may be significantly less expensive than others. Travel agents, especially low-fare specialists (⇨ Discounts and Deals), are helpful.

Consolidators are another good source. They buy tickets for scheduled flights at reduced rates from the airlines, then sell them at prices that beat the best fare available directly from the airlines. Sometimes you can even get your money back if you need to return the ticket. Carefully read the fine print detailing penalties for changes and cancellations, purchase the ticket with a credit card, and **confirm your consolidator reservation with the airline.**

When you **fly as a courier,** you trade your checked-luggage space for a ticket deeply subsidized by a courier service. There are restrictions on when you can book and how long you can stay. Some courier companies list with membership organizations, such as the Air Courier Association and the International Association of Air Travel Couriers; these require you to become a member before you can book a flight.

Many airlines, singly or in collaboration, offer discount air passes that allow foreigners to travel economically in a particular country or region. These visitor passes usually must be reserved and purchased before you leave home. Information about passes often can be found on most airlines' international Web pages, which tend to be aimed at travelers from outside the carrier's home country. Also, try typing the name of the pass into a search engine, or search for "pass" within the carrier's Web site.

If you plan to fly around the country, ask about any type of "Visit Peru" fares that can be purchased in conjunction with your international ticket, making flying to several destinations within the country more affordable. And if you have frequent flyer miles with an airline that doesn't fly to Peru, bear in mind that it may have an agreement with an airline that does.

₪ Consolidators AirlineConsolidator.com ☎ 888/468-5385 ⊕ www.airlineconsolidator.com; for international tickets. **Best Fares** ☎ 800/576-8255 or 800/576-1600 ⊕ www.bestfares.com; $59.90 annual membership. **Cheap Tickets** ☎ 800/377-1000 or 888/922-8849 ⊕ www.cheaptickets.com. **Expedia** ☎ 800/397-3342 or 404/728-8787 ⊕ www.expedia.com. **Hotwire** ☎ 866/468-9473 or 920/330-9418 ⊕ www.hotwire.com. **Now Voyager Travel** ⊠ 45 W. 21st St., 5th floor, New York, NY 10010 ☎ 212/459-1616 ⊟ 212/243-2711 ⊕ www.nowvoyagertravel.com. **Onetravel.com** ⊕ www.onetravel.com. **Orbitz** ☎ 888/656-4546 ⊕ www.orbitz.com. **Priceline.com** ⊕ www.priceline.com. **Travelocity** ☎ 888/709-5983, 877/282-2925 in Canada, 0870/876-3876 in the U.K. ⊕ www.travelocity.com.

₪ Courier Resources Air Courier Association/Cheaptrips.com ☎ 800/282-1202 ⊕ www.aircourier.org or www.cheaptrips.com. **International Association of Air Travel Couriers** ☎ 308/632-3273 ⊕ www.courier.org.

ENJOYING THE FLIGHT

State your seat preference when purchasing your ticket, and then repeat it when you confirm and when you check in. For more legroom, you can request one of the few emergency-aisle seats at check-in, if you are capable of lifting at least 50 pounds—a Federal Aviation Administration requirement of passengers in these seats. Seats behind a bulkhead also offer more legroom, but they don't have underseat storage. Don't sit in the row in front of the emergency aisle or in front of a bulkhead, where seats may not recline.

Ask the airline whether a snack or meal is served on the flight. If you have dietary concerns, **request special meals when booking.** These can be vegetarian, low-cholesterol, or kosher, for example. It's a good idea to pack some healthful snacks and a small (plastic) bottle of water in your carry-on bag. On long flights, try to maintain a normal routine, to help fight jet lag. At night, **get some sleep.** By day, **eat light meals, drink water** (not alcohol), and **move around the cabin** to stretch your legs. For additional jet-lag tips consult *Fodor's FYI: Travel Fit & Healthy* (available at bookstores everywhere).

Smoking policies vary from carrier to carrier. Many airlines prohibit smoking on all of their flights; others allow smoking only on certain routes or certain departures. Ask your carrier about its policy.

International travel between the Americas is a bit less wearing than to Europe or Asia because there's no problem with jet lag. New York, for instance, is in the same time zone as Lima. If you have a choice between day or night flights, **take a night plane if you sleep well while flying.** Especially en route to the Andean countries, you will have lovely sunrises over the mountains. Southbound, the best views are usually out windows on the plane's left side.

FLYING TIMES

Flying times are for nonstop flights to Lima: from Miami 5 hours 45 min; Dallas 7 hours 12 min; Houston 6 hours 45 min; Los Angeles 8 hours 35 min, and from

New York 7 hours. Total flying time to Lima from London, taking British Airways to Madrid to connect with Iberia's non-stop flight (including connecting time) is 16 hours.

HOW TO COMPLAIN

If your baggage goes astray or your flight goes awry, complain right away. Most carriers require that you **file a claim immediately.** The Aviation Consumer Protection Division of the Department of Transportation publishes *Fly-Rights,* which discusses airlines and consumer issues and is available on-line.

F Airline Complaints **Aviation Consumer Protection Division** ✉ U.S. Department of Transportation, C-75, Room 4107, 400 7th St. NW, Washington, DC 20590 ☎ 202/366-2220 ⊕ www.dot.gov/airconsumer. **Federal Aviation Administration Consumer Hotline** ✉ for inquiries: FAA, 800 Independence Ave. SW, Room 810, Washington, DC 20591 ☎ 800/322-7873 ⊕ www.faa.gov.

RECONFIRMING

Check the status of your flight before you leave for the airport. You can do this on your carrier's Web site, by linking to a flight-status checker (many Web booking services offer these), or by calling your carrier or travel agent. Always confirm international flights at least 72 hours ahead of the scheduled departure time.

AIRPORTS

Peru has 19 international airports. Twenty-two small regional airports are used mainly for charters and Peru's air force. Peru's main international point of entry is Lima's Jorge Chávez International Airport. The address is listed as Callao, which is the name of the port area. Scheduled flights from Miami to the Colonel Francisco Secada Vignetta international airport—usually referred to as just C. F. Secada or the Iquitos airport—are an on-again-off-again service. Flights returning to Miami from Iquitos must go through Lima until the Iquitos airport can meet new security regulations for nonstop flights to Miami.

F Airport Information **Jorge Chávez International Airport** ☎ 01/575-1434 ⊕ www.corpac.gob.pe. **Col. Francisco Secada Vignetta** ☎ 064/23-1501.

BIKE TRAVEL

Riding a bike will put you face to face with the people and landscapes of Peru. However, the rugged terrain, high altitudes, and road conditions pose considerable challenges. Don't even think about going it on your own. Join a bike tour with an experienced, reputable operator. You have the option of bringing your own or renting equipment. If you plan to bring your own bike, ask the tour organizer what type you'll need. It will probably be a mountain bike, since basic touring bikes are too fragile for off-road treks. If you do decide to pedal around on your own, wear a bike helmet and remember to **avoid riding in congested urban areas,** where it's difficult getting around by car, let alone by bike.

BIKES IN FLIGHT

Most airlines accommodate bikes as luggage, provided they are dismantled and boxed; check with individual airlines about packing requirements. Some airlines sell bike boxes, which are often free at bike shops, for about $15 (bike bags can be considerably more expensive). International travelers often can substitute a bike for a piece of checked luggage at no charge; otherwise, the cost is about $100. U.S. and Canadian airlines charge $40–$80 each way.

BOAT & FERRY TRAVEL

Travel across Lake Titicaca from Peru to Bolivia is via Puno aboard hydrofoils operated by Crillón Tours, or catamarans operated by Transturin to Copacabana and the Huatahata Harbor in Bolivia, continuing to La Paz by bus. Stops on the crossing usually include the Sun and Moon Islands. Passengers not continuing to La Paz can visit Copacabana and Sun Island, overnighting in either place before returning to Puno.

Passenger boats are the most important means of transportation in the jungle. If you visit a jungle lodge, your hosts will pick you up in an outboard-powered boat—some have thatched roofs. Larger boats make 4- to 10-day cruises on the Amazon from Iquitos traveling downriver to the Brazil border or upriver to the Pacaya-Samiria wildlife reserve. You can also make arrangements for an excursion with a native guide in a wooden dugout called a *pecku-pecka,* the nickname coming from the sound of the small motor. However, do get a reference from a reliable source in whatever river town you happen to be in. Out of Puno on Lake Titicaca, there are many entrepreneur boatmen with small boats offering taxi service to the islands. Your best bet (although not the cheapest) is to arrange your trip with a local tour agency.

Crillón Tours ⊠ Av. Camacho 1223, La Paz ☎ 02/337-533 🖶 02/391-039 ⊕ www.titicaca.com. **Transturin/Titikaka Catamarans** ⊠ Calle Alfredo Ascarrunz 2518 La Paz Bolivia ☎ 02/422-222 🖶 02/411-922 ⊕ www.transturin.com.

BUS TRAVEL

Peru's buses travel between towns and are often in better condition than the roads, especially when you turn off the Pan-American Highway, and even the highway is sometimes precarious during the December–March rainy season. However, if you stick with one of the recommended companies like Cruz del Sur or Ormeño you can usually expect a good experience. The intercity bus system in Peru is extensive, and fares are quite reasonable. If your luggage is stored underneath, try to hop off the bus before the compartment is opened so you can be there to grab it. However, unless you have unlimited time, confine bus trips to destinations you can reach during daylight hours for two reasons: **petty theft is common at bus stations** and distances between most tourist destinations are either great or rugged. Good bus runs are between Lima and Ica for the Plains of Nazca (3 hours 45 min.) and between Cusco and Puno on Lake Titicaca. The Pan-American Highway between Lima and Trujillo to the north is usually okay. (Check conditions during rainy season.) The distance is 525 km (325 mi).

Alternative forms of public transportation are the *colectivos*, small vans that follow the same routes as buses. They charge about twice as much but are usually much faster. The catch is that they often don't depart until they fill up.

CLASSES

Second-class buses (*servicio normal*) tend to be overcrowded and uncomfortable, while the more expensive first-class service (*primera clase*) is safer, more comfortable, and much more likely to arrive on schedule.

FARES & SCHEDULES

Bus fares are substantially cheaper in South America than they are in North America or Europe. Competing bus companies serve all major and many minor routes, so it can pay to shop around if you're on an extremely tight budget. Always speak to the counter clerk, as competition may mean fares are cheaper than the official price posted on the fare board.

The recommended Oremño's top service is called *Royal Class* and the one-way fare from Lima to Arequipa is around US$26, while *Business Class* is around $13 for the 1,009-km (626-mi), 14-hr trip. Recommended Cruz del Sur's fares are about the same. Their less expensive class is called *Imperial.* A one-way plane ticket is around US$59 plus taxes for a 1-hr flight.

PAYING & RESERVATIONS

Tickets are sold at bus-company offices and at city bus terminals. Note that in larger cities there may be different terminals for buses to different destinations, and some small towns may not have a terminal at all. Instead, you'll be picked up and dropped off at the bus company's office. You should **be prepared to pay with cash,** as credit cards aren't always accepted. Reservations aren't necessary except for trips to popular destinations during high season. Summer weekends and major holidays are the busiest times. You should **arrive at bus stations early** for travel during peak seasons.

Bus Information Cruz del Sur ⊠ Jr. Quilca 531, Lima ☎ 01/424-6158 ⊠ Av. Javier Prado 1109, San Isidro, Lima ☎ 01/225-6163 ⊕ www.cruzdelsur. pe/empresa.htm. **Ormeño** ⊠ Carlos Zavala 177 Lima ☎ 01/427-5679 ⊠ Av. Javier Prado Este 1059, San Isidro, Lima ☎ 01/472-1710 ⊕ www.grupo-ormeno. com.

BUSINESS HOURS

Hours vary from region to region, but office hours are usually from 8:30 AM to 5 PM Monday through Friday. Some businesses close for one to two hours for lunch, especially during the summer months.

BANKS & OFFICES

Opening hours vary among banks, but generally banking hours are from 9 AM to 4 PM Monday through Friday and 9 AM to 12 PM Saturday. ATM's are now in major cities, credit cards are widely accepted—American Express, Diners Club, Mastercard, Visa—and foreign currency can always be exchanged in hotels. Most businesses, even taxis, gladly accept U.S. dollars. **Do not exchange money on the street.**

GAS STATIONS

Most gas stations, especially in the larger cities, are now open 24 hours.

MUSEUMS & SIGHTS

Most museums are open Monday–Saturday 9–6. Some close at lunch, usually between 1 and 3, but always check hours under individual museum listings. A good source is the *Peru Guide,* published monthly in Lima and given out free in most hotels.

PHARMACIES

There is usually at least one pharmacy open 24 hours in most neighborhoods, but it may not always be the same one, so ask at your hotel desk. In San Isidro, a suburb of Lima, try **Pharmax** (✉ Av. Salavery 3100 ☎ 01/264–5782, 01/264–2989 delivery).

SHOPS

Stores are generally open Monday–Saturday 10–8. Many smaller stores close for two hours at lunchtime and are open only in the morning on Saturday. Stores that cater to tourists usually have longer hours, and many open on Sunday. In Lima, since modern shopping malls also have restaurants and theaters, they are usually open seven days a week, from 10 or 11 AM to 10 or 11 PM. When in doubt, ask a taxi driver or someone behind the hotel desk.

CAMERAS & PHOTOGRAPHY

Peru, with its majestic landscapes and varied cityscapes, is a photographer's dream. Latin Americans seem amenable to having picture-taking tourists in their midst, but you should always ask permission before taking someone's picture. **People in remote villages often don't like being photographed.** Many of the people in traditional dress hanging around heavily touristed areas expect you to pay them if you take their photo.

To avoid the blurriness caused by your hand shaking, buy a mini tripod—they're available in sizes as small as 6 inches. Get a small beanbag to support your camera on uneven surfaces. If you'll be visiting the Andes, get a skylight (81B or 81C) or polarizing filter to minimize haze and light problems. The higher the altitude, the greater the proportion of ultraviolet rays. Light meters don't read these rays and consequently, except for close-ups or full-frame portraits where the reading is taken directly off the subject, photos may be overexposed. These filters may also help with the glare caused by white adobe buildings, sandy beaches, and so on. **Bring high-speed film to compensate for low light** under the tree canopy on rain forest trips. **Invest in a telephoto lens to photograph wildlife,** as even standard zoom lenses of the 35–88 range won't capture a satisfying amount of detail.

Casual photographers should **consider using inexpensive disposable cameras** to reduce the risks inherent in traveling with sophisticated equipment. One-use cameras with panoramic or underwater functions can be nice supplements to a standard camera and its gear.

The *Kodak Guide to Shooting Great Travel Pictures* (available at bookstores everywhere) is loaded with tips. **🖪 Photo Help Kodak Information Center** ☎ 800/242-2424.

EQUIPMENT PRECAUTIONS

Don't pack film and equipment in checked luggage, where it is much more susceptible to damage. X-ray machines used to view checked luggage are extremely powerful and therefore are likely to ruin your film. Try to **ask for hand inspection of film,** which becomes clouded after repeated exposure to airport X-ray machines, and **keep videotapes and computer disks away from metal detectors.** Always **keep film, tape, and computer disks out of the sun.** Carry an extra supply of batteries, and **be prepared to turn on your camera, camcorder, or laptop** to prove to airport security personnel that the device is real.

FILM & DEVELOPING

Bring your own film. Film is readily available in all major cities, but is usually more expensive than back home and frequently stored in hot conditions. When purchasing film locally, be sure and check the expiration date. In Peru, Kodak's Advantix is available only in Lima. Plan on shooting a minimum of two 36-exposure rolls per week of travel, then toss an extra roll into your bag. If you don't want the hassle of keeping a shot log, **make a quick note whenever you start a new roll**—it will make identifying your photos much easier when you get home.

CAR RENTAL

In general, it is not a great idea to rent a car in Peru, but if you do, know that most Peruvians see traffic laws as suggestions rather than commands. Outside cities, drive only during daylight hours, fill your gas tank whenever possible, and make sure your spare tire is in good repair. You may want to carry wooden planks to help you out of muddy spots on the road. **Using cell phones while driving is discouraged.** In some areas, drivers caught using a cell phone while driving receive a hefty fine, especially on the coastal highway following the cliff along the Pacific Ocean between Lima, Miraflores, and San Isidro.

There is an area of Peru where renting a car can be a fun thing to do—between Lima, Paracas, Ica, and the Plains of Nazca, traveling south on the Pan-American Highway. The highway follows the Pacific Ocean coastline before it cuts in through the desert, and stops can be made along the way for a picnic and a swim. It's a 3–4 hour drive to Ica. The highway is good, and while there isn't too much to see along the way, it will be nice to have a car to enjoy the area when you get there.

All the major agencies listed have counters at the Lima airport, and most also have offices in San Isidro and Miraflores. Avis has offices in Lima, Arequipa, and Cusco.
🚩 Major Agencies **Alamo** ☎ 800/522-9696 ⊕ www.alamo.com. **Avis** ☎ 800/331-1084, 800/879-2847 in Canada, 0870/606-0100 in the U.K., 02/9353-9000 in Australia, 09/526-2847 in New Zealand ⊕ www.avis.com. **Budget** ☎ 800/527-0700, 0870/156-5656 in the U.K. ⊕ www.budget.com. **Dollar** ☎ 800/800-6000, 0124/622-0111 in the U.K., where it's affiliated with Sixt, 02/9223-1444 in Australia ⊕ www.dollar.com. **Hertz** ☎ 800/654-3001, 800/263-0600 in Canada, 0870/844-8844 in the U.K., 02/9669-2444 in Australia, 09/256-8690 in New Zealand ⊕ www.hertz.com. **National Car Rental** ☎ 800/227-7368, 0870/600-6666 in the U.K. ⊕ www.nationalcar.com.

CUTTING COSTS

Fly-drive packages, popular in Europe, are extremely rare in Peru. If you plan to rent a car it is best to make arrangements before you leave home, and **book through a travel agent who will shop around.** If you plan to rent during a holiday period, be

sure to reserve ahead. International car-rental agencies in Peru are operated by local businessmen. **Consider hiring a car and driver** through your hotel concierge, or **make a deal with a taxi driver** for some extended sightseeing at a longer-term rate. Drivers often charge an hourly rate regardless of the distance traveled. You'll have to pay cash, but you'll often spend less than you would for a rental car.
🚩 Local Agency **Localiza** ✉ Lima ☎ 01/242-3939.

INSURANCE

When driving a rented car you are generally responsible for any damage to or loss of the vehicle. You also may be liable for any property damage or personal injury that you may cause while driving. Before you rent, see what coverage you already have under the terms of your personal auto-insurance policy and credit cards.

Always **give the rental car a once-over** to make sure that the headlights, jack, and tires (including the spare) are in working condition. Note any existing damages to the car and get a signature acknowledging the damage, no matter how slight.

REQUIREMENTS & RESTRICTIONS

Minimum age in Peru for renting a car is 25, but there is no upper age limit. However, renting a car isn't cheap. It will average around $48 a day plus 39 cents a kilometer, and regardless of what car insurance you have there is a mandatory collision insurance of $6 to $10 a day with a $500 deductible or $18 a day with zero deductible. This charge is sometimes eliminated when you use a credit card, as is the case with American Express, but check with your own credit-card company to see what it covers.

SURCHARGES

Before you pick up a car in one city and leave it in another, **ask about drop-off charges or one-way service fees,** which can be substantial. Note, too, that some rental agencies charge extra if you return the car before the time specified in your contract. To avoid a hefty refueling fee, **fill the tank just before you turn in the car,** but be aware that gas stations near the rental outlet may overcharge. It's almost never a deal to buy the tank of gas that's in the car when you rent it; the understanding is that you'll return it empty, but some fuel usually remains.

CAR TRAVEL

In Peru, your own driver's license is acceptable identification, but an international driving permit (IDP) is good to have. They are available from the American and Canadian automobile associations and, in the United Kingdom, from the Automobile Association and Royal Automobile Club. These international permits, valid only in conjunction with your regular driver's license, are universally recognized; having one may save you a problem with local authorities.

The major highways in Peru are the Pan-American Highway, which runs down the entire coast, and the Carretera Central, which runs from Lima to Huancayo. Most highways have no names or numbers; they are referred to by destination. Due to a massive road-improvement program, conditions have improved on highways, but elsewhere, including Lima, roads tend to be littered with potholes. Outside of Lima, street signs are rare and lighting is nonexistent.

The bottom line is that **driving is the least desirable way to negotiate Peru.** Instead, fly, take a bus, a train, a guided tour with transportation provided, rent a car and driver or, in rural areas, rent a horse. Congested city streets are chaotic; country roads aren't as crowded, but poor conditions and a lack of signs are discouraging.

EMERGENCY SERVICES

The Touring and Automobile Club of Peru will provide 24-hour emergency road service for members of AAA and affiliates upon presentation of their membership cards. Members of the American Automobile Association can purchase good maps at members' prices.

🚗 Emergency Services **Touring and Automobile Club of Peru** ✉ César Vallejo 699, Lince, Lima ☎ 01/221-2432.

GASOLINE

Gas costs around $2 a gallon. Stations along the highways are few and far between, so don't pass up on the chance to gas up. Most stations are now open 24 hours.

PARKING

In the cities, parking lots that charge about $1 an hour are common and provide the best security. Parking on the street costs between 25¢ and 50¢; you should tip someone to watch your car. Theft of the entire car is not as common as the theft of the car's body parts.

RULES OF THE ROAD

You can drive in Peru with a foreign license for up to six months, after which you will need an international driver's license. Speed limits are 25 kph–35 kph (15 mph–20 mph) in residential areas, 85 kph–100 kph (50 mph–60 mph) on highways. Traffic tickets range from a minimum of $4 to a maximum of $40. The police and military routinely check drivers at road blocks, so make sure your papers are easily accessible. Peruvian law makes it a crime to drive while intoxicated, although many Peruvians ignore that prohibition. If you are caught driving while under the influence, you will either pay a hefty bribe or spend the night in jail.

CHILDREN IN PERU

As in all South American countries, children are welcome in Peru and there are many areas, like Machu Picchu, that older children 12 and up will appreciate and enjoy. One thing that never fails to delight are the llamas and alpacas. With younger children, it may be best to explore the coastal areas, where altitude and rough terrain will not be a problem. Younger children may enjoy the Amazon, especially if you are staying in one of the better lodges, but consult your child's doctor about recommended vaccinations and shots.

Let older children join in on the planning as you outline your trip. Scout your library for picture books, storybooks, and maps about places you'll be going. Try to **explain the concept of foreign language;** some kids, who may have just learned to talk, are confused when they can't understand strangers and strangers can't understand them. On sightseeing days try to schedule activities of special interest to your children.

Serious consideration should be given to not renting a car if you are traveling with small children, but if you do, don't forget to **arrange for a car seat.** Renting a car with a driver, if possible, would be a better idea. For general advice about traveling with children, consult *Fodor's FYI: Travel with Your Baby* (available in bookstores everywhere).

FLYING

If your children are two or older, **ask about children's airfares.** As a general rule, infants under two not occupying a seat fly at greatly reduced fares or even for free. But if you want to guarantee a seat for an infant, you have to pay full fare. Consider flying during off-peak days and times; most airlines will grant an infant a seat without a ticket if there are available seats. When booking, **confirm carry-on allowances** if you're traveling with infants. In general, for babies charged 10% to 50% of the adult fare you are allowed one carry-on bag and a collapsible stroller; if the flight is full, the stroller may have to be checked or you may be limited to less.

Experts agree that it's a good idea to use safety seats aloft for children weighing less than 40 pounds. Airlines set their own policies: if you use a safety seat, U.S. carriers usually require that the child be ticketed, even if he or she is young enough to ride free, because the seats must be strapped into regular seats. And even if you pay the full adult fare for the seat, it may be worth it, especially on longer trips. Do **check your airline's policy about using safety seats during takeoff and landing.** Safety seats are not allowed everywhere in the plane, so get your seat assignments as early as possible.

When reserving, **request children's meals or a freestanding bassinet** (not available at all airlines) if you need them. But note that bulkhead seats, where you must sit to use the bassinet, may lack an overhead bin or storage space on the floor.

FOOD

Children may like the nourishing soups— sans hot peppers—that are a staple in Peru. Potatoes, fixed numerous ways, as well as rice and fish, are also good bets. You'll find McDonalds and other fast food places in Lima.

LODGING

Most hotels in Peru allow children under a certain age to stay in their parents' room at no extra charge, but others charge for them as extra adults; be sure to **find out the cutoff age for children's discounts.** Large chain hotels will make arrangements for babies and small children, but if staying in pousadas or boutique hotels, be sure to inquire before making a reservation.

PRECAUTIONS

Children must have all their inoculations up to date before traveling abroad. Take mosquito repellent that is safe for small children if traveling to jungle areas. Ensure that health precautions, such as what to drink and eat, are applied to the whole family. Drink only bottled water. Not cramming too much into each day will keep the whole family healthier while on the road.

SIGHTS & ATTRACTIONS

While you can travel comfortably in Peru with small children, it is a destination they will appreciate more when they are older. There are some museums that may appeal to the entire family, but not to a very young child. While there are many public parks, it's hard to relax with small children because so often parks are surrounded by busy streets. However, the park in the center of the district of Barranco south of downtown Lima (after San Isidro and Miraflores) is a good place to take small children. The park is small, and casual restaurants, a library, a pharmacy, the city hall, and a church surround it. There's even a streetcar for a very short tour.

Places that are especially appealing to children are indicated by a rubber-duckie icon (☺) in the margin.

SUPPLIES & EQUIPMENT

Baby formula and disposable diapers are readily available in supermarkets and some pharmacies in cities. If you are traveling to an isolated area, take a supply with you, just in case. **Pack things to keep your children busy while traveling.** For children of reading age, **bring books from home;** English-language books for kids are hard to find in many places.

COMPUTERS ON THE ROAD

If you're traveling with a laptop, carry a spare battery, a universal adapter plug, and a converter if your computer isn't dual voltage. Ask about electrical surges before plugging in your computer. Keep your disks out of the sun and avoid excessive heat for both your computer and disks. As in many countries, carrying a laptop computer could make you a target for thieves; **conceal your laptop in a generic bag, and keep it close to you at all times.** In Peru, many hotels, not just those in the luxury category, have business centers, or at least offer Internet services at a reasonable charge. There are also Internet cafes in almost every city and even in small towns.

CONSUMER PROTECTION & ASSISTANCE

Whether you're shopping for gifts or purchasing travel services, **pay with a major credit card** whenever possible, so you can cancel payment or get reimbursed if there's a problem (and you can provide documentation). If you're doing business with a particular company for the first time, **contact your local Better Business Bureau and the attorney general's offices** in your state and (for U.S. businesses) the company's home state as well. Have any complaints been filed? Finally, if you're buying a package or tour, always **consider travel insurance** that includes default coverage (⇨ Insurance).

BBBs Council of Better Business Bureaus ⊠ 4200 Wilson Blvd., Suite 800, Arlington, VA 22203 ☎ 703/276-0100 🖷 703/525-8277 🌐 www.bbb.org.

TOURIST INFORMATION & ASSISTANCE

Peru's 24-hour free tourist information and assistance service is called iPerú and is indicated by a dotted "i" inside a circle. It does just what its name implies; gives out information, offers assistance in an emergency, and advises you what to do if you feel services paid for were not provided as advertised. iperú does not recommend travel agencies, lodgings, or transport service, make reservations, or file applications for customs or immigration. It can only advise you of the availability of tourist services, flight itineraries, and information on buses and trains.

iPerú will help you if you feel there are discrepancies in a bill; you feel you did not get the services you paid for; if a flight was delayed or canceled and the airline did not provide the necessary compensation and information, or if an airline or overland company refuses to take responsibility for loss of luggage. Advice is also given on what to do if you have lost documents or valuable objects have been stolen.

There are iPerú offices in Arequipa, Ayacucho, Cusco, Iquitos, Lima, Puno and Trujillo. In Lima, the office at Jorge

Chávez International Airport, in the main part of the terminal, is open 24 hours.
iPerú Contacts Arequipa ⊠ Rodríguez Ballón Airport ☎ 054/44-4564 ⊠ Plaza de Armas (Main Square ☎ 054/22-1228.

Ayacucho ⊠ Portal Municipal 48 - Plaza Mayor (Main Square). ☎ 066/82-8305.

Cusco ⊠ Velasco Astete Airport. ☎ 084/23-7364 ⊠ Portal de Carrizos 250 - Plaza de Armas (Main Square). ☎ Daily 8:30-7:30.

Lima ⊠ Jorge Chávez International Airport (Main Hall). ☎ 01/574-8000 (24-hr hot line; outside Lima, 001/574-8000) ⊠ Jorge Basadre 610, San Isidro. ☎ 01/421-1627 ⊠ Larcomar Entertainment Center Module 14, Plaza Gourmet.

Iquitos ⊠ Col. F. S. Vignetta Airport (Main Hall). ☎ 094/26-0251.

Trujillo ⊠ Jr. Pizarro 412, Municipalidad de Trujillo (Town Hall). ☎ 044/29-4561.

CUSTOMS & DUTIES

When shopping abroad, **keep receipts** for all purchases. Upon reentering the country, **be ready to show customs officials what you've bought.** Pack purchases together in an easily accessible place. If you think a duty is incorrect, appeal the assessment. If you object to the way your clearance was handled, note the inspector's badge number. In either case, first ask to see a supervisor. If the problem isn't resolved, write to the appropriate authorities, beginning with the port director at your point of entry.

IN PERU

When you check through immigration upon arrival in Peru be sure to put the white International Embarkation/Disembarkation form you filled out in a safe place when it is returned to you. You will need it when you leave the country. If you lose it, in addition being delayed, you may have to pay a fine of around US$4. You may bring into Peru up to $1,000 worth of goods and gifts, which are taxed 20% (excluding personal and work items); everything thereafter is taxed at a flat rate of 25%. You may also bring a total of three liters of liquor; jewelry or perfume worth less than $300; and 20 packs of cigarettes or 50 cigars.

IN AUSTRALIA

Australian residents who are 18 or older may bring home A$400 worth of souvenirs and gifts (including jewelry), 250 cigarettes or 250 grams of cigars or other tobacco products, and 1,125 ml of alcohol (including wine, beer, and spirits). Residents under 18 may bring back A$200 worth of goods. Members of the same family traveling together may pool their allowances. Prohibited items include meat products. Seeds, plants, and fruits need to be declared upon arrival.

7 **Australian Customs Service** ☜ Regional Director, Box 8, Sydney, NSW 2001 ☎ 02/9213-2000 or 1300/363263, 02/9364-7222 or 1800/803-006 quarantine-inquiry line ☐ 02/9213-4043 ⊕ www.customs.gov.au.

IN CANADA

Canadian residents who have been out of Canada for at least seven days may bring in C$750 worth of goods duty-free. If you've been away fewer than seven days but more than 48 hours, the duty-free allowance drops to C$200. If your trip lasts 24 to 48 hours, the allowance is C$50. You may not pool allowances with family members. Goods claimed under the C$750 exemption may follow you by mail; those claimed under the lesser exemptions must accompany you. Alcohol and tobacco products may be included in the seven-day and 48-hour exemptions but not in the 24-hour exemption. If you meet the age requirements of the province or territory through which you reenter Canada, you may bring in, duty-free, 1.5 liters of wine *or* 1.14 liters (40 imperial ounces) of liquor *or* 24 12-ounce cans or bottles of beer or ale. Also, if you meet the local age requirement for tobacco products, you may bring in, duty-free, 200 cigarettes and 50 cigars. Check ahead of time with the Canada Customs and Revenue Agency or the Department of Agriculture for policies regarding meat products, seeds, plants, and fruits.

You may send an unlimited number of gifts (only one gift per recipient, however) worth up to C$60 each duty-free to Canada. Label the package UNSOLICITED GIFT—VALUE UNDER $60. Alcohol and tobacco are excluded.

7 **Canada Customs and Revenue Agency** ✉ 2265 St. Laurent Blvd., Ottawa, Ontario K1G 4K3 ☎ 800/461-9999, 204/983-3500, 506/636-5064 ⊕ www.ccra.gc.ca.

IN NEW ZEALAND

All homeward-bound residents may bring back NZ$700 worth of souvenirs and gifts; passengers may not pool their allowances, and children can claim only the concession on goods intended for their own use. For those 17 or older, the duty-free allowance also includes 4.5 liters of wine or beer; one 1,125-ml bottle of spirits; and either 200 cigarettes, 250 grams of tobacco, 50 cigars, *or* a combination of the three up to 250 grams. Meat products, seeds, plants, and fruits must be declared upon arrival to the Agricultural Services Department.

7 **New Zealand Customs** ✉ Head office: The Customhouse, 17–21 Whitmore St., Box 2218, Wellington ☎ 09/300-5399 or 0800/428-786 ⊕ www.customs.govt.nz.

IN THE U.K.

From countries outside the European Union, including Peru, you may bring home, duty-free, 200 cigarettes or 50 cigars; 1 liter of spirits or 2 liters of fortified or sparkling wine or liqueurs; 2 liters of still table wine; 60 ml of perfume; 250 ml of toilet water; plus £145 worth of other goods, including gifts and souvenirs. Prohibited items include meat products, seeds, plants, and fruits.

7 **HM Customs and Excise** ✉ Portcullis House, 21 Cowbridge Rd. E, Cardiff CF11 9SS ☎ 0845/010-9000 or 0208/929-0152, 0208/929-6731 or 0208/910-3602 complaints ⊕ www.hmce.gov.uk.

IN THE U.S.

U.S. residents who have been out of the country for at least 48 hours may bring home, for personal use, $800 worth of foreign goods duty-free, as long as they haven't used the $800 allowance or any part of it in the past 30 days. This exemption may include 1 liter of alcohol (for travelers 21 and older), 200 cigarettes, and 100 non-Cuban cigars. Family members from the same household who are traveling together may pool their $800 personal exemptions. For fewer than 48 hours, the duty-free allowance drops to $200, which may include 50 cigarettes, 10 non-Cuban cigars, and 150 ml of alcohol (or 150 ml of perfume containing alcohol). The $200 allowance cannot be combined with other individuals' exemptions, and if you exceed it, the full value of all the goods will be taxed. Antiques, which the U.S. Bureau of Customs and Border Protection defines as objects more than 100 years old, enter duty-free, as do original works of art done entirely by hand, including paintings, drawings, and sculptures. This doesn't apply to folk art or handicrafts, which are in general dutiable.

You may also send packages home duty-free, with a limit of one parcel per addressee per day (except alcohol or tobacco products or perfume worth more than $5). You can mail up to $200 worth of goods for personal use; label the package PERSONAL USE and attach a list of its contents and their retail value. If the package contains your used personal belongings, mark it AMERICAN GOODS RETURNED to avoid paying duties. You may send up to $100 worth of goods as a gift; mark the package UNSOLICITED GIFT. Mailed items do not affect your duty-free allowance on your return.

To avoid paying duty on foreign-made high-ticket items you already own and will take on your trip, register them with Customs before you leave the country. Consider filing a Certificate of Registration for laptops, cameras, watches, and other digital devices identified with serial numbers or other permanent markings; you can keep the certificate for other trips. Otherwise, bring a sales receipt or insurance form to show that you owned the item before you left the United States.

🔲 **U.S. Bureau of Customs and Border Protection** ✉ for inquiries and equipment registration, 1300 Pennsylvania Ave. NW, Washington, DC 20229 🌐 www.customs.gov ☎ 202/354-1000 ✉ for complaints, Customer Satisfaction Unit, 1300 Pennsylvania Ave. NW, Room 5.5D, Washington, DC 20229.

DINING

The cost and quality of dining out in Peru can vary widely, but a modest restaurant may serve as splendid a meal as one with elegant furnishings. Most smaller restaurants offer a lunchtime *menú*, a prix-fixe meal ($2–$5) that consists of an appetizer, a main dish, dessert, and a beverage. Peru is also full of cafés, many with a selection of delicious pastries. Food at bars is usually limited to snacks and sandwiches.

There are few complaints about food in Peru, as it is hearty and wholesome. Thick soups made of vegetables and meat are excellent. Try *chupes*, soups made of shrimp and fish with potatoes, corn, peas, onions, garlic, tomato sauce, eggs, cream cheese, milk and whatever else happens to be in the kitchen. Corvina, a sea bass caught in the Pacific ocean, is superb, as is a fish with a

very large mouth, called *paiche,* that is found in jungle lakes and caught with spears. Or try piranha—delicious, but full of bones. *Anticuchos* (marinated beef hearts grilled over charcoal) are a staple. Peru's large-kernel corn is very good, and it is claimed there are over 100 varieties of potatoes, served in about as many ways. And there is always *ceviche,* raw fish marinated in lemon juice and white wine then mixed with onions and red peppers and served with sweet potatoes, onions, and sometimes corn. It is almost considered a staple.

Top-notch restaurants serve lunch and dinner, but most Peruvians think of lunch as the main meal of the day, and many restaurants open only at midday. Served between 1 and 3, lunch was once followed by a siesta, though the custom has largely died out. Dinner can be anything from a light snack to another full meal. Peruvians tend to dine late, between 7 and 11 PM.

The restaurants we list are the cream of the crop in each price category. Properties indicated by an ✕🍽 are lodging establishments whose restaurant warrants a special trip.

RESERVATIONS & DRESS

Peruvians dress quite informally when they dine out, and often a jacket is sufficient for men even at the most expensive restaurants. A smart pair of slacks or a skirt is always appropriate for women. Shorts are frowned upon everywhere except at the beach, and T-shirts are appropriate only in very modest restaurants.

Reservations are always a good idea; we mention them only when they're essential or not accepted. Book as far ahead as you can, and reconfirm as soon as you arrive. (Large parties should always call ahead to check the reservations policy.) We mention dress only when men are required to wear a jacket or a jacket and tie.

WINE, BEER & SPIRITS

Peru's national drink is the pisco sour, made with a pale grape brandy—close to 100 proof—derived from grapes grown in vineyards around Ica, south of Lima. Added to the brandy are lemon juice, sugar, bitters, and egg white. It is a refreshing drink and one that nearly every bar in Peru claims to make best. Tacama's Blanco de Blancos from Ica is considered the country's best wine. Ica's Vintage (Wine Tasting) Festival is in March.

Peruvian beer (*cerveza*) is also very good. In Lima, try Cristal and the slightly more upscale Pilsen Callao, both produced by the same brewery. In the south it's Arequipeña from Arequipa, Cusqueña from Cusco, and big bottles of San Juan from Iquitos, where the warm climate makes it taste twice as good. In Iquitos they also make Chuchuhuasi from the reddish-brown bark of the canopy tree that grows to 100 feet high in the Amazon rain forest. The bark is soaked for days in rum *aguardiente* and is claimed to be a cure-all for everything—very good for colds. However, in Iquitos, it has been bottled and turned into a pretty tasty drink for tourists.

DISABILITIES & ACCESSIBILITY

Peru, as in most of South America, is not yet well equipped to handle travelers with disabilities, especially those in wheelchairs. Adding to the problem is the terrain. Many of Peru's prime attractions are in areas difficult to reach, and high altitudes may also be a problem for some. However, a new disability law has been passed and PromPeru is working in coordination with SATH (Society for Accessible Travel & Hospitality) in the United States and with hotels and transportation companies to improve facilities.

One company that is trying to open up Peru's attractions to people with disabilities is Apumayo Expeditions. General Manager Juan José López has already taken small groups to Cusco, Machu Picchu, and the Amazon, with a great deal of cooperation from the tourism sector. The company has offices in Lima and in Cusco.
F Local Resources **Apumayo Expeditions.**
⊠ Bellavista 518 Miraflores, Lima, ☎ 01/444-2310, ⊕ www.apumayo.com

RESERVATIONS

When discussing accessibility with an operator or reservations agent, **ask hard questions.** Are there any stairs, inside *or* out? Are there grab bars next to the toilet *and* in the shower/tub? How wide is the doorway to the room? To the bathroom? For the most extensive facilities meeting the latest legal specifications, **opt for newer accommodations.** If you reserve through a toll-free number, consider also calling the hotel's local number to confirm the information from the central reservations office. Get confirmation in writing when you can.

TRANSPORTATION

PeruRail, now run by Orient Express hotels, goes the extra mile to accommodate travelers with disabilities. Their on-board staff will help board people using wheelchairs, and will store the wheelchairs. With advance notice, seats with the most leg room can be reserved. Also, 83 rooms in their Hotel Monasterio in Cusco have been equipped with an oxygen enrichment system to aid in adjusting to the high altitude.

The two train routes now being operated by PeruRail are between Cusco–Juliaca–Puno on Lake Titicaca and Cusco–Machu Picchu. (The train between Ariquipa and Puno is available only for groups.) The Cusco–Puno sector is not a problem for travelers with disabilities, but on the Cusco–Machu Picchu trip, people using wheelchairs would have to arrange transportation from the train station to the ruins. There is also helicopter service from Cusco to Aguas Calientes (the Machu Picchu train station) for around $150 round-trip.
F **PeruRail** ⊠ Arequipa General Office, Av. Tacna y Arica 200, ☎ 054/215-350, ⊟ 054/231-603, ✍ info@perurail.com, ⊕ www.perurail.com.
F Transportation Complaints **Aviation Consumer Protection Division** (⇨ Air Travel) for airline-related problems. **Departmental Office of Civil Rights** ⊠ for general inquiries, U.S. Department of Transportation, S-30, 400 7th St. SW, Room 10215, Washington, DC 20590 ☎ 202/366-4648 ⊟ 202/366-9371 ⊕ www.dot.gov/ost/docr/index.htm. **Disability Rights Section** ⊠ NYAV, U.S. Department of Justice, Civil Rights Division, 950 Pennsylvania Ave. NW, Washington, DC 20530 ☎ ADA information line 202/514-0301, 800/514-0301, 202/514-0383 TTY, 800/514-0383 TTY ⊕ www.ada.gov. **U.S. Department of Transportation Hotline** ☎ for disability-related air-travel problems, 800/778-4838 or 800/455-9880 TTY.

TRAVEL AGENCIES

In the United States, the Americans with Disabilities Act requires that travel firms serve the needs of all travelers. Some agencies specialize in working with people with disabilities.
F Travelers with Mobility Problems **Access Adventures** ⊠ 206 Chestnut Ridge Rd., Scottsville, NY 14624 ☎ 585/889-9096 ✍ dltravel@prodigy.net, run by a former physical-rehabilitation counselor. **CareVacations** ⊠ No. 5, 5110-50 Ave., Leduc, Al-

berta, Canada, T9E 6V4 ☎ 780/986-6404 or 877/ 478-7827 🖷 780/986-8332 ⊕ www.carevacations. com, for group tours and cruise vacations. **Flying Wheels Travel** ✉ 143 W. Bridge St., Box 382, Owatonna, MN 55060 ☎ 507/451-5005 🖷 507/451-1685 ⊕ www.flyingwheelstravel.com.

DISCOUNTS & DEALS

Be a smart shopper and **compare all your options** before making decisions. A plane ticket bought with a promotional coupon from travel clubs, coupon books, and direct-mail offers or purchased on the Internet may not be cheaper than the least expensive fare from a discount ticket agency. And always keep in mind that what you get is just as important as what you save.

DISCOUNT RESERVATIONS

To save money, **look into discount reservations services** with Web sites and toll-free numbers, which use their buying power to get a better price on hotels, airline tickets (⇨ Air Travel), even car rentals. When booking a room, always **call the hotel's local toll-free number** (if one is available) rather than the central reservations number—you'll often get a better price. Always ask about special packages or corporate rates.

When shopping for the best deal on hotels and car rentals, **look for guaranteed exchange rates,** which protect you against a falling dollar. With your rate locked in, you won't pay more, even if the price goes up in the local currency. **🛈 Airline Tickets Air 4 Less** ☎ 800/AIR4LESS; low-fare specialist. **🛈 Hotel Rooms Accommodations Express** ☎ 800/444-7666 or 800/277-1064 ⊕ www. accommodationsexpress.com. **Steigenberger Reservation Service** ☎ 800/223-5652 ⊕ www.srs-worldhotels.com. **Travel Interlink** ☎ 800/888-5898 ⊕ www.travelinterlink.com. **Turbotrip.com** ☎ 800/ 473-7829 ⊕ www.turbotrip.com.

PACKAGE DEALS

Don't confuse packages and guided tours. When you buy a package, you travel on your own, just as though you had planned the trip yourself. Fly/drive packages, which combine airfare and car rental, are often a good deal. In cities, ask the local visitor's bureau about hotel packages that include tickets to major museum exhibits or other special events.

SOUTH AMERICAN EXPLORERS

In Lima and Cusco, a helpful organization for anyone on a budget or traveling solo is the South American Explorer's Club, founded in Lima in 1977. The club offers advice, recommendations, and help, as well as a place to hang out if you're a member. Membership is tax deductible. **🛈 Club Locations Lima** ✉ Calle Piera 135, Miraflores ✎ Mailing address: Casilla 3714, Lima 100, Peru. ☎ 01/445-3306. ✐ limaclub@saexplorers.org **Cusco** ✉ Choquechaca 188, No. 4 ✎ Apartado 500 ☎ 84/245-484. ✐ cuscoclub@saexplorer.org **United States** ✉ 126 Indian Creek Rd., Ithaca, New York 13850 ☎ 607/277-0488, 🖷 607-277-6122, ✐ explorer@samexplo.org.

ECOTOURISM

Ecotourism is loosely defined as tourism that is interesting and entertaining, but also protects the environment and includes and benefits local communities. For Peru, the strong push toward ecotourism is extremely important, as tourism is one of the country's top income producers. But Peru's tourism appeal and very life depend on a successful juggling act—the natural attractions must be kept pristine while at the same time the country and its people must progress and prosper. Keeping the popular Inca Trail to Machu Picchu clean of litter has been a real challenge, but with new, stricter regulations things are looking up. Private companies are also pitching in to help clean up rivers and keep the countryside free of trash in the Sacred Valley of the Incas, so it is not only more attractive for tourists but also a better place for the people who live there. PeruRail, the operator of the south and southeast rail services owned by Orient-Express Hotels Ltd.; its Peruvian partner, Peruval Corp., and Auqui S.R.L, a local travel agency, are now supporting an annual clean-up campaign of the Urubamba River, working with the cooperation of the villagers.

Tour operators within Peru and in other countries promoting ecotourism are finding most travelers to be enthusiastic participants. The movement has been especially strong among companies offering adventure tourism.

ELECTRICITY

To use electric-powered equipment purchased in the U.S. or Canada, **bring a converter and adapter.** The electrical current in Peru is 220 volts, 50 cycles alternating current (AC). An adapter is needed for appliances requiring 110 voltage. U.S.-style flat prongs are used.

If your appliances are dual-voltage, you'll need only an adapter. Don't use 110-volt outlets marked FOR SHAVERS ONLY for high-wattage appliances such as blow-dryers. Most laptops operate equally well on 110 and 220 volts and so require only an adapter.

EMBASSIES & CONSULATES

For additional information on Australian, Canadian, New Zealand, U.K., and U.S. embassies and consulates in Peru, *see* the individual country A to Z section at the end of each chapter.

🛂 Australia Peru ⊠ 40 Brisbane Ave., Barton, ACT 2600 ☎ 02/6273-8752.

🛂 Canada Peru ⊠ 130 Albert St., Suite 1901, Ottawa, Ontario K1P 5G4 ☎ 613/238-1777.

🛂 New Zealand Peru ⊠ 40 Mercer St., Wellington ☎ 04/499-8087.

🛂 United Kingdom Peru ⊠ 52 Sloane St., London SW1X 9SP ☎ 020/7235-1917.

🛂 United States Peru ⊠ 1700 Massachusetts Ave. NW, Washington, DC 20036 ☎ 202/833-9860.

🛂 Embassies in Peru Canada ⊠ F. Gerdes 130, Miraflores Lima ☎ 01/444-4015. New Zealand ⊠ Av. Natalio Sánchez 125, Floor 12, Plaza Washington, Lima ☎ 01/433-4738. United Kingdom ⊠ Edificio El Pacífico, Arequipa, 5th block, Plaza Washington, Lima ☎ 01/433-4738 or 01/433-4839. United States ⊠ Encalada, Cuadra 16, Monterrico, Lima ☎ 01/434-3000.

EMERGENCIES

The fastest way to connect with the police is to dial 105—for fire, dial 116. Lima and other cities have a 24-hr hot line.

The Tourism Police, a body of the National Police of Perú, exists for the security and protection of visitors. Officers are usually found in main commercial areas, hotels, archaeological centers, museums, or any place that is frequently visited by tourists. They usually speak English.

🛂 Hot Lines Arequipa ⊠ Jerusalen 315–A Street. ☎ 054/23-9888. Cajamarca ⊠ Pl. Amalia Puga, ☎ 076/82-3438. Chiclayo ⊠ Av. Saenz Peña N. 830, ☎ 074/22-7615. Cusco ⊠ Av. El Sol, Templo Coricancha, ☎ 084/22-1961. Huaraz ⊠ Plaza de Armas-Municipalidad de Huaraz, ☎ 044/72-1341. Ica ⊠ Av. Arenales, Urb. San Joaquin, ☎ 056/22-4553. Iquitos ⊠ Airport, Col. FAP Francisco

Secada, ☎ 065/23-7067. Lima ⊠ 2465 Javier Prado Este ☎ 02/225-8698. Nazca ⊠ Los Incas, Cuadra 1, ☎ 056/52-2105. Puno ⊠ Jr. Deustua N. 538 ☎ 051/35-7100. Trujillo ⊠ Independencia Cuadra 6–Casa Goicochea, ☎ 044/24-3758.

ENGLISH-LANGUAGE MEDIA

Most major hotels in Lima will carry the international edition of *The Miami Herald* in English. Peru's principal Spanish-language newspapers are *El Comercio*, and *El Sol*. For books, *Epoca* has stores in Miraflores and Lima and *El Virrey* in San Isidro. Ask around for a copy of *Rumbos*, an interesting magazine focusing on travel and culture published twice a month in English and Spanish.

🛂 Resources Epoca ⊠ Av. Comandante Espinar 864, Miraflores ☎ 01/447-8907, ⊠ Jr. Belén 1072, ☎ 01/424-9545, El Virrey ⊠ Miguel Dasso 141, San Isidro, ☎ 01/440-0607

ETIQUETTE & BEHAVIOR

Peru is one of South America's most hospitable nations. Even in the overburdened metropolis of Lima, people are happy to give directions, chat, and ask a question you'll hear a lot in Peru, *De dónde vienes?* (Where are you from?). Peruvians are quite knowledgeable and proud of the history of their country. Don't be surprised if your best source of information isn't your tour guide but your taxi driver.

In the cities women who know each other often greet each other with a single kiss on the cheek, which actually lands in the air—while men shake hands. However, this is not a custom among the conservative Indian population. It was apparently introduced by the Spaniards. Except in small villages, Peruvians really are living in the 21st century with a knowledge of the world. Their customs, except for the kiss on the (one) cheek greeting, do not differ that much from those of towns in the U.S. midwest—never flamboyant and a little on the conservative side. No special "etiquette" is required, just be polite and friendly.

To feel more comfortable, **take a cue from what the locals are wearing.** Except in beach cities, men typically don't wear shorts and women don't wear short skirts. Bathing suits are fine on beaches, but cover up before you head back into town. People dress nicely to enter churches.

GAY & LESBIAN TRAVEL

Gay and lesbian travel can be difficult due to conservative political and religious norms. Homosexual acts are illegal in Peru and public attitudes toward homosexuality are generally negative. Police harassment of gays still occurs.

7 Gay- & Lesbian-Friendly Travel Agencies Different Roads Travel ✉ 8383 Wilshire Blvd., Suite 520, Beverly Hills, CA 90211 ☎ 323/651-5557 or 800/429-8747 (Ext. 14 for both) 🖷 323/651-3678 ✎ lgernert@tzell.com. Kennedy Travel ✉ 130 W. 42nd St., Suite 401, New York, NY 10036 ☎ 212/840-8659, 800/237-7433 🖷 212/730-2269 ⊕ www.kennedytravel.com. Now, Voyager ✉ 4406 18th St., San Francisco, CA 94114 ☎ 415/626-1169 or 800/255-6951 🖷 415/626-8626 ⊕ www.nowvoyager.com. Skylink Travel and Tour ✉ 1455 N. Dutton Ave., Suite A, Santa Rosa, CA 95401 ☎ 707/546-9888 or 800/225-5759 🖷 707/636-0951; serving lesbian travelers.

GAY & LESBIAN WEB SITES

For information about South America's gay scene, check out the Internet. The best site online for general information about gay travel is Out and About (⊕ www.outandabout.com). You can scour though the back issues for information on gay-friendly destinations. You also can try PlanetOut (⊕ www.planetout.com/travel) and Gay.Com (⊕ www.gay.com), two general-interest gay sites.

HEALTH

ALTITUDE SICKNESS

Soroche (altitude sickness) affects most visitors to Cusco, Puno, and other high-altitude cities. Headache, dizziness, nausea, and shortness of breath are common. When you visit areas over 10,000 ft above sea level, take it easy on your first day. Avoid alcohol and drink plenty of liquids. To fight soroche, Peruvians swear by *mate de coca,* a tea made from the leaves of the coca plant.

Soroche may also be a problem when you visit the Andes. Slow down, and spend a few nights at lower elevations before you head higher. If you must fly directly to higher altitudes, plan on doing next to nothing for the first day or two. Drinking plenty of water or coca tea or taking frequent naps may also help. If symptoms persist, return to lower elevations.

If you have high blood pressure or a history of heart trouble, check with your doctor before traveling to such heights as those at Cusco 3,490 m (11,444 ft) and Puno, above 3,660 m (12,000 ft). Most hotels in high-altitude areas have oxygen tanks for emergencies and the Orient Express Ministerio Hotel in Cusco pipes oxygen directly into the room.

DIVERS' ALERT

Do not fly within 24 hours of scuba diving. Neophyte divers should have a complete physical exam before undertaking a dive. If you have travel insurance, **make sure your policy applies to scuba-related injuries,** as not all companies provide this coverage.

FOOD & DRINK

The major health risk in Peru is traveler's diarrhea, caused by eating contaminated fruit or vegetables or drinking contaminated water. So **watch what you eat.** Do not eat anything from pushcart vendors. Avoid ice, uncooked food, and unpasteurized milk and milk products, and **drink only bottled water** or water that has been boiled for several minutes, even when brushing your teeth. Mild cases may respond to Imodium (known generically as loperamide) or Pepto-Bismol, both of which can be purchased over the counter; or Lomotil, also known as paregoric, that can be purchased in Peru without a prescription. Drink plenty of purified water or tea—chamomile (*manzanilla*) is a good folk remedy. In severe cases, rehydrate yourself with a salt-sugar solution (½ teaspoon salt (*sal*) and 4 tablespoons sugar (*azúcar* per quart of water).

The number of cases of cholera has dropped dramatically in recent years, but you should still take care. Even Peruvians tell you to stick to bottled water. Anything raw, including ceviche, should only be eaten only in the better restaurants, or ones that have been recommended. In Lima, you can buy solutions, such as Zonalin, to disinfect fresh fruit and vegetables.

Immunizations can help prevent some types of food- and water-borne diseases, such as for hepatitis A. Check with health authorities about which vaccinations they feel are necessary and which are only recommendations. Other possibilities include vaccinations for typhoid, polio, and tetanus-diphtheria. If you intend to travel in the jungle, you'll need a yellow fever vaccination and malaria prophylactics.

MEDICAL PLANS

No one plans to get sick while traveling, but it happens, so **consider signing up with a medical-assistance company.** Members get doctor referrals, emergency evacuation or repatriation, hot lines for medical consultation, cash for emergencies, and other assistance.

🔢 Medical-Assistance Companies **International SOS Assistance** ⊕ www.internationalsos.com ✉ 8 Neshaminy Interplex, Suite 207, Trevose, PA 19053 ☎ 215/245-4707 or 800/523-6586 🖷 215/244-9617 ✉ Landmark House, Hammersmith Bridge Rd., 6th floor, London, W6 9DP ☎ 20/8762-8008 🖷 20/8748-7744 ✉ 12 Chemin Riantbosson, 1217 Meyrin 1, Geneva, Switzerland ☎ 22/785-6464 🖷 22/785-6424 ✉ 331 N. Bridge Rd., 17-00, Odeon Towers, Singapore 188720 ☎ 6338-7800 🖷 6338-7611.

OVER-THE-COUNTER REMEDIES

Over-the-counter analgesics may curtail soroche symptoms, but consult your doctor before you take these, as well as any other medications you may take regularly. Always carry your own medications with you, including those you would ordinarily take for a simple headache, as you will usually not find the same brands in local pharmacies. However, if you forgot, for a headache, Tonopan is a local brand frequently recommended or try asking for *aspirina.* Use the English word "pharmacy" not "drug store" when inquiring where to go, as it is easily recognized, since the Spanish word is *pharmacia.* Also, try writing down the name of your local medication, because in many cases, the druggist will understand.

PESTS & OTHER HAZARDS

"Don't drink the water " is probably the most-heard precaution when traveling in Peru, and that includes drinks with ice cubes. However, use your own judgement on ice cubes, especially if staying in a well-known or chain hotel. Mosquitos will be encountered in jungle areas, especially at dusk. Take repellent with you, although you may not get through airport screening with a spray, so take a liquid or rub-on; however, repellent is readily available in pharmacies and usually in food stores. Chiggers are sometimes a problem in the jungle or where there are animals. Red, itchy spots suddenly appear, most often *under* your clothes. Not to worry, take clear nail polish (though any color will do) with you and dab it on the spot. It apparently suffocates them.

SHOTS & MEDICATIONS

No vaccines are required to enter Peru, however, it is a good idea to have up-to-date tetanus boosters, and a hepatitis A inoculation can prevent one of the most common intestinal infections. If you're heading to tropical regions, you should get yellow fever shots. Children traveling to Peru should have their vaccinations for childhood diseases up to date.

According to the Centers for Disease Control (CDC) there's a limited risk of cholera, typhoid, malaria, hepatitis B, dengue, and Chagas' disease. While a few of these you could catch anywhere, most are restricted to jungle areas. If you plan to visit remote regions or stay for more than six weeks, **check with the CDC's International Travelers Hot Line.**

In areas with malaria and dengue, both of which are carried by mosquitoes, take mosquito nets, wear clothing that covers the body, apply repellent containing DEET, and use a spray against flying insects in living and sleeping areas. Chloroquine (Aralen) is prescribed as a preventative antimalarial agent; there is no vaccine against dengue.

🔢 Health Warnings **National Centers for Disease Control and Prevention** (CDC) ✉ National Center for Infectious Diseases, Division of Quarantine, Travelers' Health, 1600 Clifton Rd. NE, Atlanta, GA 30333 ☎ 877/394-8747 international travelers' health line, 800/311-3435 other inquiries 🖷 888/232-3299 ⊕ www.cdc.gov/travel.

HOLIDAYS

New Year's Day; Easter holiday, which begins midday on Maundy Thursday and continues through Easter Monday; Labor Day (May 1); St. Peter and St. Paul Day (June 29); Independence Day (July 28); St. Rosa of Lima Day (August 30); Battle of Angamos Day, which commemorates a battle with Chile in the War of the Pacific, 1879–81 (October 8); All Saints' Day (November 1); Immaculate Conception (December 8); Christmas.

INSURANCE

The most useful travel-insurance plan is a comprehensive policy that includes coverage for trip cancellation and interruption, default, trip delay, and medical expenses (with a waiver for preexisting conditions).

Without insurance you'll lose all or most of your money if you cancel your trip, regardless of the reason. Default insurance covers you if your tour operator, airline, or cruise line goes out of business. Trip-delay covers expenses that arise because of bad weather or mechanical delays. Study the fine print when comparing policies.

If you're traveling internationally, a key component of travel insurance is coverage for medical bills incurred if you get sick on the road. Such expenses aren't generally covered by Medicare or private policies. U.K. residents can buy a travel-insurance policy valid for most vacations taken during the year in which it's purchased (but check preexisting-condition coverage). British and Australian citizens need extra medical coverage when traveling overseas. Always **buy travel policies directly from the insurance company**; if you buy them from a cruise line, airline, or tour operator that goes out of business you probably won't be covered for the agency or operator's default, a major risk. Before making any purchase, **review your existing health and home-owner's policies** to find what they cover away from home.

🚹 Travel Insurers In the U.S.: **Access America** ✉ 6600 W. Broad St., Richmond, VA 23230 ☎ 800/284-8300 🖷 804/673-1491 or 800/346-9265 ⊕ www.accessamerica.com. **Travel Guard International** ✉ 1145 Clark St., Stevens Point, WI 54481 ☎ 715/345-0505 or 800/826-1300 🖷 800/955-8785 ⊕ www.travelguard.com.

🚹 In the U.K.: **Association of British Insurers** ✉ 51 Gresham St., London EC2V 7HQ ☎ 020/7600-3333 🖷 020/7696-8999 ⊕ www.abi.org.uk. In Canada: **RBC Insurance** ✉ 6880 Financial Dr., Mississauga, Ontario L5N 7Y5 ☎ 800/565-3129 🖷 905/813-4704 ⊕ www.rbcinsurance.com. In Australia: **Insurance Council of Australia** ✉ Insurance Enquiries and Complaints, Level 3, 56 Pitt St., Sydney, NSW 2000 ☎ 1300/363683 or 02/9251-4456 🖷 02/9251-4453 ⊕ www.iecltd.com.au. In New Zealand: **Insurance Council of New Zealand** ✉ Level 7, 111-115 Customhouse Quay, Box 474, Wellington ☎ 04/472-5230 🖷 04/473-3011 ⊕ www.icnz.org.nz.

INTERNET

E-mail has come to Peru in full force. Even in Puno on Lake Titicaca you can stop in a small shop and send an e-mail message back home for about $2. A bank of computers in Lima's Jorge Chávez International Airport departure area lets you surf the Internet while awaiting a flight. Many hotels have equally inexpensive services for guests.

Internet access is surprisingly widespread. In addition to full-fledged cyber cafés, look for machines set up in phone offices. Rates range from $1 to $10 an hour. Many upscale hotels catering to business travelers offer Internet access to their guests among their amenities. If you're logging on to one of the Web-based e-mail sites, late afternoon is an especially sluggish time because of high usage.

Computer keyboards in South America resemble, but aren't exactly the same as, the ones in English-speaking countries. Your biggest frustration will probably be finding the @ symbol to type an e-mail address. If you need to ask, it's called *arroba* in Spanish and Portuguese.

LANGUAGE

Spanish is Peru's national language, but many indigenous languages also enjoy official status. Many Peruvians claim Quechua, the language of the Inca, as their first language, but most also speak Spanish. Other native languages include the Tiahuanaco language of Aymará, which is spoken around Lake Titicaca, and several languages in the rain forest. Wealthier Peruvians and those who work with tourists often speak English, but they are the exception. If you speak any Spanish at all, by all means use it. Your hosts will appreciate the effort, and any laughter that greets your words will be good-natured rather than mocking.

A word on spelling: since the Inca had no writing system, Quechua developed as an oral language. With European colonization, words and place-names were transcribed to conform to Spanish pronunciations. Eventually, the whole language was transcribed, and in many cases words lost their correct pronunciations. During the past 30 years, however, national pride and a new sensitivity to the country's indigenous roots have led Peruvians to try to recover consistent, linguistically correct transcriptions of Quechua words. As you travel, you may come across different spellings and pronunciations of the same name. An example is the city known as Cusco. The city government uses "Qosqo" as the official spelling, though most Peruvians still use "Cusco."

LANGUAGES FOR TRAVELERS

A phrase book and language-tape set can help get you started. *Fodor's Spanish for*

Travelers (available at bookstores everywhere) is excellent.

LODGING

It's always good to take a look at your
room before accepting it; especially if
you're staying in a budget hotel or hostal.
If it isn't what you expected, you might
have several others from which to choose.
Expense is no guarantee of charm or
cleanliness, and accommodations can
vary dramatically within a single hotel.
Many older hotels in some of the small
towns in Peru have rooms with charming
balconies or spacious terraces; ask if
there's a room *con balcón* or *con terraza*
when checking in.

An unfortunate number of South American hotels have electric-powered heaters
attached to the shower heads, referred to
as a "suicide shower" by some irreverent
budget travelers. In theory, you can adjust
both the temperature and the pressure. In
practice, if you want hot water, you have
to turn the water pressure down very low;
if you want pressure, expect a brisk rinse.
Don't adjust the power when you're under
the water—you can get a little shock.

If you ask for a double room, you'll get a
room for two people, but you're not guaranteed a double mattress. If you'd like to
avoid twin beds, you'll have to **ask for a
cama matrimonial** (no wedding ring seems
to be required).

The lodgings we list are the cream of the
crop in each price category. We always list
the facilities that are available, but we
don't specify whether they cost extra;
when pricing accommodations, always ask
what's included and what costs extra.
Properties are assigned price categories
based on the range between their least and
most expensive standard double room at
high season (excluding holidays) to the
most expensive. Properties marked
✕ are lodging establishments whose
restaurants warrant a special trip.

Assume that hotels operate on the **European Plan** (EP, with no meals) unless we
specify that they use the **Continental Plan**
(CP, with a Continental breakfast), **Modi-
fied American Plan** (MAP, with breakfast
and dinner), or the **Full American Plan**
(FAP, with all meals).

APARTMENT & HOUSE RENTALS

If you want a home base that's roomy
enough for a family and comes with cooking facilities, **consider a furnished rental.**
These can save you money, especially if
you're traveling with a group. Home-exchange directories sometimes list rentals as
well as exchanges.

🏠 International Agents **Hideaways International**
✉ 767 Islington St., Portsmouth, NH 03802 ☎ 603/
430–4433 or 800/843–4433 🖷 603/430–4444
⊕ www.hideaways.com, membership $129. **Villas
International** ✉ 4340 Redwood Hwy., Suite D309,
San Rafael, CA 94903 ☎ 415/499–9490 or 800/221–
2260 🖷 415/499–9491 ⊕ www.villasintl.com.

CAMPING

Peru is conducive to camping, but don't
just grab a tent and take off. Contact a
tour operator that specializes in adventure
tourism and go with a group or at least a
recommended guide. The camping trip between Cusco and Machu Picchu is the most
famous, but its popularity has led the Peruvian government to slap some new regulations on trekkers or risk destroying the
area. The entrance fee is now $50; no more
than 500 hikers a day are permitted on the
trail, and only with a government-autho-
rized guide. An improvement has been the
installation of portable toilets about every
two miles. Sometimes you'll see 20 in a
row. There are still no showers, so you will
arrive in Machu Picchu rather grimy.

A 20-year-old adventure-tour company in
Gainesville, Florida, PeruPeru (➪ Sports
and Outdoors), has an interesting trip that
includes traveling from Cusco to the Manu
BioStation and camping along the way.

HOME EXCHANGES

If you would like to exchange your home
for someone else's, **join a home-exchange
organization,** which will send you its updated listings of available exchanges for a
year and will include your own listing in at
least one of them. It's up to you to make
specific arrangements.

🏠 Exchange Clubs **HomeLink International**
🏠 Box 47747, Tampa, FL 33647 ☎ 813/975–9825 or
800/638–3841 🖷 813/910–8144 ⊕ www.homelink.
org; $110 yearly for a listing, on-line access, and cat-
alog; $40 without catalog.

HOSTELS

No matter what your age, you can **save on
lodging costs by staying at hostels. In**

some 4,500 locations in more than 70 countries around the world, Hostelling International (HI), the umbrella group for a number of national youth-hostel associations, offers single sex, dorm style beds and, at many hostels, rooms for couples and family accommodations. Membership in any HI national hostel association, open to travelers of all ages, allows you to stay in HI-affiliated hostels at member rates; one-year membership is about $28 for adults (C$35 for a two-year minimum membership in Canada, £13.50 in the U.K., A$52 in Australia, and NZ$40 in New Zealand); hostels charge about $10–$30 per night. Members have priority if the hostel is full; they're also eligible for discounts around the world, even on rail and bus travel in some countries.

⏹ Organizations Hostelling International–USA ✉ 8401 Colesville Rd., Suite 600, Silver Spring, MD 20910 ☎ 301/495-1240 🖷 301/495-6697 ⊕ www.hiayh.org. **Hostelling International–Canada** ✉ 400-205 Catherine St., Ottawa, Ontario K2P 1C3 ☎ 613/237-7884 or 800/663-5777 🖷 613/237-7868 ⊕ www.hihostels.ca. **YHA England and Wales** ✉ Trevelyan House, Dimple Rd., Matlock, Derbyshire DE4 3YH, U.K. ☎ 0870/870-8808 🖷 0870/770-6127 ⊕ www.yha.org.uk. **YHA Australia** ✉ 422 Kent St., Sydney, NSW 2001 ☎ 02/9261-1111 🖷 02/9261-1969 ⊕ www.yha.com.au. **YHA New Zealand** ✉ Level 3, 193 Cashel St., Box 436, Christchurch ☎ 03/379-9970 or 0800/278-299 🖷 03/365-4476 ⊕ www.yha.org.nz.

HOTELS

Peru uses a star rating system, and by government decree has established a set list of services that accommodations must possess to be categorized as a *Hotel, Hostal or Motel, Apart Hotel,* or *Lodge or Aubergue.* A hotel can have one to five stars, a hostal one to three, an apart hotel three to five, and a lodge doesn't qualify for any.

Hotels with few stars are not necessarily inferior; they may only be missing an amenity or two that may or may not be important to you. Accommodations in Peru come under many names that do not necessarily have anything to do with the category. An *Inn* or a *Posada* can be at the high end, middle, or low end.

⏹ Toll-Free Numbers Best Western ☎ 800/528-1234 ⊕ www.bestwestern.com. **Choice** ☎ 800/424-6423 ⊕ www.choicehotels.com. **Clarion** ☎ 800/424-6423 ⊕ www.choicehotels.com. **Comfort Inn** ☎ 800/424-6423 ⊕ www.choicehotels.com. **Days Inn** ☎ 800/325-2525 ⊕ www.daysinn.com. **Four Sea-**sons ☎ 800/332-3442 ⊕ www.fourseasons.com. **Hilton** ☎ 800/445-8667 ⊕ www.hilton.com. **Holiday Inn** ☎ 800/465-4329 ⊕ www.sixcontinentshotels.com. **Howard Johnson** ☎ 800/446-4656 ⊕ www.hojo.com. **Hyatt Hotels & Resorts** ☎ 800/233-1234 ⊕ www.hyatt.com. **Inter-Continental** ☎ 800/327-0200 ⊕ www.intercontinental.com. **La Quinta** ☎ 800/531-5900 ⊕ www.laquinta.com. **Marriott** ☎ 800/228-9290 ⊕ www.marriott.com. **Le Meridien** ☎ 800/543-4300 ⊕ www.lemeridien-hotels.com. **Quality Inn** ☎ 800/424-6423 ⊕ www.choicehotels.com. **Radisson** ☎ 800/333-3333 ⊕ www.radisson.com. **Sheraton** ☎ 800/325-3535 ⊕ www.starwood.com/sheraton.

MAIL & SHIPPING

Airmail letters and postcards sent within the Americas cost S/2.70 for less than 20 grams; anything sent from Peru to the United States, Canada, the United Kingdom, Australia, or New Zealand costs S/3.30. Bring packages to the post office unsealed, as you must show the contents to postal workers. Mail service has been steadily improving, and a letter should reach just about anywhere in a week from any of the main cities, but for timely delivery or valuable parcels, use Federal Express, United Parcel, or DHL International.

The main post office (*correo*) in downtown Lima is open Monday–Saturday 8–8 and Sunday 9–1. Hours vary at the branches and in cities and towns outside Lima, but most are closed Sundays.

⏹ Post Offices Jorge Chávez International Airport ☎ 01/575-11434. **Oficina Principal de Correos** ✉ Conde de Superunda 170, Pl. de Armas, Lima ☎ 01/428-6200. **Arequipa** ✉ Moral 118, ☎ 054/21-5247. **Cusco** ✉ Av. El Sol and Garcilaso, ☎ 084/22-3701,. **Iquitos** ✉ Av. Arica 402, ☎ 094/23-1915. **Puno** ✉ Moquegua 269, ☎ 054/35-1141. **Trujillo** ✉ Independencia 286, at Bolognesi. ☎ 044/24-5941.

OVERNIGHT SERVICES

DHL Worldwide and Federal Express are available in Peru; FedEx is represented by Scharff International Courier and Cargo, S.A.

⏹ Couriers DHL Worldwide Express ✉ Los Castaños 225, San Isidro, Lima, ☎ 01/221-2474. **Federal Express** ✉ Av. Elmer Faucett 3350, Callao (Lima airport area), ☎ 01/575-1884.

RECEIVING MAIL

If you don't know where you will be staying in advance, you can have mail sent to you (mark the letters "poste restante") at Correo Central. American Express cardholders can receive mail at the company's Lima office. South American Explorers Club members can receive mail at the club address in Lima; the club will also forward mail for members.

American Express ✉ Belén 1040 ☎ 01/330-4481. **South American Explorers Club** ✉ Calle Piura 135, Miraflores, ☎ 01/445-3306. ✉ Choquechaca 188, No. 4, Cusco, ☎ 084/245-484.

MONEY MATTERS

Prices throughout this guide are given for adults. Substantially reduced fees are almost always available for children, students, and senior citizens. For information on taxes, *see* Taxes.

ATMS

ATMs (*cajeros automáticos*) are widely available, especially in Lima, and you can get cash with a Cirrus- or Plus-linked debit card or with a major credit card.

The bank networks aren't evenly dispersed, so to be on the safe side, carry several cards. Note also that **if your PIN code is more than four digits long it might not work in some countries.** Check with your bank for details. For your card to work on some ATMs, you may need to hit a screen command that roughly translates to "foreign client."

ATM Locations **MasterCard Cirrus** ☎ 800/424-7787 🌐 www.mastercard.com. **Visa Plus** ☎ 800/843-7587 🌐 www.visa.com/atm.

CREDIT CARDS

For costly items, try to **use your credit card whenever possible**—you'll come out ahead, whether the exchange rate at which your purchase is calculated is the one in effect the day the vendor's bank abroad processes the charge or the one prevailing on the day the charge company's service center processes it at home.

Major credit cards, especially Visa, are accepted in most hotels, restaurants, and shops in tourist areas. If you're traveling outside major cities, always check to see whether your hotel accepts credit cards. You may have to bring enough cash to pay the bill. Throughout this guide, the following abbreviations are used: **AE,** American Express; **DC,** Diners Club; **MC,** MasterCard; and **V,** Visa.

If your credit card has been lost or stolen, credit-card company representatives in Peru will usually accept a collect call; dial 108 and ask the operator for a *por cobrar.* Through its Global Customer Assistance system, Visa has a representative on call 24 hours a day; you can request a collect call to one of its help lines.

Before leaving home make copies of the back and front of your credit cards; keep one set of copies with your luggage, the other at home.

Reporting Lost Cards **American Express** ✉ Pardo y Aliaga 698 (Lima Tours) San Isidro ☎ 01/222-2525. **Diners Club** ✉ Canaval y Moreyra 535, San Isidro, ☎ 01/221-2050 or 01/442-6572. **MasterCard** ✉ Av. Paseo de la República 3505 (Banco Latino), Lima ☎ 01/222-4242, 0800-40190 (toll free outside Lima). **Visa** ☎ 410/581-9754, 410/581-0120, 410/581-7931.

CURRENCY

Peru's national currency is the nuevo sol (S/). Bills are issued in denominations of 5, 10, 20, 50, and 100 soles. Coins are 1, 5, 10, 20, and 50 céntimos, and 1, 2, and 5 soles.

At press time, the exchange rate was S/3.45 to the U.S. dollar, S/2.27 to the Canadian dollar, S/4 to the pound sterling, S/.456 to the Australian dollar, and S/1.78 to the New Zealand dollar.

CURRENCY EXCHANGE

You can safely exchange money or cash traveler's checks in a bank, at your hotel, or at *casas de cambio* (exchange houses). The rate for traveler's checks is usually the same as for cash, but many banks have a ceiling on how much they will exchange at one time.

For the most favorable rates, **change money through banks.** Although ATM transaction fees may be higher abroad than at home, ATM rates are excellent because they're based on wholesale rates offered only by major banks. You won't do as well at exchange booths in airports or rail and bus stations, in hotels, in restaurants, or in stores. To avoid lines at airport exchange booths, **get a bit of local currency before you leave home.**

Exchange Services **International Currency Express** ✉ 427 N. Camden Dr., Suite F, Beverly Hills, CA 90210 ☎ 888/278-6628 orders 📠 310/278-6410 🌐 www.foreignmoney.com. **Thomas Cook Currency**

Services ☎ 800/287-7362 orders and retail locations ⊕ www.us.thomascook.com.

TRAVELER'S CHECKS

Do you need traveler's checks? It depends on where you're headed. If you're going to rural areas and small towns, go with cash; traveler's checks are best used in cities. Lost or stolen checks can usually be replaced within 24 hours. To ensure a speedy refund, buy your own traveler's checks—don't let someone else pay for them: irregularities like this can cause delays. The person who bought the checks should make the call to request a refund.

PACKING

If there's a general rule for what to wear in Peru, it's to dress more conservatively than you ordinarily might while vacationing. In the Andean countries avoid wearing short shorts or halter tops. If you're doing business in Peru, you'll need the same attire you would wear in U.S. and European cities: for men, suits and ties; for women, suits for day wear or pants, and for evening, depending on the occasion—do ask your host or hostess—a cocktail dress or just a nice (but not austere) business suit with a dressy blouse.

For sightseeing and leisure, casual clothing and good walking shoes are both desirable and appropriate, and most cities don't require very formal clothes, even for evenings. For beach vacations, you'll need lightweight sportswear, a bathing suit, a sun hat, and lots of sunscreen. Travel in rain-forest areas will require long-sleeve shirts, long pants, socks, sneakers, a hat, a light waterproof jacket, a bathing suit (if you want to swim), and insect repellent. Light colors are best, since mosquitoes avoid them. You can never have too many large resealable plastic bags (bring a whole box), which are ideal for storing film, protecting things from rain and damp, and quarantining stinky socks.

If you're visiting the Andes, bring a jacket and sweater, or plan to acquire one of the hand-knit sweaters or ponchos crowding the marketplaces. Evening temperatures in Cusco are rarely above the 50s.

Please note: While a Swiss Army knife, listed below, is a useful item, it must be put in your checked luggage. If you take a compass, as benign as that may sound, put

it in your carry-on luggage in plain sight or risk being taken off the plane to have your checked baggage inspected. The moving needle apparently can be taken for a ticking time bomb.

Other useful items include a screw-top bottle that you can fill with purified water, a money pouch, a travel flashlight and extra batteries, a Swiss Army knife with a bottle opener, a medical kit, binoculars, and a pocket calculator to help with currency conversions. A sarong or light cotton blanket can have many uses: beach towel, picnic blanket, and cushion for hard seats and, most important, always travel with tissues or a roll of toilet paper as sometimes it's difficult to find in local rest rooms.

In your carry-on luggage, **pack an extra pair of eyeglasses or contact lenses and enough of any medication** you take to last a few days longer than the entire trip. You may also ask your doctor to write a spare prescription using the drug's generic name, as brand names may vary from country to country. In luggage to be checked, **never pack prescription drugs, valuables, or undeveloped film.** And don't forget to carry with you the addresses of offices that handle refunds of lost traveler's checks. Check *Fodor's How to Pack* (available at on-line retailers and bookstores everywhere) for more tips.

To avoid customs and security delays, carry medications in their original packaging. Don't pack any sharp objects in your carry-on luggage, including knives of any size or material, scissors, and corkscrews, or anything else that might arouse suspicion.

To avoid having your checked luggage chosen for hand inspection, don't cram bags full. The U.S. Transportation Security Administration suggests packing shoes on top and placing personal items you don't want touched in clear plastic bags.

CHECKING LUGGAGE

You're allowed to carry aboard one bag and one personal article, such as a purse or a laptop computer. Make sure what you carry on fits under your seat or in the overhead bin. Get to the gate early, so you can board as soon as possible, before the overhead bins fill up.

Baggage allowances vary by carrier, destination, and ticket class. On international flights, you're usually allowed to check two bags weighing up to 70 pounds (32 kilograms) each, although a few airlines allow checked bags of up to 88 pounds (40 kilograms) in first class. Some international carriers don't allow more than 66 pounds (30 kilograms) per bag in business class and 44 pounds (20 kilograms) in economy. On domestic flights, the limit may be 50 pounds (23 kilograms) per bag. Most airlines won't accept bags that weigh more than 100 pounds (45 kilograms) on domestic or international flights. Check baggage restrictions with your carrier before you pack.

Airline liability for baggage is limited to $2,500 per person on flights within the United States. On international flights it amounts to $9.07 per pound or $20 per kilogram for checked baggage (roughly $640 per 70-pound bag) and $400 per passenger for unchecked baggage. You can buy additional coverage at check-in for about $10 per $1,000 of coverage, but it often excludes a rather extensive list of items, shown on your airline ticket.

Before departure, **itemize your bags' contents** and their worth, and label the bags with your name, address, and phone number. (If you use your home address, cover it so potential thieves can't see it readily.) Include a label inside each bag and **pack a copy of your itinerary.** At check-in, **make sure each bag is correctly tagged** with the destination airport's three-letter code. Because some checked bags will be opened for hand inspection, the U.S. Transportation Security Administration recommends that you leave luggage unlocked or use the plastic locks offered at check-in. TSA screeners place an inspection notice inside searched bags, which are re-sealed with a special lock.

If your bag has been searched and contents are missing or damaged, file a claim with the TSA Consumer Response Center as soon as possible. If your bags arrive damaged or fail to arrive at all, file a written report with the airline before leaving the airport.
⨳ Complaints **U.S. Transportation Security Administration Consumer Response Center** ☎ 866/289-9673 ⊕ www.tsa.gov.

PASSPORTS & VISAS

Visitors from the United States, Canada, the United Kingdom, Australia, and New

Zealand require only a valid passport and return ticket to be issued a 60-day visa at their point of entry into Peru.

When traveling internationally, **carry your passport** even if you don't need one (it's always the best form of I.D.) and **make two photocopies of the data page** (one for someone at home and another for you, carried separately from your passport). While sightseeing in Peru it's best to carry the copy of your passport and leave the original hidden in your hotel room or in your hotel's safe; if you're not confident about leaving it behind, store it in a hidden money belt on your person. If you lose your passport, promptly call the nearest embassy or consulate and the local police. Also, never, ever, leave one city in Peru to go to another city (even for just an overnight or two) without carrying your passport with you—in a safe place, of course.

U.S. passport applications for children under age 14 require consent from both parents or legal guardians; both parents must appear together to sign the application. If only one parent appears, he or she must submit a written statement from the other parent authorizing passport issuance for the child. A parent with sole authority must present evidence of it when applying; acceptable documentation includes the child's certified birth certificate listing only the applying parent, a court order specifically permitting this parent's travel with the child, or a death certificate for the non-applying parent. Application forms and instructions are available on the Web site of the U.S. State Department's Bureau of Consular Affairs (⊕ www.travel.state.gov).

PASSPORT OFFICES

The best time to apply for a passport or to renew is in fall and winter. Before any trip, check your passport's expiration date, and, if necessary, renew it as soon as possible.
⨳ Australian Citizens **Passports Australia** ☎ 131-232 ⊕ www.passports.gov.au.
⨳ Canadian Citizens **Passport Office** ✉ to mail in applications: 200 Promenade du Portage, Hull, Québec J8X 4B7 ☎ 819/994-3500 or 800/567-6868 ⊕ www.ppt.gc.ca.
⨳ New Zealand Citizens **New Zealand Passports Office** ☎ 0800/22-5050 or 04/474-8100 ⊕ www.passports.govt.nz.
⨳ U.K. Citizens **U.K. Passport Service** ☎ 0870/521-0410 ⊕ www.passport.gov.uk.

U.S. Citizens National Passport Information Center ☎ 900/225-5674 or 900/225-7778 TTY (calls are 55¢ per minute for automated service or $1.50 per minute for operator service), 888/362-8668 or 888/498-3648 TTY (calls are $5.50 each) ⊕ www.travel.state.gov.

REST ROOMS

In Lima and other cities, your best bet for finding a rest room while on the go is to walk into a large hotel as if you're a guest and find the facilities. The next best thing is talking your way into a restaurant bathroom; buying a drink is a nice gesture if you do. Unless you are in a large, usually chain hotel, don't throw toilet paper into the toilet—use the basket provided—as unsanitary as this may seem. And always carry your own supply of tissues or toilet paper, just in case.

SAFETY

Be street-smart in Peru and trouble generally won't find you. Don't wear a money belt or a waist pack, both of which peg you as a tourist. Distribute your cash and any valuables (including your credit cards and passport) between deep front pockets, inside jacket or vest pockets, and a concealed money pouch. Do not reach for the money pouch once you're in public. If you carry a purse, choose one with a zipper and a thick strap that you can drape across your body; adjust the length so that the purse sits in front of you at or above hip level. Store only enough money in the purse to cover casual spending. If you must carry a camera bag, keep it close to your body; backpacks are best worn on your front. And at all times, avoid wearing flashy jewelry and wristwatches.

Many streets throughout Peru are not well lit, so avoid walking anywhere at night by yourself or even with a friend, and certainly avoid deserted streets, day or night. Always walk "with a purpose" as if you know where you're going, even if you don't—stay alert.

Use only "official" taxis: don't get into a car just because there's a taxi sign in the window, although it may be just a businessman on his way home with the hope of making some extra money. Especially at night, call a taxi from your hotel or restaurant.

Refer to individual chapters for any area-specific precautions.

LOCAL SCAMS

Do not let anyone distract you. Beware of someone "accidentally" spilling food or liquid on you and then offering to help clean it up; the spiller might have an accomplice who's trying to lift your purse or wallet while your guard is down.

TRAVEL ADVISORIES

Peru has had its share of political struggle and drug-related strife, and although the turmoil and crime have abated, research the latest travel warnings and advisories before you go, and before traveling outside the usual tourist circuits once you're there. The United States, Canada, United Kingdom, Australia, and New Zealand all maintain hot lines, fax lines, and Internet sites with this information for their citizens.

Government Advisories U.S. Department of State ✉ Overseas Citizens Services Office, Room 4811, 2201 C St. NW, Washington, DC 20520 ☎ 202/647-5225 interactive hot line or 888/407-4747 ⊕ www.travel.state.gov; enclose a cover letter with your request and a business-size SASE. **Consular Affairs Bureau of Canada** ☎ 800/267-6788 or 613/944-6788 ⊕ www.voyage.gc.ca. **U.K. Foreign and Commonwealth Office** ✉ Travel Advice Unit, Consular Division, Old Admiralty Building, London SW1A 2PA ☎ 020/7008-0232 or 020/7008-0233 ⊕ www.fco.gov.uk/travel. **Australian Department of Foreign Affairs and Trade** ☎ 02/6261-1299 Consular Travel Advice Faxback Service ⊕ www.dfat.gov.au. **New Zealand Ministry of Foreign Affairs and Trade** ☎ 04/439-8000 ⊕ www.mft.govt.nz.

WOMEN IN PERU

Women, especially blondes, can expect some admiring glances and perhaps a comment or two, but outright come-ons or grabbing are rare. Usually all that is necessary is to keep eyes-front and walk down the street. Unless you speak Spanish you won't understand what they're saying anyway. Peruvian men in the cities are used to women in the workforce and are more reserved than men in some other Latin American countries. Outside the cities, men are even more reserved. Just take the same precautions you would at home.

SENIOR-CITIZEN TRAVEL

Peru is a very interesting destination for senior citizens, whether on an independent vacation, an escorted tour, or an adventure trek. Before you leave home, however, determine what medical services your health insurance will cover outside the United States; note that Medicare doesn't provide for payment of hospital and medical services outside the United States. If you need additional travel insurance, buy it (⇨ Insurance, *above*).

Peru is full of good hotels and excellent ground operators who will meet your flights and organize your sightseeing. To qualify for age-related discounts, **mention your senior-citizen status up front** when booking hotel reservations (not when checking out) and before you're seated in restaurants (not when paying the bill). Be sure to have identification on hand. When renting a car, ask about promotional car-rental discounts, which can be cheaper than senior-citizen rates.

Orient Express operates PeruRail, a vastly improved train service to Machu Picchu and Puno. The Rail Travel Center in Putney, Vermont, operates a group train tour. **⛅** Adventure Travel **Overseas Adventure Travel** ✉ Grand Circle Corporation, 625 Mt. Auburn St., Cambridge, MA 02138 ☎ 617/876-0533 or 800/221-0814 🖷 617/876-0826 ⊕ www.oattravel.org. **Rail Travel Center** ✉ 125 Main Putney, Vermont 05346 ☎ 800/458-5394 (U.S./Canada) ⊕ www.railtravelcenter.com.

⛅ Educational Programs **Elderhostel** ✉ 11 Ave. de Lafayette, Boston, MA 02111-1746 ☎ 877/426-8056, 978/323-4141 international callers, 877/426-2167 TTY 🖷 877/426-2166 ⊕ www.elderhostel.org. **Interhostel** ✉ University of New Hampshire, 6 Garrison Ave., Durham, NH 03824 ☎ 603/862-1147 or 800/733-9753 🖷 603/862-1113 ⊕ www.learn.unh.edu. **Folkways Institute** ✉ 14600 S.E. Aldridge Rd., Portland, OR 97236-6518 ☎ 503/658-6600 or 800/225-4666 🖷 503/658-8672 ⊕ www.folkwaysinstitute.org.

SHOPPING

Perhaps the biggest bargains in Peru are hand-knitted alpaca sweaters, shawls, and textiles made from alpaca or vicuña wool. Llamas are the pack animals and their wool is often too coarse for fine garments. And if you're looking for art, it isn't unusual to see paintings for sale lining sidewalks, parks, or hotel lobbies. Some of the more interesting portraits are of faces—of Indian children and elderly men and women. Upscale shops selling jewelry, silverware, pottery, handicrafts, and clothing are plentiful in Lima's Miraflores district.

In Cusco, the San Blas area near the Main Square is the art center, where many craftsmen have settled. Here on the cobblestone streets you can find it all—sculptures, wood carvings, silver work, masks, and religious art.

KEY DESTINATIONS

One of the best artisan markets for prices, quantity, and quality is Feria Artesanal (Artisans Market) in the Lima suburb of Pueblo Libre, about 8 km (5 mi) northwest of Miraflores at Avenida La Marina 998. Market stalls have alpaca-wool sweaters, rugs, weavings, Indian masks, jewelry, wood carvings, paintings, and mirrors with intricately designed gilt frames that only look heavy (a typical Peruvian craft); a 61 by 43 cm (24 by 17 in) frame might take four days to make and sells for around US$35. Another good artisan market is in Miraflores at Petit Thouars 5321, called Mercado Indio. There are 100 stalls with handcrafted goods from all over Peru, open 9–9 daily.

The best prices on hand-knit alpaca wool sweaters are at the street market near the train station in Puno and at Artesanias Puno on Calle Lima 549. There is usually an Indian woman sitting in a corner of the shop knitting away. If you are in the Amazon town of Iquitos, look for artisan shops along the waterfront selling Shipibo pottery and hand-painted cloth from Pucallpa, a small town upriver from Iquitos on the Ucayali river.

WATCH OUT

To discourage the killing of exotic animals for their feathers or as stuffed souvenirs, the export of any live or any part of a live or dead endangered species (including feathers) is against the law. And unless you have a permit from Inrena, the state natural resources entity, you cannot bring out live animals or birds. There are no restrictions on bringing home the dead piranha souvenirs sold in gift shops in Iquitos, as that ferocious little fish isn't endangered; you cannot, however, bring live ones into your own country. Nothing of archaeological value may be taken out of Peru.

SIGHTSEEING GUIDES

Unless you have already charted your course and know exactly where you're going and what you want to see, sign up for a city tour, either at the travel desk in your hotel or with a local travel agency. The agencies are not difficult to find; they will usually have signs in the window listing their tour offerings. Many major sites, especially museums, have English-speaking guides at the entrance who will take you around. They work for tips. It is prudent not to hire a guide who approaches you on the street.

SPORTS & OUTDOORS

Peru is not big on spectator sports, but its spectacular outdoor adventures pack appeal for both the tame and the extreme. The best time for most adventure sports is between May and December.

RAFTING

There are tame rafting trips on the Urubamba River (year-round) near Cusco or extreme Class IV, V, and VI rafting adventures through the Colca Canyon (May through Sept.) near Arequipa operated by Apumayo Expediciones Peru.

🛈 Rafting Resources **Apumayo Expediciones Peru** ✉ Garcilazo 265, Int. 3, Cusco ☎🖷 084/ 24-6018, ⊕ www.apumayo.com, ✑ apumayo@hotmail.com.

MOUNTAIN CLIMBING

Wilderness Travel leads mountain climbers up the Cordillera Blanca Range, where you'll find Peru's highest peak, the Huascarán at 6,772 m (22,204 ft). For a tamer adventurer, Wilderness has a Peru Llama Trek that follows an off-Inca trail route to Machu Picchu where llamas carry your gear and you have the trail to yourself until near the end.

🛈 Mountain Climbing Resources **Wilderness Travel** ✉ 1102 Ninth St., Berkeley, Ca., 94710. ☎ 800-368-2794, ⊕ www.wildernesstravel.com.

SURFING

With Surf Express, surfers ride with some of the best left-breaking waves in the world, such as at Punta Rocas south of Lima or Cabo Blanco north of Trujillo. Surfing is good all year in Peru.

🛈 Surfing Resources **Surf Express** ✉ 568 Highway A1A, Satellite Beach, Florida, 32937 ☎ 321-779-2174, 🖷 321-779-0652, ⊕ www.surfex.com.

CAMPING

PeruPeru runs camping trips for birders and wilderness enthusiasts in the National Park Tourist Reserve in Manu National Park, with screened, hermetically sealed walk-in tents, hinged, lockable doors, and solid wooden floors. This is luxury tenting.

🛈 Camping Resources **PeruPeru (World Class Travel)** ✉ 808 N.W. 13th, Gainesville, Florida, 32601, ☎ 800-771-3100, ⊕ peruperu.com, ✑ info@peruperu.com.

EXPLORING

Adventure Specialists and Chachapoyas Tours lead explorations of the Chachapoyas, Kuelap, and Gran-Vilaya ruins northeast of Trujillo

🛈 Exploring Resources **Adventure Specialists** 🏠 Bear Basin Ranch Copper Canyon, Colorado ☎ 719/783-2076 (summer) 🖷 719-783-2076, 🖷🖷 719/630-7687. ⊕ www.adventurespecialists. org ✑ discovery@adventurspec.com. **Chachapoyas Tours** 🏠 1805 Swann Av., Orlando, Florida, 32809, ☎ 800-743-0995, ⊕ www.kuelap.org, ✑ info@kuelap.org ✉ Jr. Grau 534, Main Plaza Chachapoyas ☎ 044/77-8078.

STUDENTS IN PERU

Although airfares to and within the continent are high, you can take buses to most destinations in Peru for mere dollars, and you can usually find safe, comfortable (if sparse), affordable hostals, small hotels, and other accommodations for a fraction of what it might cost back home. All students should procure an international student ID card and should consider joining the South American Explorers Club (⇨ Discounts and Deals).

🛈 I.D.s & Services **STA Travel** ✉ 10 Downing St., New York, NY 10014 ☎ 212/627-3111 or 800/777-0112 🖷 212/627-3387 ⊕ www.sta.com. **Travel Cuts** ✉ 187 College St., Toronto, Ontario M5T 1P7, Canada ☎ 416/979-2406, 800/592-2887, 866/246-9762 in Canada 🖷 416/979-8167 ⊕ www.travelcuts.com.

TAXES

Peru's economy has stabilized after the chaos of the 1980s and '90s. Although the basics are reasonably cheap, anything that might loosely be called a luxury tends to be expensive. An 18% sales tax, known as *impuesto general a las ventas*, is levied on everything except goods bought at open-air markets and from street vendors. It is usually included in the advertised price of merchandise and should be included with food and drink.

Restaurants have been ordered to publish their prices—including taxes and a 10% service charge that is sometimes added on—but they do not always do so. They are also prone to levy a cover charge for anything from live entertainment to serving you a roll with your meal. It is best to check before you order. Hotel bills may also have taxes and a 10% service charge added on.

Airport taxes are $28 for international and $5 for domestic flights.

TELEPHONES

For numbers anywhere in Peru, dial "103" for Telefónica del Perú. For assistance from an international operator to place a call, dial "108" or place your call through your hotel's front desk, which is usually more expensive. To place a direct call, dial "00" followed by the country and city codes.

COUNTRY & AREA CODES

To call Peru direct, dial 011 followed by the country code of 51, then the city code, then the number of the party you are calling. (When dialing a number from abroad, drop the initial 0 from the local area code.)

INTERNATIONAL CALLS

For international calls you should dial 00, then 1 for the United States and Canada or 44 for the United Kingdom. To make an operator-assisted international call, dial 108.

LOCAL CALLS

Telefónica del Peru, the country's newly privatized telephone company, has invested a hefty sum in Peru's phone system. New, "intelligent" pay phones require a coin or phone card instead of the old token system. Unless you're making many calls, using coins is much easier than purchasing cards.

LONG-DISTANCE SERVICES

To call another region within the country, first dial 0 and then the area code. Long-distance calls are easy to make from Lima and the coast, more difficult in the highlands, and sometimes impossible in the jungle. Hotels add hefty surcharges to long-distance calls made from rooms, so you may want to call from a pay phone.

AT&T, MCI, and Sprint access codes make calling long-distance relatively convenient,

but you may find the local access number blocked in many hotel rooms. First ask the hotel operator to connect you. If the hotel operator balks, ask for an international operator, or dial the international operator yourself. One way to improve your odds of getting connected to your long-distance carrier is to travel with more than one company's calling card (a hotel may block Sprint, for example, but not MCI). If all else fails, call from a pay phone. To reach an AT&T operator, dial 171. For MCI, dial 190. For Sprint, dial 176.

☎ Access Codes **AT&T Direct** ☎ 800/225-5288. **MCI WorldPhone** ☎ 800/444-4444. **Sprint International Access** ☎ 800/793-1153.

TIME

Peru shares the Eastern Standard Time zone with New York and Miami when the U.S. East Coast is not on Daylight Savings Time. For example, when it is 12 noon in Lima it will be 11 AM in Dallas and Houston; 9 AM in Los Angeles, and in Sydney, 3 AM the following day.

TIPPING

A 10% tip is sufficient in most restaurants unless the service has been exceptional. Porters in hotels and airports expect S/2–S/3 per bag. There is no need to tip taxi drivers. At bars, tip 20 céntimos–50 céntimos for a beer, more for a mixed drink. Bathroom attendants get 20 céntimos; gas station attendants get 50 céntimos for extra services such as adding air to your tires. Tour guides and tour bus drivers should get S/5–S/10 each per day.

TOURS & PACKAGES

Because everything is prearranged on a prepackaged tour or independent vacation, you spend less time planning—and often get it all at a good price.

BOOKING WITH AN AGENT

Travel agents are excellent resources. But it's a good idea to collect brochures from several agencies, as some agents' suggestions may be influenced by relationships with tour and package firms that reward them for volume sales. If you have a special interest, **find an agent with expertise in that area**; the American Society of Travel Agents (ASTA; ⇨ Travel Agencies) has a database of specialists worldwide.

Make sure your travel agent knows the accommodations and other services of the place being recommended. Ask about the hotel's location, room size, beds, and whether it has a pool, room service, or programs for children, if you care about these. Has your agent been there in person or sent others whom you can contact?

Do some homework on your own, too: local tourism boards can provide information about lesser-known and small-niche operators, some of which may sell only direct.

BUYER BEWARE

Each year consumers are stranded or lose their money when tour operators—even large ones with excellent reputations—go out of business. So **check out the operator.** Ask several travel agents about its reputation, and try to **book with a company that has a consumer-protection program.** (Look for information in the company's brochure.) In the United States, members of the National Tour Association and the United States Tour Operators Association are required to set aside funds to cover payments and travel arrangements in the event that the company defaults. It's also a good idea to choose a company that participates in the American Society of Travel Agents' Tour Operator Program; ASTA will act as mediator in any disputes between you and your tour operator.

Remember that the more your package or tour includes, the better you can predict the ultimate cost of your vacation. Make sure you know exactly what is covered, and **beware of hidden costs.** Are taxes, tips, and transfers included? Entertainment and excursions? These can add up.

¶ Tour-Operator Recommendations **American Society of Travel Agents** (⇨ Travel Agencies). **National Tour Association (NTA)** ✉ 546 E. Main St., Lexington, KY 40508 ☎ 859/226-4444 or 800/682-8886 🖷 859/226-4404 ⊕ www.ntaonline.com. **United States Tour Operators Association** (USTOA) ✉ 275 Madison Ave., Suite 2014, New York, NY 10016 ☎ 212/599-6599 or 800/468-7862 🖷 212/599-6744 ⊕ www.ustoa.com.

TRAIN TRAVEL

Peru's rail system is called PeruRail, and is operated by Orient-Express Hotels Ltd., the same company that runs one of the most luxurious and famous trains in the world, the Venice Simplon Orient Express

between London and Venice. Its Peruvian partner is Peruval Corporation. Since the company took over in 1999 it has been making constant improvements. First-class cars have been added to most trains, with dining services, improved washroom facilities, and observation cars for unhindered viewing of the passing landscape. The improved train service is between Cusco and Machu Picchu and Cusco, Juliaca, and Puno on Lake Titicaca. The line between Puno and Arequipa is operated for charters or groups only. Tickets can be purchased either at train stations or through travel agencies, but during holidays or high season it is best to get your tickets in advance.

PeruRail is also continuing to operate two local trains a day between Cusco and Machu Picchu, as it is the only means of transportation for the local residents.

Round-trip fare on the Vistadome Service between Cusco and Machu Picchu is US$86 plus tax and for the Backpacker, US$58 plus tax. Rates one-way on the "Andean Explorer" (Cusco-Lake Titicaca (Juliaca-Puno) route are US$81 plus tax for First Class, including lunch and US$14 plus tax for Tourist/Backpacker service. Taxes fluctuate, but add around 28% total.

CLASSES

PeruRail operates four classes between Cusco and Machu Picchu for the 3-hr 25-min trip; the local, the backpacker, Vistadome and, introduced in 2003, the "Hiriam Bingham," the most deluxe service, with four carriages, two dining cars, a bar car with observation deck, and a kitchen car. It carries 84 passengers.

The "Hiram Bingham" departs from Cusco later in the morning and leaves Machu Picchu at 7 PM, allowing day-trippers more time to enjoy the ruins without the crowds. Brunch is served enroute to Machu Picchu, and on the return, dinner is offered from a five course à la carte menu.

¶ Train Information **Estación San Pedro (Cusco-Machu Picchu)** ✉ Cascaparo s/n, near the Mercado Central (Central Market) ☎ 084/23-5201 or 004/22 1352. **Estación Wanchaq (Cusco-Juliaca-Puno)** ✉ Av. Pachacutec 503 ☎ 084/23-8722 or 084/221-992. 🖷 084/221-114.

PAYING

Credit cards, especially AE, DC, MC, and V, are acceptable forms of payment as are U.S. dollars. Other foreign currency may be hard to use or exchange except in banks in Lima. Traveler's checks are not readily accepted, especially outside of Lima.

RESERVATIONS

Reserve and purchase your ticket as far ahead as possible, especially during holidays or festival times. Reservations can be made directly with PeruRail through their Web site, or through a travel agency or tour operator at home or in Peru. **PeruRail Reservations** ⊠ Wanchaq Station, Av. Pachacutec s/n, Cusco. ⊕ www.perurail.com ✎ reservas@perurail.com.

TRANSPORTATION AROUND PERU

The great distance and difficult terrain between towns and tourist attractions in Peru are drawbacks to surface travel, even though there is good bus service. Flying is the better alternative, in addition to being a time saver. Also, it is not advisable to travel on Peru's roads at night, especially if you are driving alone. Consider buying a package that at least includes accommodations and airport transfers.

Having someone meet you at the airport when you arrive to fend off the overly eager taxi drivers is a great comfort. If you are "doing it yourself," before exiting the airport there is an official taxi desk where you can pay for a taxi and be escorted out to the car. It may cost a little more, US$20–US$25, but it is worth it.

TRAVEL AGENCIES

A good travel agent puts your needs first. Look for an agency that has been in business at least five years, emphasizes customer service, and has someone on staff who specializes in your destination. In addition, **make sure the agency belongs to a professional trade organization.** The American Society of Travel Agents (ASTA)—the largest and most influential in the field with more than 20,000 members in some 140 countries—maintains and enforces a strict code of ethics and will step in to help mediate any agent-client disputes involving ASTA members if necessary. ASTA (whose motto is "Without a travel agent, you're on your own") also maintains a Web site that includes a directory of agents. (If a travel agency is also acting as your tour operator, *see* Buyer Beware *in* Tours and Packages.)

Local Agent Referrals American Society of Travel Agents (ASTA) ⊠ 1101 King St., Suite 200, Alexandria, VA 22314 ☎ 703/739–2782 or 800/965–2782 24-hr hot line 🖷 703/739–3268 ⊕ www. astanet.com. **Association of British Travel Agents** ⊠ 68–71 Newman St., London W1T 3AH ☎ 020/7637–2444 🖷 020/7637–0713 ⊕ www.abtanet.com. **Association of Canadian Travel Agents** ⊠ 130 Albert St., Suite 1705, Ottawa, Ontario K1P 5G4 ☎ 613/237–3657 🖷 613/237–7052 ⊕ www.acta.ca. **Australian Federation of Travel Agents** ⊠ Level 3, 309 Pitt St., Sydney, NSW 2000 ☎ 02/9264–3299 🖷 02/9264–1085 ⊕ www.afta.com.au. **Travel Agents' Association of New Zealand** ⊠ Level 5, Tourism and Travel House, 79 Boulcott St., Box 1888, Wellington 6001 ☎ 04/499–0104 🖷 04/499–0786 ⊕ www. taanz.org.nz.

VISITOR INFORMATION

Learn more about foreign destinations by checking government-issued travel advisories and country information. For a broader picture, consider information from more than one country.

Peru no longer has tourist offices in other countries. **PromPeru** (Comisión de Promoción del Peru) is Peru's official tourism information agency in Lima and it has an information Web site in English and Spanish, ⊕ www.peru.org.pe.

See the A to Z sections at the end of each chapter for area-specific visitor information.

WEB SITES

Do check out the World Wide Web when planning your trip. You'll find everything from weather forecasts to virtual tours of famous cities. Be sure to **visit Fodors.com** (⊕ www.fodors.com), a complete travel-planning site. You can research prices and book plane tickets, hotel rooms, rental cars, vacation packages, and more. In addition, you can post your pressing questions in the Travel Talk section. Other planning tools include a currency converter and weather reports, and there are loads of links to travel resources.

Another Web site to try is the Latin American Network Information Center at the University of Texas, with country-specific sections and exhaustive links to tourism, history, culture, business, and academic sites, ⊕ www.lanic.utexas.edu.

LIMA

1

FODOR'S CHOICE

Astrid y Gaston, *continental fare in Miraflores*

Country Club Lima Hotel, *San Isidro*

El Cartujo, *fine fish and wine in San Isidro*

Gran Hotel Bolívar, *El Centro*

Hotel Antigua Miraflores, *Miraflores*

Huaca Pucllana, *temple in Miraflores*

Iglesia de San Francisco, *El Centro*

L'eau Vive, French cuisine, *El Centro*

La Castellana, *hotel in Miraflores*

Museo Arqueológico Rafael Larco Herrera, *Pueblo Libre*

Museo Pedro de Osma, *Barranco*

HIGHLY RECOMMENDED

RESTAURANTS   Bircher-Benner, *Miraflores*

Las Mesitas, *Barranco*

Lima de Antaño, *El Centro*

HOTELS   Hotel San Blas, *San Isidro*

Sonesta Posada del Inca El Olívar, *San Isidro*

SIGHTS   Plaza de Armas, *El Centro*

Puente de los Suspiros, *Barranco*

NIGHTLIFE   Downtown Todo Vale, *Miraflores*

Kafé Kitsch, *Barranco*

Updated by
Mark Sullivan

IT WON'T BE LOVE AT FIRST SIGHT when you are introduced to Lima. Peru's capital—clogged with traffic and choked with fumes—doesn't make a very good first impression. But spend a few days wandering around the regal edifices surrounding the Plaza de Armas, among the gnarled olive trees of San Isidro, or along the winding lanes in the coastal community of Barranco and you might find yourself charmed.

After two unsuccessful attempts, Francisco Pizarro finally found the perfect place for the capital of Spain's colonial empire in 1535. On a natural port, the so-called "Ciudad de los Reyes" was the perfect place from which to ship home all the gold the conquistador plundered from the Inca. Lima served as the capital of Spain's South American empire for 300 years, and it is safe to say that no other colonial city enjoyed such power and prestige during this period.

When Peru declared its independence from Spain in 1821, the declaration was read in the square that Pizarro had so carefully designed. Many of the colonial-era buildings around the Plaza de Armas can still be seen today. Walk a few blocks in any direction to find graceful churches and elegant houses that reveal just how wealthy this city once was.

But liberated from its chains, Lima soon had growing pains. The walls that once surrounded the city were demolished in 1870, making way for unprecedented growth. A former hacienda became the graceful residential neighborhood of San Isidro. In the early 1920s, with the construction of tree-lined Avenida Arequipa, people pushed farther south to neighborhoods like bustling Miraflores and bohemian Barranco.

Lima continues to grow, which causes city officials to shake their heads in frustration. Almost a third of the country's population of 8 million now lives here, many of them in poverty-stricken *pueblos jóvenes* on the outskirts of town. Many residents of these "new towns" come from mountain villages, desperate for any kind of work. The lack of jobs led to a dramatic increase in crime during the '80s and '90s.

Things have improved since those depressing days. Residents who used to steer clear of the historic center now stroll along its streets. And many travelers who once would have avoided the city altogether now plan to spend a day here and end up staying two or three. Not surprising, after all, since Lima has the country's finest museums, swankiest shops, and most dazzling restaurants. It turns out that there really is a reason to fall in love with Lima.

Exploring Lima

Most of Lima's colonial-era churches and mansions are found in the historic center, along the streets surrounding the Plaza de Armas. From El Centro, a highway called Paseo de la República whisks you south to residential areas like San Isidro, Miraflores, and Barranco. The charms of these neighborhoods are simpler—a tree-lined park, a bluff overlooking the sea, a wooden bridge filled with young couples.

Museums are more difficult to reach, as they are scattered around the city. Pueblo Libre, a neighborhood west of San Isidro, has two of the best, the Museo Arqueológico Rafael Larco Herrera and the Museo Nacional de Antropología, Arqueología, e Historia del Perú. In the other direction from San Isidro is the Museo de la Nación, in the residential area of San Borja. Monterrico, east of Miraflores, is the site of Lima's most popular museum, the glittering Museo de Oro.

Spend at least a day touring the sights in the historic center, with an additional day devoted to whichever museums strike your fancy. Bargain

Numbers in the text correspond to numbers in the margin and on the Lima, Centro, Miraflores, San Isidro, and Barranco maps.

If you have 1 day

If you have just a day—or even less—in the capital, focus on the historic center. Start in the vast **Plaza de Armas,** 1 the square where the city was founded and the call for independence was made. If you made arrangements in advance, you can view the imperial splendor of the **Palacio de Gobierno** 2. Afterwards duck into the **Catedral** 4, where the city's founder, Francisco Pizarro, is buried. More than 75,000 people are buried in the catacombs below the nearby **Iglesia de San Francisco** 6. Take a guided tour to wander through the dusty vaults. After lunch, visit the **Museo de la Inquisición** 7, which chronicles the efforts of the Spanish to root out heretics.

If you have 3 days

If you have three days, spend your first day in the historic center. On your second morning head to the neighborhood of Pueblo Libre to bone up on Peruvian history with a visit to the **Museo Arqueológico Rafael Larco Herrera** 40 and the **Museo Nacional de Antropología, Arqueología, e Historia del Perú** 39. Pick up some sandwiches and a bottle of wine for lunch in **Parque El Olívar** 27, a former olive grove in the heart of San Isidro. In the afternoon explore the nearby temple of **Huaca Huallamarca** 28, built hundreds of years before the arrival of the Inca. On day three head to Miraflores, where you can spend most of the morning shopping. Stroll down Avenida José Larco to **Parque del Amor** 33, where you just might see paragliders sailing through the sky. In the afternoon head to Barranco, where the **Museo Pedro de Osma** 37 displays a matchless collection of colonial-era religious art. Don't miss a stroll across the **Puente de los Suspiros** 38, a wooden bridge favored by cooing couples.

If you have 4 days

If you're lucky enough to have more time in Lima, follow the above itinerary for the first three days. On day four, drive south of the city to **Pachacámac,** the area's most impressive archaeological site. If that's not your thing, consider a lazy day on the beach at the fishing village of **Pucusana.**

---

hunters should do some window-shopping in Miraflores. Take one evening to wander through laid-back Barranco, at one time a seaside retreat for wealthy *Limeños*. The café scene here is lively, attracting artists and those who would like to be.

Timing

If you visit Lima between December and March, chances are good that you'll see some sunny days. Otherwise you'll encounter the thick, dank fog called *garúa* that blankets the city day and night. The good news is that this coastal region never gets very much rain.

El Centro

When Francisco Pizarro sketched out his plans for the "City of Kings" in 1535, he drew an area that would forever define the capital. Although the official boundaries have pushed outward over the years, most of residents still consider these narrow streets to be the city proper. When you ask someone from a far-flung neighborhood like Miraflores or San

Isidro where you might find the Plaza de Armas, they will undoubtedly tell you "Lima."

This was more than a capital—it was the seat of power for the viceroyalty of Peru. It held sway over a swath of land that extended from Panama to Chile. With power came money, as is evident by the grand scale on which everything was built. The finely carved doorways of many private homes reach two or three stories high. And there are at least half a dozen churches that in any other city would be called cathedrals.

But history has not always been so kind to this neighborhood. Earthquakes struck in 1687 and 1746, leveling many of the buildings surrounding the Plaza de Armas. Many other landmarks, such as the Iglesia de San Augustín, were nearly destroyed by artillery fire in the numerous skirmishes that have plagued the capital, and many other buildings have suffered from neglect. It is heartbreaking to see a stone wall on a colonial-era building buckling, or an intricately carved balcony that is beyond repair. But the city government has devoted quite a bit of effort to restoring its historic center. After years of decline, things are slowly changing for the better.

Numbers in the text correspond to numbers in the margin and on the El Centro and Rímac map.

a good
walk

Almost all Lima's most interesting historic sites are within walking distance of the **Plaza de Armas** ❶ ▶, one of the grandest central squares in all South America. The lovely fountain in the center can be used as a slightly off-center compass. The trumpet of the bronze angel points due north, where you'll see the **Palacio de Gobierno** ❷. To the west is the neo-colonial **Municipalidad de Lima** ❸, while the **Catedral** ❹ and the adjoining Palacio Episcopal are to the east. Head north on Jirón Carabaya, the street running beside the Palacio de Gobierno, until you reach the butter-yellow **Estación de Desamparados** ❺, the municipal train station. Follow the street as it curves to the east. In a block you'll reach the **Iglesia de San Francisco** ❻, the most spectacular of the city's colonial-era churches. Plan to send some time here, as you'll want to explore the catacombs.

Follow Jirón Ancash one block east to reach Avenida Abancay, a major thoroughfare. One block south you'll see the imposing structure that corrals the country's congress. On the street that runs along the southern edge is the **Museo de la Inquisición** ❼, where you can explore one of the more gruesome aspects of the country's history. Head two blocks south to Jirón Ucayali, where a block west is the rather plain exterior of the **Iglesia de San Pedro** ❽. Just beyond, marvel at the facades of two of the city's finest private homes, **Casa Goyeneche** ❾ and **Casa Torre Tagle** ❿. There are two other stunning residences within a few blocks of the Plaza de Armas. **Casa Aliaga** ⓫ is a block north of the square on Jirón de la Union, which runs along the western side of the Palacio de Gobierno. **Casa Riva-Agüero** ⓬ is on Jirón Camaná, one block west and two blocks south of the square.

If you can't get enough of colonial-era churches, a cluster can be found south and west of the Plaza de Armas. From the Plaza de Armas, head one block west past the **Correo Central** ⓭ to the **Convento de Santo Domingo** ⓮, with the tomb of San Martín de Porras. Continue three blocks west to the **Santuario de Santa Rosa de Lima** ⓯, where locals pray to South America's first saint. Head south along bustling Avenida Tacna to the imposing **Iglesia de las Nazarenas** ⓰. From here, head four blocks east on Jirón Huancavelica to the **Iglesia de la Merced** ⓱. Walk a block west to Jirón Camaná, then two blocks south to the **Iglesia de Jesús, María y José** ⓲.

Archaeological Treasures Most people come to Peru to see the stone fortress of Machu Picchu, but few are aware that in and around the capital are more than 30 archaeological digs. Several of these excavations are well worth visiting. In the neighborhood of Miraflores, a pre-Inca temple called Huaca Pucllana soars above the nearby apartment buildings. In San Isidro is another temple called Huaca Huallamarca. Constructed entirely of mud bricks, these fragile structures have survived 1,500 years of wind and rain. The region's most impressive site, however, is a short drive south of the city. Pachacámac was begun nearly 2,000 years ago, and its plazas, pyramids, and palaces are worthy of a city with such a long history.

1

Colonial Charm Earthquakes and other natural disasters have devastated this city, sometimes leveling entire neighborhoods. Much of what you see in the historic center has had to be rebuilt time and time again. But the streets surrounding the Plaza de Armas are full of buildings dating back to the time when this was the most important city on the continent. Impossible to miss are the churches, many of which were built in the 16th and 17th centuries. Especially noteworthy is the Iglesia de San Francisco, whose facade is considered the height of the "Lima Baroque" style of architecture. On many streets you'll still see mansions that belonged to the city's upper classes. Look for the elegant enclosed balconies, all carved by hand. A few of these homes, such as Casa Goyeneche and Casa Torre Tagle, have been lovingly restored. Many others are still waiting to be returned to their original splendor.

Heart & Sole Lima gazes down at the ocean, so it should be no surprise that fish figures prominently on almost every menu. You won't be here long before encountering *cebiche,* an incredible dish in which chunks of raw fish or shellfish are marinated in lemon juice and covered with onions. It will undoubtedly be accompanied by fried kernels of corn called *canchas.* There's plenty of other fish on the menu, although most common are *corvina* (sea bass) and *lenguado* (sole). The manner in which it is prepared—fried, steamed, or with some succulent sauce—is up to you.

But the capital's restaurants don't forget the cuisine found in the rest of the country. The more creative chefs put a new spin on old recipes in a style of cooking called *novo andino.* Hearty dishes that once sustained farmers living far up in the Andes have become more heart-healthy. Gone are the thick sauces and the piles of potatoes. The result is much more palatable for nine-to-fivers in a hot coastal city.

It would be a shame to leave Lima without stepping into a *chifa,* one of the hundreds of restaurants serving Chinese food with a Peruvian flair. Use of local ingredients such as the *ají,* a thin pepper used in many Peruvian dishes, gives familiar dishes a distinctive taste. This exchange works both ways, of course. Peruvian standbys such as *lomo saltado* (beef stir-fried with onions and peppers) now often include soy sauce.

Aeropuerto Internacional Jorge Chavéz

CALLAO

Río Rímac

CARMEN DE LA LEGUA REYNOSO

Av. Perú

Av. Caquetá

N. Dueñas

Colonial

Av. República de Argentina

Zorritos

Av. Colonial

Ugarte

BELLAVISTA

Ciudad Universitaria

Av. Arica

Av. Elmer Faucett

Av. República de Venezuela

BREÑA

Av. Riva Agüero

Parque las Leyendas

Universitaria Católica del Peru

Av. Tingo Maria

LA PERLA

Av. de la Marina

Av. Bolívar

PUEBLO LIBRE

Av. Brasil

SAN MIGUEL

Av. Universitaria

40

JESÚS MARIA

Av. la Paz

His

39

Museo de la República

Av. Sucre

Av. Salaverry

Av. Sanchez Carrión

Playa Mar Bella

MAGDALENA

Av. Javier

Prad

S ISI

Campo de Golf

27 - 29 see detail map

Playa los Delfines

San Isidro

S

PACIFIC OCEAN

Playa la Pampilla

Av. Jo

M FLO

Playa Makah

Pl Es

E

Lima

0 ————— 1 mile

0 ————— 1 km

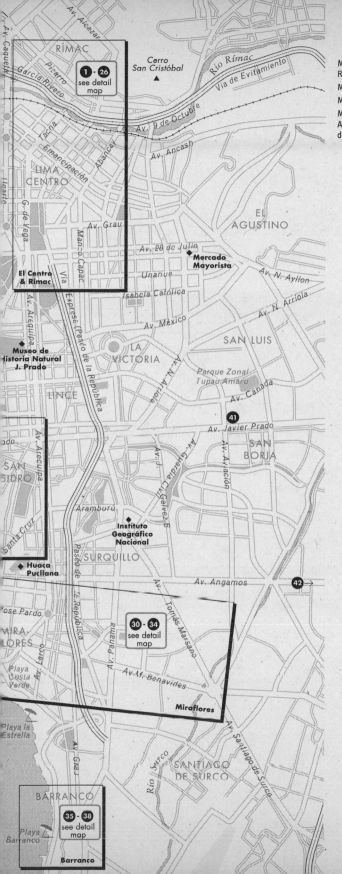

RÍMAC

1 - **26**
see detail map

Cerro
San Cristóbal ▲

Río Rímac

Vía de Evitamiento

Av. Alcazar

Pizarro

García Rivero

Av. Caquelpi

Av.

Tacna

Emancipación

Abancay

Av. 9 de Octubre

Av. Ancash

LIMA
CENTRO

G. de Vega

Av. Grau

EL
AGUSTINO

Man-o Capac

El Centro
& Rímac

Av. 28 de Julio

♦ Mercado
Mayorista

Unanue

Av. N. Ayllon

Vía

Isabela Católica

Av. Arequipa

Av. México

SAN LUIS

Av. N. Arriola

♦ Museo de
Historia Natural
J. Prado

LA
VICTORIA

Av. N. Arriola

Parque Zonal
Tupau Amaru

Av. Canada

LINCE

Vía Express (Paseo de la República)

41

Av. Javier Prado

Av. Aviación

SAN
BORJA

Av. Arequipa

SAN
SIDRO

Av. J. Galvez B

Av. J. Galvez B

SAN
BORJA

Santa Cruz

Aramburú

Instituto
Geográfico
Nacional

♦ Huaca
Pucllana

SURQUILLO

Paseo de la República

Av. Angamos

42 →

ose Pardo

30 - **34**
see detail map

Av. Tomás Marsano

Av. Panama

MIRA-
FLORES

Av. Larco

Playa
Costa
Verde

Av. M. Benavides

Miraflores

Playa la
Estrella

Av. Grau

Av. Surco

Río Surco

SANTIAGO
DE SURCO

Av. Santiago de Surco

BARRANCO

35 - **38**
see detail map

Playa
Barranco

Barranco

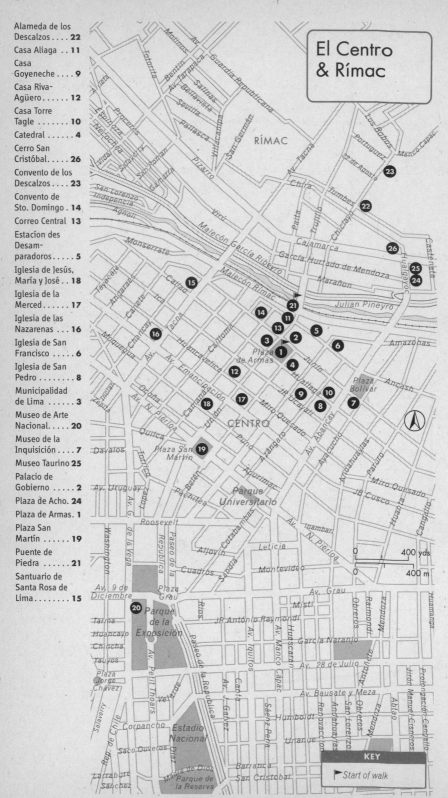

El Centro & Rímac

Up for a bit more walking? Head south on Jirón de la Unión to **Plaza San Martín** ⑲, one of the city's best-preserved squares. The neoclassical splendor of the Gran Hotel Bolívar presides over the western edge. Continue south on Jirón de la Unión, passing the Paseo de la República, until you reach the pretty green park called the Parque de la Exposición. Here, at what most people consider the gateway to the historic district is the **Museo de Arte Nacional** ⑳.

TIMING & PRECAUTIONS
An unhurried visit to the historic district's main attractions takes a full day, with at least an hour devoted to both the Museo de Arte Nacional and the Museo de la Inquisición. Even if you're short on time, don't bypass the guided tour of the underground catacombs of the Iglesia de San Francisco. Also, spend some time just sitting on the cathedral steps, as the locals do.

As the locals begin to head home for the day, so should you. This neighborhood can be a bit dicey in the evening. If you find yourself on the street in the late afternoon, it's probably wise to take a taxi to your destination.

What to See

⑪ **Casa Aliaga.** Said to be the oldest colonial mansion in South America, the Aliaga House has been owned and occupied by the same family since Francisco Pizarro granted the land to Jerónimo de Aliaga in 1535. An impressive wooden staircase in the tree-shaded courtyard leads up to the elaborate rooms, many of which are decorated with colonial furnishings. Visitors must arrange trips in advance through Lima Tours. ✉ *Jr. de la Unión 224, El Centro* ☎ *01/424–5110.*

⑨ **Casa Goyeneche.** Although it strongly resembles nearby Casa Torre Tagle, the 40 or so years between them are evident. While the 1730 Casa Torre Tagle has a baroque style, the 1771 Casa Goyeneche has clearly been influenced by the rococo movement. Sadly, the house is not open to the public. ✉ *Jr. Ucayali 360, El Centro.*

⑫ **Casa Riva-Agüero.** A matched pair of balconies with *celosías*—intricate wood screens through which ladies could watch passersby unobserved—grace the facade of this mansion dating from 1760. Ornately carved wooden balconies overlook the front and back courtyards of this typical colonial house. An interesting museum of folk art is on the second floor. ✉ *Jr. Camaná 459, El Centro* ☎ *01/427–9275* 🎟 *Free* ⊙ *Tues.–Sat. 10–12:30 and 2–7:30.*

⑩ **Casa Torre Tagle.** Considered one of the most magnificent structures in South America, this mansion sums up the grace and elegance of the early 18th century. The coat of arms of the original owner, the Marquis of Torre Tagle, is still visible above the door. Flanked by a pair of elegant balconies, the stone entrance is as expertly carved as that of any of the city's churches. It currently serves as a governmental building and is not open to the public, but you can often get a peek inside. You might see the tiled ceilings, carved columns, or 16th-century carriage. ✉ *Jr. Ucayali 363, El Centro.*

④ **Catedral.** The layout for this immense structure was dictated by Francisco Pizarro himself, and his basic vision has survived even though earthquakes in 1746 and 1940 required it to be completely rebuilt. The first church on the site was completed in 1625. Inside are some impressive Baroque appointments, especially the intricately carved choir stalls. Because of changing tastes, the main altar was replaced around 1800 with one in a neoclassical style. At about the same time the towers that flank the entrance were added. A highlight of a visit to the church is seeing the chapel where Pizarro is entombed. There is also a small museum of religious art and artifacts. ⊠ *East side of the Plaza de Armas, El Centro* ☎ *01/427–9647* ⊠ *S/5* ☉ *Mon.–Sat. 10–4:30.*

⑭ **Convento de Santo Domingo.** The 16th-century Convent of Saint Dominic clearly shows the different styles popular during the colonial era in Lima. The bell tower, for instance, has a Baroque base built in 1632, but the upper parts rebuilt after an earthquake in 1746 are more rococo in style. The church is a popular one, as it holds the tombs of the first two Peruvian saints, Santa Rosa de Lima and San Martín de Porres. The pair of cloisters in the convent are worth a look, as they are decorated with yellow-and-blue tiles imported from Spain in the early 17th century. ⊠ *Conde de Superunda and Camaná, El Centro* ☎ *01/427–6793* ⊠ *S/3* ☉ *Mon.–Sat. 8:30–12:30 and 3–6, Sun. 9–12:30 and 3–6.*

⑬ **Correo Central.** Inaugurated in 1897, this regal structure looks more like a palace than a post office. You can certainly buy a stamp or send a package, but most people come here to admire the exuberance of an era when no one thought twice about placing bronze angels atop a civic building. A narrow passage filled with vendors splits the building in half. The Museo Postal y Filatélico, a tiny museum of stamps, is just inside the front entrance. ⊠ *Conde de Superunda, between Jr. de la Unión and Jr. Camaná, El Centro* ☎ *01/427–9370* ⊠ *Free* ☉ *Mon.–Sat. 8–8, Sun. 9–2.*

❺ **Estación de Desamparados.** Inaugurated in 1912, Desamparados Station was the centerpiece for the continent's first railway. The building itself, using lots of glass to make use of the natural light, was based on styles popular in Europe. Trains no longer run from this station. ⊠ *Jr. Carabaya and Jr. Ancash, El Centro.*

⑱ **Iglesia de Jesús, María y José.** The 1659 Church of Jesus, Mary and Joseph may have a plain facade, but inside is a feast for the eyes. Baroque retables representing various saints grace the main altar. ⊠ *Jr. Camaná and Jr. Moquegua, El Centro* ☎ *01/427–6809* ⊠ *Free* ☉ *Mon.–Sat. 7–noon, 3–8.*

⑰ **Iglesia de la Merced.** The first house of worship to be built in Lima, Our Lady of Mercy was commissioned by Hernando Pizarro, brother of the city's founder. He chose the site because it was here that services were first held in the city. The current structure, with an unusual Baroque facade, was finished in 1704. Inside are a series of retables that gradually change from Baroque to rococo styles. The intricately carved choir stalls, dating from the 18th century, have images of cherubic singers. ⊠ *Jr. de la Unión at Jr. Miro Quesada, El Centro* ☎ *01/427–8199* ⊠ *Free* ☉ *Tues.–Sun. 8–12, 4–8.*

⑯ **Iglesia de las Nazarenas.** This rococo church has become the repository of the *Señor de los Milagros* (Lord of the Miracles). When an earthquake destroyed much of the city in 1655, a wall with an image of Christ remained standing. When it survived subsequent tremors in 1687 and 1746, people believed it to be miraculous. The church was built to house the now famous icon. Every year on October 18, 19, and 28 and November 1, purple-robed devotees carry an oil copy of the mural, resplendent in a gold frame, through the streets of Lima. ⊠ *Jr. Tacna at Jr. Huancavelica, El Centro* ☎ *no phone* ⊠ *Free* ☉ *Daily 6:30–noon, 5–8:30.*

♻ ❻ **Iglesia de San Francisco.** The Church of Saint Francis is the most visited in Lima, and with good reason. The 1674 structure is the best example of what is known as "Lima Baroque" style of architecture. The handsome carved portal would later influence those on other churches, including the Iglesia de la Merced. The central nave is known for its beautiful ceilings painted in a style called *mudejar* (a blend of Moorish

FodorsChoice
★

and Spanish designs). On a tour, peruse the adjoining monastery's immense collection of antique texts, some dating back to the 17th century. But the best part of a tour is a visit to the vast catacombs. The city's first cemetery, these underground tunnels contains the bones of some 75,000 people. In many places the bones have been stacked in eerie geometric patterns. Tours are available in English. ⊠ *Jr. Ancash 471, El Centro* ☎ *01/427–1381* ⌦ *S/5* ⊙ *Daily 9:30–5.*

8 **Iglesia de San Pedro.** The Jesuits built three churches in rapid succession on this corner, the current one dating from 1638. It remains one of the finest examples of early colonial religious architecture in Peru. The facade is remarkably restrained, but the interior shows all the extravagance of the era. The interior is richly appointed with a series of Baroque retables thought to be the best in the city. Don't miss the side aisle, where gilded arches lead to chapels decorated with beautiful hand-painted tiles. Many have works by Italians like Bernardo Bitti, who arrived on these shores in 1575. His style influenced an entire generation of painters. In the sacristy is *The Coronation of the Virgin,* one of his most famous works. ⊠ *Jr. Ucayali at Jr. Azángaro, El Centro* ☎ *01/428–3010* ⌦ *Free* ⊙ *Mon.–Sat. 7–noon and 5–8.*

3 **Municipalidad de Lima.** Although it resembles the colonial-era buildings surrounding it, the City Hall was actually constructed in 1944. Step inside to see the stained-glass windows above the marble staircase. Running beside the building is a lovely pedestrian walkway called the Paseo Los Escribanos, or Passage of the Scribes, lined with inexpensive restaurants. On the south side of the building is the tourist information office. ⊠ *West side of the Plaza de Armas, El Centro.*

20 **Museo de Arte Nacional.** Built in 1872 as the Palacio de la Expedición, this mammoth neoclassical structure now houses the National Museum of Art. It has a bit of everything, from pre-Columbian artifacts to colonial-era furniture to contemporary paintings. One of the highlights is the collection of 2,000-year-old weavings from Paracas. Make sure to leave time to wander around the extensive gardens outside. ⊠ *Paseo Colón 125, El Centro* ☎ *01/423–6332* ⌦ *S/6* ⊙ *Thur.–Tue. 10–1 and 2–5.*

7 **Museo de la Inquisición.** A massive mansion that belonged to the one of the first families to arrive in Lima served as the headquarters of the Spanish Inquisition. Visit the original dungeons and torture chambers, where stomach-churning, life-size exhibits illustrate methods of extracting information from prisoners. The residence later served as the temporary home of Congress, which found a permanent home in the neoclassical structure across the street. The guided tour lets you admire the beautiful building, especially the coffered ceilings dating from the 18th century. ⊠ *Jr. Junín 548, El Centro* ☎ *01/428–7980* ⌦ *Free* ⊙ *Mon.–Sat. 9–5.*

2 **Palacio de Gobierno.** Built on the site where Francisco Pizarro was murdered in 1541, the Palacio de Gobierno was completed in 1938. The neo-Baroque palace is the official residence of the president. The best time to visit is at noon, when soldiers in red-and-blue uniforms conduct an elaborate changing of the guard. Guided tours, which include visits to many of the rooms where the president conducts affairs of state, must be arranged at least two days in advance. To do so, bring your passport to the unmarked side door on Jirón de la Unión, across from the statue of a conquistador on horseback. ⊠ *North side of the Plaza de Armas, El Centro* ☎ *01/426–7020* ⌦ *Free* ⊙ *Weekdays 10–12:30.*

★ ⌐ **1** **Plaza de Armas.** This massive square has been the center of the city since 1535. Over the years it has served many functions, from an open-air theater for melodramas to an impromptu ring for bullfights. Huge fires once burned in the center for people sentenced to death by the Spanish Inquisition. Much has changed over the years, but one thing remaining is the bronze fountain unveiled in 1651. It was here that José de San Martín declared the country's independence from Spain in 1821. ✉ *Jr. Junín and Jr. Carabaya, El Centro.*

⑲ **Plaza San Martín.** This popular plaza is unlike any other in the city. It is surrounded on three sides by French-style buildings—all of them an oddly appealing shade of pumpkin—dating from the 1920s. Presiding over the western edge is the Gran Hotel Bolívar, a pleasant place to stop for afternoon tea. Several restaurants on the periphery let you enjoy the view of the statue of San Martín in the center. ✉ *Between Jr. de la Union and Jr. Carabaya, El Centro.*

⑮ **Santuario de Santa Rosa de Lima.** Inside the 17th-century Sanctuary of St. Rose, the tiny adobe cell that was her hermitage keeps alive the memory of the region's first saint. Here you'll find a well where every August 30 thousands of the faithful leave notes requesting that she hear their prayers. In the church next door is the Museo Etnográfico, where exhibits detail the lives of Peru's jungle peoples. ✉ *Jr. Tacna and Conde de Superunda, El Centro* ☎ 01/425–0143 ✉ *Free* ⊙ *Tues.–Sun. 9–1 and 3 to 6.*

Rímac

In the beginning of the 17th century, the neighborhoods around the Plaza de Armas were bursting at the seams. The construction of the Puente de Piedra, which literally means "Stone Bridge," meant people were soon streaming over the Río Rímac. Among those who crossed the river were members of the upper classes who saw the newly christened Rímac as the perfect place to construct their mansions. It wasn't long before there were tree-lined promenades like the Alameda de los Descalzos and aquatic gardens like the Paseo de las Aguas. The neighborhood has fallen on hard times, but the faded facades are among the loveliest in the city.

Numbers in the text correspond to numbers in the margin and on the El Centro and Rímac map.

a good tour

Like thousands of other people each day, you'll probably reach Rímac by crossing the historic **Puente de Piedra** ㉑ ▶. A few blocks north of the bridge is a strip of green called the **Alameda de los Descalzos** ㉒. You'll notice small churches like the Iglesia de Nuestro Señora de Patrocinio along on either side. At the far end of the alameda is a massive monastery called the **Convento de los Descalzos** ㉓.

As you head south, you'll probably notice another narrow park to the east. The Paseo de las Aguas, commissioned in 1770, is guarded at one end by a graceful arcade. The park, once a popular place for an evening promenade, has been badly neglected. A few blocks south of the Paseo de las Aguas is the city's bull ring, the **Plaza de Acho** ㉔. If you can't make it to a bullfight, get a peek inside the massive structure by visiting the adjacent **Museo Taurino** ㉕. Should you wish to get a bird's-eye view of the Plaza de Acho, as well as the rest of Rímac, hop in a taxi and head to the top of **Cerro San Cristóbal** ㉖.

TIMING & PRECAUTIONS   A tour of the sights won't take more than an hour or two, but know that Rímac is not a place where you want to walk; don't let that stop you from visiting, however. The best way to see the neighborhood is by taxi; hire one in the Plaza de Armas. Any driver will be happy to wait as you explore sights like the Convento de los Descalzos. Negotiate a price in advance.

What to See

㉒ Alameda de los Descalzos. The tree-lined Promenade of the Discalced Brothers, a reference to the monks at the nearby monastery, was constructed in 1610. A dozen marble statues representing the signs of the zodiac were added in 1858. On sunny afternoons ice-cream vendors blow little whistles as they pass. ⊠ *Northern end of Jr. Chiclayo, Rímac.*

㉖ Cerro San Cristóbal. Rising over the northeastern edge of Rímac is this massive hill, recognizable from the cross at its peak that is a replica of the one placed there by Pizarro. If the air is clear—a rarity in Lima—you'll see most of the city spread out below. It's not so easy to get here, but many tour companies include a visit here on their itineraries. ⊠ *Calle San Cristóbal, Rímac.*

㉓ Convento de los Descalzos. The rose-colored Monastery of the Discalced Brothers has been converted into a fascinating repository of colonial-era religious art. Room after room of this maze-like structure is filled with paintings dating back to the 16th century. There are four cloisters and two chapels, so it's easy to get lost here—in fact, it's practically guaranteed. A highlight is the Capilla de la Virgen Carmen, entered through a doorway decorated to resemble a bright blue Baroque church. Inside is an altar that gleams with gold leaf. The kitchen still contains antique wine-making equipment, and the pharmacy is filled with glass-stoppered bottles of unidentifiable liquids. English-speaking guides are available. ⊠ *Northern end of the Alameda de los Descalzos, Rímac* ☎ *01/481–0441* ⌫ *S/5* ☼ *Tues.–Sun. 10–6.*

㉕ Museo Taurino. Stuffed heads of several bulls stare down at you from the walls of the tiny Museum of Bullfighting. There are plenty of examples of the colorful costumes worn by the matadors, letting you see how styles have changed over the years. Perhaps most interesting are the posters from around the world. An 1899 advertisement from Barcelona shows women attending a bullfight in all their frills and finery. If there is no one around, the guard will let you see the Plaza de Acho. ⊠ *Jr. Hualgayoc 332, Rímac* ☎ *01/482–3360* ⌫ *S/5* ☼ *Tues.–Sun. 10–6.*

㉔ Plaza de Acho. Up until 1766, bullfights were held in the Plaza de Armas. They were moved across the river to this structure, which at the time was the largest bull ring in the world. It was originally octagonal, but in 1946 it was given its current circular shape. Matches were originally held on Sundays, but church leaders complained that attendance at services was getting sparse. ⊠ *Jr. Hualgayoc 332, Rímac* ☎ *01/481–1467* ⌫ *S/5* ☼ *Tues. Sun. 10 6.*

▶ **㉑ Puente de Piedra.** Across the nearly dry Río Rímac is this 17th-century stone bridge, whose builders strengthened their mortar with thousands of egg whites. From the bridge is a nice view of the Palacio de Gobierno and other grand structures along the river's edge. ⊠ *Northern end of Jr. de la Union.*

San Isidro

Many frequent visitors to Lima find themselves drawn to the residential neighborhood of San Isidro. Like nearby Miraflores, it has plenty of boutiques selling designer goods, bars serving up the latest cocktails, and restaurants dishing out cuisine from around the world. What it lacks is the hustle and bustle. While strolling through Parque El Olívar you might be shocked to realize that there's not a single car in sight.

Numbers in the text correspond to numbers in the margin and on the San Isidro map.

San Isidro

a good tour

Start in **Parque El Olívar** ㉗ ►, a swath of green that runs through the center of San Isidro. Head north along any of the paths and you'll soon find yourself on Pancho Fierro, a block-long strip of cafés and restaurants. At the end you'll catch sight of the steeple crowning the Iglesia de la Virgen del Pilar. Go west on Avenida Victor A. Belaunde, then south on Avenida El Rosario. Soon you'll catch sight of the perfectly preserved pyramid that forms the centerpiece of the **Huaca Huallamarca** ㉘. Spend an hour or so clambering around the ruins, then continue south on Avenida El Rosario to Avenida El Golf, where you'll head west. After five blocks you'll reach the **Country Club Lima Hotel** ㉙, a lovely reminder of the city's glittering past. Stop for lunch here or double back to Parque El Olívar for an impromptu picnic.

TIMING & PRECAUTIONS Unless you have your own wheels, the best way to travel between San Isidro's widely dispersed attractions is by taxi. Taking things at a leisurely pace, this tour will take a few hours.

What to See

㉙ **Country Club Lima Hotel.** Two magnificent palms stand guard at the entrance to this 1927 hotel, widely regarded as the most elegant hotel in the city. If you're here in the afternoon, you might want to stop by for the English-style tea. ✉ *Los Eucaliptos 590, San Isidro* ☎ *01/211–9000.*

㉘ **Huaca Huallamarca.** The sight of this flat-topped temple catches many people off guard. The structure, painstakingly restored on the front side, certainly seems out of place among the neighborhood's towering hotels and apartment buildings. The upper platform affords some nice views of San Isidro. There's a small museum with displays of objects found at the site, including several mummies. ✉ *Av. El Rosario and Av. Nicolás de Rivera, San Isidro* ☎ *01/224–4124* 💷 *S/5* 🕓 *Tues.–Sun 9–5.*

When strolling through Parque El Olívar, stop by **Pasteleria Monserrat** (✉ Pancho Fierro 131, San Isidro ☎ 01/440–0517) for some of the neighborhood's most fanciful pastries, including little cupcakes shaped like mice.

▶ ㉗ **Parque El Olívar.** This was once an olive grove, so it's no surprise that you'll find an old olive press in this pretty park. The gnarled old trees, some more than a century old, still bear fruit. Yellow and red irises line the walkways, adding a splash of color. ✉ *East of Av. La República, San Isidro.*

Miraflores

The seaside suburb of Miraflores has become the city's main destination for tourists, and it's easy to see why. Next to the relentless right angles of El Centro, the fan-like diagonals extending out from Ovalo José Pardo are a relief. For a complete change of place, wander through the neighborhood's flower-filled parks or along the cliffs overlooking the ocean. But Miraflores is also the city's cultural hub, which means there are plenty of boutiques, galleries, and museums, as well as bars, cafés, and restaurants. Some people who find themselves in Lima for a short time never leave this little haven.

Numbers in the text correspond to numbers in the margin and on the Miraflores map.

Any tour of Miraflores begins in **Parque Miraflores** ㉚ ▶, which sits like a slice of pie between Avenida José Larco and Avenida Diagonal. On the eastern side is the Parroquia Virgen Milagrosa, the neighborhood's largest church. The colonial-style building next door is the Municipalidad de Miraflores, where most governmental business takes place. Where you go next depends on your areas of interest. If you don't have time to venture outside the city to archaeological sites such as Pachacámac, head east along Avenida José Pardo then north on Miguel Grau to the towering temple of **Huaca Pucllana** ㉛. Continue east on Avenida José Pardo, then north on Avenida Santa Cruz to the **Museo Amano** ㉜. This tiny museum has one of the city's best collections of ancient artifacts.

More interested in shopping? Head south along Avenida José Larco, where you'll find many interesting shops. If antiques are your passion, take a detour a few blocks east to Avenida La Paz. At the tip of Avenida José Larco you'll find Larcomar, one of the city's best shopping centers. Cool off here with a pisco sour as you enjoy the ocean views. If you have romance on your mind, head south along Avenida Diagonal—also known as Avenida Oscar Benevidas—to reach **Parque del Amor** ㉝. You won't be alone, as this waterfront park attracts young lovers all day. If it's too crowded for your taste, stroll east to **El Faro de la Marina** ㉞, a lovely little lighthouse that dates back to the beginning of the last century.

TIMING & PRECAUTIONS Good times to stroll Miraflores are mid-morning, when the heat is not yet overbearing, or mid-afternoon, when you can escape the sun by ducking into a bar or café. If shopping is your goal, arrive after sunset when things have cooled down. All the stores along Avenida José Larco stay open for early-evening window shoppers. About a half hour of walking will lead you to the ocean, where you'll want to spend another hour or so strolling along the cliff.

Miraflores is a very safe neighborhood, but keep your wits about you in the markets and parks. Pickpockets sometimes target tourists distracted by a street performer or a good bargain.

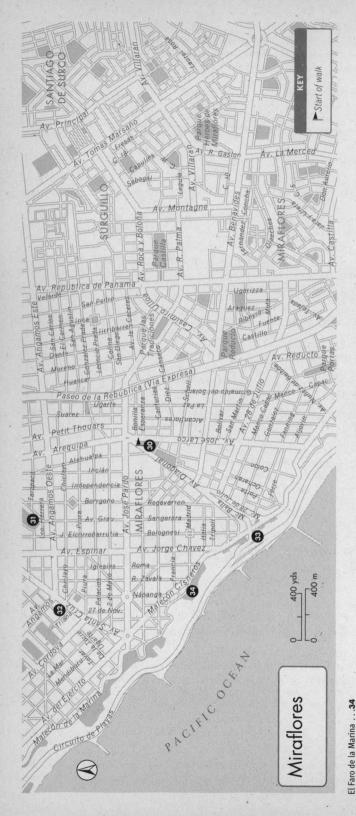

Miraflores

What to See

34 El Faro de la Marina. Constructed in 1900, this little lighthouse has steered ships away from the coast for more than a century. The classically designed tower is still in use today. ⊠ *Malecón Cisneros and Madrid, Miraflores.*

31 Huaca Pucllana. Rising out of a nondescript residential neighborhood is this mud-brick pyramid. The pre-Inca *huaca,* or temple, dates back to at least the 4th century. Archaeologists are still working on the site, and are usually happy to share their discoveries about the people who lived in this area hundreds of years before the Inca. A tiny museum highlights some of their recent finds. Knowledgable guides are available in Spanish and English. ⊠ *Av. Larco Herrera at Elías Aguirre, Miraflores* ☎ *01/445–8695* 🖭 *Free* ⊙ *Daily 9–5.*

32 Museo Amano. Although it consists of only two rooms, this museum packs a lot into a small space. The private collection of pre-Columbian artifacts includes one of the best displays of ceramics in the city. Imaginative displays reveal how cultures in the northern part of the region focused on sculptural images, while those in the south used vivid colors. In between, around present-day Lima, the styles merged. A second room holds an impressive number of weavings, including examples from the Chancay people, who lived in the north between 1000 and 1500. Some of their work is so delicate that it resembles the finest lace. Call ahead, as you need an appointment to join one of the Spanish-language tours. ⊠ *Retiro 160, Miraflores* ☎ *01/441–2909* 🖭 *Free* ⊙ *Weekdays; by appointment only.*

need a break?

A few steps from the biggest swath of green in Miraflores is aptly named **El Parque** (⊠ East of Parque Kennedy, Miraflores ☎ 01/326–0206), an old-fashioned ice-cream parlor that's always a hit with kids. Delicious desserts include a cherry-nosed clown and a pair of cookie-eared mice with the oddly familiar names Miky and Miny.

33 Parque del Amor. You might think you're in Barcelona when you stroll through this pretty park. Like Antonio Gaudí's Parque Güell, the park that provided the inspiration for this one, the benches are decorated with broken pieces of tile. Here, however, they spell out silly romantic sayings like *Amor es como luz* ("Love is like light"). The centerpiece is a controversial statue of two lovers locked in a rather lewd embrace. ⊠ *Av. Diagonal, Miraflores.*

▶ **30 Parque Miraflores.** What locals call Parque Miraflores is actually two parks. The smaller section is shady Parque Central, where you'll find frequent open-air concerts. Shoeshine boys will ask whether you need a *lustre* when you stop to listen to the music. The honking noise you hear is probably the ice-cream vendors that patrol the park on bright yellow bicycles. A friendly tourist information kiosk sits on the south side. Across a pedestrian street always full of local artists showing off their latest works is Parque Kennedy, where the babble from a lively crafts market fills the air each evening. A few sidewalk cafés are found on the eastern edge. ⊠ *Between Av. José Larco and Av. Diagonal, Miraflores.*

Barranco

With a bohemian feel found nowhere else in the city, Barranco is a magnet for young people, who come to carouse in its bars and cafés. A bit sleepy during the day, the neighborhood comes to life around sunset when artists start hawking their wares and its central square and bars begin filling with people ready to party. Founded toward the end of the 19th century, Barranco was where wealthy Limeños built their summer residences. The weather proved so irresistible that many eventually constructed huge mansions on the cliffs above the sea. Many of these have fallen into disrepair, but little by little they are being renovated into funky restaurants and hotels.

Numbers in the text correspond to numbers in the margin and on the Barranco map.

a good walk

To get your bearings, start in **Parque Municipal** 35 ▶, one of the prettiest parks in the city. To the south, the brick-red building with the tower is the Biblioteca Municipal, or Municipal Library. Stop by the tourist office on the ground floor to pick up a map of the neighborhood. To the north is the parish church called La Santisima Cruz. Across Avenida Pedro de Osma is a wonderful little museum called the **Museo-Galería Arte Popular de Ayacucho** 36. Continue down Avenida Pedro de Osma for about three blocks to the **Museo Pedro de Osma** 37. Backtrack to Parque Municipal, then head east to is Lima's own Bridge of Sighs, the **Puente de los Suspiros** 38. Directly below is the the Bajada de Baños, lined with wonderful old houses. Head down this cobblestone street and soon you'll find yourself walking in the waves at Playa Barranquito. If it's late afternoon, you might want to watch the sunset from the deck of the elegant Costa Verde.

TIMING & PRECAUTIONS

All the major sights in Barranco are within a block or two of Parque Municipal. Depending on how long you linger, the walk should take no more than a few hours. Don't walk down deserted streets, especially at night.

What to See

36 **Museo-Galería Arte Popular de Ayacucho.** Its unassuming facade makes it easy to miss this little gem. Inside you'll find one of the country's best collections of folk art. One especially interesting exhibit in the bright, airy gallery is an explanation of *cajones San Marcos,* the boxlike portable altars that priests once carried as they moved from village to village. Peasants began to make their own, placing scenes of local life inside. These dioramas, ranging in size from less than an inch to more than a foot wide, are still made today. ⊠ *Av. Pedro de Osma 423, Barranco* ☎ *01/ 247–0599* ☞ *Free* ⊗ *Tues.–Sat. 9–6.*

37 **Museo Pedro de Osma.** If there were not one piece of art hanging inside this museum, it would still be worth the trip to see the century-old mansion that houses it. The mansard-roofed structure—with inlaid wood floors, delicately painted ceilings, and breathtaking stained-glass windows in every room—was the home of a wealthy collector of religious art. The best of his collection is now permanently on display. The finest of the paintings, the 18th-century *Virgen de Pomato,* represents the earth, with her mountain-shaped cloak covered with garlands of corn. The former dining room, in a separate building, contains some fine pieces of silver, including a lamb-shaped incense holder with shining ruby eyes. ⊠ *Av. Pedro de Osma 423, Barranco* ☎ *01/467–0141* ☞ *S/10* ⊗ *Tues.–Sun. 10–1:30 and 2:30–6.*

FodorśChoice
★

need a break?

Along a walkway leading past La Ermita is the unassuming **La Flor de Canela** (⊠ Ermita 102, Barranco ☎ no phone), a sweet little café with a porch overlooking much of Barranco. The dimly lit space inside is a great place to escape the midday heat.

▶ 35 **Parque Municipal.** Elegant swirls of colorful blooms make this park stand out from others in Lima. Here you'll find locals relaxing on the

benches, their children playing nearby. At about 6 PM every evening you'll find artists who live in the nearby streets showing off their latest works. ⊠ *Between Av. Pedro de Osma and Av. Grau, Barranco.*

★ ❸❽ **Puente de los Suspiros.** The romantically named Bridge of Sighs is a lovely wooden walkway shaded with flowering trees. You won't have to wait long to see couples walking hand in hand. The bridge crosses over the the Bajada de Baños, a cobblestone walkway that leads to Playa Barranquito. On the far side is La Ermita, a lovely little chapel painted a dazzling shade of red. ⊠ *East of Parque Municipal, Barranco.*

Pueblo Libre

You may find yourself longing to linger in Pueblo Libre, which manages to retain a sense of calm not found elsewhere in the capital. Instead of hurrying past, residents often pause to chat with friends. This neighborhood northwest of San Isidro has two of the city's finest museums, the Museo Nacional de Antropología, Arqueología, e Historia del Perú and the Museo Arqueológico Rafael Larco Herrera.

Start at Plaza Bolívar, the pretty park that is the heart of Pueblo Libre. It's surrounded by colonial era buildings, many of which have shops and restaurants. On the south side is the Municipalidad de Pueblo Libre, with governmental offices. A small gallery on the ground floor sometimes hosts exhibitions of painting and photography. Directly across the square is the **Museo Nacional de Antropología, Arqueología, e Historia del Perú** ❸❾, a mustard-colored building that takes up an entire block. A blue line painted on the sidewalk traces a 15-minute walk to the **Museo Arqueológico Rafael Larco Herrera** ❹❶. The sun can be brutal, so in the summer you should take advantage of the taxis lined up outside either museum.

TIMING   If you get an early start, this walk will take up most of a morning. Plan to spend an hour or two in each of the museums.

What to See

☺ ㊴ **Museo Nacional de Antropología, Arqueología, e Historia del Perú.** The country's most extensive collection of pre-Columbian artifacts can be found at this sprawling museum. Beginning with 8,000-year-old stone tools, Peru's history comes to life through the sleek granite obelisks of the Chavín culture, the intricate weavings of Paraca peoples, and the colorful ceramics of the Moche, Chimú, and Inca civilizations. Fascinating are a pair of mummies from the Nazca region that are thought to be more than 2,500 years old; they were so well preserved that you can still see the grim expressions on their faces. Not all the exhibits are labeled in English, so you might want to hire a guide to negotiate your way around the museum's twin courtyards. ⊠ *Plaza Bolívar, Pueblo Libre* ☎ *01/463–5070* ☜ *S/10* ☾ *Daily 9–5.*

> **need a break?** Saloon-style doors lead you into the **Antigua Taberna Queirolo** (⊠ Jr. San Martín 1090, Pueblo Libre ☎ 01/463–8777), a charming little bar about a block west of Plaza Bolívar. Locals lean against round tables as they sample the pisco that is bottled at the bodega next door.

㊵ **Museo Arqueológico Rafael Larco Herrera.** Fuchsia bougainvillea tumbles
Fodor'sChoice over the white walls surrounding Museo Arqueológico Rafael Larco Her-
★ rera, home of the world's largest private collection of pre-Columbian art. The oldest pieces here are crude vessels dating back several thousand years. Most intriguing are the thousands of ceramic "portrait heads" crafted more than a millennium ago. Some owners commissioned more than one, allowing you to see how they changed over the course of their lives. The famous *sala erótica* reveals that these ancient artists were surprisingly uninhibited. Everyday objects are adorned with images that are frankly sexual and frequently humorous. As this gallery is across the garden from the rest of the museum, you'll be able to distance the kids from it if necessary. ⊠ *Av. Bolívar 1515, Pueblo Libre* ☎ *01/461–1835* ☜ *S/20* ☾ *Mon.–Sat. 9–6, Sun. 9–1.*

Elsewhere in Lima

A few of Lima's most interesting museums are in outlying neighborhoods such as Monterrico and San Borja. The most convenient way to reach them is a quick taxi ride.

What to See

㊶ **Museo de la Nación.** If you know little about the history of Peru, a visit to this fortress-like museum is likely to leave you overwhelmed. The number of cultures tracked over the centuries makes it easy to confuse the Chimú, the Chincha, and the Chachapoyas. The three floors of artifacts end up seeming repetitious. The museum is more manageable if you have a specific interest, say, if you're planning a trip north to Chiclayo and you want learn more about the Moche people. Except for a pair of scale models of Machu Picchu, the pair of rooms dedicated to the Inca is disappointing. ⊠ *Av. Javier Prado Este 2465, San Borja* ☎ *01/476–9878* ☜ *S/6* ☾ *Tues.–Sun. 9–5.*

㊷ **Museo de Oro.** All that glitters is not gold at this extremely popular museum. There's plenty of silver and other precious metals in this collection of Inca and pre-Inca treasures. When you see examples of how gold was used in these societies—from a mantle made of postage-stamp-sized pieces worn by a Lambayeque priest to an intricately designed sheet that once decorated an entire wall of the Chimú capital of Chán Chán—you can begin to imagine the opulence of these ancient cities. The museum has other interesting items, including a child's poncho of yellow feathers and a skull with a full set of pink quartz teeth. Upstairs are military uniforms and weapons. None of the displays are particularly well marked, either in English or Spanish, so you might want to see the museum as part of a city tour; it's a pretty good deal, as you'll save the cost of a taxi. At any rate, be prepared to pay one of the highest admissions of any of South America's museums. ⊠ *Alonso de Molina 1100, Monterrico* ☎ *01/345–1271* ☞ *S/30* ☉ *Daily 11:30–7.*

WHERE TO EAT

There's no need to get dressed for dinner in the capital. The heat and humidity dictate a casual dress code at all but the top restaurants. Even at trendy places like Huaca Pucllana and Costa Verde there's no reason for men to put on a necktie. You will, however, get a few odd looks if you show up in shorts or with a baseball cap. Reservations are required if you hope for a table at a popular restaurant in Miraflores or San Isidro, especially on the weekend. Otherwise, you can simply show up at most places and be seated immediately. You may have to wait a few minutes at lunch if you have picked a place that is popular with business executives.

Eating out in Lima need not cost a lot. One of the best deals is lunch in any of the hundreds of storefront restaurants scattered around the city. For a few bucks you get soup, a main dish, and even a dessert. How to pick among these no-name establishments? Just look for a crowd.

WHAT IT COSTS In Nuevo Soles					
	$$$$	$$$	$$	$	¢
AT DINNER	over 65	50–65	35–50	20–35	under 20

Restaurant prices are per person, for a main course.

Barranco

In keeping with its reputation as a bohemian neighborhood, Barranco has a slew of cozy cafés where you can while away an afternoon. Look for these around the Puente de los Suspiros. For more substantial fare, head to those facing Parque Municipal.

Peruvian

$–$$ ✕ **Manos Morenas.** A century-old house behind an iron gate has one of the most atmospheric restaurants in Barranco. The tables scattered around the front porch are so inviting that you might not get farther than the front door. Inside is a warmly lit dining room bustling with women in colorful headwraps serving up tasty Peruvian fare. The *ají de gallina*, a spicy stewed hen, is the best you'll find anywhere. If you're brave, sample the *anticuchos*, skewers of beef hearts. At night the place bursts to life with music and dancing from the coastal regions. ⊠ *Av. Pedro de Osma 409, Barranco* ☎ *01/467–0421* ☜ *Reservations essential* ☱ *AE, MC, V.*

$ ✕ **Las Terrazas de Barranco.** If you're standing in Parque Municipal, you won't miss this restaurant. Bright pink geraniums tumble down the series of terraces that give the place its name. The open-air dining room, big enough for half a dozen tables, lets you enjoy the cool ocean breezes. The specialty here is *cebiche* (chunks of raw fish marinated in lemon juice and topped with onions), and the spicy fish dish is served several ways. Drop by for lunch and for about $3, sample all of them. There is plenty on offer for meat eaters as well. ⊠ *Av. Grau 290, Barranco* ☎ *01/247–1477* ☱ *MC, V.*

★ ¢ ✕**Las Mesitas.** Filled with a dozen or so marble-topped tables, Las Mesitas is an old-fashioned café a block north of Parque Municipal. The constant stream of Limeños lets you know that the food is first rate. You couldn't do better than share a few *humitas,* steamed tamales that you season with pickled onions or bright yellow hot sauce. The best are those stuffed with chicken, onions, and green corn. If the café's pinwheel design doesn't make you feel a bit off balance, then the spinning desert display certainly will. Try the *mazamorra morada,* a sweet pudding of cornmeal and candied fruit. ⊠ *Grau 341, Barranco* ☎ *01/477–1346* ▱ *MC, V.*

Seafood

$$$–$$$$ ✕**Costa Verde.** The pink and gold hues of the sunset make people return again and again to this seaside standout. Order a pisco sour—one of the best in the city—and no matter where you sit in the glassed-in dining room you'll have a front-row seat. Highlights include the lobster, which arrives steaming. Locals with a lot of cash on hand come for brunch on weekends, when there's a buffet so expansive it holds a place in the *Guinness World Records* book. It's a bit touristy, especially when your server places a flag from your home country in the middle of your table. ⊠ *Playa Barranquito, Barranco* ☎ *01/477–2424* ⌕ *Reservations required* ▱ *AE, DC, MC, V.*

$–$$ ✕**La Ermanita.** Facing a cobblestone street leading down to the ocean, this butter-yellow building has an unbeatable location. Wide windows in the dining room let you watch young lovers stroll across the Puente de los Suspiros. With the ocean practically at the door, it's no surprise the focus here is seafood. You must decide between several types of freshly caught fish, then from a dozen or so sauces. You might try your sole prepared *pulpa de cangrejo gratinado,* or stuffed with shredded crab. If you arrive a bit early, enjoy a pisco sour at the beautifully polished outdoor bar. ⊠ *Bajada de Baños 340, Barranco* ☎ *01/247–0069* ⌕ *Reservations essential* ▱ *AE, DC, MC, V.*

El Centro

If you're looking for a fancy meal, you'll be hard pressed to find it in El Centro. But if you want a cheap, filling meal, you've come to the right place. A highlight of a visit to the neighborhood is the Barrio Chino, packed with dozens of Chinese-Peruvian restaurants called *chifas*.

Cafés

$ ✗ **Estadio.** If you want to watch the big game—and in this country that can only mean one thing—you couldn't do better than this neighborhood hangout. Soccer paraphernalia covers just about every square inch of the wood-paneled dining room. It's a pretty sedate place during the day, making it the perfect place for a lunch of typical dishes like *ají de gallina* (chicken in a spicy sauce). On game day things can get out of hand. If it gets too noisy inside, head outside to one of the tables facing Plaza San Martín. ⊠ *Av. Nicolás de Piérola 926, El Centro* ☎ *01/428–8866* ▭ *AE, MC, V.*

¢–$ ✗ **Restaurante Cardano.** This isn't the kind of old-fashioned café that has been gussied up to attract tourists. In fact, nobody seems to have done much straightening up at all since two Italian brothers opened for business in 1905. But that's the charm. You enter through swinging doors, and a waiter in a long white apron waves you over to an empty table. There's even a huge mirror hanging over the curved wooden bar. The *menú economico,* which rings up for less than two bucks, is one of the city's great bargains. With three courses, you certainly won't go away hungry. ⊠ *Av. Ancash 202, El Centro* ☎ *01/427–0187* ▭ *AE, V.*

Chinese

$–$$$ ✗ **Wa Lok.** Of the dozens of *chifas* in Chinatown, none comes close to Wa Lok. Attention to the smallest detail makes every meal memorable; *kun pou kay tien*—bits of chicken stir-fried with asparagus and yellow peppers—arrives garnished with an impossibly elaborate hibiscus flower carved from a carrot. Vegetarians won't have a problem here, as more than 30 dishes are made without meat. No matter what you order, do as the locals do and enjoy it with a glass of chartreuse-colored Inca Cola. If the dining room is full, don't fret; there's another branch in town. ⊠ *Jr. Paruro 864 El Centro* ☎ *01/427–2656* ⊠ *Av. Anamos 700, Miraflores* ☎ *01/447–1329* ▭ *AE, DC, MC, V.*

French

$–$$ ✗ **L'eau Vive.** Calling to mind *The Sound of Music,* a group of nuns sings **Fodor'sChoice** "Ave Maria" every night at this elegant eatery. You just might join ★ them, as the French fare prepared by the holy sisters is simply heavenly. Trout baked in cognac is but one of the many dishes that bring locals back again and again. In a beautifully restored mansion directly across from Palacio Torre Tagle, the restaurant is worth a visit just for a peek inside the centuries-old rooms. The nuns, members of a French order, run the place as a charity, so all profits are given to the poor. ⊠ *Ucayali 370, El Centro* ☎ *01/427–5612* ▭ *AE, MC, V* ☉ *Closed Sun.*

Peruvian

★ **¢–$** ✗ **Lima de Antaño.** Tucked into the courtyard of a beautiful colonial-era building, this is one of the prettiest restaurants in the historic district. Tables with chocolate-colored umbrellas are set beneath flower-covered colonnades. The food, creative takes on old recipes, is just as appealing. Start with a spinach salad tossed with bacon, walnuts, and slices of apples, then move on to roast pork with apple sauce made from scratch. For something special, order the *paríhuela,* a tasty seafood soup. The staff is eager to please, sometimes even running from the kitchen to deliver a dish while it's still hot. ⊠ *Jr. Ucayali 332, El Centro* ☎ *01/426–2372* ☉ *Closed Sun. No dinner* ▭ *AE, DC, MC, V.*

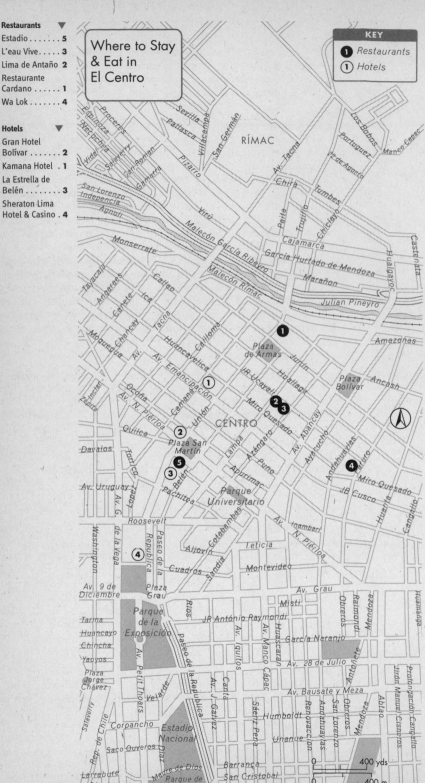

Where to Stay & Eat in El Centro

KEY
❶ *Restaurants*
① *Hotels*

Miraflores

Although inexpensive eateries are clustered around Parque Miraflores, the more elegant ones are scattered about, so plan on reaching them by taxi. If you want to dine with a view of the ocean, Miraflores has more options than any other neighborhood.

Cafés

¢–$ ✕ **Café Café.** Irish coffee is too tame for this jazzed-up java joint. Here the drink of choice is the cappuccino calypso, combining a jolt of joe with frangelica, Kahlua, and rum. Don't worry—you can still order your espresso straight up. Most people forgo the food, but that's a shame, as the roast-beef sandwich is a sizzling slab of meat atop a wedge of crusty bread. This is definitely a see-and-be-seen kind of place. Tables on the second level let you check out the crowd below, while those on the street give you an unobstructed view of Parque Central. ⊠ *Martir Olaya 250 Miraflores* ☎ *01/445–1165* ⊠ *Malecón de la Reserva and Av. José Larco, Miraflores* ☎ *01/445–1165* ⊟ *AE, DC, MC, V.*

¢ ✕ **La Buena Esquina.** If you're planning a picnic, you couldn't do better than stop by this little corner bakery. It has tempting pre-prepared sandwiches, such as the *tres jamones*, piled high with three kinds of ham. If you're a do-it-yourselfer, buy a big baguette and some cheese and you're all set. The Good Corner is also a good spot for afternoon coffee, as the selection of pastries can't be beat. If you happen by late at night, you'll smell the next day's offerings in the oven. ⊠ *José Galvez and Jorge Chavez, Miraflores* ☎ *01/241–8603* ⊟ *AE, DC, MC, V.*

¢ ✕ **4d.** An emerald-green awning won't allow you to miss this oddly named café, a favorite among young couples on dates and harried parents with children in tow. It's also a good choice for those headed to the nearby archaeological site of Huaca Pucllana. Grab one of the tables by the window and a member of the charming staff will appear to recite the daily specials. Most people, however, head to the counter in back to choose from the 20 or so varieties of gelato. Among the sassier tropical flavors are tamarindo and guanabana. ⊠ *Av. Angamos Oeste 408, Miraflores* ☎ *01/447–1523* ⊟ *No credit cards.*

Continental

$$–$$$$ ✕ **Astrid y Gaston.** You can't help but watch the kitchen door at this el-
Fodor'sChoice egant restaurant, as each dish the waiters carry out is a work of art. Take
★ the eye-catching *pato asado con mil especies* (roast duck with 1,000 spices). The honey-brown breast is accompanied by a steamed pear and a pepper bubbling over with basil risotto. Other dishes, like the pasta with squid and artichokes, are just as astonishing. Make sure to peruse the wine list, one of the best in town. In a colonial-style building on a quiet street, the restaurant itself is lovely, with pumpkin-colored walls covered with original artwork. ⊠ *Cantuarias 175, Miraflores* ☎ *01/444–1496* ⊟ *AE, MC, V.*

Italian

$–$$$ ✕ **Trattoria di Mambrino.** You don't even have to walk through the door to know that this trattoria's pasta is fresh. Passersby pause by a window to watch cooks stuff the ravioli and drape the fettuccini on long wooden rods. But the proof is on the plate: delicious dishes like tortellini tossed with chunks of beef, mushrooms, and a bit of cream leave you satisfied but not stuffed. That means you are able to save room for desert, so you can be tormented by the *tormento de chocolate*. The only caveat here is the service, which at times can be lackadaisical. ⊠ *Manuel Bonilla 106, Miraflores* ☎ *01/446–7002* ⌲ *Reservations essential* ⊟ *AE, MC, V.*

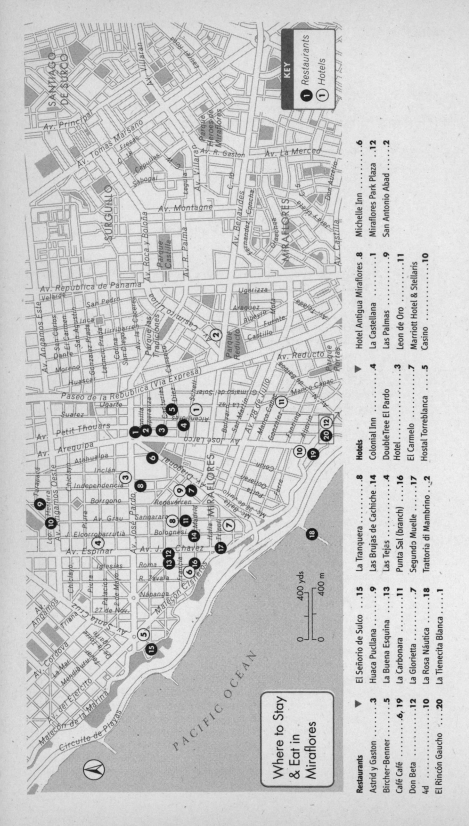

¢–$ ✕ **La Carbonara.** Bow-tied waiters greet you wit[h] this friendly neighborhood trattoria. All the d[etails—] the checked napkins, the towering windows, t[he ...] ing across one of the sun-dappled walls—cons[pire to make you feel at] home. There are countless varieties of pizzas, [...] as well as a selection of mix-and-match pastas [...] order the marvelous lasagna with artichokes. W[hile you wait,] munch on *pan a la plancha,* grilled flatbread that becomes something wonderful when dipped into extra-virgin olive oil. ✉ *Av. Grau and Calle Francia, Miraflores* ☏ *01/241–7201* ⊘ *Closed Mon.* 🖃 *AE, DC, MC, V.*

¢–$ ✕ **La Glorietta.** Locals refer to the alley west of Parque Kennedy as "La Calle de Pizza," and with good reason—it's packed with nearly identical pizza parlors. The best of the bunch is this popular place, as relaxed as the others are rowdy. There are wooden tables instead of plastic, and attentive waiters instead of disinterested teens. Best of all, the pizza isn't half bad. Enjoy it with a free beer or pisco sour as one of the wandering musicians plays "My Way" on the Pan flute. ✉ *Juan Figari 181, Miraflores* ☏ *01/445–0498* 🖃 *AE, MC, V.*

Peruvian

$$–$$$ ✕ **Huaca Pucllana.** You feel like a part of history at this beautiful restau-
Fodor'sChoice rant, which faces the ruins of a 1,500-year-old pyramid. Excavations
★ are ongoing, so you can watch archaeologists at work as you enjoy the breezes on the covered terrace. Rough-hewn columns hold aloft the dining room's soaring ceiling. This is *novo andino* cuisine, which puts a new spin on old recipes. Yellow peppers stuffed with shrimp are a great way to start, while grilled scallops tossed with fried potatoes and covered with a spicy chili sauce are a work of art. Wash it all down with one of many pisco preparations. ✉ *Av. General Borgoña, 2 blocks north of Av. Angamos Oeste, Miraflores* ☏ *01/445–4042* ⬧ *Reservations essential* 🖃 *AE, DC, MC, V.*

$–$$$ ✕ **El Señorío de Sulco.** It's no surprise that the food here is so good when you learn that owner Isabel Alvarez authored several cookbooks. The antique cooking vessels hanging on the walls reveal her passion for Peruvian cuisine. Start with *chupe de camerones,* a hearty soup combining shrimp and potatoes, then move on to *arroz con pato,* duck stewed in dark beer and seasoned with coriander. For desert there's the meringue-topped *suspiro de limeña,* which literally means "sigh of a lady of Lima." Arrive early to watch the sun set over the ocean. ✉ *Malecón Cisneros 1470, Miraflores* ☏ *01/441–0389* 🖃 *AE, DC, MC, V* ⬧ *Reservations essential* ⊘ *No dinner Sun.*

$–$$$ ✕ **Las Brujas de Cachiche.** Although the name conjures up a haunted house, The Witches of Cachiche is actually a modern space with huge windows, soaring ceilings, and lots of interesting modern art. The magic here is the cooking, which draws on Peru's traditional cuisines. Don't expect dishes like baby goat roasted with herbs to be just as they were handed down from *abuela,* as the chef often adds interesting touches from other cultures. The lunch buffet, a favorite of local business executives, includes dizzying dishes. The wine list offers several of the top South American vintages. ✉ *Bolognesi 460, Miraflores* ☏ *01/444–5310* 🖃 *AE, DC, MC, V* ⬧ *Reservations essential* ⊘ *No dinner Sun.*

$–$$ ✕ **Las Tejas.** As it's a few steps down from the street, it would be easy to pass by this family-run restaurant. That would be a shame, as it serves up some of the neighborhood's tastiest traditional cuisine. The staff is happy to explain each dish, what part of the country it comes from, and how it is made. This is the best place to sample *lomo saltado,* slices of pork sautéed with tomatoes and onions and served over fried potatoes. You know the food is fresh, as it is prepared in the open-air kitchen just inches away from the tables scattered around the covered terrace. ⊠ *Av. Diez Conseco 340, Miraflores* ☎ *01/444–4360* ⊟ *AE, DC, MC, V.*

Seafood

$–$$$ ✕ **La Rosa Náutica.** One of the most recognizable landmarks in Miraflores, La Rosa Náutica is at the end of a prominent pier. The blue slate roof of the rambling Victorian-style building is unmistakable. Take a seat in the gazebo-like dining room, where you'll have a view of the entire coast. Signature dishes include grilled scallops topped with a hearty cheese, but you might not be able to resist the succulent sea bass or the sole. The chef will prepare your selection *a su gusta.* For dessert, try the *crepes suchard* filled with ice cream and topped with hot fudge. ⊠ *Espigón 4, Miraflores* ☎ *01/447–0057* ⊟ *AE, DC, MC, V.*

$ ✕ **Don Beta.** You'll feel like you're at sea when you step into this neighborhood hangout. The dining room's slanted roof is held aloft by wood columns tied off with thick rope. Above your head an armada of model boats floats on a sea created by light from the blue-and-green lanterns. You won't find a more extensive selection of cebiches—more than a dozen versions make choosing difficult. For a heartier meal, try the *lenguado royal,* sole covered with a creamy sauce of shrimp and mushrooms. To make the evening more romantic, ask for one of the tables on the patio under the papaya trees. ⊠ *José Galvez 667, Miraflores* ☎ *01/445–8370* ⊟ *AE, DC, MC, V.*

$ ✕ **Segundo Muelle.** Plenty of restaurants can be found along the ocean, but the crowds keep coming to this cheerful little spot. The reason is the seafood, specifically the lip-smacking cebiche. Choose from 10 different versions, each with some type of fish, shrimp, squid, or octopus; the *mixto* lets you sample them all. For something a little different, there's the tiradito, which livens up the traditional recipe by omitting the onions in favor of peppers and garlic. There are plenty of other fish dishes on the menu, all cooked any way you like. ⊠ *Malecón Cisneros 156 Miraflores* ☎ *01/241–5040* ⊠ *Av. Conquistadores 490, San Isidro* ☎ *01/421–1206* ⊟ *AE. DC, MC, V* ☉ *No dinner.*

Steak

$$$–$$$$ ✕ **El Rincón Gaucho.** The cowhides on the floors and the photos of prize heifers on the walls don't let you forget that this is the place for steaks. Even the menus are made of hand-tooled leather. The Argentine beef, always sliced to order, is on display just inside the front door. The best bet for the indecisive is the *parrillada,* a mixed grill of steaks, kidneys, livers, pork chops, chicken legs, and blood pudding. The order for two will satisfy three or four people. Although the restaurant overlooks the ocean, only a handful of tables have a view. ⊠ *Av. Armendariz 580, Miraflores* ☎ *01/447–4778* ⊟ *AE, DC, MC, V.*

$$–$$$ ✕ **La Tranquera.** A butcher's front window couldn't display more cuts of meat than the glass case along the wall of this local landmark. Check out the different cuts, then inform your waiter which one you want and how it should be cooked. It will arrive at your table atop a charcoal brazier, still sizzling from the grill. If you have a lighter appetite, the *costillas a la barbacoa* are basted with a tangy barbecue sauce that doesn't overwhelm the flavor of the ribs. Hearty eaters will appreciate all 26 ounces of short ribs that make up the *asado de tira.* ⊠ *Av. José Pardo 285, Miraflores* ☎ *01/447–5111* ⊟ *AE, DC, MC, V.*

Swiss

$–$$$ ✕ **La Tiendecita Blanca.** A shiny brass espresso machine is the only modern touch at this old-fashioned eatery that first flung open its doors in 1937. The fancifully painted woodwork on the doors and along the ceiling and the honey-colored baby grand conjure up the Old Country. Crepes

A FINE KETTLE OF FISH

AS THE WAITER PLACED the steaming bowl of sopa de mariscos on the table between us, my dining companion leaned forward and breathed in deeply. A huge smile crept across her face.

"Why isn't there food like this anywhere else in the world?" she asked, gesturing at the thick seafood soup. "Because the fish needs to be fresh. You can't make a dish like this with frozen fish."

I didn't doubt that the fish was fresh. As we walked through the door of the restaurant we stopped to chat with Papo, who was helping to repair the net that had delivered the catch of the day. Isabel, slicing some slender strips of sea bass, waved merrily from the kitchen. It was interesting to see how this husband and wife team had divided up the duties. She made sure the fish was expertly prepared, and he made sure there was fish.

Their restaurant happened to be in the coastal community of Chorillos, but there are hundreds of similar places scattered around Lima. They range from single-room shacks on the beach where a piece of perfectly prepared pescado costs a few dollars to domed dining rooms in upscale neighborhoods where the exact same dish sets you back ten times that amount. All of them are packed with Limeños who wouldn't think of spending their weekend any other way. Many people bring their children to the same spot where their parents took them years before.

The basic dish in all of these restaurants is cebiche, chunks of raw fish marinated in lemon juice and topped with onions. You'll almost always find sweet potatoes and steamed corn piled on the plate as well. But I soon found that there are innumerable variations to the recipe. Some cooks squeeze in limes or another type of citrus. Others substitute shellfish such as conchitas (scallops) or camarones (shrimp). The more adventurous add sauces that completely transform the dish.

The menu at any of these cebicherías is likely to includes dozens of other dishes, which can be intimidating to those who who can't tell lenguado (sole) from langosta (lobster). I was relieved when my friend suggested we order a series of dishes that we could share. This is exactly what local families do—pass around huge platters of pescado until they are picked clean, then gesture to the server to bring out the next course.

We started off with the fragrant sopa de mariscos, overflowing with chorros (mussels) still in their shells. We moved on to tiradito, which is similar to cebiche but leaves off the onions and adds a spicy yellow-pepper sauce. It's one of the most colorful dishes you are likely to run across. A platter of chicharrones de calamar, little ringlets of deep-fried squid, arrived next. A squeeze of lime makes them irresistible. The grand finale, as always, was a nice piece of fish. Many restaurants suggest a dozen or more ways you might like to have it prepared. We had it grilled, or a la plancha.

By the time we were leaving at about 3 PM, Isabel was already scrubbing out the pots and pans and Papo was rolling up the net to bring back to the boat. Their shop, like most cebicherías, would be closed long before sunset. I asked my friend why they wouldn't stay open for dinner."I told you already, " she replied. "The fish has to be as fresh as possible. If not, why bother?"

— Mark Sullivan

suzette and cheese fondue are among the traditional choices, but you may want to fast-forward to dessert, as the glass case is filled with eye-popping pies and pastries. You can also do as the locals do and buy a few crusty rolls and sit outside in Parque Miraflores. ⊠ *Av. Larco Herrera 111, Miraflores* ☎ *01/445–9797* ☱ *AE, DC, MC, V.*

Vegetarian

★ ¢–$ ✕ **Bircher-Benner.** In a colonial-style house painted a very appropriate shade of green, this vegetarian eatery is always packed. The food—like the fish-free cebiche made with mushrooms and sweet potatoes—is just that tasty. Peruvian dishes such as lomo saltado are expertly prepared. The menu has pages of fresh fruit salads, including a few with unusual ingredients, such as figs. If you want to take home some of this goodness, there's a little grocery just inside the front door. ⊠ *Av. Diez Canseco 487, Miraflores* ☎ *01/444–4250* ☱ *AE, DC, MC, V.*

San Isidro

Most of San Isidro's restaurants are on or near Avenida Conquistadores, the neighborhood's main drag. This is one of the only places in the city where you can stroll around in search of the perfect meal.

Cafés

¢–$ ✕ **Café Olé.** Locals start their day at this cheerful little café, sipping coffee and nibbling pastries under the eye-catching red-and-yellow awnings. It's also a great place to stop for lunch or dinner, especially on weekends, when there's less competition for the tables. Sandwiches are a big hit here; one of the best is the *lomo humito*, consisting of smoked ham with a dash of honey. ⊠ *Pancho Fierro 115, San Isidro* ☎ *01/221–8288* ☱ *AE, DC, MC, V.*

Continental

$–$$ ✕ **El Cartujo.** With a tree-shaded park at its doorstep, El Cartujo feels
Fodor'sChoice miles away from the busy streets of San Isidro. Sit outside under honey-
★ color canopies or in the dining room dominated by a painting of the obscure order of monks that gave the place its name. The salads are excellent; the *ensalada flamenco* has smoked salmon, plump olives, and buttons of caviar atop fresh greens. Save room for seafood, especially the sole stuffed with lobster or the sea bass topped with crab. There's a top-notch wine list, and the steward is happy to help you make the perfect selection. ⊠ *Calle Los Libertadores 108, San Isidro* ☎ *01/222–2323* ⌕ *Reservations essential* ☱ *AE, DC, MC, V.*

French

$–$$ ✕ **Le Bistrot de Mes Fils.** You can get raw fish in numerous restaurants along Avenida Los Conquistadores, but Le Bistrot de Mes Fils is probably the only place with raw beef. Steak tartare, prepared with raw egg just as they do it in Paris, is one of the specialties of this homey little place. Also order other delicacies you thought you'd never find in Peru, such as foie gras. Blue-and-white-checkered curtains give the place an authentic bistro feel. If a glass of French wine is what you had in mind, the pleasantly dim bar opens at 8 PM. ⊠ *Av. Conquistadores 510, San Isidro* ☎ *01/422–6308* ☱ *AE, MC, V.*

Japanese

$–$$$ ✕ **Matsuei.** Chefs shout out a greeting as you enter the teak-floored dining room of this San Isidro standout. Widely considered the best Japanese restaurant in town, Matsuei specializes in sushi and sashimi. If that's not your thing, the menu offers pages of fish dishes that are broiled, steamed, and fried. The tasty *kushiyaki,* one of the specialities, is a broiled fillet with a ginger-flavored sauce. There is plenty for vegetarians. Japa-

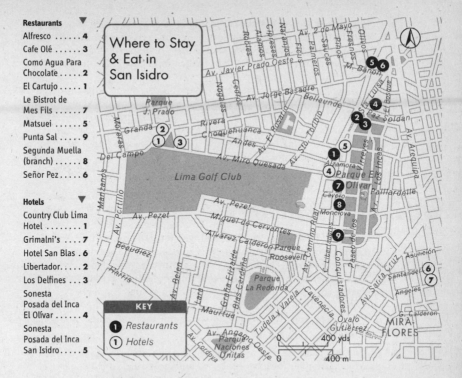

Where to Stay & Eat in San Isidro

KEY

1 *Restaurants*

1 *Hotels*

nese eggplant is grilled to perfection and served with a sweet sesame glaze in the *goma nasu*. The building is shaded by a cluster of slender trees. ✉ *Manuel Bañon 260, San Isidro* ☎ *01/422–4323* ▭ *AE, DC, MC, V.*

Mexican

$ ✕ **Como Agua Para Chocolate.** You can't miss this cantina, as the three-story structure is painted an eye-catching royal blue. Once you duck under the star-shaped piñata hanging just inside the front door you'll realize that the dining rooms are in equally vivid shades of gold and green. Happily, the food doesn't pale in comparison. Among the specials are *barbacoa de cordero,* which is lamb steamed in avocado leaves, and *albóndagas al chipotle,* a plate of spicy meatballs served with yellow rice. If you want to take home a bit of the magic, there's even a stand selling the namesake sweets ✉ *Pancho Fierro 108, San Isidro* ☎ *01/222–0174* ▭ *AE, DC, MC, V.*

Seafood

$–$$ ✕ **Alfresco.** If this popular place reminds you of an oceanfront seafood shack, you're not alone. Plastic tables and chairs under a yellow and orange canopy call to mind a dinner by the docks. The fish is among the best the city. Start with the excellent cebiche, available at a reasonable price. If you have room for more, try the *pulpo a la brasa* (grilled octopus) or *fetuccini negro con camarones* (squid ink pasta tossed with shrimp). Accompany your meal with a selection from the long list of South American wines. ✉ *Santa Luisa 295, San Isidro* ☎ *01/422–8915* ⊙ *No dinner* ▭ *AE, DC, MC, V.*

$–$$ ✕ **Punta Sal.** There are a few splashes of color in the dining room—the royal blue of the tablecloths, for example—but the real excitement is on the platters streaming out of the kitchen. Order the tiradito criollo, for example, and the slices of fish arrive covered in a vivid sauce made from yellow peppers. This place has won every award in the book, undoubtedly because the chefs constantly look to other countries for in spiration. This is one of the few *cebicherías* with carpaccio. Should you prefer, you can ask that your sole or sea bass be cooked one of 10 different ways. ⊠ *Av. Conquistadores 948, San Isidro* ☎ *01/441–7431* ⊠ *Malecón Cisneros at Av. Tripoli Miraflores* ☎ *01/242–4524* ☐ *AE, DC, MC, V* ⊘ *No dinner.*

$ ✕ **Señor Pez.** Locals can't get enough of this restaurant—maybe because the fish dishes are so good, or maybe because the prices, including the lunch specials, are so reasonable. The popularity might also stem from the place's not taking itself too seriously. One platter of *cau cau* is labeled "King Kong" because of its size. Some people just stop by for a beer in the afternoon, as the sun streaming through the huge windows is incredibly inviting. ⊠ *El Bosque 170, San Isidro* ☎ *01/921–1458* ☐ *AE, MC, V* ⊘ *No dinner.*

WHERE TO STAY

Lima isn't lacking in terms of lodging—you can't go far before you see the flurry of flags above a doorway indicating that international travelers are welcome. If you have a bit of money to spend, the capital has some astonishing accommodations. For something special, pass by the gleaming towers of glass and steel and head to such charmers as the Miraflores Park Plaza, the Country Club Lima Hotel, or the Gran Hotel Bolívar. This trio of luxury hotels, so notable that tour guides point them out, offers a taste of the city's rich history.

There are plenty of low-cost lodgings, but they are not clustered together as in many other cities. Budget hotels and most others are on quiet streets in the mostly residential neighborhoods of Miraflores, San Isidro, and Barranco. These areas are safe and secure, so you don't have to worry about taking a stroll during the day. Because many streets are deserted after dark, it's usually better to take a taxi at night. Travelers looking for something a little different should look at Barranco, which has a bohemian flavor. There are no big resorts here, just small hotels with a funky flavor. All of these neighborhoods are linked to El Centro by the Paseo de la República, so getting to the major sights is a snap.

While the historic center is much safer than it once was, it still has few decent hotels. A few holdouts, such as Gran Hotel Bolívar, are outstanding. If you decide to stay near the heart of the city, remember that you have far fewer options in terms of bars and restaurants than in other neighborhoods.

WHAT IT COSTS In Nuevo Soles				
$$$$	**$$$**	**$$**	**$**	**¢**
FOR 2 PEOPLE over 500	375–500	250–375	125–250	under 125

Hotel prices are for a standard double room, excluding tax.

Barranco

$ ▥ **Hostel Domeyer.** A friendly labrador retriever greets you at the gate of this funky find. Barranco is the artist hangout, so it's no surprise that the hotel's common areas are furnished in what might called "thrift store chic." Bronze sculptures are scattered about and paper lanterns hang from above. It all somehow works with the old house's vividly colored tile floors. Rooms have high ceilings and tall windows with shutters you can throw open to catch the ocean breezes. The only problem is the baths, which lack a bit of privacy. ⊠ *Jr. Domeyer 296, Barranco* ☎ *01/247–*

1413 ⊕ *page.to/domeyerhostal* ⇔ *8 rooms* ⚲ *Cable TV, in-room VCRs, bar, laundry service* ⊟ *AE, DC, MC, V.*

¢ ▦ **La Quinta Allison.** On a quiet side street in Barranco, this unassuming hotel doesn't shout to get your attention. But you should take a second look, especially because it's by far the cheapest place in the neighborhood. Rooms are on the small side, but are more than comfortable. All of the neighborhood sights are within a few blocks. ⊠ *Jr. 28 de Julio 281, Barranco* ☎ *01/247-1515* ⊠ *01/247-6430* ⊕ *www. hotel-laquinta.com.pe* ⇔ *20 rooms* ⚲ *Restaurant, room service, cable TV, fans, bar* ⊟ *MC, V.*

El Centro

$$$$ ▦ **Sheraton Lima Hotel & Casino.** The country's largest casino can be found in the lobby of downtown's most distinguished hotel. You might call it a landmark, except for the fact that its concrete facade makes it fade into the background. Perfectly serviceable rooms have subdued colors and surround an open atrium. This is a good choice for business travelers, as it has eight large meeting rooms and a convention center. Tourists appreciate that it's within walking distance of the city's historical district. The hotel is near the expressway, so it's also a short drive to San Isidro and Miraflores. ⊠ *Paseo de la República 170, El Centro* ☎ *01/315-5000* ⊠ *01/315-5015* ⇔ *438 rooms, 21 suites* ⚲ *3 restaurants, coffee shop, in-room data ports, in-room safes, minibars, cable TV, tennis court, pool, bar, casino, shops, laundry services, Internet, business services, convention center, meeting rooms, airport shuttle* ⊟ *AE, DC, MC, V.*

$$ ▦ **Gran Hotel Bolívar.** Tastes may have changed since it was built in 1924,
Fodor'sChoice but this grand dame retains the sumptuousness of the days when guests
★ included Ernest Hemingway. As you enter the marble-columned rotunda, your eyes are drawn upward to the magnificent stained-glass dome. Off to one side is the bar, which remains as popular as ever. The tables on the terrace are the perfect place to enjoy the best pisco sours in town. A grand staircase sweeps you up to the rooms, which retain lovely touches like parquet floors. Pull back the curtains for an unforgettable view of Plaza San Martín. ⊠ *Plaza San Martín, El Centro* ☎ *01/428-7672* ⊠ *01/428-7674* ⊕ *www.hotelbolivar.com* ⇔ *272 rooms, 5 suites* ⚲ *2 restaurants, room service, in-room safes, cable TV, bar, convention center, meeting rooms* ⊟ *AE, DC, MC, V.*

$ ▦ **Kamana Hotel.** Less than three blocks from the Plaza de Armas, this hotel puts you right in the middle of things. All the sights in downtown are a short walk away. The best part is that you don't have to pay a lot for this prime spot. Rooms are quite comfortable, and the locally made textiles make each feel a little different. Although rooms facing the street are sunnier, ask for an inside room if traffic noise bothers you. The improbably named café, Mr. Koala, specializes in Italian fare. ⊠ *Jr. Camaná 547, El Centro* ☎ *01/426-7201* ⊠ *01/426-0790* ⊕ *www. hotelkamana.com* ⇔ *44 rooms* ⚲ *Café, room service, cable TV, in-room safes, minibars, bar, laundry service, Internet, meeting rooms* ⊟ *AE, DC, MC, V* ⎢⊙⎢ *CP.*

¢ ▦ **La Estrella de Belén.** There aren't many bargains like this left: for less than you'll probably spend on dinner, get clean, comfortable accommodations on one of the safest streets in downtown. The staff works hard, so you can be sure the wood floor in each of the sunny rooms shines. The café in the lobby, where a brooding mural dominates, serves up incredibly inexpensive traditional fare. The majestic Plaza San Martín is less than a block away. ⊠ *Jr. de la Union 1051, El Centro* ☎ *01/428-6462* ⇔ *20 rooms* ⚲ *Café, fans, cable TV* ⊟ *MC, V.*

Miraflores

$$$$ ⊡ **Miraflores Park Plaza.** Surprisingly few of the city's hotels are near the ocean, which is why this hotel is in such demand. If you think the views from your room are breathtaking, just head up to the rooftop pool overlooking the entire coastline. Rooms have sitting areas that make them as big as suites, and computer connections and fax machines that make them perfect for business travelers. Better suited for couples are the suites, which have hot tubs strategically placed beside the beds. Don't miss the Dr. Jekyll and Mr. Hyde bar, which has a hidden mezzanine for romantic rendezvous. ⊠ *Malecón de la Reserva 1035, Miraflores* ☎ *01/242–3000* 🖷 *01/242–3393* ⊕ *www.mira-park.com* 📣 *64 rooms, 17 suites* ♧ *2 restaurants, room service, in-room data ports, in-room safes, minibars, cable TV with movies, in-room VCRs, pool, health club, squash, 2 bars, shops, laundry services, Internet, business services, meeting rooms, airport shuttle* ⊟ *AE, MC, V.*

$$$$ ⊡ **Marriott Hotel & Stellaris Casino.** This isn't a hotel—it's a small city. Just about anything you long for, whether it's a chocolate-chip cookie or a pair of diamond earrings, can be had in the shops downstairs. If not, there's the Larcomar shopping center across the street. The views are spectacular from the glass tower, which forever altered the skyline of Miraflores when it opened at the turn of the millennium. On clear days the entire coastline is visible. The only disappointment is the rooms, which are luxuriously appointed but lack the slightest hint that you're in Peru. The Stellaris Casino, one of the city's most glittery, is a winner. ⊠ *Malecón de la Reserva 615, Miraflores* ☎ *01/217–7000* 🖷 *01/217–7002* ⊕ *www.marriotthotels.com* 📣 *288 rooms, 12 suites* ♧ *2 restaurants, café, in-room data ports, in-room safes, minibars, cable TV with movies, 2 tennis courts, pool, health club, hair salon, bar, piano bar, casino, shops, dry cleaning, laundry service, Internet, business services, convention center, meeting rooms, airport shuttle* ⊟ *AE, DC, MC, V.*

$$ ⊡ **DoubleTree El Pardo Hotel.** This is one hotel where you won't want to go to your room. The open-air café on the ground floor is a great place for a cocktail, while the rooftop pool and hot tub have a view that will leave you breathless. The high-tech health club, with all the latest equipment, is among the best in the city. This is primarily a business hotel, so there is a well-stocked business center and half a dozen meeting rooms that can be configured for just about any purpose. It's fair rate makes it a good deal for pleasure travelers as well. ⊠ *Jr. Independencia 141, Miraflores* ☎ *01/241–0410* 🖷 *01/444–2171* ⊕ *www.doubletreepardo. com.pe* 📣 *92 rooms, 18 suites* ♧ *Restaurant, café, room service, in-room data ports, in-room safes, minibars, cable TV with movies, pool, hot tub, health club, bar, laundry service, Internet, business services, convention center, meeting rooms, airport transfers* ⊟ *AE, DC, MC, V.*

$$

Fodor's Choice

★

⊡ **Hotel Antigua Miraflores.** In a salmon-colored mansion dating back more than a century, this elegantly appointed hotel is perhaps the city's loveliest lodging. Black-and-white marble floors greet you as you stroll through the antiques-filled lobby. Up the wooden staircase are guest rooms with hand-carved furniture. Those in front have more character, while those in the newer section curve around a graceful fountain. Known for its impeccable service, the hotel sees repeat business year after year. The original art that adorns the dining room is for sale, so you may want to take home a souvenir of your stay. ⊠ *Grau 350, Miraflores* ☎ *01/241–6116* 🖷 *01/241–6115* ⊕ *www.peru-hotel* 📣 *15 rooms* ♧ *Restaurant, fans, cable TV, gym, hot tub, bar, Internet meeting rooms* ⊟ *AE, DC, MC, V.*

$

Fodor's Choice

★

⊡ **La Castellana.** A favorite for years, this exuberantly neoclassical structure resembles a small castle. The foyer, where wrought-iron lanterns cast a soft glow, is a taste of what is to come. Beyond are lovely touches like stained-glass windows and a towering turret. All the wood-shuttered rooms are lovely, but especially nice are No. 10, which overlooks the sunny courtyard, and No. 15, which has a private balcony facing the front. The friendly staff goes above and beyond the call of duty, even helping with things like airplane reservations. This inn remains immensely popular, so reservations should be made far in advance. ⊠ *Grimaldo del Solar 222, Miraflores* ☎ *01/444–3530* 🖷 *01/446–8030* ⊕ *www.hotel-lacastellana.com* ⇗ *29 rooms* ⚹ *Restaurant, fans, in-room safes, cable TV, bar* ⊟ *AE, DC, MC, V.*

$ 🖵 **Colonial Inn.** Elaborately carved wooden balconies accentuate the facade of this mustard-colored colonial-style edifice. A huge fireplace dominates the lobby, where a graceful arch leads to the airy restaurant serving traditional fare. Religious relics such as heavy iron crosses decorate the common areas found on every floor. Rooms leading off the wrought-iron staircase have nice touches like wood wainscoting and beamed ceilings. One especially nice touch is the minuscule bar, with a vault ceiling and padded wallpaper on the walls. Here, beside the antique upright piano, chat with other guests as you enjoy a pisco sour. ⊠ *Commandante Espinar 310, Miraflores* ☎ *01/241–7471* 🖷 *01/445–7587* ⊕ *www.hotelcolonialinn.com* ⇗ *34 rooms* ⚹ *Restaurant, room service, fans, in-room safes, minibars, 2 bars, laundry service, Internet, airport transfers* ⊟ *AE, DC, MC, V.*

$ 🖵 **Leon de Oro.** A statue of a lion stands guard at this boutique hotel. Don't expect the usual bright colors and colonial-style furniture. Instead you'll find muted shades and crisp lines in the generously sized rooms. The butter-soft linens on the queen-size beds and polished marble in the baths will leave you feeling pampered. For real luxury, spend a bit more on a suite and settle into your own hot tub. On a quiet street in Miraflores, the hotel is an easy walk from dozens of shops and restaurants. ⊠ *Av. La Paz 930, Miraflores* ☎ *01/242–6200* 🖷 *01/444–9805* ⊕ *www.leondeoroperu.com* ⇗ *42 rooms, 2 suites* ⚹ *Restaurant, room service, fans, in-room safes, cable TV, lounge, laundry service* ⊟ *AE, DC, MC, V.*

$ 🖵 **San Antonio Abad.** Cool breezes blow through the arches at this mansion on the eastern edge of Miraflores. Common areas decorated with colonial-style furniture are found throughout the rambling old building. The wood staircase that dominates the lobby leads up to cozy rooms, many of which have wood floors and beamed ceilings. Some have balconies that overlook the sunny patio. The hotel is nestled in a quiet residential area, so nothing is likely to disturb your slumber. Three parks, including the lovely Parque Reducto, are within a few blocks. The shops and restaurants of Miraflores are a 10-minute walk away. ⊠ *Ramón Ribeyro 301, Miraflores* ☎ *01/447–6766* 🖷 *01/446–4208* ⇗ *24 rooms* ⚹ *Dining room, cable TV, Internet, meeting rooms* ⊟ *AE, DC, MC, V* ⫟⫠ *BP.*

¢–$ 🖵 **Hostal Torreblanca.** With a name that refers to the gleaming white tower on its top floor, you can guess that this butterscotch-colored building is distinctive. All budget hotels should have little touches like the beamed ceilings and red-tile floors found in the sunny rooms. The best of the bunch has a roaring fireplace and a balcony overlooking a circular park covered with flowers. Although the hotel is a bit far from the center of Miraflores, it is just a block from the beach. Many people from the neighborhood are regulars at the restaurant, which has a huge grill for sizzling steaks. ⊠ *Av. José Pardo 1453, Miraflores* ☎ *01/242–1876* 🖷 *01/447–0142* ⊕ *www.torreblancaperu.com* ⇗ *30 rooms* ⚹ *Restaurant, room service, fans, minibars, cable TV, bar, laundry service, airport transfer* ⊟ *AE, DC, MC, V* ⫟⫠ *BP.*

¢ 🖵 **El Carmelo.** A stone's throw from Parque del Amor, this little inn is on one of the neighborhood's quietest streets, yet all the hustle and bustle of Parque Miraflores is merely four blocks away. Simply furnished rooms, some with nice touches like wood floors, are clean and comfortable. Some have interior windows, so ask for one facing the street. There's a little bar in the lobby where guests mingle. ⊠ *Bolognesi 749, Miraflores* ☎ *01/446–0575* ☒ *01/249–9029* ⤴ *31 rooms* ⚬ *Restaurant, dining room, room service, fans, TV with cable, bar, Internet, laundry service* ⊟ *AE, DC, MC, V* ⏃⏃ *CP.*

¢ 🖭 **Michelle Inn.** You won't come any closer to staying in a private home than this little bed and breakfast. On a quiet street, it's a favorite of people in town for a month or more. It's half a block from the seaside cliffs, so some rooms have views of a sliver of the ocean. Paragliders often sail past the windows. Gazing down from the second floor, the señora keeps the staffers on their toes. The wood-floored rooms are large and sunny, and the baths are sparkling. It's not fancy, but it's one of the cheapest places to stay in Lima. ⊠ *Av. de la Aviación 565, Miraflores* ☎ *01/446–9381* ☒ *01/444–5047* ⊘ *hostalmichel@terra.com.pe* ⤴ *8 rooms* ⚬ *Dining room, fan, cable TV, pool* ⊟ *MC, V* ⏃⏃ *CP.*

¢ 🖭 **Las Palmas.** A block from Parque Miraflores, this apricot-colored building puts you in the heart of things. The paneled lobby and wood staircase call to mind an older European pension. Upstairs, however, things are completely modern. Many of the comfortably furnished rooms are a bit on the small side, so ask to see a few before you decide. Calle Berlín, which runs along the side, is lined with several friendly little cafés serving incredibly inexpensive lunches. ⊠ *Calle Bellavista 320, Miraflores* ☎ *01/444–6033* ☒ *01/444-6036* ⊕ *www.hotellaspalmas.com* ⤴ *66 rooms, 3 suites* ⚬ *Restaurant, room service, fans, cable TV, bar, Internet* ⊟ *AE, DC, MC, V.*

San Isidro

$$$$ 🖭 **Country Club Lima Hotel.** Priceless paintings from the Museo Pedro de
Fodor'sChoice Osma hang in each room in this luxurious lodging. The hacienda-style
★ hotel, dating from 1927, is itself a work of art. Just step into the lobby, where hand-painted tiles reflect the yellows and greens of the stained-glass ceiling. The air of refinement continues in the rooms, all of which are draped with fine fabrics. Many have private balconies that overlook the oval-shaped pool or the well-tended gardens. Locals frequently come by for high tea in the atrium or traditional fare in the elegant restaurant. The outdoor terrace is perfect for romantic dinners. ⊠ *Los Eucaliptos 590, San Isidro* ☎ *01/211–9000* ☒ *01/211–9002* ⤴ *75 rooms* ⚬ *Restaurant, room service, in-room data ports, in-room safes, minibars, cable TV with movies, pool, hair saloon, gym, sauna, shops, laundry services, Internet, business services, meeting rooms, airport shuttle* ⊟ *AE, DC, MC, V.*

$$$$ 🖭 **Libertador Hotel.** When you want to relax, this high-rise hotel knows how to accommodate you. The staff greets you in voices barely above a whisper as you stroll through the understated lobby. Although the hotel is in the heart of San Isidro's business district, the rooms are surprisingly quiet. No bland furnishings here, as bright fabrics and original artwork make you doubt that this is a chain hotel. The top-floor restaurant, the Ostrich House, specializes in dishes made from that odd bird. The dining room has views of Club Lima Golf. ⊠ *Los Eucaliptos 550, San Isidro* ☎ *01/421–6666* ☒ *01/442–3011* ⊕ *www.libertador.com.pe* ⤴ *53 rooms* ⚬ *2 restaurants, room service, minibars, cable TV with movies, health club, bar, laundry service, Internet, business services, convention center, meeting rooms, airport transfer* ⊟ *AE, DC, MC, V.*

$$$$ 🖭 **Los Delfines.** It's not every day that a pair of dolphins greets you near the entrance of your hotel. Yaku and Wayra do just that in the lobby of

this high-rise. Kids love to help feed them as their parents look on from the adjacent café. Although they're a bit on the small side, the rooms are bright and comfortably furnished, and many have sweeping views of the adjacent Club Lima Golf. Downstairs, the beautifully decorated Knossos restaurant serves up delicious Indian fare. ⊠ *Los Eucaliptos 555, San Isidro* ☎ *01/211–9000* 🖷 *01/211–9002* ⊕ *www.losdelfineshotel.com.pe* ⏎ *207 rooms, 24 suites* 🔥 *Restaurant, café, room service, in-room data ports, in-room safes, minibars, cable TV with movies, pool, hair saloon, gym, sauna, bar, casino, shops, laundry services, Internet, business services, convention center, meeting rooms, airport shuttle* ⊟ *AE, MC, V.*

★ **$$$$** 🏨 **Sonesta Posada del Inca El Olívar.** Stretching along an old olive grove, this luminous hotel has one of the most relaxed settings in San Isidro. This is especially true as you avail yourself of the sundeck and pool on the top floor. Rooms are amply proportioned, especially those with private balconies overflowing with greenery. The clientele is mostly business travelers, so the rooms have computer connections and lots of space to spread out. Refined Italian cuisine is served at I Vitrali, where you're treated to a view of the park. Ichi Ban serves up a vast selection of sushi and sashimi. ⊠ *Pancho Fierro 194, San Isidro* ☎ *01/221–2121* 🖷 *01/221–2141* ⊕ *www.sonesta.com* ⏎ *134 rooms, 11 suites* 🔥 *2 restaurants, café, room service, in-room dataports, in-room safes, minibars, cable TV with movies, pool, hair salon, health club, bar, shops, laundry services, Internet, business services, convention center, meeting rooms, airport transfer* ⊟ *AE, DC, MC, V.*

$$ 🏨 **Sonesta Posada del Inca San Isidro.** With dozens of bars and restaurants within walking distance, this hotel puts you right in the middle of the action. It has all the amenities—except a pool—of its more upscale sibling, but the price tag is considerably less. Rooms are quite large, with pairs of tables to spread out your work on. Sun streams through the windows, double paned to keep out the noise from the street. Relax with a pisco sour in Inkafé, the modern café in the corner of the lobby. Wheelchair ramps allow free movement for those who can't manage steps. ⊠ *Av. Libertadores 490, San Isidro* ☎ *01/222–4373* 🖷 *01/222–4370* ⊕ *www.sonesta.com* ⏎ *45 rooms, 5 suites* 🔥 *Restaurant, in-room data ports, in-room safes, minibars, cable TV, bar, Internet, business services, laundry services, airport shuttle* ⊟ *AE, DC, MC, V.*

★ **$** 🏨 **Hotel San Blas.** The best deal in San Isidro—maybe in the entire city—is this little gem. Its price tag is below that of many budget hotels, while its amenities are equal to those of quite a few resorts. The bright, airy rooms are as big as suites and have niceties like modem connections and sound-proof windows. Jacuzzis turn the baths into spas. A well-equipped meeting room on the ground floor that accommodates 30 people opens out into a sunny patio. The café in the lobby is on call if you order up a midnight snack, even if it's three in the morning. ⊠ *Av. Arequipa 3940, San Isidro* ☎ *01/222-2601* 🖷 *01/222-0516* ⊕ *www.hotelsanblas.com. pe* ⏎ *30 rooms* 🔥 *Café, room service, in-room safes, in-room hot tubs, minibar, hair salon, laundry service, Internet, business center, meeting rooms, airport shuttle* ⊟ *AE, DC, MC, V.*

¢ 🏨 **Grimalni's.** This is extremely rare in upscale San Isidro—a real budget lodging. Even better, this seven-story building is not on some dimly lit street but right in the middle of things. In a few minutes you can walk to dozens of shops and restaurants. For this price you don't get luxury—the rooms are on the small side, and some have windows that face the inside of the building. What you do get is a comfortable bed and a sparkling bath. The glassed-in bar on the second floor is a good place to relax after a day of sightseeing. ⊠ *Av. Arequipa 3960, San Isidro* ☎ *01/ 222-1847* 🖷 *01/222-1846* ⏎ *14 rooms* 🔥 *Coffee shop, room service, cable TV, bar, laundry service* ⊟ *MC, V.*

NIGHTLIFE & THE ARTS

Lima may not be the city that doesn't sleep, but it certainly can't be getting enough rest. Limeños love to go out on the town, as you'll notice on any Friday or Saturday night. Early in the evening they are clustered around movie theaters and concert halls, while late at night they are piling into taxis headed to the bars and clubs of Miraflores and Barranco. For more details on the city's cultural offerings, check newsstands on Fridays for the English-language *Lima Herald*. Ask at your hotel for a free copy of *Peru Guide*, an English-language monthly full of information on bars and clubs as well as galleries and performances. For the latest hot spots, peruse the Spanish-language *El Comercio*.

The Arts

Film

In addition to the latest Latin American hits, movie theaters in and around Lima screen all the Hollywood blockbusters. Unless you can deal with a film that has been *doblada* (dubbed) into Spanish, make sure your selection is in English with *subtituladas* (subtitles). Complete listings are found each Friday in *El Comercio*.

In Lima's Museo de Arte is a small art house called **Filmoteca de Lima** (✉ Paseo Colón 125, El Centro ☎ 01/423–4732). Many of the classics screened here have been dubbed into Spanish, so check ahead if you aren't fluent. **Multicines Starvisión El Pacífico** (✉ Av. José Pardo 121, Monterrico ☎ 01/445–6990) always has a line of people waiting to get into its twelve theaters. It is conveniently across from Parque Miraflores. **Cinemark Perú Jockey Plaza** (✉ Av. Javier Prado 4200, Miraflores ☎ 01/435–9262) has a dozen theaters. It's inside the city's most popular shopping mall. **UVK Multicines Larcomar** (✉ Malecón de la Reserva and Av. José Larco, Miraflores ☎ 01/446–7336) has a whopping 14 screens. It's in the Larcomar shopping center, so expect lots of noisy teenagers.

Galleries

Miraflores is full of art galleries that show the works of Peruvian and occasionally foreign artists. In the rear of the Municipalidad de Miraflores, the **Sala Luis Miró Quesada Garland** (✉ Av. Larco Herrera and Calle Diez Canseco, Miraflores ☎ 01/444–0540) sponsors exhibits of sculpture, painting, and photography. **Trapecio** (✉ Av. Larco Herrera 743, Miraflores ☎ 01/444–0842) shows works by contemporary Peruvian artists. **Corriente Alterna** (✉ Av. de la Aviación 500, Miraflores ☎ 01/242–8482) often has works by notable new artists.

In San Isidro, **Artco** (✉ Calle Rouad and Paz Soldán, San Isidro ☎ 01/221–3579) sponsors cutting-edge art, sometimes involving different mediums such as painting and video. **Praxis** (✉ Av. San Martín 689, at Diez Canseco, Barranco ☎ 01/477–2822) has constantly rotating exhibits of international artists experimenting with different forms.

Music

The Orquestra Sinfónica Nacional, ranked one of the best in Latin America, performs at the Museo de la Nación's **Auditoria Sinfónica** (✉ Av. Javier Prado Este 2465, San Borja ☎ 01/476–9878). In the heart of Barranco, the **Centro Cultural Juan Parra del Riego** (✉ Av. Pedro de Osma 135, Barranco ☎ 01/477–4506) sponsors performances by Latin American musicians.

In the Municipalidad de Miraflores, the **Centro Cultural Ricardo Palma** (✉ Av. Larco Herrera 770, Miraflores ☎ 01/446–3959), sponsors cultural events throughout the week, including films, poetry readings, and concerts. The **Instituto Cultural Peruano Norteamericano** (⊠ Av. Angamos Oeste and Av. Arequipa, Miraflores ☎ 01/446–0381) offers music ranging from jazz to classical to folk.

Nightlife

The most popular weekend destinations are *peñas,* bars that offer *música criolla,* a breathless combination of Peruvian, African, and other influences. The music is accompanied by flashily costumed dancers whipping themselves into a frenzy. Depending on the venue, these shows can be exhilarating or just plain exhausting. Ask locals to recommend one not geared toward tourists. Most peñas start the show at 10:30 or 11 and continue until the wee hours of the morning.

There are plenty of other options. A handful of establishments offer live music that might include rock, reggae, or regional favorites. These clubs, which run from claustrophobic to cavernous, are popular with a surprisingly broad segment of the population.

Bars

When you're in Barranco, a pleasant place to start off the evening is **La Posada del Mirador** (⊠ Ermita 104 Barranco ☎ 01/477–9577). The bar has a second-story balcony that looks out to sea, making this a great place to watch the sunset. There's often a crowd at **Mochilero's** (⊠ Av. Pedro de Osma 135, Barranco ☎ 01/477–4506), in the hotel of the same name. Bands perform on the weekends.

Facing Barranco's main square is **Juanito's** (⊠ Grau 274, Barranco ☎ no phone), one of the neighborhood's most venerable establishments. Built by Italian immigrants in 1905, the former pharmacy retains its glass-front cabinets. Today, however, the bottles inside are filled with wine and spirits. **Posada del Ángel** (⊠ Av. Pedro de Osma 164, Barranco ☎ 01/247–0341) retains its Victorian-era warmth. It's one of the few bars in Barranco where you can actually hold a conversation.

Miraflores lets you sample beers from around the world. If you're longing for a pint of Guinness, head to **Murphy's Irish Pub** (⊠ Schell 627 Miraflores ☎ 01/242–1212). The wood paneling and the well-worn dart board may convince you that you're in Ireland. If you prefer a good pilsner, try **Freiheit** (⊠ Lima 471, Miraflores ☎ 01/247–4630). The second-story establishment is a favorite among college students.

In San Isidro, toss back a Sapporo or any other Japanese beer at the sleek **Osaka** (⊠ Av. Conquistadores 999 San Isidro ☎ 01/222–0405). French wine would be apropos at the pleasantly dim **Le Bistrot de Mes Fils** (⊠ Av. Conquistadores 510, San Isidro ☎ 01/422–6308).

Dance Clubs

★ It's not really a dance club, but the patrons of **Kafé Kitsch** (⊠ Bolognesi 742, Barranco ☎ 01/242–3325) simply push back the tables so they can show off their moves. Busts of Elvis and statuettes of the Virgin Mary gaze down in astonishment. The crowd is mostly straight, but there's usually a contingent of gays as well. A triangular wood staircase leads up to **Déjà Vu** (⊠ Av. Grau 294, Barranco ☎ 01/247–3742), a collection of odd-shaped rooms where little tables are pushed together to accommodate big groups. The dance floor, off to one side, is a bit of an afterthought. Should the noise get to you, head out to the balcony overlooking the central square. An upscale crowd heads to **Costa Verde** (⊠ Playa Barranquito, Barranco ☎ 01/441–3367) when the city's most elegant restaurant transforms itself into the most elegant dance club. Don't even think about wearing shorts here.

Near Parque Miraflores is **Tequila Rocks** (✉ Calle Diez Canseco 146, Miraflores ☎ 01/444–3661), a downtown *discoteca* that's been popular for years. Drinks specials bring in the crowds seven nights a week.

Gay & Lesbian Clubs

Early in the evening you might want to stop for a drink at **La Sede** (✉ Av. 28 de Julio 441, Miraflores ☎01/242–2462). The candy apple–red walls give the place a funky feeling. After midnight you should head to the ★ most popular disco, **Downtown Todo Vale** (✉ Pasaje Los Pinos 160, Miraflores ☎ 01/444–6433). A balcony filled with comfy couches overlooks the cavernous dance floor. Psychotic drag queens dressed as hula dancers or space mutants shout epithets from the stage at the crowd of men and women.

In San Isidro, the place to be is **Mykonos** (✉ Av. Conquistadores 392, San Isidro ☎ 01/987–0848). This sleek little bar keeps the decibel level low enough that you can talk without shouting. The most fun to be had is at **Minotauro** (✉ Manuel Del Piño 694, Santa Beatriz ☎ 01/471–8141), a gay men's club in what was once a grand house. It feels slightly naughty, as if you invited a bunch of friends to party while your parents were out of town.

Live Music

Clubs offering live music are scattered all over Miraflores. It's easy to miss the **Jazz Zone** (✉ Av. La Paz 656, Miraflores ☎ 01/241–8139), as the unassuming little club is down an alley. You head up a bright red stairway to the dimly lit second-story lounge. Expect jazz flavored with local rhythms. As overblown as the Jazz Zone is understated **Satchmo's** (✉ Av. La Paz 538, Miraflores ☎ 01/444–4957). Flashing lights let you know you've arrived. The music, from all around Latin America, attracts a slightly older crowd. From the slender green facade, you'd never guess how many people can fit into **El Cocodrilo Verde** (✉ Francisco de Paula Camino 226, Miraflores ☎ 01/242–7583). Dozens of round café tables are scattered around the main room as well as the upstairs mezzanine. A younger crowd enjoys everything from jazz to rock.

In Barranco, **El Ekeko** (✉ Grau 266, Barranco ☎ 01/477–5823) is the most elegant of the live music venues. Head upstairs to the main room, where tall windows crowned with yellow and green stained glass recall when this neighborhood was a retreat for the rich and powerful. Locals who pack the place enjoy Latin-flavored music, from calypso to cha-cha-cha. Slightly more sedate than most clubs is **La Estación de Barranco** (✉ Av. Pedro de Osma 112, Barranco ☎ 01/467–8804). In an old train station, the warmly lit space specializes in folk music. **La Noche** (✉ Bolognesi 307, Barranco ☎ 01/477–4154) is at the far end of a pedestrian street called Bulevar Sánchez Carrión. The rock and jazz bands booked here appeal to a youthful, noisy crowd. Escape to an outdoor patio or a second-story balcony to check out who is coming and going.

Peñas

The most upmarket of the peñas is found in Barranco at **Manos Morenas** (✉ Av. Pedro de Osma 409, Barranco ☎ 01/467–0421). Extravagantly costumed performers hardly seem to touch the ground as they recreate dances from around the region. The musicians, switching instruments half a dozen times during a song, are without equal. The place feels like a theme park, though, perhaps because of the long tables of picture-taking tourists. Vying for the tourist market is **La Candelaria** (✉ Av. Bolognesi 292, Barranco ☎ 01/247–1314), which is immediately recognizable from the fiery torches flanking the front door. A series of small spaces leads to the main room, where the dancers have plenty of room to show off their steps. The facade may be dull, but the attitude is anything but at **De Rompe y Raja** (✉ Jr. Manuel Segura 127, Barranco ☎ 01/247–3271). Slightly off the beaten path, this peña attracts mostly locals to its shows with *música negra,* a black variant of *música criolla.*

In Miraflores, an older crowd heads to **Sachún** (✉ Av. del Ejército 657, Miraflores ☎ 01/441–4465). The draw, it seems, are the sentimental favorites played by the band. **Zeñó Manué** (✉ 2 de Mayo 598, Miraflores ☎ 01/444–9049) offers traditional folk shows most nights.

SPORTS & THE OUTDOORS

Participant Sports

Athletic Clubs

The residents of the capital are a health-conscious bunch, which accounts for the number of health clubs scattered around the city. As you drive down the avenues of Miraflores, you'll spot long lines of Limeños on treadmills. One of the best gyms is the sleek **Las Americas** (✉ Calle Bellavista 216, Miraflores ☎ 01/242-6600). After working out on the state-of-the-art machines or taking an aerobics class, soak your tired muscles in the hot tub. Forgot your shorts? There's a shop on the premises that sells the latest styles and colors. A day pass costs about $6. You may never get around to working out at **Milenium Sports Club** (✉ Jr. Independencia 145, Miraflores ☎ 01/242-8557). Atop this three-level club is a sun deck with twin hot tubs. Locker rooms have saunas and steam rooms. The exercise rooms have huge windows facing the street, so there's plenty of natural light.

Golf

The best course in the city is **Club Lima Golf** (✉ Camino Real 720, San Isidro ☎ 01/442-6006). Unfortunately, it's not open to nonmembers. If you're determined to get some time on the links while in Lima, stay at Country Club Lima Hotel or Sonesta Posada del Inca El Olívar, both of which offer passes to their guests.

Paragliding

If you walk along the ocean on a sunny day, you'll doubtless see a dozen or so brilliantly colored swaths of cloth in the sky above you. Suspended from one is likely to be Luis Munarriz, an instructor of *paradente,* or paragliding. His school, called **Fly Adventure** (✉ Av. Jorge Chavez 658, Miraflores ☎ 01/241–5693 ⊕ www.yalatina.com/flyadventure) offers a six-day course for about $360.

Tennis

Right in the middle of Miraflores are the city's best tennis courts. **Club Tennis Terrazas** (✉ Malecón 28 de Julio 390, Miraflores ☎ 01/445-1984) is perched on the side on a hill leading down to the ocean, so you can enjoy the lovely views as you wait for one of the clay or grass courts. The cost for nonmembers is about $5 an hour.

Spectator Sports

Bullfighting

Bullfighting remains exceedingly popular in Peru. The spectacle, with all the pomp and circumstance of similar events in Spain, takes place in October and November at the **Plaza de Acho** (✉ Jr. Hualgayoc 332, Rímac ☎ 01/482-3360). Even if you have no interest in the actual event, it's worth getting a peak inside the bull ring that was once one of the largest in the world. Ticket prices depend on the event, but always expect to pay more for a seat in *sombra* (shade) than *sol* (sun).

Soccer

Soccer—or *fútbol*, as it's known in this part of the world—reigns supreme in Peru. When there's a highly contested match being televised, don't be surprised to see dozens of people in the street outside a bar or restaurant that happens to have a television. Peru's leading teams are Alianza, Universitario, Sport Boys, and Cristal. Matches are played year-round at the imposing **Estadio Nacional** (⊠ Jr. José Díaz, El Centro ☎ 01/433–6366). Tickets for most matches range from $5 to $25.

SHOPPING

Because most travelers must pass through on their way home, the capital has handicrafts from around the country. The prices are a bit higher than in Cusco or Arequipa, but so is the quality. Instead of schlepping around that adorable doll from Machu Picchu, you just might want to wait to buy one when you get back to Lima. Looking for an alpaca sweater or scarf? These items are found elsewhere in the country, but you won't find the selection you will in Lima. Hundreds of stores offer goods of the highest quality. The same goes for silver and gold jewelry. Wander down Avenida La Paz in Miraflores and you'll be astounded at the number of shops selling one-of-a-kind designs; the street also yields clothing and antiques at reasonable prices. Miraflores is also full of crafts shops, many of them along Avenida Petit Thouars. For upscale merchandise, many people now turn to the boutiques of San Isidro. For original works of art, the bohemian neighborhood of Barranco has many small galleries.

Malls

Limeños love to shop, as you'll discover when you walk through any of the city's massive malls. With more than 200 shops, **Jockey Plaza** (⊠ Av. Javier Prado 4200, Surco ☎ 01/435–1035) is by far the largest in Lima. Just about every chic boutique has opened a branch here, so it's the place to come for one-stop shopping. The only trouble is that it's in Surco, a hike from most hotels. Right in the heart of things is **Larcomar** (⊠ Larcomar Malecón de la Reserva and Av. José Larco, Miraflores ☎ 01/620–7583), a surprisingly appealing shopping center in Miraflores. It's built on a bluff below Parque Salazar, so it's almost invisible from the street. Its dozens of shops, bars, and restaurants are terraced so they all have views of the ocean. Kids like it because there's a movie theater, bowling alley, and several places to play video games.

Markets

On the northern edge of Miraflores, Avenida Petit Thouars has at least half a dozen markets crammed with vendors. No need to hit more than one or two, as they all carry the same merchandise. To get a rough idea of what an alpaca sweater or woven wallet should cost, head to **Artesanías Miraflores** (⊠ Av. Petit Thouars 5541, Miraflores ☎ no phone). It's small, but has a little of everything. Better-quality goods can be found at **La Portada del Sol** (⊠ Av. Petit Thouars 5411, Miraflores ☎ no phone). In this miniature mall the vendors show off their wares in glassed cases lit with halogen lamps. Some even accept credit cards. Ask a local about the best place for handicrafts and you'll probably be told to go to **Mercado Indios** (⊠ Av. Petit Thouars 5245, Miraflores ☎ no phone). Among the mass-produced souvenirs are a few one-of-a-kind pieces.

For rock-bottom prices, many people make a pilgrimage to Pueblo Libre. Several mazelike markets stand side by side on Avenida de la Marina near the corner of Avenida Sucre. As you browse, you'll be rubbing elbows with staffers from specialty shops who come here to replenish their stock. **Gran Mercado Inka** (✉ Av. de la Marina 884, Pueblo Libre ☏ no phone) has perhaps the best selection.

In El Centro there aren't as many souvenir shops as you might think. Most people head to **Artesanías Santo Domingo** (✉ Conde de Super and Jr. Camaná, Miraflores ☏ 01/242–2871), a cluster of shops in a pretty colonial-style building. If you get tired of shopping, the plaza outside overlooks the pretty Iglesia de Santo Domingo.

Specialty Shops

Antiques

Dozens of shops selling *antigüedades* crowd Avenida La Paz, making this street in Miraflores a favorite destination for bargain hunters. Toward the back of a little cluster of shops, **El Arcón** (✉ Av. La Paz 646, Miraflores ☏01/447–6149) packs an incredible variety into a small space. Head to the rooms in back for fearsome masks and colorful weavings dating back almost a century. **Antigüedades Siglo XVIII** (✉ Av. La Paz 661, Miraflores ☏ 01/445–6530) specializes in precious metals. Don't miss the case full of silver *milagros*, or miracles. These heart-shaped charms were once placed at the feet of religious statues in gratitude for answered prayers. Brooding saints dominate the walls of **El Armario** (✉ Av. La Paz 668, Miraflores ☏ 01/444–2502). They seemingly have no interest in the elaborately carved armoires that give the place its name.

Clothing

Lots of stores stock clothing made of alpaca, but one of the few to offer articles made from vicuña is **Alpaca 111** (✉ Av. Larco 671, Miraflores ☏ 01/447–1623 ✉ Larcomar Malecón de la Reserva and Av. José Larco, Miraflores ☏ 01/241–3484). This diminutive creature, distant cousin of the llama, produces the world's finest wool. It is fashioned into scarves, sweaters, and even knee-length coats. There are branches of the store in Hotel Los Delfines, Miraflores Park Hotel, and Sonesta Posada del Inca El Olívar.

There are several shops specializing in alpaca on Avenida La Paz in Miraflores. **Royal Alpaca** (✉ Av. La Paz 646, Miraflores ☏ 01/444–2150) sells sweaters and other pieces of clothing in sophisticated styles. Bright colors reign at **La Casa de la Alpaca** (✉ Av. La Paz 665, Miraflores ☏ 01/447–6271). The patterns are updated takes on Andean designs.

Fabric

Inspired by Peru's proud past, Silvia Lawson has created a line of fine fabrics. The wonderful weaves at **Silvania Prints** (✉ Calle Diez Canseco 378, San Isidro ☏ 01/242–2871) are printed by hand on the finest cotton. Buy them already fashioned into everything from scarves to tablecloths. **Lanifico** (✉ Av. Alberto del Campo 285, San Isidro ☏ 01/264–3186) offers fine fabrics made from baby alpaca—wool from animals no older than two years old.

Handicrafts

For beautiful pottery, head to **Antisuyo** (✉ Tacna 460, Miraflores ☏ 01/447–2557), which sells only traditional pieces from around the country. Tiny *retablos* (boxes filled with scenes of village life) are among the eye-catching objects at **Raices Peru** (✉ Av. La Paz 588, Miraflores ☏ 01/447–7457) For one-of-a-kind pieces, **Coral Roja** (✉ Recavarren 269, Miraflores ☏ 01/447–2552) sells work made on the premises. The little red building is known for its original designs.

Jewelry

It's unlikely you'll find gold jewelry elsewhere in designs as distinct as those at **H. Stern** (⊠ Museo de Oro Alonso de Molina 1100, Monterrico ☎ 01/345–1350) The well-regarded South American chain is savvy enough to know that people head to Peru for a taste of the culture. Many of their designs are influenced by the art of pre-Colombian peoples. One especially lovely piece is a vividly colored pin shaped like a Paracas warrior. Look for branches in top hotels, including Hotel Los Delfines, Hotel Marriott, and Sheraton Lima Hotel & Casino. For one-of-a-kind gifts, try **Migue** (⊠ Av. La Paz 311, Miraflores ☎ 01/444—0333), where you'll find jewelers fashioning original pieces in gold and other precious metals.

For sterling silver, you can't beat the classic designs at **Camusso** (⊠ Av. Oscar Benavides 679, El Centro ☎ 01/425–0260 ⊠ Av. Rivera Navarrete 788, San Isidro ☎ 01/442–0340), a local *platería* that opened its doors in 1933. Call ahead for a free guided tour of the factory, which is a few blocks west of El Centro. Whimsical designs fashioned in silver are the trademark of **Ilaria** (⊠ Av. Dos de Mayo 308, San Isidro ☎ 01/221–8575 ⊠ Los Eucaliptos 578, San Isidro ☎ 01/440–4875). The store has two branches in San Isidro.

Wine & Spirits

Winning the 2002 prize for the country's best pisco was **Santiago Queirolo** (⊠ Av. San Martín 1062, Pueblo Libre ☎ 01/463–1008). It has had years to practice, as the company was founded in 1880. Besides four types of pisco, also sample seven types of wine and two champagnes. Take a peek at how they are brewed and bottled at the factory in Pueblo Libre.

On a quiet street near Parque El Olívar, **Daily Care** (⊠ Calle Pancho Fierro 129, San Isidro ☎ 01/440–1235) stocks many wines. It also has plenty of savories in case you want to put together an impromptu picnic in the park.

SIDE TRIPS FROM LIMA

Pachacámac

31 km (19 mi) south of Lima on the Carretera Pan-American Highway.

While Machu Picchu in the east and Chán Chán in the north get the vast majority of visitors, this lesser known archaeological site is well worth seeing. Dating back to the first century, this city of plazas, palaces, and pyramids, many of them painstakingly restored, was for centuries a stronghold of the Huari people. Here they worshipped Pachacámac, creator of the world. It was a pilgrimage site, and people from all over the region came to worship here. In the 15th century the city was captured by the Inca, who added structures such as the *Acllahuasi*, the well-known Palace of the Chosen Women. When the Spanish heard of the city, they dispatched troops to plunder its riches. In 1533, two years before the founding of Lima, they marched triumphantly into the city, only to find a few remaining objects in gold. The site has an excellent small museum displaying discoveries made here. Although it's a quick drive from the city, the easiest way to see Pachacámac is by a half-day guided tour offered by Lima Tours and several other agencies in Lima. The cost is about $25 per person. ⊠ *Carretera Panamericana Sur* ☎ *01/430–0168* 🎫 *S/6* ⊙ *Daily 9–4.*

Pucusana

60 km (37 mi) south of Lima on the Carretera Panamericana Sur.

South of Lima you'll find a string of sandy beaches, most of them backed with massive, glistening sand dunes. The water is cold and rough, and lifeguards are nonexistent. Most have kiosks where you can buy cold drinks. The names can be wonderfully evocative. El Silencio, 42 km (26 mi) south of Lima, is known for its tranquil waters. Punta Rocas 50 km (31 mi) south of Lima does indeed have a rocky point, popular with surfers. Continue south along the Panamericana Sur to the last beach to reach Pucusana, a cliff-top fishing village that wraps around a little bay. You won't have to guess the livelihood of the town, as dozens of little boats bob and up and down with the waves. On weekends it's filled with day-trippers from Lima. There are vendors selling fried fish along the shore, or, wander into town to find any of dozens of cebicherías.

LIMA A TO Z

To research prices, get advice from other travelers, and book travel arrangements, visit www.fodors.com.

AIR TRAVEL

Numerous airlines handle domestic flights, so getting to any of the major tourist destinations is no problem. You can often find space at the last minute, especially outside of high season. Aero Continente has the most domestic flights, stopping in Arequipa, Chiclayo, Cusco, Iquitos, Juliaca, Trujillo, and other cities. LanPeru flies to Arequipa, Cusco, Juliaca, Puerto Maldonado, and Trujillo. Aero Cóndor flies to Trujillo, while Taca Peru flies to Cusco.

⁊ Carriers Aero Cóndor ☎ 01/442-5215 in Lima ⊕ www.aerocondor.com.pe. **Aero Continente** ☎ 888/586-9400 in North America; 01/242-4242 in Lima ⊕ www.aerocontinente.com. **LanPeru** ☎ 800-735-5590 in North America; 01/221-3764 in Lima. ⊕ www.lanperu.com. **Taca Peru** ☎ 01/446-0033 or 01/446-0033 ⊕ grupotaca.com.

AIRPORT

Aeropuerto Internacional Jorge Chávez is on the northwestern fringe of the city. A taxi to most places in the city should cost no more than $10. It is 10 km (6 mi) southeast and a 20-minute drive to El Centro, and a 30-minute drive to Miraflores and San Isidro.

⁊ Airport Information Aeropuerto Internacional Jorge Chávez ⊠ Av. Faucett s/n ☎ 01/575-1712 international, 01/574-5529 domestic.

BUS TRAVEL

There's no central bus terminal in Lima. Buses generally depart for the northern regions along Avenida Alfredo Mendiola in San Martín de Porres. Buses to the southern regions line up along Avenida Carlos Zavala, while buses to the central part of the country can be found at Montevideo, Lima, and Nicolás Ayllon. Recommended bus companies in Lima include Cruz del Sur, Ormeño, and Tepsa.

⁊ Bus Information Cruz del Sur ⊠ Jr. Quilca 531, El Centro ☎ 01/424-1005 or 01/424-0589. **Ormeño** ⊠ Javier Prado Este 1059, San Isidro ☎ 01/472-1710. **Tepsa** ⊠ Jr. Lampa 1337, El Centro ☎ 01/427-5642.

BUS TRAVEL WITHIN LIMA

Two types of buses—regular-size *micros* and the van-size *combis*—patrol the streets of Lima. You won't have to wait long for a bus; on major thoroughfares it is not uncommon to have half a dozen or more waving you aboard. You simply hop on at any intersection and pay the conductor as you leave. Fares are cheap, usually S/1.20, or 35¢ for a ride of any distance. It is difficult to tell where buses are headed. The conductors hang out the door and announce the route with the speed of an auctioneer, all but impossible to understand. A better way to discern the route is by the signs in the windshield or along the sides. The names of the major streets traveled will be listed. If a bus travels on a section of Avenida Arequipa, the sign will say "Arequipa." If it travels the entire distance, it will say "Todo Arequipa." When you want to get off, simply tell the conductor "la proxima esquina," meaning "the next corner." Give him plenty of notice, as it sometimes takes a while for the speeding buses to slow down.

CAR RENTAL

Most rental agencies also offer the services of a driver, a good solution for those who want the freedom of a car without the hassle of driving on Lima's busy streets. The agencies below all have branches at Jorge Chávez International Airport that are open 24 hours.

🚗 Major Agencies **Avis** ⌧ Av. Larco 1080, Miraflores ☎ 01/446-4533. **Budget** ⌧ Moreyra 569, San Isidro ☎ 01/442-8703. **Hertz** ⌧ Av. Cantuarias 160, Miraflores ☎ 01/447-2129. **National** ⌧ Av. España 453, El Centro ☎ 01/433-3750.

CAR TRAVEL

Lima's main streets are in pretty good condition, but heavy congestion and the almost complete absence of traffic lights make driving a harrowing experience. Better to leave the hassle to a taxi driver. However, a car is a great way to see the sights outside the city. The highways surrounding the capital are reasonably well maintained. In the city, always park in a guarded lot. If you can't find one, hire someone who offers "*cuidar su carro*" ("to take care of your car"). Pay about S/5 when you return and find your car intact.

EMBASSIES

🏢 **Canada** ⌧ Jr. Libertad, Miraflores ☎ 01/444-4015. **New Zealand** ⌧ Av. Natalio Sánchez 125, El Centro ☎ 01/433-4738. **United Kingdom** ⌧ Av. Larco 1301, Miraflores ☎ 01/617-3050. **United States** ⌧ Av. La Encalada, Cuadra 17, Monterrico ☎ 01/434-3000.

EMERGENCIES

For robberies and other petty crimes, contact the Tourist Police. English-speaking officers will help you negotiate the system. For more urgent matters, call the police and fire emergency numbers.

There are several clinics with English-speaking staff, including the Clinica Anglo-Americana and Clinica Ricardo Palma. Both are in San Isidro. There are pharmacies operating around the clock across the city. Look for Farmacia Deza, Farmacia Fasa, and InkaFarma.

🚑 Emergency Numbers **Fire** ☎ 116. **Police** ☎ 105. **Tourist Police** ☎ 01/225-8698 or 01/225-8699.

🏥 Hospital **Clinica Anglo-Americana** ⌧ Av. Alfredo Salazar, San Isidro ☎ 01/221-3656. **Clinica Ricardo Palma** ⌧ Av. Javier Pardo Este 1066, San Isidro ☎ 01/224-2224. 💊 Pharmacy **Farmacia Deza** ⌧ Av. Conquistadores 144, San Isidro ☎ 01/441-5860. **Farmacia Fasa** ⌧ Av. Benavides 487, Miraflores ☎ 01/475-7070 ⌧ Av. Larco 129, Miraflores ☎ 01/619-0000. **InkaFarma** ⌧ Av. Benavides 425, Miraflores ☎ 01/314-2020.

ENGLISH-LANGUAGE MEDIA

The *Lima Herald,* an English-language weekly published every Friday, is available at newsstands all over the city. There are several English-language guides available, including the monthly *Peru Guide.*

Ibero, a popular bookstore chain, has several branches around the city. You'll find a small selection of books in English, especially travel guides.

📚 Bookstores **Ibero** ⌧ Av. Diagonal 500, Miraflores ☎ 01/242-3152 ⌧ Av. Larco 199, Miraflores ☎ 01/445-5520 ⌧ Las Begonias 526, San Isidro ☎ 01/421-1214.

INTERNET

Get on-line at any of the city's dozens of Internet cafés, which usually charge S/2.50–S/3 an hour. In El Centro, Cybersandeg is open Monday–Saturday 8:30 AM–10 PM and Sunday 10:30–6. In Miraflores, Click. Com and Econovisis are open 24 hours.

🔢 Internet Cafés **Cybersandeg** ✉ De la Union 853, El Centro 📠📠 01/427-1695. **Click. Com** ✉ Av. Diagonal 218, Miraflores 📠 01/447-9290. **Econovisos** ✉ Av. Benavides 455, Miraflores 📠 01/444-4099.

MAIL & SHIPPING

The Correo Central, the city's main post office, is in an incredibly ornate building just off the Plaza de Armas. It's open Monday through Saturday 8–8 and Sunday 9–1. There are also branches in Miraflores and San Isidro. It's best to send important packages from the Federal Express office in Miraflores or the DHL and UPS offices in San Isidro. DHL is open weekdays 8:30–1 and 2–9, Saturday 9–5, and Sunday 9–1. Federal Express is open weekdays 8:30–6. UPS is open weekdays 8–6:30.

🔢 Post Offices **Centro** ✉ Av. Conde de Superunda, between Jr. de al Unión and Jr. Camaná 📠 01/427-0370. **Miraflores** ✉ Av. Petit Thouars 5201 📠 01/445-0697. **San Isidro** ✉ Av. Libertadores 325 📠 01/422-0981.

🔢 Shipping Services **DHL** ✉ Calle Los Castaños 225, San Isidro 📠 01/517-2500. **Federal Express** ✉ Martín Olaya 260, Miraflores 📠 01/242-2280. **UPS** ✉ Av. Perez Aranibar 2107, San Isidro 📠 01/264-0105.

MONEY MATTERS

Automatic teller machines have become ubiquitous in Lima. On Avenida José Pardo, the main commercial street in Miraflores, there's a bank on nearly every block. Banco Continental has branches all over Lima, but its ATMs accept only cards linked with Visa. Banco de Credito, Banco Santander, and Interbank accept all cards. Currency exchange offices include P&P, which has an office in Miraflores that is open weekdays 9:30–5. The company's downtown branch is also open Saturday 10–1. When exchanging money, you will usually be asked to show your passport.

🔢 Banks **Banco Continental** ✉ Av. Grau and Unión, Barranco ✉ Av. José Pardo and Jorge Chavez, Miraflores ✉ Av. Conquistadores and Conde de la Monclova, San Isidro. **Banco de Credito** ✉ Av. José Larco and Schell, Miraflores ✉ Av. José Pardo between Recavarren and Libertad, Miraflores. **Banco Santander** ✉ Carabaya and Ucayali, El Centro. **Interbank** ✉ Av. José Larco and Schell, Miraflores ✉ Jr. de la Unión and Huancavelica El Centro.

🔢 Currency Exchange **P&P** ✉ Av. Benavides 735, Miraflores ✉ Av. La Colmena 805, El Centro.

SAFETY

Although El Centro is safe for daytime strolls, at night you'll want to take a taxi to your destination. In Rímac you should take a taxi day or night. Residential neighborhoods like Miraflores, San Isidro, and Barranco have far less street crime, but you should be on your guard away from the main streets. Always be alert for pickpockets in crowded parks and markets.

TAXIS

Locals warn you that hailing taxis on the street can be dangerous. In truth, robberies by cab drivers are rare. To be on the safe side, only use those taxis that are painted yellow and that have the driver's license prominently displayed. It's best to negotiate the fare before you get in. A journey between two adjacent neighborhoods should cost between S/4 and S/7, while longer trips should be about S/10. If you call a taxi, the price will be roughly double. Well-regarded companies include Taxi Metro, Taxi Seguro, and Taxi Móvil.

🔢 Taxi Companies **Taxi Metro** 📠 01/437-3689. **Taxi Seguro** 📠 01/438-7210. **Taxi Móvil** 📠 01/422-6890.

TELEPHONES

Peruvian coins are used in public phones, but you can also make local or international calls with phone cards. Telefónica del Perú has branches throughout the city that sell phone cards. The main office is in El Centro near Plaza San Martín.

🔊 **Telefónica del Perú** ⊠ Carabaya 933 El Centro ☎ 01/433-1616.

TOURS

Lima has many top tour operators with experienced English-speaking guides that can arrange local sightseeing as well as tours throughout the country. The most professional is Lima Tours, which offers tours of the city and surrounding area as well as the rest of the country. Other well-regarded companies include Condor Travel, Kinjyo Travel, Puma Tours, Setours, and Solmartour.

🔊 **Condor Travel** ⊠ Av. Mayor Amando Blondet 249, San Isidro ☎ 01/442-3000. **Kinjyo Travel** ⊠ Las Camelias 290, San Isidro ☎ 01/212-1111 ⊕ www.kinjyo.com.pe. **Lima Tours** ⊠ Belén 1040, El Centro ☎ 01/424-5110 ⊕ www.limatours.com.pe. **Puma Tours** ⊠ Bolognesi 147, Miraflores ☎ 01/441-1279 ⊕ www.pumatours.net. **Setours** ⊠ Av. Comandante Espinar 229, Miraflores ☎ 01/447-1190. **Solmartour** ⊠ Av. Grau 300, Miraflores ☎ 01/444-1313.

TRAVEL AGENCIES

If you need help mid-trip, Costasol is an excellent agency that is willing to do as much or as little of the planning as you want. Another well-regarded agency is Coltur.

🔊 **Costasol** ⊠ Av. José Pardo 620, Miraflores ☎ 01/445-4635. **Coltur** ⊠ Av. José Pardo 138, Miraflores ☎ 01/241-5551 ⊕ www.coltur.com.pe.

VISITOR INFORMATION

PromPerú, the national tourism organization, has English- and Spanish-language information for travelers. The two offices in San Isidro are open weekdays 9–6. An information booth at Jorge Chávez International Airport is open 24 hours. The most thorough information about Lima, as well as the rest of Peru, is available at South American Explorers. This nonprofit organization dispenses a wealth of information. You can also call ahead with questions, or just show up at the beautiful clubhouse in Miraflores and browse through the lending library or read through trip reports filed by members. It costs $50 to join, but you'll probably make up for that with discounts offered to members by hotels and tour operators.

🔊 **PromPerú** ⊠ Calle 1 Oeste 50 13th floor, San Isidro ☎ 01/224-9355 ⊠ Jorge Basadre 610, San Isidro ☎ 01/421-1627 ⊕ www.peru.org.pe. **South American Explorers** ⊠ Calle Piura 135, Miraflores ☎ 01/445-3306 ⊕ www.saexplorers.org.

THE SOUTH

2

FODOR'S CHOICE

Apu Salkantay, *vegetarian cuisine in Puno*

Colca Lodge, *Arequipa*

Colon Inn, *Puno*

Convento de la Santa Catalina, *Iberian-style convent in Arequipa*

El Griego Restaurant, *Nazca*

Hostal Alegría, *Nazca*

Hostal Santa Catalina, *Arequipa*

Hotel de la Borda, *Nazca*

Hotel Mossone, *Huacachina*

Hotel Nazca Lines, *Nazca*

La Casona, *steak and soup in Puno*

La Plaza, *kid-friendly sandwich spot in Puno*

La Posada del Puente, *lodging in Arequipa*

La Taberna, *Peruvian fare in Ica*

Le Bistrot, *French cuisine in Arequipa*

Mixto's Cebichería, *seafood in Arequipa*

Museo Histórico Regional, *Ica*

Posada del Inca, *modern hotel in Puno*

Pukara, *bargain hostal in Puno*

HIGHLY RECOMMENDED

RESTAURANTS   El Rincon Norteno, *Arequipa*

HOTELS   Hotel Las Dunas, *Huacachina*

Hotel Libertador, *Arequipa*

La Casa de Melgar, *Arequipa*

Libertador Hotel Isla Esteves, *Puno*

Qelgatani, *Puno*

SIGHTS   Molino de Sabandía, *Arequipa*

Museo Santuarias de Altura, *Arequipa*

Updated by
Holly S. Smith
and Joan
Gonzalez

AS YOU HEAD SOUTH FROM LIMA, the road stretches ahead into an ice-blue sky that hangs wide and cloudless above soft, rolling dunes. Only nubs of cactus and wind-torn brush cling to this stark, desolate land of sandstorms and rugged, rocky earth. Even the climate is ruthless, rising to 40°C (10°F) by day and plunging to below freezing in darkness. But keep traveling and you'll find a surprising number of oases scattered through the barren land. Fertile river valleys tuck swatches of green into the grey folds of the mountains, where rows of blossoming fruit trees take a fragrant, plucky stand amid their barren surroundings. This is where ancient cultures once set up farming communities, creating a string of thriving settlements in the desert. Today the region is famous for crops as varied as asparagus, avocados, cotton, grapes, olives, and rice. Some of the country's best wines and pisco are also produced here.

The coastal region was home to the Paracas, who established a line of fishing villages that now depend as much on the profits of nearby fish-meal factories as on their seafaring traditions. Arriving as early as 1300 BC and surviving through around 200 AD, the Paracas created some of Peru's most advanced weavings, ceramics, stone carvings, metal jewelry, and implements of the time. The Moche (or Mochica), who came to power around 500–650 AD along the north coast, also lived in this region. In the southern desert, the Nazca culture was ascending at the same time, leaving its mark on such ruins as the temple complex at Cahuachi. This was also the era of the Tiahuanaco, who lived by Lake Titicaca, and who developed into the aggressive Huari-Tiahuanaco tribe that domi-nated the east between 650 and 1100 AD. The tribe then broke into smaller groups that developed on their own for the next 400 years, until the Inca conquered most of Peru in the early 16th century. But then came the Spanish conquistadors, who by 1540 had made it to Arequipa, then a gathering of Aymará Indians and Inca. They gradually worked their cus-toms and aesthetics into the lifestyle of the south over the next 300 years. However, in 1821, fresh from liberating Chile and Argentina from Span-ish rule, General José de San Martín landed at Paracas Bay to do the same for Peru.

The region survived political and economic struggles over the next 50 years, until the 1879 War of the Pacific. Chile was at odds with Bolivia over rich nitrate deposits found in what was then Bolivia's western desert and coast. Peru sided with Bolivia and both lost to Chile, which took Bolivia's coastline and the Tacna area of southern Peru in the Treaty of Anco. The Tacna area, however, was ceded back into Peru in 1929. Since then, left in peace for the most part, the region has survived bouts of economic strife and political changes, as well as natural up-heavals. Settled above the Nazca and South American tectonic plates, southern Peru is a land of major earthquakes—including an 8.4 tem-blor in 2001 that leveled much of Arequipa. Tsunamis, some 7 m (23 ft) high, often accompany the quakes and can splash in as much as 1 km (½ mi) from the coast. Another danger is landslides, which can cause an avalanche of sand and rocks to slide down over villages and major highways.

Still, it's a beautiful, fascinating slice of Peru, and if you're not pressed for time, the way to explore it is via the Pan-American Highway. From Lima, it leads to Pisco, where you can choose side trips southwest to Paracas National Reserve, the Islas Ballestas, or east to Ayacucho. Con-tinuing south, you'll pass through the desert towns of Ica and Nazca, take-off point for flights over the Nazca Lines as well as trips east to Cusco and Machu Picchu. Farther south still is the lovely colonial town of Arequipa, the largest settlement in the region, as well as the gateway

Numbers in the text correspond to numbers in the margin and on the South; Paracas Peninsula; Ica; Arequipa; Around Lake Titicaca; and Puno maps.

2

If you have
5 days

Fly from Lima to ▥ **Pisco ⑥** ► and spend the first day exploring the town and the nearby wineries. Stay in Pisco for two nights while touring **Paracas National Reserve ⑧**, including the **Islas Ballestas ⑦** on day two. On day three fly to ▥ **Nazca ㉑** and tour the Nazca Lines and some of the area's other sights. Head for ▥ **Arequipa ㉜ – ㊽** on day four, touring the city all day as well as part of day five; try to take in the **Convento de la Santa Catalina ㉟**, the **Museo Histórico Municipal ㊱**, and the many fine colonial homes before heading back to Lima.

If you have
8 days

On day one fly from Lima to ▥ **Pisco ⑥** ► and tour the local vineyards and bodegas. On day two, head to Paracas to explore the ▥ **Paracas National Reserve ⑧** and the **Islas Ballestas ⑦**. On day three fly to ▥ **Nazca ㉑** to tour the Lines. On your fourth day take a river-rafting trip on the Río Cotahuasi or the Río Colca, spending the night in ▥ **Camaná ㉗**. On day five head to ▥ **Arequipa ㉜ – ㊽** (where you'll spend the next two nights) and tour the town's famous **Convento de la Santa Catalina ㉟**, its many small museums, and its attractive colonial neighborhoods. On day six choose one of Arequipa's outer sights: tour the **Molina de Sabandía ㊽** flour mill, take a drive through the **Valley of the Volcanoes ㉙**, or even make a day climb up the El Misti volcano. On day seven head to Lake Titicaca, spending the night in ▥ **Puno ㊾ – ㊼** before heading back to Arequipa and flying back to Lima on day eight.

If you have
2 weeks

From Lima, drive on day one to the beach resort town of ▥ **San Vicente de Cañete ②** ►, stopping to visit the ruins and wineries at **Lunahuaná ③** on the way. Spend the night in Lunahuaná. On day two drive to ▥ **Pisco ⑥** to tour a few more wineries and sample the country's famed beverage. On day three head to Paracas and tour the ▥ **Paracas National Reserve ⑧** and the **Islas Ballestas ⑦**, and take day four to see what you missed the previous afternoon. Spend another night in Paracas, then drive to ▥ **Nazca ㉑** on day five, breaking for lunch in **Ica ⑨ – ⑲**. Overnight in Nazca, and on day six fly over the Nazca Lines in the morning and take an archeological tour in the afternoon. Spend another night in Nazca, and on day seven drive to ▥ **Camaná ㉗** on the coast. On day eight, take a river-rafting or kayaking trip on the Río Cotahuasi or the Río Colca, overnighting in Camaná again. On day nine drive to ▥ **Arequipa ㉝ – ㊽** and take an afternoon walking tour. Head for Lake Titicaca on day ten, staying in ▥ **Puno ㊾ – ㊼** for two nights so you can explore the region on day eleven as well. On day twelve, drive back west for a mid-morning break in Arequipa, than head south to spend the night in Moquegua. On day thirteen keep driving south to ▥ **Tacna ㉛** and cross the border over to Arica, Chile; return to Tacna for the evening. On the last day you can fly back to Lima from Arica, Tacna, or Arequipa.

to some of the world's deepest canyons and Lake Titicaca. From Arequipa, it's a long, parched desert drive to Tacna at the Chilean border.

Exploring the South

Southern Peru is connected to Lima by the Pan-American Highway, which runs down the coast to Pisco and the Paracas Peninsula before cutting inland to Ica and Nazca. The road then splits, heading east to Cusco or west again to the coast and then south to Arequipa at Tacna, at the Chilean border. Several roads between these two towns turn due east through the Andes to Lake Titicaca and the Bolivian border. Although mountains dominate the eastern horizon, the terrain here is mostly arid, sandy, and endless—except where green river valleys and farmlands are nourished by snowmelt from the Andes. This is a scorching section of country by day, particularly around Lake Titicaca, where the wind and sun can singe your nose cherry-red in just an hour on the chilly sapphire waters. The landscape is equally dramatic in the region's stark central desert, where the Río Cotahuasi, Río Colca, and other swift streams have scraped the earth into some of the world's deepest canyons. The best way to enjoy this amazing region's history is to travel through it in your own vehicle. Those pressed for time and on a budget can easily catch buses between major destinations, or fly between towns for a spectacular overview of the land and then take day trips to nearby attractions.

About the Restaurants

As in virtually every other part of Peru, casual dress is the order of the day. Reservations are seldom necessary at either lunch or dinner, where multicourse meals are plentiful and reasonable. Throughout the south seafood is key, and your chef might might blend local farm goods and the catch of the day with international seasonings.

Ica has a fair number of restaurants. Sample the *chifas* (Chinese restaurants) along Calle Lima, especially if you're on the leanest of budgets. While you're here, be sure to try *tejas,* candies made of *manjar blanco,* a sweet, pudding-like milk spread. A treat available only during harvest festivals is *cachina,* a partially fermented wine.

About the Hotels

Accommodations in southern Peru range from luxury resorts to spartan *hostals* that run less than S/10 per night. Hotels rated **$$$$** usually have more than standard amenities, which might include such luxury on-site extras as a spa, sports facilities, and business and travel services, and such room amenities as minibars, safes, faxes, or data ports. Hotels rated **$$$** and **$$** are recommended but might have only some of the extras. Accommodations rated ¢–$ are basic and may have shared baths or be outside the central tourist area. If you're arriving without a reservation or you're on a budget, most towns have accommodations around the Plaza de Armas or transport stations.

WHAT IT COSTS In Nuevo Soles				
	$$$$	**$$$**	**$$**	**$**	**¢**
RESTAURANTS	over 65	50–65	35–50	20–35	under 20
HOTELS	over 500	375–500	250–375	125–250	under 125

Restaurant prices are per person, for a main course at dinner. Hotel prices are for two people in a standard double room, excluding tax.

Archeology

Cultural relics are a highlight of this region, which is littered with crumbled religious sites, old roads, and ravaged cemeteries. You can explore Inca ruins at Pachacamac, the Cañete valley, and Lunahuaná, all day trips from Lima. Closer to Pisco, you'll also find Inca relics at Tambo Colorado and Huaytara. The most famous archaeological sights are the Nazca Lines, in the middle of the desert near Nazca.

2

Arts & Crafts

Textiles, ceramics, metal implements, and jewelry from the Paracas, Nazca, Moche, and Inca cultures have been found throughout southern Peru. Some of the best examples are in the small-town museums near where they were uncovered, while others still lie intact where they were discovered.

Beaches

The coast of southern Peru is a mix of attractive tourist beaches, pleasant lesser-known hideaways, and rough and rugged stretches with rocks and rip tides. Just an hour south of the capital, Pucusana is a charming, cliffside resort town where Limeños flock for top-notch seafood and weekend socializing. Other popular southern beaches nearby are Las Niñas and Naplo. Seaside settlements around Pisco, Chala, Camaná, Matarani, and Mollendo are also lined with brown-sand, palm-fringed beaches that attract the crowds on holidays.

Festivals

If you can't be in Lima, then southern Peru is the next best place to celebrate the country's numerous religious holidays. The region also hosts local festivals that keep each town hopping year-round; parades, fireworks, music, dancing, bullfights, and athletic competitions are the typical highlights.

River Exploring

The Río Cañete, about two hours south of Lima, is a good spot to try white-water rafting on Class II rapids. You can also raft and kayak near Lunahuaná at San Jerónimo on Class IV–V rapids. There's top-rate kayaking here, too, and an adventure-sports festival every February. Colca Canyon and Cotahuasi Canyon are probably the best-known spots in the region for kayaking and rafting.

Southern Savories

Seafood is the speciality of coastal towns, where you'll dine in cebecherías, as well as more upscale marisquerías (seafood restaurants). Ceviche (fish or shellfish marinated in lime juice, cilantro, onions, tomatoes, and chilis) is always on the menu, served raw as a salad or cocktail and usually accompanied by canchas (toasted corn kernals sprinkled with salt). Escabeche (fish and prawns with chilis, cheese chunks, sliced eggs, olives, and onions) is another raw entrée.

Regional favorites include lomo saltado (sautéed beef strips with garlic, tomatoes, onions, chilis, and fried potatoes), lomo a la huancaina (beef strips with egg and cheese sauce), and cuy chactado (roasted guinea pig). Soups and stews include chupe verde (with potatoes, cheese, eggs, and herbs), hualpa chupe (with chicken, chilis, and spices), chupe de camarones (spicy shrimp stew), and sopa a la criolla (with thin noodles, diced beef heart, and potatoes). Mollejitas (chicken innards) are the specialty in Arequipa.

Panaderías (bakeries) and pastelerías (pastry shops) are places to find fresh-baked rolls and pan integral (grain bread); wheat bread is a cousin. Try alfajores (shortbread) and cócadas al horno (macaroons) at the bakeries, or ganja blanco (boiled evaporated milk and sugar mixed with pineapple or peanuts), churros (fried dough sprinkled with sugar), and mazamorra morada (purple maize, cinnamon, milk, and sugar) from small street stands.

The Mountain Dew–like Inka Cola is the local soda brand. Regional beers includes Cusqueña and Arequipa. Chicha or chicherias (a fermented corn drink) is the national beverage for fiestas and celebrations, not to be confused with chicha morada (a nonalcoholic drink from purple corn). If you need a caffeine fix, you'll find local and international coffees, cappuccino, espresso, and mate (tea), the latter a high-altitude headache reliever made from coca leaves.

Wineries

The South has fertile vineyards that produce notable crops for some of the country's best bodegas (traditional wineries). Many are near Lunahuaná and Pisco, which are both in fertile grape-growing valleys and host a fiesta de la vendimia (grape harvest festival) each March. Cañete, Condoroy, and Chincha also have wineries and hold popular festivals each year. Pisco is the home of the country's most famous drink, and National Pisco Day is the third Saturday in September.

Wildlife

Although much of the south is barren, windy desert, there are areas of flourishing wildlife. Most notable is Paracas National Reserve, on the bay of Paracas, where you can spot thousands of flamingoes, seabirds, and coastal creatures. A short boat hop takes you to the Islas Ballestas, with condors and a raucous sea-lion colony. The Reserva Nacional Pampas Galeras east of Nazca and the Reserva Nacional Salinas y Aguada Blanca near Colca Canyon are places to observe the shy vicuña and other local species.

Timing

Although the weather in southern Peru is fairly even and arid throughout the year, the best time to visit is during the summer and autumn, November through April, when the rivers are ripe for rafting and kayaking and harvest festivals spice up the small towns. Beware, though, of the days around Christmas, Carnival, the grape harvest, Easter, the mid-June religious festivals, and Peru's independence day in July, when hotels are often booked to capacity.

Paracas National Reserve, the Nazca Lines, and other tourist sights tend to be busy year-round, but packages can be booked solid during the holidays. Make your hotel reservations, tour plans, and travel arrangements at least three months in advance if possible, six months or even a year early if you'll be there in during a festival or summer weekend.

NORTH OF PISCO

Driving south from Lima on the Pan-American Highway, you'll take in a lot of history on your way to Pisco. Relics of the pre-Inca **Pachacamac** settlement, including a reconstructed Inca mamaconas known as Templo de las Virgenes (House of the Chosen Women), are scattered across a sandy hill above the Pacific just 32 km (20 mi) south of the capital. Other important ruins and several attractive resort towns also await at regular intervals.

Pucusana

❶ *67 km (42 mi) south of Lima*

Excellent seafood restaurants are a draw in this seaside town. Have a swim at the beach here or at nearby Las Niñas or Naplo. Although you can't enter the nearby **Boquerón del Diablo** (Big Devil's Mouth) tunnel, it's fun to listen to the wind create haunting moans and shrieks through it.

San Vicente de Cañete

▶❷ *144 km (89 mi) south of Lima; 75 km (45 mi) from Pucusana*

Simply known as Cañete, this town holds one of the region's most exciting *Fiestas de la Vendimia* (grape harvest festivals) the first weekend in March. The event stems from the town's proximity to the **Valle Cañete,** best known for its fertile vineyards that produce some of Peru's greatest wines. Several small archaeological sites also remain in the valley.

Lunahuaná

❸ *150 km (93 mi) south of Lima; 83 km (51 mi) from Pucusana; 85 km (54 mi) north of Pisco*

Heading east from Cañete along the Río Cañete, the paved road cuts between vineyards toward Lunahuaná and then farther up into the mountains. Ruins are scattered through the valleys, including *anexos* around the thermal baths at **Incahuasi,** 8 km (5 mi) from Lunahuaná. Other places to explore archaeological finds are at San Jerónimo, Langla, Jita, Uchumpampa, Catapalla, the pre-Inca Cantagallo, and Paullo, with relics of the valley's first church. Situated amid the blossoming vineyards, Lunahuaná has several bustling bodegas open to visitors. Their award-winning labels are celebrated at the Fiesta de la Vendimia in March and Fiesta del Níspero (Medlar Festival), which attract both Limeños and foreign travelers. Even the small towns like Condoray have family bodegas that participate in the festivities. There are numerous small family hostals where you can sleep for under S/35, as well as several luxury-level accommodations. This is also a guinea pig–breeding region, so you'll find delicious versions of cuy on most menus.

Where to Stay

$ 🏨 **Río Grande Alto Lunahuana Hotel.** Just ½ km from Lunahuana, this popular and charming hacienda-style hotel sits amid the grasslands and blossoming vineyards that define this attractive region. The theme is classical Peruvian countryside, with local arts and crafts in the cozy public spaces. Rooms have broad windows, slightly worn but comfortable furnishings, private bathrooms, and TVs. There are also two fully equipped bungalows; one sleeps five (S/243), the other sleeps seven (S/340). The hotel's proximity to the Río Cañete attracts outdoor-sports enthusiasts, who make this their base for canoe and kayak trips, horseback rides, and hiking. ✉ *Cañete–Lunahuana Hwy., Km. 38.5* ☎ *01/463–5490 in Lima* 🛏 *23 rooms, 2 bungalows* ⚑ *Restaurant, some kitchens, some refrigerators, 2 pools, bar, laundry service, travel services, free parking* 🚗 *AE, DC, MC, V.*

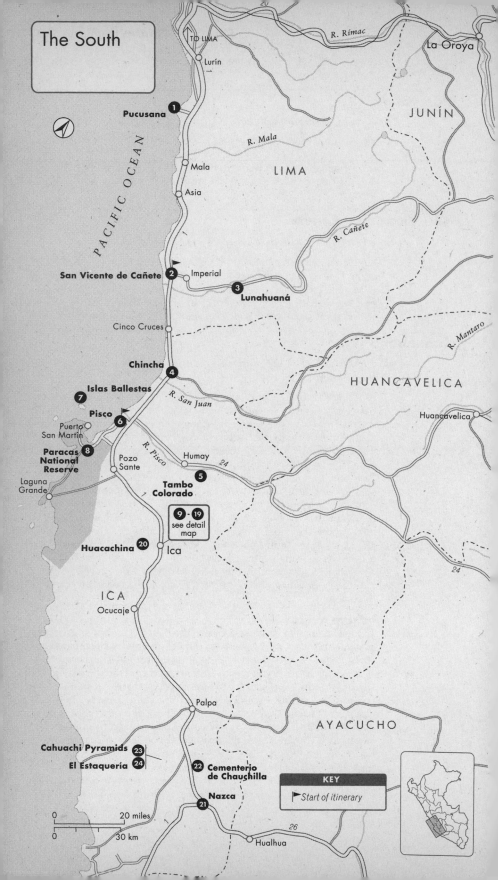

The South

PACIFIC OCEAN

TO LIMA
Lurín
Pucusana ①

Mala

Asia

LIMA

R. Mala

R. Rímac
La Oroya

JUNÍN

R. Cañete

San Vicente de Cañete ② Imperial
③ **Lunahuaná**

Cinco Cruces

R. Mantaro

Chincha ④

Islas Ballestas
⑦
Pisco ⑥
Puerto
San Martín
⑧
**Paracas
National
Reserve**
Laguna
Grande

R. San Juan

HUANCAVELICA

Huancavelica

R. Pisco

Pozo
Sante

Humay 24

⑤ **Tambo
Colorado**

⑨ · ⑲
see detail
map

Huacachina ⑳ Ica

ICA

Ocucaje

Palpa

AYACUCHO

Cahuachi Pyramids ㉓
El Estaquería ㉔

㉒ **Cementerio
de Chauchilla**

㉑ **Nazca**

KEY
▶ *Start of itinerary*

0 ——— 20 miles
0 ——— 30 km

24

26

Hualhua

Chincha

④ *93 km (58 mi) north of Pisco*

Drive 55 km (34 mi) south of Cañete and you'll reach Chincha, another wine-growing settlement founded by Spaniards as Pueblo Alto de Santo Domingo in 1571. Spread out through the valley of the Río Cochas, the town is home to many black descendents of slaves who once worked on the surrounding coastal plantations. Chincha and neighboring El Carmen are probably the best places to enjoy some of the unique Afro-Peruvian music and regional dances, particularly at the Fiesta Verano Negro in February and the Fiestas Patrias in late July. A highlight is El Alcatraz, a dance in which a hip-swiveling male dancer tries to set his partner's cloth tail on fire with a candle. These events are also a great chance to sample local wines and pisco.

Tambo Colorado

⑤ *48 km (30 mi) north of Pisco.*

A collection of ancient adobe buildings, named for the red *colorado* (colored) paint on many of the walls, Tambo Colorado is just an hour's drive from Pisco and provides a chance to view some of the country's best-preserved ruins from the pre-Columbian, pre-Inca Paracas civilization. The centuries-old burial site, discovered beneath the sand dunes by Peruvian archeologist Julio Tello in 1925, was well preserved by the dry setting. Tello's original find included funeral *fards* (burial cocoons), dating from 1300 BC to 200 AD, wrapped in bright cotton and wool textiles embroidered with detailed patterns. Some skulls showed evidence of trepanation, the insertion of metal plates to replace sections broken in battles where rocks were used as weapons. Across the road from the settlement is a public plaza, with a garrison and messengers' quarters. A limited collection of artifacts is still on-site, and the caretaker can show you around the ruins. Samples from Tello's original dig are also on display at the Museo Julio Tello near Paracas. ⊠ *Paracas Bay* ☎ *No phone* 🖃 *S/5* ⊙ *Daily 9–5.*

PISCO & THE PARACAS PENINSULA

A half-day's drive south of Lima, this region couldn't be more different from the sweltering, smog-covered capital. The relaxed, colonial-style town and deepwater port of Pisco lie just above the nub of the Paracas Peninsula, where rough-hewn rock walls are studded with shelves and crevasses with abundant wildlife. This dry, sunny region is visibly similar to the Galapagos Islands 400 km (249 mi) north, with choppy blue seas surrounding deserted islets dotted with birdlife. Head inland to the desert to find well-preserved Inca ruins at various sites.

Pisco

▶ **⑥** *30 km (19 mi) south of Chincha.*

A pleasant coastal town 235 km (148 mi) south of Lima, Pisco is the point where the Argentinian hero, General San Martín, landed with his troops to fight for Peru's freedom from Spanish rule. It's also the city where *pisco*, the clear grape alcohol that is the country's national drink, was invented. Legend actually has it that the origins of *pisco* were a goof the Spaniards made when introducing grapes and wine production into the region. However, they kept at it anyway and eventually refined to their liking this powerful but smooth version of brandy.

The city is divided into two sections that are slowly growing together, the port and fisheries at Pisco Puerto and the more colonial-looking Pisco Pueblo. The city doesn't stand on its original site, either, as an earthquake in 1687—and pirate attacks in its aftermath—damaged so many structures that viceroy Count de la Monclova decided to rebuild the city where it lies today.

In the midst of the revolutionary struggle between local cultures and Spanish conquistadors, Gen. Martín landed at Paracas Bay in 1821 aiming to free Peru from the Spanish. He made his headquarters at Club Social Pisco, near the Plaza de Armas, and a commemorative statue of Martín now stands on the main plaza. Another monument on a sandy hill keeps guard over the city.

Today this settlement of 90,000 centered around a wide Plaza de Armas is a serene getaway for many Limeños. For travelers, it's a prime location for exploring colonial architecture and history, as well as regional culture, wildlife, and wines. National Pisco Day, the third Saturday in September, draws thousands to the drink's birthplace. Paracas National Reserve and the Islas Ballestas are additional attractions, as Pisco is the jumping-off point for these parks. You may even find yourself landing here instead of the capital, for Pisco's military airport is the stand-in when it's too foggy to land in Lima.

Just a half block from the Plaza de Armas, the **Club Social Pisco** is the former headquarters of General José San Martín, who landed at Paracas Bay in 1821 and fought to free Peru from the Spaniards. ⊠ *Av. San Martín 132* ☎ *34/526413* ⌑ *Free* ☉ *Daily 9–5.*

A private research institute, **Acorema** aims to raise public awareness about the region's marine environment. Stroll around the aquarium displays to see what's underwater around the Paracas Reserve and the Islas Ballestas. Informative guides speak some English and will help explain how local residents are working to protect their marine resources and wildlife. ⊠ *Av. San Martín 1471* ☎ *34/530012* ⌑ *Free* ☉ *Daily 10–4.*

Where to Eat

¢–$ ✕**As de Oro.** Minimal furnishings and brisk service place the ultimate emphasis on the terrific local food at this small restaurant on the outskirts of town. Try the tangy ceviche or one of the seafood stews; those who like heartier fare can sample roast chicken and grilled meats. If you want to nosh between meals, there are plenty of salads, soups, coffees, and desserts. At lunch you'll mingle with locals here for a break between business meetings. ⊠ *Av. San Martín 472* ☎ *034/532010* ⊟ *No credit cards* ☉ *Closed Mon.*

¢   ✕**Panadería Pastelería.** For a mix of cheap Spanish and Western dishes at their most basic, stop in at this tiny restaurant on the Plaza. Hamburgers, hot dogs, salads, and juice are served until 10 PM, and if you want a little spice you can order empañadas, tortillas, and local specialties. There's even a bakery, which turns out all sorts of delicious breads and cakes throughout the day—but get there early (6 AM) if you want the best and the freshest selection. ⊠ *Av. San Martín 472* ☎ *034/532010* ⊟ *No credit cards* ☉ *Closed Mon.*

Where to Stay

Several upscale resorts cater to rich and famous Limeños, as well as international guests who want to explore Paracas Reserve. Budget digs are mostly divided in price and character between those that attract Western backpackers (S/35 or less per night) and those that attract Peruvian travelers (around S/100 per night).

$$ ⊞ **Hostal Suite San Jorge.** A modern hotel behind a faux hacienda exterior, with old Spanish colonial furnishings, this property is a relaxing choice regardless of your budget: there are cold-water rooms for economy travelers and larger quarters with private baths and hot water for those who want to live it up. ⊠ *Jr. Comercio 187* ☎ *034/534-2000* ⊞ *034/532-9477* ⟿ *45 rooms, 6 suites* ⚏ *Restaurant, café, 3 pools, miniature golf, 4 tennis courts, boating, water skiing, bicycles, laundry service, travel services, free parking; no phones in some rooms, no TVs in some rooms* ⊟ *AE, DC, MC, V* ⟦◯⟧ *EP.*

$ ⊞ **Hostal El Candelabro.** This quiet hotel has rooms with contemporary furnishings mixed with well-worn antiques—plus such surprising amenities as TVs and minibars. Breakfast is included. The location, just a block from the main Plaza, is convenient to everything, and the proprietors speak both Spanish and English. ⊠ *Corner Jr. Callao and Pedemonte* ☎ *034/532620* ⟿ *104 rooms* ⚏ *Restaurant, café, room service, minibars, bar, laundry service, free parking* ⊟ *AE, DC, V* ⟦◯⟧ *CP.*

¢   ⊞ **San Isidro.** Join the family in this fun, friendly house with cozy, comfortable rooms done in bright Peruvian motifs. There's hot water in the shared bath, and you can park your car or motorcycle safely outside. This is one of the best values in town, and one of the best places to pick up tips on local sites, cooking, and language. ⊠ *San Clemente 103* ☎ *034/541854* ⟿ *8 rooms* ⚏ *Dining room, free parking; no room phones, no room TVs* ⊟ *No credit cards* ⟦◯⟧ *BP.*

Islas Ballestas

❼ *15 km (10 mi) south of Pisco.*

Spectacular rocks pummeled by waves and wind into *ballestas* (arched bows) along the cliffs mark Islas Ballestas, a haven of jagged outcrops and rugged beaches that shelters thousands of marine birds and sea lions. You're not allowed to walk onshore, but you wouldn't want to—the land is calf-deep in *guano* (bird droppings). Anyway, a boat is the best place from which to view the wildlife: penguins, pelicans, seals, boobies, cormorants, and even condors, which make the most appearances in February and March. Punta Pejerrey, the northernmost point of the isthmus, is also the best spot for viewing the enormous, cactus-shaped **Candelabro** carved in the cliffs, which could be a symbol of the power of the northern Chavín culture, an image of the Southern Cross, or a pre-Inca religious figure. From the opposite side of the isthmus you can also view the sea lions from the **Mirador los Lobos** if you don't want to tackle the trek.

To visit Islas Ballestas, you must be on a registered tour, which usually means an hour or two cruising around the islands among sea lions and birds. Some companies will let you actually jump in and swim with the sea lions if you want to, but for the sake of safety and hygiene this isn't recommended. Motorboat tours usually leave from the El Chaco jetty at 8 and 10 AM. Note that you'll be in the open wind, sun, and waves during boat trips, so dress appropriately, and prepare your camera for the mists in July and August. Bring a hat, as tourists are moving targets for multitudes of guano-dropping seabirds. Also, be prepared for the smell—between the sea lions and the birds the odor can drop you to your knees. It takes about 1½ hours to reach the park from the jetty; you're close when you can see the Candelabra etched in the coastal hills.

Paracas National Reserve

8 *15 km (10 mi) south of Pisco.*

Named for the blustering *paracas* (sandstorms) that buffet the west coast each winter, the Reserva Nacional de Paracas is Peru's first park for marine conservation. Settled atop a peninsular hook of land slightly southwest of Pisco, this 280,000-hectare (700,000-plus-acre) coastal park includes a conglomeration of mountains, desert, and islands. Thin dirt tracks lead to sheltered lagoons, rugged cliffs full of caves, and small fishing villages. The pristine surroundings and lonely feeling are misleading, however—a monument marks the spot where General José San Martín first stepped into Peru nearly 200 years ago.

Wildlife is everywhere in this stunning reserve, particularly bird colonies and sea creatures. Pelicans, condors, and red-and-white flamingos congregate and breed here; the latter, in fact, are said to have inspired the red-and-white independence flag General San Martín designed when he liberated Peru. On shore you can't miss the sound (or the smell) of the hundreds of sea lions, while in the water you might spot penguins, sea turtles, dolphins, manta rays, and even hammerhead sharks.

This is prime walking territory, where you can stroll from the the bay to the **Julio Tello Museum,** and on to the fishing village of **Lagunilla** 5 km (3 mi) farther across the neck of the peninsula. Adjacent to the museum are colonies of flamingos, best seen June through July (and absent January through March, when they fly to Sierra). Hike another 6 km (4 mi) to reach **Mirador de Lobos** (Wolf Lookout) at Punta El Arquillo, along the cliffs overlooking a sea-lion colony, or to view the rock formation **La Catedral** (the Cathedral). Carved into the highest point in the cliffs above Paracas Bay, 14 km (9 mi) from the museum, is the **Candelabra.** Note that you must hire a guide to explore the land trails.

Minibus tours of the entire park can be arranged through local hotels and travel agencies for about S/15 for 5 hours. A taxi from Pisco to Paracas runs about S/14, or you can take a half-hour Chaco–Paracas–Museo *combi* to El Chaco for S/2.

Where to Stay

$$ ⊞ **Hotel Condor Club & Beach Resort.** A beach at your doorstep is the draw of this pleasant little hotel, which fronts Paracas Bay. The Spanish-style exterior fits into the surroundings, which guests can explore on guided hikes and boat trips. Comfortable rooms are done in muted shades that match the landscapes; some rooms have private terraces with ocean or lush garden views. ⊠ *Santo Domingo Urb.* ☎ *034/224531* ⤶ *10 rooms* ⚭ *Restaurant, café, room service, cable TV, 2 pools, bicycles, bar, laundry service, meeting rooms, free parking* ⊟ *AE, DC, V* ⦿❘ *CP.*

$$ ⊞ **Hotel Paracas.** Opened in the 1940s for Lima's elite, this Mediterranean-style resort—the area's largest—lies behind a wide, half-circle park and dock that juts out into the deep-blue Paracas Bay. Air-conditioned rooms have wood furnishings, private bathrooms, and TVs. Larger suites and flower-bedecked bungalows are often booked by families. An extensive Sunday buffet (S/87) draws crowds, and nonguests can use the pool (S/7). It's a convenient base from which to launch trips into the reserve, tour local ruins, or head out for some fishing (bring your own gear). ⊠ *Av. Paracas 173* ☎ *034/221736, 01/447–0781 reservations in Lima* 🖷 *034/225379* ⊕ *www.hotelparacas.com* ⤶ *95 rooms, 7 suites, 3 bungalows* ⚭ *Restaurant, cafeteria, room service, some in-room safes, some minibars, some refrigerators, cable TV, 2 tennis courts, miniature golf, 2 pools, children's pool, beach, dock, boat-*

ing, fishing, volleyball, 2 bars, shop, laundry service, meeting rooms, free parking ⊟ *AE, DC, MC, V* ⚈ CP.

¢ ⌧ **Hostería Paracas.** If you don't want to splurge on the grand Hotel Paracas, try this modest little bed-and-breakfast hidden away down the street. Rooms are compact but clean, and the friendly hosts will help you with travel arrangements to the park and local sights. It's a good place to hook up with budget travelers and exchange information. ✉ *Av. Paracas 169* ☎ *01/447–4400 reservations in Lima* ⇒ *8 rooms* ⚈ *Dining room, laundry facilities, free parking; no air-conditioning, no room phones, no room TVs* ⊟ *No credit cards* ⚈ *CP.*

Sports & the Outdoors

Most beaches at Paracas are rugged and scenic, top-notch for walking but dangerous for swimming due to rip tides and undertow. Beware in the shallows, too—there are often stingrays and giant jellyfish. Calmer stretches include La Catedral, La Mina, and Mendieta, as well as Atenas, a prime windsurfing section. Dirt roads lead farther to Playa Mendieta and Playa Carhaus. Small, open restaurant shacks line the more popular beaches.

ICA & NAZCA

Fertile green fields and vineyards nuzzle the roads around Ica, where rare, emerald patches of valley fed by Andes snowmelt make perfect grape-growing fields that are a key part of this region's economy. More than 80 bodegas tucked into Ica's outskirts are within easy walking distance of town. Many are open to visitors, who are often invited to sample their renowned wines and piscos.

A 15 minute drive southwest, Huacachina is a resort town on a wide green lake, whose mineral-rich water is reputed to have magical healing powers. The settlement also lies amid sand dunes so high you can surf them, and thus draws both the health-conscious, who enjoy the area's many spas, and the adrenaline junkies, who come for all the sports. From here, though, the thin black highway cuts through desert vast and pale as cracked parchment, and there's nothing but sand and sky as far as the eye can see. Flying over it, though, you'll notice what look like long scratches in the earth's surface. Get closer and you'll see they actually form enormous designs—a hummingbird, a llama, a condor, a whale—created by removing the uppermost layer of desert. These are the Nazca Lines, whose origin and meaning are still a mystery, a collection of unusual and giant engravings that draw thousands of visitors every year.

Today the central region's main town of Nazca is more a way station for trips to the Lines and local archaeological sites than a tourist hub. For sophistication and services, most travelers stay in Ica or the resort town of Huacachina, both about halfway between Pisco and Nazca.

Ica

⑨—⑲ *56 km (35 mi) southeast of Paracas.*

Ica was the Nazca capital between 300 and 800 AD, and the Nazca people couldn't have picked a better place to center their desert civilization. Set in a patch of verdant fields and abutted by snow-covered mountains, Ica is serene, relaxing, and cheerful, with helpful residents—likely due as much to the nearly never ending sunshine as to the vast selection of high-quality wines and piscos produced by dozens of local bodegas. This is a town of laughter and festivals, most notably the Fiesta de Vendimia, the wine-harvest celebration that takes place each year in early March.

Ica is also famous for its pecans and its high-stepping horses called *caballos de paso.*

The city's colonial look comes from its European heritage, as Ica was founded by the Spanish in 1536, making it one of the oldest towns in southern Peru. The Spaniards fought with the locals for power, though, and barely more than a century later the two groups were vying for control of the region. One who joined General San Martín's revolutionary troops was José de la Torre Ugarte, author of Peru's national anthem, who was born in Ica in 1768. Peru's first civilian president, Domingo Elass, also from Ica, ran the country when it was newly independent; he attempted to start a revolution in 1854 but failed, took control of Arequipa for a short time, and then fled to Chile.

Today this bustling oasis in Peru's richest wine-growing region is a source of national pride, and its fine bodegas are a major attraction. Most are open all year, but the best time to visit is February to April, during the grape harvest. Chilean and Argentine wines may win all the awards, but several fine labels from Ica hold their own in international competitions. The Tacama and Ocucaje bodegas are generally considered to have the best-quality wines from this region. The Peruvian autumn is the season for Ica's Fiesta de la Vendimia, where you can enjoy parades, sports competitions, local music, and dancing, and even catch beauty queens stamping grapes. It's also a great time to be introduced to the vast selection of local wines and piscos, as well as an opportunity to try homemade concoctions not yet on the market.

The city's excitement also heightens for such festivals as February's Carnival, Semana Santa in March or April, and the all-night pilgrimages of El Señor de Luren in March and October. Other fun times to visit are during Ica Week, around June 17, which celebrates the city's founding, and the annual Ica Tourist Festival in late September.

(9) A 16th-century farm hacienda hides the thoroughly modern production of the internationally renowned **Bodega Hacienda Tacama.** Some of Peru's best labels, particularly the Blanco de Blancos, are produced here. Stroll through the rolling vineyards—still watered by the Achirana irrigation canal built by the Inca—before sampling their end result. The estate is about 11 km (7 mi) from town. ⊠ *Camina a la Tinguiña s/n* ☎ *056/ 228395* ⚅ *Free* ⊘ *Weekdays 9–2.*

(10) Look for **Bodega El Carmen,** a small winery on the right side of the road, when you're driving south into Ica; it makes a good stop for a sampling of fine pisco. Look for the ancient grape press, which was made from an enormous old tree trunk. ✛ *3 km (2 mi) north of Ica* ⊠ *Guadalupe* ☎ *056/233495* ⚅ *Free* ⊘ *Mon.–Sat. 10–4.*

(11) A sunny brick archway welcomes you to the large, pleasant **Bodega Vista Alegre,** which has been producing fine wines, pisco, and sangria since it was founded by the Picasso brothers in 1857. The largest winery in the valley, it's a popular stop for tour buses and has regular tours and tastings. Get here early before the groups, but bring a friend who can translate if you don't speak Spanish. You can stroll to the estate from downtown Ica; cross the Grau Bridge, then take the second left and continue 3 km (2 mi). You can also hire a taxi or take city buses 8 or 13, which have stops near the winery. ⊠ *Camina a la Tinguiña, Km. 205* ☎ *056/232919* ⚅ *Free* ⊘ *Weekdays 9–2.*

(12) The ornate stained-glass windows make **Iglesia San Francisco** one of the city's grandest religious buildings. ⊠ *Corner Avs. Municipalidad y San Martín* ☎ *No phone* ⚅ *Free* ⊘ *Mon.–Sat. 8–12 and 2–4.*

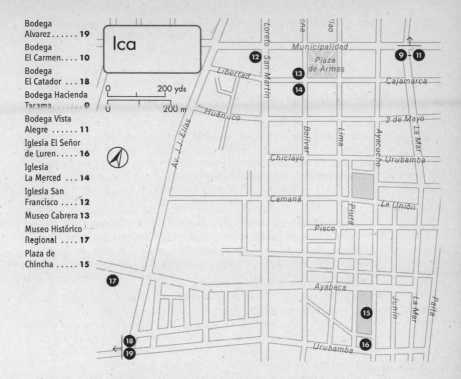

⑬ It's just a small, unmarked building on the Plaza de Armas, but the cluttered **Museo Cabrera** has regional cultural artifacts and more than 10,000 varieties of stones. The charismatic owner, Dr. Javier Cabrera, is a descendant of one of Ica's founders. Some of the rocks are etched with what might be pre-Columbian images of daily life and surgical techniques, possibly from a technologically advanced Stone Age civilization. ⊠ *Bolívar 170* ☎ *056/253576* ☞ *S/1 with guided tour* ☉ *Mon.–Sat. 9–1 and 4:30–8:30.*

⑭ The quaint **Iglesia La Merced**, built in 1874, overlooks the Plaza de Armas. Peek in for a glimpse of the delicately carved wooden altars. ⊠ *Corner Libertad y Bolívar* ☎ *No phone* ☞ *Free* ☉ *Mon.–Sat. 10–5.*

⑮ A wide, open square, **Plaza de Chincha** is surrounded by sets of red steps, with palm trees towering in neat lines around the perimeter. As it's above street level, it's a breezy place for an afternoon break or a picnic. ⊠ *Ayabaca y Ayacucho* ☎ *No phone* ☞ *Free* ☉ *Daily 24 hrs.*

⑯ Inside the pretty, colonial-style **Iglesia El Señor de Luren** is a famous Christ image that is paraded around the city all night during local religious festivals. Legend has it that the statue, purchased for the church by a friar in 1570, was transported to Peru by boat. The captain threw it overboard in a storm, but it washed up on a beach near Paracas and was miraculously carried to Ica intact. The church stands slightly southeast of town. ⊠ *Cutervo y Ayacucho* ☎ *No phone* ☞ *Free* ☉ *Mon.–Sat. 9–4.*

A vast and well-preserved collection on regional history—particularly from the Inca, Nazca, and Paracas cultures is on display in the fascinating **Museo Histórico Regional**. Note the *quipas* (Inca counting strings), ⑰ mysterious knotted, colored threads thought to have been used to count commodities and quantities of food. Head out back to view a scale model of the Nazca Lines from an observation tower. You can also buy maps (S/.50) and paintings of Nazca motifs (S/4). The museum is about 1½ km (1 mi) from town, so take a 20-minute walk, hop on Bus 17 from Plaza de Armas (S/2), or catch a *mototaxi* from the corner of the Plaza (S/2). ✉ *Ayabaca s/n* ☎ *056/234383* 🖬 *S/7, plus S/.50 camera fee* ⊙ *Mon.–Sat. 9–6:30, Sun. 9–2.*

⑱ A family-run operation 7 km (4 mi) from Ica in the Subtanjalla district, the elegant yet friendly **Bodega El Catador** produces wines and pisco. Take a free vineyard and winery tour, then shop for homemade brands and traditional wine-making paraphernalia at the museumlike shop. The excellent Taberna restaurant and bar opens in the evening for dining, dancing, and live music. Book your tour early during the February to April grape-harvest season. If you don't want to drive, take a taxi or wait at the second block of Moquegua for Bus 6 (S/1), which passes by about every half hour. ✛ *Pan-American Hwy. S, Km 296,* ✉ *Fondo Tres Equinas 102* ☎ *056/403295* 🖬 *Free.* ⊙ *Daily 8–6.*

⑲ Umberto Alvarez, who won the gold medal for the country's best pisco in 1995, owns **Bodega Alvarez**, a highly regarded winery. Be sure to ask about the rare *pisco de limón* or the special *pisco de mosto verde.* ☎ *056/254399* 🖬 *Free* ⊙ *Weekdays 9–1, Sat. 9–12.*

Where to Stay & Eat

$$ ✗ **La Taberna.** In Bodega El Catador, this elegant restaurant serves
Fodor's Choice exquisite local specialties at small, candlelit tables. Be sure to ask the
★ waiter for his recommendations on the fine wines and pisco available. If you eat elsewhere, you can always stop by the bar for drinks and dancing to live Peruvian music. ✉ *José Carrasco González, Km 296* ☎ *056/403263* 🖃 *AE, MC, V.*

¢ ✗ **Casa Naturista.** In one of Ica's best vegetarian spots, order small vegetable sandwiches, vegetarian tamales, and empañadas, or pasta and pizza. ✉ *Andahuaylas 204* ☎ *No phone* 🖃 *No credit cards.*

¢ ✗ **El Otro Peñoncito.** Friendly and relaxed, this restaurant has Peruvian and international cuisine. The fettuccine *con ajo* (with garlic) is served with a spicy sauce similar to that used in the traditional *papa a la huancaina.* Milder fare, such as sandwiches and soups, is also served. ✉ *Bolívar 255* ☎ *056/233921* 🖃 *DC, MC, V.*

¢ ✗ **Pastelería La Spiga.** Snack possibilities abound in this fragrant little pastry and sandwich shop. Display cases glisten with frosted cakes and shaped cookies, while the wall is lined with loaves of grain breads. Add a cup of coffee and make your order to go, then head for the Plaza to picnic in the fresh sunshine. ✉ *Lima 243* ☎ *No phone* 🖃 *No credit cards.*

¢ ✗ **Zambos Sandwiches.** On the south side of the Plaza, this modest restaurant is a convenient place to relax after walking through Ica's charming neighborhoods. Besides the obvious sandwiches, which you can order in just about any meat and vegetable combination, there are refreshing juice blends and light pastries. ✉ *Callao* ☎ *No phone* 🖃 *No credit cards.*

$–$$ ✗🖼 **Ocucaje Sun & Wine Resort.** The focus here is on all the best of southern Peru: sunshine and good wines. It feels like a comfortable Spanish country home, but rooms have all the amenities. At the Bodega Ocucaje slightly outside of Pisco, it's a desert resort meant to restore your spirits—which you can do by lying beside the attractive pool, getting a spa massage, or exploring the nearby historic sights. Breakfast is included. ✛ *Pan-American Hwy. S, Km. 336* ✉ *Av. Principal s/n* ☎ *056/408001* 🖷 *056/408003* ⊕ *www.ocucaje.com* 🛏 *55 rooms* ⚐ *Restaurant, minibars, room service, tennis court, pool, hot tub, massage, sauna, spa, exercise equipment, horseback riding, volleyball, bicycles, shop, bar, dance club, recreation room, baby-sitting, laundry service, business services,* *meeting rooms, travel services, car rental, free parking* ⊟ *AE, DC, MC, V* ⦿ *BP.*

$ ⊡ **El Carmelo Hotel & Hacienda.** At this colonial-style, slate-roof hotel 5 km (3 mi) from downtown Ica, rooms are in several buildings around a flower-filled courtyard. An inviting garden house has wicker furniture and a 19th-century wine press. ⊠ *Pan-American Hwy., Km 301* ☎ *056/ 232191* ⤳ *40 rooms* ⟁ *Restaurant, pool, bar, laundry service, travel services, free parking; no room phones, no room TVs* ⊟ *AE, MC, V.*

¢   ⊡ **Hostal Rocha.** Family-run, this operation provides guests with cooking and laundry facilities, hot water, and breakfast. Motorcycles are welcome, and you can grab a sand board for surfing the nearby dunes. ⊠ *Independencia 258* ☎ *056/232111* ⤳ *6 rooms* ⟁ *Dining room, kitchenettes (some), laundry facilities, travel services, free parking; no room phones, no room TVs* ⊟ *No credit cards.*

¢   ⊡ **Hostal Sol de Ica.** This lively hotel with many amenities is a great place to hook up with other budget travelers. Rooms have private baths, hot water, and TVs. You can even relax in the Turkish bath. ⊠ *Jr. Lima 265* ☎ *056/236168* ☒ *056/235169* ⤳ *70 rooms* ⟁ *Pool, Turkish bath, disco, travel services, free parking; no room phones, no room TVs* ⊟ *MC, V.*

Shopping

Ica is an excellent place to pick up Peruvian handicrafts with regional styles and motifs. Tapestries and textiles woven in naturally colored llama and alpaca wool often have images of the Nazca Lines and historical figures. In particular, look for *alfombras* (rugs), *colchas* (blankets), and *tapices* (hangings). Clay pots are often painted with *toros* (bulls), and *retablos* (wooden boxes) usually have miniature painted ceramic figures in Andean scenes. Also look for jewelry, especially silver in Nazca Lines designs.

Huacachina

⓴ *5 km (3 mi) southwest of Ica.*

Drive 10 minutes through the pale, mountainous sand dunes southwest of Ica and you'll suddenly see a gathering of attractive, pastel-colored buildings surrounding a patch of green. It's not an oasis on the horizon, but rather the lakeside resort of Laguna de Huacachina, a palm-fringed lagoon of jade-colored waters whose sulfurous properties are reputed to have healing powers. The view is breathtaking: a collection of attractive, colonial-style hotels in front of a golden beach and with a backdrop of snow-covered peaks against the distant sky. In the 1920s, Peru's elite traveled here for the ultimate holiday, and today the spacious resorts still beckon. The lake is also a pilgrimage site for those with health and skin problems, as well as sandboarders who want to tackle the 100-m (325-ft) dunes and budget travelers who pitch tents in the sand or sleep under the stars.

en route   About 40 km (27 mi) southeast of Huacachina is **Bodega Ocucaje,** a famous winery in an old Spanish mansion, whose vintages—including the famous Vino Fond de Cave—are considered among the best in the country. Also on the property is the posh Ocucaje Sun & Wine Resort, actually a charming inn that offers accommodation packages with dining, sports, and winery tours. ⊠ *Av. Principal s/n* ☎ *034/ 408001* ⛁ *S/10* ⊙ *Weekdays 9–12 and 2–5, Sat. 9–12.*

Where to Stay & Eat

★ $$$ ✕⊡ **Hotel Las Dunas.** A cluster of whitewashed buildings amid the dunes, this colonial-style holiday resort is a favorite getaway for Peruvian families. Spacious rooms have balconies overlooking lush lawns, while suites have sunny courtyards and whirlpools. The restaurant, where you can dine poolside or in a breezy gazebo, serves such dishes as flounder with seafood sauce and spicy lomo saltado. Rent sandboards, play golf on the dunes, ride horseback, or fly over the Nazca Lines (S/350) from the hotel's airstrip. Add 18% tax and service fee to the price—but book weekdays to save 20%. ✉ *La Angostura 400* ☎ *034/256224* 🖷 *034/ 256231* ⌨ *invertur@protelsa.com.pe* ⇥ *106 rooms, 3 suites* ♦ *Restaurant, cafeteria, 9-hole golf course, tennis court, 2 pools, lake, massage, sauna, gym, horseback riding, bar, dance club, laundry service, business services, travel services, airstrip, free parking* ⊟ *AE, DC, MC, V.*

$ ✕🖃 **Hotel Mossone.** A Spanish colonial–style courtyard lined with tall
Fodor'sChoice ficus trees is the focal point of this century-old mansion. Rooms look
★ out onto gardens overflowing with flowers, which partially hide the small, secluded pool and playground. The relaxed bar and restaurant have splendid lake views, and if you like the food you can book a room with full board. The hotel provides free bicycles and sandboards for guests, but if you're staying elsewhere you can still stop in for excellent comida criolla, especially *papa a la huancaina* (potatoes with cheese sauce). ✉ *Balneario de Huacachina* ☎ *034/213630, 01/442–3090 in Lima* 🖷 *034/ 236137* ⌨ *mossone@invertur.com.pe* ⇥ *53 rooms* ♦ *Restaurant, pool, lake, bicycles, bar, playground, laundry service, travel services, free parking* ⊟ *AE, DC, MC, V.*

Sports & the Outdoors

Most hotels have sandboards available, or you can rent them for about S/2 an hour. European sports fans arrive in droves every year to practice for the international sand-surfing competitions on Cerro Blanco, the massive dune 14 km (8 mi) north of Nazca. Camping and sandboarding are free around Manual's Restaurant. If you don't have a car you can reach Huacachina by bus from the Plaza de Armas in Ica (S/2) or take a taxi from town (S/1).

Nazca

㉑ *120 km (75 mi) southeast of Ica.*
Fodor'sChoice
★ A mirage of green in the desert, lined with cotton fields and orchards and bordered by crisp mountain peaks, Nazca has remained a quiet colonial town amid a cache of archaeological ruins. Set 598 m (1,961 ft) above sea level, the town has a dry climate—scorching by day, nippy by night—that was instrumental in preserving centuries-old relics from Inca and pre-Columbian tribes. Overlooking the parched scene is 2078-m (6,815-ft) Cerro Blanco, the highest sand dune in the world. In 1901 the area came came to the world's attention when Peruvian archaeologist Max Uhle excavated sites around Nazca and rediscovered this unique culture. The area also has more than 100 cemeteries, where the humidity-free climate has helped preserve priceless jewelry, textiles, pottery, and mummies.

However, this area is most famous as the site of one of the world's greatest mysteries, the giant engravings—called the Nazca Lines—on the Pampas de San José, 20 km (12 mi) north of town. Discovered by scientist Paul Kosok in 1929, the motifs were made by removing the surface stones and piling them beside the lighter soil underneath. Figures, some measuring up to 300 m (1,000 ft) across, include a hummingbird, a monkey, a spider, a pelican, a condor, a whale, and an "astronaut." Probably the most famous person to investigate the origin of the Nazca Lines was Kosok's translator, German scientist Dr. Maria Reiche, who studied the Lines from 1940 until her death in 1998.

Your best bet for exploring the area's archaeological sites and the Nazca Lines is on a set tour, which usually covers all the major areas. You can take a taxi to the *mirador* for around S/35, or catch a morning bus there for only 50¢ (then hitchhike back). Nazca Lines flights run S/104–S/180 depending on the season. Eager tour guides waiting at the bus stop in Nazca offer S/87 tours that include flights and a visit to the mummies at the Chauchilla cemetery.

Named for the German anthropologist who dedicated her life to study-ing the Nazca Lines, **Casa-Museo Maria Reiche** is considered to be one of the best museums in the country. The first floor has extensive ex-hibits of textiles, tools, musical instruments, mummies, and skeletons from the Paracas, Nazca, Wari, Chincha, and Inca cultures. Upstairs are more modern displays of colonial paintings and furniture. There's a scale model of the Nazca Lines behind the building. Take a micro from the Ormeño terminal to the Km. 416 marker (70¢) to reach the mu-seum, which is 1 km (½ mi) from town. ⊠ *Pan-American Hwy., Km. 416 San Pablo* ☎ *034/255734* ⊕ *www.magicperu.com/MariaReiche* ☒ *S/3.50* ☉ *Daily 9–4.*

The highlight of the private, Italian-run **Museo Antonini,** focusing on the Nazca culture, is its collection of painted textiles from the ancient adobe city of Cahuachi. This is also the place to see how local relics have been excavated and restored. In back is the stone Bisambra aqueduct, used for irrigating the fields of the Nazca. ☎ *034/265421* ☒ *S/5* ☉ *Mon.–Fri. 9–2, Sat. 9–12.*

㉒ In the midst of the pale, scorched desert, the ancient **Cementerio de Chauchilla** is scattered with sun-bleached skulls and shards of pottery. *Huaqueros* (grave robbers) have ransacked the site over the years, and now the mummies unearthed by their looting erupt from the earth in a jumble of bones and threadbare weavings. It's an eerie site, as the mum-mies still have hair attached, as well as mottled, brown-rose skin stretched around empty eye sockets and gaping mouths with missing teeth. Some are wrapped in tattered burial sacks, though the jewelry and ceramics with which they were laid to rest are long gone. Tours take about 3 hours and cost around S/2. Visits to the cemetery are also packaged with Nazca Lines flights. ⊠ *30 km (19 mi) from Nazca, the last 12 km (7 mi) of which is unpaved* ☎ *No phone* ☒ *Free* ☉ *Daily 8–6.*

㉓ Within a walled, 4,050-square-yard courtyard west of the Nazca Lines are the **Cahuachi Pyramids,** an ancient ceremonial and pilgrimage site. Six adobe pyramids, the highest of which is about 70 ft, stand above a network of rooms and connecting corridors. Grain and water silos are also inside, while several large cemeteries lie outside the walls. Used by the early Nazca culture, the site is estimated to have existed for about two centuries before being abandoned about 200 AD. Cahuachi takes its name from *qahuachi* (meddlesome). El Estaquería, with its mummi-fication pillars, is nearby. ⊠ *34 km (21 mi) west of Nazca* ☎ *No phone* ☒ *Free* ☉ *Daily 8–5.*

㉔ The wooden pillars of **El Estaquería,** carved of *huarango* wood and placed on mudbrick platforms, were once thought to have been an as-tronomical observatory. More recent theories, however, lean toward their use in mummification rituals, perhaps to dry bodies of deceased tribal members. The site was probably part of the last Nazca capital before the Huari culture took over the region. You can take a private tour of the site for about S/17 with a three-person minimum. ⊠ *34 km (21 mi) west of Nazca* ☎ *No phone* ☒ *Free* ☉ *Daily 8–4.*

CloseUp

THE MYSTERY OF THE NAZCA LINES

ALL SORTS OF MYTHS *are attached to the mysterious Nazca Lines, for no one knows their purpose or origin. Only a few cultures dared to brave this barren desert 20 km (12 mi) from the town of Nazca, including the Paracas, who lived here from 200 BC to AD 600. The Nazca people also flourished here from 300 BC to AD 700, and migrants from Ayacucho took over the area about AD 630. Thus theories abound about how any—or all—of these groups might have used the Lines, if indeed they made them.*

Paul Kosok, an expert in ancient irrigation, was flying over the Nazca area on June 21, 1929, to document Inca irrigation patterns when he noticed the strange designs in the desert. He only spotted them because, coincidentally, the sunlight was at the southern hemisphere's winter equinox that day and highlighted the outlines of the designs. After Kosok told of his find, the area around Nazca was flooded with archaeologists and treasure hunters eager to figure out who had created the giant drawings—and see whether they had left valuables with them.

Dubbed the "Nazca Lines" by archaeologists for their proximity to town, the motifs were made by removing stones on the desert surface and piling them beside the lighter soil beneath. There are 11 major figures—including a hummingbird, a monkey, a spider, a pelican, a condor, and a whale—plus the mysterious "astronaut" and various triangles and trapezoids. Some measure up to 300 m (1,000 ft) across and have been preserved for more than 2,000 years by an unusual combination of gentle, cleansing winds and arid climate.

Because the lines matched up to the sun at its equinox, Kosok maintained that the figures were some type of irrigation system marking the seasons. However, Kosok's translator, German scientist Dr. Maria Reiche, had other ideas, which she explored from 1940 until her death at 95 in 1998. She theorized that the Lines were made by the Nazca people as part of a vast astronomical calendar noting the rainy season in the highlands, the source of the area's water supply, and seasonal changes in the regional climate. In 1976 she paid for the mirador (platform) 20 km (12 mi) north of town, from which the lizard, arbos (tree), and manos (hands) can be seen. She opened a small museum in 1994, and her book Mystery on the Desert *is still a local bestseller.*

Other theories about the meaning of the Lines are that they are simply artwork meant to be seen from the air, based on ancient Nazca pottery and textiles depicting balloonists and local legends of flying men. Dr. Johan Reinhard proposed that because there are similar lines in Bolivia and Chile, they have to do with fertility rites throughout the Andes. British Astronomer Alan Sawyer and scientist Georg A. von Breunig both proposed that since the Nazca and other local cultures were such excellent athletes, the Lines were running tracks for sports events. Henri Stirlin offered the explanation that the patterns represent local yarns and weaving motifs. Zsoltan Zelko deducted that the pampas were a map depicting the Tiahuanaco empire, and the designs are somehow part of the story. Recent theories, however, concur with Kosok and Reiche in thinking that the Lines were related to the flow of water from the mountains to the plains.

Note that mid-morning is usually the best time to fly over the Lines, as earlier there is often a haze over the pampas, and later winds can make for a turbulent journey. The flight, which takes place in a small (and sometimes questionably rickety) propeller plane—and combines bright sunlight and strong fuel fumes with quick twists and turns, deep dives, and bumpy takeoffs and landings—is not for the queasy. Those who plan to explore this desert mystery in 2005 might also catch the rare, 12-hour phenomenon when, at the autumn equinox, Mars will appear as a red light in the sky.

— By Holly Smith

$ ✕🖻 **Hotel de la Borda.** In fragrant gardens and surrounded by cotton
Fodor'sChoice fields, this quiet 80-year-old hacienda 1½ km (1 mi) from the airport
★ offers a taste of life on a coastal farm. Rooms with hot showers overlook a lush section of colorful blossoms. The excellent restaurant serves
up local specialties, while the English-speaking staff can organize horseback rides, mountain-bike trips, or four-wheel-drive vehicle excursions.
⊠ *Pan-American Hwy. S, Km 447* 🖃🖃 *034/522576* 🖘 *39 rooms
⚘ Restaurant, room service, 2 pools, horseback riding, mountain bikes,
bar, laundry service, travel services, free parking; no room phones, no
room TVs* 🖃 *DC, MC, V.*

¢ ✕🖻 **Albergue Villa Verde.** The hook of this small hacienda set in verdant gardens is its focus on nature. The serenity and familial warmth
set it above other lodgings in the area. Small rooms painted in sunny
colors have antique furnishings and paintings by local artists. The owners will cook up local delicacies upon request, and will even wrap them
up in a picnic. ⊠ *Pasaje Angela s/n* 🖃 *34/523373* 🖘 *11 rooms ⚘ Restaurant, pool, bar, laundry service, travel services, free parking; no room
phones, no room TVs* 🖃 *AE, DC, MC, V* ⦿ *BP.*

¢ 🖻 **Hostal Alegría.** One of the most popular budget spots in town, this
Fodor'sChoice modest, clean operation has all a backpacker needs. Rooms and bun-
★ galows have private baths and hot water, plus there's a pool to cool off
in after a dusty morning flying over the Nazca Lines. After dark, dance
the night away at the adjacent disco, then take a sunrise breakfast in
the coffee shop garden. This is a good place to clean up, wash clothes,
check e-mail (S/7 per hour), exchange paperbacks, and get organized
before heading off on another adventure. Staff travel experts offer general tourist info and guide recommendations, and there's a free nightly
video on the Lines daily at 9 PM. The hostal is sometimes full or closed,
so call first—and get a free ride from the bus station. You can also store
luggage, even if you're not a guest. ⊠ *Jr. Lima 168* 🖃 *34/522702
🖃 34/522444* 🖘 *20 rooms, 4 bungalows ⚘ Coffee shop, pool, Internet, library, disco, laundry service, Internet, travel services, free parking; no room phones, no room TVs* 🖃 *AE, MC, V* ⦿ *BP.*

THE SOUTHERN COAST

Heading south toward Arequipa, the road parallels the ancient, 240-
km (149 mi) Inca footpath to Cusco, which was used to transport goods
between the mountain towns and the main shipping point of Puerto Inca.
Every 7 km (4 mi) you'll see a waiting post, where Inca runners relayed
notes and changed messengers so news could be passed from one end
of the path to the other in 24 hours. The pre-Columbian ruins of the
seaside settlement of Puerto Inca are about an hour southwest of Nazca
and 10 km (6 mi) north of Chala. On the right side of the bay is a cemetery, where a temple sits on the hill. Watch your step, as large holes in
the ground mark where drying and storage buildings once stood. You
can walk from Chala in two hours, or get dropped off at Km 603 and
hike 3 km (2 mi). Otherwise, a taxi from Chala runs about S/17, while
a colectivo from Yauca costs about S/1.75 (50¢).

Chala

㉕ *173 km (107 mi) southwest of Nazca,*

The serene coastal village of Chala is surrounded by quiet beaches that
attract international visitors and local families escaping the dry towns
for the fresh ocean breezes. The shore is lined with restaurants, where
enormous plates of fresh-cooked fish are quickly served up to hordes
of tourists on weekends and holidays. There are also many small, home-

Where to Stay & Eat

$ ✗ **La Taberna.** A fan slowly rotates above the churning bar crowd a popular criollo restaurant, *the* watering spot in which to be seen also one of the few places where you can leave your mark—litera on walls decorated with a montage of international poems, art, and vice from former diners. Nightly Andean flute groups and local ba keep the place upbeat and relaxing. Ice-cold beer and perfect p sours complement the delectable Peruvian spiced chicken, ceviche, milder pasta choices. ✉ *Jr. Lima 321* ☎ *034/522322* ⊟ *AE, MC,*

¢ ✗ **Cevichería El Tiburón II.** This lively little place serves terrific and ch ceviche at small tables crowded with laughing patrons. Most stay the music and dancing on weekends. ✉ *Callao 195* ☎ *No phone* ⊟ *credit cards.*

¢ ✗ **Chifa Nam Kug.** Near the Plaza de Armas, this well-known restaura concocts an eclectic but delicious mix of Chinese and Peruvian flavo Fried rice is the staple, but the garlic beef and grilled seafood entré are excellent. You can even sneak in back to flatter the chef as you wat him work. ✉ *Bolognesi 116* ☎ *No phone* ⊟ *MC, V.*

¢ ✗ **Concordia.** Stop here after a morning flight over the Nazca Lines f a filling, inexpensive lunch—or come later to enjoy a pisco sour. Loca swear by the *sopa criolla* (Creole soup), and if you have a sweet tootl dig into the chocolate cake. To burn off the calories, rent a bike for S/3.5 an hour. ✉ *Lima 594* ☎ *No phone* ⊟ *No credit cards.*

¢ ✗ **El Griego Restaurant.** Huge portions of Peruvian specialties are serve
Fodor'sChoice up to the backpacking crowd at this budget restaurant. It's all delicious
★ but go for the set almuerzo or one of the hearty soups. Top it off with a pisco sour in the evening. ✉ *Bolognesi 287* ☎ *No phone* ⊟ *No credit cards.*

¢ ✗ **Pin Point Café.** The after-meal crowds from La Taberna often pause at this small coffee bar, as do locals on their way to and from work. Light breakfasts, sandwiches, juices, and cappuccino are served. Late-afternoon diners receive a 15% happy-hour discount. ✉ *Jr. Lima 323* ☎ *No phone* ⊟ *No credit cards.*

$$ ✗▣ **Hotel Maison Suisse.** Comfortable, and conveniently across from the airport, this renovated hotel set amid gardens is a tour-group favorite. Old-fashioned wood furniture gives the rooms a Spanish-colonial feel, and you can upgrade to a suite with a hot tub. If you're on a quick trip, catch the daily video detailing the Nazca Lines before you take your scenic flight, then pick up local souvenirs at the well-stocked shop before you leave town. ✉ *Pan-American Hwy. S, Km 445* ☎☎ *034/522434* ☎ *32 rooms, 6 suites* ⚫ *Restaurant, pool, shop, bar, laundry service, travel services, free parking; no phones in some rooms, no TVs in some rooms* ⊟ *AE, DC, MC, V.*

$–$$ ✗▣ **Hotel Nazca Lines.** The former home of Maria Reiche, this historic
Fodor'sChoice hacienda set around a shaded, sunken courtyard with a pool is the per-
★ fect spot from which to explore local mysteries. Built in the 1940s, the hotel has long drawn international travelers and archaeologists, al-though the rooms have been updated over the decades to include air-conditioning, hot water, and sunny private patios. Attractive decorative touches such as charcoal sketches and wrought-iron headboards pre-serve the colonial feel. Delicious meals served on a tiled walkway be-side the courtyard are worth the expense, and nonguests can use the pool for S/1.50. Nazca Lines tours, including 2–3 nights at the hotel and a scenic flight, run about S/870. ✉ *Jr. Bolognesi* ☎ *034/522293, 01/ 442–3090 in Lima* 🖷 *034/522112* ☎ *34 rooms* ⚫ *Restaurant, lounge, tennis court, pool, bar, laundry service, travel services, free parking; no phones in some rooms, no TVs in some rooms* ⊟ *AE, DC, MC, V.*

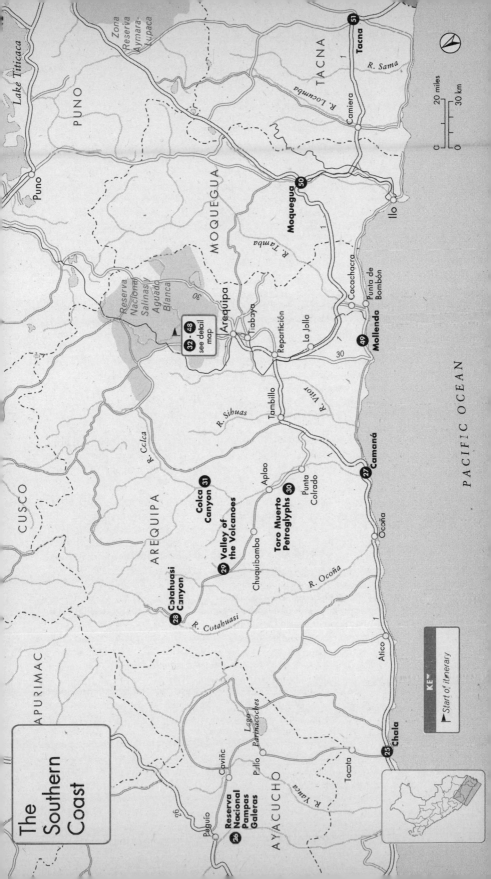

The
Southern
Coast

CUSCO

APURIMAC

AYACUCHO

AREQUIPA

PUNO

MOQUEGUA

TACNA

Lake Titicaca

Zona Reserva Aymara-Lupaca

Puno

Reserva Nacional Salinas y Aguada Blanca

30

Arequipa

see detail map

32 - 48

Yura

Tiabaya

Repartición

La Joila

30

27 Camaná

49 Mollendo

Punta de Bombón

Cacachacra

Ilo

50 Moquegua

R. Tambo

R. Locumba

R. Sama

Camiara

51 Tacna

1

R. Vítor

Tambillo

R. Sihuas

R. Colca

31 Colca Canyon

29 Valley of the Volcanoes

Chuquibamba

Aplao

Punta Colorado

30 Toro Muerto Petroglyphs

R. Ocoña

Ocoña

Atico

1

R. Cutahuasi

28 Cotahuasi Canyon

R. Yauca

Pullo

Caviñc

Puquio

26

Lago Parinacochas

26 Reserva Nacional Pampas Galeras

Tocota

Chala **25**

PACIFIC OCEAN

KEY
► Start of itinerary

0   20 miles
0   30 km

style hotels looking out onto scenic western ocean panoramas. From Nazca, you can reach Chala by car or colectivo for S/12.

Reserva Nacíonal Pampas Galeras

㉖ *50 km (30 mi) east of Nazca on Hwy. 26*

Take the paved road east from Nazca for two hours and you'll reach this nature reserve with herds of the rare, slender brown vicuña. Established in 1967, the 6,500-hectare park is composed of flat, windy grasslands where Andean condors and guanaco can also be spotted. A military base is on the site, and a park guard records all entrances and exits. Admission is S/7; the park is open daily from 8–6.

Camaná

㉗ *150 km (93 mi) south of Chala.*

This summer resort town sparkles with fun and frolicking locals, but it also played an important part in the region's history. Supplies were unloaded here before being transferred to Arequipa and the silver mines in Posotí, Bolivia, during colonial times. Peru's grand chess master, Julio Granda Zuñiga, also hails from this area. Today Camaná is known for its attractive beaches, especially La Punta. This quickly developing stretch of sand, 5 km (3 mi) from town, literally vibrates with energy and noise during the summer. Discos and bars stand edge to edge with little hotels and cafés, which provide an alternative to bronzing and bikini-watching. Bring an umbrella and strong sunscreen, as there's no shade, and don't plan to swim in the strong undertow. Shop the local market for good-quality trinkets—it's also the place to sample such local delicacies as huge freshwater *camarones* (shrimp). You can reach La Punta from Camaná by catching a colectivo (25¢) or bus from the town center. Major bus lines traveling between Lima and Arequipa also stop here.

Where to Stay

$$ ✕⊞ **Hotel Turistas.** Beautiful colonial architecture makes this bright, homey, and relaxing hacienda attractive. Spacious accommodations have high ceilings, arched doorways, and long windows overlooking pretty gardens. The first-floor restaurant serves local delicacies and desserts. ✉ *Av. Lima 138* ☎ *034/571113* ⊲ *18 rooms* ♿ *Restaurant, massage, exercise equipment, bar, library, laundry service, travel services, free parking* ⊟ *AE, DC, MC, V* ⦿ *BP.*

$$ ✕⊞ **Mountain House.** This waterfront hotel is among the most posh in town, and its graceful colonial feel attracts many upscale Arequipeños. Spacious rooms filled with antiques and local art have baths and hot water. The restaurant attracts regional diners who crave the sopa criolla and camarones. ✉ *Pan-American Hwy., Km 842* ☎ *34/522566* ⊲ *34 rooms* ♿ *Restaurant, pool, hot tub, massage, exercise equipment, bar, dance club, laundry service, travel services, free parking* ⊟ *AE, DC, MC, V* ⦿ *EP.*

$–$$ ✕⊞ **Residencial Selva.** It's surprising to find such a modern hotel so out of the way in southern Peru, but this spacious, family-run hacienda provides a relaxing Spanish-style getaway complete with 21st-century fixtures. Large rooms and updated décor mix with colonial furnishings and architectural details, making for a serene yet comfortable experience. Stroll the lush gardens, dine on the shady patios, or grab a delicious midday snack at the small restaurant. Although the hotel isn't central, you can get a free ride from Camaná, as well as a discount for stays over a week. ✉ *Prolongación 2 de Mayo 225, Urb. Granada* ☎ *034/572063* ⊲ *22 rooms* ♿ *Cafeteria, laundry service, travel services, free parking* ⊟ *AE, MC, V* ⦿ *EP.*

¢–$ ✕🖾 **Sun Valley.** This new resort near the beach is the place to go for water sports and other outdoor activities. After a day of play you can relax in a modern, if blandly decorated, room with a hot bath. The restaurant serves a mix of Peruvian and contemporary comfort foods. ⊠ *Cerrillos 11, Km 842* ☎ *034/571345* ✆ *eridv@hotmail.com* ⇦ *42 rooms* ⚘ *Restaurant, pool, hot tub, massage, sauna, gym, bar, library, shops, dance club, dry cleaning, laundry service, travel services, free parking* ▤ *AE, DC, MC, V* ❘❍❘ *BP.*

Cotahuasi Canyon

㉘ *50 km (31 mi) north of Colca Canyon.*

Fodor's Choice

★ Colca Canyon may be the region's most famous natural attraction, but at 3,354 m (11,001 ft) Cotahuasi is the world's deepest gorge. Carved by the Río Cotahuasi, which changes into Río Ocuña before connecting to the Pacific, the canyon was declared a Zona de Reserva Turística in 1988. Its deepest point is at Ninochaco, below the quaint administrative capital of Quechualla, and accessible only by kayak; in fact it was kayak explorations that first documented the area in the mid-1990s.

The gateway to the canyon is Piro, from where it's three hours to Sipia and the 150-m (462-ft) Cataratas de Sipia waterfalls. Three hours farther along a thin track against the canyon wall—which climbs 400 m (1,312 ft) above the river in some places—you'll reach Chaupo, a settlement surrounded by groves of fruit trees. You can camp here and hike through Velinga to ruins at Huña before reaching Quechualla, where you can see the ancient farming terraces of Maucullachta across the gorge. When the Inca ruled, the road between Cusco and Puerto Inca followed the canyon for much of the way.

The serene town of Cotahuasi is set high in the hills, where the clear air at the 2,600-m (8,528-ft) altitude perfectly suits its more than 4,000 residents. Their attractive, whitewashed colonial-style homes line slim, straight lanes before a backdrop of Cerro Hiunao. Winding upward ahead is the highway to Chuquibamba and the 5,425-m (17,794-ft) slopes of Nevado Coropuna.

Sports & the Outdoors

Kayakers and white-water rafters can challenge the rapids anywhere from the upper Cotahuasi, near the village, almost to the Pacific. Note that there's some portage involved, especially around Iquipi, where there's a descent of 2,300 m (7,544 ft). White-water season is May through August, when the rapids are Class III to V.

Valley of the Volcanoes

㉙ *65 km (40 mi) north of Colca Canyon.*

This spectacular, 65-km (40-mi) crevasse north of Colca Canyon includes a line of 80 extinct craters and cinder cones. Looming over the scene is active Volcán Coropuna, the highest peak in Peru and the tenth-tallest in the Andes. Andagua village, at the head of the valley, has the best tourist facilities in the area. The valley is about five hours by road from Colca Canyon. Buses from Arequipa travel here Sunday, Wednesday, and Friday. The Arequipa–Andagua bus continues to Orcopampa, from where you can also visit the thermal springs of Huancarama.

Toro Muerto Petroglyphs

③ *40 km (25 mi) northeast of Canaña.*

This is the world's largest petroglyph field, where hundreds of volcanic rocks are thought to have been painted more than 1,000 years ago by the Huari (or Wari) culture. Lifelike sketches of pumas, llamas, guanacos, and condors, as well as warriors and dancers, show what life was like during this time. Head higher for expansive views of the desert. It's hot and windy, so bring water, a hat, sunglasses, and good walking shoes. Toro Muerto is three hours by bus from Arequipa's main terminal and an hour's walk south from Corire, where hotels and restaurants cater to travelers. Agencies in Arequipa can help you organize a trip.

Colca Canyon

③ *30 km (19 mi) north of Toro Muerto.*

Named for the stone warehouses (*colcas*) used to store grain by prehistoric Indians living along the walls of this wondrous gorge, Colca Canyon is one of Peru's most amazing natural sights. Carved into the foothills of the snow-covered Andes and sliced by the silvery Río Colca, this canyon is one of the world's deepest, some 3,182 m (10,607 ft) down—twice as deep as the Grand Canyon. Flying overhead, you can't miss the green, fertile trough as it cuts through the barren terrain, but it's all an illusion; only scrub brush and cactus cling to the canyon's sheer basalt sides.

Quechua farmers once irrigated narrow, stacked terraces of volcanic earth along the rim to make this a productive farming area. These pre-Columbian fields are still used for *quinoa* and *kiwicha* grains, and barley grown here is still used to brew Arequipeña beer. With the arrival of the Inca and the Spaniards, the canyon was soon part of the route between the coast and Bolivia's silver mines. With an exodus of Colca men to the mines and a new train service that bypassed the valley for Arequipa, Colca was all but forgotten. Thanks to a controversial (ultimately scrapped) irrigation project, the canyon came into the limelight and is now one of the country's most popular tourist attractions.

Most of those who live along the rim today are Collagua Indians, whose settlements date back more than 2,000 years. It is thought that this independent people came from higher regions in the Andes and were possibly descendents of the Aymaras. Their traditions persevered through the centuries, and they even kept their way of life during Inca times; in fact, stories have it that the Inca chief Mayta Capac married a Collagua princess and built her a gracious, copper bridal home near Sibayo. In these unspoiled Andean villages you'll still see Collaguas and Cabana people wearing traditional clothing and embroidered hats. Spanish influence is also on display in such rimside towns as Achoma, Maca, Pinchollo, and Yanque, where gleaming white *sillar* (volcanic-stone) churches add a colonial feel.

You wouldn't expect much wildlife in such a stark place, but Cruz del Condor is a haunt for the giant birds, particularly at dusk and dawn, when they soar on the winds rising from the deep valley. At 1,200 m (4,000 ft), the "condor cross" precipice between the villages Pinchollo and Cabanaconde is the best place to spot them. View Colca early in the day, when it's full of low clouds, or at dusk when it glows with crimson light from the sunset. Trails are rough and unmarked, so you'll need a guide to explore, as well as good walking shoes. The most knowledgeable and experienced locals are in the villages Arequipa and Chivay on the south rim. Here you'll also find restaurants, hotels, and tourist facilities.

Where to Stay & Eat

In the small, rimside settlements of Chivay, Coporaque, Ichupampa, and Madrigal you can experience local life by staying with families. In addition to exploring ruins and historic sites with guides who know everything about this region, you'll have the opportunity to help out with daily chores and participate in seasonal festivities.

$ ✕⊞ **Rumi Llaqta.** This small hotel in Chivay has the feel of a Swiss ski lodge, with comfortable cabins made of locally quarried rock—hence the name "city of stone." Cozy rooms with comfortable, rustic furnishings have private baths with hot water. The restaurant serves excellent Peruvian fare. *⊠ Calle Huayna Capac, Chivay ☎ 054/241974 ☎☎ 054/521098 ⌂ rumillaktacolca@lared ⇩ 28 rooms �ᕤ Restaurant, room service, pool, fishing, boating, hiking, horseback riding, mountain bikes, bar, laundry service, travel services, free parking; no TVs in some rooms ▭ No credit cards.*

$ ⊞ **Colca Lodge.** The hotel's understated look, with adobe and clay walls
Fodor'sChoice and thatched roof, complement the surrounding terrain. The location
★ between Yanque and Ichupampa offers plenty to do, including daily canyon hikes, horseback rides, bike trips, trout fishing, and dips in hotel hot springs. Breakfast is included. *Reservations ⊠ Zela 212, Arequipa ☎ 054/212813 ☎ 054/220147 ⇩ 25 rooms �ᕤ Restaurant, room service, minibars, pool, boating, fishing, hiking, horseback riding, mountain bikes, bar, laundry service, travel services, free parking; no TVs in some rooms ▭ AE, MC, V ⏀ BP.*

$ ⊞ **Fundo Puye Lodge.** The newest hotel in this region is a gathering of thatch-roof bungalows with terraces that have spectacular views over the silvery Río Colca and small hot springs. Accommodations have comfortable, Western-style furnishings, bright bedspreads, and curtains with Inca geometric patterns, and baths with hot water. The wilderness location outside of Chivay ensures peace and privacy, as well as such activities as hiking and horseback riding. *⊠ Llanque ☎ 054/245199 ☎ 054/242088 ⌂ colcalodge@grupoinca ⇩ 21 rooms �ᕤ Restaurant, room service, minibars, pool, boating, fishing, hiking, horseback riding, mountain bikes, bar, laundry service, travel services, free parking; no TVs in some rooms ▭ AE, MC, V ⏀ BP.*

Sports & the Outdoors

There are plenty of places for tough hiking around the Colca Canyon, but paths aren't marked—so hire a guide. Travel agencies in Arequipa can arrange day treks and overnight adventures to the canyon for S/73–S/122, including accommodations, meals, a cultural show, and trips to hot springs and Cruz del Condor. The Río Colca is also known among kayakers and rafters for its terrific and thrilling white-water conditions. North of the canyon is a sheltered valley that runs east to west, allowing you to see the incredible changes in scenery along the way.

HIKING   For about S/100 per day you can hire **Carlos Zárate Aventuras** (⊠ Santa Catalina 204 ☎ 054/OR 263107) and his professional hiking and mountain guides, who conduct tours in Spanish, English, and French. Upscale travelers go with **Colonial Tours** (⊠ San Martín 133 ☎ 054/232461), an outfit that charges around S/87 per day for tours utilizing hotels and restaurants with better amenities. **Santa Catalina Tours** (⊠ Santa Catalina 356 ☎ 054/216994) runs slightly less expensive trips for about S/70 a day.

MOUNTAIN   **Carlos Zárate Aventuras** has a team of professionally trained and expe-
CLIMBING   rienced guides. Compare expert local mountain leaders with **Find-A-Guide** (⊕ www.findaguide.com), a service for Peru climbing experts and adventure tour companies.

SURFING Punta Hermosa, near Km 44 on the Pan-American Highway and about an hour's drive south of Lima, has reefs and coves that create prime surfing conditions. The largest waves in South America, some 7 m (20 ft), roll into nearby Pico Alto, with nearly 20 good breaks around the Pico Alto Surf Camp. Light winds and balmy water temperatures mean you can wear just a bathing suit in summer, although you'll need a wetsuit at other times. Punta Rocas, also along this section of coast, hosted the World Surfing Championships.

WHITE-WATER Below Colca Canyon, conditions on the Río Majes are superb for white-
RAFTING water rafting. The best time to hit the Río Colca rapids is during the South American summer, December through March. Most travel agencies in Arequipa can arrange trips. **Majes Tours** (⊠ Villa Flórida B-7, Cerro Colorado, Arequipa ☎ 054/255819), one of the best agencies, offers trips down this part of the river. Accommodations are at a rustic lodge in Ongoro.

Arequipa

32–48 *150 km (93 mi) south of Colca Canyon, 200 km (124 mi) south of Cotahuasi Canyon.*

Settled in a lush valley encircled by towering, snow-covered volcanoes, Arequipa glows with charm, light, and energy. The largest city between Lima and Santiago, Chile, and Peru's second-largest city after the capital, this settlement of 1 million residents grew from a collection of Spanish-colonial churches and homes constructed from brilliant white *sillar* (volcanic stone) gathered from the surrounding terrain. At an elevation of 2,300 m (7,500 ft) above sea level, the city enjoys fresh, crisp air, as well as warm days averaging 23°C (73°F) and comfortable nights at 14°C (57°F). To make up for the lack of rain, the Río Chili waters the surrounding foothills, which were once farmed by the Inca and now stretch into rows of alfalfa and onions.

The town was a gathering of Aymara Indians and Inca when Pizarro arrived to name it "Villa Hermosa" on August 15, 1540. His proud Spanish traditions have carried on through the centuries, giving the settlement a distinct European flavor in the midst of the desert. No one is quite sure how the name "Arequipa" originated, although due to the town's proximity to Volcán El Misti the Aymaras are thought to have called it *Arequipa* (the place behind the pointed mountain). After the Spanish arrived, the town grew into the region's most profitable center for farming and cattle-raising, and these businesses are still key to Arequipa's modern economy. The settlement was also an important point on the silver route linking the coast to the Bolivian mines. By the 1800s, due to its solid economy and comfortable climate, Arequipa had more Spanish settlers than any town in the south.

The city's European look has been preserved over the centuries, and today Arequipa is said to have the most colonial architecture after Cusco. Due to its bleached, white sillar structures, Arequipeños now call their home "White City." This main economic center for the south is also called the "Independent Republic of Arequipa" by its proud residents, who have made several attempts to secede from Peru and even designed the city's own passport and flag. Each August 15, parades, fireworks, bullfights, and dancing celebrate the city's founding. The combination of grace and conviviality has drawn many outsiders to move here, and the city's population has doubled in the last decade. Little wonder Arequipa received a designation as a World Cultural Heritage site by UNESCO.

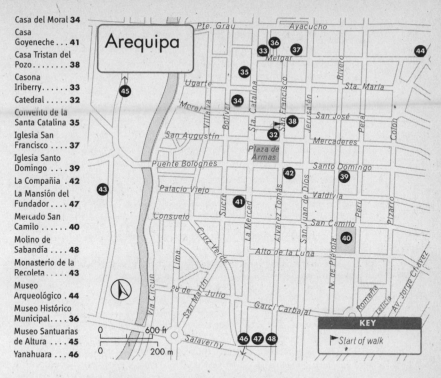

*Numbers in the text correspond to numbers in the margin and on the
Arequipa map.*

A Good Tour

Begin at the Plaza de Armas in the center of town and take a quick tour
of the elaborate, twin-towered **Catedral** ③② ▶. Head to the northwest corner of the plaza and cross the street to reach **Casona Iriberry** ③③, with its
cultural complex, set opposite at the corner of Santa Catalina and San
Augustín. Continue a block west on San Augustín, then turn right on
Bolívar to reach **Casa del Moral** ③④. Stroll a block farther on Bolívar, turn
right on Ugarte, then turn left on Santa Catalina to the **Convento de la
Santa Catalina** ③⑤; have a tour and then take a break at the café. From
here, continue on Santa Catalina, turn right on Zela, and take the first
left to the **Museo Histórico Municipal** ③⑥. On the next block of Zela you'll
see the **Iglesia de San Francisco** ③⑦. Keep going to Jerusalén, then turn
right and walk two blocks south to San José, then turn left to find the
Casa Tristan del Pozo ③⑧. Head back to Jerusalén, make a right, and
walk two blocks to Morán. Next, walk a block east, turn right on
Piérola, and you'll see the **Iglesia Santo Domingo** ③⑨. Continue two blocks
farther on Piérola, then turn left on San Camilo to reach the **Mercado
San Camilo** ④⓪. Backtrack three blocks on San Camilo, which turns into
Consuelo, to where it crosses La Merced. Take a right and walk a block
to the corner of Palacio Viejo, where you'll see the **Casa Goyeneche** ④①.
Walk a block right on Palacio Viejo and turn left on Alvarez Tomás to
the 17th-century **La Compañia** ④②, which you can tour. Finally, walk a
block north on San Francisco to return to the Plaza de Armas, where
you can have a picnic lunch or grab a meal at one of the small eateries
along the square.

In the afternoon, walk west across the Puente Grau and Ejército to the
Monasterio de la Recoleta ④③. From here you can continue west along

Ejército to explore the pretty colonial suburbs of Yanahuara and Cayma, which have lovely views of the city. Stay here for drinks and dinner, or stroll back to Arequipa's Plaza de Armas, where you can catch a bus east to the **Museo Arqueológico** ㊹ at the Universidad de San Agustín or the **Museo Santuarias de Altura** ㊺ at the Universidad Católica Santa María in Umacollo.

TIMING &
PRECAUTIONS
You can easily walk through Arequipa in a half day, but the more pleasant way to tour the neighborhoods is by stopping in the museums, churches, and colonial homes, with pauses for coffee or a cold drink and shopping. Taken leisurely, this route could easily stretch from morning into the late afternoon. For a quick, cheap tour, spend S/1 and catch a Vallecito bus for a 1½-hour circuit around Calles Jerusalén and San Juan de Díos. Most sites are open mornings and afternoons, but close for a couple of hours around midday. Churches usually open 7 to 9 AM and 6 to 8 PM, before and after services.

Wear comfortable walking shoes, and bring a hat, sunscreen, a Spanish dictionary, some small change, and a good map of town. Be street smart in the Arequipa market area—stay alert, access your cash discreetly when you need it, and keep your valuables close. For further tips, *see* Safety *in* Smart Travel Tips A to Z.

What to See

㉞ **Casa del Moral.** The Banco Sur is in one of thé town's most unusual buildings, also known as the Casa Williams. Once a lovely old colonial home, it was bought in the 1940s by the British consul and renovated to its former elegance. Above the door, a sillar portal is carved with a Spanish coat of arms, and you're welcomed to enter by a mestizo design that combines puma heads with snakes emerging from their mouths—motifs found on Nazca textiles and pottery. Inside, you'll walk through a small museum with alpaca rugs ánd soaring ceilings to view polished period furniture and a gallery of Cusco School paintings. ⊠ *Moral 318 and Bolívar* ☎ *054/213–171* ⊠ *S/7* ☉ *Mon.–Sat. 9–5, Sun. 9–1.*

㊶ **Casa Goyeneche.** Look for the Banco Central de la Reserva and you'll find this attractive Spanish-colonial home. Ask the guard for a tour, and you'll enter through a pretty courtyard and an ornate set of wooden doors to view rooms decorated in period-style antiques and paintings. ⊠ *La Merced 201 y Palacio Viejo* ☎ *054/352674* ⊠ *Free* ☉ *Mon.–Fri. 8–4, Sat. 8–1.*

㊳ **Casa Tristan del Pozo.** Also knówn as Casa Gibbs-Ricketts, this small museum and art gallery was originally built as a seminary in 1738 and is now site of the Banco Continental. Look for the elaborate puma heads spouting water. Inside you'll find colonial paintings, ornate Peruvian costumes, and furniture. ⊠ *San Francisco 108* ☎ *054/215–060* ⊠ *Free* ☉ *Weekdays 9–12 and 4–6.*

㉝ **Casona Iriberry.** This beautiful late 18th-century home is filled with colonial-period furniture, paintings, and décor. The Complejo Cultural Chaves la Rosa in back has some of the city's most important arts venues, including exhibits, concerts, and films. ⊠ *San Augustin y Santa Catalina* ☎ *054/362534* ⊠ *S/10* ☉ *Mon.–Sat. 9–4.*

▶ ㉜ **Catedral.** You can't miss the imposing twin towers of this 1612 cathedral, whose facade guards the entire eastern flank of the Plaza de Armas. The inside is spacious and light, with high, vaulted ceilings above a beautiful Belgian organ. The ornate wooden pulpit, carved by French artist Rigot in 1879, was transported here in the early 1900s by a local aristocrat's daughter. In back, look for the Virgin of the Sighs statue in her white wedding dress, and the figure of Beata Ana de Los Angeles, a nun from Santa Catalina monastery who was beatified by Pope John Paul II when he stayed in Arequipa in 1990. A fire in 1844 destroyed much of the cathedral, as did an 1868 earthquake, so parts now have a 19th-century look. ⊠ *Santa Catalina, at San Francisco* ☎ *034/533920* ☎ *S/7* ☉ *7–11 and 5–8.*

③⑤ Convento de la Santa Catalina. A five-acre complex of mud-brick, Iberian-
style buildings surrounded by fortress-like walls and separated by neat,
open plazas and colorful gardens, this working convent is a city in itself
and one of Peru's most famed cultural treasures. Founded in 1579 and
closed to the public for the first 400 years, Santa Catalina was an exclusive retreat for the daughters of Arequipa's wealthiest colonial patrons.
Narrow streets run past the Courtyard of Silence, where teenage nuns
lived during their first year, and the Cloister of Oranges, where nuns decorated their rooms with lace sheets, silk curtains, and antique furnishings. Though about 400 nuns once lived here, fewer than 30 do so today.
Admission includes a 1-hr guided tour (tip S/10–S/20) in English or most
European languages. Afterward, head to the cafeteria for the nuns' famous *torta de naranja* (orange cake), pastries, and tea. ⊠ *Santa Catalina
at Ugarte* ☎ *054/229798* ☎ *S/14* ☉ *Daily 9–5; last entry at 4.*

FodorsChoice
★

③⑦ Iglesia de San Francisco. This 16th-century church has survived numerous natural disasters, including several earthquakes that cracked its
cupola. Inside, near the polished silver altar, is the little chapel of the
Sorrowful Virgin, where the all-important Virgin Mary statue is stored.
Each year on December 8, during Arequipa's Feast of the Immaculate
Conception, the Virgin is paraded around the city all night atop an ornate carriage and surrounded by images of saints and angels. A throng
of pilgrims carrying flowers and candles takes part in the procession.
⊠ *Zela 103* ☎ *No phone* ☎ *Free* ☉ *7–11 AM and 5–8 PM.*

③⑨ Iglesia Santo Domingo. Designed with hints of Islam in its elegant brick
arches and simple stone domes, this cathedral carries an aura of elegance.
Step inside to view simple furnishings and sunlight streaming through
stained-glass windows as what seems like a thousand small silver candles flicker along the back wall near the altar. The working Dominican
monastery in back keeps the church busy at all hours. ⊠ *Santo Domingo
y Piérola* ☎ *No phone* ☎ *Free* ☉ *Mon.–Sat. 8–11 and 2–5.*

④② La Compañía. Built by the Jesuits in 1525, this beautiful, bone-white series of buildings incorporates several decorative styles and touches. The
side portal, built in 1654, and main façade, built in 1698, show examples of Andean mestizo style with carved flowers, spirals, birds—and angels with Indian faces—along gently curving archways and spiral pillars.
Inside, **Capilla St. Ignatius** (St. Ignatius Chapel) has a polychrome cupola
and original 17th-century oil paintings by Bernardo Bitti and other
Cusco School artists. Hike up to the steeple at sunset for sweeping views
of Arequipa bathed in golden light. The former monastery, now converted
into shops, contains two cloisters which can be entered from General Morán
or Palacio Viejo. The main building is on the southeast corner of the Plaza
de Armas. ⊠ *General Morán at Alvarez Tomás* ☎ *No phone* ☎ *Chapel
50¢* ☉ *Church daily 9–1 and 4–9, chapel Mon.–Sat. 9–1 and 4–9.*

④⑦ La Mansión del Fundador. Alongside the Río Sabandía, La Mansión del
Fundador is a beautifully restored colonial home and museum. First owned
by Arequipa founder Don Garcí Manuel de Carbajal, the mansion has
been painstakingly renovated into a showpiece with original furnishings
and paintings. Admission is S/8, and there's a cafeteria with a bar on-
site. To reach the home, go past Tingo along Avenida Huasacanche.

40 **Mercado San Camilo.** This jam-packed collection of shops sells everything from snacks and local produce to clothing and household goods. You can find it between Perú, San Camilo, Piérola, and Alto de la Luna. ✉ *San Camilo 352* ☎ *No phone* 🎟 *Free* ⊙ *Daily 6–4.*

★ **48** **Molino de Sabandía.** There's a colorful and complicated story behind the area's first stone *molina* (mill), 7 km (4 mi) southeast of Arequipa. Built in 1621 in the gorgeous Paucarpata countryside, the mill fell into ruin over the next century. Famous architect Luis Felipe Calle was restoring the Arequipa mansion that now houses the Central Reserve Bank in 1966 when he was asked to work on the mill project. By 1973, the restoration of the volcanic-stone structure was complete—and Calle liked the new version so much that he bought it, got it working again, and opened it for visitors to tour. Bring your swimsuit and walking shoes in good weather, as there's a pool and trails around the lovely countryside. Adjoining the site is Yumina, which has numerous Inca agricultural terraces, some of which are still in use today. Admission to the mill is S/7. If you're not driving, flag a taxi for S/14 or take a gray bus from Socabaya in Arequipa to about 2 km (1 mi) past Paucarpata.

43 **Monasterio de la Recoleta.** One of Peru's most extensive and valuable libraries is in this 1648 Franciscan monastery. With several cloisters and museums on-site, it's a wonderful place to research regional history and culture. Start in the massive, wood-paneled, wood-floored library, where monks in brown robes quietly browse among 20,000 ancient books and maps, the most valuable of which were printed before 1500 and are kept in glass cases. Pre-Columbian artifacts and objects collected by missionaries to the Amazon are on display in one area, while a selection of elegant colonial and religious artwork is in another. Guides are available (tip S/7 or so). To reach the monastery, cross the Río Chili by Puente Grau or Puente Bolognesi. ✉ *Recoleta 117* ☎ *054/270–966* 🎟 *S/7* ⊙ *Weekdays 9–12 and 3–5, Sat. 9–12.*

44 **Museo Arqueológico.** Though it's slightly out of town, this archaeology museum at the Universidad de San Augustín provides a background on local ruins. Apply to the director for an appointment to visit; once you're approved, you'll have an expert guide to tell all the stories behind the displays of textiles, pottery, and mummies. ✉ *Av. Independencia, betw. La Salle y Santa Rosa* ☎ *054/229719* 🎟 *S/4* ⊙ *Weekdays 8–2.*

36 **Museo Histórico Municipal.** In the 1804 Sala Naval building, this history museum provides an overview of Arequipa's development into a modern city, along with exhibits of local archaeology, natural history, and architecture. There are extensive displays of old photos, maps, paintings, and war memorabilia. ✉ *Betw. Zela and Francisco* ☎ *No phone* 🎟 *50¢* ⊙ *Weekdays 9–5.*

★ **45** **Museo Santuarias de Altura.** This fascinating little museum at the Universidad Católica Santa Maria holds the frozen bodies of four young girls who were apparently sacrificed more than 500 years ago by the Inca to appease the gods. "Juanita," the first, was found in 1995 near the summit of Mt. Ampato by local climber Miguel Zarate and anthropologist Johan Reinhard. When neighboring Volcán Sabancaya erupted, the ice that held Juanita in her sacrificial tomb melted and she rolled partway down the mountain and into a crater. English-speaking guides will show you around the museum, and you can watch a video detailing the expedition. No photographs are permitted. ✉ *Samuel Velarde 305 Umacollo* ☎ *054/252554* ⊕ *www.mountain.org* 🎟 *S/10* ⊙ *Mon.–Sat. 9–1 and 3–5.*

46 **Yanahuara.** The eclectic little suburb of Yanahuara, northwest of the city, makes a pleasant tour around lunch or in the late afternoon. As the neighborhood sits above Arequipa, bring your camera to capture the amazing views over the city from the platform at the end of the Plaza de Armas. Stop in at the 1783, mestizo-style sillar Iglesia Yanahuara, whose interior includes wrought-iron chandeliers and gilt sanctuaries surrounding the nave. Ask to see the glass coffin that holds a statue of Christ used in parades on holy days. There are plenty of casual *picantería* where you can grab a cup of coffee and a pastry or sandwich. To reach Yanahuara, head across the Avenida Grau bridge, then continue on Avenida Ejército to Avenida Lima, and from here, it's five blocks to the Plaza.

off the beaten path

RESERVA NACIONAL SALINAS Y AGUADA BLANCA – In the midst of the gorgeous, grassy fields that encompass, this vast nature reserve, you'll spot herds of graceful, beige-and-white vicuñas grazing on the sparse plantlife. Wear good walking shoes for the uneven terrain. Also bring a hat, sunscreen, and a warm jacket, as the park sits at a crisp 3,900 m (12,800 ft). The reserve is 5 km (3 mi) north of Arequipa, just beyond El Misti.

Where to Eat

Comida Arequipa (Arequipan cuisine) is a special version of comida criolla. Perhaps the most famous dish is *rocoto relleno,* a large, spicy red pepper stuffed with meat, onions, and raisins. Other specialties to try are *cuy chactado* (roasted guinea pig), and *adobo* (pork stew), a local cure for hangovers. Picanterías are where locals head for good, basic Peruvian meals and cold Arequipeña beer served with *cancha* (fried, salted corn).

The west side of the Plaza de Armas has dozens of food stalls along the balcony above the Portal San Augustin. Although it's crowded on Sundays after the flag-raising and parade, this is a great place to sample local fare—look around and see what everyone else is ordering. If you're really hungry, you can even get half a grilled chicken for about S/14.

The first block of Calle San Francisco, north of the Plaza de Armas, is lined with cafés, restaurants, and bars. The Mercado San Camilo carries *queso Mejía* (Mejía cheese), a local specialty. *Queso helado* (frozen, fresh milk mixed with sugar and a sprinkling of cinnamon), toffee, and chocolate is an excellent Arequipan sweet, and if you're a chocolate addict, the La Ibérica factory on Jerusalén, northeast of Plaza de Armas, gives tours on weekdays.

$$$$ ✗ **Sol de Mayo** In the colonial Yanahuara neighborhood, this charming garden restaurant is worth the expense to taste true Arequipan cooking, which has been served here for more than a century. Specialties include *ocopa arequipeña* (boiled potato slices in spicy sauce and melted cheese), rocoto relleno, and other heat-intense fare. ⊠ *Jerusalén 207, Yanahuara* ☎ *054/254148* ▤ *MC, V.*

$–$$$$ ✗ **Las Quenas.** Rustic and well-known, this restaurant filled with antiques and musical instruments offers complete immersion into Arequipan life and traditions. Lunch and tea are served daily, but set dinners are the speciality, served nightly except Sunday to the accompaniment of a live folkloric performance. Dinners start at 8, and the tourist package includes a cocktail, appetizer, main course, dessert, and a show for S/87, with tax and tip. ⊠ *San Francisco 215* ☎ *054/281115* ▤ *AE, D, MC, V* ☾ *Closed Sun.*

$ ✕ **El Conquistador Picantería.** You won't see any tourists at this tiny diner—but you will have the chance to rub shoulders (and perhaps share a pitcher of homemade sangria) with in-the-know locals who consider this the best food in Arequipa. Pork pie and pig's head salad are specialties, but you can also go for the white-vegetable soup or the ubiquitous relleno, too. ☒ *Bayoneta 106* ☎ *054/286009* ⊟ *No credit cards.*

$ ✕ **Grill de Oyague.** Elegant woodwork and muted lighting add to the romance of this spot up in Yanahuara. Dive into the salad bar, included with your entrée of grilled steaks or sausages. You can dine to live music on Friday and Saturday nights. ☒ *Alfonso Ugarte 104* ☎ *054/235542* ⊟ *D, MC, V* ☉ *No lunch Mon.–Sat.*

$ ✕ **Tradición Arequipeña.** It may be a S/7 taxi ride from town to this restaurant in Paucarpata, but locals come in droves for the fantastic Arequipan food. The décor is Peruvian country, with red-tile walls and wood floors, but the flavors lean toward Creole. Get ready for such entrées as cuy chactado and ocopa arequipeña. Diners pay S/25 to hear live music Fridays 2–7 and Saturday 4–11. ☒ *Dolores 111* ☎ *054/426467* ⊟ *MC, V.*

¢ ✕ **Aji Limón Cebichería.** It's so tiny there are just five tables, but locals line up to wait for the restaurant's famous ceviche. Other seafood dishes are served, but this is the place to come for a solid version of the local staple. ☒ *Plaza San Francisco 300* ☎ *No phone* ⊟ *No credit cards.*

¢ ✕ **Balcón Arequipa.** Overlooking the Plaza de Armas, this local favorite is a great place to start the day, with views of Arequipan life and kicky Peruvian flavors. Just make sure you're in the mood to relax, as the leisurely service encourages you to sit back and enjoy the scene. ☒ *Merced y Bolognesi* ☎ *No phone* ⊟ *No credit cards.*

¢ ✕ **Café Peña Anuschka.** European expatriates and travelers craving the bitter and sour flavorings of German cuisine frequent this busy, friendly, dinner-only restaurant. You can also drop in after supper for a fruity cocktail or coffee and a freshly baked German pastry. The café, open 6–11 PM, turns into a peña with live music Friday and Saturday nights. ☒ *Santa Catalina 204* ☎ *054/213221* ⊟ *No credit cards* ☉ *No lunch. Closed Sun.*

★ ¢ ✕ **El Rincón Norteño.** Trujillo cuisine—seafood, grilled meats, and varying local specialties—is the specialty of this attractive, wood-paneled restaurant, but you can ask the friendly owners for recommendations that aren't on the menu. Sidle up to the wood-and-brick bar for a pisco, northern style, below photos of northern Peru. There are live folk music performances on weekend evenings. ☒ *San Francisco 300-B* ☎ *054/215257* ⊟ *No credit cards* ☉ *No dinner Sun.*

¢ ✕ **Govinda.** The Hare Krishnas who run the large hall decorated with Indian motifs and textiles cook up excellent organic, vegetarian food. The tastes are Euro-inspired, with brown breads, yogurts, fruit salads, and drinks. The filling, set meal runs S/4. It's alongside the Catedral. ☒ *Santa Catalina 120* ☎ *054/285540* ⊟ *No credit cards.*

¢ ✕ **Helados Artika.** This small, retro-style *helados* (ice cream) café next to La Compañía is the perfect place to stop for a cone after shopping around the Plaza de Armas. Also sample the delicious homemade cakes and cookies. ☒ *Morán 120* ☎ *no phone* ⊟ *No credit cards.*

¢ ✕ **Ka Hing.** Fondly referred to as "El Chifa" by locals, this is *the* Chinese restaurant at which to be seen. It was the first real Chinese restaurant in town, and the food remains true to its origins. The lengthy menu includes myriad meats and seafood; lunch and dinner specials are accompanied by soup and rice. It's a favorite of families, so make reservations for weekends and holidays. ☒ *Dolores 144* ☎ *054/247500* ⊟ *No credit cards.*

¢ ✗ **La Canasta.** Follow the scent of fresh baguettes to this bright little bakery where the authentic, crusty French loaves are baked twice a day. Settle into the serene courtyard with a friend to trade tastes of grainy, buttered slices and small sweets. You'll also find such Peruvian starches as *pan de yema* (regional brioche) and *pan de tres cachets* (a croissant filled with dulce de leche). ⊠ *Jerusalén 115* ☏ *054/214–900* ▭ *AE, DC, MC, V* ⊘ *Closed Sun.*

¢ ✗ **La Casita de José Antonio Cebichería.** Imaginative combinations of sea creatures and spices result in the delicious fare at this small, cheery restaurant. *Tortilla de erizo* (sea urchin omelette) or *machitas à la criola* (pink clams in spicy sauce), anyone? Hearty entrées such as *parihuela* (seafood casserole) and *corvina la macho* (sea bass in thick broth) join the always reliable ceviche. ⊠ *Plaza San Francisco 300* ☏ *054/289327* ▭ *No credit cards.*

¢ ✗ **Laksmivan.** Beautiful watercolors by local artists decorate this harmonious little spot named for the goddess of spirits and nature. Popular with locals and budget travelers for more than 25 years, the restaurant is known for creating inexpensive vegetarian dishes that combine healthy ingredients with Peruvian flavorings. Sit outside in one of the courtyards to enjoy the lovely blossoms and birds. ⊠ *Jerusalén 402* ☏ *054/228768* ▭ *No credit cards.*

¢ ✗ **Le Bistrot.** It's a streetside café straight out of Paris, with little tables, comfortable chatting seats, and endtables scattered with board games and international magazines. But everyone comes for the crêpes, served both filled and with sauce, as entrées and desserts. On the ever-changing menu, look for such crêpe specialties as the ham and asparagus; the spinach and mozzarella; or the lighter, buttery varieties drizzled with a berry sauce or sugar. If you're in the mood for more basic fare, try a baguette sandwich or a mixed salad. High grade espresso drinks are served with such delicacies as chocolate gâteau. Look for the restaurant in the Alianza Francesa compound. ⊠ *Santa Catalina 208* ☏ *054/215579* ▭ *MC, V* ⊘ *Closed Sun.*
FodorsChoice ★

¢ ✗ **Mandala.** Innovative vegetarian cuisine is served throughout the day at this simple, Peruvian-style restaurant. The choices vary from vegetarian takes on Arequipan criolla to pastas, Chinese dishes, and desserts. The healthy, natural ingredients result in a low-calorie menu that can offset a night of empañadas and pisco. ⊠ *Jerusalén 207* ☏ *054/696562* ▭ *No credit cards.*

¢ ✗ **Mixto's Cebichería.** Above the glowing white Catedral, this lovely, romantic spot serves up some of Arequipa's best seafood dishes. Ceviche is, of course, the focus, but you'll also find shellfish empañadas and mixed stews. If you're averse or allergic to ocean fare, don't worry; the restaurant also serves pastas, salads, and grilled meats. If the weather is warm, ask for a table on the terrace above the Catedral entrance. ⊠ *Pasaje Catedral 115* ☏ *054/215325* ▭ *AE, MC, V.*
FodorsChoice ★

¢ ✗ **Sambambaias.** In a leafy suburb that's about a 10-minute walk from the center of town, this restaurant has pink decorations that may strike you as charming or kitschy, depending on your taste. A pianist serenades as the efficient staff delivers the international fare to your table. ⊠ *Luna Pizarro 304, Vallecito* ☏ *054/223657* ▭ *AE, DC, MC, V.*

¢ ✗ **Sulz.** Come hungry to this spacious, elegant restaurant that serves Arequipan food at its best. Enormous rooms packed with tables accommodate the flood of local families and tourists. If you can't decide what to order from the extensive menu, choose the Triple, which includes rocoto, *chicharran* (pork rind), and *patitas de carnero* (mutton in sauce). There's a S/25 fee for patrons on weekend and holiday nights, when the live orchestra plays to those on the dance floor. ⊠ *Progreso 202A* ☏ *054/449787* ▭ *No credit cards.*

Where to Stay

★ **$$–$$$** ╳▥ **Hotel Libertador.** Amid beautiful, sprawling gardens, this 1940 Spanish colonial villa creates an oasis of Old Arequipa in the modern city. Hand-hewn sillar arches, wrought-iron window screens, and touches of Peruvian décor give this luxury hotel the intimate feel of an old family home. Breakfast on the terrace to absorb it all, then dip in a pool overlooking Volcán Misti and the Andean panorama. Nonguests can stop in the pub-style bar or splurge on the Continental delights at Restaurant Los Robles ($$). ⊠ *Plaza Bolívar, Selva Alegre* ☏ *054/ 221–5110* 🖷 *054/442–2988* ⊕ *www.libertador.com.pe* ⌷ *92 rooms, 6 suites* ⌷ *3 restaurants, room service, minibars, refrigerators, 4 tennis courts, pool, hot tub, massage, sauna, exercise equipment, gym, shops, bar, lounge, nightclub, Internet, baby-sitting, dry cleaning, laundry service, business services, meeting rooms, travel services, car rental, free parking* ⊟ *AE, DC, MC, V.*

$–$$ ╳▥ **Hotel El Portal.** On the Plaza de Armas, this upscale hotel doesn't have the charm of some of the colonial-style hostals, but the facilities and service are top-rate. Ask for a room overlooking the square to view the activities (if you don't mind the noise). Splurge on a dinner in the excellent El Gaucho restaurant, followed by a dip in the rooftop pool. ⊠ *Portal de Flores 116* ☏ *054/215530;* 🖷 *054/234374* ⌷ *32 rooms, 4 suites* ⌷ *Restaurant, pool, bar, shop, laundry service, travel services, free parking* ⊟ *AE, DC, MC, V.*

$ ╳▥ **Hostal Casa Grande.** A family home for many years, this popular colonial structure in a quiet neighborhood has channeled its family feel into a pleasant, cozy hostal. The amicable owners will help you make travel arrangements and find fun things to do around town. ⊠ *Garcia Calderon 202, Vallecito* ☏ *054/214000* 🖷 *054/214001* ⌷ *4 rooms* ⌷ *Dining room, piano, library, travel services, free parking; no room phones, no room TVs* ⊟ *AE, MC, V.*

$ ╳▥ **Hotel Maison Plaza.** Elegant touches like hand-carved sillar walls and vaulted ceilings mark this hotel above the Plaza de Armas. This may be colonial Spanish at its best, with polished antiques and dark religious paintings, but rooms have all the modern touches, including cable TV, phones, and minibars. It's also unexpectedly quiet, considering the goings-on outside on the plaza. The price includes breakfast. ⊠ *Portal de San Agustín 143* ☏ *054/218929* 🖷 *054/218931* ⌷ *44 rooms* ⌷ *Restaurant, café, minibars, room service, bar, shop, library, laundry service, travel services, free parking* ⊟ *AE, MC, V* ⓧ *BP.*

$ ╳▥ **La Posada del Monasterio.** The hotel's colonial look and moderate size make it feel more like a grand mansion than a travelers' resting place— and the top-rated service makes you feel like the owner. Enter through a beautifully groomed courtyard to find a surprisingly modern interior accented with antique furnishings and art. The location is central to all the city's sites, as the hotel sits across from the Convento de la Santa Catalina near the Plaza de Armas. ⊠ *Santa Catalina 300* ☏🖷 *054/215705* ⌷ *52 rooms* ⌷ *Café, free parking; no room phones, no room TVs* ⊟ *AE, DC, MC, V.*

$ ╳▥ **La Posada del Puente.** Rose blossoms spill over the grounds of this
Fodor's Choice delightful hotel, set beside the Río Chili and overlooking Volcán Misti.
★ The pastel-colored rooms have charming art and antique furnishings, and two of the large suites have hot tubs. The cozy restaurant serves excellent pastas and a fine selection of Peruvian and Chilean wines. ⊠ *Bolognesi 101* ☏ *054/253132* 🖷 *054/253576* ⌷ *20 rooms, 4 suites* ⌷ *Restaurant, in-room hot tubs (some), refrigerators, bar, library, laundry service, travel services, free parking* ⊟ *AE, DC, MC, V.*

★ ¢ ╳▥ **La Casa de Melgar.** In a beautiful tiled courtyard surrounded by fragrant blossoms and dotted with trees is this 18th-century home. The magnificent double rooms have towering vaulted ceilings, as well as private baths with hot water. The single suite has an original cookstove from when this was a private house. The café serves light Continental and Peruvian meals. ✉ *Melgar 108* ☎ *054/222459* ⊕ *www.lared.net.pe/ lacasademelgar* ⇌ *6 rooms, 1 suite* ♦ *Café, laundry service, free parking; no room phones, no room TVs* ▭ *No credit cards.*

$ 🖼 **Casa Arequipa.** A young, hip, and helpful staff helps this little inn surpass the service you might encounter in the city's larger hotels. They will escort you to one of eight rooms filled with antique furnishings typical of the region. The hand-carved beds are piled high with alpaca blankets to counter the cool Andean air. A lavish breakfast buffet makes waking up here a special treat. The location, in an upscale neighborhood a short walk from the center of town, is hard to beat. ✉ *Av. Lima 409* ☎ *54/284–219* ⊕ *www.arequipacasa.com* ⇌ *8 rooms* ♦ *Breakfast room, bar* ▭ *AE, DC, MC, V.*

¢   🖼 **Hostal Santa Catalina.** A popular choice for the budget crowd, this
FodorsChoice   hostal offers both shared and private quarters. The clean rooms, friendly
★   owners, dependable hot water, and laundry facilities attract repeat customers year-round, so call far ahead for reservations. It's a pleasant and homey place; kick back in the central courtyard and read your guidebook while your clothes hang to dry in the sunshine. ✉ *Santa Catalina 500* ☎ *054/243705* ⇌ *8 rooms, 3 dorms* ♦ *Dining room, library, laundry facilities, travel services, free parking; no room phones, no room TVs* ▭ *No credit cards.*

¢   🖼 **La Casa de Mi Abuela.** An old stone wall encircles this famous budget traveler haunt. Extensive gardens frame the outside, but the English-speaking owners show their sense of humor in its centerpiece: a rusted Fiat van. Comfortable, wood-paneled rooms have well-worn furniture; some have kitchens, TVs, and private baths with hot water. It's a fun, safe place to clean up, put your feet up with a dog-eared paperback from the library, and check your e-mail. Breakfast and evening snacks are served in the garden, and you can take a dip in the pool anytime. ✉ *Calle Jerusalén 606* ☎ *054/241206* 🖷 *054/242761* ✉ *casademiabuela@LaRededu.pe* ⇌ *32 rooms* ♦ *Cafeteria, kitchenettes (some), minibars, pool, playground, library, Internet, laundry facilities, free parking; no room phones, no TVs in some rooms* ▭ *MC, V.*

¢   🖼 **La Hosteria.** For a quiet hotel with an old Spanish-colonial feel and modern amenities, try this traditional hacienda. The white sillar walls surround a central courtyard that's a riot of bright bougainvillea blossoms, a beautiful spot to have breakfast or write in your journal. Rooms have antique furnishings and such up-to-date touches as bathroom skylights; some have gorgeous stone fireplaces. The upstairs lounge has a casual arrangement of comfortable couches where you can kick back and recount the day. ✉ *Bolivar 405* ☎ *054/289269* 🖷 *054/281779* ⇌ *6 rooms* ♦ *Dining room, library, laundry service, travel services, free parking; no room phones, no room TVs* ▭ *MC, V.*

Nightlife & the Arts

Young and gorgeous Arequipeños head to the **Blues Card Club** (✉ San Francisco 319 ☎ 054/283387), where it's just S/12 cover for strong drinks and nightly live blues. **Déja Vu** (✉ San Francisco 125 ☎ 054/2538757), open 10 PM to midnight, is a popular place to have a late meal of light Continental fare while watching eclectic films and listening to DJ-spun pop fare. At the **Forum Rock Café** (✉ San Francisco 317 ☎ 054/202697) you can take your pick of six bars, enjoy live concerts, and dine among tropical furnishings. The **Instituto Cultural Peruano Norteamericano** (✉ Melgar 109 ☎ 054/243–201) hosts evening concerts of traditional and classical music. Pick up a free pass from the Arequipa tourist office for

Janízaro (✉ Melgar 119 ☎ 054/235684), a popular local bar; otherwise, pay the S/5 cover charge. Near the Plaza San Francisco, **Kibosh** (✉ Zela 205 ☎ 054/203837), is the favorite local disco. **La Troica** (✉ Calle Jerusalén 522-A ☎ 054/225690), open Monday through Saturday from 7 PM, specializes in Afro-Peruvian music, but also has groups from all over South America. A folkoloric show is the highlight on Saturdays. There's a S/6 cover charge, but the Arequipa tourist office gives out free passes. You can catch strolling Peruvian folklórico musicians—amid the hard-rock atmosphere—at **Pizzeria Los Leños** (✉ San José ☎ 054/215423). The raucous crowd at **Pub Tenzaro** (✉ Melgar 119 ☎ 054/202991) comes for the casual surroundings and ice-cold beer. A DJ is in the house on weekend nights at **Sumptuous Disco Pub** (✉ General Morán 118 ☎ 054/243880) in the back of The Cloisters hotel.

Shopping

Arequipa has the widest selection of Peruvian crafts in the south. Alpaca and llama wool is woven into brightly patterned sweaters, ponchos, hats, scarves, and gloves, as well as wall hangings, blankets, and carpets. In particular, look for *chullos* (woolen knitted caps with ear flaps and ties), transported from the Lake Titicaca region. Ceramic *toros* (bulls) are a local favorite to hold flowers or money, and you can even see them sitting in the rafters or on the roofs of homes to bring good luck and protection. *Retablos* (wooden boxes) hold tiny painted ceramic figures depicting Andean scenes. Gold and silver jewelry pieces often have Nazca motifs.

Begin shopping at the Plaza San Francisco, where the cathedral steps are the site of a daily flea market that has delicate handmade jewelry. Cross the street to find the Fundo el Fierro, where crafts vendors tout bargains on clothing, ceramics, jewelry and knickknacks in a cobblestone courtyard; deals can be had until about 8 PM. Behind the cathedral on the narrow Pasaje Catedral are boutiques selling jewelry and knickknacks made of Arequipa agate. Calle Jerusalén has several cluttered antiques shops where you can search for bargains. Across the street from Iglesia de San Francisco is a handicraft center, in a former prison— but a beautiful building nonetheless.

Alpaca 21 (✉ Jerusalén 115 ☎ 054/213425) sells high-quality clothing and accessories. **Anselmo's Baby Alpaca** (✉ Portal del Flores ☎ no phone) carries sweaters, rugs, and wall hangings, and smaller woven items such as gloves, hats, and scarves. **Arte Peru** (✉ Puente Bolognesi 147 ☎ no phone) is a virtual gallery of local antiques, including ceramics, jewelry, and carvings. In central Arequipa, **Claustros de la Compañia** (✉ General Morán 118 ☎ No phone), is an old Jesuit compound where two dozen shops sell alpaca clothing, silver jewelry, and handmade crafts. **Curiosidades** (✉ Zela 207 ☎ 054/232703) is a five-and-dime type of curiosity shop carrying everything from furniture and weapons to postcards and silver. **Galería de Arte Jericó** (✉ Santa Catalina 400 ☎ 054/228893) is a catch-all store that sells furniture, jewelry, paintings, and ceramics. For high-quality, reasonably priced jewelry, stop at **L. Paulet** (✉ General Morán 118 ☎ 054/287–786). Shop **El Zaguán** (✉ Santa Catalina 120A ☎ 054/223950) for a general selection of Peruvian crafts.

Mollendo

㊾ *45 km (28 mi) southwest of Arequipa.*

Mollendo's eastern skyline is filled with undulating fields of rice and sugarcane that spread out from the Río Tambo valley. A balmy seaside resort town, it once drew Arequipa's elite to its beautiful beaches; today, however, many prefer Meíji, 15 km (10 mi) down the coast, once a quiet fishing village but now where Peru's luxury travelers escape to their holiday homes. Matarani, 14 km (8 mi) northwest, is another developing resort area. At the nature reserve **Santuario Nacional Lagunas de Meíji**, you'll spot hundreds of coastal birds and migratory species.

Moquegua

50 *220 km (136 mi) south of Arequipa.*

The desert is at its driest near this dusty, sun-bleached town on the edge of the Río Moquegua. In just the past century, though, more than 10,000 settlers have immigrated here to jump on the copper-mining bandwagon, settling in rows of low, mud-brick homes with sugarcane-stalk roofs along the cobblestone streets. Surprisingly, there are oases of green in this vast landscape, both in the neatly trimmed city gardens and in the surrounding vineyards and avocado fields. Today Moquegua is a pretty town marked by Spanish-style churches and a plaza de armas with precisely cut topiaries of llamas. Although it's mostly a place to breeze through on the way from Lima to Arica, Chile, it's good for a break to browse the **Museo Contisuyo** for local archaeological finds. If you stay, be sure to head up to Cerro Baúl, the northern ridge, from where you'll have an amazing panorama of town and the parched landscape beyond.

Where to Stay

$ **Hotel El Mirador.** It's about 3 km (2 mi) from town, but this mini-resort is perfect for families or for budget travelers who enjoy comfort. Compact rooms have slightly worn contemporary furniture, but they have private bathrooms, hot showers, and TVs—and you'll be spending more time at the pool, playground, or local trails anyway. Larger bungalows sleep two, three, or four. The hotel's location provides easy access to nearby thermal springs and lagoons. ✉ *Alto de la Villa s/n* ☎ *054/289269* 📠 *054/281779* 🛏 *16 rooms, 12 bungalows* 🍴 *Restaurant, cafeteria, room service, pool, playground, laundry service, free parking* 🖃 *MC, V* 🍽 *CP.*

Tacna

51 *150 km (100 mi) south of Moquegua.*

This sprawling, sunny city spreads like a pool of melted butter in the Atacama desert between Moquegua and the Chilean border 36 km (23 mi) south. It's a treacherous stretch of sand, however, strewn with land mines left over from battles between Chile and Peru. It's also a region rife with desperate smugglers trying to transport all sorts of contraband—but not so much drugs as name-brand clothing, cosmetics, food, and pharmaceutical products. Tacna was actually part of Chile from 1880—when Peru lost the War of the Pacific—to 1929, when the population voted themselves back into Peru. Today this modern, if relaxed, town has been renovated with parks, promenades, and pedestrian malls to give it a cosmopolitan edge. It also has some of the country's best schools and hospitals, as well as a strong military base. The central area is lined with trees and gardens, as well as cafés, shops, and attractive restaurants. The shady Plaza de Armas is a pleasant picnic spot, with its enormous, arching monument flanked by bronze statues of Admiral Grau and Colonel Bolognesi, heroes in the War of the Pacific. The 6-m (20-ft) bronze fountain is the work of Gustave Eiffel, the designer of the Paris tower. Stop by on Sunday morning to witness the weekly flag-raising ceremony at 10 AM.

In the Casa de Cultura, the **Museo del Instituto Nacional de Culture** is the place to learn about Tacna's history. Exhibits and paintings illustrate the region's part in the War of the Pacific. Numerous local archaeological treasures are also on display. ✉ *Jr. Bolívar* ☎ *no phone* 💲 *Free* 🕙 *Mon.–Sat. 9–12.*

In one of the city's oldest buildings, the tiny **Casa de Zela** is a museum honoring Francisco Antonio de Zela, the man who began the region's quest for freedom in 1811. Displays include paintings, clothing, furniture, and photos of de Zela and his compatriots, as well as memorabilia from the War of the Pacific. ✉ *Zela 500* ☎ *No phone* 💲 *Free* 🕙 *Daily 10–1 and 3–5.*

Tacna's **Catedral** was designed by French architect and engineer Gustave Eiffel. Construction began in the 1870s but wasn't completed until almost 60 years later. The stained-glass windows are gorgeous in the afternoon light, and you can step inside to view the beautiful, high onyx altar. ✉ *Arequipa y Blondel* ☎ *no phone* 💲 *Free* 🕙 *Mon.–Sat. 8–12 and 2–5.*

Antique trains and other railway memorabilia are on display at the **Museo Ferroviario** (Train Museum), right in the Tacna train station. Exhibits range from the small—an international collection of railway-theme postage stamps—to the enormous—early 20th-century engines from British days. Head about ½ km (¼ mi) southwest along the tracks to find the Parque de la Locomotora, where you can view the British locomotive built in 1859 and used to pull troop trains in the War of the Pacific. You can even catch a train to Arica, Chile, from here. ✉ *2 de Mayo* ☎ *no phone* 💲 *S/1* 🕙 *Weekdays 9–3.*

Where to Stay

$$ 🏨 **Gran Hotel Tacna.** Enormous, leafy trees shade this sprawling hotel set amid blossoming gardens in the midst of town. Rooms show off luxurious fabrics, plush carpeting, and hand-crafted décor, and some have balconies with views over the grounds. When not touring the surrounding desert or making a jaunt into Chile, guests hang out by the pool, stroll the paths, or play tennis. ✉ *Avenida Bolognesi 300, Tacna* ☎ *054/724193* 🖷 *054/722015* 🛏 *71 rooms, 4 suites* ⚉ *Restaurant, cafeteria, room service, tennis court, pool, bar, dance club, laundry service, travel services, free parking* ▭ *AE, DC, MC, V* ⓧ *CP.*

$ 🏨 **Hotel Camino Real.** On the east side of Tacna, this tall, box-like hotel has all the comforts and cleanliness of larger places, but in a cozier setting. Plain rooms have narrow windows, TVs, minibars, and private bathrooms with hot water. As it's out of the central traffic, it's a bit quieter than other accommodations. ✉ *San Martín 855, Tacna* ☎ *054/721891* 🖷 *054/726433* 🛏 *35* ⚉ *Restaurant, room service, minibars, nightclub, laundry service, free parking* ▭ *AE, DC, MC, V.*

¢ 🏨 **Pensión Alojamiento Genova.** A haunt of world-travelers on a shoestring budget, this small, homestyle hotel has no-frills rooms and shared baths. However, it's rich in tourist resources, as the owners are happy to provide information on local sights, culture, and history. There's even a casual restaurant where you can grab a cheap, filling, Peruvian lunch. ✉ *Deustua 559, Tacna* ☎ *054/715441* 🛏 *12 rooms* ⚉ *Restaurant, laundry facilities, free parking* ▭ *No credit cards.*

The South A to Z

To research prices, get advice from other travelers, and book travel arrangements, visit www.fodors.com.

AIR TRAVEL

Aero Continente operates daily flights from Lima to Arequipa and Tacna. LanPeru has several daily flights between Lima and Arequipa. TANS Perú has one daily flight from Lima to Arequipa.

Nazca Lines tours on Aero Cóndor, which depart from the small Nazca airport, cost S/191 for a 40-minute flight plus lunch, a tour of Nazca's archaeological museum, and a trip to the *mirador.* Note that these flights are often overbooked, year-round. Less expensive flights on Aero Ica and new upstarts Aero Montecarlo, Aero Palpa, Aeroparacas, Alas Peruanas, TAE, Travel Air, and Taxi Aereo have similar services. As these latter lines are small operations with varying office hours, check at the airport for current flight schedules. Most sightseeing flights depart from Nazca, although Aero Paracas also originates in Lima and Pisco.

Daily flights between Tacna and Arequipa take about 20 minutes and run about S/140. Note that there are no airport buses from Tacna, so you'll need to take a taxi for S/14 or walk the 5 km (3 mi) to town. ✈ Carriers **Aero Condor** ✉ Juan de Arona 781, San Isidro, Lima ☎ 01/442–5215, 034/256230 in Ica, 034/522424 in Nazca ⊕ www.aerocondor.com.pe. **Aero Continente** ✉ Av. Pardo 651, Miraflores, Lima ☎ 01/242–4260 ⊕ www.aerocontinente.com.pe ✉ Portal San Agustín 113, Arequipa ☎ 054/204020 ✉ Calle Apurímac 265, Tacna ☎ 054/747300. **Aero Ica** ✉ Hotel Maison Suisse, Nazca ✉ Tudela and Varela 150, Lima ☎ 01/440–1030. **Aero Paracas** ✉ Santa Fe 270, Higuereta ☎ 01/271–6941 ✉ Hotel Paracas, Pisco ✉ Pan-American Hwy., Km 447 ☎ 034/522–688. **LanPeru** ✉ Av. José Pardo 269, Miraflores, Lima, ☎ 01/213–8200 ⊕ www.lanperu.com ✉ Portal San Agustín 109, Arequipa ☎ 054/201–100. **TANS Perú** ✉ Av. Arequipa 5200, Miraflores, Lima ☎ 01/426–8480 ⊕ www.tansperu.com.pe.

AIRPORTS
You can book a flight with any of the small companies at the Aeropuerto Nazca. Rodríguez Ballón Airport is 7 km (4½ mi) from Arequipa. Make sure you arrive early to check in for your flight, as many are full and there's a chance you'll get bumped if you're late. ✈ Airport Information **Aeropuerto Nazca** ☎ 034/523854. **Rodríguez Ballón Airport** ☎ 054/443–464.

TRANSFERS Buses along Puente Grau and Ejército will drop you less than 1 km (½ mi) from the airport; look for vehicles marked "Río Seco," "Cono–Norte," or "Zamacola." It's easiest to take a hotel shuttle or taxi (S/10) to the airport in most towns.

BOAT & FERRY TRAVEL
The deep-water Puerto General San Martín in Pisco is the major port of this region. Radisson Seven Seas Cruises runs trips along this coast, with shore excursions to Paracas Reserve and the Islas Ballestas, the Nazca Lines, Ica, Huacachina, and Tambo Colorado. Luxury travel services, including Crillón Tours, make hydrofoil trips across Lake Titicaca, including runs between the Peruvian and Bolivian borders. You take a bus from Puno to Copacabana, then catch a hydrofoil to Isla del Sol and Huatajata, Bolivia. Catamaran services, some by Transturin, also run from the dock at Chúa, Bolivia. ⛴ **Crillón Tours** ✉ 1450 Bayshore Dr., Suite 815, Miami FL 33131 ☎ 305/358–5353. **Radisson Seven Seas Cruises** ✉ Pisco ⊕ www.rssc.com. **Transturin** ✉ Libertad 176, Puno ☎ 054/352771 ✉ Portal de Panes 109, Cusco ☎ 054/222332.

BORDER CROSSINGS
The border with Chile, about 40 km (25 mi) from Tacna, is open from 9 AM to 10 PM. Buses south from Tacna run about S/10 and depart hourly; drivers will help with border formalities. It's more comfortable, however, to take a colectivo for about S/15, including the terminal tax. The road journey takes about an hour. You can also make one of four border crossings into Bolivia from Puno and Lake Titicaca. From Puno, take a bus three hours to Yunguyo, catch a colectivo for S/1 to the border,

and continue to Copacabana and La Paz. The immigration offices are open 8–12 and 2–6. You can take a colectivo or walk the ½ km (¼ mi) between the Peruvian immigration office, where you'll get an exit stamp, and Bolivian immigration, where you'll get a 30-day tourist visa.

Colectivos and buses also make the S/7, 3-hr run from Puno to Desaguadero, another crossing point into Bolivia that's open 8–12 and 2–7:30. Many tour buses stop at the famous Tiahuanico ruins along this route. A less-traveled crossing to Bolivia is via Huncané and Moho to Puerto Acosta, although buses usually only attempt this rugged road on weekends and holidays. If you make this trip, get your exit stamp in Puno. You can also enter Bolivia by hydrofoil across Lake Titicaca.

BUS TRAVEL

There is reliable, comfortable bus service throughout southern Peru, especially down the paved Pan-American Highway. From Lima to Íca it's 303 km (188 mi), and from Lima to Nazca it's 443 km (275 mi). The longest stretch, from Nazca to Arequipa, is a 566-km (351-mi) journey that takes 8–12 hours. Delays due to mud slides or sand drifts are common.

In Arequipa many bus offices are near the 600 block of San Juan de Dios. Most buses leave from modern Terminal Terrestre, 3 km (2 mi) south of the city. There is a 50¢ departure tax. Better-class buses depart from the Terrapuerto, next to the Terminal Terrestre. From Arequipa, buses run to Lima (14–16 hours, S/28 regular, S/88 luxury) on CIVA, Cruz del Sur, Flores Hermanos, Ormeño, and Sudamericano. Most buses leave in the afternoon for this long trip. Buses to Juliaca and Cusco (14 hours, S/35) run on rugged roads often washed out in bad weather, plus the night journey is bitterly cold, so dress and pack for the worst. Ormeño's international buses run to La Paz, Bolivia (12 hours, S/70), via Puno; Santiago, Chile (60 hours, S/280), via Tacna; and Buenos Aires, Argentina (110 hours, S/452).

Ormeños has the most departures from Ica, and the expense is often worth the comfort. Buses usually depart from the park at the western end of Salaverry, including to Lima (5 hours, S/16), Pisco (1 hour, S/4), Nazca (3 hours, S/10), and Arequipa (15 hours, S/42). Taxi *colectivos* to Lima (3 ½ hours, S/42) and Nazca (2 hours, S/7) leave from the southwest corner of Municipalidad and Lambayeque when full.

Buses from Nazca run all over the south, including to Lima (7 hours, S/28), Ica (3 hours, S/7), Pisco (4 hours, S/12), Camaná (7 hours, S/21), Moquegua (4 hours, S/14), Tacna (12 hours, S/42), and Arequipa (8–12 hours, S/28). Cruz del Sur and Cira have luxury service; Ormeño is also reliable. Wari Tours, on the Pan-American Highway at the junction for Puquío, makes overnight trips to Cusco (30–40 hours, S/63) that go through the Reserva Nacional Pampas Galeras vicuña reserve.

You can reach Cañete by bus from Lima in 2½ hours for S/10, and continue on to Pisco in about 1½ hours for S/6. Buses also run between Cañete and Lunahuaná. During festivals, buses run 24 hours between the partying crowds of Chincha and El Carmen; cover charges to dance events run about S/17.

From Pisco, try Paracas Express or Empresa José de San Martín for long-distance trips to Lima. Ormeños and San Martín run regular buses to Lima (4 hours, S/14), Nazca (4 hours, S/12), Ica (2 hours, S/4), and Arequipa (14 hours, S/42). Buses to Ayacucho (10 hours, S/32) leave from San Clemente, 10 km (6 mi) north of town and 20 minutes by colectivo on the Pan-American Highway. Note that Pisco is about 5 km (3 mi) off the Pan-American Highway and many bus services will drop you only at the turnoff—make sure you have booked a bus directly into town.

Unless you have your own vehicle, a taxi or colectivo is the best option from Pisco to Paracas village. Comité 9M vehicles costing S/1.75 leave from the market, while Comité 2M vehicles costing S/.70 leave for San Andrés every few minutes. Taxis to Paracas are S/10. Minibuses also go to Paracas, where you can catch a slow motorboat to the reserve and islands.

Buses from Puno take 9 hours to reach Cusco and cost S/35. It's 12 hours and S/35 to Arequipa, and 42 hours and S/70 to Lima. Cruz del Sur is the most popular company for the latter routes, while First Class makes the run to Cusco for S/87, including an English-speaking guide. It takes just an hour and S/9 to reach Juliaca on Transportes Los Angeles. Empresa San Martín buses head 12 hours south for Tacna, costing S/52.

Tacna's Terminal Terrestre is on Unanue, at the northeast end of town. There is a S/1.50 departure tax. Note that northbound buses are often stopped and searched by authorities, so pack loosely, keep your passport ready, and don't carry packages for strangers. Buses south to Arica, Chile, cost S/7 and leave hourly, and drivers help with border formalities.

🚌 Bus Lines **Cruz del Sur** ✉ Jr. Quilca 531, Lima ☎ 01/427–1311; ✉ Av. Los Incas, Nazca ☎ 034/522484 ✉ Av. El Sol 568, Puno ☎ 034/352451. **Empresa José de San Martín** ✉ 2 de Mayo y San Martín, Pisco ☎ 034/543167 ✉ Av. Titicaca 210, Puno ☎ 034/352511. **First Class** ✉ Av. Melgar 110, Puno ☎ 034/364036. **Flores Hermanos** ✉ Terminal Terrestre, Unanue, Tacna ☎ 054/726691. **Ormeños** ✉ Lambayeque 180, Ica ☎ 056/215600; ✉ Av. Los Incas, Nazca ☎ 034/561432; ✉ Av. San Francisco, Pisco ☎ 034/532764; ✉ Arias Aragues 700, Tacna ☎ 054/724401. **Paracas Express** ✉ Pan-American Hwy., Km 447, Pisco ☎ 034/533623. **San Martín** ✉ San Martín 199, Pisco ☎ 034/522743. **Transportes Los Angeles** ✉ Av. Tacna y Av. Libertad, Puno ☎ 034/357294. **Wari Tours** ✉ Pan-American Hwy., Nazca ☎ 034/534967.

CAR RENTALS

The major international car rental agencies, including Avis, Budget, and Hertz, all have branches in south Peru. Local agencies such as Exodo also provide high-quality service. Office hours are usually 8–1 and 3–6 weekdays, and 9–1 Saturdays, except at the Arequipa airport, where agencies may be open 24 hours. You can pick up your car at one end of the region and drop it off at the other, but there may be a hefty fee.

🚌 Agencies **Avis G&B** ✉ Palacio Viejo 214, Arequipa ☎ 054/443576 🌐 www.avis.com ✉ Rodriguez Ballón Airport, Arequipa ☎ 054/443576. **Exodo** ✉ Manuél Belgrado F-1, Urb. Alvarez Thomas, Arequipa ☎ 054/423756.

CAR TRAVEL

The Pan-American Highway runs down the length of southern Peru, some of it along the coast, some through desert, and some over plateaus and mountains. It's all paved and in good condition, but you should have fully equipped first-aid and repair kits packed. Besides breakdowns, hazards along this road include potholes, rock slides, sandstorms, and heat. Fortunately, you'll find many service stations along this route, most of which have clean bathrooms, convenience stores, and snack counters. Most are also full-service, meaning that your gas is pumped, your windshield cleaned, and your oil checked for free. Off the highway, however, conditions are less predictable. Roads may be in particularly poor condition in the eastern highlands and around the Paracas Reserve. Four-wheel-drive vehicles are recommended for all driving except within major cities. The Touring and Automobile Club of Peru, in Arequipa and Ica, provides maps and details on routes.

🚹 **Touring y Automóvile Club del Perú** ✉ Goyeneche 313, Arequipa ☎ 054/215-640 ✉ Manzanilla 523, Ica ☎ 056/235061.

EMERGENCIES

Peru's main cities have well-equipped emergency facilities, and local residents are nearly always willing to help. Small-town doctors usually have access to modern resources, but for complicated procedures you'll want to head for Lima (or home). If you have a medical emergency, go to the nearest hospital, and keep the name of your doctor and any pertinent records or information on chronic conditions handy. Fire brigades and police are always quick to help tourists as well.

🚹 **Emergency Services** Emergency Central: ☎105. Fire: ☎116. Medical Alert: ☎22540. Police: ☎ 105. Red Cross: ☎ 26587.🚹 **Police** ✉ Calle Jerusalén 315-A, Arequipa ☎ 054/239888. ✉ Av. Los Incas, Nazca ☎ no phone.

🚹 **Tourist Protection Oficina de Protección al Turista (24 hrs)** ✉ Jerusalén 317, Arequipa ☎ 054/212054 or toll-free 0800/45279.

🚹 **Hospitals Clinical Arequipa SA** ✉ Puente Grau y Av. Bolognesi, Arequipa ☎ 054/253424. **General Base Goyeneche** ✉ Av. Goyeneche s/n, Arequipa ☎ 054/211313. **Regional Honorio Delgado** ✉ Av. A. Carrión s/n, Arequipa ☎ 054/238465.

HEALTH

The main health advice for the rest of Peru also applies to this region: Don't drink the water (or use ice), and don't eat raw or undercooked food. Take a good look at street-vendor food before you taste it. Note that water doesn't boil sufficiently at high altitudes to rid the bacteria, so you'll have to use purification tablets. Local brands are Micropur, which dissolves the most easily, and Certimil.

Get a gamma globulin shot before traveling to Peru, as hepatitis is common throughout the country. Make sure your dishes and utensils are clean before you eat, and avoid unpasteurized products, as tuberculosis has made a comeback. Typhoid is another frequent local sickness, although travelers rarely get it if they're careful. Keep away from stray dogs, as rabies is a concern; hence, most hospitals will have anti-rabies injections.

Traveling to mountain towns and around Lake Titicaca could result in *soroche* (altitude sickness). Temporary cures include *mate de coca* (coca tea) or a small block of *chancaca* (crystallized pure cane sugar). It usually takes a day or two to shake the headaches and bloating.

MAIL & SHIPPING

Arequipa has numerous places to log on and check e-mail, notably Centro Internet UNSA, Chips Internet, Net Central, and Varnie Benavides. All are open 9–8 or later and cost about S/7 an hour. The Bill Gates Computer School in Pisco is open daily 7 AM to 11 PM (ring the bell on Sundays); surf the Web for S/10 an hour. Arequipa's most reliable Internet center is on Alvarez Thomas, near Palacio Viejo. Log on in Ica at Cetelica, between San Martín and Bolívar. Nazca's Hotel Alegria has a post office and Internet services, and you can send and receive faxes and make international calls at the Telefónica office. You can check e-mail and use the computers at Internet in Tacna, which is open 9–9 daily except Sunday.

Send regular mail from the main post office in Arequipa, which is open Monday through Saturday 8–8 and Sunday 8–2. You can send courier packages with DHL in Arequipa, Ica, and Nazca.

🚹 **Post Offices Arequipa** ✉ Calle Moral 118 ☎ 054/215247. **Ica** ✉ Lima y Moquegua ☎ 056/221958. **Nazca** ✉ Jr. F. de Castillo 300 ☎ 034/523947.

🔗 Internet Cafés **Centro Internet UNSA** ✉ San Augustín 115, Arequipa ☎ 054/218781. **Chips Internet** ✉ San Francisco 202A, Arequipa ☎ 054/226435. **Net Central** ✉ Alvarez Thomas 219, Arequipa ☎ 054/216453. **Varnie Benavides** ✉ Santa Catalina 113-A, Arequipa ☎ 054/234156.

Cetelica ✉ Huánico, Ica ☎ 056/221534. **Hotel Alegría** ✉ Lima 166, Nazca ☎ 034/522375. **Bill Gates Computer School** ✉ San Francisco 290, Pisco ☎ 034/526544. **Internet** ✉ San Martín 611, Tacna ☎ 054/723546.
🔗 Shipping Services **DHL** ✉ Av. Santa Catalina 115, Arequipa ☎ 054/234288 ✉ Av. San Martín 398, Ica ☎ 056/234549 ✉ Jr. Fermín del Castillo 379, Nazca ☎ 054/522016.
🔗 Telephone Offices **Arequipa** ✉ Alvarez Thomas 201 ☎ 054/232748. **Ica** ✉ Av. San Martín y Huánuco ☎ 056/231630. **Nazca** ✉ Lima 359 ☎ 034/522058.

MONEY MATTERS
Many international banks are found in Arequipa, Ica, Nazca, Pisco, and Tacna. Arequipa Inversiones, Banco de Crédito, Banco Continental, Banco Santander Hispano, and Interbank are realiable local places to exchange currencies, get credit-card cash advances, and cash traveler's checks; many have ATMs. Small money-changing shops can usually be found around the banks and ATMs of tourist areas. In Ica there are several moneychangers along Cajamarca.
🔗 Banks **Arequipa Inversiones** ✉ Jerusalén 109-C, Arequipa ☎ 054/238033. **Banco de Crédito** ✉ San Juan de Dios 125, Arequipa ☎ 054/222112 ✉ Av. Grau 105, Ica ☎ 056/235959 ✉ Lima y Grau, Nazca ✉ Plaza de Armas, Pisco. **Banco Continental** ✉ San Francisco 108, Arequipa. **Banco Santander Hispano** ✉ Jerusalén, Arequipa. **Interbank** ✉ Mercaderes 217, Arequipa.
🔗 Currency Exchange **Casa de Cambio** ✉ San Juan de Dios 109, Arequipa ☎ 054/282528. **Willy Cambios** ✉ San Juan de Dios 120, 3-B, Arequipa.

SAFETY
As always when traveling, be wary of your valuables. Keep your documents, credit cards, and cash, except for small change, hidden in a traveler's pouch beneath your clothing. Have copies of all traveler's checks and identification in case your lose them or they are stolen.

While on the road or rails, make sure you have a first-aid kit and any emergency supplies you might need. Take extra blankets and food when traveling through the mountains at night by car or bus, as it gets bitterly cold and vehicles often break down.

Theft can be a problem in crowded tourist areas, such as beaches, or on economy-class transport. Police are kind and extremely helpful to most foreign travelers, but procedures can be slow, so take care with your valuables. If you lose something important, like your passport, report it to the police and to your country's nearest embassy.

If you're traveling by public transport in economy class, keep a close watch on your possessions, as pickpocketing is common both on board and at the station. Purchase your tickets in advance, when you don't have to stand in line with your bags. Also note that there have been holdups on the crowded night train cars from Arequipa to Juliaca—you might want to buy a Pullman ticket (instead of just a first-class ticket) for the reclining seats, heaters, and locked doors.

TIME
Peruvian time is 1 hr behind Chilean time, and 2 hrs behind during daylight savings time. Bolivia is also an hour ahead of Peruvian time.

TOUR & TRAVEL AGENCIES

Travel agencies in Lima offer three- to seven-day tours of Arequipa, Paracas, Ica, Nazca, and Lake Titicaca. Try Explorandes, Hirca Travel, Lima Tours, Peru Chasquitur, or Receptour.

From Arequipa, tours to Colca and Cotahuasi canyons can be arranged with local operators. Try Condor Travel Arequipa, G.A. Travel Expert, Santa Catalina Tours, or Transcontinental Tours. The Arequipa office of Lima Tours offers a two-day, one-night tour of Colca Canyon. Holley's Unusual Tours runs four-wheel-drive expeditions to area sites and ruins.

In Ica, Costa Linda and Pelican Travel Service offer tours of the city and can arrange trips to Paracas National Park and the Nazca Lines. Nazca-based Alegría Tours also has tours of pre-Columbian ruins in the area. Guided tours of Paracas National Park and the Ballestas Islands are offered by Ballestas Travel Service.

Trips to from Pisco to Paracas and Islas Ballestas can be arranged by Blue Sea Tours, Paracas Islas Tours, and The Zarcillo Connection. Ballestas Travel Service represents several travel agencies who sell park packages. Larger hotels also offer travel services to the area for about S/70; other tours leave daily from the Plaza de Armas at 7 AM and cost S/28 or more, depending on length of tour and quality of vehicles and guides. Make sure your boat has life jackets available.

Most hotels can arrange tours of the Nazca Lines, but several travel companies also specialize in local explorations. The inexpensive Alegría Tours includes stops at several archaeological sites, maps, guides, and options for hiking the area. Nasca Trails arranges flights over the Nazca Lines, trips to the Pampas Galeras vicuña reserve, and tours of the Cementerio Chauchills in Spanish, Italian, French, German, and English. Nanasca Tours can arrange a taxi with a driver-guide to local sites; however, these tours are mostly in Spanish.

You can purchase general transport tickets at the local bus and train stations, but most travel agencies also sell bus and train tickets (charging a 25% commission). Although it costs more, it's often easier to let an experienced agent do the legwork, as you'll avoid wasting time standing in lines, and they often include transport from your hotel to the departure point.

Guides often hassle tired new arrivals at airports, bus stations, and hotels. Don't be pressured to book a hotel or tour right away. Ask for recommendations from other travelers, and make sure the guide or agency is licensed and experienced. Finally, professional guides must be approved by the Ministry of Tourism, so ask for identification before you hire. ⚑Arequipa Area **Condor Travel Arequipa** ⊠ Av. Puente Bolognesi 120, Arequipa ☎054/218362. **G.A. Travel Expert** ⊠ Santa Catalina 312, Arequipa ☎ 054/247722. **Lima Tours** ⊠ Belén 1040, Lima ☎ 01/424-5110 ⊠ Santa Catalina 120, Arequipa ☎ 054/242271. **Santa Catalina Tours** ⊠ Jerusalén 400-D, Arequipa ☎☎ 054/216991. **Transcontinental Tours** ⊠ Puente Bolognesi 132, Arequipa ☎ 054/213843. ⚑ Nazca Lines **Alegría Tours** ⊠ Jr. Lima 168, Nazca ☎ 034/522985. **Nasca Trails** ⊠ Ignacio Morsequi, Nazca ☎ 034/522858. **Nanasca Tours** ⊠ Lima 160, Nazca ☎ 034/522917. ⚑ Paracas & Islas Ballestas **Blue Sea Tours** ⊠ Chosica 320, San Andrés ☎ 034/533469. **Ballestas Travel Service** ⊠ San Francisco 249, Pisco ☎ 034/533095. **Costa Linda** ⊠ Prolongación Ayabaca 509, Ica ☎ 056/234251. **Paracas Islas Tours** ⊠ Comercio 128, Pisco ☎ 034/665872. **Pelican Travel Service** ⊠ Independencia 156, Galerías Siesta, Ica ☎☎ 056/225211. **Zarcillo Connection** ⊠ San Francisco 111, Pisco ☎ 034/262795.⚑ General Tours **Explorandes** ⊠ San Fernando 320, Lima ☎ 01/442-1738 or 01/445-0532. **Hirca Travel** ⊠ Bellavista 518, Miraflores Lima ☎ 01/242-0275. **Holley's**

Unusual Excursions ✉ Casilla 77, Arequipa ☎ 054/224452 **Lima Tours** ✉ Belén 1040, Lima ☎ 01/424-5110 ✉ Santa Catalina 120, Arequipa ☎ 054/242271. **Peru Chasquitur** ✉ Mariano de los Santos 183, San Isidro, Lima ☎ 01/441-1279. **Receptour** ✉ Av. Alvarez Calderón 155, Suite 304, San Isidro, Lima ☎ 01/221-3341.

TRAIN TRAVEL
Three times a week, Peru Rail runs a train between Arequipa and Puno, via Juliaca. Be sure to request the safer, more comfortable—and heated—Pullman "Inka Service," which costs about S/100 each way. The trip takes about 11 hours.

🚉 Train Information **Peru Rail** ✉ Av. Tacna and Arica 201, Arequipa ☎ 054/215-350.

VISITOR INFORMATION
Information on all areas of Peru can be obtained from PromPerú. In Arequipa, the Oficina de Información Turística is helpful. The Tourist Office on La Merced is open weekdays 8:30–12:30 and 2:30–3:30; there's also an airport office. The Oficina de Información Turística in Ica, near the intersection of Avenidas Grau and Jirón Ayacucho and a block east of the Plaza de Armas, is open weekdays 8–3:30. The Tourist Office on Cajamarca is open weekdays 7:30–3. For information on Colca Canyon or Paracas National Park, contact the Lima-based Inrena.

🏛 **Inrena** ✉ Petirrojos 355, Urbanización El Palomar, San Isidro, Lima ☎ 01/441-0425. **Oficina de Información Turística** ✉ Portal de la Municipalidad 112, Plaza de Armas, Arequipa ☎ 054/211021. **Tourist Office** ✉ La Merced 117, Arequipa. **Inrena** ✉ Petirrojos 355, Ica ☎ 01/441-0425. **Tourist Office** ✉ Cajamarca 179, Ica. **PromPerú** ☎ 01/224-3125 or 01/224-3118 📠 01/224-3323 🌐 www.peru.org.pe.

PUNO & LAKE TITICACA

Puno sits rather bleakly on the high Collao plateau along Lake Titicaca's windy shores, but with its many festivals and wealth of handicrafts, dances, songs, and parades, it has rightly earned the title of Peru's folkloric capital. Faithfully preserving the choreography of more than 140 typical dances, Puno's most memorable celebration is the *Festival of the Virgen de la Candelaria* (candle), held during the first two weeks of February. A cast of hundreds of elaborately costumed Andean singers, dancers, and bands from neighborhing communities parade through the streets for days, carrying the rosy-white complexioned statue of the Virgen. During the rest of the year, the statue rests on the altar of the San Juan Bautista Church. Some of the dances are Indian-inspired; others mock the Spanish conquistadors, while the most memorable is *La Diablada*, the legend of trapped miners saved from death and the clutches of the devil by the *Virgin of the Candelaria*. The festival was first celebrated in 1583. When Puno isn't having a celebration, it reverts to its true character, that of a small Andean agriculture town on the shore of the highest navigable lake in the world.

According to legend, under orders from their father, the Sun God, the first Inca, Manco Cápac and his sister Mama Ocllo emerged from the deep blue waters of Lake Titicaca and founded the Inca empire. There is no documentation describing when this reportedly happened, but as one watches the mysterious play of light on the water and the shadows on the mountains, the myth seems almost believable. This is the altiplano—the high plains of Peru, where the earth has been raised so close to the sky that the area takes on a luminous quality.

The legends that rise out of Lake Titicaca are no more mysterious than discoveries made in its depths. In the millennium year 2000 an international diving expedition, called Atahuallpa 2000 and backed by the

Akakor Geographical Exploring Group, bumped into what is believed to be a 1,000 year-old pre-Inca temple. The stone structure is 201 m (660 ft) long and 49 m (160 ft) wide, with a wall 793 m (2,699-ft) long. The discovery was made between the town of Copacabana on the Bolivian side and the Sun and Moon islands. A broad stone causeway leading up from the depths of the lake has also been found, lending credence to the theory that a causeway once connected Titicaca with the Pacific Ocean before a cataclysmic event dramatically raised the Andes.

Puno

52–57 *975 km (609 mi) southeast of Lima.*

Puno, the capital of the province of the same name, retains traits of the Aymará, Quechua, and Spanish cultures that settled on the northwestern shores of the lake. Their influence is evident in the art, music, dance, and dress of today's inhabitants, who call themselves "Children of the Sacred Lake." Much of the city's character comes from the continuation of ancient traditions. High-stepping young men in military uniforms present arms on the Plaza de Armas every Sunday at 11 AM in a stirring patriotic ceremony, and at least once a month there's a parade or a festival celebrating some recent or historic event.

Puno is a small town with a small-town friendliness, and chances are, whatever you need can be found along the street called Jirón Lima, between Pino Park (sometimes called Parque San Juan after the San Juan Bautista Church nearby) and the Plaza de Armas. Restaurants, shops, Internet services, banks, a laundry, and a drug store line the four-block pedestrian-only street. Coming from the airport, you enter onto Jirón Lima through a large stone arch, Arco Deustua, erected as a memorial

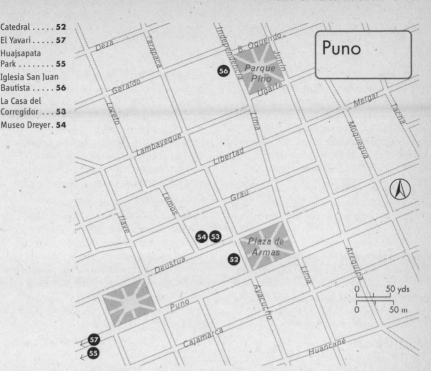

to the men who fought in the decisive battles of Junin and Ayacucho in the war of independence from Spain.

At 12,550 ft above sea level Puno will be a challenge to your system, so eat lightly, go easy on alcoholic drinks, forgo your morning jog, and take it easy for a day or two once you arrive.

The focal point on the Plaza de Armas, the Baroque-style, 18th-century stone **Catedral** has carvings at the entrance of flowers and fruits, as well as mermaids playing an Andean guitar called the *charango*. It is rather plain on the inside, with its main decoration a gilt altar and paintings from the Cusco School. In back of the cathedral, on the corner of Deustua and Conde de Lemos, is the house where the viceroy Count Lemos stayed when he arrived for a visit in 1668. No visitors are allowed in the house, but you can gaze at its intricately carved wooden balcony from the street. ✉ *Plaza de Armas*, ⊘ *Daily 8–12 and 3–5* ✎ *Free.*

In Spain, a *corregidor* was a government official who acted as judge and juror and collected taxes, a job apparently held by a Catholic priest, Silvestre de Valdés, who was also in charge of the construction of Puno's Cathedral in 1668 and lived in **La Casa del Corregidor** across the street. The house had a long history of changing owners until 1995, when its present owner, Sra. Ana Maria Piño Jordán, bought it at public auction. With the help of volunteers she converted it into a cultural center, and it is now a pleasant place to drop in for sandwiches, drinks, or light snacks served in its early 1900's-style café and bar. There's also an Internet center that charges a mere 85 (US) cents an hour. Local art displays and music events take place in the exhibition hall, and the research library has documents in Spanish on Puno, the altiplano, and the Andes. ✉ *Deustua 576*, ☎ *51/351–921*, ⊘ *Tues.–Sat. 10–10, also Sun. May–Oct.*

CloseUp
LLAMAS, VICUÑAS & ALPACAS

LLAMAS, VICUÑAS, AND ALPACAS roam the highlands of Peru, but unfortunately not in the great herds of pre-Inca times. However, there are always a few around, especially the domesticated llama and alpaca. The sly vicuña refuses domestication. Here's a primer on how to tell them apart.

The Alpaca is the cute and cuddly one, especially while still a baby. It grows a luxurious, long wool coat that comes in as many as 20 colors and its wool is used in knitting sweaters and weaving rugs and wall hangings. Its finest wool is from the first shearing and is called "baby alpaca." When full-grown it is close to 1.5 m (4.9 ft) tall and weighs about 7 kg (15 lb). Its size and the shortness of its neck distinguishes it from the llama.

The Llama is the pack animal with a course coat in as many as 50 colors, though one that's unsuitable for weavings or fine wearing apparel. It can reach almost 2 m (6 ft) from its hoofs to the top of its elongated neck and long, curved ears. It can carry between 40–60 kg (88–132 lb), depending on the length of the trip. It can also have some nasty habits, like spitting in your eye or kicking you if you get too close to its hind legs.

The Vicuña has a more delicate appearance. It will hold still (with help) for shearing, and its wool is the most desirable. It is protected by the Peruvian government, as it was almost killed off by unrestricted hunting. It is the smallest of the Andean camelids, at 1.3 m (4 ft) and weighs about 40 kg (88 lb) at maturity. It is found mostly at altitudes over 3,600 m (12,000 ft).

— By Joan Gonzalez

---

54 Puno's principal museum, **Museo Dreyer,** is a block from the Plaza de Armas, with exhibits of pre-Hispanic and colonial art, weavings, gold, silver, and copper works, a coin collection, delicate Aymará pottery, pre-Inca stone sculptures, and historical documents in Spanish on the founding of Puno. ⊠ *Conde Lemos 289,* ☉ *Mon.–Fri. 7:30–3:30* ☎ *S/3.60.*

55 The high point of the small **Huajsapata Park** (behind the Cathedral) is a monument honoring the first Inca, Manco Cápac. It also gives you an excellent overview of the city, if you're up to the walk in Puno's high altitude. ⊠ *Three blocks southwest of the Plaza de Armas.*

56 The 18th-century **Iglesia San Juan Bautista** has been entrusted with the care of the *Virgin of the Candlemas,* the focus of Puno's most important yearly celebration in February, the Festival de la Virgen de la Candelaria. The statue rests on the main altar. Also here are the Virgen's more than 100 elaborate robes and cloaks. ⊠ *Jr. Lima and Parque Pino.*

57 The restored Victorian iron ship **El Yavari** was built in Birmingham, England, in 1862. It was then dismantled, and its 1,383 pieces were loaded onto a freighter and shipped to the Port of Arica on the Pacific coast. The pieces were then carried by mules and porters across the Andes mountains to Puno. The journey took six years and it was Christmas Day, 1870, before it was reassembled and launched on Lake Titicaca. It is now a museum, docked at the end of a pier. After remaining idle for 40 years, the vessel took a trial run in 1999 after volunteers rebuilt its engine. If the ship is brought up to code, it might one day cruise the lake again. ⊠ *Pier behind the Posada del Inca Hotel, at the end of Av. El Puerto* ☎ *051/369–329,* ☎ *Donation.* ☉ *Daily 8–5* ⊕ *www.yavari.org.*

Where to Stay & Eat

Puno has many small, informal restaurants, especially along Jirón Lima. On the menu are typical Peruvian dishes: *lechón al horno o cancacho* (highly spiced baked suckling pig); *pesque o queso de quinua* (resembling ground up barley), prepared with cheese and served with fish fillet in tomato sauce; *chairo* (lamb and tripe broth cooked with vegetables, and frozen dried potato known as *chuño*). Particularly good are *trucha* (trout) and *pejerrey* (mackerel) from the lake. Also, pizza is quite popular in Puno. Always ask if the restaurant has the Menu Turistica, also known as El Menu or the set menu, which is cheaper than á là carte, but not always advertised.

Not all Puno hotels are adequately heated, and the town gets cold at night, so when you register, ask about heating. You're in luck if there's an electric space heater in your room. Prices can jump as much as 30% during the most popular festivals in February and November—reserve at least a month ahead if you're visiting then. You can bargain for a hotel room, but check it out before checking in, and ask if there's 24-hour hot water. Most hotels in the small towns outside Puno are run-down and not recommended.

¢–$$ FodorsChoice ★ ╳ **La Casona.** Walking into this restaurant along Puno's main street is like entering a museum. It's filled with antiques, with an especially interesting display of antique irons. The large space is divided into small, intimate rooms, and lace tablecloths give you the feeling of having dinner at great-grandma's. Try local fare, such as *lomo de alpaca* (alpaca steak) or one of their thick soups made with vegetables and meat or fish. Ask for the set menu and have a great meal for under US$5, and a pisco sour for under US$2. ⊠ *Av. Lima 517* ☎ *051/351–108* ▭ *MC, V.*

¢–$ FodorsChoice ★ ╳ **Apu Salkantay.** Even though it's a favorite with tourists and locals, you can usually manage to get a table. A fire is always burning in the wood stove and their set menu is a bargain. *Trucha ahumadas* (smoked trout), alpaca steaks, pizza and vegetarian dishes prepared with natural ingredients are also on the menu. Live folkloric music begins nightly at 8 PM. If the evening chill has your teeth chattering, across the street is Qori Chaska Artesanias (handicraft store) where you can pick up an inexpensive handknit alpaca sweater. ⊠ *Lima 425* ☎ *051/363–955* ▭ *MC, V.*

¢–$ ╳ **Comedor Vegetariano Delisse.** Great early breakfasts (doors open at 7 am) of pancakes and vegetable omelets with regular or espresso coffee are a speciality in this small, dark, and informal vegetarian restaurant run by Seventh Day Adventists. They also cook up fish and a few other basic Peruvian stews and soups. The restaurant is in the same block as the post office, which is at Moquequa 269. ⊠ *Jr. Moquegua 200, at Jr. Libertad.* ☎ *no phone.* ▭ *DC, MC, V.*

¢–$ ╳ **Don Piero.** Hunting trophies hanging on the walls gaze down at you as you enjoy such dishes as barbecued chicken, fresh fish (pejerrey and *trucha*—trout) fried in oil and garnished with potatoes, lettuce, and toasted chili peppers. Local musicians entertain nightly. ⊠ *Lima 360* ☎ *054/351–108* ▭ *MC, V.*

¢–$ FodorsChoice ★ ╳ **La Plaza** Prices are inversely proportional to the large portions at this kid friendly restaurant. Try hearty regional dishes like *chairo puneño* (soup with dehydrated potatoes and beef), *cuy* (guinea pig), and *trucha* (trout). Sandwiches, pasta, and chicken dishes are also available. Order ice cream for dessert. Dancers perform in the evenings, with piano music between shows. ⊠ *Jr. Puno 419, Plaza de Armas,* ☎☎ *051/351–424* ▭ *AE, MC, V.*

¢–$ ╳ **Pizzeria del Buho.** If you want a complete Italian dinner, ask for the set menu, otherwise order up the best pizza in town at this spot with red-checked tablecloths and a woodburning stove. ✉ *Lima 347,* ☎ *051/ 363-955* ▭ *DC, V.*

¢ ✕ **Rico Pan.** It's more of a bakery than a café, but you can get a good cup of cappuccino or an espresso and a pastry or fresh-baked bread to go with it. Or stop by for a sandwich at lunchtime. ✉ *Moquegua 330* ☎ *051/354-179* ♠ *No reservations.* ▭ *No.*

★ **$$$** ⊞ **Libertador Hotel Isla Esteves.** A gleaming white low-rise hotel (just four stories), the Libertador is 5 km (3 mi) from Puno—40 minutes from the Juliaca (Puno) airport, and is the area's most luxurious lodging. On Isla Esteves, an island in Lake Titicaca, it is connected to the mainland by a causeway. In back of the hotel steps lead up to a small sitting area where you can watch the sun rise over Lake Titicaca. Play billiards in the game room, go to the discotheque, or relax in the piano bar. The gift shop has beautiful alpaca wool sweaters that are more expensive than in the street market, but the quality is excellent. Taxis are the only way to get to the center of town—about US $2 and usually a little cheaper on the return. You can catch a taxi around Parque Pino on Calle Lima. ✉ *Isla Esteves* ☎ *051/367-780* 🖨 *051/367-879* ⊕ *www.libertador.com.pe* ⬁ *126 rooms, 11 suites* ♠ *Restaurant, health club, bar, dance club* ▭ *AE, DC, MC, V* ⊙ *BP.*

$$ ⊞ **Posada del Inca.** The warmth of Indian weavings, polished wood, and
Fodor's Choice native art give character to this thoroughly modern Sonesta hotel on the
★ shores of Lake Titicaca. It is 5 km (3 mi) from the center of town and has its own dock that extends out into the lake with the *El Yavari*, the world's oldest motorized iron ship anchored at the end. Hydrofoils to Copacabana and the Sun and Moon Islands on the Bolivian side of Lake Titicaca also leave from the Posada's dock. Eating in the hotel's restaurant is a pleasure, as large picture windows offer you a panoramic view of the lake. ✉ *Sesqui Centenario 610, Sector Huaje* ☎ *051/363-672* ⊕ *www.posadas.com.pe* ⬁ *62 rooms* ♠ *Restaurant, lounge, business services, meeting rooms* ▭ *AE, DC, MC, V* ⊙ *BP.*

$ ⊞ **Colon Inn.** Once a tiny 19th-century colonial house that evolved into
Fodor's Choice a mansion, this Best Western property is now a gracious inn with such
★ modern amenities as private baths with hot water, and Internet service for around US$2 an hour. The staff is fluent in English, French, and Spanish, and they also know how to make pizza. It is close to the central handicrafts market; about 5 blocks northeast of the Plaza de Armas and 2 mi west of Lake Titicaca. The inn is listed as a National Historic Monument. Airport transfers are available for US $10. ✉ *Calle Tacna 290,,* ☎ *051/351-432,* 🖨 *051/357-090,* ⊕ *www.coloninn.com.* ⬁ *21 rooms* ♠ *2 restaurants, pub, Internet Service* ▭ *AE, V, MC* ⊙ *BP.*

$ ⊞ **Hotel Ferrocarril.** The original building dates from 1899, but continuous remodeling has kept it up to date. It is near the train station, six blocks from Lake Titicaca and, in the other direction, six blocks from the Plaza. The restaurant serves good Italian and international dishes and also regional specialties. The hotel will arrange an Andino Buffet with folkloric music and dances for a minimum of eight. All rooms have private baths with 24-hour hot water, and central heating. ✉ *Av. La Torre 185,* ☎ *051/351-752* 🖨 *051/351-752* ⊕ *www.hotelferrocarril.com* ✎ *mail@hotelferrocarril.com* ⬁ *29 rooms* ♠ *Restaurant, bar, cable TV* ▭ *AE, V, MC.*

★ **$** ⊞ **Qelgatani.** The owner is always around to ensure your happiness at this small hotel on a quiet street about three blocks from the Cathedral and a five-minute walk from Jirón Lima. Rooms and private baths are large and have individual space heaters. A full breakfast in the friendly first-floor restaurant is included, and it is also open for lunch or dinner. Next door is Rey Travel Agency, where you can book tours or transfers or reconfirm your flights. ✉ *Tarapacá 355* ☎ *051/366-172* 🖨 *051/351-*

052 ◉ 20 rooms ⅍ Restaurant, coffee shop, travel services ▤ AE, MC, V ❑ BP.

¢ ☒ **Hotel Italia.** A good restaurant, a lovely courtyard, and a rooftop terrace are all pluses at this hotel just a block from Parque Pino. Rooms are simple but comfortable, with parquet floors and wood furniture; those on the fourth floor have a view of the lake. ✉ Teodoro Valcarcel 122 ☎ 051/352–521 ⎙ 051/352–131 ◉ 30 rooms ⅍ Restaurant ▤ MC, V ❑ CP.

¢ ☒ **La Casa Del Abuelo.** Abuelo translates to grandfather, and this really was the house of the owner's grandfather. Opened as a guest house in 2001 with just five rooms, it is one block from the Qelqatani Hotel. Breakfast is included, and all rooms have private baths and 24-hour hot water. ✉ Jr. Tarapaca 399, ☎ 051/352–061, ⊕ www.reytours.com/info.html, ◉ 6 ⅍ Restaurant, internet service, laundry, ▤ AE, MC, V ❑ BP.

¢ ☒ **Pukara.** This hostal is just a few steps west of Jirón Lima, where all

Fodor'sChoice the action is, but the neighborhood is quiet, so you can get a good night's
★ sleep. The hotel is casual and friendly, the staff speaks English, and all rooms, although small, have private baths with hot showers. Breakfast in the upstairs restaurant is included. An impressive, huge woven tapestry dominates the lobby. ✉ Libertad 328 ☎ 054/368–448 ◉ 10 rooms, ▤ MC, V ❑ BP.

Nightlife & the Arts

The **Apu Salkantay Café Internet Bar** (✉ Lima 425 ☎ 051/351–962) serves up nightly folk music and excellent pisco sours.

Pub Ekeko's (✉ Lima 355) If you can't do without your soccer fix, Ekeko's has a large-screen TV and shows all the games. When there are no games on, there's music and dancing.

Shopping

Model reed boats, small stone carvings, and alpaca-wool articles are among the local crafts sold at Puno's **Mercado Artesanal** (Handicrafts Market) near the train station, two blocks east of Parque Pino around Calle Arbula and Avenida Los Incas. Don't be fooled by the market's shabby appearance—some of the country's highest-quality alpaca sweaters are sold here, and if you find you aren't dressed for Puno's chilly evenings, it's the place to buy a good woolen pancho for under US$10. A miniature reed boat is a nice souvenir to take home for your younger relatives. It's also interesting to stroll by the produce section and see the many varieties and colors of potatoes. There are no set hours, but the vendors start setting up their stands daily in the early morning and stay open all day, roughly 8–6. Make sure you know where your wallet or purse is while you're snapping a photo of the colorful market.

Artesanías Puno (✉ Lima 549 ☎ 051/351–261) sells a modest selection of locally made alpaca items, including sweaters, scarfs, and ponchos. Also look for Puno's signature pottery, the Torito de Pucara (Little Bull from Pucará). The pot is a receptacle used to hold a mixture of the bull's blood with chicha (a drink), in a cattle-branding ceremony. Other popular pottery objects are churches and houses of glazed earthenware decorated with flowers. If you don't find what you want here, just walk on down Calle Lima, as there are more artisans' shops along the way.

Lake Titicaca

Forms Puno's eastern shoreline

The border between Peru and Bolivia runs right through Lake Titicaca. The largest piece of Peru's part of the lake is to the northwest, and Puno also has the largest port. Bolivia's side, however, takes in two very important islands, Isla del Sol and Isla de la Luna. Lake Titicaca draws visitors both with its scenery and with the vivid Quechua and Aymará cultures that still thrive on its shores. Surrounded by high, barren mountains, it is truly an inland sea whose opposite shores are often out of view. Some 3,845 m (12,500 ft) above sea level, it is the highest navigable lake in the world. The Bahía de Puno, separated from the lake proper by the two jutting peninsulas of Capaschica and Chucuito, is home to the descendents of the primitive Uro people, who are now mixed with the Aymará and Quechua. The lakeshores are lush with totora reeds—valuable as building material, cattle fodder, and, in times of famine, food for humans.

In 1978 most of Lake Titicaca was designated a National Reserve to help conserve the region's plant and animal wildlife while also promoting sustainable use of its resources. The 36,180-hectare (89,400–acre) reserve extends from the Bay of Puno to the peninsula of Capachica. It is divided into two sectors: one surrounds and includes the Bay of Puno and protects the resources of the Uros-Chuluni communities; the other, in the Huancané area, preserves the totora-reed water fields and protects the nesting area of more than 60 species of birds, including the Titicaca flightless grebe. Fourteen native fish and 18 amphibian species have been identified, including the giant Titicaca frog.

Sillustani

58 *30 km (19 mi) northwest of Puno.*

High on a hauntingly beautiful peninsula in Lake Umayo is the necropolis of Sillustani. Twenty-eight stone burial towers represent a city of the dead that both predated and coincided with the Inca empire. The proper name for a tower is *ayawasi* (home of the dead), but they are generally referred to as *chullpas,* which are actually the shrouds used to cover the mummies deposited inside. This was the land of the Aymará-speaking Colla people, and the precision of their masonry rivals that of the Inca. Sillustani's mystique is heightened by the view it provides over Lake Umayo and its mesa-shape island, El Sombrero, as well as by the utter silence that prevails, broken only by the wind over the water and the cries of lake birds. On your way to the chullpas, keep an eye out for shepherds watching over their sheep and alpacas.

Most of the chullpas date from the 14th and 15th centuries, but some were erected as early as AD 900. The tallest, known as the Lizard because of a carving on one of its massive stones, has a circumference of 28 ft. An unusual architectural aspect of the chullpas is that the circumference is smaller at the bottom than the top. To fully appreciate Sillustani, it is necessary to make the long climb to the top; fortunately, the steps are wide and it's an easy climb. You will be besieged at the site by young girls selling necklaces that are interesting, attractive, and inexpensive. If you take photos of mothers, children, and pet alpacas, a donation of a couple of soles will be much appreciated.

The Floating Islands
59 *10 km (6 mi) northeast of Puno.*

Even though the Uros Islands, a group of 40 floating islands in Lake Titicaca near Puno, have been called floating souvenir stands by some visitors, they still provide a glimpse of one the region's oldest cultures. The closest group of "floating museums" is 10 km (6 mi) from Puno and occupies a large part of the Lake Titicaca National Reserve. These man-made islands of woven totora reeds illustrate a form of human habitation that evolved over centuries. The islanders make their living by fishing, trapping birds, and selling visitors well-made miniature reed boats, weavings, and collages depicting life on the islands. You can walk around the springy, moist islands or hire an islander to take you for a ride in a reed boat. Progress has come to some of the islands in the form of solar-powered energy and microwave telephone stations. Seventh Day Adventists converted the inhabitants of one island and built a church and school, the only structures not made of mud and reeds.

Taquile & Amantani

60 *Taquile 35 km (22 mi) west of Puno. Amantani 45 km (28 mi) north-west of Puno, 10 km (6 mi) north of Taquile*

Unlike the floating islands, which are in the Bay of Puno, Taquile and Amantani are in Lake Titicaca proper and are surrounded by a vast, ocean-like panorama. The proud, Quechua-speaking people of Taquile, where the hills are topped with Inca and Tiahuanaco ruins, weave some of Peru's loveliest textiles. They still wear traditional dress and have successfully maintained the strong community ties and cooperative lifestyle of their ancestors, though there are signs that the island may be losing its un-spoiled character under the weight of tourism. Amantani, also with pre-Columbian ruins, has a larger, mainly agrarian society, whose traditional way of life has stood up better to outside pressure.

For a day visit to the islands, take one of the agency tours that leave at around 7:30 AM and include a trip to one of the floating islands. If you want to make an overnight stay on Taquile or Amantani (which is rec-ommended), travel instead on the slower local ferry, since there are some-times problems with the agency services if you try to break your trip and continue the next day. Lodging costs about $4, and you stay in a local home. Nights can be cold and blankets inadequate, so you may wish to take along a sleeping bag. Bring your own water or water-pu-rification tablets. There are two ways to reach the top of Taquile—you can climb up the 535 stone steps, or take the long way up a path that eventually brings you to the top.

Amantani, the lesser-known of the two islands, is 45 km (28 mi) from Puno. Travel time between the two islands is around two hours. Aman-tani has a population of 3,500 Quechua. Sacred and ceremonial rituals are held in its two pre-Inca temples, dedicated to the earth's fertility. Aman-tani also welcomes visitors for overnight home stays, but conditions are not as comfortable or as advanced as on Taquile.

Chucuito

61 *20 km (12 mi) southeast of Puno.*

Chucuito (in Aymará *Choque-Huito,* Mountain of Gold) is the first of three small towns (Juli and Pomata are the other two) that are usually visited on a bus tour enroute to the Bolivian side of Lake Titicaca. Their principal attractions are colonial churches. There's a trout hatchery at the lake, and the townsfolk are known for weaving fine reed boats.

Chucuito is surrounded by hillsides crisscrossed with agricultural ter-races on the southern shore of Chucuito (Puno) Bay, and was built on top of an Inca settlement. The main plaza has a large stone Inca sun-dial as its centerpiece. There are two Renaissance-style 16th-century churches, La Asunción alongside the plaza and the Santo Domingo on the east side of town. Chucuito was once the capital of the province and housed the Spanish mint. However, much of its fame today is due to the Temple of Inca Uyo. This "temple" doesn't quite meet the dictionary's description of a temple as a stately edifice, but that is what it is called. It is an outdoor area surrounded by a high stone wall that blocks the view of a "garden" of anatomically correct phallic stone sculptures from the nearby Santo Domingo church on the outskirts of Chucuito. It is better known as the Temple of the Phallus. In ancient times it was visited by females who would sit there for hours, believing it would increase their fertility.

Juli

62 *On Lake Titicaca, 84 km (52 mi) southeast of Puno*

At one time this village may have been an important Aymará religious center, and it has served as a Jesuit training center for missionaries from Paraguay and Bolivia. Juli is considered a sort of altiplano Rome because of its disproportionate number of churches. Four interesting churches in various stages of restoration are **San Pedro Mártir, Santa Cruz de Jerusalén, Asunción,** and **San Juan de Letrán.** The latter has 80 paintings from the highly rated Cusco School and huge windows worked in stone.

Pomata

63 *108 km (67 mi) southeast of Puno*

The main attraction in the small lakeside town of Pomata is the church of **Santiago Apóstol de Nuestra Señora del Rosario.** It was built in the 18th century of pink granite, and has paintings from the Cusco School and the Flemish School. Its mestizo baroque carvings and translucent alabaster windows are spectacular. Its altars are covered in gold leaf. Pomata is also famous for its fine pottery, especially for its Toritos de Pucará (bull figures).

Side Trip to Bolivia

A fun way to visit the Bolivian side of the lake is to take a hydrofoil trip from Puno, stopping first at the Uros floating islands before continuing to Copacabana on the Bolivian side, then on to the Sun and Moon Islands for an overnight or two on Sun Island. Time on Sun Island (Isla del Sol) can be spent walking the stone trails that were part of the Inca's trails crisscrossing the island. From the top of a ridge you have a view of the entire island, Lake Titicaca, and the Andes Mountains. You can return to Puno or continue to the Inca Utama Resort & Spa at the Huatahata harbor to spend a couple of days relaxing at the resort and visiting the Andean Roots Cultural Complex. A real treat is the observatory with a rollback roof, which gives you a real view of southern-hemisphere stars through powerful telescopes donated by NASA. You can either return to Puno by hydrofoil or fly to Cusco or Miami on Lloyd Boliviano Airlines from La Paz.

Bolivia's unit of currency is the boliviano—though Bolivians often refer to their currency as *pesos*. Price categories below are in bolivianos, though the ranges are comparable to those given for nuevo soles throughout the chapter.

WHERE TO STAY   ▣ **Inca Utama Hotel &Spa.** By far the best and most fascinating lodging
$$–$$$ on Lake Titicaca is the Inca Utama Hotel &Spa at Huatajata, home harbor for Crillón Tours' hydrofoils on Lake Titicaca. At the Kallawaya natural spa, relax through hydrotherapy with mud or salt baths, massages and treatments for stress and weight loss. There are two restaurants, Sumaj Untavi, with nightly "Pena" folkloric shows, and La Choza Nautica, where you can watch the sun set over Lake Titicaca. A second-floor bar-lounge

is also a nice place to relax, with a fireplace and educational videos about Bolivia. On premises are the Altiplano and Eco museums, with exhibits on Andean cultures; you can explore them at your own pace with a headset. In the Andean Roots Cultural Complex, learn about Andean customs and medicines and meet a natural-medicine doctor who can tell your fortune by casting sacred coca leaves. The complex also has its own herds of llamas, alpacas, and vicuñas. ✉ *Huatajata,* ☎ *02//33–/533* 🖷 *02/ 211–6481* ⊕ *www.titicaca.com* ⬙ *70 rooms* ⬥ *2 restaurants, health club, spa, bar, meeting rooms* ▭ *AE, MC, V.*

$$ 🏨 **La Posada del Inca.** Sitting high on a bluff surrounded by pine and eucalyptus trees and overlooking Lake Titicaca is this restored colonial-style hacienda on Isla del Sol. If you're not up to the climb, you can ride up on a mule, but if that seems too drastic, go up in a comfortable (by comparison) golf cart, over a new, narrow road. You can also walk up a winding stone path in 30 to 45 minutes— depending on your endurance, with llamas carrying your luggage. The Posada uses solar energy and has electric blankets and heaters in all rooms to keep you toasty. Meals are family-style around a long dining-room table, and their soups and stews are hearty and healthful. You can also have lunch or dinner in the Uma Kollo restaurant below the posada. A whimsical note at the hotel's entrance is a full-size bicycle made entirely of twigs that almost looks as if it could be ridden. In a very small town with minimal shopping just above the hacienda, you can watch the islanders planting crops on old Inca terraces. Rooms must be booked with Crillón Tours. ☎ *02/ 733–7533,* 🖷 *02/211–6481* ⊕ *www.titicaca.com* ⬙ *20 rooms (all with private bath)* ⬥ *Restaurant.* ▭ *AE, MC, V.*

Puno & Lake Titicaca A to Z

To research prices, get advice from other travelers, and book travel arrangements, visit www.fodors.com.

AIR TRAVEL

You can arrange airport transfers to your hotel in Puno from the Aeropuerto Manco Cápac in Juliaca, a commercial and industrial center 50 km (31 mi) north of town. Make arrangements through a travel agency, take a taxi, or share a minibus.

Aero Continente has daily flights from Lima and Arequipa to Juliaca. LanPeru flies from Lima to Juliaca.

🛈 **Airlines & Contacts Aero Continente** ☎ 051/242–4242. **LanPeru** ☎ 051/367–227.
🛈 **Airport Information Aeropuerto Manco Cápac, Juliaca.** ☎ 051/322–905.

BOAT & FERRY TRAVEL

Crillón Tours in La Paz, Bolivia, is once again operating its hydrofoils all the way to Puno, eliminating the bus-hydrofoil combination between Peru and Bolivia. En route to Bolivia, the hydrofoil stops at the Uros floating islands and the Sun and Moon islands before continuing to Copacabana or to the Huatajata harbor. Passengers can stay overnight on Sun Island, at Copacabana, or at the Inca Utama Hotel & Spa at Huatajata harbor in Bolivia before continuing by bus to La Paz or returning to Puno. It's possible to go by bus from Puno to La Paz, but it takes more than 12 hours and involves a ferry crossing at the border. You can also take a bus from Juliaca, 50 km (31 mi) from Puno, around the top of the lake to La Paz, but it's a long, cold trip over rough roads. Make arrangements for the crossing to Bolivia through a travel agency in Puno or Lima or with Crillón Tours.

The easiest and most pleasant way to cross the border between Peru and Bolivia is to book passage on the comfortable hydrofoils operated by

Crillón Tours between Puno on the Peruvian side and Copacabana on the Bolivian side. Hydrofoils leave Puno Tuesday, Thursday, and Saturday, and from Copacabana to Puno on Wednesday, Friday, and Saturday. Once you make the crossing, you can choose to go from Copacabana to Sun Island to spend some time, then to Huatajata harbor to relax at the Inca Utama complex before returning via the same route to Peru, or go on to La Paz for a few days. Once in La Paz, LAB, the Bolivian airline, flies three times a week to Cusco, Peru, and daily between La Paz, Santa Cruz, and Miami, Florida.

🚢 Boat & Ferry Information**Crillón Tours** ✉ Av. Camacho 1223, La Paz ☎ 02/337-533 ⊕ www.titicaca.com.

BUS TRAVEL

Peru has good bus service between cities, but think twice before embarking on a bus trip from Lima to Puno or even Arequipa to Puno. It's a long haul, with many sections of bumpy roads. However, service is good between Puno and Cusco, and so is the road between Puno and Copacabana in Bolivia. Cruz del Sur and CIVA have offices in Puno. It is best to buy your tickets ahead of time, either from the bus-company offices or—preferably—from a travel agency that can give you all the options. For your comfort and safety, take the best service you can afford. An estimate for the least expensive is US$6 for every 250 km (155 mi). The distance between Puno and Cusco is 394 km (245 mi.)

🚌 Bus Information**Cruz del Sur** ✉ Av. El Sol 568 ☎ 051/352-451**CIVA** ✉ Melgar 389 ☎ 051/356-882

EMERGENCIES

There is a tourism police office in Puno near the Plaza de Armas, and from Puno and the other provinces you can dial toll-free the **Servicio de Protección al Turista** (Tourist Protection Service) in Lima.

🚓Tourism Police Office ✉ Jr. Deustua 538 ☎ 051/357-100 **Tourist Protection Service** ☎ 0800-4-2579 🕐 Mon. to Fri. 8:30-4:30 🏥 Hospitals**Manuel Nuñez Butron National Hospital** ✉ Av. El Sol 1022 🕐 24 hours ☎ 051/369-286

HEALTH

Not only medical personnel, but even the clerk behind your hotel counter will most likely be of assistance in helping you with what may be your biggest problem in Puno and Lake Titicaca: *soroche* (high-altitude sickness). If you're coming from Cusco or La Paz, Bolivia, you will probably not be affected, but when flying in from Lima, do take a day to adjust, even if you think you're okay. Put off climbing to the top of the Sillustani ruins, for example, until at least your second day. Drink only bottled water, of course, and you may want to skip the ice cubes in your drink, unless you've been assured they were made from bottled water. Eat lightly, go easy on the alcohol, and consult your doctor before leaving for your trip if you have any health problems that high altitude may exacerbate. If the altitude is affecting you beyond a slight headache or a mild stomach upset, most hotels have access to oxygen.

MAIL & SHIPPING

Puno's post office is two blocks from the Plaza de Armas. For shipping packages, DHL is also available.

🖥 Internet Cafés**La Casa del Corregidor** ✉ Deustua 576 ☎ 051/351-921 🕐 Tues.-Sat. 10-10

📮 Post Office**Puno** ✉ Av. Moquegua 269 ☎ 051/351-141 🕐 Mon.-Sat. 8-8, Sun. 8-3.

📦 Shipping Services**DHL** ✉ Av. Lambayeque 175, Puno ☎ 051/352-001.

MONEY MATTERS

In Puno, Banco de Crédito will exchange currency and cash traveler's checks.

Banks Banco de Crédito ✉ Jr. Lima 516, Puno ☎ 051/352-119.

SAFETY

Except for trips to the islands on Lake Titicaca or the Sillustani ruins, most of the sights, restaurants, and night spots in Puno are along the pedestrian-only Jirón Lima, which is safe for strolling, even at night. Of course, watch your wallet, pocketbook, or backpack at all times.

TELEPHONES

In Puno, Telefónica del Peru is one of the best places to make calls.

Telefónica del Peru ✉ Jr. Lima Puno ☎ 051/369-180.

TOUR OPERATORS

Excursions to the floating islands of the Uros as well as to Taquile and Amantani can be arranged through tour agencies in Puno. Most tours depart between 7:30 and 9 AM, as the lake can become choppy in the afternoon. You also can take the local boat at the Puno dock for about the same price as a tour, although boats don't usually depart without at least 10 passengers.

Allways Travel ✉ Tacna 234 ☎ 051/355-552 ⊕ www.allwaystravelperu.com **Condor Travel** ✉ Jr. Melgar 173 ☎ 051/352-632 ⊟ 051/355-794 ⊕ www.condortravel.com.pe **Edgar Adventures** ✉ Jr. Lima 328 ☎ 051/353-444 ⊟ 051/354-811 **Grace Tours** ✉ Lima 385 ☎☎ 051/355-721. **Kontiki Tours** ✉ Jr. Melgar 188 ☎☎ 051/353-473. **Receptour** ✉ Lima 419, Suite 205 ☎ 051/352-391 ⊟ 051/369-941 **Rey Tours** ✉ Tarapacá 399 ☎ 051/352-061. **Solmartour** ✉ Jr. Libertad 229-231 ☎ 051/622-043. **Turpuno** ✉ Lambayeque 175 ☎☎ 054/351-431.

TRAIN TRAVEL

Passenger train service between Puno and Arequipa has been discontinued except for charters or group bookings. Trains between Puno and Cusco chug across the altiplano Monday, Wednesday, and Saturday in each direction, with additional service during high season. The first-class service, with a 3-course lunch included, operates only with a minimum of 20 passengers. First-class one-way fare is US$83. For tourist or backpacker cars, the cost is US$15. A short stop is made at La Raya, the highest point, at 4,026 m (13,200 ft), so you can snap some photos or buy handicrafts from vendors along the tracks. The trip takes about nine hours, that now includes only a 45-minute wait in Juliaca. If you have booked through a tour operator, they may offer to have a guide take you to Juliaca to board or pick you up there if you're coming from Cusco, to avoid the wait. Juliaca is about 42 km (26 mi) from Puno.

Train Information PeruRail ✉ Estacion Puno, La Torre 224 ☎ 051/351-233 ⊕ www.perurail.com.

VISITOR INFORMATION

Información Turística ✉ Lima 582 and Ayacucho 682, Puno ☎ 051/364-976, ⊟ 051/351-261. **Touring and Automobile Club of Peru** ✉ Titicaca 531, Puno ☎ 051/352-432.

CUSCO, MACHU PICCHU & THE SACRED VALLEY

(3)

FODOR'S CHOICE

Granja Heidi, *German fare in Cusco*

Inca Trail, *Machu Picchu*

Machu Picchu Pueblo Hotel, *Aguas Calientes*

Museo Hilario Mendívil, *Cusco*

Museo Inka, *Cusco*

Pisac Market, *local savories and crafts*

Qorikancha, *Inca temple in Cusco*

HIGHLY RECOMMENDED

RESTAURANTS Chez Maggy, *Cusco*

Pucará, *Cusco*

HOTELS Hotel Pakaritampu, *Ollantaytambo*

Monasterio de Cusco, *Cusco*

Sonesta Posada del Inca Valle Sagrado, *Yucay*

SIGHTS Catedral, *Cusco*

By Jeffrey Van
Fleet

IN A FERTILE VALLEY IN THE ANDES, 3,500 m (11,500 ft) above sea level, lies Cusco, the southern capital of the Inca empire and today, arguably, the southern capital of tourism in the Western Hemisphere. While the name Inca originally applied only to the royal family, in particular the emperors (e.g., the Inca Pachacutec), today it describes the indigenous people as a whole. The Inca language was Quechua in this empire they called Tawantinsuyo, the four corners of the earth. Under the rule of the legendary Pachacutec, the Inca expanded that empire as far north and south as present-day Colombia and Argentina. But today's Cusco remained the Inca Qosqo, the "Navel of the World," the glittering capital from which all power emanated.

But not all was Inca in southern Peru, a point that gets lost in the tourist trek from one Inca ruin to the next. The presence not far from Cusco of Pikillacta, a pre-Inca city constructed by the Wari culture that thrived between AD 600 and 1000, is an indication that this territory, like most of Peru, was the site of sophisticated civilizations long before the Inca appeared on the scene. Then came Francisco Pizarro and the Spanish. After the 1532 conquest of the Inca empire, the new colonists overlaid a new political system and new religion onto the old. They also literally superimposed their architecture, looting former structures of their gold, silver, and stone, grafting their own churches, monasteries, convents, and palaces onto the foundations of the Inca sites. The result throughout the region is an odd juxtaposition of imperial and colonial, indigenous and Spanish. Traditionally clad Quechua-speaking women sell their wares in front of a part-Inca, part-colonial structure as a business executive walks by carrying on a cell-phone conversation. The two cultures coexist, but have not entirely embraced each other almost five centuries after the conquest.

And not all is Cusco in this much-visited region of Peru. The warmer, fertile, lower-elevation Sacred Valley of the Inca was favored by the emperors as a place for cultivation and recreation and has many Inca ruins, too. And of course the Spanish conquerors never did find Machu Picchu, the fabled "Lost City of the Inca," whose existence remained a secret to the outside world until its rediscovery in 1911, a fact for which every pilgrim to the site gives thanks. Too often Cusco and Machu Picchu are sold as a three-day, two-night package—and sometimes even a whirlwind tour of the Sacred Valley is incorporated into the third day. That's a shame, because each is a destination in its own right. Cusco has enough to keep you occupied for at least three days and should be looked on as more than an embarkation point for the trek to Machu Picchu. The ruins should also be appreciated and absorbed on their own, and require more than the three or four hours spent at the site during a typical day tour.

Exploring Cusco & Machu Picchu

Cusco was the Inca "Navel of the World," and it remains the heart of this region and of tourism in Peru. The city nests in a high mountain valley at 3,500 m (11,500 ft). The Río Urubamba passes, at its closest, about 30 km (18 mi) north of Cusco and flows through a river basin about 300 m (980 ft) lower than the city, extending to the northwest and southeast. The northwest sector, romantically labeled the "Sacred Valley of the Inca," contains some of the region's most appealing towns and interesting pre-Columbian ruins. A car is the best option for exploring this part of the valley, but frequent buses run from Cusco and between communities. You'll likely have the towns and ruins of the less-visited southeast Urubamba Valley to yourself, but the area is well served by good roads and public transportation. The vehicular tourist route ends at Ollantaytambo, beyond which rail—most visitors board the train in Cusco, however—or a hike along the famed Inca Trail are the only options for reaching the remains of Machu Picchu.

About the Restaurants

Employees of restaurants on Cusco's Plaza de Armas and Plateros and Procuradores streets—any of these could be renamed "Restaurant Row"—stand in their doorways, touting their establishments, menus in hand, to entice you in to dine if you're an obvious visitor here. The same happens in Aguas Calientes near Machu Picchu. Lunch is served between 1 and 3. Dinner begins around 7, and most restaurants start winding down service at about 9. Most places do stay open continually throughout the afternoon if you wish to dine outside these hours.

About the Hotels

No matter what your travel budget, you won't be priced out of the market staying in this region of Peru: luxury hotels, backpackers' digs, and everything in between await. Most lodgings discount rates during the unofficial off season of September–May. With one exception, absent are the international hotel chains, but in their place you'll find some smaller, top-end, independently run lodgings offering impeccable service, even if they do lack swimming pools and concierges. Lodgings in all price ranges, whether housed in a former 17th-century convent or newly built, mimic the old Spanish colonial style of construction arranged around a central courtyard or patio. Breakfast, at least a Continental one (and usually something more ample), is included in most lodging rates.

You may have to adjust your internal thermostat if you stay in moderate or budget lodgings at this altitude, but all provide extra blankets to keep you comfy at night. And the hot water might not be on all day, or could be lukewarm at best, even though hotels in this price range say they have *agua caliente*. Many accommodations keep an oxygen supply on hand for those having trouble adjusting to the thin air. Lodgings in Cusco and Machu Picchu keep shockingly early checkout times. (Flights to Cusco arrive early in the morning, as do the Cusco–Machu Picchu trains.) Expect to have to vacate your room by 8 or 9 AM, though this is less strictly enforced in the off season. All will hold your luggage if you're not leaving town until later in the day.

WHAT IT COSTS In Nuevo Soles					
	$$$$	$$$	$$	$	¢
RESTAURANTS	over 65	50–65	35–50	20–35	under 20
HOTELS	over 500	375–500	250–375	125–250	under 125

Restaurant prices are per person, for a main course at dinner. Hotel prices are for two people in a standard double room, excluding tax.

Timing

You'll find all the high-season/low-season tradeoffs in this region. Winter (June through August) means drier weather and easier traveling, but higher lodging prices and larger crowds. (It's prime North American and European vacation time, after all.) Yet even Machu Picchu manages to absorb its up to 1,500 high-season visitors a day at this time without too much fuss. Make reservations for flights to and from Cusco, the Machu Picchu train, and hotels a few days in advance at this time of year, and

Numbers in the text correspond to numbers in the margin and on the Cusco; Sacred Valley and Southeastern Urubamba Valley; and Machu Picchu maps.

If you have 3 days

Three days approximates the standard, albeit rushed package tour sold for visiting the region. Fly into ▦ **Cusco❶ –⓱** 🏞 the first morning. Spend the day exploring the ancient capital's Inca and Spanish sights—if you visit nothing else, tackle the **Qorikan-cha⓫** (Temple of the Sun) and **Catedral❷** . Use at least part of your evening to sample the city's nightlife. Board a train early the next day for the three-hour-plus journey to **Machu Picchu㉞ –㊼** where you'll have a few hours to walk among the famed Lost City's ruins before heading back to Cusco late that afternoon. Spend your second evening in Cusco. Sign on for a tour of the Sacred Valley on your third day. Tuesday, Thursday, and Sunday are days when most agencies operate excursions to coincide with the famous market in **Pisac㉘** .

If you have 5 days

Two extra days beyond the three-day itinerary above literally give you a chance to catch your breath: Spend your first two nights in ▦ **Cusco❶ –⓱** 🏞, but take things slowly to acclimatize yourself to the city's 3,500-m (11,500-ft) altitude. Its **Museo Inka❾** and **Museo de Arte Religioso del Arzobispado❺** provide useful background on the region's history, and few activities will relax you more than a leisurely stroll through the pedestrian streets of the San Blas neighborhood. The nearby ruins of **Sacsayhuamán⓲** are second in importance to Machu Picchu in this region. Board the train to **Machu Picchu㉞ –㊼** your third day. Spend the entire afternoon at the ruins, stay the night in ▦ **Aguas Calientes** down the hill, and partake of the ruins' unforgettable early morning quiet and soft light before the day-trippers arrive from Cusco the next day. Return to Cusco yourself that afternoon. Devote your last day to exploring the charming towns of the Sacred Valley between Cusco and Machu Picchu, visit their nearby ruins, and shop at the **Pisac㉘** market.

If you have 8 days

Eight days give you ample time for altitude acclimatization and extensive, yet leisurely exploring. If your time allows, ▦ **Cusco❶ –⓱** 🏞 warrants a full three days in which to delve into the city's smaller churches and museums and Inca ruins close by. Spend your fourth and fifth days in **Machu Picchu㉞ –㊼** before returning to Cusco the fifth evening. Get out of the city and base yourself in the Sacred Valley during your extra days. **Pisac㉘** , **Ollantaytambo㉛** , **Urubamba㉚** , and **Yucay㉙** get rave reviews for their authentic small-town charm. All have wonderful lodging and make great bases for exploring the region. Juggle your itinerary a bit and plan to be in **Pisac㉘** on a Sunday, the most colorful of its three weekly market days. You can also take a day to explore the less-visited ruins of the southeastern Urubamba River valley.

---

weeks in advance if you'll be here for Cusco's famed June 24 Inti Raymi festival, or near Peru's July 28 Independence Day holiday. Prices and visitor numbers drop dramatically during the November–March summer rainy season. For near-ideal weather and manageable crowds, consider a trip during the spring and autumn months.

CUSCO

"Bienvenidos a la ciudad imperial del Cusco," intones the flight attendant's announcement as your plane touches down. "Welcome to the imperial city of Cusco." To bid you welcome to simply "Cusco" would shortchange one of the country's, and the world's, great travel destinations. Cusco is a city of terra-cotta roofs and cobblestone streets, where the blending of Inca and Spanish cultures has emerged into a distinct local style. The city has stood for nine centuries, first as the capital of the Inca empire, then as the new settlement of the conquering colonial Spanish, and finally as home to the mestizo culture of today and, of course, the centerpiece of tourism in Peru. Cusco takes its newest role all in stride, and absorbs thousands of travelers with an ample supply of lodgings, restaurants, and services. That such a polished infrastructure exists in such a remote, high-elevation locale is a pleasant surprise.

According to tradition, the Inca Manco Capac and his sister-consort Mama Occlo founded the city. They envisioned Qosqo, their capital, in the shape of a puma, the animal representation of the earth in the indigenous cosmos, a fact that is evident today if someone traces the animal outline on a city map. The Spanish arrived and built their structures on existing Inca foundations. The later Spanish architecture does appear sloppy compared with precise stonework visible in the city's early walls and foundations. The juxtaposition can be jarring as in the case of the Santo Domingo church built on top of the Qorikancha, the Temple of the Sun. And it's downright ironic to think of the cloistered convent of Santa Catalina occupying the same site as the equally cloistered Acllawasi, the home of the Inca chosen women. The cultural combination shows up in countless other ways too: witness the pumas carved into the cathedral doors. The city also gave its name to the Cusqueña school of art, in which New World artists combined Andean motifs with European-style painting, usually on religious themes. You'll chance on paintings that could be by Van Dyck but for the Inca costumes on New Testament figures.

Exploring Cusco

The visitor's Cusco centers on its central Plaza de Armas, slightly sloped, with streets heading downhill, most prominently the Avenida El Sol, leading to the more modern sectors of the city. Heading uphill takes you to the city's older neighborhoods, notably the artisan quarter of San Blas and its web of pedestrian-only walkways. The center city is most enjoyably explored on foot. In fact, even many of the streets open to vehicular traffic are so narrow that it's simply faster to walk than drive. Cusco streets have a habit of changing names every few blocks, or even every block. Many streets bear a common Spanish name that everyone uses, but have newly designated street signs with an old Quechua name in an effort by the city to highlight its Inca heritage: the Plaza de Armas is Haukaypata; the Plaza Regocijo is Kusipata; Triunfo is Sunturwasi; Loreto is Intikijlli; Arequipa is Q'aphchijk'ijllu. The list goes on.

If you haven't booked a tour of Cusco through a travel agency, purchase a *boleto turístico* (tourist ticket) for S/36 (S/18 with an international student ID). Buy these at the lobby of the **Instituto Nacional de Cultura** (✉ Garcilaso and Heladeros ☎ 084/226–919), open Monday through Friday 8 to 5, Saturday 8 to 4, and Sunday 8 to 12. The ticket is valid for 10 days for one entry each to most main attractions in Cusco, including churches, convents, museums, and archaeological sites in the nearby Sacred Valley, a total of 16 locations in all. (Machu Picchu is

3

Ultimate Archaeology

Machu Picchu, the fabled Lost City of the Inca, and arguably the most famous archaeological site in the Americas, draws huge crowds and is one of the world's must-see attractions. But don't ignore the other Inca and pre-Inca ruins near Cusco and scattered throughout the Sacred Valley. Experts vehemently dispute the function some of these places served in Inca times. A given site might get billing as a temple, *huaca* (any sacred place), fortress, burial ground, palace, or storage depot, depending on who you talk to. Current theory holds that most of these sites performed multiple functions and that an expansive interpretation of their purpose is the correct one.

Taters, Critters & Tea

Meat, potatoes, and other vegetables characterize the cuisine of this part of Peru. The agricultural terraces that are still in use today were used by the Inca to cultivate dozens of varieties of potatoes. *Papas rellenas,* or potatoes stuffed with meat or vegetables, remain a particular favorite here. *Choclo,* the region's distinctive white-kernel corn, can be eaten on the cob, as part of soups, as a side dish, or brewed into *chicha,* a corn beer drunk at room temperature and sold from rural homes that display a red flag in front. Meat is standard fare, but for two peculiarly Andean delicacies that may leave you wildly or tepidly enthused: alpaca is touted for its tender, low-fat, low-cholesterol beef-like flavor; and *cuy,* or guinea pig compares favorably to pork, at least among its fans here. Both are best when prepared in a *fogón,* an open-air oven.

Mate de coca is touted as a cure-all for your high-altitude ailments. Indigenous peoples have chewed the leaves of the coca plant for centuries to cope with Andean elevations. But the brewing of the leaves in an herbal tea is considered a more refined, and completely legal way to ingest the substance, in Andean nations at least. Most restaurants and many hotels have a pot steeping constantly.

Mysticism

Few regions of the world can match the mystique-per-square-kilometer quotient of Cusco, Machu Picchu, and the Sacred Valley that connects them. Mystics, shamans, spiritualists, astrologers, and UFO spotters, professionals and wannabes, homegrown and international, all flock to this serene region where the unknown overshadows the known and where every new discovery raises new questions. Even the most no-nonsense curmudgeons find themselves contemplating the secrets of history and the mysteries of the cosmos.

Treks

The two- to four-day hike of the Inca Trail from near Ollantaytambo to Machu Picchu is the region's best-known outdoor expedition, but other trekking options abound in the area. White-water rafting is available in Classes II through V on the Río Urubamba and nearby tributaries. Guided mountain-biking expeditions and hot-air balloon outings are the newest offerings on the slate of outdoor excursions. Cusco has plenty of outfitters dedicated to safe, friendly, professional service ready to fix you up and get you going.

not included.) This is the only way to visit any of the sites; individual admission prices are not assessed. The ticket takes the form of a color certificate that certifies that you visited each of the sites portrayed on its face. The reverse side shows a map, addresses, and opening hours. An alternative is the S/21 *boleto parcial* (partial ticket), valid for admission for one day only at Sacsayhuamán, Qenko, Puka Pukara, and Tambomachay, the four Inca ruins nearest Cusco.

Numbers in the text correspond to numbers in the margin and on the Cusco map.

a good walk

Most of Cusco's main attractions lie within its historic center, whose heart is the Haukaypata, more commonly known as the **Plaza de Armas**❶ ⌐. In the eastern corner of the Plaza de Armas are remnants of an Inca wall, part of the Acllawasi (House of the Chosen Women). The palace of Pachacutec, who turned the Inca kingdom into an empire, once stood on what is now the western corner of the plaza. The **Catedral**❷ sits on the northeast side. Rivaling the cathedral in stature is **Iglesia de La Compañía**❸, on the corner diagonally across the plaza. As you face the cathedral you will see to the right a steep, narrow street, Triunfo, now rebaptized with its original Quechua name of Sunturwasi. One block up on the right, where the street name changes to Hatun Rumiyoq, stands what is believed to have been the **Palacio de Inca Roca**❹. Today the colonial building that rests on the Inca foundations is the **Museo de Arte Religioso del Arzobispado**❺. Before heading up the hill to San Blas, a short detour on Choquechaca takes you to the **Museo Irq'i Yachay**❻, a children's art museum. The street leads up to a steep, cobblestone hill known as the Cuesta de San Blas, the entry into the traditional artists' quarter of San Blas. Continue on the same street for one block to reach the **Plazoleta de San Blas**❼. Also on the square is the **Museo Hilario Mendívil**❽.

Backtracking to again from the Plaza de Armas, the street to the left of the cathedral, called Cuesta del Almirante, will take you to a beautiful colonial mansion, the Palacio del Almirante, the site of Cusco's **Museo Inka**❾. To the left of the modern fountain in the Plazuela del Tricentenario, in front of the mansion, is a 200-m-long (656-ft-long) walkway with a fine view of the Plaza de Armas and central Cusco. Once again starting from the Plaza de Armas, follow the street named Santa Catalina Angosta along the Inca wall of the Acllawasi to the **Convento de Santa Catalina de Siena**❿. A few blocks away is one of the most splendid examples of Inca architecture, the Temple of the Sun, known as **Qorikancha**⓫, with a colonial church superimposed on it. West of the Plaza de Armas, along the Calle del Medio, is the Kusipata, still commonly referred to by its former name, Plaza Regocijo. In the municipal building on the plaza sits the **Museo de Arte Contemporáneo**⓬. Beyond it is the **Casa de Garcilaso**⓭. Walk down Heladeros to Mantas to reach the church and monastery of **La Merced**⓮. Follow Mantas to the **Plaza e Iglesia de San Francisco**⓯. From here, through the attractive Arco Santa Clara, a colonial archway, Cusco's public market area begins. Ahead are **Iglesia Santa Clara**⓰ and **Iglesia San Pedro**⓱.

TIMING & PRECAUTIONS

The city is compact, so you can visit most sites in a day. However, to fully enjoy Cusco, to have time inside the museums, and to adjust to the high altitude, you need at least two days. The churches close for a few hours in the middle of the day. Get a very early start, or split the walk in two. Most of the city's museums close on Sunday.

Be street smart in the Cusco area, especially in the bustling Plaza de Armas, the San Pedro market area, and, particularly in the evenings, the pedes-

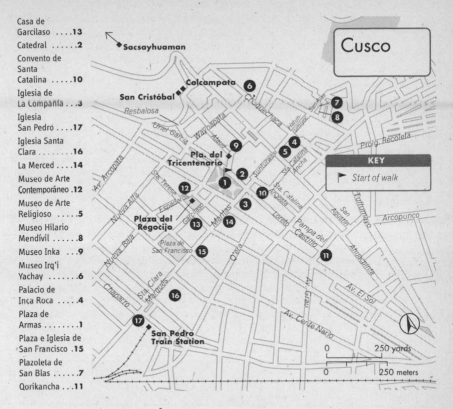

trian-only streets of San Blas. Stay alert, access your cash discreetly when you need it, and keep your valuables close. For further tips, *see* Safety *in* Smart Travel Tips A to Z.

What to See

13 **Casa de Garcilaso.** This is the colonial childhood home of Inca Garcilaso de la Vega, the famous chronicler of the Spanish conquest and illegitimate son of one of Pizarro's captains and an Inca princess. Inside the mansion, with its cobblestone courtyard, is the Museo de Historia Regional, with Cusqueña-school paintings and pre-Inca mummies—one from Nazca has a 1.5-m (5-ft) braid—and ceramics, metal objects, and other artifacts. ⊠ *Heladeros at Garcilaso* ☎ *084/223–245* 🎟 *Boleto Turístico* ⊗ *Mon.–Sat. 8–5.*

★ **2** **Catedral.** The baroque-style cathedral is built on the foundations of the palace of the Inca Wirachocha. Construction began in 1550, using many stones looted from the site of the hillside Sacsayhuamán fortress, and ended a century later. It is considered one of the most splendid Spanish colonial churches in the Americas. Within its high walls are some of the best examples of the Cusqueña school of painting, including a Marcos Zapata painting of the Last Supper with a local specialty, cuy (guinea pig), as the main dish. The cathedral's centerpieces are its massive, solid-silver altar, and the enormous 1659 María Angola bell, the largest in South America, which hangs in one of the towers. The cedar choir has carved rows of saints, popes, and bishops, all in stunning detail down to their delicately articulated hands. Five chapels flank each side of the nave; the one dedicated to Nuestro Señor de los Temblores (Our Lord of the Earthquakes) contains a solid-gold crucifix that, legend has it, minimized damage to the chapel during a 1650 earthquake. There's also non-Christian imagery here too: figures of pumas, the Inca representation of the earth, are carved on the enormous main doors. Normal access to the cathedral is not via those doors but through the adjoining Iglesia del Triunfo, the city's first Christian church. ⊠ *Haukaypata (Plaza de Armas)* ☎ *no phone* ✉ *Boleto Turístico* ⊙ *Mon.–Wed. and Fri.–Sat. 10–11:30 and daily 2–5:30.*

🔟 **Convento de Santa Catalina de Siena.** Still an active Dominican convent, Santa Catalina has a 1610 church with high and low choirs and a museum with religious art. Ironically, the site represents the change of one group of chosen women for another: the convent was built on the site of the Acllawasi, the house of some 3,000 Inca chosen women dedicated to teaching, weaving Inca ceremonial robes, and service to the sun. ⊠ *Santa Catalina Angosta s/n* ☎ *084/223–245* ✉ *Boleto Turístico* ⊙ *Mon.–Thurs. and Sat. 9–5, Fri. 9–3:30.*

③ **Iglesia de La Compañia.** The company referred to here is the Society of Jesus, the powerful Jesuit order that built this church on the foundation of the Inca Huayna Capac's palace in the late 17th century. Note the outstanding carved facade, the two Baroque towers and, inside, the Cusqueña-school paintings of the life of Jesuit patron St. Ignatius Loyola. During construction, the Archbishop of Cusco complained that the church would rival the cathedral a block away in beauty and stature. By the time the pope stepped in to rule in favor of the cathedral, it was too late; construction of the Compañia church was nearly complete. ⊠ *Haukaypata (Plaza de Armas)* ☎ *no phone* ✉ *Free* ⊙ *Masses: Mon.–Sat. 7 AM, noon, and 6 PM, Sun. 7:30, 11:30 AM, and 6 and 7 PM.*

⑰ **Iglesia San Pedro.** Stones from Inca ruins were used to construct this church. Though spartan inside, San Pedro is known for its ornately carved pulpit. The vendors you see on the front steps are a spillover from the nearby central market. Though colorful, this neighborhood shopping area is not the safest for tourists—leave important belongings in your hotel room. ⊠ *Santa Clara at Chaparro* ☎ *no phone* ✉ *Free* ⊙ *Mon.–Sat. 7–11:30 and 6–7:30.*

need a break? Half café, half cultural center, the second-floor **La Tertulia** sits just off the Plaza de Armas and is a place to curl up with a cup of coffee in front of a cozy fireplace on a chilly day. Donate the book you've just finished to the book exchange and grab another, or browse the selection of foreign newspapers, magazines, and a few travel guides, Fodor's among them. Morning means an all-you-can-eat breakfast buffet with a delicious selection of 15 varieties of crepes; lunch entails a vegetarian-friendly salad bar, a real rarity in this land of cuy and potatoes. (⊠ Procuradores 44 ☎ 084/243–062 ⊙ Daily 7–3 and 5–11)

⑯ **Iglesia Santa Clara.** This austere 1588 church, the oldest cloistered convent in Peru, was built in old Inca style, using stone looted from Inca ruins, finely hewn and tightly assembled. The inside is notable for its gold-laminated altar and thousands of mirrors. ⊠ *Santa Clara* ☎ *no phone* ✉ *Free* ⊙ *Daily 7–11:30 and 6–7:30.*

⑭ **La Merced.** Rebuilt in the 17th century, this monastery—with two stories of portals and a colonial fountain, gardens, and benches—has a spectacular series of murals that depict the life of the founder of the Mercedarian order, St. Peter of Nolasco. A small but impressive museum of the convent's treasures has, among other objects, the Custodia, a solid gold container for communion wafers encrusted with hundreds of precious stones. ⊠ *Mantas 121* ☎ *084/231–831* ✉ *S/3* ⊙ *Church: Mon.–Sat. 7–7:30 AM and 5–8 PM, Sun., 7–12 and 6:30–7:30 PM; museum: Mon.–Sat. 8–12:30 and 2–5:30.*

⑫ **Museo de Arte Contemporáneo.** Take a refreshing turn back toward the present in this city that wears its history on its sleeve. Yet even the modern-art museum, in the Cusco municipal hall, focuses on the past. Twentieth-century artists have put a modern-art spin on imperial and colonial themes. ⊠ *Kusipata s/n(Plaza Regocijo)* ☎ *084/240–006* ⬚ *Boleto Turístico* ⊗ *Mon.–Fri. 9–5:30.*

❺ **Museo de Arte Religioso del Arzobispado.** First the site of the Inca Roca's Hatun Rumiyoq palace, then the juxtaposed Moorish-style palace of the Marqués de Buenavista, the building reverted to the archdiocese of Cusco and served as the archbishop's residence. The prelate still lives in one wing of the building, which, with its elaborate gardens, doorways, and arcades is worth a look. But it now serves as the city's primary repository of religious art, mostly Cusqueña-school paintings, many by famed artist Marcos Zapata. A highlight of the collection of religious art is a series of 17th-century paintings that depict the city's Corpus Christi procession. ⊠ *Hatun Rumiyoq and Herejes* ☎ *084/ 222–781* ⬚ *Boleto Turístico* ⊗ *Mon.–Sat. 8–11:30 and 3–5:30.*

❽ **Museo Hilario Mendívil.** In the home of famous 20th-century Peruvian
Fodor'sChoice religious artist Hilario Mendívil (1929–77), this gallery displays the
★ maguey-wood and rice-plaster sculptures of the Virgin with the elongated necks that were the artist's trademark. Art has always been a family affair among this clan; Mendívil, himself the son of artists, began painting at age 10, and his wife, Georgina Dueñas, who died in 1998, also had an artistic flair. Their six children have continued the tradition since their father's death, and several budding painters and sculptors have sprung up in the fourth generation of Mendívils as well. ⊠ *Plazoleta San Blas 634* ☎ *084/226–506* ⬚ *Free* ⊗ *Mon.–Sat. 8–8.*

❾ **Museo Inka.** The draw of this archaeological museum is its collection of
Fodor'sChoice Inca mummies, but the entire facility is Cusco's best Spanish-language
★ introduction to pre-Columbian Andean culture. The ceramics, vases, and textiles provide a much-needed reminder that civilizations thrived in this region before the Inca. The building was once the palace of Admiral Francisco Aldrete Maldonado, hence its common designation as the Palacio del Almirante (Admiral's Palace). ⊠ *Ataúd at Córdoba del Tucumán* ☎ *084/237–380* ⬚ *S/5* ⊗ *Mon.–Fri. 8–5, Sat. 9–4.*

☾❻ **Museo Irq'i Yachay.** The museum's name translates as "Wisdom of the Young," and that it is. A rural-development venture, the Taller Móvil de Arte (Mobile Art Workshop), has collected children's artworks from remote Andean communities as part of an educational project to enhance young people's cultural awareness and sense of expression. ⊠ *Choquechaca and Ladrillos* ☎ *084/223–390* ⬚ *Free* ⊗ *Wed.–Sun. 11–5.*

❹ **Palacio de Inca Roca.** Inca Roca lived in the 13th or 14th century. Halfway along the palace's side wall, nestled amid other stones, is the famous 12-angled stone, an example of masterly Inca masonry. There's nothing sacred about the 12 angles, other than that today the stone is the symbol that appears on every bottle of Cusqueña beer. Inca masons were famous for incorporating stones with many more sides than 12 into their buildings. Ask one of the shopkeepers along the street to point it out. ⊠ *Hatun Rumiyoq and Palacio Herrajes.*

▶❶ **Plaza de Armas.** The imposing plaza is a direct descendant of imperial Cusco's central square, which the Inca called the Haukaypata (the only name indicated on today's street signs) and which extended beyond the area covered by the present-day square as far as the Plaza del Regocijo. According to belief, it was the exact center of the Inca empire, Tawantinsuyo, the Four Corners of the Earth. Eight *portales,* or covered arcades, now ring the plaza, one of Latin America's finest. Starting at the cathedral and going clockwise they bear religious or commercial names: Belén (Bethlehem); Carrizos (straw); la Compañía (Jesuits); Comercio (commerce); Confituría (preserves); Panes (breads); Harinas (flours); and Carnes (meats). Each Sunday morning sees a military parade on the cathedral side of the plaza that draws hundreds of spectators and, as a sign of the times in today's Peru, a few protesters.

⑮ **Plaza e Iglesia de San Francisco.** The plaza, though unimpressive, has an intriguing garden of native plants. The church has two sepulchers with arrangements of bones and skulls, some pinned to the wall to spell out morbid sayings. A small museum of religious art with paintings by Cusqueña-school artists Marcos Zapata and Diego Quispe Tito is in the church sacristy. ✉ *3 blocks south of Plaza de Armas* ☎ *084/221–361* 💳 *S/1* ⊙ *Mon.–Fri. 9–12 and 3–5.*

❼ **Plazoleta de San Blas.** The little square in San Blas has a simple adobe church with one of the jewels of colonial art in the Americas—the pulpit of San Blas, an intricately carved 17th-century cedar pulpit hewn from a single tree trunk and arguably Latin America's most ornate, dominated by the triumphant figure of Christ. ☎ *no phone* 💳 *Boleto Turístico* ⊙ *Church Mon.–Sat. 10–11:30 and 2–5:30.*

⑪ **Qorikancha.** The Temple of the Sun was built to honor Tawantinsuyos'
Fodor's Choice most important divinity and served as astronomical observatory and repository of the realm's gold treasure. (The temple's name translates as
★ "Court of Gold.") If Cusco was constructed to represent a puma, then Qorikancha was positioned as the animal's loins. Some 4,000 priests and attendants are thought to have lived within its confines. Walls and altars were plated with gold, and in the center of the complex sat a giant gold disc, positioned to reflect the sun and bathe the temple in light. At the summer solstice, sunlight reflected into a niche in the wall where only the Inca were permitted to sit. Terraces that face it were once filled with life-size gold and silver statues of plants and animals. Much of the wealth was removed to pay ransom for the captive Inca Atahualpa at the time of the conquest, blood money that was paid in vain. In the 16th century, above its looted ruins, the Spanish constructed the Dominican church of Santo Domingo using stones from the temple, perhaps Cusco's most jarring imperial-colonial architectural juxtaposition. An ingenious restoration to recover both buildings after the 1953 earthquake lets you see how the church was built on and around the walls and chambers of the temple. In the Inca structures left exposed, you can admire the mortarless masonry, earthquake-proof trapezoidal doorways, curved retaining wall, and exquisite carving that exemplify the Inca artistic and engineering skills. A small museum just down the hill with an entrance on Avenida El Sol documents the history of the site. ✉ *Pampa del Castillo at Plazoleta Santo Domingo* ☎ *no phone* 💳 *Boleto Turístico* ⊙ *Daily 9–5:30.*

San Blas. Cusco's traditional old Bohemian quarter of artists and artisans is one of the city's most picturesque districts. Recently restored, its whitewashed adobe homes with bright blue doors shine anew. The Cuesta de San Blas (San Blas Hill), one of the main entrances into the area, is sprinkled with galleries that sell paintings in the Cusqueña-school style of the 16th through 18th centuries. Many of the stone streets are built as stairs or slopes (not for cars) and have religious motifs carved into them. Avoid wandering the pedestrian-only streets here at night, but if you choose to, travel with companions.

| off the beaten path |

COLCAMPATA – For the energetic, the 15-minute walk to Colcampata offers a tour through colonial neighborhoods in the heights above the city. Following Procuradores from the Plaza de Armas to Waynapata and then Resbalosa, you'll come to a steep cobblestone staircase with a wonderful view of La Compañía. Continuing to climb, you'll find the church of San Cristóbal, which is of little intrinsic interest but affords another magnificent panorama of the city. The church stands atop Colcampata, believed to have been the palace of the first Inca ruler, Manco Capac. The Inca wall to the right of the church has 11 niches in which soldiers may once have stood guard. Farther up the road, the lane on the left leads to a post-conquest Inca gateway beside a magnificent Spanish mansion.

Where to Eat

¢–$$$ ✕ **Varayoc.** Perfect for a midday snack, this café with exposed wooden beams and whitewashed walls serves tasty pastries and huge glass mugs of freshly made *mate de coca*. It's a popular place with artsy types. Evenings transform Varayoc—the name comes from the ceremonial staff wielded by rural mayors—into the consummate Swiss restaurant. Crepes and fondues are the house specialties. ☒ *Espaderos 142* ☎ *084/232–404* ▭ *AE, MC.*

¢–$$ ✕ **Fallen Angel.** Suppress your gasps as you walk in: images of heaven, hell, earth, limbo, and purgatory, and everything in between greet you. This was one of Francisco Pizarro's houses, and it's doubtful that he envisioned anything so avant-garde. But once you've caught your breath, enjoy the menu of steaks, salads, and pastas subdued with mild spices such as rose petals or boysenberries, and top it off with white-chocolate mousse and an Italian coffee for dessert. ☒ *Plazoleta Nazarenas 221* ☎ *084/258–184* ▭ *AE, DC. MC. V* ☺ *No lunch Sunday.*

$ ✕ **Mesón de Espaderos.** You'll drink in the city's history as you dine on a rustic, second-floor terrace with stucco walls and high beamed ceilings above the Plaza de Armas. The *parrilladas* (barbecued meats) are the best in Cusco; the platter for one person is more than enough for two. But there's an ample salad bar if you're not feeling quite so carnivorous. ☒ *Espaderos 105* ☎ *084/235–307* ▭ *AE, DC, MC, V.*

$ ✕ **Paititi.** On the Plaza de Armas, this tourist-oriented restaurant that encompasses part of the original Inca wall has good fish, especially the grilled or fried trout. It's also a fine place to initiate yourself to alpaca: Paititi's specialty is this peculiarly Andean delicacy basted in a honey sauce. Additional lures are live folk-music shows nightly and a free pisco sour for all diners. ☒ *Portal de Carrizos 270, Haukaypata (Plaza de Armas)* ☎ *084/252–686* ▭ *AE, DC, MC, V.*

★ $ ✕ **Pucará.** This is the best place in Cusco to sample regional dishes, which means it's always busy. The lunch specials are ample and reasonably priced. The *ají de gallina* is outstanding but a bit heavy before an afternoon of sightseeing. On the lighter side, the fish dishes are served with a colorful assortment of vegetables. The homemade truffles are the perfect dessert. ☒ *Plateros 309* ☎ *084/222–027* ▭ *AE, MC, V.*

$ ✕ **La Retama.** A cozy fireplace, Andean tapestries, a view of the Plaza de Armas, a nightly folk music show, and vases filled with its namesake flower found in the fields around Cusco make for a charming experience. The fish dishes are delicious—try the trout in fennel cream sauce or the trout ceviche. ☒ *Portal de Panes 123, Haukaypata (Plaza de Armas)* ☎ *084/226–372* ▭ *DC, MC, V.*

$ ✕ **Tunupa.** An endless buffet with platter after platter of dessert, free pisco sours, and a nightly show to boot make this upstairs venue a popular restaurant for sampling traditional Peruvian fare. Try the carpaccio *de* *lomo* (beef marinated in herbs, olive oil and Parmesan cheese) and top it off with a rich *suspiro a la limeña*, a sweet Peruvian mousse. ⊠ *Portal de Confiturías 233, Haukaypata (Plaza de Armas)* ☎ *084/252–936* ▭ *AE, DC, MC, V.*

¢–$ ✕**Granja Heidi.** You won't offend the owner if you ask, "Are you
Fodor'sChoice Heidi?" but that's actually the name of the mule who resides on the nearby
★   farm where Gudrun and Karl Heinz get much of the produce for this
San Blas restaurant. Breakfast means crepes and farm-fresh yogurt.
Lunch and dinner yield meat and vegetarian dishes, soups and stir fries.
Try the *carapulcra* (dried potatoes served with a tangy, spicy sauce), and
save room for the Nelson Mandela cake. (The owners are great admirers.) The service is the most attentive you'll find. ⊠ *Cuesta San Blas 525*
☎ *084/238–383* ☉ *Closed Sunday.*

¢–$ ✕**Macondo.** Part art gallery, part café, and entirely hip place to hang
out, the Macondo takes its name from the land of magical realism in
Gabriel García Márquez's *One Hundred Years of Solitude*. Photos of
patrons having a good time in Cusco rest under the glass table tops,
and you'll enjoy yourself, too. Browse the magazines and paperbacks,
take in the art on display and feast on the mild alpaca or vegetable curry
dishes. ⊠ *Cuesta San Blas 571* ☎ *084/229–415* ▭ *AE, DC. MC. V*
☉ *No lunch Sunday.*

¢   ✕**Al Grano.** Don't let the Andean tapestries and replica Inca stone wall
fool you. This small restaurant off the Plaza de Armas specializes in Asian
rice plates. It offers a fantastic selection of affordable dishes from India,
Thailand, Malaysia, Sri Lanka, Vietnam, Myanmar, and Indonesia. You
have a choice of eight prix-fixe dinners every evening, each including
one of a rotating selection of entrées. The rich dessert cakes and brownies *are* Peruvian rather than Asian, however. ⊠ *Santa Catalina Ancha*
398 ☎ *084/228–032* ▭ *No credit cards* ☉ *Closed Sunday.*

¢   ✕**El Ayllu.** This café on the Plaza de Armas really comes into its own in
the morning as the consummate diner, serving hearty breakfasts accompanied by a big glass mug of *café con leche* (coffee with steamed
milk) and mouthwatering pastries, including a scrumptious apple strudel.
⊠ *Portal de Carnes 208, Haukaypata (Plaza de Armas)* ☎ *084/232–*
357 ▭ *No credit cards* ☉ *No dinner Sunday.*

¢   ✕**Bagdad Café.** There's nothing Middle Eastern here; the moniker
comes from the quirky 1988 German film of the same name. The two
main things going for this café are the location on a balcony above the
Plaza de Armas—come during non-peak hours to snag one of the six
precious outdoor tables for the best view of the plaza—and the delicious
pizzas, baked in a clay oven. Music adds to the already lively mood many
nights. ⊠ *Portal de Carnes 216, Haukaypata (Plaza de Armas)* ☎ *084/*
239–949 ▭ *MC, V.*

★ ¢   ✕**Chez Maggy.** If you find the mountain air a little chilly, warm up in
front of the open brick ovens that produce the café's great pizzas and
calzones. (There actually is Peruvian cuisine on the menu, yet everyone
comes here for the pizza.) There are two branches in Cusco within a
block of each other. The tables are smaller and more intimate at the main
location on Plateros, but you're sure to trade tales with other travelers
around the corner at Procuradores 344, as seating there is at very long
wooden tables. ⊠ *Plateros 344* ☎ *084/234–861* ▭ *AE, DC, MC, V.*

Where to Stay

$$$$ ▦**Hotel Libertador Cusco.** Close enough, but a bit removed from the hubbub of the Plaza de Armas, this hotel on the tiny Plazoleta Santo
Domingo was the last home of Francisco Pizarro, the first governor of
Peru. The glass-covered lobby is a great place to relax with a mate de

coca and soak in the antiques, fountain, and Cusqueño art that fills the lobby and courtyard. Rooms, decorated in Peruvian colonial style with views of patio gardens, all have central heating to keep out the chill. The plush bar makes a mean pisco sour. ✉ *Plazoleta Santo Domingo 259* 🕾 *084/231–961* 🖷 *084/233–152* ⊕ *www.libertador.com.pe* ⤶*254 rooms, 13 suites* ⚫ *Restaurant, café, bar, in-room data ports, in-room safes, minibars, hair salon, sauna, shops, laundry service, concierge, business services, meeting rooms; no a/c* ▭ *AE, DC, MC, V* ¶⊙¶ *BP.*

★ **$$$$** 🖾**Monasterio de Cusco.** One of Peru's loveliest hotels is in the restored 1592 monastery of San Antonio Abad, a national historic monument. Planners managed to retain the austere beauty of the complex—the lodging even counts the original chapel and its collection of Cusqueño art— and kept rooms simple and elegant with a mix of colonial and modern furnishings. At night the view of the stars from the main courtyard is truly serene. Eighty rooms can be pressurized much like an airplane cabin to duplicate conditions of those 1,000 meters (3,300 feet) lower than Cusco, the only such hotel system in the world, and an option for which you can pay a 25-percent premium. ✉ *Palacio 136* 🕾 *084/240–696, 01/221–0826 in Lima* 🖷 *084/237–111, 01/440–6197 in Lima* ⊕ *www. orient-expresshotels.com* ⤶ *127 rooms, 6 suites* ⚫ *2 restaurants, café, in-room safes, minibars, bar, shops, laundry service, dry cleaning, concierge, business services, meeting rooms; no a/c* ▭*AE, DC, MC, V* ¶⊙¶ *BP.*

$$$ 🖾**Hotel Don Carlos.** Part of a Peruvian mini-chain of hotels, the high-rise Don Carlos caters to business travelers in town from elsewhere in the country. The hotel is modern in its furnishings—all rooms are done in cream and maroon—but as with even new hotels in Cusco, rooms are arranged around a central patio, glassed-in in this case. That, and the double-paned windows, keep it comfortably warm at night. ✉ *El Sol 602* 🕾 *084/226–207* 🖷 *084/241–375* ⊕ *www.hotelesdoncarlos.com* ⤶ *50 rooms* ⚫ *Restaurant, in-room safes, minibars, hair salon, bar, shop, baby-sitting, laundry service, meeting rooms, airport shuttle, no-smoking floors; no a/c* ▭ *AE, DC, MC, V.*

$$$ 🖾**Picoaga Hotel.** The front half of this hotel consists of a colonial building with rooms arranged around an attractive arcaded courtyard, originally the 17th-century home of the Marquis of Picoaga. Behind is a modern wing with a restaurant that overlooks the Plaza de Armas. The rooms are a bit worn, but the colonial building itself is attractive. Opt for one of the older, quieter colonial rooms facing the courtyard. ✉ *Santa Teresa 344* 🕾 *084/252–330* 🖷 *084/221–246* ⊕ *www.picoagahotel. com* ⤶ *70 rooms* ⚫ *Restaurant, in-room safes, minibars, billiards, bar, laundry service, concierge; no a/c* ▭ *AE, DC, MC, V* ¶⊙¶ *BP.*

$$ 🖾**Hotel Savoy.** The Savoy, several blocks from the Plaza de Armas, has been acquired by the U.S. Howard Johnson's chain, but what other HoJo's offers you free *mate de coca* all day long? The mirrored colonial-style lobby introduces you to this hotel's conservative, yet friendly, style. Dark carved wood is everywhere: the front desk, the mailboxes, the elevators, the room doors, and the dressers and headboards inside the carpeted rooms. The rooftop Sky Room restaurant provides a panoramic view of the city. ✉ *Av. El Sol 954* 🕾 *084/224–322* 🖷 *084/221–097* ⊕ *www. cusco.net/savoyhotel* ⤶ *114 rooms, 6 suites* ⚫ *Dining room, minibars, shop, bar; no a/c* ▭ *AE, DC, MC, V* ¶⊙¶ *BP.*

$ 🖾**Hostal Tika Wasi.** On a lovely, winding street in the San Blas neighborhood, the Tika Wasi has a flower-filled garden, around which cluster modern, airy, carpeted rooms with huge windows and stupendous views. ✉ *Tanda Pata 491, San Blas* 🕾🖷 *084/231–609* ✉ *tikawasi@hotmail.com* ⤶ *20 rooms* ⚫ *Café, laundry service; no a/c, no TV in some rooms* ▭ *No credit cards* ¶⊙¶ *CP.*

$ ▥ **Hotel Incatambo Hacienda.** Here's the only lodging at the hillside Inca ruins of Sacsayhuamán, but the Incatambo maintains a discreet 200-m (650-ft) distance from the site entrance. This is the 16th-century ranch house where Francisco Pizarro once resided amid pine-forested grounds. Ample use of pine and cedar accent the stucco walls and give the place a country-style coziness, though the carpeting in the common areas is a bit worn. ⊠ *Km. 2, Carretera a Sacsayhuamán* ☎ *084/221–918* 🖷 *084/222–045* ⊕ *www.hotelesdoncarlos.com* ↩ *21 rooms, 2 suites* ⚘ *Restaurant, in-room safes, minibars, horseback riding, bar, shop, babysitting, laundry service, meeting rooms, airport shuttle, no-smoking rooms; no a/c* ⊟ *AE, DC, MC, V.*

¢ ▥ **Hostal Loreto.** You can't get much closer to the Plaza de Armas than this hostel in a colonial building around a small attractive sunlit courtyard. The tiny establishment has four rooms built against the original Inca wall. The others are nothing special, however. The friendly, eager-to-please owners live on the premises. ⊠ *Intik'ijllu 115 (Loreto)* ☎🖷 *084/ 226–352* ⊕ *www.hloreto.com* ↩ *13 rooms* ⊟ *MC, V* ⚘ *Dining room, laundry service, airport transfer; no a/c, no room TVs* ⯀ *BP.*

¢ ▥ **Hostal Los Marqueses.** Los Marqueses does business out of a 16th-century home on a quiet street, and is a cut above the standard backpackers' hostel. Rooms congregate around an arcaded courtyard and grand old staircases, and are pretty basic with beds, stucco walls, and print drapes and spreads. The breakfast room is positively Victorian with vases, pictures, and knickknacks charmingly strewn everywhere. This is one of the few businesses in town that accepts American Express traveler's checks as payment, and the owners are always open to bargaining during the off season on the already inexpensive rates. ⊠ *Garcilaso 256* ☎ *084/257–819* 🖷 *084/227–028* ↩ *22 rooms* ⚘ *Laundry service, airport shuttle; no a/c, no room phones, no room TVs* ⊟ *No credit cards* ⯀ *CP.*

¢ ▥ **Hotel Colonial Palace.** Built inside the 17th-century Convent of Santa Teresa, about a block from the Casa del Marqués de Valleumbroso, this hotel has simply furnished rooms on two floors laid out around a lovely courtyard. The staff is exceptionally friendly and eager to please. The hotel guarantees hot water from 5–10, both AM and PM. ⊠ *Quera 270* ☎ *084/232–151* 🖷 *084/232–329* ⊕ *www.colonialpalace.com* ↩ *38 rooms, 32 with bath* ⚘ *Restaurant, shop; no a/c, no TV in some rooms* ⊟ *AE, DC, MC, V* ⯀ *CP.*

¢ ▥ **Los Niños Hotel.** If you prefer lodging with a social conscience—and even if you don't—this is a great budget find; proceeds from your stay at "The Children's Hotel" provide medical and dental care, food, and recreation for 250 disadvantaged Cusqueño children who attend daycare on the premises and cheerfully greet you as you pass through the courtyard. Rooms tend toward the spartan side, with painted hardwood floors but firm, comfy mattresses and an endless supply of hot water. A few other rooms as well as four apartments with shared bath, for longer stays, are down the street on Calle Fiero. The catch? The place is immensely popular. Make reservations weeks in advance. ⊠ *Meloq 442* ☎🖷 *084/231–424* ⊕ *www.ninoshotel.com* ↩ *20 rooms, 13 with bath* ⚘ *Café, laundry service, no smoking; no room TVs, no room phones, no a/c* ⊟ *No credit cards.*

Nightlife & the Arts

The nights are chilly, the air is thin, and you need to rise early for your excursion tomorrow morning. So you'd anticipate no nightlife, right? You couldn't be more wrong. Cusco is full of bars and discos with live and recorded music, everything from U.S. rock to Andean folk. Though dance places levy a cover charge, there's usually someone out front handing out free passes to tourists—highly discriminatory, but in your favor, of course. Several restaurants also host live performances.

For a cold beer and satellite English-soccer broadcasts, try **Cross Keys** (✉ Portal Confiturías 233, Haukaypata (Plaza de Armas) ☎ 084/229–227), a pub that will make London expats homesick. Challenge the regulars to a game of darts at your own risk. **El Muki** (✉ Santa Catalina Angosta 114 ☎ 084/227–797) resembling a little cave, is popular with the younger crowd, and has the younger music to match. The second-floor, dark-wood **Paddy Flaherty's** (✉ Triunfo 124 ☎ 084/247–719) mixes pints of Guinness and old-fashioned Irish pub grub with Philly steaks, pita sandwiches, and chicken baguettes. The most polished Irish pub in town, **Rosie O'Grady's** (✉ Santa Catalina Ancha 360 ☎ 084/243–514) has the occasional Andean music show to take in while you down your pint of Guinness, and quite an extensive menu if you're hungry. The second-floor **Norton Rat's** (✉ Intik'ijllu 115 (Loreto) ☎ 084/246–204) is Cusco's answer to a U.S.-style sports bar, with billiards, burgers, darts, and a big-screen satellite TV showing sporting events from the United States.

Reputed to be Cusco's first disco, dating all the way back to 1985, **Kamikase** (✉ Kusipata 274 (Plaza Regocijo) ☎ 084/233–865) is a favorite gringo bar, though plenty of locals visit too, and has a mix of salsa, rock, and folk music for your dancing pleasure most evenings. Dance the night away at **Ukukus** (✉ Plateros 316 ☎ 084/233–445), a pub and disco that hops with a young crowd most mornings until 5 AM. **Mama Africa** (✉ Portal de Panes 109, Haukaypata (Plaza de Armas) ☎ 084/245–550), Cusco's hottest reggae and hip-hop dance venue, is also part travel agency and cyber café.

Tunupa (✉ Portal de Confiturías 233, Haukaypata (Plaza de Armas) ☎ 084/252–936) has a nightly folklore show along with fine dining. Enjoy the sounds of Andean music during dinner each evening at **La Retama** (✉ Portal de Panes 123, Haukaypata (Plaza de Armas) ☎ 084/226–372). **Paititi** (✉ Portal de Carrizos 270, Haukaypata (Plaza de Armas) ☎ 084/252–686) presents a live folklore show during dinner most nights. **Bagdad Café** (✉ Portal de Carnes 216, Haukaypata (Plaza de Armas) ☎ 084/239–949) has live music during dinner many nights of the week, but with no fixed schedule.

Shopping

Cusco is full of traditional crafts and artwork and more modern handmade goods, especially clothing made of alpaca, llama, or sheep wool. Much of what you see is factory made, despite some sellers' claims to the contrary. Several enclosed crafts markets are good bets for bargains. Vendors will approach you relentlessly on the Plaza de Armas, and if you keep your eyes open and bargain hard, you may take home something special. The municipal government operates the **Centro Artesanal Cusco** (✉ Tullumayo and El Sol ☎ no phone), containing 340 stands of artisan vendors. The **Feria Inca** (✉ Corner of San Andrés and Quera) is a small, informal affair, but bargains can be found. A nonprofit cooperative called **Antisuyo** (✉ Triunfo 387 ☎ 084/227–778) sells high-quality crafts from all over Peru. Religious art, including elaborately costumed statues of the Virgin Mary, is sold at the shop at the **Galería Mendívil** (✉ Plazoleta San Blas ☎ 084/226–506). In San Blas, the **Galería Mérida** (✉ Carmen Alto 133 ☎ 08/422–1714) sells the much-imitated ceramics of Edilberto Mérida. **Galería Latina** (✉ San Agustín 427 ☎ 084/246–588) is a reasonably priced crafts shop with many original pieces, tapestries, ceramics, and alpaca clothing among them. **Alpaca 111** (✉ Kusipata 202 (Plaza Regicijo) ☎ 084/243–233) has alpaca sweaters, and is the only authorized distributor of high-quality vicuña scarves and sweaters. In San Blas, **Hecho en Cusco** (✉ Carmen Alto 105 ☎ 084/221–948) has high-quality cotton T-shirts with simple, stylized designs of pumas, serpents, and birds, definitely a cut above the ubiquitous Cusqueña beer shirts. **Maqui Arte** (✉ Sunturwasi 118 (Triunfo) ☎ 084/246–493) has high-quality alpaca sweaters. Triunfo is lined with crafts shops as far as San Blas. One of the best, **Taller Maxi** (✉ Sunturwasi 393 (Triunfo) ☎ no phone), sells dolls in historical and local costumes. You can even have one custom made. Also on display are *retablos* (wooden boxes) that show Cusco's most popular sites and alpaca jackets decorated with local weavings.

Side Trips from Cusco

Cusco is the gateway to some of Peru's greatest historical areas and monuments, such as Sacsayhuamán, on a hill that overlooks the city, or the southeastern sector of the Urubamba River Valley. Northwest of the city, the so-called Sacred Valley, an Inca breadbasket for centuries, is still marked with the footprints of its imperial past.

Sacsayhuamán
(18) *2 km (1 mi) north of Cusco*

Fodor'sChoice ★   Dominating a hilltop north of the city are the ruins of the massive military complex of Sacsayhuamán, perhaps the most important Inca monument after Machu Picchu. The center seems to have served both religious and military ends, with zigzag walls and cross-fire parapets that allowed defenders to rain destruction on attackers from two sides. Sacsayhuamán is thought to have been a network of buildings and streets that could house up to 10,000 people at its peak. Tradition holds that the Inca designed Cusco in the image of a puma, the animal representation of the earth in the indigenous cosmos. Sacsayhuamán symbolized the animal's head, and its jagged walls, the teeth. Construction of the site began in the 1440s, during the reign of the Inca Pachacutec. Indigenous chroniclers told that 20,000 workers were needed for Sacsayhuamán's construction, cutting the astonishingly massive limestone, diorite, and andesite blocks—the largest is 361 tons—rolling them to the site, and assembling them in traditional Inca style to achieve a perfect fit without mortar. The probable translation of Sacsayhuamán, "city of stone," seems apt. The Inca Manco Capac II, installed as puppet ruler after the conquest, retook the fortress and led a mutiny against Juan Pizarro and the Spanish in 1536. Fighting raged for ten months in a valiant but unsuccessful bid by the Inca to reclaim their empire. History records that thousands of corpses from both sides littered the grounds and were devoured by condors at the end of the battle.

Today only the outer walls remain of the original fortress city, which the Spanish tore down after the rebellion and then ransacked for years as a source of construction materials for their new city down the hill, a practice that continued until the mid-20th century. Only one-fifth of the original complex is left; nonetheless, the site is impressive. Sacsayhuamán's three original towers, used for provisions, no longer stand, though the foundations of two are still visible. The so-called Inca's Throne, the Suchuna, remains, presumed used by the emperor for reviewing troops. Today those parade grounds, the Explanada, are the ending point for the June 24 Inti Raymi festival of the sun, commemorating the winter solstice and Cusco's most famous celebration.

These closest Inca ruins to Cusco make a straightforward half-day trip from the city, and provide the quintessential postcard view over Cusco's orange rooftops. If you don't have a car, the easiest way to get here is to take a taxi, but if you're feeling truly fit, the ruins are a steep 45-minute walk up from the Plaza de Armas. A large map at both entrances shows the layout of Sacsayhuamán, but once you enter, signage and explanation are minimal. Self appointed guides populate the entrances and can give you a two-hour tour for S/30. Most are competent and knowledgable, but depending on their perspective you'll get a strictly historic, strictly mystical, strictly architectural, or all-of-the-above type tour. (But all work the standard joke into their spiel that the name of the site is pronounced "sexy woman.") ☎ *no phone* ✉ *Boleto Turístico* ◷ 7–6.

Qenko

⑲ *4 km (2½ mi) north of Cusco*

Qenko, the first in a series of smaller archaeological sites beyond Sacsayhuamán, was a *huaca* (any site considered sacred) with a 19-seat amphitheater where the mummies of nobles and priests were kept and brought out on sunny days for ritualistic worship. The walls of the limestone structure contain relief carvings of animals and a centerpiece stone block representing a puma. Qenko was the site of an annual pre-planting ritual in which priests poured llama blood into the top of a ceremonial pipe, allowing it to make its way down a zigzag channel. (The name of the place translates as "zigzag.") If the blood flowed left, it boded poor fertility for the coming season. If the liquid continued the full length of the pipe, it spelled a bountiful harvest. ☎ *no phone* ✉ *Boleto Turístico* ◷ 7–6.

Puka Pukara

⑳ *10 km (6 mi) north of Cusco*

Little is known of the archaeological ruins of Puka Pukara, a pink-stone site guarding the road to the Sacred Valley. Some archaeologists believe the complex was a fort—its name means "red fort"—but others claim it served as a hunting lodge and storage place used by the Inca nobility. Current theory holds that this center, likely built during the reign of the Inca Pachacutec, served all those functions. ✉ ☎ *no phone* ✉ *Boleto Turístico* ◷ 7–6.

Tambomachay

㉑ *11 km (6½ mi) north of Cusco*

The site, whose name means "cavern lodge," is a three-tiered huaca built of elaborate stonework over a natural spring. A sophisticated system of aqueducts pumped the underground water to feed ritual showers. Interpretations differ, but the site was likely a place where water, considered a source of life, was worshiped. The huaca is almost certain to have been the scene of sacred ablutions and purifying ceremonies for Inca rulers and royal women. ☎ *no phone* ✉ *Boleto Turístico* ◷ 7–6.

Salapunco

㉒ *5 km (3 mi) northeast of Cusco*

A huaca dedicated to worship of the moon, Salapunco is a collection of small caves that held mummies of Inca priests and nobility. Inside each were altars and walls decorated with puma and snake motifs, the Inca symbols for earth and the underworld, respectively. The largest cavern saw elaborate full-moon ceremonies in Inca times. The position of the entrance allows the interior to be bathed once a month by the light of the moon. ☎ *no phone* ✉ *Free* ◷ 7–5:30.

Southeastern Urubamba Valley

The Río Urubamba runs northwest and southeast from Cusco. The northwest sector of the river basin is the romantically named "Sacred Valley of the Inca" and attracts the puma's share of visitors. But along the highway that runs southeast of Cusco to Sicuani are a number of lesser-known Inca and pre-Inca sites. You may find that you have these magnificent ruins all to yourself, as they are off the traditional tourist circuit. They are easy to visit by car during a day trip from Cusco; you'll find only very rugged lodging if you choose to linger.

TIPÓN **(23)** *26 km (15½ mi) east of Cusco*

Tipón, 23 km (14 mi) southeast of Cusco, is one of the best surviving examples of Inca land and water management. It consists of a series of terraces, hidden from the valley below, crisscrossed by aqueducts and irrigation channels that edge up a narrow pass in the mountains. A spring fed the site and continually replenished a 900-cubic-m reservoir that supplied water to crops growing on the terraces. One theory is that the Inca used Tipón as a research station to develop special agricultural products. So superb was the technology that several of the terraces are still in use today, and still supplied by the same watering system developed centuries ago. The ruins of a stone temple of undetermined function guard the system, and higher up the mountain are terraces yet to be completely excavated. Unfortunately, the rough dirt track that leads to the complex is in wretched condition. If you visit, either walk up (about two hours each way) or go in a four-wheel-drive (about 45 minutes to the site and 30 minutes back). ☎ *no phone* ☒ *Boleto Turístico* ☉ *Daily 7–6.*

PIKILLACTA **(24)** *6 km (3½ mi) east of Tipón*

About 9 km (5½ mi) down the highway from the Tipón turnoff stand the haunting ruins of Pikillacta, a vast city from the pre-Inca Wari culture, which flourished between AD 600 and 1000. Like other Andean cultures, the Wari empire—which at its height stretched from near Cajamarca to the border of the Tiahuanaco empire based around Lake Titicaca—had a genius for farming in a harsh environment and built sophisticated urban centers such as Pikillacta, the "place of the flea" in its indigenous language. The Waris' capital was at Ayacucho, but little is known about the empire. The rough ruins, once enclosed by a defensive 3-m (10-ft) wall whose remains are still visible, confirm the Inca superiority in architecture and masonry. They are spread over several acres and include many two-story buildings, which were entered via ladders to doorways on the second floor. At the thatch-roofed excavation sites, you'll see uncovered walls that show the city's stones were once covered with plaster and whitewashed. Across the road lies a beautiful lagoon, Lago de Lucre. ☒ *7 km (4 mi) south of Oropesa* ☎ *no phone* ☒ *Boleto Turístico* ☉ *7–6.*

RUMICOLCA **(25)** *3 km (2 mi) east of San Pedro de Cacha*

An enormous 12-m-tall (39-ft-tall) gate stands at Rumicolca. It served as the border checkpoint and customs post at the southern entrance to the Wari empire. The Inca enhanced the original construction of their predecessors, fortifying it with andesite stone and using the gate for the same purpose. ☎ *no phone* ☒ *Free.*

ANDAHUAYLILLAS **(26)** *80 km (48 mi) southeast of Cusco*

The main attraction of the small town of Andahuaylillas, 8 km (5 mi) southeast of Pikillacta, is a small 17th-century adobe-towered church built by the Jesuits on the central plaza over the remains of an Inca temple. The contrast between the simple exterior and the rich, expressive, colonial Baroque art inside is notable: fine examples of the Cusqueña school of art decorate the upper interior walls. Traces of gilt that once covered the church walls are still visible. The church keeps no fixed hours. Ask around town for someone to let you inside. The town's name is a corruption of *Antawaylla*, Quechua for "copper prairie." ☎ *no phone* ✉ *Free.*

TEMPLE OF RAQCHI
27
4 km (2½ mi) east of San Pedro de Cacha

Legend has it that the Temple of Raqchi was built in homage to the god Viracocha, to ask his intercession in keeping the nearby Quimsa Chata volcano in check. The ploy worked only some of the time. The site, with its 12-m-high (39-ft-high) adobe walls atop a limestone foundation, performed multiple duty as temple, fortress, barracks, and storage facility. ☎ *no phone* ✉ *S/5* ☉ *9–5:30.*

SACRED VALLEY OF THE INCA

The Sacred Valley's pleasant climate, fertile soil, and proximity to Cusco made it a favorite with the Inca nobles, many of whom are believed to have had private country homes here. Inca remains lie throughout the length of the valley, which is filled with agricultural terraces and dominated by the archaeological remains of Pisac and Ollantaytambo. The so-called Sacred Valley of the Inca, along the Río Urubamba, begins at the town of Pisac, about 30 km (18 mi) northeast of Cusco. It ends 60 km (36 mi) northwest of Pisac at Ollantaytambo, where the cliffs that flank the river grow closer together, the valley narrows, and the agriculturally rich floodplain thins to a gorge as the Urubamba begins its abrupt descent toward the Amazon basin. (Machu Picchu is farther downriver, among the cloud forests on the Andean slopes above the Amazon jungle.) Cusco is hardly the proverbial urban jungle, but the valley will captivate you with its lower elevation, fresher air, warmer temperatures, and rural charm. Every Cusco travel agency does a day tour of the Sacred Valley each Tuesday, Thursday, and Sunday, to coincide with market days in Pisac. (You can almost always sign on to one as late as early the morning of, especially if you're here in the September–May off season.) But the valley deserves more than a rushed day tour if you have the time for it. While it's not quite the frontier territory it used to be, it still doesn't have the concentration of services found in Cusco; this seems to matter little to the growing number of knowledgable travelers who are basing themselves here and making Cusco their day trip, rather than the other way around.

Pisac

28 *32 km (19 mi) north of Cusco*

The road from Cusco leads directly to the town of Pisac, a colonial town of about 4,000 people, replete with Quechua-language masses in a simple stone church, a well-known market, fortress ruins, and a small selection of hotels and restaurants that make it a good base for exploring the Sacred Valley.

Fodor'sChoice
★
Pisac's famous three-times-weekly **market** (Sunday, Tuesday, and Thursday) draws the shop-'til-you-drop crowd, local and tourist alike. Fruits, vegetables, and grains happily share the stage with ceramics, jewelry, and woolens on the central plaza and spill over into the side streets. Sellers set up shop about 8 AM on market days, and start packing up at about 3 PM. Those in the know insist that vendors, anxious to minimize the load they cart back home, offer their best bargains around closing time.

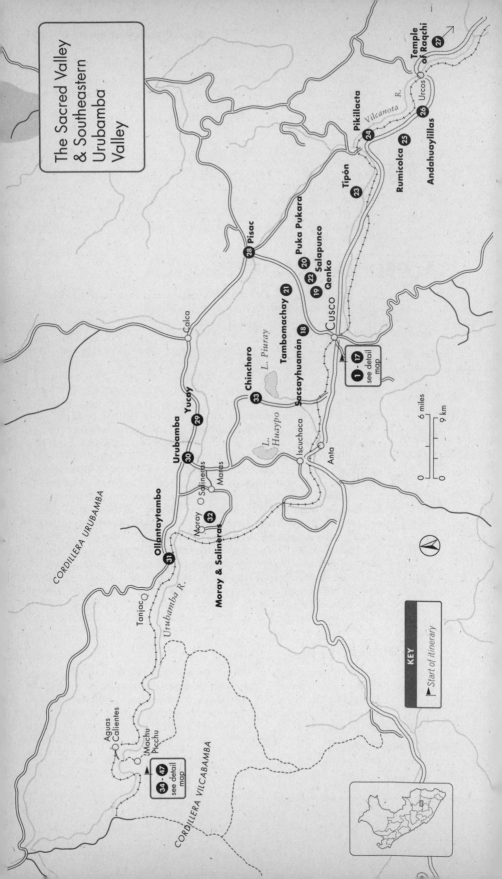

Temple of Raqchi · 27

Pikillacta · 24

Urcos · 26

Rumicolca · 25

Andahuayllilas

Vilcanota R.

Tipón · 23

Puka Pukara · 20

Salapunco · 22

Qenko · 19

Cusco

Tambomachay · 21

Sacsayhuamán · 18

Pisac · 28

Calca

L. Piuray

Chinchero · 33

L. Huaypo

Iscuchaca

Anta

1 · 17 see detail map

Yucay · 29

Urubamba · 30

Salineras

Maras

Moray · 32

Moray & Salineras

Ollantaytambo · 31

CORDILLERA URUBAMBA

Tanjac

Urubamba R.

Aguas Calientes

Machu Picchu

34 · 47 see detail map

CORDILLERA VILCABAMBA

6 miles

9 km

0

0

KEY

▲ Start of itinerary

By 5 PM even the hangers-on have filtered away from the plaza. Though the Tuesday and Thursday markets will not disappoint, go on Sunday if your schedule permits; you'll have a chance to take in the 11 AM Quechua mass at the Iglesia San Pedro Apóstolo and watch the elaborate costumed procession led by the mayor who carries his *varayoc*, a ceremonial staff, out of the church afterwards. Sunday afternoon sees bands and beer tents—this is small town Peru at its best.

From the market area, rent a horse or take a taxi up the winding but well-maintained road to the nearby Inca **ruins of Pisac**. (Visiting on market day is your best bet for finding transportation up to the ruins; the alternative is a steep two-hour walk from town.) Archaeologists think there was a fortress here to defend the empire from the fierce Antis (jungle peoples), though there is little evidence to suggest that any battles were fought here at all. The terraces and irrigation systems also support the theory that the citadel, hewn from rock, was a refuge in times of siege. The complex also contains a temple to the sun and astronomical observatory, from which priests calculated the growing season each year. The fortress is a masterpiece of Inca engineering, with narrow trails that wind tortuously between and through solid rock. You may find yourself practically alone on the series of paths in the mountains that lead you among the ruins, through caves, and past the largest known Inca cemetery (the Inca buried their dead in tombs high on the cliffs). Farther above the visitors' site are more ruins and burial grounds yet to be excavated. ☎ *no phone* ✉ *Boleto Turístico* ⊗ 7–6.

Where to Stay & Eat

¢ ✕ **Panadería.** The unnamed bakery just off the Plaza Constitución is a Pisac institution. Vegetarian empanadas and homemade breads are delivered from the clay oven fresh into your hands, but the lines are long on Tuesday, Thursday, and Sunday market days. Have patience; it's worth the wait. ✉ *Mariscal Castilla 372* ☎ *No phone* ⊟ *No credit cards* ⊗ *no dinner.*

¢ ✕ **Samana Wasi.** The Quechua name of this basic local restaurant on the central square translates as "house of rest," and the owner claims that this is Peruvian cuisine, fresh and made-to-order. It doesn't get any fresher than the trout caught in the nearby Urubamba River. These folks also dish up a spicy *cazuela de gallina* (chicken stew). If it's a nice day, grab one of the tables on the shady interior courtyard. ✉ *Plaza Constitución 509* ☎ *084/203–018* ⊟ *No credit cards.*

$ 🏨 **Hotel Royal Inka Pisac.** Just outside of town is the newest branch of Peru's Royal Inka hotel chain, and the closest lodging to the Pisac ruins. Bright, airy, carpeted rooms congregate around acres of wooded and flowered grounds, and have print spreads and drapes and white walls. All third-level rooms have a fireplace. With all the activities and facilities here, a rarity in the Sacred Valley, you really never have to leave the grounds. ✉ *Carretera a Pisac Ruinas 1.5 km* ☎ *084/203–064* ⊕ *www. royalinkahotel.com* ⊅ *76 rooms* ♨ *Restaurant, coffee shop, in-room safes, tennis, indoor pool, hair salon, hot tub, massage, sauna, bicycles, horseback riding, bar, piano bar, no smoking; no a/c* ❐ *BP.*

¢ 🏨 **Hostal Pisaq.** Here's the best budget option in town, and right on the main square. Common areas have murals crafted by the Peruvian-American owners; Andean tapestries hang in the rooms. The Continental breakfast is S/10 extra, and the Pisaq's small café dishes up pizza on market days. ✉ *Plaza Constitución 333* ☎ *084/203–062* ⊗ *hotelpisaq@terra. com.pe* ⊅ *12 rooms, 2 with bath* ♨ *Café, sauna, bicycles, laundry service; no a/c, no room phones, no room TVs* ⊟ *No credit cards.*

Yucay

㉙ *46 km (28 mi) northwest of Pisac*

Now an attractive colonial village, Yucay has the Sacred Valley's most famous lodging, the Posada del Inca, a 300-year-old monastery turned hacienda turned hotel, complete with a second-floor museum worth visiting even if you don't stay at the posada.

Where to Stay & Eat

★ $ ✕⌂ **Sonesta Posada del Inca Valle Sagrado.** In the heart of the Sacred Valley is this 300-year-old former convent (monastery). The cobblestone walkways are the perfect complement to the well-preserved colonial-era church on the grounds. A museum on the second floor of the main building has an extensive collection of pre-Inca ceramics. The rooms, with tile floors, wood ceilings, and hand-carved headboards, have balconies that overlook the gardens or the terraced hillsides. The restaurant has excellent regional fare and a popular Sunday lunch buffet. ⊠ *Plaza Manco II 123, Yucay* ☎ *084/201–107; 01/222–4777 in Lima; 800/766–3782 in North America* 🖷 *084/201–345; 01/222–3031 in Lima* ⊕ *www.sonesta.com* ⇄ *65 rooms* ⟡ *Restaurant, in-room safes, minibars, bar, shop, laundry service, business services, meeting rooms; no a/c* 🖃 *AE, MC, V.*

Urubamba

㉚ *2 km (1 mi) west of Yucay, 29 km (17 mi) northwest of Chinchero*

Urubamba is in the center of the Sacred Valley. The picturesque town is awash in flowers and pisonay trees, and has spectacular views of the nearby mountains. Spanish naturalist Antonio de León Pinedo rhapsodized that Urubamaba must have been the biblical Garden of Eden. There's little here of historic interest, per se, but the scenery, a decent selection of hotels and restaurants, and easy access to Machu Picchui rail service make the town another one of those get-out-of-the-city places in which to base yourself.

Cusco transplants and husband-and-wife team Pablo Seminario and Marilú Bejar and their German shepherds run the **Cerámica Seminario** in the center of town. They take the valley's distinctive red clay and turn it into ceramic works using modern adaptations of ancient indigenous techniques and designs. ⊠ *Berriozabal 111* ☎ *084/201–002* ⊕ *www. ceramicaseminario.com* ⊙ *Daily 8–7.*

Where to Stay & Eat

¢ ✕ **La Casa de la Abuela.** The name of this restaurant, just off Urubamba's Plaza de Armas, translates as "grandmother's house," and indeed it was the house of the proprietor's grandmother. The owners have still managed to maintain that homey feel as they stir pastas and dish up pizzas from a clay oven. ⊠ *Bolívar 272* 🖃 *No credit cards.*

$$ ⌂ **Sol y Luna Hotel.** A lovely addition to the Sacred Valley of the Inca, this hotel has bungalows surrounded by flower gardens. Nearby are the Perol Chico stables, where you can book trips through this beautiful valley on the stable's famous Peruvian *caballos de paso*. The Viento-Sur Adventure Club at the hotel also offers paragliding, biking, and walking tours. ⊠ *Fundo Huincho, 2 km west of Urubamba* 🖷🖷 *084/201– 620* ⊕ *www.hotelsolyluna.com* ⇄ *14 bungalows* ⟡ *Restaurant, pool, horseback riding, bar, laundry service, travel services; no a/c* 🖃 *AE, DC, MC, V* ⏐⏐ *BP.*

$ ⌂ **Hotel San Agustín.** The San Agustín is the quintessential two-in-one lodging. On the main road is a modern hacienda-style hotel with gleaming rooms, modern services, and all the comforts you could desire. Just up the hill is the converted Recoleta, a 16th-century Franciscan monastery with a cavernous dining room, rooms with hardwood floors, white walls, and Cusqueña paintings, and a bell tower with great views of the valley. There are fewer services at the monastery, though most guests— the Recoleta has a devoted artistic, New Age clientele—don't mind. All have access to the facilities down the hill. ⊠ *Km, 69, Carretera Pisac-Ollantaytambo* ☎ *084/201–004, 84/201–025* ⊕ *www.hotelessanagustin.com.pe* ➵ *68 rooms* ⟁ *2 restaurants, pool, hot tub, sauna, bar, meeting rooms; no a/c, no TV in some rooms* ▤ *AE, DC, MC, V* ¶◎¶ *CP.*

$ ☎ **Incaland Valle Sagrado.** Llamas and alpacas roam the Incaland's 26 wooded acres on the edge of Urubamba. Bungalows with brightly lit rooms are scattered around the grounds. All have hardwood floors, two beds, and great mountain views. The restaurant specializes in vegetarian dishes, a rarity in this part of the world, and serves freshly baked bread each morning, right out of its clay ovens. Access to the Machu Picchu trains doesn't get any better: the hotel sits right across from Urubamba's rail station. ⊠ *Av. Ferrocarril s/n* ☎ *084/201–126; 1/241–2645 in Lima* ☎ *084/201–071; 1/242–2155 in Lima* ⊕ *www.incalandperu.com* ➵ *65 rooms* ⟁ *Restaurant, minibars, tennis, 2 pools, horseback riding, bar, laundry service, business services, meeting rooms; no a/c* ▤ *AE, DC, MC, V* ¶◎¶ *BP.*

Ollantaytambo

③① *19 km (11 mi) west of Urubamba*

At the northwestern entrance to the Sacred Valley lies Ollantaytambo, perhaps the best-preserved Inca site, sitting above one of the region's loveliest towns, whose traditional air has not been stifled by the invasion of hordes of tourists. The town, pronounced "oy-yahn-tie-*tahm*-bo"—but never fear: everyone around here calls it "Ollanta" for short—was named for Ollantay, the most famous Inca general, who expanded the frontiers of Tawantinsuyo as far north as Colombia and as far south as Argentina during the reign of the Inca Pachacutec. As a reward for his military prowess, the general asked for the hand of the emperor's daughter, a request Pachacutec refused. (Accomplished though Ollantay was, he was still a commoner.) The general rebelled against the ruler and was imprisoned. Ollantay's love may have gone unrequited, but yours will not when you glimpse the stone streets and houses, superb mountain scenery, and some of the lushest territory in the valley. Ollantaytambo, whose municipal government charges a S/1 vehicular fee to enter the town, makes a superb base for exploring the Sacred Valley and has easy rail connections to Machu Picchu, without backtracking to Cusco. Ollantaytambo is also the kick-off point for the Inca Trail. You'll start here at nearby Km 82 if you wish to hike to the Lost City.

Along the Río Patacancha lies the complete Inca town of Ollantaytambo, still inhabited and with its original architecture and layout preserved. The Inca based their communities on the unit of the *cancha*, a walled city block, each with one entrance leading to an interior courtyard, surrounded by a collection of houses. The system is most obvious in the center of town around the main plaza. You'll find the most welcoming of these communities at Calle del Medio. The self-guided **Ollantaytambo Heritage Trail** allows you to tour the town, following a series of blue plaques that outline important sites.

Above the town of Ollantaytambo rises the **fortress of Ollantaytambo,** a formidable stone structure that climbs massive terraces to the top of a peak. It was the valley's main defense against the Antis from the neighboring rain forests. Construction began during the reign of Pachacutec, but for reasons unknown, was never completed. The rose-colored granite used was not mined in this part of the valley. The elaborate walled complex contained a temple to the sun, used for astronomical observation, as well as the Baños de la Ñusta (ceremonial princess baths), leading archaeologists to believe that Ollantaytambo existed for more than defense purposes. But it is most famous as the site of the greatest Inca victory over the Spanish during the wars of conquest. The Manco Inca fled here in 1537 with a contingent of troops after the disastrous loss at Sacsayhuamán and routed Spanish forces under Hernando Pizarro. The victory was short-lived: Pizarro regrouped and retook the fortress. ⊠ *Plaza Mañay Raquy* ☎ *no phone* ☒ *Boleto Turístico* ⊙ *7–6.*

The small but informative **Museo CATCO,** whose name is the Spanish abbreviation for "Andean Center for Technology and Culture of Ollantaytambo," has local history, culture, and ethnology exhibits with bilingual descriptions, one of the few such institutions around that make that concession to non-Spanish speakers. You can buy pottery at an adjoining ceramics workshop. ⊠ *Patacalle s/n* ☎ *084/204–024* ☒ *S/5* ⊙ *Tues.–Sun. 10–1 and 2–4.*

Where to Stay & Eat

★ **$$** ✕☲ **Hotel Pakaritampu.** Ollantaytambo's best lodging has a Quechua name that translates as "house of dawn." It dates only from 2000, yet is one of the coziest places around. Fireplaces, and reading rooms with Cusqueño art, invite you to settle in with a good book and a hot cup of coffee on a chilly evening. Rooms, with modern furnishings, plush blue comforters, and green-tile bathrooms, extend through two buildings. The on-grounds orchard supplies the fruit that ends up on your breakfast plate, and as accompaniment for the Peruvian cuisine served in the restaurant. ⊠ *Av. Ferrocarril s/n* ☎ *084/204–020* 🖷 *084/204–105* ⊕ *www.pakaritampu.com* ⇗ *20 rooms* ♨ *Restaurant, bar, laundry service, meeting rooms; no a/c* ☱ *AE, DC, MC, V* ⧖ *CP* ⧖ *BP.*

$ ☲ **Hotel Sauce.** The name has nothing to do with sauces used in cooking. Instead, it's a type of tree found here in the Sacred Valley. Thanks to the hotel's hillside location, half of the vaulted-ceiling rooms have a superb view of the Ollantaytambo ruins. The cozy lobby fireplace is usually stoked with a fire on brisk evenings. ⊠ *Ventideiro 248* ☎ *084/204–044* 🖷 *084/204–048* ⌨ *hotelsauce@tsi.com.pe* ⇗ *8 rooms* ♨ *Dining room, bar, laundry service; no a/c* ☱ *AE, V.*

¢ ☲ **Albergue Ollantaytambo.** Everyone in town knows the "Albergue," right at the train station, owned by exuberant longtime American resident and artist Wendy Weeks. Dark-wood rooms here are spacious but rustic, with historic black-and-white photos from the region. The lodging has homey touches that you don't find in other budget hostels, like a wood-fired sauna and a cozy sitting room. Reserve in advance: the place is popular with groups about to embark on, or just returning from, the nearby Inca Trail. ⊠ *Estación de Ferrocarril* ☎☎ *084/204–014* ⊕ *www.bed42.com/elalbergue* ⇗ *6 rooms with shared bath* ♨ *Dining room, sauna, shop; no a/c, no room phones, no room TVs* ☱ *No credit cards* ⧖ *CP.*

Moray & Salineras

③② *48 km (29 mi) northwest of Cusco.*

Scientists still marvel at the agricultural technology the Inca used at Moray, an ancestor of the modern experimental biological station. Taking advantage of four natural depressions in the ground and angles of sunlight, indigenous engineers fashioned concentric circular irrigation terraces, 150 m (500 ft) from top to bottom, and could create a difference of 15° Celsius (60° Fahrenheit) from top to bottom. The result was a series of engineered mini-climates perfect for adapting, experimenting, mixing, matching, and cultivating foods, especially varieties of maize, the staple of the Inca empire, normally impossible to grow at this stark altitude. Though the technology is attributed to the Inca, the lower portions of the complex are thought to date from the pre-Inca Wari culture. The famed terraced Inca salt pans of Salineras are still in use and also take advantage of a natural phenomenon: the Inca dug shallow pools into a sloped hillside. The pools filled with water, and upon evaporation salt crystallized and could be harvested. Neither site keeps opening hours or has an admission charge. Interesting as they are to visit, they are difficult to reach, and almost an impossibility during the rainy season. No public transportation serves Moray or Salineras. A taxi can be hired from Maras, the closest village, or from Cusco. Alternatively, you are looking at a two-hour hike from Maras to either site.

Chinchero

㉝ *28 km (17 mi) northwest of Cusco*

Indigenous lore says that Chinchero, one of the valley's major Inca cities, was the birthplace of the rainbow. Frequent sightings here during the rainy season just might convince you of the legend's truth. Chinchero is one of the few sites in the Sacred Valley that sits at a higher elevation (3,800 m or 12,500 ft) than Cusco. Tourists and locals alike frequent the small but colorful Sunday artisan market on the central plaza, an affair that gets rave reviews as being more authentic and less touristed than the larger market day in neighboring Pisac. A corresponding Chinchero produce market for locals takes place at the entrance to town.

Little remains of indigenous interest in Chinchero. After the disastrous defeat by the Spanish at Sacsayhuamán, the Inca Manco Capac passed through here in flight to the fortress at Ollantaytambo, scorching the earth in his wake, Chinchero included.

A 1607 colonial **church** is in the central plaza, built on top of the limestone remains of an Inca palace, thought to be the country estate of the Inca Tupac Yupanqui, the son of Pachacutec. ✉ *Plaza de Armas* 📷 *no phone* 🎫 *Boleto Turístico* 🕐 *7–6.*

MACHU PICCHU

㉞–㊼ *110 km (66 mi) northwest of Cusco*

Fodor's Choice
★

This mystical city, a three-hour-plus train ride from Cusco, is the most important archaeological site in South America, and one of the world's foremost travel destinations. The name itself conjures up the same magic as King Solomon's Mines or Xanadu, and Machu Picchu's beauty is so spectacular that the disappointed visitor is rare indeed. Its attraction lies in the exquisite architecture of the massive Inca stone structures and in the formidable backdrop of steep sugarloaf hills, with the winding Urubamba River—the Inca, who had a system of naming rivers by sector, called this portion of the river the Vilcanota—far below.

Ever since American explorer and Yale University historian Hiram Bingham, with the aid of local guides, "discovered" the Lost City in 1911, there have been debates about Machu Picchu's original function. Bingham himself speculated that the site was a fortress for defensive purposes, but the preponderance of religious structures here calls that theory into question. It was likely a small city of some 200 homes and 1,000 residents, with agricultural terraces to supply the population's needs and a strategic position that overlooked but could not be seen from the valley floor. Exactly when Machu Picchu was built is not known, but one theory suggests that it was a country estate of the Inca Pachacutec, which means its golden age was in the mid-15th century. Historians have discredited the romantic theory of Machu Picchu as refuge of the chosen Inca women after the conquest; analysis shows a 50/50 split of male and female remains found here.

Bingham erred in recognizing just what he had uncovered. The historian assumed he had stumbled upon Vilcabamba, the last real stronghold of the Inca, the hastily constructed fortress to which the puppet Inca Manco Capac II retreated after the battles at Sacsayhuamán and Ollantaytambo. (The actual ruins of Vilcabamba lie deep in the rain forest, forgotten and not uncovered until the 1960s. And, ironically, Bingham did stumble upon the real Vilcabamba two years before he announced his discovery, equally unaware of what he had seen.) But Machu Picchu shows no battle scars, despite Bingham's insistence that it was a citadel, or signs of having been constructed quickly the way history documents that Vilcabamba was. Bingham assigned his own English-language names to the structures within the city. Call it inertia, but those labels have stuck, even though archaeologists continue to debate the correctness of the Yale historian's nomenclature.

The site's belated discovery has led some academics to conclude that the Inca deserted Machu Picchu before the Spanish conquest. The reason for the city's presumed abandonment is as mysterious as its original function. Some archaeologists suggest that the water supply simply ran out. Some guess that disease ravaged the city. Others surmise it may have been something as basic as the death of Pachacutec, after which his estate was no longer needed. Whatever the purpose, whatever the reason, this "Lost City of the Inca" was missed by the ravaging conquistadors and survived untouched until the beginning of the 20th century, and the mystery and intrigue will certainly inspire you to devise your own theories.

Exploring Machu Picchu

Plan at least a two-day visit to Machu Picchu, staying either at the hotel near the entrance to the ruins or one below in the ruins' "metropolis," the town of Aguas Calientes, 1 km (½ mi) from the ruins. If you have only time for a day trip you'll have just a few hours at Machu Picchu, so bring a lunch with you; if you line up in the crowded cafeteria you'll have even less time, as you must leave to catch the bus back down to Aguas Calientes and the train back to Cusco. On the other hand, if you stay overnight you'll be able to wander the ruins after most tourists have gone. You'll also have time for a soak in the thermal baths in Aguas Calientes.

If you're a day-tripper, follow the crowd out of the rail station about a block away to the Consettur Machupicchu shuttle buses, which ferry you uphill to the ruins, a journey of about 20 minutes. Buy your S/32 round-trip ticket at a booth next to the line of buses before boarding. If you have the time and luxury of staying overnight, you'll first check in to your lodging and can come back later to buy a bus ticket. Buses leave Aguas Calientes for the ruins beginning at 6:30 AM and continue more or less hourly, with a big push in mid-morning as the trains begin to arrive from Cusco. The last bus up leaves about 1 PM. Buses start coming back down about 11:30 AM, with a last departure at 5:30. If you stay in Aguas Calientes overnight, you'll also have time to buy your ad-

THE AMAZON BASIN

4

mission ticket to Machu Picchu itself at the Instituto Nacional de Cultura (Av. Pachacutec s/n, open daily 6–12 and 1–5) in town just off the Plaza de Armas, thus avoiding the long high-season lines at the ticket booth at the ruins' entrance.

The illusion of being high above the valley floor makes you forget that Machu Picchu sits 2,490 meters (8,170 feet) above sea level, a much *lower* altitude than Cusco. This is semitropical highland forest. It gets warm here, and the ruins have little shade. Sunscreen, a hat, and water are musts. Officially, no food or drink are permitted within the ruins, but you can be unobtrusive with a bottle of water. Large packs must be left at the entrance. There are few signs inside to explain what you're seeing; booklets and maps are for sale at the entrance.

Within the Ruins

34 Upon entry, you first encounter the **House of the Terrace Caretaker.** Bingham surmised that Machu Picchu was divided into agricultural and urban sectors. As they did elsewhere in the empire, the Inca carved agricultural terraces into the hillsides here to grow produce and minimize erosion. Corn was the likely crop cultivated at Machu Picchu, though contemporary archaeologists wonder if the capacity and area of these terraces really could have supported a community of 1,000 residents. Absent are the elaborate irrigation systems seen at Inca ruins in the drier Sacred Valley. Machu Picchu's semitropical climate meant ample rain for most of the year.

35 About a 20-minute walk up to the left of the entrance, the **Caretaker's Hut** and **Funeral Rock** provide the quintessential vista overlooking Machu Picchu, one that you've seen in dozens of photos, and yet nothing beats seeing the view in person, especially if your schedule permits an early morning visit to catch the misty sunrise. Bodies of nobles likely lay in state at the site, where they would have been eviscerated, dried, and prepared for mummification.

36 Head back down the hill to the city itself; the **Dry Moat** separates the agricultural and urban sectors. After you enter the ruins through the terraces at the agricultural sector, you come to a series of 16 small, ritual **37** **Fountains** linked to the Inca worship of water.

38 Beyond the fountains is the round **Temple of the Sun,** a marvel of perfect Inca stone assembly. Here, on June 22 (the date of the winter solstice in the southern hemisphere), sunlight shines through a small, trapezoid-shape window and casts light into the middle of a large, flat granite stone presumed to be an Inca calendar. Prediction worked from both directions too: looking out the window, astronomers sought the perfect view of the constellation Pleiades, revered as a symbol of crop fertility. Bingham dubbed the small cave below the temple the **Royal Tomb,** though no human remains were ever found here.

39 Adjoining the temple is a two-story building Bingham called the **Palace of the Princess.** Archaeologists have doubted the accuracy of the name.
40 Up a staircase, beyond the fountains and the temple, is a **rock quarry** used **41** by Inca masons. A stone staircase leads to the three-walled **Temple of the Three Windows**—the entire east wall is hewn from a single massive rock with trapezoidal windows cut into it. Further investigation has shown that there were really five original windows.

42 Another three-walled structure, the **Principal Temple** is so dubbed because its masonry is among Machu Picchu's best, a masterpiece of fitting together many-sided stones without mortar in true Inca fashion. A secondary **43** temple abuts the primary temple. Bingham called it the **Sacristy.** It was likely the place where priests prepared themselves for ceremonies.

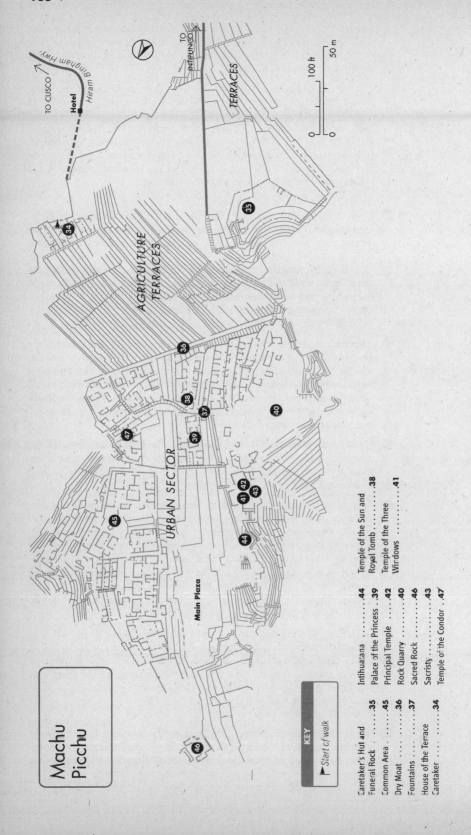

Machu Picchu

TO CUSCO ↗
Hiram Bingham Hwy.
Hotel

TO INTIPUNCO

TERRACES

34

35

AGRICULTURE TERRACES

36

47

38

37

39

40

URBAN SECTOR

45

41
42
43

44

Main Plaza

46

100 ft
0

50 m
0

44 Onward is a hillock that leads to the famous **Intihuatana,** the so-called "Hitching Post of the Sun." Every important Inca center had one of these vertical stone columns (called gnomons), but their function remains a mystery. They likely did double duty as altar and time measurement device to divine the growing seasons. The Spanish destroyed most of the hitching posts they encountered throughout the empire, deeming them to be objects of pagan worship. Machu Picchu's is one of the few to survive—partially survive at least. Shamefully, its top was accidentally knocked off in 2001 during the filming of a Cusqueña beer commercial on the site.

45 Cross a large grassy plaza toward an area of other buildings and huts.
46 Their less elaborate construction led Bingham to dub this the **Common Area.** Here you'll find the **Sacred Rock,** taking the shape in miniature of the mountain range visible behind it. Little is known of its purpose.

47 A staircase leads to the **Temple of the Condor,** so named because the positioning of the stones resembles a giant condor, the symbol of heaven in the Inca cosmos. The structure's many small chambers led Bingham to dub it a "prison," a concept that did not likely exist in Inca society. 📞 *no phone* 💲 *S/72; S/36 with International Student Identity Card* 🕐 *Daily 7–6.*

Beyond the Ruins

Several trails lead from the site to surrounding ruins. A 45-minute walk southeast of the main complex is **Intipunku,** the Sun Gate, a small ruin in a pass through which you can see the sun rise at different times of the year. It is also the gateway to the **Inca Trail.** A two- or three-hour hike beyond the Intipunku along the Inca Trail will bring you to the ruins of **Huiñay Huayna,** a complex that climbs a steep mountain slope and includes an interesting set of ritual baths.

Fodor'sChoice
★

From the cemetery at Machu Picchu, a 30-minute walk along a narrow path leads to yet another example of Inca ingenuity and engineering skills: the **Inca Bridge,** built rock by rock up a hair-raising stone escarpment.

The **Huayna Picchu** trail, which follows an ancient Inca path, leads up the sugarloaf hill in front of Machu Picchu for an exhilarating, if challenging, trek. Climbers must register at the entrance to the path behind La Roca Sagrada (the Sacred Rock), where locals often pray.

At the top and scattered along the way are Inca ruins and the **Temple of the Moon.** The walk up and back takes at least two hours—more if you stay on the summit to enjoy the sun and drink in the marvelous view of Machu Picchu—and is only for the sure-footed. Bring insect repellent; the gnats can be ferocious.

Far below the ruins sits the slightly ramshackle, but thoroughly pleasant town of **Aguas Calientes,** sometimes called Machu Picchu Pueblo. But for the grace of Hiram Bingham, Aguas Calientes would be just another remote, forgotten crossroads. But 1911, and the tourist boom decades later forever changed the community. There are but two major streets—Avenida Pachacutec leads uphill from the Plaza de Armas, and Avenida Imperio de Los Incas isn't a street at all, but the railroad tracks; there's no vehicular traffic on the former except the buses that ferry tourists to the ruins. You'll have little sense of Aguas Calientes if you do the standard day trip from Cusco: train station, bus, ruins, bus, train station. But the town pulses to a very lively tourist beat with hotels, restaurants, Internet cafés, hot springs, and a surprising amount of activity even after the last afternoon train has returned to Cusco.

Aguas Calientes takes its name from the thermal springs, the **Aguas Termales,** that sit above town. Don't expect facilities and conditions to rival those at Baden Baden, but if you aren't too fussy, this can be a refreshing dip at the end of a hot day. ⊠ *Top of Av. Pachacutec* ☎ *no phone* 💺 *S/5* ⊙ *Daily 5 AM–9 PM.*

Whoro to Stay & Eat

Pizza has taken Aguas Calientes by storm, though the town's ubiquitous pizzerias *do* offer other items on their menus. The pies are slid in and out of traditional Peruvian wood-burning clay ovens. The end product is a moist, cheesy baked pie with your favorite toppings.

¢–$ ✕**Indio Feliz.** An engaging French-Peruvian couple manage the best restaurant in Aguas Calientes, and this pink bistro is possibly the only restaurant in town *not* to have pizza on its menu. Quiche lorraine, ginger chicken, and spicy *trucha macho* (trout in hot pepper and wine sauce) are favorites here, and are usually available as part of the more reasonably priced prix-fixe menu. Top it off with a fine coffee and apple pie or flan for dessert. ⊠ *Lloque Yupanqui 4* ☎ *084/211–090* ⊟ *AE, MC, V* ⊙ *No dinner Sunday.*

¢–$ ✕**Pueblo Viejo.** Lively conversation fills this restaurant a quarter block off the Plaza de Armas as everyone gathers around the grill where cuts of beef are prepared Argentine parrillada style. Off to the side is the requisite clay oven where pizzas are baked. ⊠ *Pachacutec s/n* ☎ *084/211–193* ⊟ *AE, DC, MC, V* ⊙ *No lunch Sunday.*

¢–$ ✕**Toto's House.** Long tables are set up in the center of the restaurant to accommodate the tour groups who flock here for the huge buffet lunch, and Toto's does it up big. Grab one of the smaller tables with a river view by the window or out on the front patio if you come on your own. Evenings are more sedate, with such dishes as ceviche and *chicharrón* (pork rinds and cabbage), all to the accompaniment of a folklore music show. ⊠ *Av. Imperio de los Incas Aguas Calientes* ☎ *084/211–020* ⊟ *AE, DC, MC, V.*

¢ ✕**Chez Maggy.** A branch of the well-known Maggy's in Cusco is the best of the ubiquitous pizzerias in Aguas Calientes, and this branch even delivers its fare fresh out of the requisite clay oven for no extra charge. ⊠ *Pachacutec 156 Aguas Calientes* ☎ *084/211–006* ⊟ *AE, MC, V.*

$$$$ ✕🏨**Machu Picchu Pueblo Hotel.** This stunningly beautiful ecolodge is
FodorsChoice in a high tropical cloud forest just off the twisting road leading up to
★ the ruins. The stone bungalows, none with the same design, have a rustic elegance, with exposed beams and cathedral ceilings. Activities include a one-day Inca Trail trek, bird-watching excursions, and orchid tours. Dining in the restaurant overlooking the surrounding hills is first-rate—try the delicious *crema de choclo* (corn chowder). ⊠ *Av. Imperio de los Incas s/n Aguas Calientes* ☎ *084/211–032, 01/610–0404 in Lima* 🖷 *084/211–124, 01/422–4701 in Lima* ⊕ *www. inkaterra.com* 🛏 *76 rooms, 9 suites* ⚘ *2 restaurants, dining room, pool, spa, bar, shop, laundry service, travel services; no a/c* ⊟ *AE, DC, MC, V* ⦿⦿ *BP.*

$$$$ ✕🏨**Machu Picchu Sanctuary Lodge.** If you can get a reservation, this hotel at the entrance to Machu Picchu puts you closest to the ruins, a position for which you admittedly pay dearly. Not only will you have the thrill of watching the sun rise over the crumbling stone walls, but you'll have the ruins to yourself after most of the tourists depart each afternoon. The lodge has been completely renovated by Orient Express, which has taken over the property. The restaurant has an excellent international menu that makes it worth a special trip. ⊠ *Machu Picchu*

THE INCA TRAIL

THE INCA TRAIL, *a 50-km (31-mi) section of the stone path that once extended from Cusco to Machu Picchu, is one of the most popular hikes in South America. Nothing matches the sensation of walking over the ridge that leads to the Lost City of the Inca just as the sun is casting a yellow glow over the ancient stone buildings. U.S. historian Hiram Bingham announced his discovery of the Inca Trail in 1915. As with Machu Picchu itself, his discovery was a little disingenuous. Locals knew about the trail, and parts of it were used during the colonial and early republican eras. In fact, the Spanish used some of the roads constructed by the Inca when they were conquering the indigenous peoples. The trail begins outside the Sacred Valley town of Ollantaytambo at a place called Km 88. It takes you past ruins and through stunning scenery that starts in the thin air of the highlands and ends in cloud forests. The best months to make the four-day trek are May through September; rainy weather is more likely in April and October and a certainty the rest of the year.*

You must use a licensed tour operator, one accredited by the Unidad de Gestión Santuario Histórico de Machu Picchu, the organization that oversees the trail, and which limits the number of hikers to 500 per day. (There are some 30 such licensed operators in Cusco.) Regulations require each agency to submit its group list to the Unidad five days in advance of departure. In practice this requirement is sometimes reduced to two days, especially in the low season, but advance reservations are essential any time of year. Groups may not exceed 16 people; for more than 9 a second guide is required. The trail closes for cleaning and maintenance at least one week each February, the lowest of the low season. If you've never been backpacking, try to get some practice before you set out. You must be in decent shape, even if your agency supplies porters to carry your pack—current regulations limit your load to 20 kg (44 lb)—as the trail is often narrow and hair-raising. As the mountains sometimes rise to over 4,200 m (13,775 ft), you should be aware of the dangers of altitude sickness.

Your gear should include sturdy hiking boots, a sleeping bag, clothing for cold, rainy weather, a hat, and a towel. Also bring plenty of sunblock and mosquito repellent. Toilet paper is another essential on this rustic trail with few comfort stations. Avoid cutting flowers and vegetation. There are seven well-spaced, designated campsites along the trail.

You'll cross several rivers and lakes as you ascend the trail using suspension bridges, log bridges, or causeways constructed by the Inca. You'll also encounter fantastic ruins almost immediately. The first is Llactapata, not far from the start of the trail. The best might be Phuyupatamarca, a beautifully restored site where you'll find ceremonial baths. The grand finale, of course, is Machu Picchu, the reason the trail was constructed in the first place. Your choice of operator will result in a "you get what you pay for" experience. Check closely what you get for the price. Several agencies, usually catering to a student clientele, offer trips for under S/700, and if you're up to carrying your own equipment and eating more basic rations they are fine options. Higher fees—and they range up to S/1,400—get you porters, more luxurious tents, and meals, and likely include rail transportation between Cusco and Ollantaytambo. All operators offer a 4-day/3-night package for the entire trail, as well as an abbreviated 2-day/1-night version beginning at Km 104.

▣ **Operators Instinct** ✉ *Procuradores 50 Cusco* ☎ *084/233–451* ⊕ *www. instinct-travel.com.* **Mayuc** ✉ *Portal de Confiturías 211, Haukaypata (Plaza de Armas) Cusco* ☎ *084/232–666* ⊕ *www.mayuc.com.* **SAS Travel** ✉ *Portal de Panes 143, Haukaypata (Plaza d e Armas) Cusco* ☎ *084/237–292* ⊕ *www.sastravelperu.com.*

— By Joan Gonzalez and Jeffrey Van Fleet

☎ *084/211–038; 084/241–777* 🖷 *084/211–053; 084/237–111* ⊕ *www. orient-expresshotels.com* ⟿ *29 rooms, 2 suites* ⚭ *Restaurant, snack bar, minibars, massage, bar, laundry service; no a/c* ⊟ *AE, DC, MC, V* ⊠ *FAP.*

$ ⊞ **Hostal Presidente.** Orange, open and airy, the Presidente is one of the best moderately priced hotels in Aguas Calientes. Carpeted rooms have modern furnishings, and about half overlook the Río Vilcanota. ⊠ *Av. Imperio de los Incas s/n Aguas Calientes* ☎ *084/211–034* 🖷 *084/229– 591* ⊕ *www.presidente.com.pe* ⟿ *23 rooms* ⚭ *Dining room, laundry service; no a/c, no room TVs* ⊟ *DC, MC, V* ⊠ *BP.*

¢ ⊞ **Gringo Bill's Hostal.** Bill has hosted Machu Picchu travelers for almost a quarter century, and his was one of the first lodgings in town. Rooms are bright and airy in this rambling house with stone walls chock full of plants just off the Plaza de Armas. The corner rooms with balconies and windows get the best ventilation and have the greatest views. The small restaurant downstairs will even prepare a box lunch for your day's excursion. ⊠ *Colla Raymi 104 Aguas Calientes* 🖀🖷 *084/ 211–046* ⊕ *www.machupicchugringobills.com* ⟿ *18 rooms* ⚭ *Restaurant, massage, billiards, bar, laundry service; no a/c, no room phones, no room TVs* ⊟ *AE, MC, V* ⊠ *CP.*

¢ ⊞ **Hostal Continental.** This old budget standby is the best of the rock-bottom lodgings in Aguas Calientes, and a cut above the standard backpacker digs—and the place was completely refurbished and expanded in 2003 to boot. Rooms are small and basic, but so are the prices. All have white walls, two beds, a table and chair, and an abundant supply of hot water. ⊠ *Av. Imperio de los Incas 165 Aguas Calientes* ☎ *084/ 211–078* ⟿ *12 rooms* ⚭ *Laundry service; no a/c, no room phones, no room TVs* ⊟ *DC, MC, V* ⊠ *CP.*

CUSCO, MACHU PICCHU & THE SACRED VALLEY A TO Z

To research prices, get advice from other travelers, and book travel arrangements, visit www.fodors.com.

AIR TRAVEL

Aero Continente and its subsidiary Aviandina fly to Lima, Arequipa, and Puerto Maldonado. LanPeru connects Cusco with Lima, Arequipa, Juilaca, and Puerto Maldonado. TANS Perú flies to Lima and Puerto Maldonado. TACA Peru flies to Lima.

🛂 **Carriers Aero Continente/Aviandina** ⊠ Portal de Carnes 254, Haukaypata (Plaza de Armas) Cusco 🖀 084/243-031. **LanPeru** ⊠ Av. El Sol 627 Cusco 🖀 084/255-552. **Taca Peru** ⊠ Av. El Sol 602 Cusco 🖀 084/249-921. **TANS Perú** ⊠ San Agustín 315 Cusco 🖀 084/242-727.

AIRPORTS

Cusco's Aeropuerto Internacional Teniente Alejandro Velasco Astete (CUZ), about 15 minutes from the center of town, receives international flights only from Bolivia. You'll likely arrive from elsewhere in Peru.

🛂 Airport Information **Aeropuerto Internacional Teniente Alejandro Velasco Astete** ⊠ Av. Velasco Astete s/n 🖀 084/222-622.

BUS TRAVEL

The bus trip from Lima to Cusco is recommended only for the adventurous. The same goes for the road trip from Pisco through Ayacucho, which runs right through the adobe Colorado ruins. The bus terminal in Cusco is at the Terminal Terrestre on Pachacútec, not far from the airport. To book a comfortable bus trip from Cusco, ask for Ormeño's Royal Class service, which includes comfortable seats, air-conditioning,

toilets, and snacks. Another dependable bus service is Cruz del Sur, which travels to Arequipa from Cusco.

🚌 Bus Information **Cruz del Sur** ✉ Pachacutec 510 Cusco ☎ 084/221-909. **Ormeño** ✉ San Juan de Dios 657 Cusco ☎ 084/218-885.

CAR RENTAL

If you want to explore the Sacred Valley by car, which is advised, Cusco is the only place to rent a vehicle. However, you won't need or want to drive in the city itself; heavy traffic, lack of parking, and narrow streets, many of them pedestrian only, make a car an unnecessary burden. Avis has a branch here, as do local firms Explores Transportes and OSDI Rent-a-Car.

🚗 Agencies **Avis** ✉ Aeropuerto Velasco Astete ☎ 084/248-800 **Explores Transportes** ✉ Plateros 356 ☎ 084/261-640 **OSDI Rent-a-Car** ✉ Urb. Mateo Pumacahua B-10 ☎ 084/251-616

CAR TRAVEL

Although it's possible to drive from Lima to Cusco, or beyond Cusco to Puerto Maldonado or Puno, poor road conditions make it highly inadvisable. To visit remote sights in the Sacred Valley of the Inca, however, you must travel by car. Or, for about $50 a day, you can hire a taxi.

EMBASSIES & CONSULATES

The United Kingdom maintains an honorary consulate in Cusco, open Mon.–Fri. 9–1 and 3–6.

🏛 Consulate **United Kingdom** ✉ Pardo 895 ☎ 084/239-974.

EMERGENCIES

Most hotels have oxygen available for anyone having trouble with the altitude. The main hospital in Cusco is the Hospital Regional. Cusco's Tourist Police are part of the Policia Nacional and are specially trained to deal with visitor concerns.

🚨 Emergencies **Tourist Police** ✉ Monumento a Pachacutec, Av. Saphi s/n Cusco ☎ 084/249-654.

Policia Nacional ☎ 084/252-222 **Aguas Calientes** ☎ 084/211-178 **Ollantaytambo** ☎ 084/204-086 **Urubamba** ☎ 084/201-092🏥 Hospital **Hospital Regional** ✉ Av. de la Cultura s/n ☎ 084/227-661.

ENGLISH-LANGUAGE MEDIA

Bookshop, Cusco's bookstore with two branches and a utilitarian name, keeps a great selection of reading material in English, and other languages, too.

📚 English Speaking Bookstores **Bookshop** ✉ Maruri 276 ☎ 084/241-911; ✉ Plazoleta Santo Domingo 250 ☎ 084/248-350.

HEALTH

You might manage just fine, but altitude effects, locally known as *soroche,* are the health concern you'll likely encounter at Cusco's 3,500-m (11,500-ft) elevation. Avoid playing the crazed tourist and take things slowly your first couple of days here. Get an ample intake of fluids, but eliminate or minimize alcohol and caffeine consumption. (Both can cause dehydration, already a problem at high altitudes.) Locals swear by mate de coca, an herbal tea brewed from coca leaves that helps with altitude acclimatization. Most large hotels have an oxygen supply for their guests' use. The prescription drug acetazolamide can help offset the alkalosis caused by low oxygen at high elevations. Check with your physician about this, and also about the advisability of travel here if you have a heart condition or high blood pressure, or are pregnant. Tap water is generally not

safe to drink here. Stick with the bottled variety, *con gas* (carbonated) or *sin gas* (plain). The San Antonio brand is for sale everywhere.

LANGUAGE

Those connected with the tourist industry likely speak English, almost a guarantee in Cusco, but less so in smaller towns. The unfamiliar-sounding language you'll hear is the indigenous Quechua, which has semi-official status in Peru. Don't forget that many of the people you encounter here also speak Spanish as their second language. The Quechua-to-Spanish-to-English transformation of place names means that spelling variations abound in this part of Peru. *C* becomes *K* or changes to *Q*, *S* varies with *Z*, and *hua* interchanges with *wa*, depending on who painted the sign or printed the brochure. Cusco, the region's hub, is frequently spelled *Cuzco*, and a former municipal government really stirred the alphabet soup when it officially adopted *Qosqo*, the ancient Quechua name for the city, a change the present government rescinded.

LODGING

The Association of Family Lodgings has a listing of 192 rooms in 32 private homes in Cusco and the Sacred Valley that are near archaeological sites, historical monuments, natural attractions, and Quechua settlements. There are three categories: *inti*, which has a private bathroom; *quilla*, which shares a bathroom with another room; and *chaska*, which shares a bathroom with the family. Breakfast is included, and lunch and dinner are also available. For prices and reservations, contact Ampeeh-Cusco.
🚩 **Ampeeh-Cusco** ✉ Calle San Agustín 415 ☏☏ 084/229-227.

MAIL & SHIPPING

Post mail from Cusco, where SERPOST, the national post office, is open Monday through Saturday 7:30 AM–8 PM and Sunday 8–2. Many tourist-oriented shops in the Sacred Valley and Aguas Calientes near Machu Picchu do sell stamps and have a SERPOST mailbox to drop off your cards and letters. For important packages, DHL has an office in Cusco. Scharff International is the local representative for FedEx. You can't go wrong with Cusco's Internet cafés. They are everywhere in the Old City—all display an @ sign—connection times are fast, hours are late, and the price is dirt-cheap at S/2.50 per hour. Intinet and Telser are two of the many good bets. Public Internet access is not as widespread in the Sacred Valley as it is in Cusco. The Museo CATCO in Ollantaytambo has computers for public use. The number of Internet cafés is growing in Aguas Calientes, the fastest of which is Inkanet, along the railroad tracks. Expect to pay about S/6 per hour.
🚩 **Post Office SERPOST** ✉ Av. El Sol 800 ☏ 084/225-232.
🚩 **Shipping Services DHL** ✉ Av. El Sol 627 ☏ 084/244-167. **Scharff International/ FedEx** ✉ Pardo 978 ☏ 084/226-162.
🚩 **Internet Cafés Inkanet** ✉ Av. Imperio de los Incas s/n Aguas Calientes ☏ 084/ 211-077 **Intinet** ✉ Choquechaca 115 ☏ 084/245-157 **Telser** ✉ Calle del Medio 117 ☏ 084/242-424

Museo CATCO ✉ Patacalle s/n Ollantaytambo ☏ 084/204-024

MONEY MATTERS

Take care of money exchange, traveler's checks, and ATM transactions in Cusco. A few hotels and shops outside the city do change dollars for soles, but at a less favorable rate than you can get at a Cusco bank.

Most banks will exchange U.S. dollars, the only real useful foreign currency here. Traveler's checks are becoming easier to change for soles in Cusco, but virtually no business accepts them as payment. Try the

downtown branches of Banco de Crédito and Banco Wiese Sudameris. (The lines only look horrendous, they move quickly.) Casas de cambio bear a yellow MONEY EXCHANGE—TRAVELERS CHEQUE sign and populate the side of the Plaza de Armas opposite the cathedral and the first block of Avenida El Sol between Mantas and Almargo. Casas are open well into the evening, and rates are similar to those of banks, but they charge a two-percent commission. American Express and Diners Club both have offices in Cusco. An ATM in the luggage-claim area of Cusco's Velasco Astete airport gives cash against Plus, Cirrus, and American Express cards, as do those at Banco de Crédito offices.

🏦 **Banks American Express** ✉ Portal de Harinas 177, Haukaypata (Plaza de Armas), ☎ 084/ 235–241. **Banco de Crédito** ✉ Av. El Sol 189, ☎ 084/235–255. **Banco Wiese Sudameris** ✉ Maruri 315, ☎ 084/264–297. **Diners Club** ✉ Av. El Sol 615, ☎ 084/234–051.

SAFETY

As elsewhere in Peru, security has improved dramatically in this region in recent years, but the standard travel precautions apply. The potential for pickpocketing and robbery is greatest in situations where confusion reigns: use extra vigilance in crowded markets or when embarking and disembarking from buses and trains. Picturesque though Cusco's San Pedro market is, tales of tourist robbery there are legion.

TAXIS

Cusco's licensed taxis bear a black-and-gold checkered rectangle on each side. Fares are a standard S/2 within the central city and S/3 after 10 PM. "You should choose your taxi, rather than the driver choosing you," counsels one longtime hotel owner. Have your hotel or restaurant call a taxi for you if you are out late at night.

TELEPHONES

The area shares Peru's 084 area code. To call from abroad, drop the zero from the area code. To call within the region, dial only the six-digit number. Telefónica del Perú, the national telephone company, has an office in Cusco from which you can make international calls. Telefónica's Hola Perú phone cards can be used to place national or international calls from most telephones.

Telefónica del Perú (✉ Av. El Sol 382 ☎ 084/221–231)

TOURS

There are many excellent tour operators and travel agents in Cusco, some also with offices in Lima that can help you with accommodations, transportation, and tours around Cusco. Several companies specialize in adventure tours, including Enigma, Explorandes, Mayuc, Peruvian Andean Treks, SAS Travel, and X-treme Tourbulencia. Globos de los Andes floats you above the Sacred Valley with accompanied hot-air balloon tours. Tranvía de Cusco offers a twist on the guided city tour using an old wooden streetcar, now motorized, departing several times daily from the Plaza de Armas.

🏦 **Tour Operators Enigma** ✉ Garcilaso 132 ☎ 084/222–155. **Explorandes** ✉ Garcilaso 316-A ☎ 084/620–717, 01/992–5060 in Lima ⊕ www.explorandes.com. **Globos de los Andes** ✉ Q'apchik'ijllu 271 (Arequipa) ☎ 084/232–352 ⊕ www.globosperu.com. **Instinct** ✉ Procuradores 50 ☎ 084/233–451 ⊕ www.instinct-travel.com. **Mayuc** ✉ Portal de Confiturías 211, Haukaypata (Plaza de Armas) ☎ 084/232–666 ⊕ www.mayuc. com. **Peruvian Andean Treks** ✉ Pardo 705 ☎ 084/225–701. **SAS Travel** ✉ Portal de Panes 143, Haukaypata (Plaza de Armas) ☎ 084/237–292 ⊕ www.sastravelperu.com. **Tranvía de Cusco** ✉ Parque Industrial G-1 ☎ 084/224–377. **X-treme Tourbulencia** ✉ Plateros 358 ☎ 084/245–527 ⊕ www.x-treme_tourbulenicaperu.com.

TRAIN TRAVEL

The privatized Peru Rail's *Andean Explorer* departs from Cusco Monday, Wednesday, and Saturday at 8 AM for Puno, with a stop in Juliaca. The scenic journey takes 10 hours. The train arrives and departs from the Wanchaq Station on Pachacutec. The return trip from Puno also leaves at 8 AM on Monday, Wednesday, and Saturday.

Three Peru Rail trains depart from Cusco's San Pedro station daily for Aguas Calientes. The Vistadome leaves at 6 AM and arrives in Aguas Calientes at 9:15. It returns from Aguas Calientes at 3 PM, arriving in Cusco at 6:50. The fare is S/300. Snacks and beverages are included in the price, and the cars have sky domes to enhance your view of the scenery.

The Backpacker train leaves Cusco at 6:15 AM, arriving in Aguas Calientes at 10:10. It leaves Aguas Calientes at 3:25 PM, getting back to Cusco at 7:45. A second Backpacker train departs from Cusco at 6:35 AM and gets to Aguas Calientes at 10:35. The return from Aguas Calientes is at 3:50 PM, with arrival in Cusco at 8:10. The fare is S/205. Attendants sell snacks and beverages in Backpacker Class. Conditions are comparable to second-class trains in Western Europe and are quite comfortable.

All trains make an exaggerated series of zigzag switchbacks, climbing elevation as they leave from Cusco before descending into the lower-altitude Sacred Valley. Trains stop at Poroy, Ollantaytambo, and Km 88, the start of the Inca Trail. Arrival is in Aguas Calientes, where you disembark to catch the buses up to the ruins.

The return trip actually takes longer, but you can make up that time by disembarking in Poroy, about 15 minutes by highway from Cusco, where an Asociación de Agencias de Turismo de Cusco bus meets every Cusco-bound train. The fare is a time-saving S/5, and the bus deposits you on Cusco's Plaza de Armas.

Trains depart from Cusco's San Pedro station, where tickets can be purchased before morning departures. Your best bet is to purchase tickets in advance—that's a necessity during the June–August high season—from the Peru Rail sales office at Cusco's Wanchaq Station, daily from 8–6—note that Peru Rail does not accept credit cards—or from a travel agency. There may be fewer trains per day to choose from during the December–March low season.

If you're using the Sacred Valley as your base, the Sacred Valley Railway, a Peru Rail subsidiary, operates a Vistadome train departing from Urubamba at 6 AM, and Ollantaytambo at 7, with arrival in Machu Picchu at 8:10. The return train leaves Machu Picchu at 5 PM, with arrival in Ollantaytambo at 6:20 and Urubamba at 7:10. Round-trip fare is S/190. Shuttle buses connect the Urubamba station to a few hotels in the valley.

Tourists are not permitted to ride the Tren Local, the less expensive, but slower train intended for local residents only.

🚆 Train Information **Asociación de Agencias de Turismo de Cusco** ✉ Nueva Baja 424 Cusco ☏ 084/222-580. **Peru Rail** ✉ Cusco (San Pedro) ☏ 084/233-551 ⊕ www.perurail.com ✉ Cusco (Wanchaq), Pachacutec near Tullumayo ☏ 084/238-722 ⊕ www.perurail.com. **Sacred Valley Railway** ✉ El Sol 803 Cusco ☏ 084/249-076 ⊕ www.sacredvalleyrailway.com ✉ Av. Ferrocarril s/n Urubamba ☏ 084/201-071 ✉ Pardo 329 Miraflores Lima ☏ 01/241-2645.

VISITOR INFORMATION

Cusco has three official tourist information offices. All provide information not just about the city, but also the surrounding Cusco department. The Dirección Regional de Industria y Turismo (DRIT) provides reliable information on the city and the surrounding area. A branch at the airport is open daily for all incoming flights. iPerú has helpful information on Cusco and the region and can provide assistance if you feel you've received inadequate service from a tourist establishment. An airport branch is open daily for all incoming flights. The Instituto Nacional de Cultura sells the 10-day boleto turístico, valid for admission to 16 museums and archaeological sites in the region. A private office of note is South American Explorers, a membership organization. Its $50 annual dues get you a quarterly magazine subscription and access to a wealth of information at its clubhouse here in Cusco, as well as in Lima and in Quito, Ecuador.

🚹 Tourist Information **Dirección Regional de Industria y Turismo** ✉ Mantas 117 Cusco ☎ 084/263-176 ⏱ Mon.-Fri. 8-7, Sat. 8-12. **Instituto Nacional de Cultura** ✉ Garcilaso and Heladeros Cusco ☎ 084/226-919 ⏱ Mon.-Fri. 8 to 5, Sat. 8-4, Sun. 8-12. **iPerú** ✉ Portal de Carrizos 250, Haukaypata (Plaza de Armas) Cusco ☎ 084/234-498 ⏱ Daily 8:30-7:30. **South American Explorers** ✉ Choquechara 188 Cusco ☎ 084/245-484 ⏱ May-Sept, Mon.-Fri. 9:30-5 and Sun. 9:30-1; Oct.-Apr., Mon.-Fri., 9:30-5.

Updated by
Gregory
Benchwick and
Jeffrey Van
Fleet

PERU'S LEAST-KNOWN REGION, its road less traveled—actually it's the *river* less traveled; roads are few and far between here—occupies some two-thirds of the country, an area the size of California. The *selva* (jungle) of the Amazon Basin, watered by the world's second longest river and its tributaries, lies a world away from the Machu Picchu and Lake Titicaca of tourist brochures. The Amazon has a natural infrastructure to form the foundation of a growing ecotourism industry. What eastern Peru lacks in human population it makes up for in sheer plant and animal numbers, more than you knew could exist, all yours for the viewing. And there are lodges and guides to house and host the growing number of people who arrive to see the spectacle.

The northern Amazon, anchored by the port city of Iquitos, can claim the river itself in its territory. Iquitos is the gateway to the world's largest and most diverse natural reserve, the Amazon Rain Forest. From Iquitos you can visit Amazonian tribesmen, head for the jungle to explore the flora and fauna to be found, or drift through an enchanted floating city in Iquitos's Belén neighborhood.

Though the area has been inhabited by small indigenous tribes for more than 5,000 years, it wasn't "civilized" until Jesuit missionaries arrived in the 1500s, bringing with them Christianity, original sin, and a dislike for the aesthetic, natural equilibrium of the indigenous population. The Spanish conquistador Francisco de Orellana was the first white man to see the Amazon. He came upon the great river, which natives called Tunguragua (King of Waters), on his trip down the Río Napo in search of El Dorado. He dubbed it Amazonas after he met with extreme opposition from female warriors along the banks of the river.

The area was slow to convert to modern ways, and remained basically wild until the 1880s, when there was a great rubber boom. The boom changed the town of Iquitos overnight, and rubber barons installed themselves in lavish palaces and the city's population exploded. The natives were put to work as rubber tappers—at the time, rubber was a natural commodity that was hunted rather than farmed, and the tappers would head into the jungle and draw the sap from rubber trees. The boom upset the natives' natural balance and traditional culture, until the boom went bust in the first part of the 20th century, when a clever British entrepreneur smuggled some seeds out of Brazil and began building plantations on the Malay Peninsula. The remnants of the boom are still evident in the area. You can see it in the somewhat dilapidated palaces in Iquitos and along the banks of the Amazon and its tributaries, where Rivereños (the river people) live simply, eking their survival from the river and small plots of farmland.

Most of the native tribes—there are many small tribes in the region, the Boras, Yaguas, and Orejones being the most prevalent—have given up their traditional hunter-gatherer subsistence and now live in small communities along the backwaters of the great river. You will not see naked "pygmies" unless you travel far from Iquitos and deep into the jungle, a harrowing and dangerous undertaking. What you will see are simple, kind people, living along with nature, with traditions that date back thousands of years: a common sight might be a fisherman paddling calmly up the Amazon in his dugout canoe, angling to reel in something substantial upriver. An almost unimaginable contrast is that less than a mile away, in Iquitos, *motocarros* zoom by as pedestrians jabber on their cell phones, striving to keep pace with the 21st century.

The lesser-known southern Amazon region has to be satisfied with the big river's tributaries. Few travelers spend much time in Puerto Maldonado, the capital of Madre de Dios department, using the city instead as a jumping-off point to the Manu and Tambopata reserves. Manu is the less accessible but more pristine of the two Madre de Dios reserves, but Tambopata will not disappoint if time constrains you.

The region is remote by Peru's standards, but the Amazon is more accessible here than in the eight other South American countries that form its watershed. Just be prepared to spend some extra soles to get here. Roads, when they exist, are rough-and-tumble, and often impassible during the November–April rainy season. Rivers also overflow at this time. A dry-season visit entails the least muss and fuss. You'll most likely jet into Iquitos or Puerto Maldonado, respectively the northern and southern gateways to the Amazon. Each receives several daily flights from Lima. From each it's a trek, usually by boat, to reach the region's famed lodges.

Exploring the Amazon Basin

Logistics of travel and isolation make it unlikely that you could visit both the northern and southern Amazon regions—separated by 600 km (360 mi) at their nearest point—during one trip to Peru. The city of Iquitos is the jumping-off point for the northern Amazon; Puerto Maldonado, for the south. Some 1,200 km (720 mi) and connecting flights back in Lima separate the two cities. Choose one sector or the other for your visit. Neither will disappoint, and both are dotted with the region's famed jungle lodges, usually just a river journey away.

About the Restaurants

You can dine out at restaurants only in Iquitos and Puerto Maldonado, the Amazon basin's two cities. Meal times are the same as they are in the rest of Peru—*el almuerzo* (lunch) is the most important meal of the day, normally eaten around 2 pm. *La cena* (dinner) is normally lighter and less formal. Dinner service begins around 8 PM. Your sole dining option is your lodge if you stay in the jungle. Meals are served family-style at fixed times with everyone seated around a big table, and you can swap stories with your fellow lodgers about what you saw on your day's excursion. The food, usually making ample use of local ingredients, is quite tasty.

About the Hotels

Puerto Maldonado and Iquitos have typical, albeit small hotels, ones where, presuming availability, you can show up on a moment's notice, sign in, and secure a room. Iquitos also has a few hotels geared toward business travelers. Beyond the Amazon's two cities lie the region's jungle lodges. They vary in degree of rusticity and remoteness, usually reachable only by boat. They range from camping sites a cut above the norm, where your tent is pitched on a covered wooden platform, to full-fledged eco-lodges with private, tiled baths and solar-powered lighting. Most make do without electricity however. Showers will be refreshingly or bracingly cold depending on your needs, though some lodges are installing systems to heat the water.

All lodges offer some variation on a fully escorted tour, with packages from one to several nights including all meals and guided wildlife-viewing excursions. Many lodges quote rates per person for tours that typically last more than one day—it's not realistic to stay at most of these places for just one night.

4

The remoteness of this region and the scarcity of roads mean you sacrifice spontaneity when you visit the jungle lodges in Madre de Dios and Iquitos. In exchange, most provide fully escorted tours, transporting you to and from their sites, and taking you on guided excursions during your stay. Several of the companies in Manu divide your time between stays at two different lodges, depending on the specifics of the tour. Bear in mind that the Manu lodges tend to have specific departure dates. Advance planning is imperative.

Numbers in the text correspond to numbers in the margin and on the Madre de Dios, Iquitos, and Iquitos Environs & Where to Stay maps.

If you have 4 days

Four days is ample time to stay at one of the Tambopata lodges, especially those on the Madre de Dios River east of and closer to **Puerto Maldonado ❶ ➤**. Lodges on the Tambopata River south of the city are farther away, but can still be reached on your first day. On day one, fly into Puerto Maldonado, where a representative of your lodge will greet you at the airport and transport you to the docks for your boat ride to the lodge. You'll arrive at most lodges by afternoon and still have time for a wildlife-viewing tour. Any remaining days are jam-packed with guided activities, or yours to laze around your lodge. Day two at a Tambopata lodge will likely include a visit to one of the reserve's famous macaw clay licks. The remainder of the day will be spent traveling by catamaran or dugout, viewing river otters, caimans, and monkeys. Day three could entail a white-water rafting side excursion on the Tambopata River or if sedate is more your style, a guided boat trip to one of the reserve's oxbow lakes and their abundant waterfowl spectacle, or to one of the nearby indigenous communities. Be prepared to depart very early your final day to catch one of the morning flights out of Puerto Maldonado. Or if you have the time, spend the day in town, explore the market, stay the night, and depart the next morning.

If you plan to cover Iquitos and the surrounding area in four days, you will probably want to focus on exploring the jungle, staying all four nights out on the river in one of the many jungle lodges. A normal itinerary begins with an airport pick-up by your lodge. From there you may have time to visit the **Malecón Tarapacá ❼ ➤** riverwalk before heading out onto the river. On days two and three explore the channels, trails, and natural beauty offered by the Amazon Basin. Most lodges have complete, day-long itineraries that will keep you busy from sunrise to sundown. Activities include piranha fishing, morning birding tours, jungle hikes, nighttime canoe excursions, and visits to nearby indigenous villages. On day four, try to hit Iquitos's **Belén ❻** district, the Laguna Quistococha, and the rubber-barons' mansions in the town's center.

If you have 6 days

Six days in Madre de Dios gives you sufficient time for the more-remote Manu lodges. Your trip will begin in Cusco rather than Puerto Maldonado. Though it increases tour costs greatly, consider taking the 45-minute flight to the Boca Manu airstrip just outside the reserve. The overland trip is spectacular but can eat up anywhere from 12 to 24 hours, depending on the remoteness of your lodge. Once you arrive at Boca Manu you'll reach your lodging by boat, a journey of 90 minutes to several hours. At your lodge, your days will be structured with guided excursions.Many Manu tour operators own more than one property, so your tour might entail a split stay. After arrival, your second day will likely be spent in an orientation hike around your lodge with the opportunity for wildlife viewing. Day three could entail a visit to one of Manu's macaw or tapir clay licks, followed by a cloud-forest hike. Climb one of the rain-forest canopy viewing towers on your fourth day for that proverbial bird's eye view you can't get from down below. Spend your fifth day on a white-water rafting excursion down the Upper Madre de Dios River or its tributaries, or perhaps take a mountain-biking trip. You begin your final day early embarking on the trip back to Cusco.

For Iquitos and its environs, six days will permit a more expansive jungle trip. Building on the four day itinerary, you can add another night on the river and a full day and night in Iquitos at the end. Spend your first day seeing Iquitos sights, checking out **Belén ⑥ ☞**, the Quistococha tourist area, and the rubber-barons' mansions. Spend your first night in ▩ **Iquitos ⑥–⑪**. On day two head into the jungle, spending the next three nights in jungle lodges. Days three through five should be spent exploring the natural beauty of the Amazon Basin. All of the lodges have excellent naturalist guides and fun day-long itineraries. Your typical day on the river will consist of a morning hike or bird-watching trip. After lunch, you'll have just enough time for a short siesta in a hammock before you head out to go look for dolphins, visit an indigenous village, check out a canopy walkway, or fish for piranha. When darkness comes you can relax and recount the day's events or head out for a nighttime canoe trip, during which you might spot frogs, snakes, and sleeping butterflies. Stay in Iquitos on your last night, taking advantage of the city's good food and nightlife.

WHAT IT COSTS In Nuevo Soles				
$$$$	$$$	$$	$	¢
RESTAURANTS over 65	50–65	35–50	20–35	under 20
HOTELS over 500	375–500	250–375	125–250	under 125

Restaurant prices are per person, for a main course at dinner. Hotel prices are for two people in a standard double room, excluding tax.

Timing

The best time to visit the Amazon Basin is during the "dry season." While there is no true dry season in a rain forest, it does rain less during the months of July and August; it rains most in January and February, and it is hotter than usual between February and June. While there is also no true high tourist season, plan well in advance anyway; as some jungle lodges often take in large groups.

All southern Amazon basin reserves are best visited between May and October, the driest months; the lodges, however, are open year-round, though rivers may overflow and mosquitoes are voracious during the worst of the rainy season. Tambopata sees a well-defined wet season/ dry season distinction; Manú's rainfall is more evenly dispersed throughout the year. During the dry season, especially July, sudden *friajes* (cold fronts) bring rain and cold weather to Madre de Dios, so be prepared for the worst. Temperatures can drop from 32°C (90°F) to 10°C (50°F) overnight, so bring at least one jacket or warm sweater. No matter when you travel, bring a rain jacket or poncho and perhaps rain pants, since rain may come at any time, with or without friajes.

MADRE DE DIOS

Do the math: 20,000 plant, 1,200 butterfly, 1,000 bird, 200 mammal and 100 reptile species (and many more yet to be identified). The national parks, reserves, and other undeveloped areas of the southern department of Madre de Dios are among the most biologically diverse in the world. The southern sector of Peru's Amazon Basin, most readily approached via Cusco, is famous among birders, whose eyes glaze over in amazement at the dawn spectacle of macaws and parrots visiting the region's famed *ccollpas* (clay licks); ornithologists speculate that the birds must ingest clay periodically to detoxify other elements in their diet. Madre de Dios also offers a rare chance to see large mammals, such as tapirs and, if the zoological fates smile upon you, jaguars. Groups such as the Nature Conservancy and Conservation International view the region as one of the world's natural arks, a place where the endangered Amazon rain forest has a real chance for survival. Animal and plant life may abound, but this is the least populated of Peru's departments in terms of human population: a scant 76,000 people reside in an area slightly smaller than South Carolina, and almost two-thirds of them in the sultry capital, Puerto Maldonado. Thoughtful conservation and planning here, coupled with keeping the humans at bay, has allowed the plant and animal population to thrive.

Madre de Dios began recorded history as part of the Inca empire, though far-off Cusco exerted limited control over this region the Inca called the Antisuyo, populated by indigenous forest peoples, the difficult-to-subdue Antis. The southern Amazon saw little incursion at the time of the Spanish conquest. The discovery in the late 19th century of the *shiringa,* known in the English-speaking world as the rubber tree, changed all that. Madre de Dios saw outside migration for the first time with the arrival of the *caucheros* (rubber men) and their minions staking out claims. The discovery of gold in the 1970s drew new waves of fortune seekers to the region. You can still see dreamers panning for gold in area rivers, hoping against hope to strike it rich.

Tourism and conservation have triggered the newest generation of explorers to the species-rich southern Amazon. Two areas of Madre de Dios are of special interest. One is around the city of Puerto Maldonado, including the Tambopata National Reserve and the adjoining Bahuaja-Sonene National Park; easily accessible, they offer lodges amid primary rain forest and excellent birding. Tambopata also exists for sustainable agriculture purposes: some 1,500 families in the department work to extract Brazil nuts from the reserve, an economic incentive to keep the forest intact, rather than cut it down for its lumber. The Manu Biosphere Reserve, directly north of Cusco, though more difficult and expensive to reach, provides unparalleled opportunity for observing wildlife in one of the largest virgin rain forests in the New World.

Puerto Maldonado

1 *500 km (305 mi) east of Cusco.*

The metropolis of the southern Amazon region and inland port city of Puerto Maldonado lies at the meeting point of the Madre de Dios and Tambopata rivers. The capital of the department of Madre de Dios is a rough-and-tumble town with 46,000 people and nary a four-wheeled vehicle in sight, but with hundreds of motorized two- and three-wheeled motorbikes jockeying for position on its few paved streets.

The city is named for two explorers who ventured into the region 300 years apart: Spanish conquistador Juan Álvarez de Maldonado passed through in 1566; Peruvian explorer Faustino Maldonado explored the still-wild area in the 1860s, never completing his expedition, drowning in the nearby Madeira River. Rubber barons founded this youngster of Peruvian cities in 1912, and its history has been a boom-or-bust roller-coaster ride ever since. The collapse of the rubber industry in the 1930s gave way to decades of dormancy ended by the discovery of gold in the 1970s and the opening of an airport 10 years later.

Tourism is the new cause for economic hope here. Puerto Maldonado bills itself as the "Biodiversity Capital of the World," and makes the best jumping-off point for visiting the Tambopata National Reserve sector of Peru's Amazon rain forest. But in fact, few travelers spend any time in the city, heading from the airport directly to the municipal docks where they board boats to their respective jungle lodges. If you have a day to tack on to the beginning or end of your lodge stay, Puerto Maldonado is a beguiling town with a frontier feel; it also has a handful of decent hotels, a couple of which do provide an in-town jungle experience if you're pressed for time. As expected in such a remote region, this is the only place to use an ATM machine, cash a traveler's check, or log on to the Internet.

The southern Amazon actually has a skyscraper, the 45-m (158-ft) **Mirador de la Biodiversidad,** a few blocks north of Puerto Maldonado's downtown. Bas-relief scenes from the history of Madre de Dios decorate the lookout tower's base, and the top provides a commanding vista of the nearby rain forest. As Puerto Maldonado doesn't quite glitter in the evening, the best views from here are during the day. ⊠ *Fitzcarrald and Madre de Dios* ☎ *082/572–993* ⊙ *Daily 7–1 and 3–10* ☜ *S/1.*

Where to Stay & Eat

¢ ✕⊞ **Hotel Cabaña Quinta.** The rambling chestnut-wood Victorian-style house, the tropical veranda, the arched doorways, the latticework, and the red-and-green *sangapilla* plants in the garden could come right out of a Graham Greene novel. Rooms are a little less evocative but pleasantly furnished with wood paneling, print spreads, and drapes. The restaurant is one of Puerto Maldonado's best and serves a small menu of fish, meats, and soups, with plenty of *yuca* (cassava) chips on the side. ⊠ *Cusco 535* ☎☎ *082/571–045* ☜ *51 rooms, 3 suites* ↻ *Restaurant, pool, bar, meeting room, airport shuttle* ▤ *AE, MC, V* ⧉ *BP.*

$ ⊞ **Hotel Don Carlos.** On the bank of the Tambopata River just a few blocks from the center of town, this Don Carlos is a bit more rustic than the other modern business-class hotels in this small Peruvian chain. Wood-paneled rooms with high ceilings and tile floors enclose a pleasant garden and a much appreciated pool, one of the few around. ⊠ *León Velarde 1271* ☎ *082/571–029* ⊟ *082/571–323* ⊕ *www.hotelesdoncarlos.com* ☜ *15 rooms* ↻ *Restaurant, minibars, pool, laundry service, meeting room, airport shuttle* ▤ *AE, DC, MC, V* ⧉ *BP.*

$ ⊞ **Wasai Maldonado Lodge.** If you're pressed for time, the Wasai gives you that jungle-lodge feel right in town, just a block from the Plaza de Armas. Bungalows on stilts scatter on a hill leading down from the lobby toward the pool and gazebo-style restaurant. The shady grounds overlook the Madre de Dios River and the well-ventilated thatched-roof, tornillo-wood bungalows make for a surprisingly cool place in the

4

Crocodile Nuggets, Anyone? Amazonian cuisine, with its jungle game meats and off-color local dishes, is truly far-out. Try *chicharron de lagarto* (crocodile nuggets), *venado a la Loretana* (Loretan-style venison), *paiche* (a giant lake fish) or *suri* (palm-tree grubs). *Sarapatera* is a turtle plantain stew cooked in the turtle's shell. *Ensalada de chonta* (heart of palm salad) is also quite popular.

Fruit and fish preparations evoke neighboring Brazil more than the high-mountain cuisine found elsewhere in Peru. Try *pataraschca* (steamed fish wrapped in banana leaves). *Timbuche* is a tasty catch-all fish soup made from the catch of the day. Try *tacacho,* bananas baked over coals and spiced up with a bit of pork and onion, and top it off with the ubiquitous *juanes* (rice cakes). Brazil nuts, locally called *castañas,* make a tasty snack. Their purchase helps support a sustainable eco-friendly use of the southern Amazon rain forest.

Sadly, some city restaurants incorporate endangered turtle species into their offerings. You'll see *sopa de motelo* (turtle soup served in the shell) and *muchangue* (turtle eggs) on the menu. Don't support further elimination of an already vanishing species by ordering them.

Chapo, a sweet banana-milk-and-sugar drink, is popular, as is *mazato,* a fermented yuca beverage. For a thirst quencher that also packs a punch, look no further than *Cashasa,* a liquor concocted from sugarcane. Other local drinks include *siete raizes* (seven roots), said to be a potent aphrodisiac, and *masato,* prepared by chewing yuca and then fermenting the spit.

Wildlife Watching The numbers tell the story: Peru's Amazon basin has 50,000 plant, 1,700 bird, 400 mammal, and 300 reptile species. The region hosts a ninth of all the avian species on earth. Mammals, reptiles, and amphibians prove a bit more elusive, though the farther you venture from Iquitos and Puerto Maldonado, the greater your chances of seeing more wildlife. Regardless of who and what is on your list, a good guide—most of the lodges have experienced personnel—and a pair of binoculars are essential.

---

otherwise sweltering center of Puerto Maldonado. ⊠ *Bellinghurst s/n* ☎ *082/572–290* 📠 *082/571–355* ⊕ *www.wasai.com* 🖨 *18 cabins* ⚐ *Restaurant, refrigerator, pool, bar, travel services; no a/c in some rooms, no room phones* ☰ *AE, DC, V* �‖ *BP.*

¢ 🏨 **Iñapari.** A charming Spanish-Peruvian couple owns this budget lodging in the middle of a forest just outside of town near the airport. Cedarwood cabins are cozy but spartan, yielding beds, a table, a mosquito net, and not much else, but the rates can't be beat if you're not too fussy. The owners and their staff of knowledgeable guides offer optional three- to six-day excursions to Lago Sandoval and the Tambopata Reserve. ⊠ *Av. Aeropuerto, Km 5.5* 📠 *082/572–575* ⊕ *www. puertomaldonado.com* 🖨 *7 rooms with shared bath* ⚐ *Dining room, travel services; no a/c, no room phones, no room TVs* ☰ *No credit cards* �‖ *CP.*

Near Puerto Maldonado

The Madre de Dios River heads from Puerto Maldonado east to the Bolivian border. The river itself defines the northern boundary of the Tambopata National Reserve and passes some nearby, easy-to-reach jungle lodges.

On your way down the river, tour guides will dutifully point out Madre de Dios's best-known faux site, the abandoned ship of Carlos Fermín Fitzcarrald, the most famous of the 19th-century *caucheros* (rubber barrons). The wreckage is not Fitzcarrald's vessel, in fact, but that of a hospital ship that ran aground in the 1960s. ⊠ *4 km (2½ mi) east of Puerto Maldonado.*

Changes in the course of the Río Madre de Dios have formed several so-called oxbow lakes. Riverbeds shift and the former bed fills with water. ❷ **Lago Sandoval** east of Puerto Maldonado in the Tambopata National Reserve is the most famous of these. It brims with the requisite parrots and macaws, but also plenty of waterfowl, most notably herons and kingfishers. The lake lies a 30-minute boat ride from Puerto Maldonado; once you disembark there is an easy 2-km (1-mi) hike to the lake itself. ⊠ *9 km (5½ mi) east of Puerto Maldonado.*

❸ **Lago Valencia** is two hours northeast of Puerto Maldonado, just outside the boundaries of Tambopata. You can make it an all-day journey in a dugout locals call a *pequepeque*. Regardless of your transport, expect to see abundant wildlife, avian (herons, cormorants, and flamingos) and otherwise. Turtles abound, and your best chance of glimpsing caimans is around sunset. An indigenous Ese'eja native community is also nearby. This section of the river is a favorite lucky site for Madre de Dios's gold panners. Carry your passport on the trip to Valencia; you'll be a mere

5 km (3 mi) from the Bolivian border, and Peruvian authorities inspect documentation for those who pass this close. ✉ *23 km (14 mi) east of Puerto Maldonado.*

Where to Stay

$$$
Fodor'sChoice
★

🏨 **Sandoval Lake Lodge.** InkanaturaTravel operates this lodge, the closest to Puerto Maldonado. It's accessible by an easy 30-minute boat ride east on the Madre de Dios River and a short hike or rickshaw ride, and it's actually feasible to do a one-night stay here. (Allow for more if your schedule permits.) The lodge is in the middle of forested grounds overlooking Lago Sandoval. *Reservations:* ✉ *Plateros 361 Cusco* ☎ *082/ 255–255; 877/827–8350 in the U.S.* 🖷 *082/251–173* ⊕ *www.inkanatura. com* ↩ *25 rooms* ♿ *Dining room, bar; no a/c, no room phones, no room TVs* ¶◎¶ *All-inclusive.*

$$

🏨 **Cusco Amazónico.** A 45-minute boat ride downriver from Puerto Maldonado on the Madre de Dios River, this is the most accessible of the jungle lodges. Each of its private bungalows, set amid trees beside the river, has a flush toilet, a shower, and a porch hammock. Because the lodge is relatively close to Puerto Maldonado, large mammals are rare, but visitors often see smaller ones, such as anteaters and agoutis. For wildlife-viewing, consider a day trip to Lago Sandoval. On very rare occasions, the giant Amazon river otter may be seen. A typical jungle dinner—fried bananas, *pacamoto* (fish or chicken cooked inside bamboo over coals), and fresh papaya for dessert—is very good here. *Reservations:* ✉ *Andalucía 174, Miraflores, Lima* ☎ *01/446–2775* 🖷 *01/445– 5598* ✉ *Procuradores 48, Cusco* ☎ *084/232–161* ↩ *43 cabins* ♿ *Restaurant, bar* ▬ *AE, MC, V.*

Tambopata National Reserve & Bahuaja-Sonene National Park

❹ *5 km (3 mi) south of Puerto Maldonado*

Up the Tambopata River from Puerto Maldonado is the Tambopata National Reserve, a 3.8-million-acre primary humid-tropical-forest reserved zone about the size of Connecticut, and overlapping Madre de Dios and Puno departments. Officially separate from the reserve, but usually grouped for convenience under the "Tambopata" heading, is the Bahuaja-Sonene National Park, created in 1996 and taking its moniker from the names in the local indigenous Ese'eja language for the Tambopata and Heath rivers respectively. (The Río Heath forms Peru's southeastern boundary with neighboring Bolivia.) The former Pampas de Río Heath Reserve along the border itself is now incorporated into Bahuaja-Sonene, and encompasses a looks-out-of-place secondary forest more resembling the African savannah than the lush tropical Amazon.

Peru works closely on joint conservation projects with Bolivia, whose adjoining Madidi National Park forms a grand cross-border 7.2-million-acre reserve area. Only environmentally friendly activities are permitted in Tambopata. The area functions partially as a managed tropical forest reserve. The reserve's shiringa trees are an extraction source for latex. And cultivation here of *castañas,* or Brazil nuts, keeps thousands employed. Both activities provide an alternative incentive to conserving the forest rather than chopping it down. Tourism is the other major source of income for the reserve.

Elevations here range from 500 meters (1,640 feet) to a lofty 3,000 meters (9,840 feet), providing fertile homes for an astounding number of animals and plants. The area holds a world record in the number of butterfly species (1,234) recorded by scientists. Within the reserve, the Explorer's Inn holds the world-record bird-species sighting for a single lodge: 600 have been recorded on its grounds, 331 of those sighted within a single day, also a score no other lodging can top. Tambopata is the site of the most famous and largest of Madre de Dios's *ccollpas* (clay licks) visited daily by 15 species of parrots and macaws, who congregate at dawn to collect a beakful of mineral-rich clay, an important but mysterious part of what they eat.

The Tambopata jungle lodges are much easier—and much less expensive—to reach than those in the Manu Biosphere Reserve, Madre de Dios's more famous ecotourism area. And Tambopata is no poor man's Manu either—its sheer numbers of wildlife are impressive in their own right. A half-hour, early-morning flight from Cusco at S/350 round-trip takes you to Puerto Maldonado, the Tambopata jumping-off point. And in a few hours or less you can arrive by boat at most lodges here and be bird-watching that afternoon. (You'd still be on your way to Manu at that point.) Some of the lodges here offer two-day/one-night packages that amount to little more than 24 hours. You need to depart very early to make it back to Puerto Maldonado for your morning flight out. Opt for at least three days here if your schedule permits.

Where to Stay

The listings below are for lodges comprised of wooden huts raised on stilts. All provide rustic but more than adequate accommodations. Rates include river transportation from Puerto Maldonado, guides, and meals. For properties where a minimum stay is indicated, the price category is based on the per-night cost.

$$$ ⊞ **Tambopata Research Center.** A six-hour upriver boat journey from the Posada Amazonas lodge brings you to this Amazon base. Here you'll see several kinds of monkeys and other rain-forest wildlife, including hundreds of macaws and parrots at the nearby clay lick. The twin rooms at the lodge don't have private baths but instead share a separate room with four showers and another with four toilets. One current research project allows you to interact with macaws. The minimum stay is five days/four nights. *Reservations:* ✉ *Av. Aramburu 166, Miraflores, Lima* ☎ *01/421–8347, 877/905–3782 in the U.S.* ☎ *01/421–8183* ✉ *Sunturwasi 350 (Triunfo), Cusco* ☎☎ *084/232–772* ✉ *Arequipa 401, Puerto Maldonado* ☎☎ *082/571–056* ⊕ *www.perunature. com* ⊷ *13 rooms with shared bath* ⚒ *Dining room, bar; no a/c, no room phones, no room TVs* ⊟ *MC, V* ⦿| *All-inclusive.*

$$ ⊞ **Explorer's Inn.** No place in the world tops this one for number of bird species (600, and 330 of those in one fortuitous day) sighted at a single lodge. Explorer's is managed by Peruvian Safaris, and accommodates tourists and visiting scientists in its thatched-roof bungalows. All can be seen navigating the lodge's 30 km (18 mi) of trails. The minimum stay is three days/two nights. *Reservations:* ✉ *Alcanfores 459 Miraflores Lima* ☎ *01/447–8888* ☎ *01/241–8427* ⊕ *www.peruviansafaris.com* ⊷ *30 rooms* ⚒ *Dining room; no a/c, no room phones, no room TVs.*

$$ ⊞ **Posada Amazonas.** This comfortable lodge is owned jointly by Rainforest Expeditions and the Ese'eja Native Community of Tambopata. The property defines "jungle chic," with mosquito nets over the beds and wide, screenless windows to welcome cooling breezes. A canopy tower provides a great view of the rain forest. Transportation to the lodge is usually by a combination of a thatch-roof truck and a large wooden boat with drop-down rain curtains. A visit to a local village is made en route. Packages include all transport, lodging, meals, and guides. The minimum stay is three days/two nights. *Reservations:* ✉ *Av. Aramburu 166,*

Fodor'sChoice
★

Miraflores, Lima ☎ *01/421–8347; 877/905–3782 in the U.S.* 🖷 *01/421–8183* ✉ *Sunturwasi 350 (Triunfo), Cusco* ☎☎ *084/232–772* ✉ *Arequipa 401, Puerto Maldonado* ☎☎ *082/571–056* ⊕ *www.perunature.com* ⇆ *30 rooms* ♨ *Dining room; no a/c, no room phones, no room TVs* ▤ *MC, V* ¶◎¶ *All-inclusive.*

$$ ▦ **Tambopata Lodge.** Peru's Libertador chain operates this lodge four hours south of Puerto Maldonado on the Tambopata River. Spacious cabins have two bedrooms each, with porches and comfy hammocks in which to curl up at the end of day of sightseeing on the lodge's 25 km (15 mi) of trails. More expensive cabins use a solar-power system for light and hot water. The minimum stay is three days/two nights. ✉ *Suecia 343 Cusco* ☎☎ *084/245–645; 084/245–695 for reservations* ⊕ *www. tambopatalodge.com* ♨ *Dining room, bar, meeting room, no a/c, no room phones, no room TVs* ▤ *AE, MC, V* ¶◎¶ *All-inclusive.*

Manu Biosphere Reserve

⑤ *90 km (54 mi) north of Cusco*

Fodor'sChoice ★

Readers of the British children's series *A Bear Called Paddington* know that the title character "came from darkest Peru." The stereotype is quite outdated, of course, but the Manu Biosphere Reserve, often called "the most biodiverse park on earth," will conjure up the jungliest Tarzan-movie images you can imagine. And the reserve really does count the Andean spectacled bear, South America's only ursid, and the animal on which Paddington was based, among its 200 mammals.

This reserve area half the size of Switzerland is Peru's largest protected area and straddles the boundary of the Madre de Dios and Cusco departments. Manu encompasses more than 4½ million acres of pristine primary tropical forest wilderness, ranging in altitude from 3,450 m (12,000 ft) down through cloud forest and into a seemingly endless lowland tropical rain forest at 300 m (less than 1,000 feet). Not surprisingly, this geographical variety shelters a stunning biodiversity, and a near total absence of humans and hunting has made the animal life here less skittish and more open to observation. The reserve's 13 monkey species scrutinize visitors with the same curiosity they elicit. White caimans sun themselves lazily on sandy riverbanks, while the larger black ones lurk in the oxbow lakes. And expect to see tapirs at the world's largest tapir ccollpa. Giant Orotongo river otters and elusive big cats such as jaguars and ocelots sometimes make fleeting appearances. But it's the avian life that has made Manu world famous. The area counts over 1,000 bird species, fully a ninth of those known. Some 500 species have been spotted at the Pantiacolla Lodge alone. Birds include macaws, toucans, roseate spoonbills, and 5-ft-tall wood storks.

Manu was declared a national park in 1973, and a biosphere reserve in 1977. Ten years later, UNESCO designated it a World Heritage Site. It is divided into three distinct zones. The smallest is the so-called "cultural zone" (Zone C), with several indigenous groups and the majority of the jungle lodges. Access is permitted to all, even to independent travelers in theory, though vast distances make this unrealistic for all but the most intrepid. About three times the size of the cultural zone, Manu's "reserve zone" (Zone B) is uninhabited but contains one of the lodges. Access is by permit only, and you must be accompanied by a guide from one of the 10 agencies authorized to take people into the area. The western 80 percent of Manu is designated a national park (Zone A). Authorized researchers and indigenous peoples who reside there are permitted in this zone; visitors may not enter.

A Manu excursion is no quick trip. Overland travel from Cusco, the usual embarkation point, takes up to two days, in a thrilling trip over the mountains and down into the lowland plains. A charter flight in a twin-engine plane to the small airstrip at Boca Manu shaves that time down to 45 minutes but adds a few hundred dollars onto your package price. From Boca Manu you'll still have several hours of boat travel to reach your lodge. The logistics of travel to this remote part of the Amazon mean you should allow at least five days for your excursion. A week is more manageable.

Where to Stay

For properties where a minimum stay is indicated, the price category is based on the per-night cost.

$$$$ ☒ **Cock of the Rock Lodge.** Higher elevation means fewer mosquitoes, and this lodge perches along the Kosñipata River in the cloud forest of Manu's cultural zone. This venture of the respected Inkanatura Travel takes its name from Peru's red-and-black national bird, found in abundance on the grounds. Bungalows are basic, furnished with two beds, tables, and mosquito nets, and there's an ample supply of hot water. The minimum stay is three days/two nights. *Reservations:* ☒ *Plateros 361 Cusco* ☎ *084/255–255; 877/827–8350 in U.S.* ☎ *084/251–173* ⊕ *www. inkanatura.com* ⇝ *5 cabins with bath, 8 rooms with shared bath* ⛄ *Dining room, bar; no a/c, no room phones, no room TVs* ⊟ *AE, MC, V* ◯ *All-inclusive.*

$$$$ ☒ **Manu Cloud Forest Lodge.** High in the cloud forest of Manu's cultural zone, this lodge sits on grounds blooming with orchids and overlooking the rushing Río Unión. Rooms are rustic and spartan, with beds and tables, but all have a private bath and plenty of hot water. The highly respected Manu Nature Tours operates the lodge. The minimum stay is three days/two nights. *Reservations:* ☒ *Av. Pardo 1046 Cusco* ☎ *084/ 252–721* ☎ *084/234–793* ☒ *Conquistadores 396, San Isidro, Lima* ☎ *01/ 442–8980* ⊕ *www.manuperu.com* ⇝ *8 rooms, 4 cabins* ⛄ *Dining room, bar, sauna, mountain bikes; no a/c, no room phones, no room TVs* ⊟ *AE, MC, V* ◯ *All-inclusive.*

$$$$ ☒ **Manu Lodge.** Built by Manu Nature Tours from mahogany salvaged from the banks of the Manu River, the lodge is set deep in the reserve zone, the only such accommodation, overlooking the 2-km-long (1-mi-long) oxbow lake called Cocha Juárez. Frequently seen in the lake are giant river otters and black and white caimans. The comfortable, screened-in lodge has a two-story dining area, and guests have access to three habitats: the lakes, the river, and a trail network that spans 10 square km (4 square mi) of rain forest. The lodge also has tree-climbing equipment to lift visitors up onto canopy platforms for viewing denizens of the treetops. The minimum stay is four days/three nights. *Reservations:* ☒ *Av. Pardo 1046, Cusco* ☎ *084/252–721* ☎ *084/234– 793* ☒ *Conquistadores 396, San Isidro, Lima* ☎ *01/442–8980* ⊕ *www. manuperu.com* ⇝ *12 rooms* ⛄ *Restaurant, bar; no a/c, no room phones, no room TVs* ⊟ *AE, MC, V* ◯ *All-inclusive.*

$$$$ ☒ **Manu Wildlife Center.** As the name suggests, this is a great place for wildlife viewing, as it sits close to Manu's macaw and tapir ccollpas and encompasses 48 km (30 mi) of trails. The MWC, as it is known, is jointly owned by Cusco's Inkanatura Travel and Manu Expeditions, and services are top-notch. Raised thatched-roof bungalows have screens and wooden latticework walls as well as tiled hot-water baths. *Reservations:* ☒ *Plateros 361; Pardo 895 Cusco* ☎ *084/255–255; 084/226–671; 877/ 827–8350 in the U.S.* ☎ *084/251–173; 084/236–706* ⊕ *www.inkanatura. com; www.manuexpeditions.com* ⇝ *22 cabins* ⛄ *Dining room, bar, meet-*

ing room; no a/c, no room phones, no room TVs ⊟ *AE, MC, V* †◎† *All-inclusive.*

$$$ ⊞ **Manu Cloud Forest Tented Camp.** In the cloud forest overlooking the Río Unión, this camp has four-person tents with mattresses for two on a covered A-frame platform. Shared toilets and showers are nearby. The minimum stay is seven days/six nights. *Reservations:* ⊠ *Av. Pardo 1046 Cusco* ☎ *084/252–721* 🖷 *084/234–793* ⊠ *Conquistadores 396, San Isidro, Lima* ☎ *01/442–8980* ⊕ *www.manuperu.com* ↫ *5 tents with shared bath* ♿ *Dining room; no a/c, no room phones, no room TVs* ⊟ *AE, MC, V* †◎† *All-inclusive.*

$$$ ⊞ **Pantiacolla Lodge.** Named for the mountain range that forms this portion of the Andes, the Pantiacolla sits in Manu's cultural zone near the border of the national park. Rooms are basic, with beds, mosquito netting, tables, and wooden floors. The company specializes in excursions to nearby indigenous Yine communities. All-inclusive package tours are available. *Reservations:* ⊠ *Plateros 360 Cusco* ☎ *084/238–323* 🖷 *084/252–696* ⊕ *www.pantiacolla.com* ↫ *14 rooms with shared bath* ♿ *Dining room; no a/c, no room phones, no room TVs* ⊟ *AE, MC, V* †◎† *FAP.*

Madre de Dios A to Z

To research prices, get advice from other travelers, and book travel arrangements, visit www.fodors.com.

AIR TRAVEL
Starting in Lima and stopping in Cusco, Aero Continente, LAN Peru, and TANS Perú each have once-daily flights to Aeropuerto Padre Aldámiz (PEM), 5 km (3 mi) from Puerto Maldonado. All flights arrive and depart early in the morning.

Several of the Manu lodges fly their passengers to the small airstrip at Boca Manu on a charter basis.

🛈 Carriers **Aero Continente** ⊠ León Velarde 584 Puerto Maldonado ☎ 084/572-004. **LAN Peru** ⊠ Puerto Maldonado. **TANS Perú** ⊠ León Velarde 151 Puerto Maldonado ☎ 082/57-3861.

AIRPORTS
🛈 Airport Information **Aeropuerto Padre Aldámiz** ☎ 084/571-531.

EMERGENCIES
The Policia Nacional, Peru's national police force, handles emergencies in this region. At jungle lodges minor emergencies are handled by the staff. For serious emergencies, the camp must contact medical services in Puerto Maldonado or Cusco. Puerto Maldonado's Hospital de Apoyo handles medical emergencies.

🛈 Emergency Services **Policia Nacional** ☎ 084/571-022.

🛈 Hospitals **Hospital de Apoyo** ⊠ Cajamarca 171 Puerto Maldonado ☎ 082/571-126.

HEALTH
Peru does not require immunization against yellow fever for travelers coming directly from North America and Europe, but recommends that those visiting jungle areas below 2,300 m (7,500 ft), including the entire Amazon Basin, be vaccinated. Most patients nine months and older can receive the vaccination. Immunity takes effect 10 days after the vaccination and lasts 10 years. Though cases of yellow fever in recent years have occurred only near Iquitos, southern Amazon lodges in Manu and Tambopata tend to be sticklers about asking to see your yellow fever vaccination certificate. Carry it with you.

There is no vaccine against malaria, the Amazon's other prominent mosquito-borne illness risk, but there are prescription drugs to help minimize your likelihood of contracting the disease. As in most areas of tropical South America, strains of malaria here are resistant to the traditional regimen of chloroquine. There are three recommended alternatives: a weekly dose of mefloquine; a daily dose of doxycycline; or a daily dose of Malarone (atovaquone/proguanil). Any regimen must be started before arrival in the malarial area and continued beyond departure. Your physician can recommend the best course of prevention. Also, wear long sleeves and pants if you're out in the evening, the time of day of greatest risk, and use a mosquito repellent containing DEET. Most jungle lodges provide mosquito netting and coils to burn.

Bring all necessary medical supplies and take extra medicine with you in case you're delayed in the area. Only drink bottled water.

LANGUAGE
Guides and staff at the jungle lodges speak English. The person on the street in this remote region probably knows only Spanish. You'll hear unfamiliar indigenous languages like Ese'eja in remote areas.

MAIL & SHIPPING
In Puerto Maldonado, SERPOST, the national post office, is open Monday through Saturday 7:30 AM–8 PM and Sunday 8–2. Transtours is the local agency for DHL in Puerto Maldonado, and can ship important packages. A few public Internet cafés are scattered around Puerto Maldonado. Connection times are slower than those in Cusco. Expect to pay about S/5 per hour.

🛈 **Post Office SERPOST** ✉ León Velarde 675 Puerto Maldonado ☎ 082/571-088.

🛈 **Shipping Services Transtours/DHL** ✉ González Prada 341 Puerto Maldonado ☎ 082/572-606.

MONEY MATTERS
The Banco de Crédito on the Plaza de Armas in Puerto Maldonado changes U.S. dollars and traveler's checks for nuevo soles, and has an ATM machine that gives cash against Plus- and Cirrus-affiliated cards. Since trips into this area are usually booked through travel agents, you shouldn't need much extra cash beyond any tips you leave for the staff. Don't count on your lodge's cashing traveler's checks or accepting credit cards.

🛈 **Banks Banco de Crédito** ✉ Arequipa 334 ☎ 082/571-001.

TELEPHONES
The Madre de Dios area code is 082; Cusco's is 084. To call from abroad, drop the zero from the area code. To call within the region or from Cusco, dial only the six-digit number. Telefónica del Perú, the national telephone company, has an office in Puerto Maldonado from which you can make international calls. Telefónica's Hola Perú phone cards can be used to place national or international calls from most telephones. Most of the remote lodges communicate via radio with their offices in Puerto Maldonado, Cusco, or Lima.

🛈 **Telephones Telefónica del Perú** ✉ Puno 670 Puerto Maldonado ☎ 082/571-600.

TAXIS
It's fun to get around town in Puerto Maldonado's fleet of Honda Motokar taxis, semi-open three-wheeled motorized vehicles with room for two passengers in the back seat. Every motorbike in town also provides taxi service. You may define that as "fun" or "danger." Hold on for dear life, and don't expect a helmet.

TOURS

Those who wish to reach the more isolated parts of Madre de Dios should contact one of the agencies that conduct camping trips in Manu Biosphere Reserve. They provide all equipment and food, but you must bring your own sleeping bag. One of the most experienced guide services, the Cusco-based Manu Expeditions, offers trips that last five to nine days. Manu Nature Tours, Pantiacolla, and Inkanatura Travel operate lodges in Manu. Inkanutura also manages lodges in the Tambopata National Reserve, as do Rainforest Expeditions and Peruvian Safaris. Another reliable agency, Hirca Travel, operates five- and nine-day trips to Manu. **☎ Tour Companies Hirca Travel** ✉ Bellavista 518, Miraflores, Lima ☎☎ 01/447-3807 ✉ Retiro 128, Cusco ☎ 084/225-384. **Inkanatura Travel** ✉ Plateros 361 Cusco ☎ 084/255-255; 877/827-8350 in U.S. ☎ 084/251-173 ⊕ www.inkanatura.com. **Manu Expeditions** ✉ Procuradores 50, Cusco ☎ 084/226-671. **Manu Nature Tours** ✉ Av. Pardo 1046 Cusco ☎ 084/252-721 ☎ 084/234-793 ✉ Conquistadores 396, San Isidro, Lima ☎ 01/442-8980 ⊕ www.manuperu.com. **Pantiacolla** ✉ Plateros 360 Cusco ☎ 084/238-323 ☎ 084/252-696 ⊕ www.pantiacolla.com. **Peruvian Safaris** ✉ Alcanfores 459 Miraflores Lima ☎ 01/447-8888 ☎ 01/241-8427 ⊕ www.peruviansafaris.com. **Rainforest Expeditions** ✉ Av. Aramburu 166, Miraflores, Lima ☎ 01/421-8347; 877/905-3782 in the U.S. ☎ 01/421-8183 ✉ Sunturwasi 350 (Triunfo), Cusco ☎☎ 084/232-772 ✉ Arequipa 401, Puerto Maldonado ☎☎ 082/571-056 ⊕ www.perunature.com.

TRUCK TRAVEL

A long, rough jungle road leads to Puerto Maldonado from Cusco, but it is a grueling two- to three-day truck ride, and takes well over a week during the rainy season. The overland trip from Cusco to Manu, 12 hours over rugged terrain, is via a road called the Carretera a Shintuya, which plunges spectacularly from the *páramo* (highlands) down into the cloud forests at Atalaya. Here or at Shintuya, farther down the river, you take a boat along the Alto Madre de Dios River deep into the rain forest.

VISITOR INFORMATION

The Dirección Regional de Industria y Turismo (DRIT) has an office in Puerto Maldonado and serves as the government tourist office. It provides reliable information on the city and Madre de Dios. A branch at the airport is open daily for all incoming flights. The Conservation Association of the Southern Rain Forest has details about parks in the region. Dirección de Areas Protegidas y Fauna Silvestre offers information about Manu National Park. **☎ Dirección Regional de Industria y Turismo** ✉ Fitzcarrald 411 ☎ 084/571-164. **Conservation Association of the Southern Rain Forest** ✉ Portal los Panes 123, Haukaypata (Plaza de Armas), Cusco ☎ 084/240-911. **Dirección de Areas Protegidas y Fauna Silvestre** ✉ Petirrojos 355, Urbanización El Palomar, San Isidro, Lima ☎ 01/441-0425 ✉ Urbanización Mariscal Gamarra 4-C, Apartado 1057, Cusco ☎ 084/223-633.

IQUITOS & ENVIRONS

Founded by Jesuit priests in the 1500s, Iquitos was once called the "Pearl of the Amazon." It isn't quite that lustrous today, but it's still a pleasant, friendly town on the banks of the Amazon River, situated in Peru's northeastern jungle. The jungle port, which sits near the confluence of the Río Nanay and the Río Amazonas, is only accessed by water and by air. Motor scooters outnumber cars, and the typical family transportation is a three-wheeler with a canvas top. When the river is high, the picturesque waterfront district of Belén actually floats; when the river is low, Belén is about a half-mile out and sits in mud. It rises and falls from season to season by as much as 50 feet. The region has cycled through booms and busts since the great rubber boom of the late 1800s. The boom lasted about 30 years and brought great richness to the region. With the bust, the economy collapsed and remained stagnant for nearly 50 years. Iquitos, which had seen unprecedented growth and opulence during the rubber boom, became an Amazonian backwater overnight. The economy slouched along, barely sustaining itself with logging, exotic animal exports, and tobacco, banana, and Brazil-nut farming. In the early 1970s foreign interests began to explore the region for petroleum, and found it. The black gold, along with ecotourism and logging, have since become the backbone of the region's economy. While the main reason to drop into town is to explore the surrounding rain forest, given a chance, Iquitos will grow on you as you become accustomed to the humid climate and relaxed, easy ways of its citizens. A revamped riverwalk is the popular place for an evening stroll, followed by entertainment in the riverside plaza.

Iquitos

❻-⓫ *1,150 km (719 mi) northeast of Lima.*

A sultry port town on the Río Amazonas, Iquitos is quite probably the world's largest city that cannot be reached by road. The city has some 350,000 inhabitants and is the capital of the vast Loreto Department. The area around Iquitos was first inhabited by small, independent Amazonian tribes. In the 1500s Jesuit missionaries began adventuring in the area, trying to Christianize the local population, but the city wasn't officially founded until 1757.

☝ ▶ ❻   One of Iquitos's most fascinating sights is the **Distrito de Belén** (Belén District). In the market itself you will find sundry items from love potions
Fodor'sChoice   to fresh *suri* (palm-tree worms). It is not the cleanest or sweetest-smelling
★   market you'll encounter, but it's well worth the visit. From the center of the market you come to the port, where you can head out on a canoe trip through the floating Belén District. This slum area is often called the Venice of the Amazon (a diplomatic euphemism), but paddling by canoe through the floating "neighborhoods" is really a kick. The houses here are built on rafts. Most of the year they float placidly on the Amazon, though during the low-water season (June–Nov.) they sit in the mud and can attract disease-carrying mosquitoes. During high-water season (Dec.–May), guides hire out their services for one- to two-hour trips, which normally cost around S/7. Negotiate the price beforehand. Be street smart in Belén—evening muggings have been reported in this area, so it is best avoided at night. Also be wary of pickpockets at all times. Stay alert, access your cash discreetly when you need it, and keep your valuables close. For further tips, *see*Safety*in* Smart Travel Tips A to Z.

▶ ❼   You can take an afternoon stroll along the **Malecón Tarapacá,** the pleasant riverfront walk. There are a number of good restaurants here, as well as some well-maintained rubber-boom-era architecture.

❽   The **Museo Amazónico** gives a unique look into the rich indigenous culture of the region, with bronzed statues of local tribesman. ✉ *Malecón Tarapacá 386* ☎ *094/242–353* 🎫 *Free* 🕐 *Daily 9–6.*

Iquitos enjoyed its heyday as a port during the rubber boom a century ago. Some of the wealth of that time can still be detected in the *azulejos* (imported tiles) that face many buildings along the riverbank, notably the former **Hotel Palacio,** now converted into an army barracks and looking a little worn around the edges. The hotel was built in 1908. ✉ *Putumayo and Malecón Tarapacá* ☎ *no phone* 🎫 *Free* 🕐 *Daily.*

An example of the interesting architecture in the center of town is the **Casa de Fierro** (iron house), designed by Gustave Eiffel (of Eiffel Tower fame) and forged in Belgium. A wealthy rubber baron bought the house at the Parisian International Exposition of 1889 and had it shipped to Iquitos, where it was reassembled. Lunching at The Regal is the best way to visit the iron house. ⊠ *Putumayo 180, on the Plaza de Armas* ☎ *no phone* ☝ *Free* ⏱ *Daily 8 AM–12 PM.*

From the small **Port Bellavista Nanay,** 1.2 km (.75 mi) north of downtown Iquitos on Avenida La Marina, you can hire boats to take you to the Boras and Yaguas villages. Bringing a donation of school supplies (pencils, crayons, and notebooks) is a kind gesture and much appreciated by the Boras and Yaguas, who live in small communities near the pueblo San Andrés. A 20-minute boat ride will get you to **Pilpintuwasi Butterfly Farm,** which hosts some 42 butterfly species and also has macaws, a jaguar, and a tapir. During the dry season you'll need to walk along a forest path for 15 minutes to get to the farm. It is best to go with a guide. ⊠ *Near the village of Padre Cocha on the Nanay River, 5 km (3 mi) from downtown Iquitos* ☎ *094/232–665* ☝ *S/18 without transportation* ⏱ *Tues.–Sun. 9–4.*

off the beaten path

COMPLEJO TURÍSTICO QUISTOCOCHA – Rarely seen jungle animals roam in these small zoological gardens. You will see *otorongo* (a large jungle cat akin to the jaguar), pumas, jaguars, tapirs, river otters, and monkeys. The tourist complex sits at the edge of a jungle lagoon surrounded by verdant rain forest. Local conservationists have criticized the zoo for not feeding the animals and for keeping them in cages too small for their specific breeds. While these magnificent jungle animals do seem out of place in their tiny pens, they all seem relatively fit and well fed. There are nature trails, a swimming area, and a snack bar. At the park's entrance are murals recounting stories from local mythology: the toad-headed El Mayantu is the patron saint of lost travelers; the fierce, fire-spouting horseman La Runa Mula comes when one commits adultery. To get here, hire a motocarro in Iquitos for around S/15. ⊠ *13.5 km (8.5 mi) south of Iquitos on the Carretera Iquitos–Nauta* ☎ *no phone* ☝ *S/3* ⏱ *Daily 7–6.*

Where to Stay & Eat

¢–$ ✕ **El Mesón.** On the riverwalk, this restaurant serves ample potions of regional specialties. Try the delicious *paiche,* a giant fish found in jungle lakes. Tapestries and paintings depicting scenes from traditional Amazonian life adorn the walls. With good views of the Amazon and the easy-paced life of the paseo, this is an excellent sunset joint. ⊠ *Av. Malecón Maldonado 153* ☎ *094/231–857* ☐ *AE, MC, V, DC.*

¢–$ ✕ **Fitzcarraldo.** The colonial elegance of this riverwalk eatery shines
Fodor'sChoice through, from the antique firearms to the iron terrace chairs. The ex-
★ tensive menu has international essentials like pizza and pasta, but the Amazonian specialties are the real draw. Try the *chicharrón de lagarto* (crocodile nuggets), topping off the meal with a frothy *caipirinha* (a Brazilian drink with lime, sugar, and the sugar cane liquor cachaça). ⊠ *Napo 100, at El Boulevard* ☎ *094/243–434* ☐ *V, MC, AE, DC.*

★ $ ✕ **Gran Maloca.** This most elegant of the city's restaurants is in a lovely building encrusted with colorful *azulejos* (glazed tiles). The international fare is excellent, and the lobster and shrimp in pepper sauce is especially good. Try the *suri al ajo* (palm-tree grubs cooked in wine and garlic sauce) for an appetizer. They have an extensive wine and spirits list, with locally made fruit liqueurs. ⊠ *Sargento Lores 170* ☎ *094/233–126* ☐ *AE, DC, MC, V.*

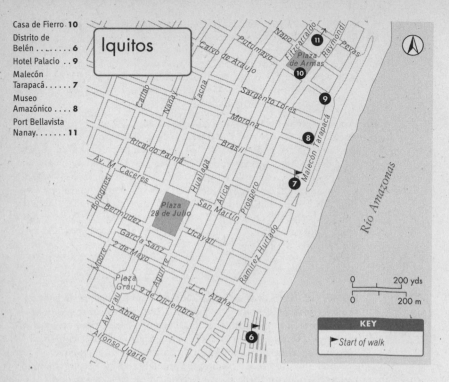

¢–$ ✕ **La Noche.** Big windows smile onto the Amazon River from this azule-jos-facaded bistro. The menu is varied and has de-riguer international standards as well as some excellent local alternatives. The *venado a la Loretana* (Loretan-style venison) is tender and yummy. This is also an excellent night spot, as the restaurant sits right on the Malecón Maldonado riverwalk. ✉ *Malecón Maldonado 177* ☎ *094/222–373* 🖃 *AE, MC, V.*

¢–$ ✕ **The Regal.** More of a cultural curiosity than a culinary one, The Regal is on the second story of Gustave Eiffel's landmark Iron House. To sit on The Regal's terrace overlooking the Plaza de Armas, one can't help but wax atavistic: dreams of scores settled and millions lost and sold in the great rubber boom haunt the imagination. The terrace can be quite noisy because of the passing motocarros. The menu tends towards the international side of the spectrum, and the steak-and-kidney pies are not to be missed. ✉ *Putumayo 180, Altos* ☎ *094/222–732* 🖃 *AE, DC, MC, V.*

★ $$$$ 🏨 **El Dorado Plaza Hotel.** This modern hotel, the best in Iquitos, richly deserves the praise it wins from guests. All rooms center around the grand entryway, which has a large fountain and a glass elevator. Behind the hotel you will find a pool with a swim-up bar. A bridge arches over the pool, leading you to the Jacuzzi. The rooms have all the modern conveniences and are equipped with soundproof glass to protect you from the incessant cacophony of central Iquitos. The hotel sits in the heart of the city on the Plaza de Armas. ✉ *Napo 258* ☎ *094/222–555* 📠 *94/224–304* ⊕ *www.eldoradoplazahotel.com* ⤶ *56 rooms, 9 suites* ⚐ *Restaurant, cafeteria, room service, in-room safes, minibars, cable TV, pool, health club, outdoor hot tub, 2 bars, shop, laundry service, business services, meeting rooms, airport shuttle, free parking* 🖃 *AE, MC, V* ⚏ *CP.*

$ 🏨 **Hotel El Dorado.** A small, grotto-like pool and a pleasant patio are a few of the charming amenities of this hotel a few blocks off the main square. The rooms have seen better days—the bedspreads are slightly dank from non-stop air-conditioning and the cheap wood furniture is becoming nicked in places. A heavy tropical odor pervades most rooms: the sweet smell of the tropics, a strange mix of sweat, overripe fruit, earth, and ozone is at first repellent and overwhelming, but you will quickly adapt and may even find the aroma alluring and exotic after a day or two. The hotel's restaurant, Las Rocas, is quite good. ⊠ *Napo 362* ☎ *094/221–985 or 094/232–574* 🖷 *094/221–985* 🖉 *dorado@TUS.com.pe* ⇆ *57 rooms, 3 suites* ♿ *Restaurant, room service, minibars, cable TV, pool, outdoor hot tub, bar, laundry service, meeting rooms, airport shuttle* 🖃 *AE, DC, V, MC* 🍴 *CP.*

★ $ 🖥 **Victoria Regia Hotel.** This modern, airy lodging has rooms dressed in cool colors that surround a courtyard with a small swimming pool. Rooms in the back are less noisy but darker. Most rooms have Impressionist and Expressionist prints adorning the walls, blond-wood furniture, and large, comfy beds. ⊠ *Ricardo Palma 252* ☎ *094/231–983 or 01/241–9195* 🖷 *094/232–499* ⊕ *www.victoriaregiahotel.com* ⇆ *34 rooms, 8 suites* ♿ *Restaurant, room service, in-room safes, minibars, cable TV, pool, bar, laundry service, business services, meeting rooms, airport shuttle, travel services* 🖃 *AE, DC, V, MC* 🍴 *CP.*

¢–$ 🖥 **Hotel Sandalo.** The hotel is a converted casona, but retains little of the original charm, with fluorescent lights and dank bedcovers. The suites facing the street are the nicest, with dolphin stencils adorning the walls and pleasant terraces. Rooms without air-conditioning go for around $10, a great break for budget travelers willing to sweat out a night. There's a little pond and rain forest–like garden at the hotel's entrance. ⊠ *Jr. Próspero 616* ☎ *094/234–761* 🖷 *094/234–643* 🖉 *sandalohotel@hotmail.com* ⇆ *31 rooms* ♿ *Cafeteria, room service, some fans, some minibars, cable TV, bar, laundry service, airport shuttle; no a/c in some rooms* 🖃 *V, MC, AE, DC* 🍴 *CP.*

¢ 🖥 **Florentina Hostal.** A bare-bones budget alternative in the center of Iquitos, La Florentina has simple, clean rooms in a more-than-100-year-old house. Two rooms come with air-conditioning; the others have fans and can get quite hot. All rooms have soft beds and thin sheets. ⊠ *Jr. Huallaga 212* ☎☎ *094/221–299* ⇆ *19 rooms* ♿ *Cafeteria, fans, cable TV, laundry service; no room phones, no a/c in some rooms* 🖃 *No credit cards.*

¢ 🖥 **Hotel Marañon.** There's a slightly institutional feel to this ultra-clean, relatively inexpensive newcomer, thanks mostly to the tiled floors, high ceilings, and unadorned walls. The front of the hotel faces a busy street; rooms in the back are quieter. The pool and small terrace in the back are a nice addition. ⊠ *Nauta 285* ☎ *094/242–673* 🖷 *094/231–737* ⊕ *www.amarillastelefonica.com/hotelmaragnon* 🖉 *hotel.maranon@terra.com.pe* ⇆ *24 rooms* ♿ *Restaurant, cafeteria, room service, cable TV, pool, laundry service, airport shuttle* 🖃 *V, MC* 🍴 *CP.*

Nightlife & the Arts

Maybe it's the heat or the humidity, maybe it's the proximity to the jungle, darkness, and its innate, inexplicable sensuality. Whatever the reason, Iquitos heats up after dark, and the dancing and bar scene here is spectacular. The revelry goes on into the wee hours. You should begin your night at one of the many bars along the Malecón. **Arandú Bar** (⊠ Malecón Maldonado 113 ☎ no phone) is one of the riverwalk's best bars, mainly because you get to choose the music; ask the waiter for the CD case and pick from a wide selection of modern pop and Latino disks. **La Noche** (⊠ Malecón Maldonado 177 ☎ 094/222–373) is another popular spot on the river. The music tends toward world-music favorites like Marley and Manu Chau. The ultra-funky **Café Teatro Amauta**

(⊠ Amauta 250 ☎ 094/233–109) has live music and performances every night. The stage faces the road and sidewalk café. This bohemian gathering spot serves local cocktails like *siete raizes* and *chuchuwasa*. **Discoteque Piraña** (⊠ Loreto 222 ☎ no phone) caters to a younger, twenty-and-under crowd and has loud Latino music. **Discotec Noa** (⊠ Fitzcarraldo 298 ☎ 094/222–993) charges a cover and is the biggest disco in town. They play mostly Latino pop, peppering the selection with the occasional techno or modern music favorite.

Shopping

There are many stores and souvenir stands along the Malecón and the streets leading off the Plaza de Armas. Look for pottery, hand-painted cloth from Pucallpa, and jungle items such as preserved piranhas, seed necklaces, fish and animal teeth, blowguns, spears, and balsa-wood parrots. The **Mercado Belén** is a riot of colors and smells. You can buy everything from souvenirs to love potions to fresh-made *masato* in the market. Beware, as there are many pickpockets in the close-quartered market. Many people will offer to sell souvenirs made from snake and caiman skins and toucan beaks, but buying these only encourages the further decimation of these at-risk animal populations. For cool T-shirts emblazoned with Federación de Borrachos de Iquitos (Federation of Drunks of Iquitos) or "FBI" logos, among others, try **Mad Mike's Trading Post** (⊠ Putumayo 184–B ☎ 094/222–372). The money goes to benefit street children and to provide medical supplies for local hospitals.

Into the Jungle

The Amazon Rain Forest is perhaps the world's last frontier. It is so immense that parts have yet to be explored by non-indigenous people. About 50 km (31 mi) from Iquitos are vast tracks of primary rain forest that seem to stretch forever, where the only intrusion from humans has been hunting and gathering. Sadly, even this light touch has had an effect, as hunting has all but eliminated large animals from the region. However, visitors are likely to see birds, monkeys, pink freshwater *bufeos* (dolphins), and caimans along the Amazon River and its tributaries. You're sure to spot large blue morpho butterflies.

The Amazon Basin is the world's most diverse ecosystem. The numbers of catalogued plant and animal species are astronomical, and scientists are discovering new species all the time. There are more than 25,000 classified species of plants in the Peruvian Amazon (and 80,000 in the entire Amazon Basin), including the 2-meter-wide Victoria Regia water lilies. Scientists have catalogued more than 4,000 species of butterfly and more than 2,000 species of fish—a more diverse aquatic life than that of the Atlantic Ocean. Scientists estimate that the world's tropical forests, while comprising only 6 percent of the Earth's landmass, may hold up to 75 percent of the planet's plant and animal species. This land is not only beautiful, with numerous indigenous populations, but is also the largest natural pharmacy in the world: one-fourth of all modern medicines have botanical origins in tropical forests.

It's interesting and worthwhile to visit the small villages of indigenous people. When the boat stops at these settlements, you'll usually find half the village waiting to trade handicrafts for whatever you have with you; items perpetually in demand include umbrellas, hammers, fishing hooks, flashlights, sewing supplies, lipstick, and clothing.

The best way to visit the jungle is with a pre-arranged tour with one of the many jungle lodges. All the lodges have highly-trained naturalist guides.

CloseUp

JUNGLE JOURNEYS

THE KNOCK AT THE DOOR COMES EARLY. *"¡Buenos días! Good morning!"* It's 5 AM and your guide is rousing you for the dawn excursion to the nearby ccollpa de guacamayos. He doesn't want you to miss the riotous, colorful spectacle of hundreds of macaws and parrots descending to the vertical clay lick to ingest a beakful of mineral-rich earth. Roll over and go back to sleep? Blasphemy! You're in the Amazon.

A stay at any of the remote Iquitos or Madre de Dios lodges is not for the faint of heart, and you'll need to gear up for a different type of vacation experience. Relaxing and luxuriating it will not be, although you might be surprised at how comfortable facilities out here can be. Your days will be packed with activities that, depending on the nature of your tour and lodge, will include: bird- and wildlife-watching, boat trips, rain-forest hikes, visits to indigenous communities, mountain biking, or white-water rafting. You'll be in the company of guides from the minute you're picked up in Iquitos, Puerto Maldonado, or Cusco. Most lodges here hire top-notch guides who know their areas well, and you'll be forever amazed at their ability to spot that camouflaged howler monkey from a hundred paces. There is downtime for curling up in a hammock with a good book, yet few visitors here want to spend their time so idly.

The lodge itself should provide mosquito netting and sheets or blankets, as well as some type of lantern for your room for the evening. (Don't expect electricity at most of these places.) But always check with the your tour operator for a list of what to bring and what the lodge itself provides. Your required inventory will vary proportionally by just how much you have to rough it. Pack sunscreen, sunglasses, insect repellent, a hat, hiking boots, and sandals or light shoes. Also, a light, loose-fitting, long-sleeve shirt and equally loose-fitting long trousers and socks are musts for the evening when the mosquitoes come out. Carry your yellow fever vaccination certificate and prescription for malaria

prevention and, of course, an extra supply of any prescription you might be taking. Bring along an antidiarrheal medication, too. You'll need a small daypack for the numerous guided hikes you'll go on, but don't forget to bring some plastic bags to protect your belongings from the rain and humidity. Also bring binoculars and plenty of film.

There is little to buy out here; everything is usually included in the package price, though you'll probably be caught off guard by the extra price you're charged for beverages. Soft drinks and, especially, beer carry a hefty markup, understandable given the cost of transporting them out here, and are almost never included in the quoted price.

Few things are more enjoyable at a jungle lodge than dinner at the end of the day. Food could be served at a buffet, or everyone might dig in and dine family style around a common table. Either way, you're sure to excitedly discuss the day's sightings and events, comparing notes with your fellow travelers well into the evening, knowing full well there will be another 5 AM knock at the door tomorrow morning.

— By Jeffrey Van Fleet

Among the activities offered at these lodges are nature walks, birding tours, nighttime canoe outings, fishing, and trips to indigenous villages. Some lodges have canopy walkways that take you into the seldom-explored rain-forest canopy.

Around Iquitos there are large tracks of virgin rain forest and several reserves worth visiting. The hard-to-reach **Reserva Nacional Pacaya Samiria** is found at the confluence of the Maranon and Ucayali rivers. The reserve is Peru's second largest and encompasses more than 2 million hectares of land, about the size of El Salvador. As with many reserves in South America, there are a number of people living in Pacaya Samiria, around 30,000 according to recent estimates. Park rangers try to balance the needs of these local communities while still trying to protect the environment, and occasionally request a minimal S/10 entrance fee. It takes at least five days to visit the park. ✉ *Confluence of the Marañón and Ucayali Rivers, 5-hr boat ride from Iquitos* ☎ *no phone* ☉ *Daily.*

There are several smaller private rain-forest reserves northeast of Iquitos near the confluence of the Napo and Amazon Rivers. **CONAPAC** (Peruvian Amazon Conservation Organization) has a large 100,000-hectare, multi-use reserve known as the CONAPAC (or Sucusuri) Biological Reserve. The Orejones tribe, whose name refers to the tribe's ritual practice of ear piercing and lobe enlargement, also has a reserve of about 5,000 hectares. ✉ *Near the confluence of the Napo and Amazon rivers, 70 km (43 mi) downriver from Iquitos* ☎ *Contact Explorama to visit the reserve: 094/252–526, 800/707–5275 in the U.S.* ☎ *094/252–533* ⊕ *www.explorama.com* ✉ *Free* ☉ *Daily.*

Where to Stay

Rates for the rain-forest lodges near Iquitos include transportation, meals, and guided walks. Transportation to the lodges is either by *palm-caris* (large wooden boats with thatched roofs) or speedboats. Four lodges—Ceiba Tops, Explorama Lodge, ExplorNapo, and ExplorTambos—are owned and operated by Explorama Tours. Explorama also takes bookings for ACEER, the Amazon Center for Environmental Education and Research. For properties where a minimum stay is indicated, the price category is based on the per-night cost.

$$$$ 🏨 **ACEER.** Rooms at the Amazon Center for Environmental Education and Research are usually reserved by scientists or special groups. The lodge, which opened in 1993, includes 43 beds in a large, thatch-roof building. The Canopy Walkway, which allows you to walk 120 ft above the ground, was the first facility of its kind in South America. Hike the "Medicine Trail" to observe how rain-forest plants are used in modern pharmaceuticals. ✉ *Reservations: Av. de la Marina 340, Iquitos* ☎ *094/252–526, 800/707–5275 in the U.S.* ☎ *094/252–533* ⊕ *www.explorama.com* ✑ *43 beds with shared bath* ⚐ *Restaurant, boating, fishing, hiking, airport shuttle, travel services, some no-smoking rooms; no room phones, no room TVs, no a/c* ☰ *MC, V, AE, DC* ☉ *FAP.*

$$$$ 🏨 **Ceiba Tops.** Explorama's newest luxury lodge, with large picture windows overlooking the Amazon, is just 45 minutes downriver from Iquitos. After a jungle trek, plunge into the pool, take a nap in your air-conditioned room, or relax with a book in a hammock. You can even take a hot shower before dinner. The restaurant has international cuisine and Peruvian wines. The hotel is on a 40-hectare private rain-forest reserve. All meals are included in the rate. ✉ *Reservations: Av. de la Marina 340, Iquitos* ☎ *094/252–526, 800/707–5275 in the U.S.* ☎ *094/252–533* ⊕ *www.explorama.com* ✑ *50 rooms, 3 suites* ⚐ *Restaurant, fans, pool, boating, fishing, hiking, bar, shop, airport shuttle,*

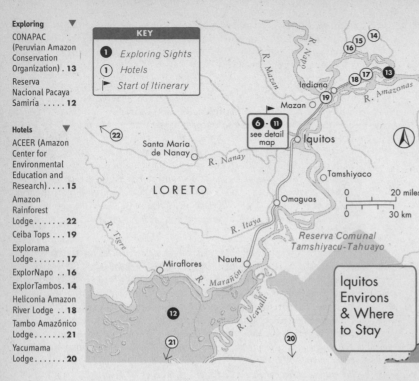

KEY
1 Exploring Sights
1 Hotels
► Start of Itinerary

Iquitos Environs & Where to Stay

travel services, some no-smoking rooms; no room phones, no room TVs ▤ MC, V, AE, DC ◉ FAP.

$$$$ Explorama Lodge. Explorama's first lodge, built in 1964, is 80 km (50 mi) down the Amazon in pristine rain forest. Under palm-thatched roofs are several houses with a total of 60 rooms. Kerosene lamps light up the covered walkways between them. Many walks are offered, including one to the Seven Bridges Trail. The rooms are extremely simple, as they are in most jungle lodges, and the requisite mosquito nets ensure a night's sleep relatively free from bites. There are cold-water shower facilities. The minimum stay is two nights. ✉ Reservations: Av. de la Marina 340, Iquitos ☎ 094/252–526, 800/707–5275 in the U.S. 🖷 094/252–533 ⊕ www.explorama.com ⬗ 63 rooms with shared bath ⌂ Restaurant, boating, fishing, hiking, bar, airport shuttle, travel services, some no-smoking rooms; no room phones, no room TVs, no a/c ▤ MC, V, AE, DC ◉ FAP.

$$$$ ExplorNapo. The remote camp is set deep in the middle of the Sucusari
Fodor'sChoice Nature Reserve, 70 km (43 mi) up the Napo River and 1½ hours by
★ boat from the Explorama Lodge. There is a large canopy walkway here for exploring the seldom-seen upper-reaches of the Amazon, as well as an informative enthnological garden. Because of the distance, many people spend a night at the Explorama Lodge en route to ExplorNapo. Facilities are rustic, with kerosene lighting and separate cold-water shower facilities. There's a screened dining room, with occasional music performed by local people. This is a prime place for spotting wildlife, so guided walks and canoe trips are daily activities. The minimum stay is four nights. ✉ Reservations: Av. de la Marina 340, Iquitos ☎ 094/252–526, 800/707–5275 in the U.S. 🖷 094/252–533 ⊕ www.explorama.com ⬗ 30 rooms with shared bath ⌂ Restaurant, boating, fishing, hiking, bar, airport shuttle, travel services, some no-smoking rooms; no room phones, no room TVs, no a/c ▤ MC, V, AE, DC ◉ FAP.

$$$$ ExplorTambos. This very primitive lodge is a three-hour hike from ExplorNapo. There are no rooms here—you sleep on mattresses on platforms under mosquito netting. Visits here are usually an extension of trips to Explorama Lodge or ExplorNapo. Being the most remote lodge in the region, the chances of seeing wildlife are quite good. But this is definitely a place for serious explorers who don't mind a little discomfort. The minimum stay is four nights. ✉ Reservations: Av. de la Marina 340, Iquitos ☎ 094/252–526, 800/707–5275 in the U.S. 🖷 094/252–533 ⊕ www.explorama.com ⬗ space for 16 people ⌂ Restaurant, boating, fishing, hiking, airport shuttle, travel services, some no-smoking rooms; no room phones, no room TVs, no a/c ▤ MC, V, AE, DC ◉ FAP.

$$$$ Tambo Amazónico Lodge. A very basic lodge near the Pacaya Samiria Nature Reserve, the Tambo Amazónico is the best lodge near this immense track of virgin rain forest. The lodge has small, thatched-roof bungalows with no electricity. It sits just at the park's entrance on the Río Yarapa. The rate includes guided tours of the park, all meals, and transportation. The minimum stay is three nights. ✉ Reservations: Calle Pevas 246, Iquitos ☎ 094/231–618 or 094/233–110 ⊕ www.paseosamazonicos.com ⬗ 10 rooms with shared bath ⌂ Restaurant, boating, fishing, hiking, airport shuttle, travel services, some no-smoking rooms; no room phones, no room TVs, no a/c ▤ V, MC ◉ FAP.

$$$$ Yacumama Lodge. Alongside the Yarapa River, a tributary of the Amazon, this beautiful complex is three to four hours from Iquitos. Raised bungalows with screened porches (widely spaced for maximum privacy) are connected to the main lodge by covered walkways. All buildings are constructed using natural materials. Most of the property is solar powered, with an emphasis on recycling, composting, and organic farming—all part of the goal of minimum impact on the surrounding environment. Although rooms don't have private baths, there are two modern buildings with showers and flush toilets. A screened "hammock room" overlooking the river is great for afternoon naps, especially after swinging from tree to tree on the "canopy skyline." Pink river dolphins are often spotted in the area. The minimum stay is five nights. Reservations: ✉ Sgto. Lores 149, Iquitos ☎ 094/235–510, 800/854–0023 in the U.S. ⊕ www.yacumama.com ⬗ 31 bungalows with shared bath ⌂ Restaurant, boating, fishing, hiking, bar, airport shuttle, meeting rooms, travel services, some no-smoking rooms; no room phones, no room TVs, no a/c ▤ AE, DC, MC, V ◉ FAP.

$$ Amazon Rainforest Lodge. Only an hour by speedboat from Iquitos, this cluster of thatch-roof bungalows sits on the Momon River. The attractive structures center around the greenish colored pool, have twin beds and private baths, and are lit by gas lanterns. Activities include guided walks, piranha fishing, night canoeing, ayahuasca ceremonies, and visits to Yagua villages. They cater to a much younger crowd than most of the jungle lodges in the area. Reservations: ✉ Putomayo 159, Iquitos ☎ 094/233–100 or 01/445–5620 🖷 094/242–231 or 01/447–2651 ⊕ www.amazon-lodge.com ⬗ 14 bungalows with shared bath ⌂ Restaurant, pool, boating, fishing, hiking, bar, shop, laundry services, airport shuttle, travel services, some no-smoking rooms; no room phones, no room TVs, no a/c ▤ MC, V ◉ FAP.

$$ Heliconia Amazon River Lodge. An hour downriver from Iquitos you'll find the Heliconia, which sits on the large Yanamono reserve. The lodge has a big thatched-roof dining area. Rooms have twin beds, private bathrooms, and hot-water showers. Guides are available for fishing, night canoeing, and bird-watching. ✉ Reservations: Av. Ricardo Palma 242, Iquitos ☎ 094/231–959 or 01/421–9195 🖷 094/231–983 or 01/442–4338 ⊕ www.amazonriverexpeditions.com ⬗ 21 rooms ⌂ Restau-

THE CENTRAL HIGHLANDS

5

FODOR'S CHOICE

Convento de Santa Rosa de Ocopa, *former mission in Concepción*

Grand Hotel Huánuco, *Huanuco*

Hostal El Marqués de Valdelirios, *Ayacucho*

La Cabaña, *Peruvian fare in Huancayo*

La Florida, *bed-and-breakfast in Tarma*

Pampas de Quinua, *battlefield in Ayacucho*

Restaurant Urpicha, *Ayacucho*

HIGHLY RECOMMENDED

RESTAURANTS La Casona, *Ayacucho*

Restaurant Olímpico, *Huancayo*

HOTELS Andino Lodging and Excursions, *Huancayo*

Hostal Residencial Huánuco, *Huanuco*

SIGHTS Kotosh, *Huanuco*

rant, boating, fishing, billiards, hiking, bar, shop, airport shuttle, travel services, some no-smoking rooms; no room phones, no room TVs, no a/c ⊟ V, MC ¶Ol FAP.

Iquitos & Environs A to Z

To research prices, get advice from other travelers, and book travel arrangements, visit www.fodors.com.

AIR TRAVEL

From Lima, Aero Continente has several flights a day to Iquitos. Taca Peru has daily flights to Iquitos, and TANS Perú has two flights a day between Iquitos and Lima. Aerocontinente offers round-trip flights from Miami on Sunday.

🚹 Carriers **Aero Continente** ☎ 094/243-489 in Iquitos, 01/242-4260 in Lima, 877/359-7378 in the U.S. **Taca Peru** ☎ 094/242-448 in Iquitos or 01/446-0033 in Lima. **TANS Perú** ☎ 094/231-071 in Iquitos, 01/575-3842 in Lima.

AIRPORTS

Iquitos's Aeropuerto Internacional Francisco Secada Vignetta is 8 km (5 mi) from the city center. There is a S/12 airport tax for domestic flights and a S/36 tax for international flights. A taxi to the airport should cost around S/10.

🚹 Airport Information **Aeropuerto Internacional Francisco Secada Vignetta** ☎ 094/260-151 in Iquitos.

BORDER CROSSINGS

It is a two-day boat ride to the Brazilian border. As of press time American citizens do not need a special visa to enter Brazil, though these policies change quite often; check with the Brazilian Embassy before heading there. For the most part, Peruvian boats operate only in Peruvian waters. You will need to change boats in Brazil. **Brazilian Embassy** (⊠ Sgto. Lores 363, Iquitos). **Iquitos Customs Office** (☎ 094/251-957).

BOAT & FERRY TRAVEL

There are a number of national and international ferry lines that operate from Iquitos, taking you to the town of Pucallpa and as far as the Atlantic Ocean in Brazil. These boats are often quite run-down and few have staterooms. You'll need to bring a hammock and lots of bug spray. Passage to Pucallpa takes four to eight days and costs around $40. Jungle Exports offers cruises to the Reserva Nacional Pacaya Samiria. Cruceros offers very expensive Amazon cruises. Most boats leave from Puerto Masusa, about 3 km north of the city center on Ave. La Marina.

🚹 Boat & Ferry Lines **Jungle Exports** ⊠ Puerto Masusa, Iquitos ☎ 094/231-870. **Cruceros** ⊠ Requena 336, Iquitos ☎ 094/231-611 in Iquitos, 01/265-9524 in Lima.

CAR RENTAL

Though there isn't much reason to rent a car in Iquitos (everything is so close), though you may want to rent one for an afternoon to check out the areas immediately surrounding town. Motos y Autos JB rents 4 x 4s and motorcycles by the day and by the hour.

🚹 Agencies **Motos y Autos JB** ⊠ Yavari 702, Iquitos ☎ 094/222-389.

CAR TRAVEL

The most common mode of transportation in the Iquitos area is the *motocarro*, a three-wheeled motorcycle with a canvas top. Service in town costs around S/1.50, while going to the outskirts you will pay around S/9 an hour. Always negotiate the price beforehand. There aren't many places to go by road, but exploring the outskirts and tiny hamlets around Iquitos—during the day—can be fun.

EMERGENCIES

In case of an accident or emergency, call the local authorities immediately, especially the tourist police if there is a branch in your particular town. Contacting your embassy is also a good idea. iPerú has a 24-hour emergency hot line. In smaller towns and in the wilderness you will probably need to arrange for transportation to Iquitos. Some of the equipment in the hospitals may not be up-to-date, but doctors are knowledgeable.

🖪 Emergency Services **General emergency** ☎ 105 throughout Peru. **Police** ☎ 094/260-361. **Tourist Police** ☎ 094/242-081. **iPerú** ☎ 094/260-251, 0800/42-579 throughout Peru. **Fire Department** ☎ 116.
🖪 **Clinica Adventista Ana Stahl** ✉ Av. de la Marina 285, Iquitos ☎ 094/252-518 or 094/252-535. **Hospital Regional de Iquitos** ✉ Av. 28 de Julio, Cuadra 15, Iquitos ☎ 094/252-743 or 094/251-882.

HEALTH

The biggest health concerns for travelers in the Amazon Basin are traveler's stomach (persistent diarrhea) and malaria. Traveler's stomach is not easy to avoid; fasting while maintaining a strict regimen of hydration (bottled water only) is the quickest way to cure traveler's stomach. When entering a questionable restaurant, check out the bathroom first; it's a good sign if it is clean and has soap. Peeling fruits and vegetables before you eat them can also help reduce your chances of having an upset stomach.

You are not required to get any vaccinations to enter Peru, but it is advisable to check with the World Health Organization before your visit. The Peruvian Embassy recommends getting a yellow fever vaccine at least 10 days before visiting the Amazon. Avoid malaria by taking precautions against the mosquitoes: use an insect repellent with high DEET concentration, wear pants and light long-sleeved shirts, tucking your pant legs into your socks, and ensure the mosquito netting over your bed is secure before you head off to bed.

MAIL & SHIPPING

Iquitos has a post office; there is no mail service available from the lodges.
🖪 Post Office **Iquitos** ✉ Av. Arica 402 ☎ 094/231-915.

MONEY MATTERS

All banks in Iquitos can exchange money and cash traveler's checks. Try the local branches of Banco de Crédito, Banco Continental, or Banco Wiese.
🖪 Banks **Banco de Crédito** ✉ Av. Putumayo 202, Iquitos ☎ 094/233-838. **Banco Continental** ✉ Sgto. Lores 171, Iquitos ☎ 094/235-421. **Banco Wiese** ✉ Av. Próspero 282, Iquitos ☎ 094/232-350.

TELEPHONES

Telephone service is very good in Iquitos, with public phones using either phone cards or coins. At remote lodges, communication is by radio.

TOURS

In Iquitos, Amazon Tours and Cruises specializes in river cruises using boats with anywhere from 8 to 21 cabins. The longest and most comprehensive cruise includes a 6-day trip on the Amazon and a 10-day journey to Manaus, Brazil. All the boats have comfortable, air-conditioned cabins with private facilities. The boats stop at various points for nature hikes and visits to villages. International Expeditions has four of the most colorful and luxurious boats on the Amazon. Boats headed up the river to the Pacaya-Samiria National Reserve have accommodations for between 8 and 26 passengers. Cruises can be booked only from the

company's offices in the United States. Jungle Exports and Cruceros also offer boat tours through the region. Emily Tours, Explorama Tours, Paseos Amazonicos, and Turismo Pacífico Iquitos arrange trips throughout the region.

🖪 Fees & Schedules **Amazon Tours and Cruises** ✉ Requeña 336, Iquitos ☎ 094/231-611 ⊕ www.amazontours.net ✉ 8700 W. Flagler St., Miami, FL 33174 ☎ 305/227-2266 or 800/423-2791. **Cruceros** ✉ Requena 336, Iquitos ☎ 094/231-611 in Iquitos, 01/265-9524 in Lima. **Emily Tours** ✉ Jr. Progreso 268-270, Iquitos ☎ 094/235-273. **Explorama Tours** ✉ Av. de la Marina 350, Iquitos ☎ 094/252-530, 800/223-6764 in the U.S. **International Expeditions** ☎ 800/633-4734 🖷 205/428-1714 ⊕ www.internationalexpeditions.com. **Jungle Exports** ✉ Puerto Masusa, Iquitos ☎ 094/231-870. **Paseos Amazonicos** ✉ Calle Pevas 246, Iquitos ☎ 094/233-110 🖷 094/231-618. **Turismo Pacífico Iquitos** ✉ Calle Ricardo Palma 180, Iquitos ☎ 094/231-627.

TRANSPORTATION AROUND IQUITOS & ENVIRONS

The best way to travel around the Iquitos area is by boat. There are huge oceangoing boats that will take you all the way to the Atlantic Ocean in Brazil, tiny dugout canoes to take you deep into the jungle, and swift launches with outboard engines and canvas tops to keep you dry. It takes several days by boat to get to any large communities near Iquitos.

VISITOR INFORMATION

There are tourist information offices in downtown Iquitos and at the airport.
🖪 **iPerú** ✉ Airport ☎ 094/260-251. **Tourist Information Office** ✉ Napo 226 ☎ 094/235-621.

Updated by
Holly S. Smith

THE CENTRAL HIGHLANDS ARE THE HEART OF PERU, a crossroads between the best of the country's scenic and cultural pleasures. Here the massive Andes mesh into the impenetrable South American rain forest, and winding, cloud-covered mountain roads eventually dip down into stark desert terrain. It's where the smog of crowded, metropolitan Lima drifts east onto vast, barren highland plains. Given the region's surrounding attractions—Machu Picchu to the southeast, Manu National Park to the northeast, and Paracas National Reserve and the Nazca Lines to the southwest—it's no mystery why the Central Highlands have been largely overlooked by travelers.

There are other reasons the region has been avoided as well, and not just for the lack of transport and travel resources. The Central Highlands have long been a major coca-growing area, and it was home to the *Sendero Luminoso* (Shining Path) terrorists and the Tupac Amaru Revolutionary Movement for almost two decades. The Sendero Luminoso, which arose in the 1960s around Ayacucho, was finally dismantled in 1992 with the arrest of its leader, Abimaél Guzman Reynoso. In 1999 then-president of Peru Alberto Fujimori led a successful manhunt for the leader of the Sendero Rojo terrorist faction, Oscar Alberto Ramírez Durand, shutting down the region's revolutionary stronghold for good.

Now calm, stable, and for the most part safe for travelers, this beautiful region is quickly gaining prominence—particularly due to tight military checkpoints that have put drug trafficking on the decline. It's one of the few truly remote regions left in the world, although improvements in road, rail, and air services have made traveling a bit less challenging than it was even five years ago.

Because it has been sheltered from the outside for so long, the Central Highlands still hold many mysteries. No one knows, for example, when the first cultures settled here on the *puna* (highland plains), or how long they stayed. Archaeologists found what they believe to be the oldest village in Peru at Lauricocha, near Huánuco, and what is thought to be the oldest temple in North or South America in the north of this region, at Kotosh. Other nearby archaeological sites at Tantamayo and Garu also show that local Indian cultures thrived here long before the Inca or Spanish conquistadors ever reached the area.

Cave sites in the puna are particularly rich with artifacts, as local cultures used them as shelters from the frigid nighttime temperatures and whipping winds. Human relics at Pachamachay, a 4,300-m (14,104-ft) cave near lake Junín, show that hunter-gatherer tribes lived in this region from around 800 through AD 1200. These pre-ceramic peoples stayed year-round in base camps, harvesting the indigenous berries and grasses and hunting llamas and vicuñas for meat. About AD 1600 these groups developed pottery-making skills, allowing them to store large quantities of food and thus rely more on herding and farming than hunting as a way of life.

When the Inca did arrive, sometime in the late 1400s, they took the already stable northern settlement of Huánuco into their empire. It eventually became an important stop along their famed route between the capital at Cusco and the northern hub of Cajamarca, and today you can see thousands of Inca ruins scattered along the Huánuco pampas. The city was finally officially founded by the Spanish in 1539 and remained a major cultural center for colonial settlers. Mineral wealth was another attraction for the Spanish explorers, who turned Cerro de Pasco's buried gold, silver, copper, and coal into the center of the mining industry north of the Amazon basin. They ruled the region—and the country—until 1824, when Simon Bolívar's troops reclaimed Peru's autonomy by defeating the Spanish on the Quinua pampas near Huánuco.

Today most of those who live in the Central Highlands are subsistence farmers whose lives depend on the crops they grow and the animals they breed—including guinea pigs and rabbits. Traditions are little changed from centuries ago, so you'll see local festivals, taste unique village cuisine, and find craft workshops much the same as they have been for years. Outside of the towns natural beauty abounds, with thundering rivers, winding trails, and hidden waterfalls tucked into the mountainous terrain. Lago Junín, the country's second-largest lake, is found in the north.

Aside from exploring the region's history, cultures, and crafts, the main attraction here is its scenery. From Lima you can drive or catch a train east through the mountains toward Huancayo through a string of small towns set high in the mountains amid misty forests overlooking smooth river valleys carpeted with olive and gold grasses. One of the most spectacular journeys in South America is the 335-km (207-mi) train route that twists through the Andes at an elevation of 4,782 m (15,685 ft). The engine chugs its way up a slim thread of rails that hugs the slopes, speeding over 59 bridges, around endless hairpin curves, and through 66 tunnels—including the 1,175-m-long (3,854-ft-long) Galera Tunnel, which, at an altitude of 4,758 m (15,606 ft), is the world's highest railway. A second uniquely amazing journey is from Tarma to Chanchamayo, on which the road descends almost 2,500 m (8,200 ft) from mountains into the jungle in less than 70 km (43 mi).

Exploring the Central Highlands

A mere hour east of Lima puts you in the foothills of the Andes, a windy, barren landscape where llamas and alpacas wander upon wide, puddled fields. Roads and rails twist around the peaks and pass by ramshackle mountain towns before gradually sliding down from the highlands into muggy, eastern rain-forest jungle. As you travel southwest past Ayacucho, the climate gets warmer and the land becomes drier, eventually smoothing out into the central deserts and plains around Nazca. Southeast of Ayacucho is more mountain terrain, where over the centuries jagged stubs of forested stone protected such great archeological finds as Machu Picchu.

You can reach the Central Highlands by air, road, or rail, but the train journey from the capital will be your most memorable option. The 335-km (207-mi) railway cuts through the Andes, through mountain slopes and above deep crevasses where thin waterfalls plunge down into icy streams far below. The most logical route is from Lima to Huancayo, then south to Huancavelica and Ayacucho. You can drive or take the train as far as Huancavelica, but from here the rails end and the road gets rugged. Except for the highway, there are mostly dirt roads in this region, so be prepared for rough travel if you're going by bus or car. Those pressed for time can fly from Lima to Ayacucho and take tours or rent a car to cover sights in between.

About the Restaurants

Dining out in the Central Highlands is a very casual experience. Breakfast is simple, usually bread and jam or butter with some fruit, while the midday lunch combines soup, salad, and a rice and meat dish for the largest meal of the day. You'll find snacks everywhere, from nuts and fruit to ice cream and sweet breads, which are popular for after-

Among the activities offered at these lodges are nature walks, birding tours, nighttime canoe outings, fishing, and trips to indigenous villages. Some lodges have canopy walkways that take you into the seldom-explored rain-forest canopy.

⑫ Around Iquitos there are large tracks of virgin rain forest and several reserves worth visiting. The hard-to-reach **Reserva Nacional Pacaya Samiria** is found at the confluence of the Marañón and Ucayali rivers. The reserve is Peru's second largest and encompasses more than 2 million hectares of land, about the size of El Salvador. As with many reserves in South America, there are a number of people living in Pacaya Samiria, around 30,000 according to recent estimates. Park rangers try to balance the needs of these local communities while still trying to protect the environment, and occasionally request a minimal S/10 entrance fee. It takes at least five days to visit the park. ✉ *Confluence of the Marañón and Ucayali Rivers, 5-hr boat ride from Iquitos* ☎ *no phone* ◷ *Daily.*

★ ⑬ There are several smaller private rain-forest reserves northeast of Iquitos near the confluence of the Napo and Amazon Rivers. **CONAPAC** (Peruvian Amazon Conservation Organization) has a large 100,000-hectare, multi-use reserve known as the CONAPAC (or Sucusuri) Biological Reserve. The Orejones tribe, whose name refers to the tribe's ritual practice of ear piercing and lobe enlargement, also has a reserve of about 5,000 hectares. ✉ *Near the confluence of the Napo and Amazon rivers, 70 km (43 mi) downriver from Iquitos* ☎ *Contact Explorama to visit the reserve: 094/252–526, 800/707–5275 in the U.S.* 🖷 *094/252–533* ⊕ *www.explorama.com* ✇ *Free* ◷ *Daily.*

Where to Stay

Rates for the rain-forest lodges near Iquitos include transportation, meals, and guided walks. Transportation to the lodges is either by *palmcaris* (large wooden boats with thatched roofs) or speedboats. Four lodges—Ceiba Tops, Explorama Lodge, ExplorNapo, and ExplorTambos—are owned and operated by Explorama Tours. Explorama also takes bookings for ACEER, the Amazon Center for Environmental Education and Research. For properties where a minimum stay is indicated, the price category is based on the per-night cost.

$$$$ 🛏 **ACEER.** Rooms at the Amazon Center for Environmental Education and Research are usually reserved by scientists or special groups. The lodge, which opened in 1993, includes 43 beds in a large, thatch-roof building. The Canopy Walkway, which allows you to walk 120 ft above the ground, was the first facility of its kind in South America. Hike the "Medicine Trail" to observe how rain-forest plants are used in modern pharmaceuticals. ✉ *Reservations: Av. de la Marina 340, Iquitos* ☎ *094/ 252–526, 800/707–5275 in the U.S.* 🖷 *094/252–533* ⊕ *www.explorama. com* ✇ *43 beds with shared bath* ⚭ *Restaurant, boating, fishing, hiking, airport shuttle, travel services, some no-smoking rooms; no room phones, no room TVs, no a/c* ⊟ *MC, V, AE, DC* ⑩ *FAP.*

$$$$ 🛏 **Ceiba Tops.** Explorama's newest luxury lodge, with large picture windows overlooking the Amazon, is just 45 minutes downriver from Iquitos. After a jungle trek, plunge into the pool, take a nap in your air-conditioned room, or relax with a book in a hammock. You can even take a hot shower before dinner. The restaurant has international cuisine and Peruvian wines. The hotel is on a 40-hectare private rain-forest reserve. All meals are included in the rate. ✉ *Reservations: Av. de la Marina 340, Iquitos* ☎ *094/252–526, 800/707–5275 in the U.S.* 🖷 *094/252–533* ⊕ *www.explorama.com* ✇ *50 rooms, 3 suites* ⚭ *Restaurant, fans, pool, boating, fishing, hiking, bar, shop, airport shuttle,*

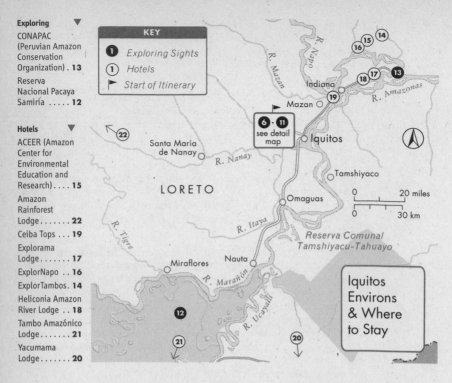

travel services, some no-smoking rooms; no room phones, no room TVs
⊟ *MC, V, AE, DC* |O| *FAP.*

$$$$ 🏠 **Explorama Lodge.** Explorama's first lodge, built in 1964, is 80 km (50 mi) down the Amazon in pristine rain forest. Under palm-thatched roofs are several houses with a total of 60 rooms. Kerosene lamps light up the covered walkways between them. Many walks are offered, including one to the Seven Bridges Trail. The rooms are extremely simple, as they are in most jungle lodges, and the requisite mosquito nets ensure a night's sleep relatively free from bites. There are cold-water shower facilities. The minimum stay is two nights. ⊠ *Reservations: Av. de la Marina 340, Iquitos* 🕾 *094/252–526, 800/707–5275 in the U.S.* 🖷 *094/252–533* 🌐 *www.explorama.com* ⇆ *63 rooms with shared bath* ⚐ *Restaurant, boating, fishing, hiking, bar, airport shuttle, travel services, some no-smoking rooms; no room phones, no room TVs, no a/c* ⊟ *MC, V, AE, DC* |O| *FAP.*

$$$$ 🏠 **ExplorNapo.** The remote camp is set deep in the middle of the Sucusari
Fodor's Choice   Nature Reserve, 70 km (43 mi) up the Napo River and 1½ hours by
★   boat from the Explorama Lodge. There is a large canopy walkway here for exploring the seldom-seen upper-reaches of the Amazon, as well as an informative enthnological garden. Because of the distance, many people spend a night at the Explorama Lodge en route to ExplorNapo. Facilities are rustic, with kerosene lighting and separate cold-water shower facilities. There's a screened dining room, with occasional music performed by local people. This is a prime place for spotting wildlife, so guided walks and canoe trips are daily activities. The minimum stay is four nights. ⊠ *Reservations: Av. de la Marina 340, Iquitos* 🕾 *094/252–526, 800/707–5275 in the U.S.* 🖷 *094/252–533* 🌐 *www.explorama.com* ⇆ *30 rooms with shared bath* ⚐ *Restaurant, boating, fishing, hiking, bar, airport shuttle, travel services, some no-smoking rooms; no room phones, no room TVs, no a/c* ⊟ *MC, V, AE, DC* |O| *FAP.*

CloseUp

JUNGLE JOURNEYS

THE KNOCK AT THE DOOR COMES EARLY. "¡Buenos días! Good morning!" It's 5 AM and your guide is rousing you for the dawn excursion to the nearby ccollpa de guacamayos. He doesn't want you to miss the riotous, colorful spectacle of hundreds of macaws and parrots descending to the vertical clay lick to ingest a beakful of mineral-rich earth. Roll over and go back to sleep? Blasphemy! You're in the Amazon.

A stay at any of the remote Iquitos or Madre de Dios lodges is not for the faint of heart, and you'll need to gear up for a different type of vacation experience. Relaxing and luxuriating it will not be, although you might be surprised at how comfortable facilities out here can be. Your days will be packed with activities that, depending on the nature of your tour and lodge, will include: bird- and wildlife-watching, boat trips, rain-forest hikes, visits to indigenous communities, mountain biking, or white-water rafting. You'll be in the company of guides from the minute you're picked up in Iquitos, Puerto Maldonado, or Cusco. Most lodges here hire top-notch guides who know their areas well, and you'll be forever amazed at their ability to spot that camouflaged howler monkey from a hundred paces. There is downtime for curling up in a hammock with a good book, yet few visitors here want to spend their time so idly.

The lodge itself should provide mosquito netting and sheets or blankets, as well as some type of lantern for your room for the evening. (Don't expect electricity at most of these places.) But always check with the your tour operator for a list of what to bring and what the lodge itself provides. Your required inventory will vary proportionally by just how much you have to rough it. Pack sunscreen, sunglasses, insect repellent, a hat, hiking boots, and sandals or light shoes. Also, a light, loose-fitting, long-sleeve shirt and equally loose-fitting long trousers and socks are musts for the evening when the mosquitoes come out. Carry your yellow fever vaccination certificate and prescription for malaria

prevention and, of course, an extra supply of any prescription you might be taking. Bring along an antidiarrheal medication, too. You'll need a small daypack for the numerous guided hikes you'll go on, but don't forget to bring some plastic bags to protect your belongings from the rain and humidity. Also bring binoculars and plenty of film.

There is little to buy out here; everything is usually included in the package price, though you'll probably be caught off guard by the extra price you're charged for beverages. Soft drinks and, especially, beer carry a hefty markup, understandable given the cost of transporting them out here, and are almost never included in the quoted price.

Few things are more enjoyable at a jungle lodge than dinner at the end of the day. Food could be served at a buffet, or everyone might dig in and dine family style around a common table. Either way, you're sure to excitedly discuss the day's sightings and events, comparing notes with your fellow travelers well into the evening, knowing full well there will be another 5 AM knock at the door tomorrow morning.

— By Jeffrey Van Fleet

$$$$ ⬚ **ExplorTambos.** This very primitive lodge is a three-hour hike from ExplorNapo. There are no rooms here—you sleep on mattresses on platforms under mosquito netting. Visits here are usually an extension of trips to Explorama Lodge or ExplorNapo. Being the most remote lodge in the region, the chances of seeing wildlife are quite good. But this is definitely a place for serious explorers who don't mind a little discomfort. The minimum stay is four nights. ✉ *Reservations: Av. de la Marina 340, Iquitos* ☎ *094/252–526, 800/707–5275 in the U.S.* 🖷 *094/252–533* ⊕ *www.explorama.com* ➪ *space for 16 people* ⚒ *Restaurant, boating, fishing, hiking, airport shuttle, travel services, some no-smoking rooms; no room phones, no room TVs, no a/c* ▭ *MC, V, AE, DC* ⍾ *FAP.*

$$$$ ⬚ **Tambo Amazónico Lodge.** A very basic lodge near the Pacaya Samiria Nature Reserve, the Tambo Amazónico is the best lodge near this immense track of virgin rain forest. The lodge has small, thatched-roof bungalows with no electricity. It sits just at the park's entrance on the Río Yarapa. The rate includes guided tours of the park, all meals, and transportation. The minimum stay is three nights. ✉ *Reservations: Calle Pevas 246, Iquitos* ☎ *094/231–618 or 094/233–110* ⊕ *www.paseosamazonicos. com* ➪ *10 rooms with shared bath* ⚒ *Restaurant, boating, fishing, hiking, airport shuttle, travel services, some no-smoking rooms; no room phones, no room TVs, no a/c* ▭ *V, MC* ⍾ *FAP.*

$$$$ ⬚ **Yacumama Lodge.** Alongside the Yarapa River, a tributary of the Amazon, this beautiful complex is three to four hours from Iquitos. Raised bungalows with screened porches (widely spaced for maximum privacy) are connected to the main lodge by covered walkways. All buildings are constructed using natural materials. Most of the property is solar powered, with an emphasis on recycling, composting, and organic farming—all part of the goal of minimum impact on the surrounding environment. Although rooms don't have private baths, there are two modern buildings with showers and flush toilets. A screened "hammock room" overlooking the river is great for afternoon naps, especially after swinging from tree to tree on the "canopy skyline." Pink river dolphins are often spotted in the area. The minimum stay is five nights. *Reservations:* ✉ *Sgto. Lores 149, Iquitos* ☎ *094/235–510, 800/854–0023 in the U.S.* ⊕ *www.yacumama.com* ➪ *31 bungalows with shared bath* ⚒ *Restaurant, boating, fishing, hiking, bar, airport shuttle, meeting rooms, travel services, some no-smoking rooms; no room phones, no room TVs, no a/c* ▭ *AE, DC, MC, V* ⍾ *FAP.*

$$ ⬚ **Amazon Rainforest Lodge.** Only an hour by speedboat from Iquitos, this cluster of thatch-roof bungalows sits on the Momon River. The attractive structures center around the greenish colored pool, have twin beds and private baths, and are lit by gas lanterns. Activities include guided walks, piranha fishing, night canoeing, ayahuasca ceremonies, and visits to Yagua villages. They cater to a much younger crowd than most of the jungle lodges in the area. *Reservations:* ✉ *Putomayo 159, Iquitos* ☎ *094/233–100 or 01/445–5620* 🖷 *094/242–231 or 01/447–2651* ⊕ *www.amazon-lodge.com* ➪ *14 bungalows with shared bath* ⚒ *Restaurant, pool, boating, fishing, hiking, bar, shop, laundry services, airport shuttle, travel services, some no-smoking rooms; no room phones, no room TVs, no a/c* ▭ *MC, V* ⍾ *FAP.*

$$ ⬚ **Heliconia Amazon River Lodge.** An hour downriver from Iquitos you'll find the Heliconia, which sits on the large Yanamono reserve. The lodge has a big thatched-roof dining area. Rooms have twin beds, private bathrooms, and hot-water showers. Guides are available for fishing, night canoeing, and bird-watching. ✉ *Reservations: Av. Ricardo Palma 242, Iquitos* ☎ *094/231–959 or 01/421–9195* 🖷 *094/231–983 or 01/442–4338* ⊕ *www.amazonriverexpeditions.com* ➪ *21 rooms* ⚒ *Restau-*

THE CENTRAL HIGHLANDS

5

FODOR'S CHOICE

Convento de Santa Rosa de Ocopa, *former mission in Concepción*

Grand Hotel Huánuco, *Huanuco*

Hostal El Marqués de Valdelirios, *Ayacucho*

La Cabaña, *Peruvian fare in Huancayo*

La Florida, *bed-and-breakfast in Tarma*

Pampas de Quinua, *battlefield in Ayacucho*

Restaurant Urpicha, *Ayacucho*

HIGHLY RECOMMENDED

RESTAURANTS La Casona, *Ayacucho*

Restaurant Olímpico, *Huancayo*

HOTELS Andino Lodging and Excursions, *Huancayo*

Hostal Residencial Huánuco, *Huanuco*

SIGHTS Kotosh, *Huanuco*

company's offices in the United States. Jungle Exports and Cruceros also offer boat tours through the region. Emily Tours, Explorama Tours, Paseos Amazonicos, and Turismo Pacífico Iquitos arrange trips throughout the region.

🔲 Fees & Schedules **Amazon Tours and Cruises** ✉ Requeña 336, Iquitos ☎ 094/231-611 ⊕ www.amazontours.net ✉ 8700 W. Flagler St., Miami, FL 33174 ☎ 305/227-2266 or 800/423-2791. **Cruceros** ✉ Requena 336, Iquitos ☎ 094/231-611 in Iquitos, 01/265-9524 in Lima. **Emily Tours** ✉ Jr. Progreso 268-270, Iquitos ☎ 094/235-273. **Explorama Tours** ✉ Av. de la Marina 350, Iquitos ☎ 094/252-530, 800/223-6764 in the U.S. **International Expeditions** ☎ 800/633-4734 🖷 205/428-1714 ⊕ www.internationalexpeditions.com. **Jungle Exports** ✉ Puerto Masusa, Iquitos ☎ 094/231-870. **Paseos Amazonicos** ✉ Calle Pevas 246, Iquitos ☎ 094/233-110 🖷 094/231-618. **Turismo Pacífico Iquitos** ✉ Calle Ricardo Palma 180, Iquitos ☎ 094/231-627.

TRANSPORTATION AROUND IQUITOS & ENVIRONS

The best way to travel around the Iquitos area is by boat. There are huge oceangoing boats that will take you all the way to the Atlantic Ocean in Brazil, tiny dugout canoes to take you deep into the jungle, and swift launches with outboard engines and canvas tops to keep you dry. It takes several days by boat to get to any large communities near Iquitos.

VISITOR INFORMATION

There are tourist information offices in downtown Iquitos and at the airport.

🔲 **iPerú** ✉ Airport ☎ 094/260-251. **Tourist Information Office** ✉ Napo 226 ☎ 094/235-621.

EMERGENCIES

In case of an accident or emergency, call the local authorities immediately, especially the tourist police if there is a branch in your particular town. Contacting your embassy is also a good idea. iPerú has a 24-hour emergency hot line. In smaller towns and in the wilderness you will probably need to arrange for transportation to Iquitos. Some of the equipment in the hospitals may not be up-to-date, but doctors are knowledgeable.

🖪 Emergency Services **General emergency** ☎ 105 throughout Peru. **Police** ☎ 094/260-361. **Tourist Police** ☎ 094/242-081. **iPerú** ☎ 094/260-251, 0800/42-579 throughout Peru. **Fire Department** ☎ 116.

🖪 **Clinica Adventista Ana Stahl** ✉ Av. de la Marina 285, Iquitos ☎ 094/252-518 or 094/252-535. **Hospital Regional de Iquitos** ✉ Av. 28 de Julio, Cuadra 15, Iquitos ☎ 094/252-743 or 094/251-882.

HEALTH

The biggest health concerns for travelers in the Amazon Basin are traveler's stomach (persistent diarrhea) and malaria. Traveler's stomach is not easy to avoid; fasting while maintaining a strict regimen of hydration (bottled water only) is the quickest way to cure traveler's stomach. When entering a questionable restaurant, check out the bathroom first; it's a good sign if it is clean and has soap. Peeling fruits and vegetables before you eat them can also help reduce your chances of having an upset stomach.

You are not required to get any vaccinations to enter Peru, but it is advisable to check with the World Health Organization before your visit. The Peruvian Embassy recommends getting a yellow fever vaccine at least 10 days before visiting the Amazon. Avoid malaria by taking precautions against the mosquitoes: use an insect repellent with high DEET concentration, wear pants and light long-sleeved shirts, tucking your pant legs into your socks, and ensure the mosquito netting over your bed is secure before you head off to bed.

MAIL & SHIPPING

Iquitos has a post office; there is no mail service available from the lodges.
🖪 Post Office **Iquitos** ✉ Av. Arica 402 ☎ 094/231-915.

MONEY MATTERS

All banks in Iquitos can exchange money and cash traveler's checks. Try the local branches of Banco de Crédito, Banco Continental, or Banco Wiese.
🖪 Banks **Banco de Crédito** ✉ Av. Putumayo 202, Iquitos ☎ 094/233-838. **Banco Continental** ✉ Sgto. Lores 171, Iquitos ☎ 094/235-421. **Banco Wiese** ✉ Av. Próspero 282, Iquitos ☎ 094/232-350.

TELEPHONES

Telephone service is very good in Iquitos, with public phones using either phone cards or coins. At remote lodges, communication is by radio.

TOURS

In Iquitos, Amazon Tours and Cruises specializes in river cruises using boats with anywhere from 8 to 21 cabins. The longest and most comprehensive cruise includes a 6-day trip on the Amazon and a 10-day journey to Manaus, Brazil. All the boats have comfortable, air-conditioned cabins with private facilities. The boats stop at various points for nature hikes and visits to villages. International Expeditions has four of the most colorful and luxurious boats on the Amazon. Boats headed up the river to the Pacaya-Samiria National Reserve have accommodations for between 8 and 26 passengers. Cruises can be booked only from the *rant, boating, fishing, billiards, hiking, bar, shop, airport shuttle, travel services, some no-smoking rooms; no room phones, no room TVs, no a/c* ⊟ *V, MC* ¶⊙¶ *FAP.*

Iquitos & Environs A to Z

To research prices, get advice from other travelers, and book travel arrangements, visit www.fodors.com.

AIR TRAVEL
From Lima, Aero Continente has several flights a day to Iquitos. Taca Peru has daily flights to Iquitos, and TANS Perú has two flights a day between Iquitos and Lima. Aerocontinente offers round-trip flights from Miami on Sunday.

🖪 Carriers **Aero Continente** ☎ 094/243-489 in Iquitos, 01/242-4260 in Lima, 877/359-7378 in the U.S. **Taca Peru** ☎ 094/242-448 in Iquitos or 01/446-0033 in Lima. **TANS Perú** ☎ 094/231-071 in Iquitos, 01/575-3842 in Lima.

AIRPORTS
Iquitos's Aeropuerto Internacional Francisco Secada Vignetta is 8 km (5 mi) from the city center. There is a S/12 airport tax for domestic flights and a S/36 tax for international flights. A taxi to the airport should cost around S/10.

🖪 Airport Information **Aeropuerto Internacional Francisco Secada Vignetta** ☎ 094/260-151 in Iquitos.

BORDER CROSSINGS
It is a two-day boat ride to the Brazilian border. As of press time American citizens do not need a special visa to enter Brazil, though these policies change quite often; check with the Brazilian Embassy before heading there. For the most part, Peruvian boats operate only in Peruvian waters. You will need to change boats in Brazil. **Brazilian Embassy** (⊠ Sgto. Lores 363, Iquitos). **Iquitos Customs Office** (☎ 094/251–957).

BOAT & FERRY TRAVEL
There are a number of national and international ferry lines that operate from Iquitos, taking you to the town of Pucallpa and as far as the Atlantic Ocean in Brazil. These boats are often quite run-down and few have staterooms. You'll need to bring a hammock and lots of bug spray. Passage to Pucallpa takes four to eight days and costs around $40. Jungle Exports offers cruises to the Reserva Nacional Pacaya Samiria. Cruceros offers very expensive Amazon cruises. Most boats leave from Puerto Masusa, about 3 km north of the city center on Ave. La Marina.

🖪 Boat & Ferry Lines **Jungle Exports** ⊠ Puerto Masusa, Iquitos ☎ 094/231-870. **Cruceros** ⊠ Requena 336, Iquitos ☎ 094/231-611 in Iquitos, 01/265-9524 in Lima.

CAR RENTAL
Though there isn't much reason to rent a car in Iquitos (everything is so close), though you may want to rent one for an afternoon to check out the areas immediately surrounding town. Motos y Autos JB rents 4 x 4s and motorcycles by the day and by the hour.

🖪 Agencies **Motos y Autos JB** ⊠ Yavari 702, Iquitos ☎ 094/222-389.

CAR TRAVEL
The most common mode of transportation in the Iquitos area is the *motocarro*, a three-wheeled motorcycle with a canvas top. Service in town costs around S/1.50, while going to the outskirts you will pay around S/9 an hour. Always negotiate the price beforehand. There aren't many places to go by road, but exploring the outskirts and tiny hamlets around Iquitos—during the day—can be fun.

Numbers in the text correspond to numbers in the margin and on the Central Highlands and Ayachucho maps.

5

If you have
3 days

On day one, fly from Lima to ⊞ **Ayacucho** ⑮ – ㉔ ► and take a walking tour of the town and its museums, churches, and colonial mansions. On day two head out on a tour of historical sights, including the famous battlefield at **Pampas de Quinua**, ⑭ the ruins at Huari, and the former Inca settlements of Vilcashuamán and Intihuatana. Spend another night in Ayacucho, then on your third day take the morning to shop the markets before flying back to Lima.

If you have
7 days

Fly from Lima to ⊞ **Huánuco** ❶, taking the afternoon to stroll through the town. Spend the night, then on the morning of day two explore the ruins on the surrounding pampas, including the ancient temple at **Kotosh** ❷ and the crumbled villages of Tomayquichua and **Tantamayo** ❹. Head south via Cerro de Pasco, Junín, and La Oroya toward ⊞ **Huancayo** ⑫ in the afternoon. On your third day, explore the town and its surroundings in the beautiful Valle de Mantaro, including the ruins at Warvilca, and the Convento de Santa Rosa de Ocopa in **Concepcion** ⑪. Overnight again in Huancayo, and rise early on day four and take the spectacular train journey to **Huancavelica** ⑬, where you can wander through the markets and plazas or head out to the thermal baths before settling down for the night. On day five, drive to ⊞ **Ayacucho** ⑮ – ㉔, then take an afternoon walking tour of the town. On day six tour the outer sights—including the famous battlefield at **Pampas de Quinua** ⑭, the ruins at Huari, and the former Inca settlements of Vilcashuamán and Intihuatana. On your final day, spend a little time browsing for clothes and crafts at the local shops before flying back to Lima.

---

noon breaks. Dinner is usually after 7 PM. Don't worry about dressing up or making reservations, although you're expected to dress smart-casual for the larger hotel restaurants and weekend peñas. Tipping isn't customary, but waiters appreciate the extra change. This is a poor region, so meat can be tough and bony. Rabbit and guinea pig farming are among the more profitable occupations here, so grilled cuy is a menu staple. Heartier fare comes in stews, which have spices and heat to stave off the mountain chill. Your best strategy is to look around and order as the locals do.

About the Hotels

Accommodations in the Central Highlands lean toward the very basic. Only the largest properties have hot water, TVs, phones, and private baths or on-site facilities like a hot tub, pool, or exercise room. If you don't need pampering, and you don't expect top-quality service, you'll travel easily—and cheaply. The majority of hotels have very clean, if spare, rooms with simple Andean-motifs. Bathrooms usually have showers only, and if hot water is available it's only in the morning or evening. Most hotels have a restaurant, or at least a dining room with some type of food service. If you want a homestay experience, ask your hotel or a local travel company, who can often hook you up with hosts in the area.

WHAT IT COSTS In Nuevo Soles				
	$$$$	$$$	$$	$	¢
RESTAURANTS	over 65	50–65	35–50	20–35	under 20
HOTELS	over 500	375–500	250–375	125–250	under 125

Restaurant prices are per person, for a main course at dinner. Hotel prices are for two people in a standard double room, excluding tax.

Timing

The best weather for this region is May through October, during winter and spring, when the skies are clear and daytime temperatures are moderate (although nights can be frigid). The rainy season is November through April, when many roads are inaccessible. If you'll be traveling in these months, plan on flying between major towns. Book tours and hotels six months early if possible, especially if you'll be traveling during the region's popular Semana Santa or anniversary festivities. Accommodations are particularly difficult to get in Ayacucho at these times, so confirm your reservations if you'll be staying for the celebration. Also book early around the anniversary of the Battle of Ayacucho in mid-December.

HUÁNUCO SOUTH TO TARMA

Heading east, the road from modern, sprawling Lima climbs through the Andes, then splits in north and south routes through the highlands. Working its way through the narrow crevasses and up the rugged hillsides of the Valle Mantaro, the northern road then spreads endlessly forward at an elevation of 4,250 m (13,940 ft) atop the earth's largest high-altitude plains. This route north connects the mountain towns of La Oroya, Junín, Cerro de Pasco, Huánuco, and Tingo María, where local customs have been preserved even amid battles for independence and intrusions of modern technology. Set at 3,755 m (12,316 ft) by the confluence of the Río Mantaro and Río Yauli, La Oroya is a town of 36,000 and a main smelting center for the region's mining industry. From here you can head due east to Tarma or continue north by road or rail to the village of Junín. Still farther northwest along the eastern shores of Lago de Junín are Tambo del Sol and Cerro de Pasco.

At an elevation of 4,333 m (14,212 ft), with more than 30,000 residents, Cerro de Pasco is the world's highest town of its size. It's also the main center for copper, gold, lead, silver, and zinc mining north of the Amazon basin. Coal is excavated from the Goyllarisquisga canyon 42 km (26 mi) north of town, the highest coal mine in the world. From here the road leads over pale, soggy Pampas de Quinua, where Simon Bolívar's troops outfought Spain in 1824.

Eighty kilometers (50 mi) east of town, the Valle de Huachón provides gorgeous mountains for hiking and camping, while the trail north toward Huánuco is along a spectacular road that plunges nearly 2,500 m (8,200 ft) in the first 30 km (19 mi). Overlooking the land from an elevation of 1,849 m (6,065 ft), Huánuco is a pleasant stopover between Lima and the eastern rain forests of Pucullpo, or before heading south toward Huancayo and into the highlands. Farther north, spread between the Andean slopes and the Peruvian jungle, Tingo María is a jumping-off point for land adventures.

Note that from Huánaco north to Pucullpo is a major coca-growing region, so the area has a strong military presence and there are numerous police checkpoints to combat illegal drug trafficking along this route.

Crafts & Textiles

Woven cloth is a major industry here, and you can find inexpensive alpaca and llama-wool coats, hats, scarves, ponchos, blankets, and rugs in nearly every market. Silver jewelry, especially filigree, is another specialty of the Central Highlands, particularly around San Jerónimo near Huancayo. Also keep an eye out for gourds carved with religious and historical scenes and belts with Andean images. *Retablos*—the multi-tiered, three-dimensional ceramic scenes of religious and historical events—are a main craft around Ayacucho. Although the larger towns have extensive craft markets, many of the textiles and much of the jewelry are machine-made. Search the back streets or smaller villages for home workshops, where you can see the artists at work and buy directly from them.

5

Rib-Sticking Stuff

Huancayo's local specialty is *papa a la huancaína* (boiled potato covered in white milk-cheese sauce), served cold with a sliced egg and an olive. *Pachamanca* (marinated meat, vegetables, potatoes, and spices), another regional specialty, is wrapped in leaves, then slow-cooked in an underground oven. Huánuco favorites include *picante de cuy* (guinea pig in hot pepper sauce), pachamanca, fried trout, humitas, tamales, and sheep's-head broth. Ayacucho is famous for its filling, flavorful *puca picante* (a peanutty pork-and-potato stew), served with rice and topped with a parsley sprig. The city's favorite drink is the hot, pisco-spiked *ponche* (flavored with milk, cinnamon, cloves, sesame, peanuts, walnuts, and sugar).

At press time, Huánuco, Tingo Maria, and Pucullpo were considered to be safe for travelers, but it's best to explore in a group, with a knowledgeable guide, and only in daylight.

Huánuco

▶ ❶ *365 km (226 mi) northeast of Lima, 105 km (65 mi) north of Cerro de Pasco*

At first glance, Huánuco is just a picturesque collection of colonial buildings and churches along the Rio Huallaga amid rocky, forested mountains, but it's actually one of the most important historical spots on the continent. The earliest evidence of human settlement in South America, and some of the oldest ruins in the country, were found nearby at Lauricocha and Kotosh. Pre-Inca ruins have turned up throughout these mountains, notably at Tantamayo and Garu. Huánuco was also a key Inca stronghold as a convenient stopover on their route from Cusco north to Cajamarca, and thousands of Inca relics still litter the surrounding pampas.

Huánuco's cool, 1,894-m (6,212-ft) elevation makes for pleasant winter days and crisp nights, but in the rainy summer it's just low enough to become immersed in the thick mountain fog. The Spanish-style architecture reflects the town's 1539 founding by the conquistadors, and later buildings tell the story of Huánuco's importance as a main cultural hub for the region. Still, the original Peruvian traditions run deep, particularly during the annual Huánuco anniversary celebrations. The availability of mountain hikes, swims in natural pools, and dips in nearby hot springs add to the area's natural appeal.

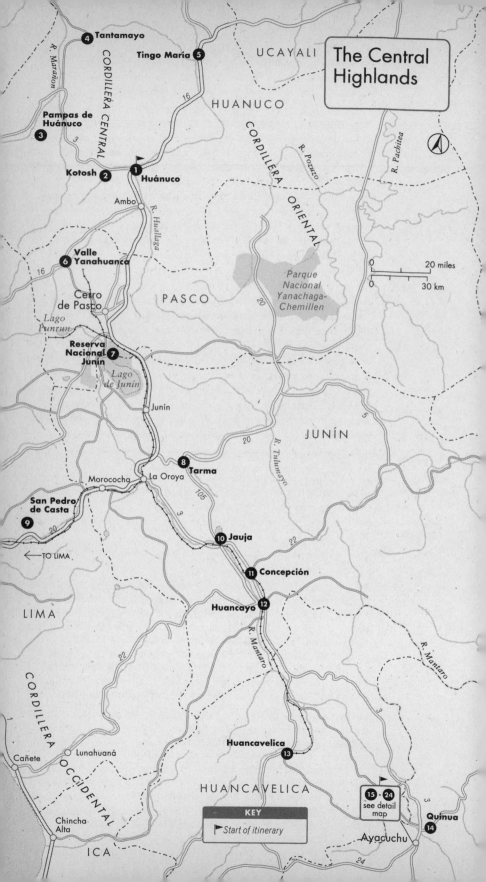

The Central Highlands

UCAYALI

4 Tantamayo

Tingo Maria 5

R. Marañón

16

HUANUCO

CORDILLERA CENTRAL

R. Pozuzo

R. Pachitea

Pampas de Huánuco 3

CORDILLERA ORIENTAL

1 ▶

Kotosh 2 Huánuco

Ambo

R. Huallaga

20 miles

30 km

Valle 6 Yanahuanca

Cerro de Pasco

PASCO

Parque Nacional Yanachaga-Chemillen

16

Lago Punrun

Reserva Nacional Junín 7

Lago de Junín

Junín

JUNÍN

20

R. Tulumayo

5

8 Tarma

Morococha La Oroya

105

San Pedro de Casta

9

20

3

10 Jauja

22

← TO LIMA

11 Concepción

LIMA

Huancayo 12

R. Mantaro

22

CORDILLERA

Cañete

Lunahuaná

1

OCCIDENTAL

R. Mantaro

3

Huancavelica 13

Chincha Alta

HUANCAVELICA

15 · 24 ▶ see detail map

Quinua 14

Ayacuchu

ICA

24

KEY
▶ *Start of itinerary*

A block from the Plaza de Armas, the small **Museo de Ciencias** is a nat-ural-history museum with multilingual displays of local crafts and weav-ing, shells, fossils, stuffed wildlife, Inca tools, and Spanish artwork. ⊠ *Gen. Prado 495* ☎ *no phone* ✉ *S/2* ⊘ *Weekdays 9–noon and 3–6, week-ends 10–12.*

The 16th-century **Iglesia San Francisco** has Cusco School paintings and a few colonial-era antiques. It's worth a peek inside just to see the spec-tacularly gilt wall and arches behind the altar. ⊠ *2 de Mayo y Beruan* ☎ *no phone* ✉ *Free* ⊘ *Mon.–Thurs. 9–1 and 4–6, Fri. and Sat. 9–12.*

Fronting a landscape of steep, grassy mountain slopes, the **Iglesia San Cristobal**, with its three-tiered bell tower, was the first local church built by the Spanish settlers. Inside are a valuable collection of colonial-era paintings and Baroque wood sculptures of San Agustín, the Virgen de la Asuncion, and the Virgen Dolorosa. ⊠ *San Cristobal y Beruan* ☎ *no phone* ✉ *Free* ⊘ *Mon.–Sat. 3–6.*

★ ❷ In the Andean foothills at 1,812 m (5,943 ft), **Kotosh**, a 4,000-year-old archaeological site, is most famous for the Templo de las Manos Cruzadas (Temple of the Crossed Hands). The oldest Peruvian pottery relics were discovered below one of the niches surrounding the main room, and the partially restored ruins are thought to have been constructed by one of the country's earliest cultures. Inside the temple you'll see images of the crossed hands, the original mud set of which is dated 3000–2000 BC and on display in Lima's Museo de Arqueología and Antropología. The site was named Kotosh (pile) in reference to the piles of rocks found strewn across the fields. Taxi fare is S/10 for the return journey from Huánuco, including a half-hour to sightsee. ✛ *5 km (3 mi) west of Huánuco* ☎ *No phone* ✉ *S/3.50* ⊘ *Daily sunrise–sunset.*

❸ **Pampas de Huánuco.** Also called Huánuco Viejo, these fields along the highland pampas near the town of La Unión are a major site of Inca ruins. ✛ *10 km (6 mi) northwest of Huánuco* ☎ *No phone* ✉ *Free* ⊘ *Daily 24 hrs.*

❹ The fields around **Tantamayo** are rich with pre-Inca ruins, some from the oldest cultures to settle in Peru. Most notable are the thick, seven-story stone skyscrapers of the Yarowilca, who flourished from AD 1200 to 1450. Finds at Susupio, Hapayán, Piruro, and Selmín Granero are the best-preserved. The ruins are within easy walking distance of Tan-tamayo village, where there are a hostel and basic restaurants; or catch a bus to Tantamayo and visit the ruins without a guide. ✛ *158 km (98 mi) northwest of Huánuco* ☎ *No phone* ✉ *Free* ⊘ *Daily 8–6.*

off the
beaten
path

TOMAYQUICHUA – This small village was the birthplace of Micela Villegas, a.k.a. La Perricholi—the famous lover of Viceroy Amat. A festival in July with parades, music, and dancing celebrates his vitality. Beautiful mountain views are the main attraction of the 2,000-m (6,500-ft) area. San Muguel Arcangel, one of the first churches built in the Huánuco area, is also here. ✛ *30 km (19 mi) from Huánuco* ☎ *No phone* ✉ *Free* ⊘ *Daily 8–6.*

Where to Stay & Eat

Restaurants in Huánuco are simple and small, mostly offering local cui-sine with a smattering of Chinese and Continental selections. *Almuerzo* (lunch) is the largest meal, and most residents don't have dinner until after dark. There are numerous little diners around the Plaza and its neigh-borhoods, as well as around the markets. Most hotels have a small restau-rant, but if yours does not, your host will usually fix a meal on request.

Hotels, too, are basic, with shared cold-water baths at most budget places. Spend a little more and you'll get lots more comfort, including a private bath, hot water, a better mattress, more room amenities, and more attentive service.

$ ×🖭 **Grand Hotel Huánuco.** Although its elegant beige, colonial-style architecture looks swanky, the hotel is both comfortable and welcoming.
Fodor's Choice Rooms, with private baths and hot water, have modern pieces and
★ touches of local art and antiques. Some have windows overlooking the Plaza, but beware the noise in the morning and on weekends. Public areas are opulent yet intimate, with corners to relax in and have a quiet conversation or meeting. The pool, sauna, and gym provide stress outlets for those here on business, or respite for those returning from long day tours of the surrounding pampas. ⊠ *Beraun 775* ☎ *062/514222* 🖷 *064/512410* ⚬ *Restaurant, cable TV, pool, sauna, gym, travel services, free parking* 🖃 *AE, DC, MC, V.*

¢ ×🖭 **Gran Hotel Cusco.** Its age shows here and there in chipped paint, squeaky pipes, and ceiling cracks, but overall this local favorite has held up well over the decades. Rooms have all the modern needs: TV, phone, and hot shower. It's a popular place for visiting businessmen, so book early if you'll be here on a weekday. The restaurant serves tasty Peruvian grilled meats and stews, as well as soups, salads, and *tallarines* (noodles). ⊠ *Huánuco 614–616* ☎ *022/443263* ⤴ *50 rooms* ⚬ *Cafeteria, cable TV, laundry service, business services, travel services, free parking* 🖃 *AE, DC, MC, V.*

¢ ×🖭 **Hotel Reál.** This modern hotel with faux colonial architecture is in the middle of town on the Plaza. Spacious rooms done in muted pastels have comfortable, contemporary furnishings. The inexpensive restaurant, serving a mix of Andean and Continental fare, is a favorite haunt of local notables. ⊠ *Huánuco 1125* ☎ *062/513411* 🖷 *064/512765* ⤴ *95 rooms* ⚬ *Restaurant, pool, sauna, laundry service, travel services, free parking* 🖃 *AE, MC, V.*

★ ¢ 🖭 **Hostal Residencial Huánuco.** It's the town's favorite backpacker hangout, where you can kick off your hiking boots and chat with new friends over a cup of *maté* (tea) in the garden. Shop the food market, then whip up your meal in the kitchen—the owners will even give cooking lessons. Hot water and laundry facilities also set this hostal above other budget options. ⊠ *Huánuco 775* ☎ *062/513096* ⤴ *28 rooms* ⚬ *Laundry facilities, travel services, free parking; no room phones, no room TVs* 🖃 *AE, MC, V.*

Tingo María

❺ *129 km (80 mi) north of Huánuco*

The warmth and humidity of this town in the Andean foothills hit you as you descend from the Huánuco highlands. Not many travelers visit this settlement at the border between mountains and jungle, as it's in the midst of the country's coca-growing core. It's a shame, though, to miss Tingo María's vibrance and beauty, seen in its colorful, bustling markets and frenzied festivals. It's a place to find peace, particularly given the strong military presence on hand to keep out illegal drug smugglers from the Río Huallaga valley to the north.

Set before a backdrop of mountains shaped like *La Belle Durmiente* (Sleeping Beauty), Tingo María is a safe haven of 21,000 residents who make their living tending the surrounding coffee, rubber, and sugarcane farms. Banana and tea plantations also wind their way up the slopes, while less than 15 km (11 mi) farther out there are hidden lakes, waterfalls, and caves to explore. There are plenty of small Peruvian restaurants and inexpensive hotels—most with cold water, but some with private baths and cable TV.

Most travelers come here to visit **Parque Nacional Tingo María,** in the midst of the Pumaringri mountains. Many highland and rain-forest species live here, including parrots, primates, and bats. This is also the home of the rare, nocturnal *guacharo* (oilbird), a black and brown, owl-like bird with a hooked beak and a three-foot wingspan. Also explore the famed **Cueva de las Lechuzas** (Las Lechuzas Cave), on the skirts of the Bella Durmiente, an enormous limestone cave which shelters an important colony of *guacharos* (a.k.a. *santanas*).

Tingo María is about three hours north of Huánuco on a paved road. You'll pass through several military checkpoints along the way, which are precautions to prevent drug trafficking and intermittent guerrilla activity. Note that summer and autumn rains often cause landslides, and the road is frequently under repair. If you're at all hesitant about driving, fly.

Valle Yanahuanca

6 *35 km (22 mi) west of Tingo María, 73 km (45 mi) north of Huánuco*

One of the longest surviving stretches of Inca road, the *Camina Incaico,* passes through the massive rocky outcrops and deep meadows of the Valle Yanahuanca. Forested hills threaded by shallow, pebbled rivers lead 4 km (2 ½ mi) farther to the village of Huarautambo, where pre-Inca ruins are treasures to search for in the rugged terrain. Continue along the 150-km (93-mi) Inca track and you'll pass La Union, San Marcos, Huari, Llamellin, and San Luis.

Reserva Nacional Junín

7 *238 km (148 mi) south of Yanahuanca, 165 km (102 mi) north of Huánuco,*

This park is at the center of the Peruvian puna, the high-altitude cross section of the Andes, which, at 3,900 to 4,500 m (12,792 to 14,760 ft), is the highest region in which humans can live. Its boundaries begin about 10 km (6 mi) north of town along the shores of Lago Junín, which, at 14 km (9 mi) wide and 30 km (19 mi) long, is Peru's second-largest lake after Titicaca.

Flat, rolling fields cut by clear, shallow streams characterize this cold, wet region set between the highest Andes peaks and the eastern rain forest. Only heavy grasses, hearty alpine flowers, and tough, tangled berry bushes can survive in this harsh climate, although farmers have cultivated the warmer, lower valleys into an agricultural stretch of orchards and plantations. The mountains are threaded with cave networks long used as natural shelters by human inhabitants, who hunted the durable llamas, alpacas, and vincuñas that graze on the plains. The dry season here is June through September, with the rains pouring in between December and March.

The 2,500-hectare reserve is also the site of the **Santuario Histórico Chacamarca** (Chacamarca Historical Sanctuary), an important battle site where local residents triumphed over the Spanish conquistadors. A monument marks the victory spot. The sanctuary is within walking distance of Junín, and there are several trails around the lake and across the pampas.

Tarma

❽ *350 km (217 mi) east of Lima, 25 km (16 mi) southeast of Junín*

The hidden mountain town known as "The Pearl of the Andes" has grown into a city of 155,000 whose Peruvian roots are held close in its traditions and sights. Long before the Spanish arrived, local tribes built homes and temples in the hills that frame the town, the ruins of which are still being turned up by local farmers who have plowed much of the terrain into flower and potato fields, coffee plantations, and orchards. The town's look is all Spanish, though, with a small Plaza de Armas and several colonial-style churches and mansions.

At an elevation of 3,050 m (10,004 ft), Tarma has a cool and breezy climate, with crisp nights any time of year. Be prepared to get out in these nights, too, as candlelight processions are a major part of the town's many festivals—notably the Fiesta San Sebastián in January, Semana Santa in April, Semana de Tarma in July, and Fiesta El Señor de Los Milagros in October. Tarma is definitely not a tourist town, but rather a place to visit if you want to be part of true Peruvian traditions.

Sights to visit include the village of Acobamba, a 10-km (6-mi) drive from town, where you can tour the famous **El Señor de Muruhuay** sanctuary. About 15 km (9 mi) northwest is the town of **San Pedro de Cajas,** well known for its exquisite weaving and as an excellent place to buy good-quality, locally made wall hangings and rugs. You can also head northwest 28 km (17 mi) to Palcamayo, then continue 4 km (2 mi) west to explore the **Gruta de Guagapo** limestone cave system that's a National Speleological Area. Guides live in the village near the entrance and can give you a basic short tour, but you'll need full spelunking equipment for deep cavern trips.

Where to Stay & Eat

¢–$ ✕ **Restaurant Señorial.** Tarma's classiest restaurant is still casual and chic, the place where the top of the townsfolk dine with fresh-pressed attire and just-shined shoes. The chefs show off their Andean flavorings in such local dishes as *pachamanca* (marinated, slow-cooked meat, vegetables, potatoes, and spices) and *picante de cuy* (guinea pig in hot pepper sauce). You can also order pastas and sauces, grilled meats, and seafood. ✉ *Huánuco 138* ☎ *064/323334* 🗐 *MC, V.*

¢ ✕ **Restaurant Chavin.** This popular travelers' hangout is right on the plaza on the first floor of the Galaxia backpacker hotel. Kitschy Andean decor—pictures of snow-covered mountains, patterned wall hangings—adds spunk to a bustling lunchtime background. Hearty stews and rice dishes are the midday specials; at dinner you'll find grilled meat and even fish. ✉ *Lima 262* ☎ *064/321449* 🗐 *MC, V.*

$ 🏨 **Los Portales.** Considered by locals to be the best hotel in town, this colonial-style mansion surrounded by gardens offers more warmth than grandeur. Rooms, which have modern amenities and private baths with hot water, are decorated with a mix of real and reproduction antiques that complement the elegant architecture. The friendly staff is very helpful with advice for regional sightseeing. ✉ *Castilla 512* ☎ *064/321411* 🖷 *064/321410* 🛏 *45 rooms* ♨ *Restaurant, cable TV, bar, shop, laundry service, free parking* 🗐 *AE, DC, MC, V* ❄️ *BP.*

¢ 🏨 **Hostal Internacional.** The Plaza has a bunch of budget hotels, but this is the best pick. Never mind the plain decor—rooms have private baths, hot water, and even TVs. ✉ *2 de Mayo 307* ☎ *064/321830* 🛏 *24 rooms* ♨ *Laundry service, travel services* 🗐 *No credit cards.*

¢   ▣ **La Florida.** Experience life at a Spanish hacienda at this charming bed-
Fodor'sChoice   and-breakfast about 10 minutes' drive from Tarma. Rooms, which sleep
★   up to four guests, are furnished with period pieces, local art, and handmade textiles to complete the 18th-century feel. There's even a camping section with a bathroom (S/10), and hiking trails that lead to ruins
and highland villages. ✦ *6 km (4 mi) north of Tarma* ☎ *01/424–6969
in Lima* ✉ *kreida@peru.itt.com.pe* ⌦ *5 rooms, 6 campsites* ⚐ *Dining room, hiking, laundry service, travel services, free parking* ▤ *AE,
MC, V* ⎊ *BP.*

San Pedro de Casta

❾ *120 km (74 mi) northeast of Lima*

This compact Andean village is a collection of mud-brick and clap-
board homes and shops where you can watch craftsmen and farmers
at work as life drifts by on the highland plains. The town is actually
more an acclimatization point for the three-hour, uphill hike to the
unusual rock formations at **Marcahuasi,** 3 km (2 mi) from San Pedro,
where winds and weather have worn the earth into a menagerie of animal shapes. There are other hiking trails through the grasslands
around San Pedro, but you'll need to spend at least one night to get
used to the high altitude. Carry a water filtration kit to drink from
the lakes. San Pedro is about 40 km (25 mi) north of Chosica, on the
main highway between Lima and La Oroya. You can catch a bus or
drive from either endpoint.

TARMA, SOUTH TO AYACUCHO

The road from Tarma continues beside the spine of the mountains, alternating between cutting through high-altitude plains and winding in
coils alongside steep crevasses. The thin air can be biting in the shade
and scorching in the mid-afternoon sunlight beating down on a dry, barren landscape pounded into rough grasslands between the peaks. Look
for spots of black, brown, and white—wild llamas and alpacas that roam
this cold, rocky range. Near Pucapampa, the road rises to 4,500 m (14,760
ft), often causing *soroche* (altitude sickness) in travelers but quite comfortable to the resident (and rare) grey alpaca.

Still the road rises, passing tiny Santa Inés and Abra de Apacheta, the
latter set at 4,750 m (15,580 ft). And somehow the scenery continues
to be even more spectacular, for oxides in the earth here have tainted
the rocks and creeks in a wash of vibrant colors. One of the highest roads
in the world is just 14 km (9 mi) farther, the 5,059-m (16,594-ft) pass
3 km (2 mi) north of Huachocolpa. From here the journey is downhill
into the wide, windy Valle Huanta, where lakes and hot springs comin-
gle with caverns and ruins.

Jauja

❿ *280 km (174 mi) southeast of San Pedro de Casta, 60 km (37 mi) south
of Tarma*

Jauja has the distinction of having been Peru's original capital, as declared by Pizarro when he swept through the region; he changed his mind
in 1535 and transferred the title to coastal Lima, a better strategic location for the wary Spanish conquistador. Jauja still has many of the
ornate 16th-century homes and churches that mark its place in the
country's history. The Wednesday market, when Andean traditions are
at their most colorful, shows the other side of life in this mountain town.

Although there are several moderately priced hotels, many travelers just come here on a day trip from Huancayo. Those who stay usually head to the lakeside **Laguna de Paca** resort area 4 km (3 mi) from town.

Concepcíon

⓫ *25 km (15 mi) northwest of Huancayo*

FodorśChoice
★   The village of Concepcíon is the site of the 1724 **Convento de Santa Rosa de Ocopa**. Originally a Franciscan foundation whose role was to bring Christianity to the Amazon tribes, the building now has a reconstructed 1905 church and a massive library with more than 25,000 books—some from the 15th century. The natural history museum has a selection of regional archaeological finds, old native costumes, and local crafts. There's a restaurant serving excellent, if simple, Andean food, as well as several sparse but comfortable accommodations in the former monks' quarters. Admission includes a guided tour. ☎ *No phone* 🖃 *S/5* ☽ *Wed.–Mon. 9–12 and 3–6.*

Huancayo

⓬ *40 km (25 mi) south of Jauja*

It's not hard to see how the modern city of Huancayo, which has close to 260,000 residents, was once the capital of pre-Inca Huanca (Wanka) culture. In the midst of the Andes and straddling the verdant Río Mantaro valley, the city has been a source of artistic inspiration from the days of the earliest settlers, and thus has thrived as the region's center for culture and wheat farming. As a major agricultural hub, Huancayo was linked by rail with the capital in 1908, making it an endpoint on the world's highest train line. Although it's a large town, its little shops, small restaurants, blossoming plazas, and broad colonial buildings give it a comfortable, compact feel.

Huancayo has also been a stronghold for the toughest Peruvian tribes, including the Huanca, who out-fought both the Inca and the Spanish. Little wonder that Peru finally gained independence in this region, near Quinua, in 1824. Still, the Spanish left their mark with the town's collection of hacienda-style homes and businesses, most with arching windows and fronted by brick courtyards with carefully groomed gardens. For an overview of the city, head northeast 4 km (1 ½ mi) on Giráldez, 2 km (1 mi) past Cerro de la Libertad park, to the eroded sandstone towers in the hillsides at Torre-Torre.

The drive from Lima to Huancayo is breathtaking, with the road rising to more than 4,700 m (15,416 ft) before sliding down to the valley's 3,272-m (10,731-ft) elevation. As you enter the city, four-lane Calle Real is jammed with traffic and crammed with storefronts—but look more closely and you'll see the elegant churches and colorful markets tucked into its sidestreets, hallmarks of local life that make the city so charming. Women with long black braids beneath black felt hats still dress in multi-tiered skirts and blouses with *mantas* (bright, square, striped cloths) draped over shoulders. Note the intricate weavings here—particularly the belts with the famous train worked into the pattern.

In front of the Río Shulcas, the **Capilla de la Merced** is a national monument marking where Peru's Constitutional Congress met in 1830. In addition to information about this historic gathering, the Chapel of Mercy also exhibits Cusqueño paintings. ⊠ *Real y Ayacucho* ☎ *No phone* 🖃 *Free* ☽ *Weekdays 8–noon.*

The **Museo Salesiano** (Salesian Museum) has more than 5,000 objects. In particular, look for the well-preserved rain-forest creatures and butterflies from the northern jungles. Local fossils and archaeological relics are also displayed. ✢ *2 blocks west of Real, across Río Shulcas* ☎ *064/ 247763* ✑ *S/3* ✆ *Weekdays 9–noon and 3–6.*

Ⓒ Affectionately known as Torre-Torre, the **Parque del Cerro de la Libertad** is an all-in-one amusement site 1 km (½ mi) east of the city. You can picnic in the grass, watch the kids at the playground, swim in the public pool, dine at the restaurant, or stroll through the zoo. Folkloric dancers and musicians perform at the Liberty Hill Park amphitheater on weekends. ✉ *Giraldez* ☎ *No phone* ✑ *Free* ✆ *Daily 24 hours.*

off the beaten path

WARVILCA – This ruined temple was built by the pre-Inca Huanca culture. The closest village is Huari, which has a little museum on the main square with ceramic figures, pottery, and a few bones and skulls. ✢ *15 km (9 mi) from Huancayo* ☎ *No phone* ✑ *.15* ✆ *Ruins: daily 10–12 and 3–5; museum: daily 10–12.*

Ⓒ The focus of the beautiful **Parque de la Identidad Huanka** (Huanka Identity Park) is on the pre-Inca Huanka culture, which occupied the area but left few clues to its lifestyle. Pebbled paths and small bridges meander through blossoming gardens and past a rock castle just right for children to tackle. The enormous sculpture honors the local artists who produce the city's famous *mates burilados* (carved gourds). ✉ *Giraldez San Antonio* ☎ *No phone* ✑ *Free* ✆ *Daily 24 hrs.*

When the Spanish founded the city in 1572, the **Plaza Huamanmarca** was the city center and the site of the weekly *Feria Dominical* (Sunday market). Today Huamanmarca Square is a center for communications, fronted by the post office, the telephone agency, and the Municipal Hall. ✉ *Calle Real, between Loreto and Piura* ☎ *No phone* ✑ *Free* ✆ *Daily 24 hrs.*

Wali Wali, the home of artist Pedro Marticorena Oroña Laya, is a small arts and crafts gallery, as well as a gathering place for local medicine men. Marticorena's sculptures, statues, and masks reflect unusual—and sometimes frightening—Andean gods and images, some taken from his own visions. You can even take Quecha lessons. Arrange a guided visit through a local tour operator, as unscheduled viewings are discouraged. ✉ *Hualahoyo 2174, off Av. Los Angeles* ☎ *No phone* ✑ *Donations accepted* ✆ *By appointment.*

en route

Valle de Mantaro. The wide Mantaro Valley stretches northwest of Huancayo, embracing not only the Río Mantaro but also a vast area of highlands lakes and plains. Trails run along the jagged mountainsides to archaeological sites and crafts villages where you can explore the region's arts and history firsthand. By road, you'll reach Cochas Chicas and Cochas Grandes, gourd-carving centers 11 km (7 mi) north of Huancayo, with some of the most talented *mate burilado* artists in the country. The road west leads 10 km (6 mi) to Hualhaus, a weaving village where you can watch blankets and sweaters being crafted from alpaca and lamb's wool dyed with local plants. Five km (3 mi) north is San Jerónimo de Tunan, where the Wednesday market specializes in gold and silver filigree. Cross the Río Mantaro and head 10 km (6 km) west to Aco, a village of potters and ceramics artists. Group tours from Huancayo cover the valley, but the roads are good enough that you can drive on your own— although you won't have a guide or a translator. Minibuses from the Plaza Constitución also reach these villages.

Where to Stay & Eat

The local specialty is *papa a la huancaína* (boiled potato covered in a milky cheese sauce), served cold with an olive. Budget restaurants with set lunch menus are gathered on Arequipa south of Antojitos, as well as along Giráldez. You can pick up a quick morning meal at the Mercado Modelo after 7 AM.

¢ ✗ **Antojitos.** The succulent grilled meats, wood-smoked pizzas, and hearty sandwiches at this renowned backpacker restaurant draw more than just the budget crowd. The elite meet here for a glass of local wine; businessmen snack on the filling lunch specials; and there's always a crowd for the live bands each weekend. ⊠ *Puno 599* ☎ *064/237950* ▭ *AE, DC, MC, V* ☺ *Closed Sun.*

¢ ✗ **La Cabaña.** There's a romantic air to this cozy, charming restaurant
FodorśChoice that has long been a travelers' favorite. The cuisine combines such Pe-
★ ruvian specialties as anticuchos and calentitos with basic Continental fare like pasta, pizza, and grills. Dine in the garden on balmy days, or around the fireplace on chilly evenings. There's live music Thursday through Saturday, and the owners can arrange cooking classes, Spanish lessons, music instruction, and long-term local homestays. Two hostel rooms, a book exchange, and numerous maps are available. ⊠ *Giráldez 652* ☎ *064/223303* ▭ *MC, V.*

¢ ✗ **Panadería Koky.** Petite tables swathed in rippling cloth are arranged in tea-party style in the airy dining room. It's a perfectly elegant way to sample the pretty cakes and pastries while sipping espresso. Hungrier patrons can get pizza and sandwiches. Afterward, wander into the liquor shop to check out the local specialties. ⊠ *Puno 298* ☎ *064/234707* ▭ *AE, MC, V.*

★ ¢ ✗ **Restaurant Olímpico.** This upmarket restaurant, open for more than 60 years, still serves a downtown lunch crowd with cheap, hearty Andean specials. It's popular and always crowded, but good food is guaranteed. For a basic selection of soup, salad, meat, rice, and dessert, try the daily special. Otherwise, you can order a mix of Peruvian delicacies, including cuy, off the à la carte menu. ⊠ *Giráldez 199* ☎ *064/234181* ▭ *AE, DC, MC, V.*

¢ ✗ **Restaurant Vegetariano.** Health food has arrived in the Andes at this vegetarian spot. Pastas, soups, and rice dishes with vegetable bases are all on the menu. The kitchen whips up yogurt, soy milk, and fruit drinks as well. This is also the place to stock up on organic products and vitamins. ⊠ *Cajamarca 379* ☎ *no phone* ▭ *No credit cards.*

$ ▦ **Hotel Turismo Huancayo.** The hacienda-style exterior of this elegant hotel gives it a worldly charm that sets it above the younger options. Public areas are ornate, with Peruvian paintings and accented with local crafts and textiles. Rooms are sparkling clean, and many have TVs, phones, and private baths with hot water. Ask to see several different options before you agree to stay, as rooms vary in size, decor, view, and amenities. Although the neighborhood is quieter than those around the plaza, the hotel is still conveniently in the middle of town. ⊠ *Ancash 729* ☎ *064/ 231072* ▧ *064/231072* ⇗ *64 rooms* ⚬ *Restaurant, room service, cable TV, laundry service, business services, travel service, free parking; no phones in some rooms, no TV in some rooms* ▭ *AE, DC, MC, V.*

★ ¢ ▦ **Andino Lodging and Excursions.** Trekkers and mountaineers favor this out-of-the-way, rustic Ahdean hotel 3 km (2 mi) from town. There are cozy rooms with chunky modern furniture and private bathrooms with hot showers. You can cook your own meals and do your own laundry after exploring the surrounding peaks. The English-speaking owner can set up hiking and mountain-bike excursions. ⊠ *San Antonia 113–115* ☎ *064/223956* ⇗ *15 rooms* ⚬ *Restaurant, mountain bikes, hiking, bar,* *laundry facilities, Internet, travel services, free parking; no room phones, no room TVs* ⊟ *AE, DC, MC, V.*

¢ ⊞ **Casa Alojamiento Bonilla.** When you're a guest of artists Aldo and Soledad Bonilla, you can't help but become a part of local life. The colonial-style hacienda harks back to Spanish conquistador days, and you can take your meals on the sunny patio amid lush gardens. Rooms have a mix of contemporary furnishings and period antiques accented with local art and crafts. The English-speaking staff makes it all too easy to stay longer than planned. There's a laundry, and breakfast is included. ✉ *Huánuco 332* ☎ *064/232103* ➥ *12 rooms* ♦ *Restaurant, dining room, laundry facilities, travel services, free parking* ⊟ *No credit cards* ⦿ *FAP.*

¢ ⊞ **Hotel Olímpico.** This central hotel has more charm than its larger competitors, and it's close to the center of town. Cozy rooms with modern furniture have all the amenities, including TVs, phones, and bathrooms with hot water. ✉ *Ancash 408* ☎ *064/214555* 🖷 *064/215700* ➥ *32 rooms* ♦ *Restaurant, room service, cable TV, laundry service, travel services, free parking* ⊟ *AE, DC, MC, V.*

¢ ⊞ **Hotel Presidente.** The most popular hotel with visiting Limeños has the comforts of a modern hotel, and a bland 20th-century exterior to match. Rooms, with contemporary furnishings and Andean fabrics and accents, have TVs, phones, private baths with hot water—and thin walls. There's a wheelchair-accessible elevator. ✉ *Real 1138* ☎ *064/231736* 🖷 *064/231275* ➥ *88 rooms* ♦ *Cable TV, laundry service, business services, travel services, free parking* ⊟ *AE, DC, MC, V* ⦿ *BP.*

¢ ⊞ **La Casa de Mi Abuela.** Hot showers, hearty Peruvian home cooking, and a sunny garden gathering spot attract budget travelers to this old colonial mansion. Rooms have a mix of contemporary, colonial, and comfortably worn pieces; some are dorms, and some have private bathrooms. The shared laundry and kitchen are often busy. A Continental breakfast is included. ✉ *Giráldez 691* ☎ *064/238224* 🖷 *064/222395* ➥ *4 rooms, 3 dormitories* ♦ *Laundry facilities, travel services, free parking; no room phones, no room TVs* ⊟ *No credit cards* ⦿ *BP.*

Nightlife & the Arts

Huancayo's nightlife is surprisingly spunky, particularly on weekends and holidays. Many restaurants turn into peñas with dancing, live music, and folkloric performances from Friday to Sunday between 7 PM and midnight (though some may start and end earlier). If you arrive around or after the time the show begins, expect to pay a cover of about S/7. Dance clubs usually open from about 10 PM to 2 AM and have a cover charge of S/10–S/14.

The **A1A** (✉ Bolognesi 299 ☎ No phone) is the city's hot disco for teens and twentysomethings. **La Cabaña** (✉ Giráldez 652 ☎ 064/223303) has rollicking live folklórico and pop bands Thursday through Saturday. Former hippies, flower children, and Beatles fans head to the compact **La Chiminea** (✉ Lima 253 ☎ no phone) for live rock-and-roll from the '60s. **El Coconut** (✉ Huancavelica 430 ☎ No phone) has a crowded dance floor and bar on weekends. The second-floor **Marisquería** (✉ Giráldez ☎ No phone) disco has a mix of modern pop and old dance hits. Video karaoke is the main attraction at the **Taj Mahal** (✉ Huancavelica 1052 ☎ No phone) when you're not dancing. Sing and dance to international pop tunes at **Taki Wasi** (✉ Huancavelica y 13 de Noviembre ☎ No phone).

Shopping

Huancayo and the towns of the surrounding Valle del Mantaro are major craft centers. The region is famous for its *mate burilado* (large, intricately carved and painted gourds depicting scenes of local life and historic events), many of which are made 11 km (7 mi) outside of town in the villages of Cochas Grande and Cochas Chico. Silver filigree and utensils are the specialties of San Jerónimo de Tunán, while exquisite knitwear, woolen sweaters, scarves, wall hangings, and hats are produced in San Agustín de Cajas and Hualhaus.

Elegant, high-quality textiles are woven and sold at **Artesanía Sumaq Ruray** (⊠ Brasilia 132 ☎ 064/237018).

You'll find top-quality, locally made goods near the Plaza Constitución at **Casa de Artesana** (⊠ Real 495 ☎ no phone), where artists sit shop-by-shop working on their various crafts.

Artists' shops and stalls line the **Centro Commerical Artesanal El Manatial** (⊠ Ancash 475 ☎ no phone), where you can browse for clothing, textiles, ceramics, woodcarvings, and many other crafts.

The city's main shopping venue is the weekend **Mercado** (⊠ Av. Huancavelica ☎ no phone), which is spread down one of the city's main thoroughfares and its side streets. In particular, look for *mate burilado, mantas* (straw baskets), and *retablos* (miniature scenes framed in painted wooden boxes).

Mercado Mayorista (⊠ Prolongación Ica ☎ no phone), stretching around the blocks near the train station, is the daily produce market. You'll need several hours to wander through the stalls of local crafts and foodstuffs, where you'll find traditional medicines and spices among such local delicacies as gourds, guinea pigs, fish, and frogs.

The **Sunday crafts market** (⊠ Calle Huancavelica ☎ no phone) has textiles, sweaters, embroidery, woodcarvings, and ceramics. This is a good place to shop for the town's famous carved gourds.

Huancavelica

⑬ *147 km (91 mi) south of Huancayo*

Spread out high in the Andes, Huancavelica was founded in the 16th century by Spanish conquistadors, who discovered the rich streaks of silver and mercury threaded through the rocky hillsides. Although mining was difficult at 3,680 m (12,979 ft), the Spanish succeeded in making the city a key profit center that today has grown to a population of around 40,000. Although the narrow, cobbled streets are lined with elegant, colonial-style mansions and 16th-century churches, you'll still see traditional costumes worn by women in the markets and shops.

This scenic town is sliced by the Río Huancavelica, which divides the commercial district on the south and the residential area in the north. The road here is rough, but the surroundings are beautiful, a mix of quiet, clapboard-style villages fronting vast sheep pastures and snow-capped mountains. As many of those who live here are too poor to own a car, the train is the vital link between Huancavelica and other mountain towns. Residents from all over the region crowd the sprawling Sunday market, as well as the daily food market at the corner of Muñoz and Barranca.

Most crafts and clothing are made in the villages on the outskirts of Huancavelica, and you're welcome to visit the artisans' shops. Other neighboring explorations include the viewpoints from Potaqchiz, just a short stroll up the hill from San Cristóbal. Thermal baths are on the hillside across from town.

Huancavelica's **Plaza de Armas** is, naturally, the main gathering place. Across from the plaza is the restored 17th-century Cathedral. ⊠ *Toledo y Segura* ☎ *No phone* ⊠ *Free* ☉ *Daily 24 hrs.*

THE QUECHUA OF THE ANDES

THE QUECHUA ARE THE ORIGINAL MOUNTAIN HIGHLANDS DWELLERS, whose strong traditions and beliefs have survived even Inca domination, Spanish conquests, and the beginning influences of modern technology. In towns throughout the region, Quechua is still the first language spoken, even before Spanish, and traditional costumes are still woven on backstrap looms and worn at the markets. Many Quechua make their living by farming maize and coca in the valleys or potatoes and quinoa in the higher altitudes, while other families herd llamas and alpacas on the cold, windy puna.

Walk through the narrow, cobbled streets of any village and you'll see Quechua men and women dressed in colorful woolen outfits as they have for hundreds of years. You'll spot Quecha men by the large, patterned, fringed ponchos draped over their shoulders, their heads topped by matching tasseled cloths beneath big, cone-shape, felt hats. Knee-length pants are held up with a wide, woven belt that often has a local motif—such as the famous mountain train. Despite the cold, men usually wear rubber sandals, often fashioned from old tires. Quechua men are usually clean-shaven, too, since most can't grow facial hair.

Quechua women's attire is equally bright, with modern knit sweaters and a flouncing, patterned skirt over several petticoats (added for both warmth and puff). Instead of a poncho, women wear an aguayo, a length of sarong-like fabric that can be tied into a sling for carrying a baby or market goods, or wrapped around their shoulders for warmth. Hats for the women differ from village to village; some wear black felt caps with neon fringe and elaborate patterns of sequins and beads, while others wear a plain brown felt derby. Women also wear rubber sandals for walking and working in the fields, but often go barefoot at home.

The Morochuco are a unique group of formerly nomadic Quechua who live near Ayacucho on the Pampas de Cangallo. They are distinguished by their light skin and blue eyes, and, unlike other Quechua, many Morochuco men wear beards. Cattle breeding and horse training are the main occupations rather than llama herding or farming. Renowned for their fearlessness and strength, the Morochuco fought for Peru's independence on horseback with Simón Bolívar, and local lore has it that they are the descendents of the army of Diego de Almagro, a Spanish hero killed by Pizzaro.

The Morochuco are first-rate horseback riders—women and children included—who use their swiftness and agility to round up bulls on the highland pampas. Women ride in long skirts and petticoats, while men don thick wool tights and dark ponchos. Both men and women wear chullos, a wool hat with ear flaps, beneath a felt hat tied under the chin with a red sash.

Look for gatherings of stone or adobe-brick homes with thatched roofs as you travel through the mountains. These are typical Quechua homes, which are basic inside and out. Cooking is done either in an adobe oven next to the dwelling or over an open fire inside. Mud platforms with llama wool or sheepskin blankets make do for beds; occasionally a family will have the luxury of a wooden bedframe and grass mattress. There is little else but cooking implements inside, as the entire family works in the fields as soon as they are able. The ayllu (extended family) is also expected to contribute their strengths and skills to major projects like harvesting the fields or building a new home.

— By Holly S. Smith

The **Iglesia de San Francisco** was begun in 1673, but it took six more decades to complete. Its dual white towers and red stone doorway—carved with regional motifs—make the San Francisco Church one of the most attractive buildings in town. ⊠ *Goodos y Tagle* ☏ *No phone* ⊠ *Free* ☉ *Mon.–Sat. 4–6.*

The Sunday **Feria Dominical** market attracts artists and shoppers from all the mountain towns. It's a good place to browse for local crafts—although you'll get better quality (and sometimes better prices) in the villages. ⊠ *Garma y Barranca* ☏ *no phone* ⊠ *Free* ☉ *Sunday 8–3.*

off the beaten path

SAN CRISTÓBAL – Locals believe that these hot-spring mineral baths, found in the tree-covered slopes north of town, have healing powers. Hundreds of pilgrims come from the surrounding villages during holy days. (⊠ *5 de Agosto* ☏ *no phone* ⊠ *S/.50 private room, S/.35 public area* ☉ *Daily 6 AM–3 PM*).

Where to Stay & Eat

Several Peruvian and international restaurants line Barranca, Toledo, and the streets around the Plaza de Armas. All are casual and have a mix of Andean and Continental cuisine. Almuerzo is the midday budget set meal; dinners are more expensive. Most restaurants also have an à la carte menu useful for sampling several dishes. Hotels usually have restaurants, or at least a small café or dining room.

¢ ✕▦ **Hotel Presidente Huancavelica.** The town's top hotel is right on the plaza in an attractive, Spanish-colonial building. Rooms have bland modern furnishings, but they're good-sized and comfortable, with phones and hot showers. Rooms with shared baths are cheaper. The restaurant offers several international choices at lunch and dinner when the hotel is busy; otherwise, it's open for breakfast only. ⊠ *Carabaya y Muñoz* ☏ *064/952760* 🖷 *064/752760* ⟿ *65 rooms* ⚭ *Restaurant, laundry service, free parking; no phones in some rooms, no TV in some rooms* ▭ *AE, DC, MC, V* ⏍ *BP.*

¢ ✕▦ **Mercurio.** It's another colonial-style hotel on the plaza, but the modestly furnished rooms are spic and span, with private bathrooms—some with tubs—and hot water. The restaurant, one of the top spots to dine, serves hearty portions of Peruvian cuisine, as well as pastas. ⊠ *Torre Tagle 455* ☏ *064/752438* ⟿ *45 rooms* ⚭ *Restaurant, laundry service, free parking* ▭ *AE, DC, MC, V.*

¢ ▦ **Hotel Tahuantinsuyo.** Old colonial architecture and a quiet neighborhood make this hotel seem more like a large home, and the price is a bargain for the small rooms with private baths and hot water. Besides the bed and nightstand, there's even a desk and chair for writing postcards. Save even more by staying in the shared rooms with cold showers. ⊠ *Carabaya y Muñoz* ☏ *064/952968* ⟿ *22 rooms* ⚭ *Laundry service, free parking; no phones in some rooms, no TV in some rooms* ▭ *MC, V* ⏍ *BP.*

Quinua

🄫 *37 km (22 mi) northeast of the Ayachuco*

Fodor'sChoice **Pampas de Quinua.** The Battle of Ayacucho took place on the grasslands
★ 37 km (22 mi) northeast of the city, near the village of Quinua, on December 9, 1824. Today a white obelisk rises 44 m (144 ft) above the pampas to commemorate how the locals firmly cemented Peru's independence here when they defeated the Spanish. You can follow the surrounding events through exhibits in the compact Quinua museum (S/5). Come the first week in December to celebrate the town's role in Peru's

democracy, when you'll see extravagant local performances, parties, parades, and crafts fairs. There's a little local market on Sunday. The town is also known for its pottery, and you'll find ceramics adorning the windowsills and rooftops. Miniature churches, delicately painted with ears of corn or flowers, are frequently-seen symbols of good luck. The ubiquitous bulls are figures once used in festivities associated with cattle-branding ceremonies. Tours of Huari, Vilcashuaman, and Vischongo often include Quinua, but you can also get here by bus.

Ayacucho

⑮–㉔ *114 km (71 mi) south of Huancavelica, 364 km (226 mi) northeast of Pisco*

Tucked into the folds of the Andes, 2,740 m (8,987 ft) up on the slopes, Ayacucho is a colorful, colonial-style town. Though its looks are Spanish—all glowing white alabaster mansions with elegant columns and arches—it's primarily still an Indian town inhabited by a proud culture that still speaks Quechua as a first language and dons traditional costume for the daily routine. Visitors are still greeted with some amazement (and lots of warmth) in this city of 120,000 where artists are revered and celebrations like Carnaval and Semana Santa take place in a frenzy of activity and energy. Religion is a serious pursuit, too, in this city of churches, where more than 50 sanctuaries beckon worshipers at all hours.

Civilization of Peru began in the valleys around Ayacucho about 20,000 years ago. Dating back this far are the oldest human remains in the country—and perhaps in the Americas—found in a cave network at Piquimachay 24 km (15 mi) west of the city. Over the centuries, the region was home to many pre-Hispanic cultures, including the Huari (Wari), who set up their capital of Huari 22 km (14 mi) from Ayacucho some 13,000 years ago. When the Inca arrived in the 15th century, they ruled these lands from Vilcashuamán.

When the Spanish came, they won hard-fought battles with the reigning Inca tribes, and none other than Francisco Pizarro finally founded Ayacucho in 1540. First named Huamanga for the local *huamanga* (alabaster) used in handicrafts, Ayacucho grew from a small village into a broad city known for its many colonial-style churches. Nearly 300 years later it was the center of Peru's rebellion for independence from the Spanish, when locals defeated the last Spanish army at Quinua in 1824. The first bells of Peru's independence were sounded at the Iglesia Santo Domingo in Ayacucho.

It took a century more before the city built its first road links west to the coast, and the road to Lima went unpaved through the 1960s. It might have opened to tourism then, but for the influence of Abimael Guzmán, a philosophy teacher at the University of Huamanga who set up the Sendero Luminoso (Shining Path) here. From March 1982, when bombs and gunfire first sounded through the cobbled streets, thousands of Ayacuchanos fled or were killed during the war between the terrorists and the government. The city was placed under military control, and Guzmán was finally arrested in 1992. You can still feel the army's presence, but with the Sendero Luminoso dismantled, Ayacucho is now considered to be a safe town.

Ayacucho's resulting isolation from the modern world means that to visit is to step back into colonial days. Elegant white *huamanga* buildings glow in the sunlight, bright flowers spilling out of boxes lining high, narrow, wooden balconies. Beyond the slim, strait roads and terra cotta roofs, cultivated fields climb the Andes foothills up to the snow. Electricity,

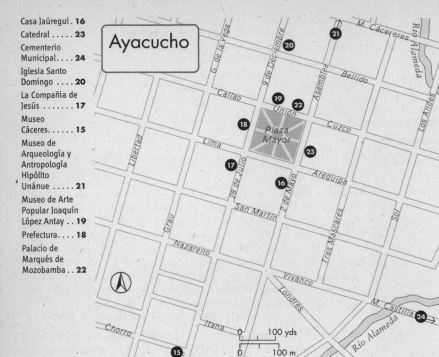

running water, and phones are unreliable, if even available. Banks and businesses are hidden in 16th-century *casonas* (colonial mansions). Women in traditional Quecha shawls draped over white blouses, their black hair braided neatly, stroll through markets packed with small fruit, vegetable, and craft stalls.

⑮ In Casona Vivanco on the Plaza Mayor, the 17th-century **Museo Cáceres** honors Andrés Cáceres, an Aycucho resident and former Peruvian president best known for his successful guerrilla leadership during the 1879–83 War of the Pacific against Chile. His Cáceres Museum is one of the city's best-preserved historic mansions, which today protects a mix of military memorabilia and ancient local artifacts, including stone carvings and ceramics. Note the gallery of colonial-style paintings. ⊠ *28 de Julio 500* ☎ *No phone* 🖂 *S/4* ⊙ *Mon.–Sat. 8–1 and 3–5.*

⑯ Across from the Iglesia Merced on the Plaza, you'll see the colonial-style **Casa Jaúregui.** The Jaúregui House is an art gallery with paintings, sculptures, and local crafts by Peruvian artists. ⊠ *Plaza Mayor* ☎ *No phone* 🖂 *S/4* ⊙ *Weekdays 9–12 and 3–5, Sat. 9–1.*

⑰ You can't miss the ochre-colored, baroque-style exterior of **La Compañia de Jesús.** The towers were added a century after the main building, which has religious art and a gilt altar. ⊠ *Jr. 28 de Julio y Lima* ☎ *No phone* 🖂 *Free* ⊙ *Weekdays 9–1 and 4–6, Sat. 9–12.*

⑱ The **Prefectura** is tucked into a 1748, two-story *casona historica* (historic mansion). Local independence-era heroine María Prado de Bellido was held prisoner in the Prefecture's patio room until her execution by firing squad in 1822. ⊠ *28 de Julio* ☎ *No phone* 🖂 *S/2* ⊙ *Weekdays 9–noon and 3–5.*

⑲ The **Museo de Arte Popular Joaquín López Antay,** in the Casona Chacón on the Plaza Mayor, has some of the region's best local art. The exquisite and valuable collections include clay sculptures, silver filigree, retablos, and paintings. Trace the town's history, as well as the craftsmanship behind many pieces, through photo exhibits. Note the gathering of looms used to weave lamb and alpaca wool into textiles and clothing. The Museum of Popular Art shares the Casona with the Banco de Credito in one of the city's best-preserved colonial-style mansions. ⊠ *Unión 28* ☎ *066/812467* ✆ *Free* ☉ *Mon.–Sat. 9–12:30 and 2–5.*

㉠ The 1548 **Iglesia Santo Domingo** is now a national monument, for the first bells ringing out Peru's independence from the Spanish after the Battle of Ayacucho were sounded from here. Byzantine towers and Roman arches mark the façade of the church, while inside there are such surprises as a gilt altar. ⊠ *Jr. 9 de Diciembre y Bellido* ☎ *No phone* ✆ *Free* ☉ *Mon., Tues., and Sat. 9–12 and 3–5, Fri. 9–12 and 4–7.*

> **off the beaten path**

HUARI – The wide plains that make up the 300-hectare Santuario Histórico Pampas de Ayacucho are scattered with relics of the Huari culture, which evolved 500 years before that of the Inca. Huari was its capital, thought to have once been home to 60,000 or more residents, and its surrounding fields contain a maze of tumbled stone temples, homes, and 12-m (39-ft) walls. This is believed to have been the first urban walled settlement in the Andes, created by a civilization whose livelihood was based on such metalworking feats as bronze weapons and gold and silver jewelry. A small museum displays skeleton bits and samples of ceramics and textiles; opening times are at the whim of the workers. You can get here cheaply from Barrio Magdalena via irregular buses, which continue to La Quinua and Huanta for less than S/2.50. Most travel agents in town offer guided tours to the site for around S/58. ✛ *22 km (14 mi) southeast of Ayacucho* ☎ *No phone* ✆ *Site: free; museum: S/3* ☉ *Ruins: daily 8–6; museum: hrs vary.*

㉑ On display at the **Museo de Arqeología y Antropología Hipólito Unánue,** at the Centro Cultural Simón Bolívar, are regional finds from the Moche, Nazca, Ica, Inca, Canka, Chavín, and Chimu cultures. Highlights of the Hipólito Unánue Archeology and Anthropology Museum include ceremonial costumes, textiles, everyday implements, and even artwork from some of the area's oldest inhabitants. The museum is locally referred to as Museo INC. ⊠ *Av. Independencia* ☎ *066/812360* ✆ *S/4* ☉ *Mon.–Sat. 8:30–11 and 2–5.*

㉒ Built in 1550 and now the home of the Escuela de Bellas Artes (School of Fine Arts), the **Palacio de Marqués de Mozobamba** is the city's oldest structure. The colonial-era, baroque-style architecture of this palace includes *portales* (stone arches) in front. ⊠ *Unión 37* ☎ *No phone* ✆ *Free* ☉ *Weekdays 10–4.*

㉓ Walk through the Plaza gardens and you'll immediately spot the twin brick bell towers of the 1612 Ayacucho **Catedral,** built by Bishop Don Cristóbal de Castilla y Zamora. Step inside to view the Cathedral's carved altars with gold-leaf designs, a silver tabernacle, and an ornate wooden pulpit. Look for the plaque inside the entrance that quotes from Pope John II's speech during his visit in 1985. The **Museo de Arte Religioso** exhibits antique objects from the sanctuary's early days, carvings of saints, and religious paintings; ask for visiting privileges if the doors are locked. During Semana Santa, the church hosts an extremely popular Palm Sunday candlelight procession with a statue of Christ transported on the back of a white donkey. ⊠ *Asemblea* ☎ *No phone* ✆ *Free* ☉ *Church and museum: Mon., Tues., and Sat. 9–12 and 3–5, Fri. 9–12 and 4–7.*

② At the end of the airport runway, the enormous **Cementerio Municipal** looks like a huge condo with multiple walls of crypts. Many of the sites date from the 1970s and 1980s, when the Sendero Luminoso rained terror on the region. ✉ *End of airport runway* ☎ *No phone* ✉ *Free* ⊘ *Daily 8–6.*

> off the
> beaten
> path

VILCASHUAMÁN AND INTIHUATANA – Four hours south of Ayacucho is the former Inca provincial capital of Vilcashuamán, set where the north–south Inca highway crossed the east–west trade road from Cusco to the Pacific. You can still see the double-seated throne and a five-tiered platform surrounded by stepped fields once farmed by Inca. An hour's walk from Vilcashuamán (or a half-hour's walk south past the main road from Ayacucho) is Inhuatana, where Inca ruins include a palace and tower beside a lagoon. Former Inca baths, a sun temple, and a sacrificial altar are also on the grounds. Check out the unusual 17-angled boulder, one of the odd building rocks that are an Inca hallmark. Ayacucho travel agencies can organize tours of both sites (S/96), or you can catch a bus or colectivo from Avenida Castilla on Tuesday, Thursday, and Saturday. If you take public transport, you'll have to stay overnight, as vehicles return on alternate days.

Where to Stay & Eat

Ayacucho is famous for its filling, flavorful *puca picante* (a peanutty pork-and-potato stew), served with rice and topped with a parsley sprig. The city's favorite drink is the hot, pisco-spiked *ponche* (flavored with milk, cinnamon, cloves, sesame, peanuts, walnuts, and sugar). The best time to sample these popular concoctions is during Semana Santa. In the beginning of November, the Ayacuchans are also busy baking sweet breads shaped like horses and babies to place in baskets for the spirits at the family gravesites. You'll find inexpensive restaurants where you can grab a cheap *almuerzo* along Jirón San Martin. Note that many restaurants are closed on Sunday.

¢-$$ ✕ **Restaurant Plaza Ayacucho.** You can dress up for dinner at this elegant restaurant, one of the town's finest, with shining brass chandeliers and crisp tablecloths. The set menu offers a rotating sample of local delights, or you can order Peruvian fare à la carte. Those who like it bland can stick with the pastas or grilled meats. Desserts include a changing selection of cakes, fruit mixes, and chocolates. ✉ *Jr. 9 de Diciembre 184* ☎ *066/812202* ✉ *MC, V.*

¢-$ ✕ **Del Morochucos.** The building is old Spanish style, but the food is all modern, ranging in flavors from the meaty Andes *parrillada* (grill) to pasta and sandwiches. Come on weekends to catch bands that rock the crowd. The restaurant is across the street from the Iglesia Santo Domingo ✉ *9 de Diciembre 205* ☎ *No phone* ✉ *No credit cards.*

★ ¢-$ ✕ **La Casona.** Dining in this Spanish-style home is like attending an intimate, upscale party in a fine hacienda. Soft music wafts between high walls lined with paintings and woven textiles, while conversations ebb and flow at a low hum. The scent of fresh flowers decorating the glass-topped tables mixes with the delicious aromas of such Peruvian specialties as *puca picante* (pork and potatoes in red sauce) and *tortas* (sweet cakes). ✉ *Bellindo 463* ☎ *No phone* ✉ *MC, V.*

¢-$ ✕ **Restaurant Los Portales.** Set above the Plaza de Armas, this Peruvian restaurant offers a taste of the Andes surrounded by a thriving local panorama. Big portions are the norm at lunch and dinner, when you can sample grilled chicken, hearty beef stews, and combination rice and vegetable dishes. Snackers can try sandwiches, soups, and fruit salads. ✉ *San Martín 406* ☎ *No phone* ✉ *No credit cards.*

¢ ✕ **Chifa El Dorado.** This tiny restaurant with stark lighting and metal tables and chairs has a basic but tasty selection of Chinese dishes, including stir-fried beef and vegetables, stir-fried noodles, hot-and-sour soup, and spicy chicken. Peruvian stews and seafood are also on the menu. ⊠ *Cusco 144* 🕾 *No phone* ⊟ *No credit cards.*

¢ ✕ **Max Max.** At this charming little coffee shop with tall windows and crowded tables, grab a cappuccino and a biscuit or sit down for a sandwich and soda. Top off a walking tour with one of the sweet iced *tortas* (cakes) or a big cookie. ⊠ *Jr. 9 de Diciembre* 🕾 *066/817567* ⊟ *No credit cards.*

¢ ✕ **Mia Pizza.** You'll make friends fast at this dinner-only spot where patrons sit side-by-side at wooden tables to snack on Italian fare. You can't miss with the pizza, cooked in an authentic wood-burning oven. The cheesy cannelloni and hearty spaghetti are also good bets. ⊠ *San Martín 420* 🕾 *066/815407* 🕙 *No lunch* ⊟ *No credit cards.*

¢ ✕ **Restaurant Cámara Comercio.** This popular lunch place hones in on the budget crowd with its inexpensive set menus. You'll fill up fast with the meal of the day, which includes soup or stew, a rice and meat dish, and a salad or bread. ⊠ *San Martín 400* 🕾 *No phone* 🕙 *No dinner* ⊟ *No credit cards.*

¢ ✕ **Restaurant La Tradición.** Another cheapie that's been a hometown favorite since 1967, this Peruvian budget restaurant has a daily choice of two set meals and extensive à la carte choices. It's the place to try cuy, or such Andean specialties as grilled or stewed beef parts. Still, if you're here more to save money than try local fare, you can always cop out and order spaghetti. ⊠ *San Martín 406* 🕾 *No phone* ⊟ *MC, V.*

¢ ✕ **Restaurant Los Alamos.** This popular backpacker hangout begins the day with serious breakfasts: hearty egg and meat dishes, pancakes, sweet breads, and the like. After dark, huge dinners are often accompanied by the music of local bands crooning crowd favorites. ⊠ *Cusco 215* 🕾 *No phone* ⊟ *No credit cards.*

¢ ✕ **Restaurant Urpicha.** Eating here feels like you're having dinner at
Fodor'sChoice grandma's—if grandma served meals in her quaint Spanish home on a
★ blossoming terrace. Meals are lovingly (if slowly) prepared, and the wait is worth it. The kitchen turns out such traditional Andean specialties as barbecued cuy. Drop by on a weekend to hear the best local folk groups. ⊠ *Londres 272* 🕾 *066/913905* ⊟ *No credit cards.*

$ 🏨 **Ayacucho Hotel Plaza.** The city's most expensive hotel is in a gracious colonial building overlooking the Plaza. Spacious gardens and opulent sitting areas bely the modest rooms with worn carpet and nicked modern furnishings. The best (and quietest) accommodations are on the second floor, where there's a view of the terra cotta roofs and the courtyard. You can request a balcony over the Plaza, but beware the ever-present commotion outside—especially on Sundays and during festivals. ⊠ *9 de Diciembre 184* 🕾 *066/912202* 🖨 *066/912314* 🛌 *84 rooms* 🕭 *Restaurant, room service* ⊟ *AE, MC, V* ⎮◯⎮ *BP.*

$ 🏨 **Hostal El Marqués de Valdelirios.** Stroll through a quiet residential neigh-
Fodor'sChoice borhood to this 1940s casona that welcomes you into the colonial era.
★ The wide, elegant courtyard is flush with blossoms year-round, making it a favorite place for local celebrations. Inside, lace curtains, crocheted bedspreads, gently polished wood accents, and antiques here and there provide the feel of a comfortable hacienda. You can order meals, served in the formal dining room. ⊠ *Bolognesi 720* 🕾 *066/913908* 🖨 *066/914014* 🛌 *14 rooms* 🕭 *Restaurant, dining room, bar, dance club, laundry service, free parking* ⊟ *AE, MC, V* ⎮◯⎮ *BP*

¢ 🏨 **Hostal Samary.** To those asking around for a good budget hotel, this one is continually recommended by travelers. The rooftop patio is a main hub for travel gossip, and the central location and cheap, clean rooms provide backpackers with all they need. Showers are hot in the morning and evening. Ask about the discount for foreign visitors. ⊠ *Callao 335* ☎ *066/912442* ⟋ *14 rooms* ⟡ *Free parking; no room phones, no TV in some rooms* ⊟ *No credit cards.*

¢ ⊞ **Hostelería Santa Rosa.** Near the Plaza, this pleasant little hotel encircles a pretty courtyard with gardens and a brick walkway. Rooms have a mix of antiques, handmade fabrics, and contemporary furnishings, plus unexpected modern amenities like TVs and phones. Private bathrooms have hot water only morning and evening. ⊠ *Lima 166* ☎ *066/914614* 🖷 *066/912083* ⟋ *26 rooms* ⟡ *Restaurant, bar, laundry service, free parking* ⊟ *No credit cards* ⟦◯⟧ *BP.*

¢ ⊞ **Hotel San Blas.** This colonial hotel has a mix of room styles and prices, ranging from basic, inexpensive quarters with shared bath to private accommodations with baths and hot water. Local ceramics and textiles add a familial flavor that's enhanced when travelers gather in the shared kitchen or laundry. On balmy afternoons the courtyard becomes a lounge for snacking and travel gossip; you can order cheap, filling Peruvian fare here as well. Ask for a discount if you plan to stay a few days. ⊠ *Chorro 161* ☎ *066/910552* ⟋ *45 rooms* ⟡ *Restaurant, laundry facilities, free parking; no room phones, no room TVs* ⊟ *No credit cards.*

¢ ⊞ **Hotel San Francisco.** At this Spanish mansion, local charm is threaded throughout the winding rooms and public areas, decorated with folk-art pieces, textiles, and crafts. Antique furnishings bring the colonial era to life, but modern room amenities like TVs and refrigerators pour on 21st-century comfort. Book a room with a balcony to enjoy the local street scene below, or dine at the rooftop restaurant for views of the city and mountains. ⊠ *Callao 290* ☎ *066/912959* 🖷 *066/914501* ⟋ *45 rooms* ⟡ *Restaurant, refrigerators, bar, lounge, meeting rooms, laundry service, free parking* ⊟ *AE, DC, MC, V* ⟦◯⟧ *BP.*

¢ ⊞ **La Colmena Hotel.** Though the rooms are small, the all-round quiet and pleasant courtyard make this one of the city's most popular budget options. Rooms, with plain furniture and local art, come with or without baths; hot water runs only in the morning. ⊠ *Cusco 140* ☎ *066/912146* 🖷 *No phone* ⟋ *18 rooms* ⟡ *Dining room, free parking* ⊟ *No credit cards.*

Nightlife & the Arts

Peña Macha (⊠ Grau 158 ☎ no phone) is a disco during the week but has folkloric shows and live music on weekends. **Punto Caliente Video Pub** (⊠ Asemblea 131 ☎ no phone) is open daily except Monday. Sample pizza and Quecha rock at **Taberna Liverpool** (⊠ Cáceres 620 ☎ no phone), which—naturally—also has lots of Beatles music. At **Taberna Madero Viejo** (⊠ Asamblea 131 ☎ No phone), patrons drink and dance to rock-music tapes. Stroll through the art gallery, then grab a drink at the **Taberna Magia Negra** (⊠ Cáceres y Vega ☎ no phone).

Shopping

Ayacucho is the home of many of Peru's best artists, whom you can often visit at work in their neighborhood shops or galleries. Look for retablos, the multitiered, three-dimensional displays of plaster characters in scenes of the city's famed religious processions and historic battles. Good markets are found in the city's outskirts, such as the busy Mercado Domingo (Sunday Market) in Huanta, an hour north.

Ayacucho's produce and meat market is the **Mercado Andrés Vivanco** (⊠ Jr. 28 de Julio ☎ No phone), found behind the main brick arch in a one-story building. Pick up bouquets of mums and gladiolas out front, or head inside to peruse the stacks of fruits and vegetables; afterward you can join the locals on the steps to snack on your purchases. Shops continue for several streets behind the main building.

The Santa Ana neighborhood is a famous weaving area, where you can visit local artists and their galleries. In particular, look for the complex *tejidos* (textiles), which have elaborate—and often pre-Hispanic—motifs that can take more than a half-year to design and weave. These creations, made of natural fibers and dyes, can cost $200 or more for high-quality work. **Galería Latina** (⊠ Plazuela Santa Ana 105 ☎ 066/818616) is the workshop of world-renowned weaver Alejandro Gallardo. Internationally famous weaver Edwin Sulca Lagos works out of **Las Voces del Tapiz** (⊠ Plazuela Santa Ana 82 ☎ 066/914242). **Familia Sulca** (⊠ Cáceres 302 ☎ No phone) is known for its beautiful carpets.

Santa Ana also has a collection of other craft workshops where families sit side-by-side carefully fashioning silver filigree and painting miniature retablos. In other corners you'll see mothers and daughters knitting tapestries, rugs, and cold-weather clothing. The **Mercado Santa Ana** (⊠ 1 block south of San Martín ☎ no phone) is a rabbit warren of tables covered with handicrafts, vegetables, and clothing.

Many famous retablo artists also live in Ayacucho, particularly around the Barrio La Libertad neighborhood. **Artesanías Helme** (⊠ Bellido 463 ☎ no phone) has a selection of retablos and other art with delicate depictions of Andean life and religious scenes. **Artesanías Huamanguina Pascualito** (⊠ Cusco 136 ☎ 066/811013) has an extensive collection of carvings. **Ohalateria Artesanías** (⊠ Plaza de Armas ☎ no phone), in the center of town, is a good place to begin studying the delicate collections. Workshops owned by the artist family **Urbano** (⊠ Peru 308 and 330 ☎ no phone) are among the best places to find finely crafted retablos. In Barrio Belén, members of the **Familia Pizarro** (⊠ San Cristóbal 215 ☎ no phone) carve *piedra huamanga* (alabaster) sculptures and weave fine textiles.

At the **Mercado Quinua** (⊠ Quinua ☎ no phone), a half-hour's drive from town, you can pick up such unique local items as chunky ceramic bulls, once created for cattle-branding festivities; miniature ceramic churches, which top many homes in Quinua; carved stone figures; and handmade musical instruments.

THE CENTRAL HIGHLANDS A TO Z

To research prices, get advice from other travelers, and book travel arrangements, visit www.fodors.com.

AIR TRAVEL

AeroContinente has daily 35-minute flights from Ayacucho to Lima ($48). AeroPeru also has weekly flights. On Tuesday, Thursday, and Sunday, AeroCóndor flies between Lima and Huánuco, where you can catch flights to Pucullpa, Trujillo, Chiclayo, and other northern towns. You can also check TANS for flights from Lima and other major cities outside of the central highlands. Flights between Ayacucho and Cusco, which were put on hold during the violence of the 1980s, still have not resumed. Note that flights are often canceled in the rainy season. Always reconfirm your flight in good weather, too, as flights can be canceled if there aren't enough passengers.

🖪 Carriers **AeroCóndor** ☎ 01/442-5215 in Lima ⊕ www.aerocondor.com.pe. **Aero Continente** ☎ 064/912816; 01/242-4242 in Lima ⊕ www.aerocontinente.com.pe. **Lan Peru** ☎ 01/213-8200 in Lima ⊕ www.lanperu.com. **TACA** ☎ 01/213-7000 in Lima ⊕ www.grupotaca.com. **TANS** ☎ 01/213-6000 in Lima ⊕ www.tansperu.com.pe.

AIRPORTS

Ayacucho's Alfredo Mendivil Airport is 4 km (2 ½ mi) from the city. You can take a taxi (about S/4), or catch a bus or colectivo from the

Plaza de Armas, which will deliver you about a half-block from the airport. David Figueroa Fernandini Airport is 8 km (5 mi) away from Huánuco. Tingo Maria Airport is about 1 ½ km (1 mi) west of town. Taxis run from most airports into town, and many hotels have transport service.

🛈 Airport Information **Alfredo Mendivil Duarte Airport** ⊠ Ejercito 950 Ayacucho ☎ 066/812088. **David Figueroa Fernandini Airport** ⊠ Airport Hwy., Km. 6 Huánuco. **Tingo María Airport** ⊠ Capitan FAP José Quiñones s/n ☎ 062/562003.

BUS TRAVEL

Buses from Ayacucho run to Lima (S/24, 10 hours), including overnight services on Andía, Los Libertadores, Transportes Antezana, and Transportes Molina. You can also reach Huancayo from Ayacucho (S/21, 10 hours) by overnight service on Andía, Antezana, and Molina—but prepare for a very rough road pockmarked with holes. Routes to Cusco (S/48, 24 hours) are covered by Ayacucho Tours and Transportes Chanka, which depart at 6 AM. Andía and Ayacucho Tours also make the 252-km (156-mi) journey to Andahuaylas (S/21, 10 hours). From here it's 135 km (84 mi) to Abancay and 195 km (121 mi) farther to Cusco. Ayacucho Tours also covers this route, but it's a tough, indirect trip.

Because Ayacucho is at a crossroads between major towns, you can often flag down local pickup trucks headed into the mountains. The best place to catch a ride is at the Grifo Chakchi petrol station. You can also take a local bus to several sites on the outskirts of Ayacucho, including Huari and Quinua. Buses depart from Paradero Magdalena at the east end of Avenida Centenario. Of course, always be cautious and trust your instincts before you hitchhike.

From Huancayo, Mariscal Cáceres has seven daily buses to Lima (S/24–S/31). ETUCSA, Cruz del Sur, Empresa Molina, and Roggero (S/1)—which has a bus departing nightly at 10 PM and is the least expensive service—also go to Lima. Comité 12 has cars to Lima (S/41, 5 hours). Empresa Molina Trans Nacional and Empresa Hidalgo have buses to Huancavelica (S/1, 6 hours). Empresa Molina and Empresa Ayacucho have buses to Ayacucho (S/21, 10–20 hours). Turismo Central and Empresa de Transportes San Juan have minibuses to Tarma (S/.75), some continuing to Chanchamayo, and buses to Satipo and other rain-forest towns. These two lines have several routes north as well. You can get to Jauja in an hour by colectivo from the corner of Huamaumarca and Amazonas.

Buses in Huancavelica depart from Avenida. M. Muñoz, including those to Huancayo (S/1, 6 hours) and Lima (S/31, 14 hours). Note that there's no direct service to Ayacucho. Oropesa buses make overnight runs from Huancavelica to Pisco (S/24, 12 hours) and Ica (S/27, 15 hours), arriving around 3 and 6 AM, respectively.

From Huánuco, León de Huánuco and Transportes Rey have buses to Lima (S/32, 9 hours). The latter company also runs north to Tingo María (S/.50, 4 hours) and Pucallpa (S/42, 15 hours), and south to Cerro de Pasco (S/.50, 5 hours). Expreso Huallaga and Turismo Central travel to Huancayo (S/21, 8 hours).

You can reach Tarma by road from Lima via Transportes DASA and Transportes Chanchamayo buses. You can also take a Comité taxi colectivo to Chanchamayo (S/1) from the market.

🛈 Bus Information **Andía** ⊠ Cáceres 896, Ayacucho ☎ 066/815376. **Ayacucho Tours** ⊠ Cáceres 880, Ayacucho ☎ 066/813532. **Cruz del Sur** ⊠ Ayacucho 281, Huancayo ☎ 064/235-6501. **Empresa Molina** ⊠ Angaraes 334, Huancayo ☎ 064/224501. **ETUCSA** ⊠ Puno 220, Huancayo ☎ 064/232638. **Expreso Huallaga** ⊠ Puente Calicanto,

Huánuco ☎ No phone. **León de Huánuco** ✉ Robles 821, Huánuco ☎ No phone. **Los Libertadores** ✉ Máscaras, Ayacucho ☎ 066/813614. **Mariscal Cáceres** ✉ Real 1217, Huancayo ☎ 064/216633. **Roggero** ✉ Hostal Rogger, , Huancayo ☎ 064/. **Transportes Chanchmayo** ✉ Callao 1002, Tarma ☎ 064/321882. **Transportes Antezana** ✉ Cáceres y Máscaras, Ayacucho ☎ 066/811235. **Transportes DASA** ✉ Callao 1012, Tarma ☎ 064/321843. **Transportes Molina** ✉ Cápac 273, Ayacucho ☎ 066/812984. **Transportes Rey** ✉ 28 de Julio 1201, Huánuco ☎ no phone. **Turismo Central** ✉ Ayacucho 274, Huancayo ☎ 066/223128 ✉ Puente Calicanto Huánuco ☎ No phone.

Ayacucho Express Bus Station ✉ Libertad 257 ☎ No phone **Main Bus Stations** ✉ San Francisco Ayacucho ☎ No phone ✉ Zavala Ayacucho ☎ No phone.

CAR RENTALS

The Central Highlands have some of the country's most scenic driving routes, and roads are paved from the capital north to Huánuco and south to Huancayo. It's five hours to La Oroya, from where a gorgeous Andes panorama stretches in three directions: north toward Huánuco, east toward Tarma, and south to Huancayo. Most sights around Huancayo in the Valle del Mantaro are accessible by car if you prefer traveling alone to taking a group tour. The rugged road from Huancayo to Ayacucho, which takes around 10 hours, should be traveled only by four-wheel-drive vehicles equipped for emergencies.

EMERGENCIES

Call the emergency services number for an ambulance, the fire department, or the police. For general traveler questions and concerns, call the 24-hour Peru Tourist Hotline. In Ayacucho, the Tourism Police can help visitors with safety and travel problems.

🛈 **Peru Tourist Hot Line** ☎ 064/224–7888. **Tourism Police Ayacucho** ✉ Arequipa 100, Ayacucho ☎ 066/812179.

🛈 **Emergency Services Ambulance, Fire, Police** ☎ 105

HEALTH

Altitude sickness, or *soroche*, is a common risk of the roads and towns in the Andes. When adjusting to higher altitudes, drink plenty of water, move slowly, and avoid alcohol for the first couple of days.

MAIL & SHIPPING

You'll usually find the main post office around the Plaza de Armas, although larger hotels will often mail letters and receive packages for you. Ayacucho has reliable Internet service at Instituto Pacifico. You can check your e-mail at Huancayo Internet, open 9 to 8:30, for $1.50 per hour. There are also numerous Internet cafés in Huancayo around the Plaza Constitución that charge around S/4 an hour for computer use. Tarma's Colegio Santa Rosa has public Internet access daily from 4 to 8 PM. You can make international calls from the Telefónica offices in the main towns; Ayacucho's has postal services, too.

🛈 **Internet Cafés Colegio Santa Rosa** ✉ Amazonas 892, Tarma ☎ 064/321457. **Huancayo Internet** ✉ Loreto 337, Huancayo ☎ 064/233856. **Instituto Pacifico** ✉ Callao 106, Ayacucho ☎ 066/814299.

🛈 **Post Offices Central Post Office** ✉ Asamblea y Cáceres, Ayacucho ☎ 066/814254. **Central Post Office** ✉ Muñoz y Segura, Huancavelica ☎ No phone. **Central Post Office** ✉ Centro Civico, Real y Loreto, Huancayo ☎ 064/233752. **Central Post Office** ✉ Beruan y 2 de Mayo, Huánuco ☎ No phone. **Central Post Office** ✉ Paucartambo y Callao, Tarma ☎ No phone.

🛈 **Telephone Information Directory Assistance** ☎ 103 **International Operator** ☎ 108 **Operator** ☎ 100.

Telefónica del Perú ✉ Asamblea 293 Ayacucho ☎ 066/812624 ✉ Carabaya y Toledo, Huancavelica ☎ 064/233754 ✉ 28 de Julio 1157, Huánuco ☎ 064/233970.

MONEY MATTERS

In Ayacucho, Huancayo, and Huánuco, Banco de Crédito has the best rates for traveler's checks; in Huancayo, also try Banco Wiese. Banco de Crédito offices usually have ATMs. Look on the 400 and 500 blocks of Calle Real for banks and *casas de cambio* in Huancayo. It's best to bring U.S. cash to the smaller towns of this region, as traveler's checks and credit cards usually aren't accepted. Travel agencies or larger hotels might change money if you're in a pinch.

🚩 Currency Exchange **Banco de Crédito** ✉ 28 de Julio y San Martín Ayacucho ⊕ www.bcp.com.pe ✉ Real 1039 Huancayo ✉ Toledo 300, Huancavelica ✉ 2 de Mayo 1005, Huánuco ✉ Huánuco 699, Huánuco.

SAFETY

Because this region still sees so few foreigners, you have little to worry about with safety or crime. Take the usual traveling precautions in your hotel and when walking or driving, and you shouldn't have any trouble. Carry your passport and other important identification at all times, and make multiple copies to store in your luggage and leave with friends at home.

Huánaco north to Pucullpo is a major coca-growing region, so the area has a strong military presence and there are numerous police checkpoints to combat illegal drug trafficking along this route. At press time, Huánuco, Tingo María, and Pucullpo were considered to be safe for travelers, but it's best to explore in a group, with a knowledgeable guide, and only in daylight.

Although the Shining Path terrorists were eradicated from the Ayacucho area more than a decade ago, you will notice the military in large numbers. To avoid confusion, don't wear camouflage-pattern clothing, and carry your passport and other identification at all times. There are still a few military checkpoints outside of town.

TOUR & TRAVEL AGENCIES

Ayacucho is surrounded by archaeological ruins and natural wonders, all of which can be viewed on a package tour. Morochucos Travel Service has city excursions and routes to Huari, Quinua, Valle Huanta and Vilcashhuamán. Quinua Tours specializes in Ayacucho's outer ruins but also runs city tours. Wari Tours Ayacucho offers explorations of the famous ruins, as well as tours of town.

Around Huancayo you can hike, bike, and explore local villages with the amazing Incas del Perú, which also has a Spanish-language school, book exchange, and folk art collection. Murikami Tours and Wanka Tours are among the better options from the numerous package-tour offices in town. Turismo Huancayo organizes trips to local ruins and natural wonders.

Servicios Turísticos in Tarma has several tour packages, as well as local maps and information.

🚩 **Incas del Perú** ✉ Giráldez 652, Huancayo ☎ 064/223303 🖥 064/222395. **Morochucos Travel Services** ✉ Constitución 14, Ayacucho ☎ 066/912261. **Murikami Tours** ✉ Jr. Lima 354, Huancayo ☎ 064/234745. **Quinua Tours** ✉ Asemblea 195, Ayacucho ☎ 066/912191. **Servicios Turísticos** ✉ 2 de Mayo 547, Tarma ☎ No phone. **Turismo Huancayo** ✉ Real 517, Huancayo ☎ 064/233351. **Wanka Tours** ✉ Real 565, Huancayo ☎ 064/231778. **Wari Tours** ✉ Independencia 70, Ayacucho ☎ 066/913115.

TRAIN TRAVEL

The Central Highlands are one of the country's most scenic areas, and tracks cut through the mountains and plains all the way from Lima to Huancavelica. Unfortunately, parts of the line often aren't running, so check first at the station. Also, these are old cars, so don't expect plush seats, clean windows, or first-class service. The most reliable section is from Huancayo to Huancavelica, a spectacular journey that's worth the discomfort.

Huancayo has two train stations, one in the town center serving Lima and one in the Chilca suburb serving Huancavelica. When it's running, the Lima train departs from the capital the last Saturday of the month at 7:40 AM and arrives in Huancayo at 6 PM. The return journey departs on Monday. Snacks and lunch are included in the price (S/68 round-trip). You can request oxygen if you get short of breath over the high passes.

The Huancavelica *Tren Expreso* departs from Huancayo Monday through Saturday at 6:30 AM and Sunday at 2 PM (S/9, 4 ½ hours). You can upgrade to the *Tren Extra*, which departs at 12:30 PM Monday through Saturday, 7 AM on Sunday, and includes a buffet in the top-class service (S/14, 6 ½ hours). Purchase advance tickets at the station.

TRANSPORTATION AROUND THE CENTRAL HIGHLANDS
You can travel by train or road from Lima to La Oroya, and then north past Cerro de Pasco to Goyllarisquisga or south to Huancavelica. A good road connects Cerro de Pasco with Huánuco and Tingo María in the north. Aside from these routes, there is no railway and roads are in poor condition. No buses run between Huancavelica and Ayacucho, so you'll need to fly, drive yourself, or catch a series of local buses and trucks via Santa Inés and Rumichaca, Izcuchaca, or Mejorada. You can fly—although not always direct—between Lima and Huánuco, Tingo María, Huancayo, and Ayacucho.

VISITOR INFORMATION
In Ayacucho, La Dirección General de Industria y Turismo has maps and information for visitors, and it's open weekdays 8 to 3. The Ministeria de Turismo is open weekdays 8–1. The best place for contacts on local culture in Huancavelica is the Instituto Nacional de la Cultura, which offers language, music, and dance lessons, cultural talks, and details on historic sights and regional history. It's open Monday through Saturday 10 to 1 and 3 to 7. Huancavelica's Ministerio de Industria y Comercio, Turismo, y Artesanías is open weekdays 7:30 to 2. Citaq, also in Huancavelica, is an ecotourism organization that focuses on appreciating the region's nature and cultures. Huancayo's Oficina de Turismo, in the Casa de Artesana, is open weekdays 7:30 to 1:30 and 4–6. In Huánuco, the Oficina de Turismo is on the main plaza. Tarma's tourist office, on the Plaza de Armas, can help you find qualified local guides for sights in the region.

🇮🇹 **Citaq** ✉ Plaza de Armas, Huancavelica ☎ No phone. **La Dirección General de Industria y Turismo** ✉ Asamblea 481, Ayacucho ☎ 066/812548. **Instituto Nacional de Cultura** ✉ Plaza San Juan de Dios, Huancavelica ☎ No phone. **Ministerio de Industria y Comercio, Turismo, y Artesanías** ✉ Nicolás de Piérola 180, Huancavelica ☎ No phone. **Ministerio de Turismo Ayacucho** ✉ Asamblea 400, Ayacucho ☎ 066/912548. **Oficina de Turismo Huancayo** ✉ Real 481, Huancayo ☎ 064/233251. **Oficina de Turismo Huánuco** ✉ Prado 714, Huánuco ☎ 064/512980. **Oficina de Turismo Tarma** ✉ 2 de Mayo y Lima, Tarma ☎ 064/321010.

THE NORTH COAST & NORTHERN HIGHLANDS

6

FODOR'S CHOICE

Club Colonial, *savory seafood in Huanchaco*

El Cuarto del Rescate, *Inca "jail" in Cajamarca*

El Patio de Monterrey, *Huaraz-area hotel*

Hotel Caballito de Mar, *Punta Sal*

Hotel Laguna Seca, *Cajamarca*

La Santitos, *bistro in Piura*

Laguna Llanganuco, *ancient lake*

Museo Brüning, *Lambayeque*

Siam de Los Andes, *Thai food in Huaraz*

HIGHLY RECOMMENDED

RESTAURANTS De Marco, *Trujillo*

El Querubino, *Cajamarca*

La Parra, *Chiclayo*

La Tushpa, *Chachapoyas*

Las Bóvedas, *Trujillo*

Monte Rosa, *Huaraz*

HOTELS Casa Suiza, *Huanchaco*

Garza Hotel, *Chiclayo*

Hostal Casa Vieja, *Chachapoyas*

Hotel Costa Del Sol, *Tumbes*

Hotel Libertador, *Trujillo*

La Posada del Puruay, *Cajamarca*

Los Frailones, *Cajamarca*

Steel Guest House, *Huaraz*

By Gregory
Benchwick

IT IS MORE THAN A PLACE OF INCREDIBLE NATURAL BEAUTY, of mountains, rivers, steep sea cliffs, and vast desert. Verdant and varied, the landscape of Peru's north coast and northern highlands is also the womb, cradle, and burial site of some of South America's oldest and most resplendent indigenous cultures. The region's ancestral roots reach back more than 5,000 years, when simple hunters and gatherers lived by the sea, scrabbling their sustenance from the dry desert ground. Later, the Chavín and Moche civilizations developed, building cities and ritual sites near the coasts, only to be conquered over time. More advanced civilizations like the Chimú were formed, grew, and withered. Finally, the Inca conquered Peru's North, connecting a vast empire that stretched across most of South America. But the Inca reign was short-lived, abbreviated by the arrival of the Spanish conquistadors; the seeds of the Inca downfall were sown in present-day Cajamarca, where Pizarro and his rowdy cohorts captured the heir apparent to the Inca throne. The remnants of the conquest are evident throughout the towns and cities of the North. Elaborate colonial buildings and churches, some dating back more than 400 years, add color and beauty to the otherwise bleak, run-down streets. But much of the region clings to its pre-Colombian past. Shamans still perform ancient rites high in the Andes, campesinos cultivate the land much as their ancestors did thousands of years ago, and life moves at the sure, steadfast speed of nature.

In the large cities of the coast, where the pace of life has caught up with the 21st century, the world moves faster each day, taxis blast their horns as they pass quiet colonial mansions and pre-Inca ruins, cell phones ring, people keep and break appointments, commerce and industry thrive as people struggle for survival. But the earth abides, and the land remains much as it was thousands of years ago when the first settlers set out their fishing nets and began to cultivate the ground.

Along the coast you will find less-than-stunning but nonetheless serviceable beaches, and many archaeological sites, such as Trujillo's Chán Chán and Huaca de la Luna, and the Tomb of Sipán, near present-day Lambayeque. As you head toward the highlands, the pace slows appreciably, and the pre-Colombian ruins are less impressive; the steep, forested hills of the highlands are the real draw, and trekkers and climbers from around the world converge to hike the green valleys and ascend the rocky, snow-capped peaks towering more than 6,000 m (19,500 ft) above the sea. Much of the North's charm stems from its situation far from the beaten path. Most travelers ignore the area, opting instead for visits to Machu Picchu, Puno, and Lake Titicaca. The lack of tourism is both a blessing and a curse. In the smaller towns, where tourists seldom set foot, service, accommodations, and hospitality are lacking. The blessing is the opportunity to explore relatively virgin territory that provides a rich peek into the cultural, historical, and physical landscape of Peru.

Exploring the North Coast & Northern Highlands

Almost all of the north coast's worthy sights sit on the Panamericana, a.k.a. the Pan-American Highway or Route 1, which runs almost entirely along the Pacific Ocean up the coast to the Ecuadorian border. Focus on Trujillo for your archaeological pursuits, as ruins give way to beaches as you head north. The sandy stretches of the far North between Piura and Tumbes are some of the best in Peru. While driving in Peru in general can be dangerous—Peruvian drivers rarely obey the rules of the road—a car is the best way to explore the coast, though another caveat is that rental-car agencies in the region are sparse. Bus drivers tend to be more careful than motorists, making bus travel a safe, somewhat slow transportation option. Taxis will hire out their services for some treks, up to $100 for a 10-hr ride. A good bet might be to catch a bus from one of the major cities, some of which also have airports, should you want to add a time-saving flight to your itinerary.

Exploring the highlands is more difficult. The verdant Andean hills, while beautiful, are also steep, and road conditions vary greatly; ask locals about the roads before striking out for any point along the highlands. Reaching Huaraz, the outdoor adventure-sports hot spot of the North, requires a 6- to 10-hr drive or bus ride from Lima along a twisty, but well-maintained road (Route 109). A 7- to 9-hr bus or car ride from Trujillo or Chiclayo will get you to Cajamarca, but it is far easier to fly to Cajamarca from Trujillo or Lima. Chachapoyas and its environs are the trickiest areas to reach; by land it's a 10- to 15-hr bus ride (depending on weather conditions) from Chiclayo, and there are flights from Lima to Chachapoyas once a week. Chachapoyas is a good starting place for investigating some of the country's seldom-visited pre-Inca ruins, but only patient and intrepid travelers should consider it.

About the Restaurants

While some of Trujillo's fancier restaurants expect dressy attire and reservations, most spots along the north coast and in the northern highlands are quite casual. Depending on the restaurant, the bill sometimes includes a 10-percent service charge, and tipping is more of an oddity than the norm. If the service is especially good, consider leaving a 10-percent tip. Throughout the North, *el almuerzo* (lunch) is the most important meal of the day, normally eaten around 2 PM. *La cena* (dinner) is normally lighter and less formal. The larger cities along the north coast have the best choices, including excellent seafood dishes.

About the Hotels

The north coast's larger towns all have good hotels, including large business properties with modern amenities and classy converted colonial mansions. The latter, called *casonas,* offer a more holistic lodging experience, with personalized service and attention to detail not found in the larger hotels. In the smaller towns, such as Barranca and Casma, luxury lodging does not exist, but the rooms are typically clean and safe. The northern Highlands have excellent country lodges on large tracts of land and properties with horse stables and hot springs; on the lower end there are cut-rate motel-style lodgings, many serviceable, with simple rooms suited to laid-back backpackers, or those with a backpacker spirit.

WHAT IT COSTS In Nuevo Soles				
	$$$$	$$$	$$	$	¢
RESTAURANTS	over 65	50–65	35–50	20–35	under 20
HOTELS	over 500	375–500	250–375	125–250	under 125

Restaurant prices are per person, for a main course at dinner. Hotel prices are for two people in a standard double room, excluding tax.

Timing

The weather along the coast is always pleasant, though sunnier during the summer months of November through May. Finding a hotel room throughout the coastal and highlands areas ought to be painless year-round, though coastal resorts like Máncora and Punta Sal are often jammed in the summer. Highlands weather is more capricious—November through early May is its rainy season, while it's drier and more pleasurable mid-May through mid-September. In September and October you are likely to have fairly good weather, but occasional storms frighten off most would-be trekkers and mountaineers. The dry season draws

Numbers in the text correspond to numbers in the margin and on the North Coast and Northern Highlands; Trujillo; Huaraz; and Cajamarca maps.

If you have 3 days

Depart from Lima on day one and head up the Pan-American Highway to 🗺 **Trujillo** ④–⑬ ➤, stopping at the **Sechín** ② ruins near Casma around lunchtime. Arriving in Trujillo in the early evening, you'll have time to walk through the town's pleasant colonial center. Spend the night in Trujillo. On day two, explore the pre-Inca ruins around Trujillo, visiting Chán Chán, Huacas del Sol y de la Luna (Temples of the Sun and Moon), and Huaca Arco Iris (Rainbow Temple). Just 12 km (7 mi) north of Trujillo you'll find the pleasant beach town of 🗺 **Huanchaco** ⑭. Overnight in either Trujillo or Huanchaco. On day three, take the Pan-American north up to 🗺 **Chiclayo** ⑯, visiting **Sipán** ⑮ and the excellent Museo Tumbas Reales de Sipán.

If you have 5 days

If you want to explore the mountains, head from Lima to 🗺 **Huaraz** ㉓–㉘ ➤. You'll need at least two days to explore the mountains and ruins surrounding this little Andean hamlet. Stay both nights in Huaraz or in the nearby hot-springs oasis of 🗺 **Monterrey** ㉙. From there, travel by land to 🗺 **Trujillo** ④–⑬, spending night three there. On day four visit the ruins around Trujillo, overnighting in Trujillo or neighboring 🗺 **Huanchaco** ⑭. On your last day, travel up the coast to **Chiclayo** ⑯, and visit the Tomb of Sipán and the Museo Tumbas Reales de Sipán.

If you have 8 days

Eight days is ample time to explore most of northern Peru. Begin in 🗺 **Cajamarca** ㉟–㊶ ➤, spending the day at the **Baños del Inca** ㊶. Get an early start on day two for a 9-hr bus ride to 🗺 **Chiclayo** ⑯. You may have time that afternoon to visit the Museo Tumbas Reales de Sipán. On day three, visit the Tomb of Sipán and explore Chiclayo's Museo Brüning. From there, take a 5-hr bus ride or half-hour flight to 🗺 **Trujillo** ④–⑬, spending your third night there. Take at least two days and nights to see Trujillo and its surrounding ruins; stay in town, at one of the lovely casona hotels, or in nearby 🗺 **Huanchaco** ⑭. On day six, take a 6- to 8-hr car or bus ride to 🗺 **Huaraz** ㉓–㉘ (best done during the day, as the mountain views are incredible and the road twists and turns) stopping at the **Sechín** ② ruins along the way. Spend the next two days exploring the extraordinary mountains, valleys, and ruins around Huaraz.

6

---

climbers and other trekkers to Huaraz and Cajamarca, so plan at least a few weeks ahead for adventuring there; for serious treks or mountaineering expeditions from these cities, plan several months ahead, as expeditions fill up quickly. Plan at least two months in advance if you want to be anywhere in the North during Easter Week and around Christmas, when Peruvians take their holidays.

THE NORTH COAST

More than five thousand years ago, civilizations flourished in the fertile river valleys of Peru's north coast. The Huaca Prieta were some of the first to settle in the region. Archaeologists have discovered the remnants of their simple hunter-gatherer civilization, dating back to 3500 BC, near present-day Trujillo. From here there is a large blank spot in the history books, and the next major culture in northern Peru, the cat-worshiping Chavín, doesn't pop up until around 850 BC. Archaeologists often refer to this period as the Early Horizon. The Chavín empire stretched through much of Peru's northern highlands and along the northern and central coasts. The Chavín were excellent artisans, and their pottery, with its jaguar motifs, can still be seen in the museums of Trujillo and Lima.

About the time of Christ, a new culture emerged, the Moche. Many of its carefully planned irrigation systems that turned the desert into productive agricultural land are still in use today. The name "Moche" is a derived from Muchik or Mochica, an ancient language spoken on the north coast. This highly advanced civilization had a stratified class system and made great advances in both artisanry and architecture. As a written language had yet to develop, much of what's known about the culture today is based on the Moche's fine ceramics, which depict scenes from both ceremonial and everyday life. The large Moche pyramids near present-day Trujillo and Chiclayo include such oddities as dragon motifs, perhaps a testament to continued commerce and intercultural exchange between South America and Asia. Although voracious *huaqueros,* or looters, have stolen many of the gold and silver treasures left in the ruins, archaeologists sifting through the sand still occasionally make unbelievable finds. The tomb of the Lord of Sipán, discovered intact in 1987, is the most famous example.

The next important civilization of Peru's north coast, the Chimú, came on the scene around 1000 AD. That civilization flourished until around 1470, when it, like most other South American cultures, was assimilated by the huge Inca Empire. The awe-inspiring, must-see Chimú city of Chán Chán is near present-day Trujillo. While the Inca center of power lay further south in the Cusco–Machu Picchu area, their cultural influence stretched far beyond the northern borders of Peru. It was along the Inca Coastal Road, near present-day Tumbes, that Pizarro, the Spanish pig farmer–turned-conquistador, first caught site of the glory and riches of the Inca Empire, which fell all too quickly. The Spanish who settled these lands built their own cities—Trujillo, Chiclayo, and Lambayeque, among others—ignoring the spectacular agricultural and architectural achievements of earlier days. The colonial and republican mansions of the north coast are a lasting testament to the determination and avarice of these early settlers, as is Peru's tacit class system that puts Spanish descendants on the top rung of a still highly stratified society.

The north coast is largely ignored by most foreign tourists, but all the way up this sun-drenched stretch of coastal desert you will find plenty of places to explore and relax. The barren, rocky landscape may seem austere and impenetrable at first glance, but on closer inspection you will find that it has not only a vast and fascinating history, but also a natural beauty found almost nowhere else in the world.

Paramonga

❶ *200 km (124 mi) northwest of Lima on the Pan-American Highway*

Heading north from Lima on the Pan-American Highway through the bleak, empty coastal desert, you pass several shanty towns before arriving in Barranca, the most important town in the immediate region. Though Paramonga itself has few sights or restaurants that warrant lingering, there is a large Chimú temple nearby that merits an afternoon visit.

The large **Paramonga** archaeological site sits just off the Pan-American Highway, about 3 km (2 mi) north of the Huaraz turnoff. The gigantic

Archeology

Archeology There are dozens of archaeological sites throughout the North. Along the coast you'll find Chavín, Moche, and Chimú ruins, dating from as far back as 3,000 BC. The most impressive ruins are around Trujillo and Lambayeque. In the highlands are Wari and other pre-Inca sites, which are less awe-inspiring than their coastal cousins but nevertheless worth the visit. Many of the more popular ruins are being destroyed by heavy traffic and litter: tread softly.

6

Savories

Savories Regional specialties along the north coast include *cabrito con tacu tacu* (kid with grilled rice), *cangrejo reventado* (boiled crab with eggs), *ceviche de mococho* (algae ceviche), *cuy* (guinea pig), and *shambar* (a bean stew particular to Trujillo). At restaurants serving *parrilladas* (barbecues) you will find every imaginable cut of beef, including *anticuchos* (cow heart) and *ubre* (cow udder). In the highlands, the food focuses less on seafood (though you can still find excellent fish dishes here) and more on beef and chicken. Here you will find *charqui* (jerked beef or pork), *trucha* (trout), and *cuy* in abundance. In the larger towns, especially Huaraz, there's good international cuisine. Heading to a *chifa* (Chinese restaurant) is always a good alternative. Sample interesting *aguardientes* (homemade liqueurs) throughout the region. Aguardientes come in sundry flavors, including *mora* (blackberry), *maracuyá* (passion fruit), *café* (coffee), and *leche* (milk).

Treks

Treks In the highlands you will find a smorgasbord of trekking and climbing, especially in Huaraz, often called the Switzerland of Peru. From there you can head off on 1- to 20-day treks through the steep hills and valleys of the Andes, climb a 6,000-m (19,500-ft) peak (for experienced mountaineers only), or go on an afternoon horseback ride. It is best to go with a guide. Guided treks range from four-star catered affairs to bare-bones, carry-your-own-weight romps through the hills. Women should not hike alone, as violent assaults have been reported here. There are also several good river runs with Class 3 and 4 rapids near Huaraz. Keep in mind that Huaraz sits at a dizzying 3,090 m (10,042 ft) above sea level: allow yourself time to acclimatize and drink lots of water to avoid dehydration and altitude sickness. The best season for trekking and climbing is June through August. Rafting is better during the rainy season, but it can be hard to find an outfitter.

---

temple has seven defensive walls easily visible from the highway. This is a good lunch stopover on your way up to Trujillo and Chiclayo further north. There is a small museum here as well, which has some good displays on Chimú culture for those who speak Spanish. Take a taxi to the Paramonga ruins from nearby Barranca for a few dollars. The budget-minded can get here from Barranca by taking a microbus to the port of Paramonga and then hiking the 3 km to the entrance. ⊠ *3 km (2 mi) north of the Huaraz turnoff from the Pan-American Highway, it is clearly visible to the east of the highway* ☎ *no phone* 💲 *S/5* ⊙ *Daily 8–6.*

Where to Stay & Eat

¢ ✕ **Pizza Don Goyo.** Simple Don Goyo serves pizza, pasta, and the requisite *pollo a la brasa* (rotisserie chicken). The special with garlic bread, two slices, and a soda is an especially good deal. ⊠ *Jr. Gálvez 506* ☎ *no phone* 🚫 *no credit cards.*

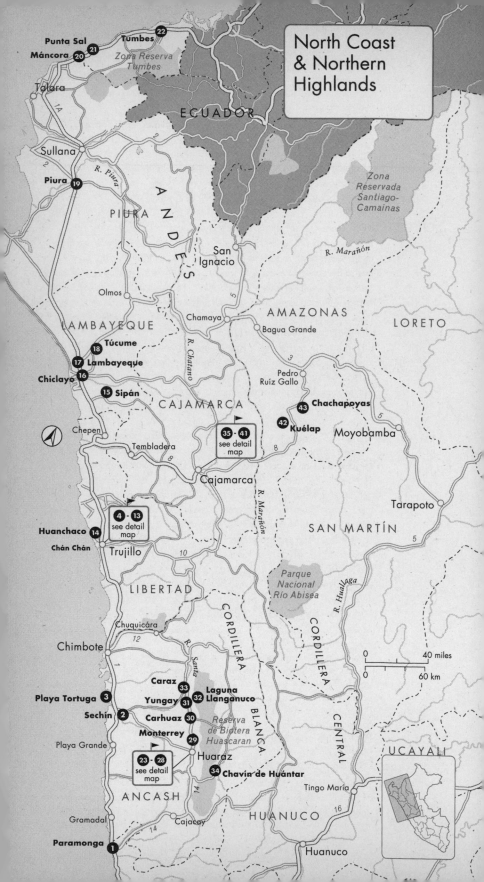

North Coast & Northern Highlands

ECUADOR

Punta Sal ㉑
Máncora ⑳ Tumbes ㉒
Zona Reserva Tumbes

Talara

1A

Sullana

2

Piura ⑲

R. Piura

PIURA

A N D E S

San Ignacio

Zona Reservada Santiago-Camainas

R. Marañón

1

Olmos

LAMBAYEQUE

Chamaya

AMAZONAS

Bagua Grande

LORETO

R. Chatano

5

Túcume ⑱
Lambayeque ⑰
Chiclayo ⑯

Pedro Ruíz Gallo

3

Sipán ⑮

CAJAMARCA

Chachapoyas ㊸
Kuélap ㊷

Chepen

㉟ - ㊶
see detail map

Moyobamba

5

Tembladera

R. Marañón

8

Cajamarca

④ - ⑬
see detail map

Huanchaco ⑭
Chán Chán
Trujillo

8

10

Tarapoto

SAN MARTÍN

5

LIBERTAD

Parque Nacional Río Abisea

R. Huallaga

Chuquicára

12

CORDILLERA

Chimbote

1

R. Santa

CORDILLERA CENTRAL

Caraz
Yungay ㉛ ㉜
Playa Tortuga ③
Sechín ②
Carhuaz ㉚
Monterrey
Playa Grande ㉝

Laguna Llanganuco

Reserva de Biotera Huascaran

BLANCA

UCAYALI

0   40 miles
0   60 km

㉙
㉝ - ㉘
see detail map

Huaraz

Chavin de Huántar ㉞

ANCASH

Tingo María

Gramadal

14

Cajacay

HUANUCO

16

Paramonga ①

Huanuco

¢ 🏨 **Hotel Chavin.** While slightly musty and worn, this property, in a six-story unfinished concrete building, is the best bet in town. The wood-floored rooms all have private baths, and there's a decent restaurant serving criollo food on the premises. ✉ *Jr. Gálvez 222,* ☎ *01/235–2358 or 01/235–2253* 🖷 *044/235–2480* 🛏 *73 rooms* ⚐ *Restaurant, cafeteria, cable TV, meeting rooms, free parking; no a/c* ▭ *DC, V.*

Nightlife

If you find yourself in Barranca for the evening, head to **eXcesos** (✉ Jr. Gálvez 525 ☎ no phone). Upstairs are pool tables and racy pictures of semi-naked models; downstairs is a boisterous discoteque catering to Barranca's 25-and-under crowd.

Sechín

❷ *170 km (105 mi) north of Paramonga*

One of the oldest archaeological sites in Peru, Sechín dates to around 1600 BC. It is not quite clear what culture is responsible for this coastal temple, which sits near the port town of Casma, but the bas-relief carvings ringing the main temple indicate that they may have been a war-like people; the carvings, some up to four meters high, graphically depict triumphant warriors and their conquered, often beheaded enemies. The site was first excavated in 1937 by the prolific and world-renowned Peruvian archaeologist J. C. Tello. Since then the site has suffered some damage from looters and natural disasters. They are still excavating here, and access to the central temple's plaza is not permitted, but a trail leads you up the neighboring hill, providing good views of the inner temple and surrounding valley. A simple museum at the site has a good collection of Chavín ceramics and a mummy found in the Trujillo area. To get to the ruins, head southeast from Casma along the Pan-American for about 3 km (2 mi), turning east on a paved road to Huaraz. The ruins sit about 2 km (1¼ mi) from the turnoff. ☎ *no phone* 💶 *S/5 (also good at the Pañamarca ruins)* ⊗ *Daily 8–6.*

There are several other ruins near Casma, including the unexcavated **Sechín Alto,** visible from the museum. **Chanquillo,** with several towers surrounded by concentric walls, is best appreciated from the air. The heavily weathered Mochica ruins of **Pañamarca,** 10 km (6 mi) inland from the Pan-American on the road to Nepeña, have a few worthy murals. There are no true tour guides in the area, but a moto-taxi will take you to the ruins surrounding Casma for about S/10 an hour. Negotiate the price before you leave. The town of Casma is the best place to stay if you want to visit the ruins. The nearby beach town of Playa Tortuga is a good alternative for those wishing to stay overnight in the area.

Where to Stay & Eat

¢–$ ✕ **Restaurant El Tio Sam.** Casma's best restaurant, Uncle Sam's has every imaginable fish combo. The *arroz chaufa con mariscos* (shellfish with Chinese-style fried rice) is especially good. With its brick facade and cement floor, the restaurant is pleasantly run down but astonishingly clean. ✉ *Av. Huarmei 138* ☎ *044/711–447* ▭ *AE, V.*

¢ ✕🏨 **Hostal El Farol.** Sheltered gardens and a gazebo are a welcome respite from the cacophony of Casma's busy streets. The rooms have unsightly green comforters and fluorescent lights, but are, nevertheless, comfortable and affordable. The bamboo-walled restaurant specializes in seafood and looks onto the center gardens. ✉ *Av. Tupac Amaru 450,* 🖷 *044/711–064 or 01/421–3819* 🖃 *hostalfarol@terra.com.pe* 🛏 *24 rooms, 1 bungalow, 4 suites* ⚐ *Restaurant, some rooms with cable TV, pool, gym, playground, laundry service, meeting rooms, free parking; no a/c, no room phones* ▭ *AE, DC, V.*

Playa Tortuga

❸ *20 km (12 mi) north of Casma*

The only worthwhile beach in the Sechín area and a good base for overnighting in the region, Playa Tortuga is in a protected bay surrounded by brown hills. The black-sand beach is rather unattractive, but the bay, with its fleet of fishing boats and pleasant lapping waves, is relaxing.

Where to Stay

★ ¢   🏨 **Hotel Terraza.** Hands down, this is the area's best hotel. A stone walkway leads to cheery and airy bamboo-ceilinged rooms. All have private terraces overlooking the bay, making for exhilarating sunset viewing, but also take in the sunset view at the back of the hotel, where the black hills turn an eerie orange. ⊠ *Caleta Norte, Playa Tortuga,* ☎ *044/619– 042* ⊕ *www.lasterrazas.com* ⇘ *8 rooms* ⚐ *Restaurant, playground, laundry service, free parking; no a/c, no room phones, no room TVs* ⊟ *no credit cards* ¶⊙¶ *CP.*

Trujillo

❹–⓭ *561 km (350 mi) northwest of Lima on the Pan-American Highway.*

A lively metropolis that competes with Arequipa for the title of Peru's "Second City," Trujillo was founded in 1534. The Spanish named it in honor of conquistador Francisco Pizarro's hometown. More than any other city in Peru, Trujillo maintains much of its colonial charm, especially along Avenida España, which encircles the heart of the city. This thoroughfare replaced a 9-m-high (30-ft-high) wall erected in 1687 to protect the city from pirates. A piece of the wall still stands at the corner of Estete and España. There are several Moche and Chimú archaeological sites in and around Trujillo, and the huge pyramids and ceremonial centers are some of the most impressive in all of northern Peru.

Considered the cultural capital of Peru, the city is known for its many festivals, including an international ballet festival, a contemporary art biennial, and the *caballos de paso* (Peruvian pace horse) show. Consider coming to town for the Festival Internacional de la Primavera (International Spring Festival), held every year during the last week of September. Trujillo is also quite busy during the last week of January, when it holds the National Fiesta de La Marinera dance competition. These events provide glimpses of traditional *criollo* culture.

Numbers in the text correspond to numbers in the margin and on the Trujillo map.

a good tour

The best way to explore Trujillo is on foot. Almost all the town's museums and historic casonas lie in the colonial center of town and can easily be reached from the Plaza de Armas. Begin your walk in the **Plaza de Armas** ❹ ▶. The ornate and beautiful **Casa Urquiaga** ❺ sits next to the plaza on the corner of Pizarro and Orbegoso. From here, head northeast on Pizarro. Just after Gamarra, you will come across the **Casa de la Emancipación** ❻, where Trujilleños declared independence in 1820. Continuing up Pizarro for half a block you'll hit the monstrous **Palacio Iturregui** ❼. Go right on Jirón Junín; on the corner of Junín and Ayacucho is the **Museo de Arqueología** ❽. From the museum, head northwest on Ayacucho, taking a right on Colón. On the corner of Colón and Bolívar is the **Monasterio El Carmen** ❾. From the monastery head to **Plazuela el Recreo** ❿ on the corner of Estete and Pizarro. There are a few artisan stalls here. From the plazuela, take a right on Estete and walk one block to Independencia. Walk back toward the Plaza de Armas on Independencia, stopping at the **Museo del Juguete** ⓫ to check out a large toy col-

Trujillo

KEY

▶ *Start of walk*

0 — 300 ft
0 — 100 m

lection. From the toy museum, head back to the Plaza de Armas via Pizarro. Continuing on Pizarro one block past the Plaza de Armas you come to **Casa del Mayorazgo de Facala** ⑫. If you still have energy, take a cab to the privately owned **Museo Cassinelli** ⑬ (Av. Nicholás de Piérola 607), in the northern sector of the city in the basement of a gas station. After this tour you'll need a break; take a taxi or minibus from the city center to Huanchaco and relax in the sun while watching the fisherman surf in on their *caballitos de totora* (boats made from totora weeds).

TIMING &
PRECAUTIONS

The walking tour will take you about half a day, depending on how long you spend in each place. Many of the museums and casonas are closed at lunchtime, so plan accordingly. It can be quite hot around midday in summer, so do the ruins in the morning and the city tour in the afternoon. It's easy to get a taxi in Trujillo's city center, and the in-town fare (S/2) is quite reasonable, so consider cabbing part of the tour if you wish.

Be street smart in the Trujillo market area—stay alert, access your cash discreetly when you need it, and keep your valuables close. For further tips, *see* Safety *in* Smart Travel Tips A to Z.

What to See

❻ **Casa de la Emancipación.** Trujillo declared its independence from Spain on December 29, 1820, in the Emancipation House, which has an interesting scale model of Trujillo when it was a walled city. It is now owned by Banco Continental. There are rotating art exhibits here as well. ✉ *Pizarro 610* ☎ *044/246–061* ✎ *Free* ⊘ *Mon.–Sat. 9–1 and 5–7.*

⓬ **Casa del Mayorazgo de Facala.** Constructed of thick adobe and covered with white stucco, this house is a classic example of Trujillo colonial architecture. The open courtyard of this house dating from 1709 is surrounded by cedar columns and has a colonial carriage. Don't miss the Moorish-style carved-wood ceiling. ✉ *Pizarro 314* ☎ *044/256–600* ✎ *Free* ⊘ *Mon.–Sat. 9–1 and 5–7.*

⑤ Casa Urquiaga. Like most of the other restored colonial museums in Trujillo, this house was saved by a bank whose offices now occupy part of the building. Visit this early 19th-century mansion on the Plaza de Armas, with its baroque patio and fine collection of pre-Colombian ceramics. The house was built in a neoclassical style and has lovely rococo furniture. ✉ *Pizarro 446* ☎ *044/245–382* ⌨ *Free* ☉ *Mon.–Sat. 9–1 and 5–7.*

⑨ Monasterio El Carmen. The monastery, built in 1725, has valuable altarpieces and colonial art. ✉ *Av. Colón at Av. Bolívar* ⌨ *Free* ☉ *Museum Mon.–Sat. 9–1.*

⑬ Museo Cassinelli. In the northern sector of the city, this privately owned museum is in, of all places, the basement of a gas station. Among the most spectacular objects in the 2,800-piece collection, which covers pre-Colombian ceramics that date from 1200 BC through the Inca period, are the Moche portrait vases. There are also whistling pots, which produce distinct notes that mimic bird calls. ✉ *Av. Nicolás de Piérola 607* ☎ *044/232–312* ⌨ *S/5* ☉ *Mon.–Sat. 9–1 and 3:30–6:30.*

⑧ Museo de Arqueología. In this old colonial home is this museum with pottery and other artifacts recovered from tombs. You will find reproductions of the murals found at the Huaca de la Luna as well as some artifacts recovered from the site. The original house, called the Casa Risco, was built in the 17th century. ✉ *Jr. Junín 682, at Jr. Ayacucho* ☎ *044/249–322* ⌨ *S/5* ☉ *Mon. 9–2, Tues.–Fri. 9:30–1 and 3:30–7, weekends 9:30–4.*

☝ ⑪ Museo del Juguete. The toy museum has a large private collection of toys from all over the world. There are puppets and puzzles, as well as a large selection of pull-along toys. The toys from pre-Colombian Peru are especially interesting, as they give a seldom-seen view into the world of the ancient cultures that preceded the Inca. Regrettably, you can't play with any of the toys. ✉ *Independencia 713* ☎ *044/297–200* ⌨ *S/4* ☉ *Mon.–Sat. 10–6; closed Sun.*

⑦ Palacio Iturregui. The republican Iturregui Palace is sometimes described as the most beautiful neoclassical home in South America. The mansion was built in 1842 by Juan Manuel Iturregui and has gorgeous Italian marble furnishings. It is now the private Club Central de Trujillo, and only the mansion's central plaza is accessible to visitors. ✉ *Pizarro 688* ⌨ *Free* ☉ *Weekdays 11–1 and 4–8.*

> **need a break?** Homemade gelato is just the ticket at **De Marco** (✉ Pizarro 725 ☎ 044/234–251 ▤ AE, DC, MC, V), a tiny bistro that also serves criollo food and has occasional peñas at night.

▶ ④ Plaza de Armas. In the heart of the city is this broad plaza fronted by the 17th-century cathedral and surrounded by the *casonas* (colonial mansions) that are Trujillo's architectural glory. Locals say this is Peru's largest main plaza. In the center stands the Monument to Freedom, sculpted by the German sculptor Edmundo Moeller and unveiled in 1929.

⑩ Plazuela el Recreo. A few artisan stalls and the town's old water distribution pump are nestled in this neat little square. ✉ *Corner of Pizarro and Estete.*

Where to Stay & Eat

Fish dishes are ubiquitous in Trujillo. Ceviche made with fish or shellfish is extremely popular, as is *causa,* a cold casserole of mashed potatoes molded around a filling of fish, ají, and onions and topped with slices of hard-boiled egg. Tasty *cabrito al horno* (roast kid), *seco de cabrito* (stewed kid), and *shámbar,* a bean stew, are other local specialties.

★ $–$$ ✕ **Las Bóvedas.** This quiet, elegant restaurant in the Hotel Libertador has a *bóveda*, or vaulted brick ceiling, and plant-filled wall niches. The house specialty is the local delicacy, shámbar, garnished with *canchita* (semipopped corn). ⊠ *Independencia 485* ☎ *044/232–741* ▤ *AE, DC, MC, V.*

★ ¢–$ ✕ **De Marco.** Right on the street, this noisy but cheery eatery, popular with locals and tourists for its excellent comida criolla and Italian dishes, has paneled walls with local artwork. Try the *tacu tacu*, a typical coastal dish of rice and beans, with seco de cabrito. Don't miss the homemade gelato. ⊠ *Pizarro 725* ☎ *044/234–251* ▤ *AE, DC, MC, V.*

¢–$ ✕ **El Mochica.** In a long, open hall with whitewashed walls and chandeliers, this traditional lunch spot is a satisfying stop—a typical meal starts with an industrial-size portion of spicy *ceviche de lenguado* (marinated sole), followed by rice smothered with *camarones* (shrimp) or *mariscos* (shellfish). ⊠ *Bolívar 462* ☎ *044/224–247* ▤ *AE, DC, MC, V.*

¢–$ ✕ **Romano.** Head to the back room of this restaurant, reached by a long, fluorescent-lit hallway right next to the Romano Cafetería, for a light seafood or pasta dinner. Local artwork adorns the walls, and a decidedly bohemian crowd gathers to enjoy the nightly peñas. The homemade desserts are excellent. ⊠ *Pizarro 747* ☎ *044/252–251* ▤ *DC, V.*

¢–$ ✕ **San Remo Restaurant.** Stained-glass windows greet you at this Italian ristoranti and pizzeria. The feel of provincial Italy runs throughout, with plates adorning the walls and a deer head at the entryway. The pasta-heavy menu also has meat and poultry dishes, as well as the town's best pizza. A decent wine list and good service burnish the evening. ⊠ *Av. Húsares de Junín 450* ☎ *044/293–333* ▤ *AE, DC, MC, V* ☉ *No lunch.*

★ $$ $$$ ▥ **Hotel Libertador.** The former Hotel de Turistas on the Plaza de Armas has been splendidly renovated to retain its colonial elegance while adding modern amenities. The pool, surrounded by a garden filled with hummingbirds, is especially delightful. Rooms have artwork with pre-Colombian designs, locally tooled leather and wood furniture, and wrought-iron wall lamps. ⊠ *Independencia 485* ☎ *044/232–741 or 800/ 537–8483 in U.S.* ☎ *044/235–641* ⊕ *www.libertador.com.pe* ⇆ *73 rooms, 5 suites* ♨ *Restaurant, café, room service, in-room safes, minibars, cable TV, pool, gym, sauna, bar, laundry service, meeting rooms, free parking, some no-smoking rooms* ▤ *AE, DC, MC, V* ▥ *BP.*

$$ ▥ **El Gran Marques.** Minutes from the city center is this upscale business hotel. A pool and lush gardens can be seen from most rooms. On the roof you will find a mini-spa, sauna, and a small pool. Rooms have soothing maroon carpets, wood furnishings, and paisley spreads. ⊠ *Díaz de Cienfuegos 145, Urb. La Merced,* ☎ *044/249–366* ☎ *044/249–161* ⊕ *www.elgranmarques.com* ⇆ *45 rooms, 5 suites* ♨ *Restaurant, cafetería, room service, minibars, cable TV, 2 pools, gym, hair salon, massage, sauna, spa, Ping-Pong, bar, laundry service, business services, meeting rooms, car rental, free parking* ▤ *AE, DC, MC, V* ▥ *BP.*

$$ ▥ **Los Conquistadores.** Near the Plaza de Armas, this all-suites hotel is a bit overpriced for what you're getting (decent service in a small business hotel), and the furnishings border on antiseptic. However, rooms are large, and each has its own sitting area. A Continental breakfast is included. ⊠ *Diego de Almagro 586* ☎ *044/244–505* ☎ *044/235–917* ⊕ *www.losconquistadoreshotel.com* ⇆ *50 suites* ♨ *Restaurant, room service, minibars, cable TV, exercise equipment, bar, laundry service, Internet, meeting rooms, free parking, some no-smoking rooms* ▤ *AE, DC, MC, V* ▥ *CP.*

$ ▥ **Gran Bolívar Hotel.** A modern hotel lurks behind the historic casona entryway of this centrally located lodging. The spacious, modern rooms have plaid bedcovers and look onto the center atrium. Ask to see a few rooms beforehand, as some have a musty aroma. ⊠ *Jr. Bolívar 957,* ☎☎ *044/222–090 or 044/223–521* ⊕ *www.granbolivarhotel.com* ⇆ *30* *rooms ⚇ Restaurant, cafeteria, room service, minibars, cable TV, gym, billiards, bar, laundry service, business services, meeting rooms, airport shuttle, free parking; no a/c in some rooms ⊟ AE, DC, MC, V ⊺⊙⊺ CP.*

$ ⊞ **Gran Hotel El Golf.** This low-slung lodging curves around a large pool and is surrounded by landscaped gardens. Rooms, most with views of the pool and gardens, have dark-wood furniture and rustic lamps. The hotel is 10 minutes from the center of town and 15 minutes from the airport. ⊠ *Los Cocoteros 500, El Golf* ☎ *044/282–515* 🖷 *044/282–231* ⊕ *www.granhotelgolf.com* ⤳ *112 rooms, 8 suites* ⚇ *Restaurant, cafeteria, room service, in-room safes, minibars, cable TV, 9-hole golf course, 2 pools, gym, massage, sauna, bar, playground, laundry service, meeting rooms, airport shuttle, free parking, some no-smoking rooms* ⊟ *AE, DC, MC, V* ⊺⊙⊺ *CP.*

Nightlife & the Arts

There are several art galleries near the Escuela de Bellas Artes (Calle Húsares de Junín and Av. America Sur), and the Casa Urquiaga has rotating art shows.

NIGHTLIFE **Chelsea** (⊠ Estete 675 ☎ 044/257–032) is a venerable men's club with dancing on the weekends. A flying ghost adorns a wall of the studiously funky **Haizea Pub** (⊠ Jr. Bolognesi 502 ☎ 044/392–961). There's live music on the weekends. **Las Tinajas** (⊠ Pizarro 389 ☎ 044/296–272) is a quiet, elegant evening spot in a converted casona. It is open only Thursday through Sunday. **Luna Rota** (⊠ Av. América Sur 2119 ☎ 044/228–877) has live criollo music most evenings. There is a discoteque and casino downstairs. See plays and concerts at the **Teatro Municipal** (⊠ Jr. Bolívar 753 ☎ 044/241–601). Consult local newspapers for show times.

Sports & the Outdoors

There are several *coliseos de gallos* (cockfight arenas) on the road to Huanchaco. Fights are normally held on weekend afternoons. Trujillo's soccer team, Coopsol, plays at the Estadio Mansiche on weekends.

BEACHES Peru's beaches are all on the Pacific Ocean, so the water can be on the chilly side. Cool temperatures don't deter the locals who race in their *caballitos de totora.* **Playa Huanchaco,** 15 km (9 mi) from Trujillo, is in a protected cove and is a pleasant place where many Peruvians spend their summer holidays. **Puerto Chicama,** 94 km (58 mi) north of Trujillo, has strong currents and is popular with surfers.

Shopping

Shop for ceramics along Avenida España, especially where it intersects with Junín. Stalls display the locally made leather goods for which Trujillo is famous, particularly shoes, bags, and coats. Don't hesitate to haggle. Avoid this area after dark. For made-to-order boots or belts, check out **Creaciones Cerna** (⊠ Bolognesi 567 ☎ 044/205–679). South of Huanchaco's Muelle Artesanal are several artisan stalls. Vendor's hock miniature *caballitos de totora* and other kitsch. **Los Tallanes** (⊠ Jr. San Martin 455 ☎ 044/220–274) has a wide selection of artisanal goods. **Lujan** (⊠ Obregoso 242 ☎ 044/205–092) makes stylized Peruvian jewelry.

Side Trips from Trujillo

HUACA DE LA LUNA & HUACA DEL SOL *10 km (6 mi) southeast of Trujillo*

Near the Pan-American Highway, several notable ruins stand across the Río Moche. Although monumental cities stood in the region around Trujillo more than a 1,000 years before Christ, this city built by the Moche people was the first to spread its influence over much of the north coast. Their capital city and its two enormous adobe pyramids were built around AD 100, but their influence in the region continued for 600 years.

The smaller of the two pyramids is the Huaca de la Luna. It stands across from the larger Huaca del Sol. The 500-m-wide (1,635-ft-wide) plain that sits between the two pyramids once held a bustling city. The Pyramid of the Moon is painted with anthropomorphic and zoomorphic reliefs. Many of the figures picture the Moche god Ipiec, while others depict fanciful and improbable creatures, notably dragons; the use of dragon images in the pyramid may point to continued cultural and commercial exchange between the developing cultures of South America and their more-advanced Asian ancestors. The Moche expanded the pyramid several times during their reign, covering up the original reliefs that adorned the exterior. Since 1990, archaeologists have been slowly uncovering the ancient layers of the pyramid. Walk through to its very heart to glimpse some of its first facades. Visiting on weekdays, you will likely be able to watch archaeologists as they uncover multicolored murals and friezes. A small tourist center is at the entrance. There are free guided tours on weekdays.

The Huaca del Sol (Pyramid of the Sun) stands over 40 m (130 ft) high— only half as tall as it once was. At least 150 million bricks went into building this, the largest adobe-brick structure in the New World. Scattered around the pyramid's base are "signature bricks," with distinctive hand, finger, and foot marks that identify the community whose labor produced the bricks for their Moche lords. Archaeologists believe that the pyramid served as an imperial palace and mausoleum, a center of political and religious power. Once a storehouse of untold treasures, it has been stripped clean over the centuries by huaqueros. So great were its riches that in 1610 the Spanish diverted the Río Moche to wash away the pyramid's base and lay bare the bounty within. There isn't much to see here, but a walk to its base can be quite enjoyable. ⊠ *10 km (6 mi) southeast of Trujillo* ☎ *044/291-891* ▭ *S/10* ⊙ *Daily 9–4:30.*

CHÁN CHÁN
Fodor's Choice
★

CHÁN CHÁN *4.5 km (2.8 mi) northwest of Trujillo.*

Three hundred years after the Moche civilization faded, the Chimú people took control of the region. Although less famous than the Inca, who conquered them in 1470, the Chimú were the second-largest pre-Columbian society in South America. Their empire stretched along 1,000 km (620 mi) of the Pacific, from Lima to Tumbes. Chán Chán, the sprawling adobe-brick capital city whose ruins lie 5 km (3 mi) west of Trujillo, has been called the largest mud city in the world. It once held boulevards, aqueducts, gardens, palaces, and some 10,000 dwellings. Within the city were nine royal compounds, one of which, the royal palace of Tschudi, has been partially restored and opened to the public. At Tschudi is the tomb of Señor Chimú. UNESCO declared the city of Chán Chán a World Heritage Site in 1986.

At the entrance to the Tschudi complex is the Plaza Principal, a monstrous open space where ceremonies and festivals were held. The throne of the king was in front where the ramp is found. The reconstructed walls have depictions of sea otters at their base. From here, head deep into the ruins toward the royal palace and tomb of Señor Chimú. The main corridor is marked by fishnet representations, marking the importance of the sea to these ancient people. You will also find renderings of pelicans, which served as ancient road signs, their beaks pointing to important sections of the city. Just before you arrive at the Recinto Funerario, where the tomb of Señor Chimú is found, you pass a small natural reservoir called a *huachaque*. There are 44 secondary tombs surrounding the *recinto funerario*, where the king Señor Chimú was buried. In his day it was understood that when you pass to the netherworld you can bring all your worldly necessities with you, and the king was buried with several live concubines and officials, as well as a slew of personal effects, most of which have long since been looted. Near the recinto funerario there is a large observation platform. From here there's a good view of the massive city of Chán Chán and its other royal palaces. Although wind and rain have damaged the city, its size—20 square km (8 square mi)—is still impressive.

The other eight royal compounds of Chán Chán have not been restored and are not open to the public. The **Museo del Sitio,** at the entrance to the ruins, has ceramics and textiles from the Chimú empire. It is best not to walk to the Tschudi ruins, as robberies have been reported between here and Trujillo; take a taxi. If you don't have a guide, you can hire one at the entrance for a few dollars. ⊠ *Carretera Huanchaco, 4.5 km (2.8 mi) northwest of Trujillo* ☎ *no phone* 🎫 *S/10 (includes entrance to museum and ruins at Chán Chán, Huaca Arco Iris, and Huaca Esmeralda)* ⊘ *Daily 9–4:30.*

HUACA ESMERALDA *2 km (1 mi) west of Trujillo*

Like other Chimú pyramids on the north coast, the ancient temple mound Huaca Esmeralda (Emerald Pyramid) served as a religious ceremonial center and burial site for kings. The highlights of the ruins are the two-stepped platforms and unrestored friezes of fish, seabirds, waves, and fishing nets that were central to the life of the Chimú. ⊠ *Av. Mansiche exit, Pan-American Hwy. N, 2 km (1 mi) west of Trujillo* ☎ *no phone* 🎫 *S/10 (includes entrance to museum and ruins at Chán Chán, Huaca Arco Iris, and Huaca Esmeralda)* ⊘ *Daily 9–4:30.*

HUACA ARCO IRIS *5 km (3 mi) west of Trujillo*

Jarringly out of place in an urban area north of Trujillo's center is the restored Huaca Arco Iris (Rainbow Pyramid), also know as the Huaca El Dragón (Pyramid of the Dragon). On this early Chimú structure is the repeating figure of a mythical creature who looks like a cross between a giant serpent and a rainbow, hence the name. On the walls, most of which are reconstructions, you will also see priests wielding the tumi knives used in human sacrifices. Half-moons sit at the bottom of most of the friezes. It is likely that the Chimú worshipped the moon and that this temple, with its rainbow and moon symbolism, was a temple to fertility and rain. ⊠ *Pan-American Hwy., 5 km (3.1 mi) from Trujillo's Plaza de Armas* ☎ *no phone* 🎫 *S/10 (includes entrance to museum and ruins at Chán Chán, Huaca Arco Iris, and Huaca Esmeralda)* ⊘ *Daily 9–4:30.*

EL BRUJO *60 km (37.2 mi) north of Trujillo*

The seldom-visited ruins of El Brujo (the Sorcerer) and nearby Huaca Prieta are some of the oldest in Peru. The Huaca Prieta people were the first to inhabit this seafront plot of land, around 5,000 years ago. The archaeological record from the Huaca Prieta site has given archaeologists a unique glimpse into pre-ceramic South American culture, but it doesn't hold much interest for the passing traveler, as it is not much more than an ancient garbage pile. Later, the region was taken over by the Mochica, who built the Huaca El Brujo and Huaca de Cao Viejo pyramids a little inland from the Huaca Prieta site. The pyramids have several well-preserved bas-relief images, some of which are polychrome (an oddity for Mochica culture). The area around El Brujo is shrouded in mystery and exudes a delicate energy. It was deemed the Sorcerer because shamans from the Chicama Valley used to come down to the pyramids to recharge their spiritual batteries. Visiting the ruins is easier said than done, as you need special permission from the archaeologist in charge of the excavation. The site is also quite hard to find. From the Pan-American, turn west from the town of Chocope heading toward the pueblo

Magdalena de Cao. The site is a short way from Magdalena de Cao. It is best to go with a guide from Trujillo. ⊠ *To visit the ruins, contact the Fundacíon Augusto N. Wiese, Av. Canaval y Moreyra 522, piso 16, Lima 27* ☎ *01/441–2201 Ext. 410* ☞ *Free with permission only.*

Huanchaco

🔟 *12 km (7.5 mi) northwest of Trujillo.*

The tiny fishing village of Huanchaco has a pleasant brown-sand beach and is a great alternative to staying in Trujillo for those looking for a little sand and sun. According to legend, it was here that Prince Takaynamo landed more than 800 years ago with his grand retinue to found the first Chimú dynasty, later erecting the city of Chán Chán. Sit in the sun and watch the fisherman go out in their *caballitos de totora*. Fisherman construct these small, unstable craft out of bundled reeds harvested just north of the city. Coastal fisherman have been using reed boats for more than 1,000 years, and Moche ceramics depict men riding these tiny craft—the fact that fishermen sit *on* them rather than in them accounts for the term *caballito*, or "little horse." Today, however, most fisherman along Peru's north coast have lost interest in totora boats, preferring the modern conveniences of outboard motors and sturdy wood construction, but the people of Huanchaco have held onto this tradition. Fisherman will often not go out for weeks on end when the sea is high, as they cannot paddle past the breakers. Aspiring caballito riders can negotiate rentals from local fishermen. There are several good surfing breaks near Huanchaco, too. The Festival del Mar (Festival of the Sea) is held here every other year—on even years—during the first week in May. There are surfing and dance competitions and other special events. Walking outside Huanchaco's center at night is reportedly dangerous, as there are several slums in the area.

On a hill overlooking the village is **El Santuario de Huanchaco** (The Sanctuary of Huanchaco), said to be one of Peru's oldest churches. It was built on a Chimú ruin around 1540. In the second half of the 16th century a small box containing the image of *Nuestra Señora del Socorro* (Our Lady of Mercy), floated in on the tide and was discovered by locals. The image, which is kept in the sanctuary, has been an object of local veneration ever since. ⊠ *Corner of Andrés Rázuri and Unión* ☎ *no phone* ☞ *free* ☉ *Daily 8–6.*

Where to Stay & Eat

¢–$ ✕ **Big Ben.** The second-story terrace dining area of this bristling white restaurant affords great views of the beach. Huanchaquero specialties include *cangrejo reventado* (boiled crab with eggs) and *ceviche de mococho* (algae ceviche). The restaurant is open only for lunch. ⊠ *Av. Victor Larco 836* ☎ *044/461–869* ☰ *AE, DC, MC, V* ☉ *No dinner.*

¢–$ ✕ **Club Colonial.** French and creole dishes, most with the seafood, are
FodorśChoice expertly prepared in this colonial casona across from the Plaza de
★ Armas. The garden dining area out back has a cage with six Humboldt penguins; coming at midday around feeding time is a real treat. ⊠ *Av. Grau 272* ☎ *044/461–015* ☰ *AF, MC, V.*

¢–$ ✕ **Lucho Del Mar.** This lively restaurant on Playa Huanchaco can be noisy, especially on the crowded mezzanine, but the view of the ocean is superb. Dishes are typical of the region, with plenty of seafood concoctions. The owners can arrange for tours in totora boats. ⊠ *Av. Victor Larco 600* ☎ *044/461–460* ☰ *AE, DC, MC, V.*

★ ¢ ⌸ **Casa Suiza.** Riverstone walkways lead you through this charming and extremely affordable hostel. The smallish rooms have blue walls and stenciled moons, and most have private baths. There is a youth-hostel feel, and young travelers congregate on the roof terrace to hang out and swap stories. The half-Peruvian, half-Swiss owner and his wife are glad to help with travel arrangements. ⊠ *Los Pinos 451* ☎ *044/461–285* 🖷 *044/461–302* ⊕ *www.casasuiza.com* ↩ *7 rooms, 2 dormitories* 🖎 *Laundry service, Internet, free parking; no a/c, no room TVs, no room phones* ▭ *no credit cards.*

¢ 🎬 **Hostal Bracamonte.** Across the wide boulevard from Playa Huanchaco, this pleasant hotel has a pool set in beautifully landscaped grounds and a small restaurant that excels at homemade pies. In summer this hotel is extremely popular among families with young children. ⊠ *Jr. Los Olivos 503* ☎ *044/461–162* 🖷 *044/461–266* ⊕ *www.welcome.to/hostal_bracamonte* ↩ *21 rooms, 6 bungalows* 🖎 *Restaurant, cafeteria, cable TV, pool, billiards, Ping-Pong, bar, playground, Internet, meeting rooms, free parking; no a/c* ▭ *AE, DC, MC, V.*

¢ 🎬 **Hostal El Ancla.** A nautical theme runs throughout this stonework hotel just across from Huanchaco's beach. Antique phonographs and sewing machines add to the allure. The rooms are simple, and the price is right. ⊠ *Av. La Rivera 101* ☎ *044/461–030 or 044/461–596* ↩ *11 rooms* 🖎 *Cafeteria, cable TV, laundry service, free parking; no a/c, no room phones* ▭ *no credit cards.*

Nightlife & the Arts

Mama Mia (⊠ Av. Victor Larco 538 ☎ no phone) serves homemade ice cream and is a pleasurable place to be at sunset. The town's only true pub, **La Tribu** (⊠ Plaza de Armas ☎ no phone), is in a converted casona, with a new-bohemian feel and a propensity for funked-out world music.

The Outdoors

Huanchaco's many beaches are good for both swimming and surfing, though the water is a bit cold. **Playa Malecon,** north of the pier, is the most popular swimming beach, where artisans hawk their goods along the beachfront walkway. **Playa Huankarote,** south of the pier, is less popular, as it's rockier, though there's good surfing here; watch the fishermen surf in on their *caballitos de totora* in the afternoon. **Lucho del Mar** (⊠ Av. Victor Larco 600 ☎ 044/461–460) can arrange for *caballito de totora* rentals. **Casa Suiza** (⊠ Los Pinos 451 ☎ 044/461–285 ⊕ www.casasuiza.com) rents surfboards.

Sipán

⑮ *35 km (21 mi) south of Chiclayo.*

The **Tumba del Señor de Sipán** (Tomb of the Lord of Sipán), saved from huaqueros in 1987 by renowned archaeologist Walter Alva, is within the Huaca Rajada, a pyramid near the town of Sipán. The trip here takes you past sugar plantations and through the fertile Chancay Valley to a fissured mud hill that is all that remains of the Huaca Rajada. The three major tombs in the smaller mound date from about AD 290 and earlier, and together they form one of the most complete archaeological finds in the Western Hemisphere. The tombs have been attributed to the Moche culture, who were known for their ornamental pottery and fine metalwork. The most extravagant funerary objects were found in the tomb, now filled with replicas placed exactly where the original objects were discovered. The originals are now on permanent display in the Museo Brüning and Museo Tumbas Reales de Sipán in Lambayeque. The Lord of Sipán did not make the journey to the Great Beyond alone—he was buried with at least eight living people: a warrior guard (whose feet were amputated to ensure that he didn't run away), three young women, two assistants, a servant, a child, a dog, and two llamas. The lord also got to bring gold and jewelry and hundreds of ceramic pots containing snacks for the long journey. It is best to stay in Chiclayo and visit the ruins early in the morning. The dig is ongoing, as other tombs are still being excavated. ☎ *no phone* ✉ *S/7* ⊙ *Daily 9–4:30.*

A 15-minute drive east from Sipán is the 8th-century Moche capital **Pampa Grande**, a 6-square-km (2½-square-mi) archaeological complex that contains one of the largest pyramids ever built in the Andes, the 55-m-high (178-ft-high) Huaca Fortaleza (Pyramid of Strength). Pampa Grande was constructed in the final years of the Moche empire. For unknown reasons the city was torched and abandoned near the beginning of the 9th century. ☎ *no phone* ✉ *S/7* ⊙ *Daily 9–4:30.*

Chiclayo

⑯ *219 km (131 mi) north of Trujillo.*

A lively commercial center, Chiclayo is both prosperous and easygoing. Although it doesn't have much colonial architecture, it is surrounded by numerous pre-Columbian sites. The Moche and Chimú people had major cities in the area, as did the Lambayeque, who flourished here from about 700 to 1370. Tourists flocked here after the 1987 discovery of the nearby unlooted tomb of the Lord of Sipán. Chiclayo now provides a comfortable base from which to visit the tomb and other archaeological sites. The enormous **Cathedral**, dating back to 1869, is worth a look for its neoclassical facade on the Plaza de Armas. ⊠ *Plaza de Armas* ✆ *Free.*

For a bit of fresh air, head to the **Paseo Las Musas.** The pedestrian walk borders a stream and has classical statues depicting scenes from mythology. ⊠ *La Florida and Falques.*

The closest beach to Chiclayo is in the port town of Pimentel, 14 km (8½ mi) west of Chiclayo. The beach itself is unattractive, but a pretty curved pier more than 100 years old is easy on the eyes.

Where to Stay & Eat

Chiclayo is most famous for a pastry called *kinkón* (pronounced much like "King Kong"), a large, round, crumbly cookie. It's filled with *manjar blanco,* a very sweet filling made of condensed milk and cinnamon boiled down until it is very thick and caramel-color. Another local specialty is the *pescado seco* (dried fish) used in stews.

¢–$$ ✕ **Restaurante Típico Fiesta.** The furnishings might seem garish at this restaurant in the 3 de Octubre district, but the main attraction is the food. The chef is known for serving up delicious *comida norteña* (typical food of northern Peru). The *cabrito* (kid) is especially good. ⊠ *Salaverry 1820* ☎ *074/201–970* ⊟ *AE, DC, MC, V.*

¢–$ ✕ **El Huaralino.** Alacritous bow-tied waiters serve up criollo specialties here. The dining area feels like a candy shop, from the pink ceiling to the pink tablecloths—it shouts *la vie en rose*—even the flowers are pink. Meals begin with complimentary fried yucca with an excellent ají sauce. From there, move on to provincial specialties like *cuy* (guinea pig) and *pato con tacu-tacu* (duck and grilled rice). ⊠ *La Libertad 155, Urb. Santa Victoria* ☎ *074/270–330* ⚇ *Reservations recommended* ⊟ *AE, DC, MC, V.*

★ ¢–$ ✕ **La Parra.** Though the brightly lit dining room lacks intimacy, this is one of Chiclayo's better restaurants. This spot specializes in *parrilladas* (barbecues), with tantalizing cuts from every imaginable part of the cow. Try such delicacies as *anticuchos* (cow heart) and *ubre* (cow utter). There's also a chifa (Chinese) menu here. ⊠ *Manuel Maria Izaga 752* ☎ *074/227–471* ⊟ *AE, DC, MC, V*

¢ ✕ **Pizzeria Nueva Venecia.** A hugely popular pizzeria, Nueva Venecia has fantastic pizza and a couple tried-and-true pasta favorites. The thick-walled country charm of this restaurant makes it worthwhile despite the stifling heat produced by the pizza oven. The service during the dinner rush is excruciatingly slow. ✉ *Av. Balta 365* ☎ *074/233–384* 🖃 *AE, DC, MC, V.*

¢ ✕ **Pueblo Viejo.** There is a refreshing airiness to this corner restaurant. Fans on the high ceiling in the downstairs dining area keep you cool. The upstairs has a skylight that brings in a lot of sunlight. The criollo food is widely lauded by locals. Try the *tacu-tacu relleno de mariscos* (shellfish-stuffed grilled rice). There are occasional art exhibitions with the work of local painters. ✉ *Manuel María Izaga 900* ☎ *074/734–583* 🖃 *no credit cards.*

★ **$$** 🏨 **Garza Hotel.** A pleasant poolside patio and bar, a friendly staff, and a central location make this one of the nicest hotels in Chiclayo. The restaurant, with stucco walls, a fireplace, and brass chandeliers, serves excellent regional cuisine. A Continental breakfast is included in the rate. ✉ *Bolognesi 756* ☎ *074/228–172* 🖨 *074/228–171* ⊕ *www.chiclayo. net/garzahotel* ⇔ *91 rooms, 4 suites* ☖ *2 restaurants, room service, mini-bars, cable TV, pool, gym, bar, casino, laundry service, business services, meeting rooms, car rental, free parking* 🖃 *AE, DC, MC, V* ❧ *CP.*

$$ 🏨 **Gran Hotel Chiclayo.** Near the Plaza de Armas, this modern lodging is popular with business travelers as well as tourists. Rooms have large windows that let in a lot of light. There is a small collection of pre-Columbian art. A buffet breakfast is included in the rate. ✉ *Federico Villareal 115* ☎ *074/234–911* 🖨 *074/223–961* ⇔ *129 rooms, 16 suites* ☖ *2 restaurants, room service, minibars, cable TV, pool, hair salon, bar, casino, dance club, shop, laundry service, business services, meeting rooms, free parking* 🖃 *AE, DC, MC, V* ❧ *BP.*

$ 🏨 **Inca Hotel.** A decent budget alternative, this hotel's rooms are rather dark and bring one back to the era of shag rugs and big hair. The recently remodelled bathrooms are modern, however. Rooms facing the road are noisy, but have noise-proof glass to protect you from the din of Chiclayo's streets. ✉ *Av. Luis Gonzales 622* ☎ *074/235–931* 🖨 *074/ 227–651* ⊕ *www.incahotel.com* ⇔ *62 rooms, 2 suites* ☖ *Restaurant, room service, minibars, cable TV, bar, casino, laundry service, meeting rooms, free parking* 🖃 *AE, DC, MC, V* ❧ *CP.*

$ 🏨 **Las Musas.** A waterfall and koi pond greet you at the entrance of this hotel at the end of Paseo Las Musas. Some rooms have funky, oh-so-seventies flower-petal lampshades, and all have big windows looking onto the paseo. The sixth-floor Mirador restaurant has great views of the city and specializes in parrilladas. ✉ *Los Faiques 101, Urb. Santa Victoria* ☎ *074/239–884* 🖨 *074/273–450* ⊕ *www.lasmusashotel.com* ⇔ *43 rooms, 3 suites* ☖ *Restaurant, room service, minibars, cable TV, bar, casino, dance club, laundry service, business services, meeting rooms, free parking* 🖃 *AE, DC, MC, V* ❧ *CP.*

Nightlife & the Arts

Nightlife in Chiclayo moves along at a decent clip, especially on week-ends. The most popular spot in town for peñas is the spirited **El Señorío** (✉ Balta and Manuel María Izaga ☎ no phone). It opens nightly at 10:30. **La Herradura** (✉ Av. Los Incas 193 ☎ 074/35–859) is a drive-in discoteque, complete with gas-station-style, jumpsuit-wearing waiters. There is a small dance floor in the back of **Premium Chopperia** (✉ Av. Balta 323 ☎ 074/ 228–850). They play mostly Latin pop and cater to an older crowd. The Gran Hotel Chiclayo's discoteque and bar **Solid Gold** (✉ Av. Federico Villarreal 115 ☎ 074/234–911) attracts an older crowd.

Shopping

Chiclayo's **Central Market** on Avenida Balta is famed for its ceramics, weavings, and charms made by local *curanderos* (folk healers). Ask at any of the stalls for an evening session with a local shaman. The **Paseo Artesenal 18 de Abril** (⊠ Calles Colon and Bolognesi) has a few artisan kiosks that sell souvenirs and other local goods.

Lambayeque

⑰ *12 km (7 mi) north of Chiclayo.*

Lambayeque has some preserved colonial architecture and two notable museums. It is often called the "Cradle of Peruvian Liberty," because it was here, on December 27, 1820, that Peru declared its independence from the Spanish crown.

The Moche, Lambayeque, and other pre-Inca cultures such as the Cupisnique, Chavín, Moche, Chimú, and Sicán are explored at the **Museo Brüning.** Run by Walter Alva, who saved the marvelous tombs of Sipán, the museum has one of the finest archaeological collections in Peru. Among the highlights are the treasures taken from the Tomb of the Lord of Sipán; a group of ceramic frogs dating from 1200 BC; a small gold statue of a woman known as the Venus de Frías; and Moche and Sicán ceramics. The museum has excellent interpretive displays with text in Spanish. There is a small gift shop that sells replicas of the antiquities found at the Tomb of Sipán. ⊠ *Huamachuco and Atahualpa* ☎ *076/282–110* 🖃 *S/7, S/10 with guide* ⊙ *Daily 9–5.*

Fodor'sChoice The **Museo Tumbas Reales de Sipán,** offers a deeper look into the culture
★ and everyday life of the Moche. The exhibits lay out where every jewel, ceramic, and other artifact was found in the Tomb of Sipán. Most of the Señor de Sipán artifacts are now found here. ⊠ *Av. Juan Pablo Vizcardo and Guzmán* ☎ *076/283–077* 🖃 *S/7* ⊙ *Tues.–Sun. 9:30–1 and 4–8; closed Mon.*

Túcume

⑱ *35 km (21 mi) northwest of Chiclayo.*

With the decline of the Moche civilization, legend has it that a lord called Naymlap arrived in the Lambayeque Valley, and with his dozen sons founded the Lambayeque dynasty, whose cities included the immense pyramid complex of Túcume. Here you'll find the Huaca Larga, one of the largest adobe pyramids in South America. From the heights of the hill called El Purgatorio, see 26 giant pyramids and dozens of smaller ones spread across a desert sprinkled with hardy little *algarobo* (mesquite) trees. Late Norwegian explorer Thor Heyerdahl, of *Kon-Tiki* fame, directed the excavations of the pyramids. There is a small **Museo de Sitio** 1 km east of Túcume with a small collection of artifacts and some displays recounting the history of the nearby ruins. The museum's interesting architecture — it is made from mud, adobe, cane, and mesquite wood, resembling the chapels around Lambayeque — is the real draw. ☎ *076/800–052 or 074/422–027* 🖃 *S/7* ⊙ *Daily 9–5.*

Piura

⑲ *269 km (167 mi) north of Chiclayo.*

Often called the oldest colonial city in Peru, Piura was founded in 1532 by Francisco Pizarro before he headed inland to conquer the Inca. The young colonial city changed sites three times, before settling down in 1578 next to the Río Piura. The Piura of today is Peru's fifth-largest city, with more than 300,000 people. Around the area, with the help of intense irrigation projects, citizens cultivate corn, rice, cotton, and bananas. Although the town is a bit run-down—an earthquake destroyed many of the original buildings in 1912—it is for many a necessary stopover en route to the pleasant beach towns to the north.

Take in the nice colonial architecture around the pleasantly shaded **Plaza de Armas.** ⊠ *Jr. Tacna and Jr. Huancavelica.*

Piura's **Catedral** is worth a visit. It was built in 1588 and is one of Peru's oldest churches. You will find an altarpiece dedicated to the Virgen de Fátima dating back more than 350 years. ⊠ *Plaza de Armas* 🎫 *Free.*

The **Museo Municipal** focuses on the area's natural history. There is also a small collection of pre-Columbian ceramics. ⊠ *Avs. Sullana and Huánuco* ☎ *no phone* 🎫 *S/5* ⊗ *Tues.–Sun. 9–1 and 4–7; closed Mon.*

Where to Stay & Eat

¢-$$ ✕ **La Santitos.** This bistro's tiny dining room with its wood roof, seashell
Fodor's Choice wind chimes, and provincial Spanish feel is superlatively intimate,
★ though it can get quite hot at lunch time. The menu focuses on criollo fish specialties and parrilladas. Try the *langosta a la parmesana* (Parmesan lobster), topping the meal off with homemade ice cream. ⊠ *Libertad 1014* ☎ *073/332–380* 🖃 *V, MC, AE.*

¢-$ ✕ **El Arrecife.** A nautical theme runs through this locally recommended seafood restaurant. From the rope chairs to the plentiful fish tanks, this is a seafood restaurant through and through. Start with the signature Arrecife ceviche and move on to one of the many other fish dishes. There is also a chifa menu for those who fancy Chinese food. ⊠ *Jr. Inca 610* ☎ *073/584–107* 🖃 *no credit cards.*

$$ 🏨 **Los Portales Hotel.** A venerable hotel sitting on Piura's tree-shaded Plaza de Armas, Los Portales has rooms surrounding a lovely center courtyard, highlighted with a fountain and umbrella tables. The pool has its own waterfall and palm-tree island. Rooms are large, with original oil paintings, though the bathrooms are small and dimly lit. ⊠ *Libertad 875* ☎ *073/323–3072* 🖷 *051/321–161* ⊕ *www.hoteleslosportales.com* ⇨ *35 rooms, 2 suites* ⚖ *Restaurant, room service, minibars, cable TV, pool, billiards, bar, casino, laundry service, business services, meeting rooms, airport shuttle, free parking* 🖃 *AE, DC, MC, V* ⦿ *BP.*

$ 🏨 **Hotel Costa Del Sol.** Modern abstract oil paintings by Piura artists adorn the common areas of this new business hotel. There is a small, kidney-shaped pool in the center terrace area. Every room looks onto the center atrium; they come with small, extremely firm beds and modern amenities. The rooms in back are less noisy. ⊠ *Av. Loreto 649* ☎ *073/302–864* 🖷 *073/302–546* ⊕ *www.costadelsolperu.com* ⇨ *32 rooms, 2 suites* ⚖ *Restaurant, room service, minibars, cable TV, pool, gym, bar, casino, laundry service, business services, meeting rooms, free parking, some no-smoking rooms* 🖃 *AE, DC, MC, V* ⦿ *CP.*

Shopping

The tiny pueblo of **Catacaos,** 12 km (7 mi) southwest of Piura, is famous for its artisanry. The local craftsmen make excellent textiles and are especially known for their gold and silver figurines. To get there take the Catacaos exit after the Puente Grau on the Pan-American highway. **Artisanías Lucas** (⊠ Jr. Comercio 629) sells a wide selection of artisanal goods.

The Outdoors

It's a bit of a haul to get to the beach from Piura. **Paita,** 57 km (35 mi) west of Piura, has a large fishing port and a few decent beaches. **Playa Colán** is a bleached-brown beach that lies just 10 minutes south of Paita.

Máncora

⑳ *229 km (142 mi) north of Piura*

Once a small fishing village, Máncora is now a popular vacation destination for Peruvian and international travellers alike. The laid-back beach
town is becoming famous for its good surf, white-sand beach, and tranquility. Surfing is best between November and March. The beaches are
also good for swimming and fishing. About 2 km (1¼ mi) south of town,
Las Pocitas is a lovely beach with rocky outcrops that hold tiny pools of
seawater at low tide.

Where to Stay

¢–$ 🏨 **Los Corales.** Rooms are appointed with bamboo furniture, tile floors,
and colorful tropical bedspreads, and all have terraces with hammocks,
ideal for relaxing with a drink come sunset. All rooms and the pool overlook the beach. ⊠ *Km 1215 Old Pan-American Hwy. N, Máncora*
☎ *074/858-309* 🖷 *074/858-124* ⊕ *www.vivamancora.com/loscorales*
🛏 *8 rooms* ⚑ *Restaurant, pool, beach, bar, laundry service, free parking; no a/c, no room phones, no room TVs* ⊟ *AE, DC, V* ⊚ *CP.*

Punta Sal

㉑ *25 km (15 mi) north of Máncora, 70 km (43 mi) south of Tumbes*

Sit on the beach, go for a swim, and while away the hours in the afternoon sun — not a bad combination for a beach resort. That's probably
why Punta Sal has become such a popular vacation spot in recent years.
In summer, droves of vacationing Limeños flock here for the blond-sand
beach, comfortable ocean breezes, and relatively sunny climate.

Where to Stay & Eat

$$ ✕🏨 **Hotel Caballito de Mar.** This top-notch beach resort has an ocean-
Fodor'sChoice front, seahorse-shaped pool. Rooms, with pitched cane roofs and big
★ comfy beds, climb up the neighboring cliff, giving you excellent ocean
views from every window. Each room comes with a private terrace. All
meals are included in the room price. The restaurant also has good à la
carte specialties. Start with *palta rellena con langostinos* (avocado
stuffed with shrimp), moving on to myriad seafood main courses. The
hotel can arrange fishing trips and four-wheeler (ATV) excursions.
⊠ *Punta Sal, Km 1187 Pan-American Hwy. N* ☎ *074/800-814 or 01/
241-4455* 🖷 *01/447-6562* ⊕ *www.hotelcaballito.com.pe* 🛏 *23 rooms*
⚑ *Restaurant, pool, massage, beach, jet skiing, fishing, bar, playground,
laundry service, Internet, travel services, free parking; no a/c, no room
phones, no room TVs* ⊟ *AE, DC, V* ⊚ *FAP.*

$ 🏨 **Sunset Hotel.** A relatively affordable beachfront hotel, the Sunset has
simple, clean rooms with cane accents, cold water showers, and rain-
bow pastel bedspreads. Some rooms have terraces with ocean views. The
hotel is a little rough around the edges, but a good value for the price.
There is a tiny pool that sits literally right above the Pacific. All meals
are included in the rates during high season. ⊠ *Punta Sal, Km 1187 Pan-
American Hwy. N, just south of Caballito de Mar* ☎ *074/540-041 or
074/688-413* ✉ *puntasal@hotmail.com* 🛏 *10 rooms* ⚑ *Restaurant,
pool, beach, fishing, bar, laundry service, free parking; no a/c, no room
phones, no room TVs* ⊟ *no credit cards* ⊚ *FAP in high-season only.*

Tumbes

㉒ *280 km (173 mi) north of Piura*

More of a way station than a destination, Tumbes sees most people head-
ing for Ecuador by land. But if you want to stay in the beach towns to

the south of here, you might end up staying the night. Tumbes has been inhabited since pre-Inca times, and it was here that Pizarro first saw the riches of the vast Inca Empire that he would later conquer. Modern Tumbes once belonged to Ecuador, until Peru's victory in the 1940–41 border war. It now sits a comfortable 30 km from the border and has numerous military barracks and forts. Hang around the central Plaza de Armas and visit the numerous pedestrian walks, including Paseo La Concordia and Paseo Jerusalén, that radiate out from the plaza.

Where to Stay

★ $$ ✕⊡ **Hotel Costa Del Sol.** It's hard not to like the "like totally eighties"–style rooms, most with pitched ceilings, blocky orange armchairs, and white bubble lamps. The circular pool in the back garden area offers a delicious break from the heat. Another treat is the El Manglar restaurant, the town's finest eatery. ⊠ *San Martin 275* ☎ *072/523–991* 🖷 *072/525–862* ⊕ *www.costadelsolperu.com* ↪ *51 rooms, 3 suites* ♦ *Restaurant, cafeteria, room service, in-room safes, minibars, cable TV, pool, gym, bar, casino, playground, laundry service, business services, meeting rooms, free parking* ▭ *AE, DC, MC, V* ⵏ⧫⧸ *CP.*

$ ⊡ **Chilimasa.** Though it's quite far from the city center and the service is a bit slow and lacks bounce, this is probably Tumbes's second-best hotel. The big, white hotel centers around a shallow pool and courtyard. The rooms are spartan and super clean. The restaurant focuses on local seafood dishes. ⊠ *Urb. Andrés Araujo MZ. 2A Lt 16* ☎ *072/ 524–555* 🖷 *072/521–946* ↪ *16 rooms* ♦ *Restaurant, cable TV, pool, bar, laundry service, Internet, meeting rooms, free parking; no a/c in some rooms* ▭ *AE, MC, V* ⵏ⧫⧸ *CP.*

Nightlife & the Arts

There are a number of restaurants with terraces looking onto the town's Plaza de Armas. These make for pleasant watering holes and good people-watching perches. **El Latino** (⊠ Plaza de Armas s/n ☎ no phone) has a terrace dining area. A younger crowd heads to **Reflejos** (⊠ Calle Andes and Calle Grau ☎ 072/969–198) on the weekend to dance. The blaring music tends toward Latin pop, though they play American music on occasion. During the week you can sing karaoke here.

The Outdoors

Puerto Pizarro has a decent beach and is just 15 km (9 mi) northwest of Tumbes. Zorritos, 27 km (17 mi) south of Tumbes, has a better blond-colored beach. There are also several nature sanctuaries and reserves in the region. North of Tumbes, near the Ecuadorian border, the **Santuario Nacional Los Manglares de Tumbes** (⊠ Access by canoe from the town of Bendito, 25 km (15 mi) north of Tumbes ☎ 044/721–551 ⧉ free, S/10 per hour canoe rental) is a mangrove reserve with crocodiles and diverse bird species. It is best visited with a guided tour. By land, head north towards Playa Pizarro, and from there head northwest on a dirt road for a few kilometers to the small hamlet of Bendito. In Bendito it may be possible to hire a canoe to visit the neighboring reserve. Inland from Tumbes, the remote **Parque Nacional Cerros de Amotape** (⊠ Access from the village of Rica Playa, 37 km (23 mi) south of Tumbes ☎ no phone ⧉ free) is a tropical dry-forest reserve with many species of wildlife. **Zona Reservada de Tumbes** (⊠ Access from the village of El Caucho, 56 km (35 mi) south of Tumbes on a rough dirt road ☎ no phone ⧉ free) is a tropical dry-forest reserve that is home to sundry species of wildlife and flora. Here, you may see monkeys, peccaries, deer, and parrots.

HUARAZ & THE CORDILLERA BLANCA

The Cordillera Blanca is one of the world's greatest mountain ranges. The soaring, glaciated Andean peaks strut more than 6,000 m (19,500 ft) above sea level and are some of the highest in the world—only Asia's mountain ranges are higher. Their tremendous glaciers carve their lonely way into the green of the Río Santa valley, forming streams, giant gorges, and glorious grey-green alpine lagoons. On the western side of the valley is the Cordillera Negra. Less impressive than the Cordillera Blanca, its steep mountains have no permanent glaciers and are verdant and brooding. The valley between these two peaks follows the Río Santa and is often called the *Callejon de Huaylas*. It is named after the district of Huaylas at the northern terminus of the valley. Driving along this paved stretch of road offers spectacular views of both mountain ranges. You will find an abundance of flora and fauna along the Callejón de Huaylas and in the narrow gorges that come snaking their way down from the high mountains. Deer, *viscacha* (alpine rodents), vicuñas, puma, bear, and condors count among the area's numerous species. You will also find the 10-m-tall (32-ft-tall) *puya raimondii* (the world's largest bromelaid), whose giant spiked flower recalls that of a century plant.

The town of Huaraz is the center of activity, and quite possibly the most important climbing and trekking destination in all of South America. From here, arrange to go white-water rafting; head out on a ten-day trek through the vast wilderness; or stay closer to home, taking a one-day excursion to local hot springs, the 3,000-year-old ruins at Chavín de Huántar, a nearby glacier, or an alpine lagoon. Packs of adventurous climbers come here during the dry season to test their iron on the numerous 6,000-m (19,500-ft) peaks in the area. The broad-peaked summit of Huascarán is the highest in Peru at 6,768 m (21,996 ft) and is clearly visible from Huaraz on sunny days. To the south of Huaraz, the remote and beautiful Cordillera Huayhuash offers numerous trekking and climbing excursions as well. The trekking, biking, and climbing options in the area are truly limitless.

The area has been inhabited since pre-Inca times, and Quechua-speaking farmers still toil on the land, planting and harvesting crops much as they did thousands of years ago. The land in the valley is quite fertile, and corn and oranges are grown there. Up above, potatoes and other heartier crops grow on the steep Andean mountainsides. Mother Earth or *Pachamamma* has always provided, but she can be iron-willed and even angry at times; every now and then she will shake her mighty tendrils and a section of one of the glaciers will cave, creating a giant rock and ice fall called an *aluvión* and destroying everything in its path. In 1970 one such aluvión resulted from a giant earthquake, destroying the town of Yungay and almost all its 18,000 inhabitants. Most of the towns throughout the area have suffered some damage from the numerous earthquakes, and not much colonial architecture is left. What remains are friendly, somewhat rugged-looking towns that serve as excellent jumping-off points for exploration of the area's vast wilderness and mountain ranges, hot springs, and 3,000-year-old ruins.

Huaraz

▶ **23** **28** *400 km (248 mi) north of Lima*

Huaraz is Peru's number-one trekking and adventure-sports destination, and it is the best starting point for those wishing to explore the Cordillera Blanca's vast wilderness. Unfortunately, the town has been repeatedly leveled by natural disasters. Records of earthquakes and the resulting debris slides, or aluvións, go back more than 300 years in the region. In the later part of the 20th century three large earthquakes and their resulting aluvións destroyed much of Huaraz, claiming more than 20,000 lives.

Despite the setbacks and death toll, Huaraz rallied, and today it is a pleasant town with outstanding views and friendly people. Being the most popular tourist destination in North Peru, Huaraz also has a great international scene; while the town has few attractions, the restaurants and hotels can be counted as some of the North's best. Many restaurants close during the rainy season, between September and May, when Huaraz practically shuts down without its hoards of climbers and trekkers. It can also be hard to find an outfitter at this time; call ahead if you plan a rainy-season visit.

㉓ While in Huaraz most of your exploration will begin in the **Plaza de Armas**, on the corner of Luzuriaga, the town's main drag, and José Sucre. There are several *ferias artesenales* (artisanal kiosks) bordering the plaza.

㉔ Although many of the pre-Columbian ruins around Huaraz have been destroyed by natural disasters, there's a lot of local history at the **Museo Arqueológico de Ancash**, just north of the Plaza de Armas. The museum has Chavín textiles and ceramics, as well as a mummified baby and ghoulishly deformed skulls. Mummies were preserved by covering the dead with salt, *muña* (wild mint), *quinua* (a corn-like plant), and *izura* (pink earth). ✉ *Av. Luzuriaga 762* ☎ *044/721–551* 💲 *S/5, S/6 with a guide* ◷ *Mon.–Sat. 8:30–5, Sun. 8:30–2.*

㉕ For a pungent look at Andean culture, head to the **Mercado Central**. Note that the market's vendors do not ice their meats. ✉ *Jr. de la Cruz Romero and Av. Cayetano Requena.*

㉖ For a look at Huaraz's colonial remnants head to **Jirón José Olaya**. ✉ *East of the town center on the right-hand side of Raimondi and a block behind Confraternidad Inter Este.*

㉗ There are good views of the Río Santa valley and Huaraz from the **Mirador de Retaquenua**, about a 45-minute walk up the hill southeast of the city. Getting there is a little complicated; ask for directions or hire a local guide. ✉ *Av. Confraternidad Inter Sur and Av. Confraternidad Inter Este.*

㉘ North of Huaraz is a small Wari temple, **Wilcahuaín**. The site dates back to AD 1100 and resembles the larger Chavín temple at Chavín de Huantar. Each story of the crumbling three-tiered temple has seven rooms. Children will show you around for a small tip. Get here on foot or by taxi. On foot, head north out of town on Avenida Centenario. A couple of hundred yards after the Real Hotel Huascarán and just before a gas station, there is a dirt road climbing eastward to your right. Walk up this road through the tiny communities of Jinua and Paria until you arrive at the ruins. Twenty kilometers (12 miles) up from here is the Laguna Llaca, which has nice mountain views and is a good place for a swim if the weather is good. From the ruins, take a 20-minute trail back to Monterrey, catching a bus back to Huaraz from there. ✉ *8 km (5 mi) north of Huaraz* ☎ *no phone* 💲 *S/5* ◷ *Daily 6–6.*

off the beaten path

GLACIAR PASTORURI – Heading south from Huaraz, a popular day trip in the town of Recuay is a visit to the glacier, where you'll have a chance to hike around on the ice and visit a large, glowing blue ice cave. Along the way it is likely that you will see the world's largest bromelaid, the Puya Raimondii. On this trip you will be going well

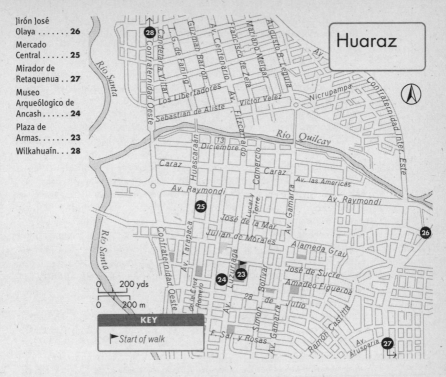

Huaraz

KEY

⊢ *Start of walk*

above 4,000 m (13,000 ft). Wear warm clothing, sunscreen, and
sunglasses—the sun is intense at this altitude—drink lots of water (to
avoid altitude sickness), and hike at a moderate pace. The easiest and
safest way to get here is with a tour company from Huaraz. The tour
costs about S/20 and take 8 hours. Admission to the glacier is S/5.
You can also hire horses to take you there for about S/10.

Where to Stay & Eat

$–$$
Fodor'sChoice
★

✕ **Siam de Los Andes.** Who would have thought—a Thai restaurant high
in the Peruvian Andes. Siam de Los Andes is a true non-sequitur in the
land of ceviche and pollo a la brasa, and therein lies its charm. The light,
delicate, and at times extremely spicy food delivers. It's the real deal;
from the chicken satay to the *kai pad prik king,* the food is authentic;
the Thailand-born owner's secret? He takes regular trips to the home-
land, importing those hard-to-find ingredients. ⊠ *Augustin Gamarra
560* ☎ *044/728–006* ▤ *no credit cards* ☯ *No lunch.*

¢–$

✕ **Creperie Patrick.** With its rooftop dining area and provincial French-
bistro coziness downstairs, Patrick's is an excellent lunch choice. The
menu has such international delights as couscous and fondue, but the
real stars are the dessert crepes. There is also a decent wine list. ⊠ *Av.
Luzuriaga 122* ☎ *011/692–474* ▢ *no credit cards* ☯ *Closed for lunch
and on Sun. during low season.*

★ **¢–$**

✕ **Monte Rosa.** With the cozy feel of a Swiss chalet, this bistro serves up
international specialties like fondue and pasta. Their pizza is lauded as
the best in Huaraz. The open kitchen and sundry decorations add to the
casual, friendly feel. They have excellent Argentine-style parrilladas, grilled
on the open *fogata.* There are also criollo and chita dishes. ⊠ *Jr. José de
la Mar 661* ▣ *044/721–447* ▤ *AE, DC, MC, V* ☯ *Closed for lunch Mon.*

¢–$

✕ **Piccolo Ristorante.** There are an abundance of potted plants on Piccolo's
sidewalk dining area, adding a splash of green to the otherwise bleak streets
of Huaraz. The ristorante specializes in pastas and pizza, but the inter-

national specialties like *filete de trucha a la piamontesa* (trout in herb sauce) and filet mignon round out the menu nicely. The breakfasts are especially good. ⊠ *Jr. Julián de Morales 632* ☏ *044/727–306* ➡ *AE, DC, V.*

$–$$ 🖭 **Hotel Andino.** A Swiss-style chalet set high on the hill above Huaraz, Hotel Andino is lauded as the town's best lodging. The clean, modern rooms have Andean wool bedspreads and funky gauze lamps; some have terraces with excellent views of the valley and mountains. ⊠ *Pedro Cochachín 357, casilla 24* ☏ *044/721–662* 🖷 *044/722–830* ⊕ *www.hotelandino.com* ⤶ *37 rooms, 3 rooms with shared bath* △ *Restaurant, in-room safes, some in-room minibars, cable TV, laundry service, Internet, meeting rooms, travel services, free parking; no a/c* ➡ *AE, DC, MC, V.*

$ 🖭 **Hotel Colomba.** There are lush, well-tended gardens in the center of this hacienda turned hotel. The rooms and bungalows have quaint lace-and-wool bedcovers and all look onto the center gardens. There is a large aviary here with indigenous eagles and falcons. Seeing these beautiful, sleek birds up close in their five-by-seven cages is both awe-inspiring and troubling. As with many haciendas in the area, there is a small chapel on the grounds. ⊠ *Jr. Francisco de Zela 278, Independencia* ☏ *044/ 721–501 or 044/722–273* ⊕ *www.bed42.com/hotelcolomba* ⤶ *22 rooms* △ *Cafeteria, room service, cable TV, playground, laundry service, meeting rooms, free parking; no a/c* ➡ *no credit cards.*

¢ 🖭 **Hotel Casablanca.** In a colonial-style building, the Casablanca is a good budget alternative. There is a small courtyard with a fountain. The rooms are a bit dark and dank, but are, nevertheless, immaculately clean. The service is quite friendly. ⊠ *Av. Tarapacá 138* ☏ *044/722–602* 🖷 *044/724– 801* ✉ *cashotel@terra.com.pe* ⤶ *27 rooms* △ *Cafeteria, room TVs, bar, laundry service, travel services, free parking; no a/c* ➡ *MC, V* ⦿ *CP.*

★ ¢ 🖭 **Steel Guest House.** This Israeli-owned guest house is probably Huaraz's best budget alternative. The simple, ultra-clean rooms have good views and down comforters to keep you cozy. Downstairs there is a common area with a kitchen, book exchange, television, and pool table. There is a rooftop terrace for afternoon sunbaths and a steam bath to fend off evening chills. ⊠ *Pasaje Alejandro Maguiña 1467* ☏ *044/724–849 or 044/729–709* ✉ *steelguesthouse@yahoo.com* ⤶ *8 rooms, 2 rooms with shared bath* △ *Steam room, billiards, laundry service, Internet; no a/c, no room phones, no room TVs* ➡ *no credit cards* ⦿ *CP.*

Nightlife & the Arts

There are a number of cool bars and discoteques in Huaraz. As in most Peruvian towns, the nightlife is most boisterous on the weekend. The ever-popular **Tambos** (⊠ José de la Mar 776 ☏ 044/723–416) has been around forever, with its low ceilings and funky, curvy walls. There is a large dance floor in the back where you can get down to international favorites and the occasional salsa tune. Just down the street is **Makondos** (⊠ Corner of Simon Bolívar and José de la Mar ☏ 044/623–629). Makondos has curving adobe walls, and the music here tends towards the modern, poppy edge of the spectrum. For a taste of modern, backpacker bohemia head to **Vagamundo** (⊠ Julían de Morales 753 ☏ 044/614–374). Play foos-ball and other games while listening to Manu Chau, Marley, and other international vagabond standards. **Las Kenas** (⊠ Gabino Uribe 620 ☏ 044/728–383) is a smallish disco that plays mostly Latino rhythms.

Sports & the Outdoors

Most of the mountain biking in Huaraz takes place on horse trails or gravel roads passing through the Cordilleras Blanca and Negra. There is good rafting on the Río Santa. Run anything from flat water to heart-pumping, Class-5 rapids. The most-often-run stretch of river runs between Jangas and Caraz. The river can be run year-round, but is at its best during the wettest months of the rainy season, between December and April.

If high adventure is what you seek, and dreams of bagging a 6,000-m (19,500-ft) peak, trekking, and climbing haunt your nights, Huaraz is the place for you. Though you can rent all the equipment necessary to do these sports in town, it is best to bring your own. Keep in mind that Huaraz sits at a lofty 3,090 m (10,042 ft), and the surrounding mountains are even higher. Allowing time to acclimatize is not an option but a life-saving necessity. Drinking lots of water and pacing yourself can also help avoid high-altitude pulmonary edema (more commonly known as altitude sickness). The climbing and trekking season runs from June through August during the area's driest months. You can trek during the off-season, but drudging everyday through thick rain just isn't that much fun. Climbing during the off-season can be downright dangerous, as crevasses get covered up by the new snow. Only experienced hikers and climbers should venture into the backcountry without a guide.

Check with the guiding agencies about conditions and maps before you head out. The guided treks in the region vary from three-day, five-star catered affairs, to bare-bones, if-you-can't-carry-it-you-can't-bring-it, 20-day marches. There are so many outfitters in the area that it can become quite overwhelming looking for a qualified company. Shop around and visit a few shops, talk with the guides, and make sure you are getting what you really want. **Mountain Bike Adventures** (⊠ Jr. Lucar and Torre 530 ☎ 044/724–259 ⊕ www.chakinaniperu.com) rents bikes and has experienced guides to take you to the good single-track spots. **Monttrek** (⊠ Av. Luzuriaga 646, upstairs ☎ 044/721–124 ⊕ www.monttrek. com) is one of the best rafting outfitters in Huaraz. They have very friendly and experienced guides for trekking, mountaineering, and rafting. **La Casa de Guias** (⊠ Parque Ginebra 28-G ☎ 044/721–811) is the area's professional organization. They can arrange for a guide. **Sechin Tours** (⊠ Av. Luzuriaga 772 ☎ 044/721–577 ⊕ www.huaraz.net/sechintours) offers simple day tours throughout the region. They also offer rafting, climbing, and trekking trips.

Shopping

There are a ton of T-shirt and souvenir shops along Avenida Luzuriaga. There are ferias artesenales on either side of the Plaza de Armas, with Andean textiles and other good kitsch. **Andes Souvenirs** (⊠ Parque Ginebra ☎ no phone) has a decent selection of textiles, handicrafts, jewelry, and pan-pipe CDs.

Around Huaraz

Monterrey

29 *5 km (3.1 mi) north of Huaraz*

Heading north from Huaraz on a paved road that stretches for some 67 km (41 mi) to the intact colonial village of Caraz, along what is popularly called the Callejón de Huaylas, you will pass many scenic villages and take in some of the area's most spectacular scenery from the comfort of your car. Five kilometers (3 mi) north of Huaraz you'll come to the pleasant hot-springs oasis of Monterrey. It's a good lodging option for those looking for tranquility and a welcome escape for those staying in the grime and noise of Huaraz. There is a nice hiking trail just behind the Hotel Monterrey that leads across a stream and up into the hills and eventually takes you to the Wilcahuaín Ruins. **Los Baños Termales de Monterrey** has a large public bathing area, where you can soak in the more-than-35-degree-centigrade water. The muddy, sulfur-rich waters are quite relaxing, though the facilities are a bit dirty. There are also private baths here. Up above the swimming area is a small Inca pool and trout hatchery. ⊠ *Av. Monterrey s/n, at top of hill next to the Hotel Monterrey* ☎ *044/727–690* 🖵 *S/3, S/5 with towel* ☉ *Daily 6–6.*

Where to Stay & Eat

¢–$ ✕ **El Cortijo.** The grassed, open-air dining area of Monterrey's best restaurant is a great place for a sunny afternoon lunch—as well as a laid-back one, as service can be slow. The large barbecue pit sits next to the dining area. The parrilladas are excellent. ⊠ *Carretera Huaraz–Caraz, Monterrey s/n* ☎ *044/723–813* 🖃 *AE, DC, MC, V.*

$ 🏨 **El Patio de Monterrey.** A lovely country hacienda built in the Spanish
Fodor'sChoice   colonial style, El Patio is a great lodging option for those wishing to get
★   a bit outside the city. White walls, wood beams, Spanish tiles, and a delightful stone patio combine to make this one of the area's best choices. Its only 16 km (10 mi) from Huaraz, making it a feasible alternative for those wishing to stay near the city. The simple rooms have antiques and a clean, provincial feel. There's a small chapel here, as the hacienda was originally built by priests. ⊠ *Carretera Huaraz–Caraz Km. 206, Monterrey* ☎*044/724–965* 🖷 *044/726–967* ✐ *elpatio@terra.com.pe* ⇦*25 rooms, 3 cabañas* ⚭ *Restaurant, room TVs, laundry service, free parking; no a/c* 🖃 *AE, DC, MC, V.*

¢   🏨 **Hotel Monterrey.** Next to Monterrey's hot springs is this big old hotel with creaky wooden floors and old mattresses. While the rooms are nothing special, the property has its own private hot-springs pool and a pleasant restaurant. Staying here gives you 24-hr access to the pools. ⊠ *Av. Monterrey s/n* ☎🖷 *044/727–690* ⇦*24 rooms* ⚭ *Restaurant, room TVs, pool, laundry service, free parking; no a/c* 🖃 *AE, DC, MC, V.*

Carhuaz

③⓪ *35 km (22 mi) north of Huaraz*

The tiny, laid-back village of Carhuaz, 35 km (22 mi) north of Huaraz, is often visited by tour groups heading through the Callejón de Huaylas. A bright spot is the ice-cream shop, with excellent homemade *helado.* The town riots with bullfights, fireworks, dancing, and plenty of drinking on its Virgen de La Merced fiesta, held every year September 14–24. This is one of the best fiestas in the region.

en route   ✕ **Heladeria El Abuelo.** You won't want to miss this ice-cream shop and café, where you'll find terrifically fantastic flavors, including pisco sour and *cerveza* (beer). The owner is a good source for information about the region; he also rents nice rooms in a country lodge near town. ⊠ *Av. La Merced 727* ☎ *044/794–149.*

Yungay

③① *59 km (37 mi) north of Huaraz*

Death still haunts Yungay, which was in the path of Peru's worst natural disaster. On Sunday, May 31, 1970, a 7.7 Richter-scale earthquake unleashed some 15 million cubic meters of rock and ice that cascaded from the west wall of Huascarán Norte. Meanwhile, in the quiet village of Yungay, some 14 km (8½ mi) away, people were going about their normal Sunday activities. The 1970 World Cup in Mexico was supposed to play on the radio that day and the Verolina Circus had recently come to town and was beginning to set up in the stadium. Then the debris slammed into town at a speed of almost 350 km/hour. Almost all of Yungay's 18,000 inhabitants were buried alive. The quake ultimately claimed nearly 70,000 souls throughout Central Peru.

The citizenry never rebuilt in Yungay, but left it as a mass grave and memorial to the dead. They now call the area **Campo Santo,** and tourists visit the site daily. Walking through the ruined town, you'll see upturned-buses, occasional gravestones, and memorials, the few remaining walls of the cathedral, and, oddly, a couple of palm trees that managed to survive the disaster. There is a large white cross on top of the old cemetery on the hill south of town. It was here that the wrath of Mother Earth spared the lives of 92 people who were visiting their dead relatives and, by some act of God, on high-enough ground to miss their call. More than 100 children were in the stadium that day and their lives were also spared. You pay a nominal S/2 to enter the site.

New Yungay was built just beyond the aluvión path—behind a protective knoll. It best serves as a starting point for those visiting the spectacular Laguna Llanganuco.

Laguna Llanganuco
32 *28 km (17 mi) east of Yungay*

Coming through a giant gorge formed millions of years ago by the retreating tentacle of a glacier, you arrive at **Laguna Llanganuco.** The lake's crystalline waters shine a luminescent turquoise in the sunlight; in the shade they are a forbidding black ink. Waterfalls of glacial melt snake their way down the gorge's flanks, falling lightly into the water of the lake. There are many *quenual* trees (deciduous alpine shrubs) surrounding the lake. Up above, you'll see treeless alpine meadows and the hanging glaciers of the surrounding mountains. Hire a rowboat (S/2.50) to take you to the center of the 28-m-deep (91-ft-deep) lake, rent horses, or take a 20-minute walk on a trail following the eastern rim of the lake. There are a few trailside signs to teach you about local flora and fauna. The easiest way to get here is with an arranged tour from Huaraz (about S/25). The tours stop here and at many other spots on the Callejón de Huaylas, finishing in Caraz.

The lake is the gateway to the **Parque Nacional Huascarán,** a 340,000-hectare park created in 1975 to protect and preserve the vast natural resources, flora, and fauna in the **Cordillera Blanca**—most of which is bounded by the park—and its outlying areas. This incredible mountain range has a total of 663 glaciers and includes some of the highest peaks in the Peruvian Andes. Huascarán, at 6,768 m (21,996 ft), is Peru's highest. The smaller Alpamayo, 5,947 m (19,327 ft), is said by many to be the most beautiful mountain in the world. And her majestic flanks do inspire awe and wonder in those lucky enough to get a glimpse. The monstrous Chopicalqui and Chacraraju both sit at more than 6,000 m (19,500 ft).

Within the park's boundaries you will find more than 750 species of flora. There is a tragic scarcity of wildlife in the park—most wild populations have been decimated by hunting and the unchecked march of larger and larger civilizations. Among the 12 species of birds and 10 species of mammals you are likely to see wild ducks and condors. With a great deal of time in the mountains and a good amount of luck you may also see foxes, deer, pumas, and viscachas

The giant national park is a locus for camping, trekking, and mountain climbing. There are myriad treks through the region, varying from easy two-day affairs to 20-day marathons. The park is the trailhead for the popular **Llanganuco–Santa Cruz Loop,** a three- to five-day trek through mountain valleys, past crystalline lakes, and over a 4,750-m-high (15,437 ft high) pass. Other popular hikes include the one-day Lake Churup trek, the two-day Quilcayhuanca–Cayesh trek, and the two-day Ishinca Trek. Check with guide agencies in Huaraz for more complete information, maps, and insider advice before heading out on these trips.

FodorsChoice
★

While experienced hikers who know how to use a compass and survive in the mountains may want to head out on their own, most people should go with a guide. Many trekkers opt to have donkeys or llamas carry the heavy stuff, leaving you with just a day pack. Arrange for guides and donkey rentals in Huaraz. The most common ailments on these treks are altitude sickness and sore feet. Wear comfortable hiking shoes that have already been broken in, and take the proper precautions to avoid altitude sickness (make sure to drink lots of water along the treks, avoid prolonged exposure to the sun, and allow yourself time to acclimatize before you head out). The best time to go trekking is during the dry season, April through October. July and August are the driest months, though dry season doesn't mean a lack of rain or even snow, so dress appropriately.

Recently, many hikers have decided to enter the park at night to avoid paying the hefty S/65 for a multi-day pass. The money from these fees goes to protect Peru's natural wilderness and the wonders of the Andes; consider this before you slip in in the dead of night. ⊠ *Park entrance is 28 km (17 mi) east of Yungay on the road to Yanama* ☎ *044/721– 601* ✉ *S/5 for a day pass, S/65 for a multi-day adventure-tourism pass* ⊙ *Daily 6–6.*

Caraz
❸❸ *67 km (42 mi) north of Huaraz*

One of the few towns in the area with an intact colonial center, Caraz is a quaint little village 67 km (42 mi) north of Huaraz and is basically the northern terminus of this region—an unpaved road continues north. While in town be sure to try the ultra-sweet *manjar blanco* frosting. North of Caraz on the road to Chimbote is the Cañon del Pato, the true northern terminus of the Callejón de Huaylas.

Chavín de Huántar
❸❹ *110 km (68 mi) southeast of Huaraz*

Built by the Chavín, one of the first civilizations in Peru, Chavín de Huántar is a fascinating archaeological site and easily reached from Huaraz in a day. It lies on the southern edge of Chavín, a tiny village 110 km (68 mi) southeast of Huaraz. The village of Chavín has only bare-bones accommodations; the ruins that date back almost 3,000 years are the real draw. Archaeologists estimate that the Chavín culture flourished from 1000 to 300 BC. In its heyday, between 800 and 400 BC, it had a large empire that stretched as far north as the present-day Ecuadorian border and southward to Ica and Ayacucho. Though little is known about these ancient people, it is judged that they were a cat-worshipping people. Their main deity was always characterized as a puma or jaguar. Lesser deities, represented by condors, snakes, and humans, were also worshipped. From excavations of middens (ancient garbage dumps), archaeologists reckon that the Chavín relied heavily on corn and squash for their simple diet.

The ruins appear to be quite unimpressive on arrival, as most of the area was covered by a huge landslide in 1945. Below ground, however, you find a labyrinth of well-ventilated corridors and chambers. They are illumined by electric lights that only occasionally work—it is wise to bring a flashlight. Deep inside the corridors you'll come upon the **Lanzón de Chavín.** This 4-m-high (13-ft-high) daggerlike rock carving represents an anthropomorphic deity (complete with fangs, claws, and serpentine hair); it sits elegantly at the intersection of four corridors.

The most important structure on the site is the three-tiered, 13-m-tall (42-ft-tall) **Castillo.** The walls of the Castillo were at one time bedizened with tenons (keystones of large blocks assembled to resemble a human face). Only one of these remains; the others are guarded inside the Castillo and other museums around the country. Visit the ruins and the alpine Laguna de Querococha from Huaraz during a 10-hr tour. The tour costs about S/25 and does not include entrance into the ruins. On the drive from Huaraz you get good views of two Andean peaks, Pucaraju (5,322 m/17,296 ft) and Yanamarey (5,237 m/17,020 ft). ✉ *110 km (68 mi) southeast of Huaraz* ☎ *no phone* ✆ *S/10, ruins only* ☉ *Daily 8–4.*

THE NORTHERN HIGHLANDS

The best description of Peru's northern highlands comes from the philosopher and writer Mariano Iberico: "It is not easy to characterize the landscape as it is of an infinite variety," he wrote. "Going from desert desolation found on high mountaintops to warm greenery in the valley, from severe austerity in sad scrublands to luxuriant vegetation in divers gorges; from that variety that lies between the confines of altitudes and depths run forth plains and plunging streams during the rainy season, while in summer in the scorched erosion, something akin to a geological intimacy of the planet is made visible." The green valleys and high mountaintops that comprise the northern highlands are certainly one of the area's biggest draws, as is the area's rich history. But very few travelers venture here, as it is hard to reach and far from the "Gringo Trail" that passes through Cusco, Puno, and Machu Picchu.

There are several major archaeological sites in the northern highlands. The pre-Inca fortress of Kuélap, near Chachapoyas, is one of the region's best-preserved ruins. The region's largest town, Cajamarca, is the center for exploration and was the site of one of history's quickest and wiliest military victories. It was here in 1532 that Pizarro and his meager force of 160 Spaniards were able to kill more than 6,000 Inca warriors and capture Atahualpa, the new king of the Inca empire. Without a king and a country divided—the empire had been ravaged by civil war just before Pizarro arrived—the vast empire quickly fell. In and around Cajamarca you will find a handful of Inca and pre-Inca sites. There are also chances for horseback riding and hiking in the area's green valleys and hills.

Cajamarca

35–**41** *865 km (536 mi) northeast of Lima, 304 km 188 mi) northeast of Trujillo*

The capital of its department (or province) and the largest city in the northern highlands, Cajamarca is a tranquil town of some 70,000 people. It sits in a large green valley and is surrounded by low hills. The name Cajamarca means "village of lightning" in the Aymara language. It is especially fitting, for the ancient Cajamarcans worshiped the god Catequil, whose power was symbolized by lightning. The area around town was first populated by the Cajamarcans 3,000 years ago, whose major cultural influence came from the cat-worshiping Chavín. The Inca conquered the region in about 1460, assimilating the Chavin culture. Cajamarca soon became an important town along the *Capac Ñan* or Royal Inca Road, with more than 2,000 inhabitants.

The arrival of the Spanish conquistador Pizarro and his quick-witted deception of the Inca Atahualpa soon brought the city and much of the region into Spanish hands. The Spanish colonials dismantled many of the Inca buildings, using the blocks to build colonial churches. Very few Inca ruins remain in modern-day Cajamarca, but the well-maintained colonial center with its churches and casonas is quite charming. The town's colonial center is so well preserved that it was declared a Historic and Cultural Patrimony Site of the Americas by OAS in 1986. Cajamarca is the best place to stay for those wishing to explore the northern highlands' lovely landscape and rich history; from town there are a number of day excursions to nearby ruins and hot springs.

Numbers in the text correspond to numbers in the margin and on the Cajamarca map.

a good walk

It is easiest to explore Cajamarca's sights on foot. Begin your tour in the **Plaza de Armas** ㉟ ▶. On the plaza's northwest corner is the **Iglesia de San Francisco** ㊱. Adjoining the church, to the right, is the lovely **Capilla de la Virgen de Dolores.** From here, walk around the plaza to the **Catedral** ㊲, on the corner of Arequipa and Avenida Uma. Cross the plaza and head to **El Cuarto del Rescate** ㊳, one block east of the plaza on Jirón Amalia Puga. From there, head south on the Calle Belén. In **El Complejo de Belén** ㊴, visit the **Iglesia de Belén,** the **Museo Arqueologíco de Cajamarca,** and the **Museo Etnologico.** You'll want to spend some time around the Belén complex to take in all the museums. Finish off the walk with a heart-pounding walk up the **Cerro Santa Apolonia** ㊵. To get there, head farther south from the Complejo Belén. You'll start climbing the steps from the end of 2 de Mayo. There are pretty gardens on the top, and you'll have great views of the colonial city down below. After the exhausting climb to Santa Apolonia, your muscles and bones will surely deserve a break. From below the Cerro take a cab to the **Baños del Inca** ㊶ (6 km/3.7 mi east of town), for a relaxing soak in the hot springs.

TIMING   You can easily do the walk above in a morning, allowing the afternoon for rest or a relaxing dip at the Baños del Inca hot springs. Be sure to wear comfortable shoes and sunscreen. Cajamarca is 2,650 m (8,612 ft) above sea level. While not very high by Andes standards, it is still higher than most cities in the United States and Europe. Take your time, and drink plenty of water to avoid altitude sickness.

What to See

㊶ **Baños del Inca.** Six km (3.7 mi) east of Cajamarca are the pleasant Baños del Inca hot springs. Atahualpa and his 40,000 to 80,000 troops were camped here when Pizarro came to Cajamarca. There are several public pools and private baths, as well as the Poza del Inca, an intact Incan pool with stone banks and a clever system of aqueducts. ⊠ *6 km (3.7 mi) east of Cajamarca on Av. Manco Cápac* ☎ *no phone* ✉ *S/5* ☽ *Daily 8–6.*

㊲ **Catedral** Originally known as the Iglesia de Españoles (because only Spanish colonialists were allowed to attend church here), Cajamarca's cathedral was built in the 17th and 18th centuries. It has a pleasantly ornate Baroque facade that was sculpted from volcanic rock. Like many of Cajamarca's churches, the cathedral has no belfry; the Spanish crown levied taxes on completed churches, so the clever settlers left the churches unfinished, freeing them from the tight grip of the tax man. ⊠ *East side of Plaza de Armas, corner of Arequipa and Av. Amalia Puga* ☎ *no phone* ✉ *Free* ☽ *Daily 3–6.*

㊵ **Cerro Santa Apolonia.** South of the city, right off 2 de Mayo, are the steps leading to this hilltop *mirador,* or lookout. At the top are many carved bricks dating back to pre-Columbian times. One of the rocks has the shape of a throne and has been dubbed the Seat of the Inca. According to local legend, it was here that Inca kings would sit to review their troops. You'll find pretty gardens here and great views of the town. ⊠ *Ascend steps at the end of 2 de Mayo* ☎ *no phone* ✉ *S/2* ☽ *Daily 9–6.*

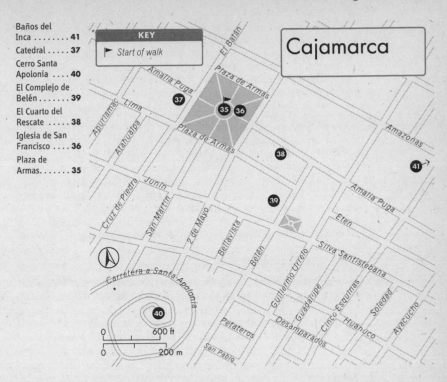

KEY

▶ *Start of walk*

Cajamarca

off the beaten path

VENTANILLAS DE OTUZCO & COMBAYO – One of the oldest cemeteries in Peru, the Ventanillas de Otuzco (Otuzco Windows), 8 km (5 mi) northeast of Cajamarca, dates back more than 3,500 years. The ancient necropolis is comprised of several large burial niches carved into a rock cliff. From afar the niches look like windows, hence the area's name. On closer inspection you see that many of the burial niches are adorned with carved decorations. The site is slowly being eroded by wind and rain. The cemetery, the Necrópolis de Combayo (Combayo Necropolis), is easily reached with a tour or on foot. About 30 km (18 mi) from Combayo in the same direction you'll find the better-preserved Ventanillas de Combayo. A guided tour costs around S/25.

★ ❸❾ **El Complejo de Belén.** Built in the later part of the 17th Century, the hospital at El Complejo de Belén now has archaeological and ethnological museums. The old kitchen and dispensary contain a small art museum, with rotating exhibitions. Next to the hospital, the **Iglesia de Belén** has an ornate facade and a polychrome pulpit and cupola. At the **Museo Arqueológico de Cajamarca**, (☎ 076/822–601), the town's only archaeological museum, are exhibits of Cajamarcan pottery and textiles. The pre-Inca Cajamarcans were especially famous for their excellent patterned textiles that were often dyed blue. The **Museo Etnologico** (☎ 076/822–601) has a few displays of everyday bric-a-brac—there's even an old saddle and a dilapidated coffeemaker—dating back to pre-colonial times. ✉ *Jr. Belén and Jr. Junín* ☎ *no phone* ✆ *S/4, includes admission to the Complejo Belén and archaeological and ethnological museums, as long as you visit them all on the same day* ⊙ *Mon.–Sat. 9–1 and 3–5:45, Sun. 9–1.*

❸❽ **El Cuarto del Rescate.** The Ransom Chamber is the only Inca building still standing in Cajamarca. Legend has it that after Pizarro and his men captured the Inca king Atahualpa, the king offered to fill the Ransom

FodorsChoice

★

Chamber once with gold and twice with silver. The ransom was met, but the war-hardened Spaniards killed Atahualpa anyway. What you see today is a big stone room with some rectangular niches in the walls, but the story itself is enough to make this worth a visit. ⊠ *Jr. Amalia Puga 750* ☎ *no phone* ⌨ *S/4, includes admission to the Complejo Belén and archaeological and ethnological museums, as long as you visit them all on the same day* ⊙ *Mon.–Sat. 9–1 and 3–5:45, Sun. 9–1.*

③⑥ **Iglesia de San Francisco.** Built in the 17th and 18th centuries, the Church of San Francisco sits proudly on the Plaza de Armas. The church's two bell towers were added in republican times and only finished in 1951. Interestingly, the church was called the Iglesia de Indios (Church of the Indians) as Indians were allowed to attend mass here but not in the main Cathedral. Inside you find catacombs and a small religious-art museum. To the right of the church, the Capilla de la Virgen de Dolores is one of Cajamarca's most beautiful chapels. There is a large statue of Cajamarca's patron saint, La Virgen de Dolores, making this a popular pilgrimage destination for local penitents. ⊠ *Northeast corner of Plaza de Armas, on 2 de Mayo* ☎ *no phone* ⌨ *S/2 for museum* ⊙ *Daily 3–6.*

▶ ③⑤ **Plaza de Armas.** Built on roughly the same spot as the great Inca plaza where the Inca Atahualpa was captured and later killed, Cajamarca's Plaza de Armas no longer shows any sign of Inca influence. It is a large, shining park and a great place for an afternoon stroll or nap. In the center there is a fountain dating back to 1692 that commemorates Columbus's landing in the Americas. ⊠ *Av. Uma and Arequipa.*

off the
beaten
path

CUMBE MAYO – This pre-Inca archaeological site, 23 km (14 mi) southwest of Cajamarca, was discovered in 1937. The famous Peruvian archaeologist J. C. Tello was the first to study it, and called it one of the most notable aqueducts in the Andes. The site surrounds a large rock outcropping, where you'll find various petroglyphs left by the ancient Cajamarcans. Constructed around 1000 BC, the aqueduct was designed to direct the ample water from the Andes into the drier area of Cajamarca, where there was a large reservoir. There are more than 8 km (5 mi) of the ancient aqueduct still intact. Also at the site you'll find petroglyph-adorned caves. Get here by road or in a fixed tour from Cajamarca. It is also fun to take the 4-hr hike from Cajamarca. There is a signposted road from the bottom of Cerro Santa Apolonia in Cajamarca. Guided tours cost around S/25.

Where to Stay & Eat

¢–$ ✕ **Cascanuez.** The name translates to "Nutcracker," and Sugar Plum Fairies would certainly dance over the desserts here. Choose from a sweet, decadent, and extensive list of homemade pastries, tortes, and other temptations. There is also a small dinner and lunch menu. With Impressionist prints on the wall, there is a certain aesthetic delicacy to this restaurant not often found in Peru's northern highlands eateries. ⊠ *Av. Puga 554* ☎ *076/826–089* ⌨ *no credit cards.*

¢–$ ✕ **El Batán.** The patio dining area of this criollo restaurant has iron chairs and a stone floor. Adding to the casona charm are a stained-glass roof and large shade tree. The menu has a fixed executive lunch that is an excellent value. ⊠ *Jr. Del Batán 369* ☎ *076/826–025* ⌨ *AE, DC, MC, V* ⊙ *Closed Mon.*

★ ¢–$ ✕ **El Querubino.** A tiny, bistro-style eatery just a block from the Plaza de Armas, El Querubino (The Cherub) has monogrammed, pastel-colored plates and Tuscan-yellow walls. The blond-wood tables lend a sense of the "institutional" to the restaurant. Nevertheless, the food is excellent—especially the brochettes and steaks—as is the service. They also have Cajamarca's most extensive wine list. ⊠ *Av. Puga 589* ☎ *076/830–900* ⊟ *AE, DC, MC, V.*

¢–$ ✕ **Restaurant Salas.** Perhaps Cajamarca's most venerable restaurant, Salas has been serving criollo specialties since 1947. The big dining room, with its fluorescent lights and cheap faux-wood chairs, leaves much to be desired, but the food hits an authentic chord with such regional specialties as *cuy* (guinea pig), *perico* (a lake fish), and Spanish-style tortillas. It's on the Plaza de Armas. ⊠ *Av. Puga 637* ☎ *076/822–867* ⊟ *AE, DC, MC, V.*

$$–$$$ ▦ **Hotel Laguna Seca.** Hot-spring pools and aqueducts run throughout
Fodor'sChoice this colonial-style hacienda, which lies just outside of town. The piping
★ hot spring water is pumped into every room, each of which comes with giant tubs big enough for two, prints depicting Peruvian country life, and wood-beam ceilings. The Laguna Seca's grounds are incredible; spring water follows the paths throughout the immaculately maintained gardens, leading you to the hot-spring pools. A bullring and chapel add to the country hacienda flavor. ⊠ *Av. Manco Cápac 1098, Baños del Inca* ☎ *076/894–600* 🖷 *076/894–646* ⊕ *www.lagunaseca.com.pe* ⛫ *25 rooms, 16 suites* ♨ *Restaurant, cafeteria, room service, minibars, cable TV, 3 pools, massage, spa, steam room, bicycles, horseback riding, 2 bars, playground, laundry service, business services, meeting rooms, airport shuttle, travel services, free parking* ⊟ *AE, DC, MC, V.*

★ $$ ▦ **La Posada del Puruay.** A true country hacienda, La Posada del Puruay sits far from the noise and bustle of Cajamarca. Here you'll find extensive gardens, a trout hatchery, and plenty of green hills for horseback riding and hiking. The hacienda was constructed in 1914. The rooms have vaulted wood-beam ceilings; large rosaries adorn the walls. ⊠ *Carretera Porcón Km 4.5* ☎ *01/336–869* 🖷 *076/827–928* ⊕ *www. puruayhotel.com.pe* ⛫ *8 rooms, 6 suites* ♨ *Restaurant, room service, room TVs, in-room VCRs, bicycles, horseback riding, Ping-Pong, soccer, bar, playground, laundry service, meeting rooms, airport shuttle, free parking* ⊟ *AE, DC, MC, V* ⦿ *BP.*

$ ▦ **Hotel El Ingenio.** A giant orange tree stands in the central courtyard of this refurbished hacienda, which has well-manicured garden areas throughout its extensive grounds. There's a large saddle in the lobby, adding to the country ranch feel. The rooms are simply decorated with antique-looking hardwood furniture and large, comfy beds. ⊠ *Av. Vía de Evitamiento 1611–1709* 🖷 *076/827–121 or 01/446–9322* ⊕ *www. iaxis.com.pe/elingenio* ⛫ *24 rooms, 6 suites* ♨ *Restaurant, room service, in-room safes, minibars, cable TV, bar, laundry service, Internet, free parking; no a/c* ⊟ *AE, DC, MC, V* ⦿ *CP.*

¢ ▦ **El Portal del Marques.** Centrally located, this lovely casona is a great value if you want to stay in Cajamarca's downtown area. You'll find simple, clean, affordable rooms and two sunny courtyards. The common areas have a colonial feel, with antique rugs and furniture, while the smallish rooms are more modern. The beds are tiny and quite soft. ⊠ *Jr. de Comercio 664* 🖷 *076/828–464* ⊕ *www.portaldelmarques.com* ⛫ *27 rooms, 3 suites* ♨ *Restaurant, some minibars, cable TV, laundry service, business services, free parking; no a/c* ⊟ *AE, DC, MC, V* ⦿ *CP.*

¢ ▦ **Hostal Portada del Sol.** This slightly run-down casona cum hotel is a decent value for the money. Rooms with beamed ceilings are pleasant despite harsh florescent lighting. Wood floors add a bit of rustic charm. The center courtyard has a stained-glass roof, a nice touch. ⊠ *Jr. Pisagua 731* ☎ *076/823–395 or 01/225–4306* ✑ *portasol@amet.com.pe* ⛫ *18 rooms* ♨ *Restaurant, room service, cable TV, laundry service; no a/c* ⊟ *AE, DC, MC, V* ⦿ *CP.*

Nightlife & the Arts

Los Frailones is the town's best nightspot. This beautifully converted casona has antiques throughout. There is an air of sophistication not often
found in these parts. The waiters dress in monks' robes, adding to the
magic. There are several levels to the house, where you'll find a grill, a
dance area, and a cozy pub. There are often *peñas* on weekends and sometimes during the week. (⊠ Av. Perú 701 ☎ 076/825–113). **Up & Down**
(⊠ Tarapacá 782 ☎ 076/827–876) has a discoteque in the basement, with
overwhelmingly loud salsa and pop music. The middle story has karaoke,
and upstairs is a quiet bar that has live peñas on weekends. **Cowboy Pub**
(⊠ Amalia Puga 298 ☎ 076/971–487) is a roughneck joint popular
with many of the town's miners. **El Muky** (⊠ José Galvez 935 ☎ 076/
699–658) is the best of several discos near Apurima and Avenida Perú.
It has lively dance music and caters to a younger, just-turning-twenty crowd.
Upstairs there is a more relaxed bar that often has live peñas.

The Outdoors

There are a number of hikes in the area around Cajamarca. These will
take you along the rivers of the region, past Inca and pre-Inca ruins. Most
follow the *Capac Ñan* or Royal Inca Road, that went from Cusco all
the way north to Quito. One of the most popular walks is to the pre-
Inca necropolis of **Combayo**. To get to the trailhead, drive 30 km (18
mi) north of the Inca baths along the Chonta River. The hike takes around
four or five hours. The **Ruta del Tambo Inca** takes you to an old Inca
tambo, or resting point. It is difficult to find this trailhead. Go 46 km
(28 mi) from Cajamarca on the road to Hualgayoc. Near Las Lagunas
turn onto a dirt road and follow the road to the milk depository at
Ingatambo. The trail begins from here. The 16-km (10-mi) trip takes about
8 hours. The best time to go trekking is during the dry season, April
through October. **APREC** (Association for the Rescue of the Cajamarcan
Ecosystem) publishes an excellent guide with maps and route descriptions of many other hikes in the region. Their office is in the Hotel Laguna Seca. (⊠ Av. Manco Cápac 1098 ☎ 076/894–600 Ext. 360 ⊕ www.
aprec.org) **Clarin Tours.** (⊠ Jr. Del Batán 161 ☎ 076/826–829) offers trips
to many of the ruins and sites around Cajamarca.

Shopping

A gift shop at the **Casa Luna** sells well-made Peruvian goods. (⊠ 2 de
Mayo 334 ☎ 076/333–072). There are also a few shops around Cajamarca selling artisanal goods. The town of **Llancanora,** 13 km (8 mi) from
the city on the road to Baños del Inca, is famous for making reed bu-
gles. There are several artisanal shops and kiosks around town.

Kuélap

★ ❷ *72 km (45 mi) south of Chachapoyas*

The most impressive archaeological site in the area, the immense pre-
Inca city of Kuélap, is the area's biggest tourist draw, and most visitors
to this region come solely to see the grand city. Little is known about
the people who built it; archaeologists have named them the Chachapoyans or Sachupoyans. They were most likely a warlike people, as the city
of Kuélap is surrounded by a massive defensive wall ranging from 6 to
12 m (20 to 40 ft) high. The Chachapoyans left many cities and fortresses
around the area. In 1472 they were conquered by the Inca Huayna Capac.

A visit to Kuélap is an all-day affair from Chachapoyas. It sits at a dizzying 3,100 m (10,075 ft) above sea level, high above the Río Utcubamba.
The oval-shaped city has more than 400 small, rounded buildings. The
city's stonework, though a bit rougher than that of the Inca, has geo-

metric patterns and designs, adding a flight of fancy to a town seemingly designed for the art of war. There are three entrances into the ruins, and the principal entryway is bordered by high walls—ideal for the town's defense. The most interesting of the rounded buildings has been dubbed El Tintero (The Inkpot). Here you'll find a large underground chamber with a huge pit. Archaeologists hypothesize that the Chachapoyans kept pumas in this pit, dumping human sacrifices into its depths.

It is best to visit Kuélap with a tour group from Chachapoyas. The trip costs around S/35. Vilaya Tours, in the Grand Hotel Vilaya, is highly recommended. Gran Vilaya also arranges tours to the remote ruins of Gran Vilaya, which requires a 31-km (19-mi) hike, and to the Pueblo de Los Muertos, which requires a 23-km (14-mi) hike. Remember to bring a hat for protection from the sun, and to take frequent rests and drink lots of water to avoid altitude sickness. Kuélap is not directly accessible by road, and you will need to walk about 12 km (7½ mi) uphill from the village of Tingo to get there. Ask the locals for directions. ✉ *72 km (45 mi) south of Chachapoyas* ☎ *no phone* ✆ *S/10, S/35 for guided trip from Chachapoyas* ⊗ *Daily 6–6.*

Chachapoyas

④③ *460 km (285 mi) east of Chiclayo*

At the *ceja de la selva* (jungle's eyebrow), Chachapoyas is the capital of Peru's Amazonas department, and is a good jumping-off point for exploring some of Peru's most fascinating and least-visited pre-Inca ruins. The giant fortress at Kuélap, and the ruins of Purunllacta and Gran Vilaya are all easily reached from town. Despite the Amazonas moniker, there is nothing junglelike about the area around Chachapoyas. The surrounding green highlands constitute what most people would call a highland cloud forest. Farther east, in the newly formed department of Loreto (a region won by Peru in the 1942 border dispute with Ecuador), you'll find true jungle. Chachapoyas is difficult to reach by land and most easily accessed from Chiclayo. There are infrequent flights here from Lima as well. Chachapoyas is a sleepy little town of some 20,000 inhabitants. It has a well-preserved colonial center and one small archaeological museum. Shopping options are few, but about 10 km (6 mi) north of Chachapoyas is the tiny pueblo of Huancas, whose citizens are well known for their pottery; this is a good place to buy artisanal goods and locally made ceramics.

The **Iglesia Santa Ana** is the town's oldest church. It was one of Peru's first "Indian churches," though Spaniards and Natives attended mass separately. The church was built in the 17th century and is on a small square of the same name. ✉ *Av. Santa Ana, on Pl. Santa Ana* ⊗ *Daily.*

There is a small display of Chachapoyan ceramics at the **Museo Arqueologico.** Here you will also find a ghoulish display of mummies lying in the fetal position. ✉ *Jr. Ayacucho 904* ☎ *044/777-045* ✆ *Free* ⊗ *Tues.–Sun. 8–1 and 2–4:45.*

There is a natural spring a few blocks west of the Plaza de Armas at the **Pozo de Yanayacu.** They say the spring magically appeared during a visit from Saint Toribio de Mogrovejo. ✉ *Jr. Salamanca, two blocks west of Jr. Puno.*

off the
beaten
path

PURUNLLACTA – About three hours and 35 km (22 mi) southeast of Chachapoyas are the ruins of Purunllacta, with pre-Inca agricultural terraces, dwellings, ceremonial platforms, and roads. The site extends for more than 420 hectares and is a good place for hiking. To get here, take a taxi to the town of Cheto. From the town it is a 1-hr walk uphill to the sight. You'll have to ask people in Cheto exactly how to get here, as it is a little hard to find the trailhead. There is no entrance fee.

Where to Stay & Eat

¢   ✕ **El Tejido.** With big picture windows overlooking the town's Plaza de Armas, this is one of Chacha's toniest eateries. The criollo food is serviceable, and the staff is most attentive when the *dueña* (owner) is around. ✉ *Jr. Grau 534* ☎ *044/777–654* ▭ *no credit cards.*

★ ¢   ✕ **La Tushpa.** Probably the best eatery in town, La Tushpa has good grilled steaks served with homemade *chimichuri* sauce and a variety of pizzas. There's also an on-site bakery. Though it feels a bit institutional, the restaurant is warmer than most in the region, with Andean textiles framed on the walls and an extremely friendly waitstaff. Ask to see the owner's orchard garden, which he keeps above the restaurant. ✉ *Jr. Ortiz Arrieta 753* ☎ *044/777–198* ▭ *no credit cards.*

¢   ✕ **Matalache.** This locally recommended restaurant offers simple, good criollo fare, and a handful of chifa offerings. The brightly lit dining area is typical of the region; pictures of scenic Peru adorn the walls. ✉ *Jr. Ayacucho 616* ☎ *044/778–325* ▭ *no credit cards.*

¢   ▤ **Gran Hotel Vilaya.** A pleasant, but slightly antiseptic hotel in Chacha's city center, the Gran Vilaya has affordable rooms with simple furnishings and wood headboards. The service here is quite friendly, and there is a good in-house travel agency. ✉ *Jr. Ayacucho 755* ☎ *044/777–506* 🖷 *044/778–154* ⊕ *www.vilayatours.com* ⮑ *20 rooms* ♤ *Cafeteria, cable TV, bar, laundry service, airport shuttle, travel services; no a/c, no room phones* ▭ *V* ❘⊙❘ *CP.*

★ ¢   ▤ **Hostal Casa Vieja.** This colorful casona, with its bougainvillea-filled courtyard, pleasant terraces, and overall attention to detail, is Chachapoya's finest. There's a charming salon, with a chimney and upright piano for evening relaxation. The hostal's rooms vary greatly; ask to see a handful before you decide. No. 3, with its large sitting area and chimney, is the nicest. ✉ *Jr. Chincha Alta 569* ☎☎ *044/777–353 or 044/999–282* ⊕ *www.casaviejaperu.com* ⮑ *8 rooms* ♤ *Restaurant, room service, cable TV, laundry service, business services, airport shuttle, travel services; no a/c* ▭ *No credit cards.*

¢   ▤ **Puma Urco.** Simple, clean rooms make this a good budget alternative. Most rooms have large beds with flowers painted over the headboards. However, the walls are paper-thin. ✉ *Jr. Amazonas 883* ☎☎ *044/777–871* 🖉 *pumaurco@peru.com* ⮑ *22 rooms* ♤ *Cafeteria, cable TV, laundry service; no a/c, no room phones* ▭ *no credit cards.*

Nightlife & the Arts

La Reina has a large selection of local *aguardientes* (locally distilled liquors), including *leche* (milk) and *mora* (blackberry). (✉ Jr. Ayacucho 520–727 ☎ 044/777–618). **La Estancia** is a friendly grill and pub. They play mostly American blues, and Johnny, the owner, loves to sit and chat with the customers about the area's history and natural beauty. (✉ Jr. Amazonas 861 ☎ 044/778–432).

THE NORTH COAST & NORTHERN HIGHLANDS A TO Z

To research prices, get advice from other travelers, and book travel arrangements, visit www.fodors.com.

AIR TRAVEL

There are daily flights from Lima to Trujillo, Chiclayo, and Tumbes. There are flights only once or twice a week from Lima to Cajamarca and

Chachapoyas. Huaraz has an airport, but there is no commercial service here. Flights cost around $60 to $100 one-way. Aero Continente is the biggest and best carrier. Tans Perú also serves some cities. Aero Cóndor flies to Cajamarca. Flights to Chachapoyas are infrequent and unreliable. From Lima they charge an airport tax of $4 for national flights and $25 for international flights

🏠 Carriers **Aero Continente** ☎ 01/242-4242 in Lima, 044/244-042 in Trujillo, 074/229-916 in Chiclayo, 073/325-635 in Piura, 072/523-892 in Tumbes, 877/359-7378 in the U.S. **Tans Perú** ☎ 044/290-005 in Trujillo, 074/226-546 in Chiclayo, 073/302-432 in Piura. **Aero Cóndor** ☎ 044/255-212 in Trujillo, 076/822-813 in Cajamarca.

AIRPORTS

There are airports in Trujillo, Chiclayo, Piura, Tumbes, Cajamarca, and Chachapoyas.

🏠 Airport Information **Carlos Martínez de Pinillos, Trujillo** ☎ 044/464-013. **Aeropuerto Internacional José Abelardo Quiñones Gonzales, Chiclayo** ☎ 074/233-192. **Aeropuerto de Piura** ☎ 073/325-635. **Aeropuerto de Tumbes Pedro Canga** ☎ 072/525-102. **Aeropuerto de Cajamarca** ☎ 076/822-813.

BORDER CROSSINGS

The best way to cross into Ecuador is via Tumbes. You will need your passport to cross the border into Ecuador. American citizens do not need a special visa to enter the country, nor do they pay an entry fee, though these rules change often; check with the Ecuadorian Embassy before making the border crossing. To get to the border from Tumbes, you will need to take a taxi or minibus 27 km (17 mi) north. Many robberies have been reported in the area, so watch your belongings carefully. Check with the **Oficina de Migracíon** (☎ 074/523-422) for up-to-date information.

BUS TRAVEL

Bus service throughout the coastal area and highlands is generally quite good. There are frequent departures from all the cities along the north coast and to Huaraz and Cajamarca. Getting to Chachapoyas is difficult (10–12 hours) and best done by direct bus from Chiclayo. Most larger cities have terminals, while the smaller towns have none. From the smaller towns, like Barranca and Casma, you just hail a bus from the Pan-American. Emtrafesa runs all the way up the coast. It is a 3- to 4-hr trip between most cities. Ormeño also runs the whole coast. Other reputable companies include Cruz del Sur and Oltursa. Tepsa uses old Greyhound buses—often called the "dirty dog"—and is probably the least desirable of all the bus lines.

🏠 Bus Information **Cruz del Sur** ✉ Jr. Quilca 531, in Lima ☎ 01/424-1005 in Lima, 044/261-802 in Trujillo, 074/225-058 in Chiclayo, 076/822-488 in Cajamarca. **Emtrafesa** ✉ Av. Miraflores 127, Trujillo ☎ 044/243-981 in Trujillo, ✉ Av. Colón at Av. Bolognesi, Chiclayo ☎ 074/234-291 in Chiclayo. **Expreso Cruz del Sur** ✉ Av. del Ejército 285, Trujillo ☎ 044/26-1801. **Expreso de Chiclayo** ✉ Grau 653, Lima ☎ 01/428-5072 in Lima, 074/233-071 in Chiclayo. **Oltursa** ✉ Av. del Ejército 342, Trujillo ☎ 044/263-055. **Ormeño** ✉ Javier Prado Este 1059, Lima ✉ Carlos Zavala 177, Lima ☎ 01/427-5679 in Lima, 044/259-782 in Trujillo, 076/829-889 in Cajamarca. **Tepsa** ✉ Paseo de la República 129, Lima ☎ 01/427-5642 in Lima, 044/205-017 in Trujillo, 074/234-421 in Chiclayo, 076/823-306 in Cajamarca.

CAR RENTAL

There are no major car rental agencies in the North, though you'll find reputable smaller ones in Trujillo, Chiclayo, and Huaraz.

🏠 Agencies **Avisacar** ✉ Av. San Martí de Porras 254, San Andres, Trujillo ☎ 044/204-170. **Rent-a-Car Trujillo** ✉ Fernando La Carrera 1080, Urb. La Merced, Trujillo ☎ 044/220-176. **Chiclayo Rent-a-Car** ✉ Av. Federico Villarreal 115, Gran Hotel Chiclayo, Chiclayo ☎ 074/237-512. **Monte Rosa** ✉ Jr. José de la Mar 691, Huaraz ☎ 044/721-447.

CAR TRAVEL

The major highway that serves the north coast is the Pan-American Highway. You will take Highway 109 to Huaraz and Highway 8 to Cajamarca. Think twice before renting a car to see the archaeological sites; some are isolated, and it's easy to get lost on the unnamed little back roads. Hiring a driver or going with a tour company is an efficient way to see the ruins throughout the north coast. Roads in the northern highlands are always in some state of disrepair, so it's wiser to travel by air or bus to get to these regions.

EMERGENCIES

iPerú has a 24-hr emergency hot line. In smaller towns and in the wilderness you will probably need to arrange for transportation to the nearest large town in case of an emergency.

🔂 Emergency Services **General emergency** ☎ 105 throughout Peru. **Police** ☎ 044/233-181 in Trujillo, 072/523-535 in Tumbes, 044/271-461 in Huaraz, 076/825-572 in Cajamarca, 044/777-176 in Chachapoyas. **Tourist Police** ☎ 044/224-025 in Trujillo, 074/236-700 in Chiclayo, 044/721-341 in Huaraz, 076/823-042 in Cajamarca. **iPerú** ☎ 01/574-8000 in Lima, 0800/42-579 throughout Peru. **High Altitude Rescue** ☎ 044/793-327 or 044/793-291 in Huaraz.

🔂 Hospitals **Belén Hospital of Trujillo** ⊠ Bolívar 350 ☎ 044/245-281. **Clinica del Pacifico** ⊠ Av. José Leonardo Ortiz 420 Chiclayo ☎ 074/233-705. **Hospital Cayetano Heredia** ⊠ Av. Independencia s/n, Urb. Miraflores Piura ☎ 073/303-208. **Ministerio de Salud Hospital** ⊠ Av. 14 de Junio 556 Tumbes ☎ 072/521-703. **Hospital Victor Ramos Guardia** ⊠ Av. Luzuriaga, Cuadra 8 Huaraz ☎ 044/721-861. **Hospital de Cajamarca** ☎ 076/822-557. **Hospital Chachapoyas** ⊠ Jr. Triunfo, Cuadra 3 Chachapoyas ☎ 044/777-354.

🔂 Pharmacy **Boticas Fasa** ⊠ Jr. Pizarro 512 Trujillo ☎ 044/899-028. **Max Salud** ⊠ Corner 7 de Enero and Bolognesi Chiclayo ☎ 074/226-215.

ENGLISH-LANGUAGE MEDIA

In Trujillo, Libreria Peruana is open daily 9–1 and 4:30–9.

🔂 Bookstores **Libreria Peruana** ⊠ Jr. Pizarro 505, Trujillo ☎ 044/232-521.

MAIL & SHIPPING

Mail can be sent or received at the post office, often called *correos* or *Serpost*. The post office is normally found in the center of town near the Plaza de Armas. Do not send important packages via Peruvian mail. DHL in Trujillo has a reliable service for important correspondence. The post offices are open during regular business hours. There are Internet cafés in almost every town along the coast and in the larger cities of the northern highlands.

🔂 Post Offices ⊠ Av. Independencia 286, Trujillo ☎ 044/245-941. ⊠ Elías Aguirre 140, Chiclayo ☎ 074/237-031. ⊠ San Martín 208, Tumbes. ⊠ Av. Luzuriaga 702, Huaraz ☎ 044/721-030. ⊠ Jr. Amazonas 443, Cajamarca. ⊠ Jr. Grau 553, Chachapoyas.

🔂 Shipping Services **DHL** ⊠ Av. Pizarro 318, Trujillo ☎ 044/233-630.

🔂 Internet Café **Power Net** ⊠ Jr. Pizarro 107 Trujillo ☎ 044/206-957.

MONEY MATTERS

Banks in the North are usually open weekdays 9–1 and 4–6:30 and Saturday 9–noon. Exchanging money in the colonial cities of Trujillo and Cajamarca can be fun, as the banks are in restored casonas. There are ATMs in almost every town except for small hamlets. The ATMs generally accept only Visa. You can normally get cash advances with American Express and MasterCard inside banks. Avoid the many money exchangers on the streets, who often pass counterfeit bills.

🔂 Banks **Banco Wiese** ⊠ Pizarro 314, Trujillo ☎ 044/256-600. **Banco de Crédito** ⊠ Av. Balta 630, Chiclayo ☎ 074/235-501. **Banco de Crédito** ⊠ Jr. J. de Sucre and Av. Luzuriaga, Huaraz. **Banco de Crédito** ⊠ Del Comercio 679, Cajamarca ☎ 076/822-680. **Banco de Crédito** ⊠ Jr. Ortiz Arrieta 580, Chachapoyas.

TELEPHONES

National or international calls can be made from from public phones using either coins or phone cards. In most cities you can also use the central office of Telefónica del Peru. Calling via Internet saves you big bucks, but it is often hard to hear and there is a long delay.

🛈 **Telefónica del Peru** ✉ Av. Bolívar 658, Trujillo ✉ Elias Aguirre 447, Chiclayo ✉ Corner Av. Simon Bolívar and J. de Sucre, Huaraz. **Telenet Center** ✉ Jr. Amazonas 676, Cajamarca.

TOURS

Condor Travel and Guía Tours both organize tours to the ruins around Trujillo. Sipán Tours is one of Chiclayo's best tour companies for trips to the Tomb of Señor Sipán. There are many tour companies in Huaraz; Monttrek is among the best, offering trips to the surrounding mountains and arranging rafting, trekking, and mountain-climbing expeditions. Clarin Tours is said to be one of Cajamarca's best, as is Chachapoya's Vilaya Tours.

🛈 **Clarin Tours** ✉ Del Batán 161, Cajamarca ☎ 076/826-829 **Vilaya Tours** ✉ Jr. Ayacucho 624, Chachapoyas ☎ 044/777-506 ⊕ www.vilayatours.com.

Sipán Tours ✉ 7 de Enero 772, Chiclayo ☎ 074/229-053. **Monte Rosa** ✉ Jr. Jose de la Mar 691, Huaraz ☎ 044/721-447 ⊕ www.andes.moto_sport.de. **Monttrek** ✉ Av. Luzuriaga 646, upstairs, Huaraz ☎ 044/721-124 ⊕ www.monttrek.com **Sechin Tours** ✉ Av. Luzuriaga 772, Huaraz ☎ 044/721-557 ⊕ www.huaraz.net/sechintours. **Piura Tours** ✉ Jr. Ayacucho 585, Piura ☎ 073/326-778. **Condor Travel** ✉ Jr. Independencia 553, Trujillo ☎ 044/254-763. **Guía Tours** ✉ Jr. Independencia 580, Trujillo ☎ 044/256-553 ⊕ www.geocities.com/guia_tours. **Trujillo Tours** ✉ Diego de Almagro 301, Trujillo ☎ 044/257-518. **Preference Tours** ✉ Calle Grau 427, Tumbes ☎ 072/524-757.

TRANSPORTATION AROUND THE NORTH COAST & NORTHERN HIGHLANDS

The easiest way to get around the north coast and northern highlands is by plane and bus. You will want to fly to the more out-of-the-way destinations like Cajamarca and Tumbes to save time. Within the cities it is easy to hail cabs or mototaxis, which cost around S/2 and S/1, respectively, within the city centers. To visit the ruins or wilderness around your destination it is easiest to go with a guided tour. More adventurous travelers can rent cars in major cities, heading out on their own, though know that it is quite easy to get lost.

Taxi rides in town centers should cost around 2 nueva soles; rates go up late at night. A longer ride to the suburbs or town environs will cost from 5 to 10 nueva soles. Negotiate the price with the cabbie before you head off.

VISITOR INFORMATION

Most larger towns will have an iPerú or Mitinci tourist information office. These offices have informative maps and guides, will help you arrange accommodations, and will point out good local restaurants and attractions.

🛈 Tourist Information **iPerú** ☎ 01/574-8000 in Lima, 0800/42-579 throughout Peru ✉ Jr. Independencia 630, Trujillo ☎ 044/224-025 ✉ Av. Sáenz Peña 830, Chiclayo ☎ 074/236-700 ✉ Av. Laredo 716, Huaraz ☎ 044/721-341 ✉ Av. 13 de Julio s/n, Cajamarca ☎ 076/823-042. **Mitinci** ✉ Jr. Ortiz Arrieta 1250, Chachapoyas ☎ 044/778-355. **General information** ✉ Av. Ayacucho 733, Piura ☎ 073/303-208 ✉ Centro Civico, 2nd floor, 204, Tumbes ☎ 052/523-699.

UNDERSTANDING PERU

CHRONOLOGY

VOCABULARY

CHRONOLOGY

About ten thousand years ago, a group of hunters and gatherers crossed the natural land bridge (Panama) between North and South America into what is now Colombia, gradually working their way southwest along the Pacific coast. They discovered the fertile river valleys of what was to become northern Peru, and as early as 2500 BC these hunters and gatherers had settled permanently in the area. They formed small villages, building houses out of sand and mud bricks and feeding their families by fishing and farming.

AD 1531 Fueled by stories of the great wealth of the Inca Empire, Francisco Pizarro and his entourage arrive in northern Peru (Cajamarca), easily capturing the great Inca, Atahualpa, devastating his army, and causing the collapse of the Empire, already weakened by a bloody civil war between the half-brothers Atahualpa, ruler of the north, and Huáar, ruler of Cusco.

1532–33 Atahualpa bargains for his release by ordering that tons of gold from all over the empire be delivered to Pizarro, who has Atahualpa killed anyway and keeps the ransom for himself and his men, giving none to his fellow conquistador, Diego de Almagro, igniting a civil war that eventually costs both men their lives. The sacking and burning of the great Inca capital of Cusco is the final death knell for the great Inca Empire.

1535 Lima is founded on January 18 at the mouth of the Rímac River and becomes the most important viceroyal capital in Spanish America. It is widely known for its regal splendor.

1536 Manco Inca leads an uprising of the natives which is easily put down, only to be followed by skirmishes between the Spanish Pizarro group and the Almargo group in Cusco.

1538 Spanish conquistador Diego de Almagro challenges Pizarro's control of Cusco; Pizarro orders him executed.

1541 Francisco Pizarro is assassinated in Lima by supporters of Diego de Almagro, sparking a long period of unrest; Spain sends more viceroys to impose order.

1542 Spain tries to repeal a decree allowing the colonists to virtually enslave the indigenous peoples in return for protecting and christianizing them. Spain views the policy as a threat, fearing the colonists are creating an elite Andes colony to challenge the crown's authority.

1544 Gonzalo Pizarro, brother of the assassinated Francisco Pizarro, assumes control of Peru, but his brutal rule causes Spain to send another representative, Pedro de la Gasca, to restore the crown's authority. Gasca executes Gonzalo Pizarro in 1548 and ends the threat of a civil war.

1555 Prosperity and calm descend on Peru, and immigrants (including slaves) start arriving from Spain, Portugal, and Italy. By now Peru is keeping Spain financially afloat, supplying two-thirds of the silver Spain needs. Peru's arts flourish between 1555 and 1700.

1572 Spain mounts one last campaign to rid the country of the last reigning Inca, Túpac Amaru, who had escaped to an Inca stronghold in

Vilcabamba, west of Machu Picchu. Túpac Amaru is captured, tried, and beheaded in a public ceremony in Cusco, putting a final, tragic touch to the great Inca Empire that existed for just one century.

1578   Spain's "ownership" of the seas goes unchallenged until 1578, when Sir Francis Drake and his galleon appear, but it is the Dutch who try to take over Lima and also Arica (now a part of Chile), with plans to take possession of Potosí (now part of Bolivia) and its silver mines.

1746   A devastating earthquake destroys 80 percent of the city of Lima, including important monuments, and Peru starts on a course of gradual decline. Uprisings by native Americans increase, owing to a scarcity of land created by illegal purchases by colonists; higher taxes levied on them by Spain; and mistreatment, even by some of their own people, who have managed to achieve a higher status and acceptance by the "elite."

1780   Uprisings and protests end when José Gabriel Condorcanqui, a wealthy mestizo with Inca ancestors, captures an official near Cusco and executes him. Condorcanqui raises an army, intent on returning Peru to its Inca past, and calls himself Túpac Amaru II. He is captured by royalist forces and executed. His brother continues the rebellion until 1782, when the royal bureaucracy finally agrees to carry out reforms.

1821–24   José San Martín, the son of a Spanish army officer stationed in Argentina, rides into Peru in 1821 after liberating Argentina and Chile; he declares Peru independent, and is named protector by an assembly of notables. However, the campaign to free Peru is stalled. A meeting is set up in Guayaquil between San Martín and Simón Bolívar Palacios, the liberator of Columbia and Venezuela, to come up with a plan to complete the liberation of Peru. Bolívar agrees to help, but insists on all the credit. San Martín abandons the talks and leaves for France. Bolívar, along with the help of San Martín's forces, rides into Peru and wins the Battle of Junín in August 1824, and his lieutenant defeats royalist forces at Ayacucho December 9, 1824. Spanish colonial rule is finally ended.

1824   Peru as a country is liberated, but for the majority of the people, independence means nothing more than changing one oppressive regime for another. Bolívar struggles to set up a liberal government, but returns to Colombia in 1826, leaving the country wide open for a succession of strongmen.

1845   General Marshal Ramón Castilla takes over the leadership of Peru, setting the country on a course of economic growth by expanding exports, especially fertilizer from guano (bird droppings) on the Chincha (Ballestas) Islands. Castilla abolishes the last vestiges of slavery, modernizes the army, and centralizes state power. Along with Peru's new economic wealth comes the ability to get large foreign loans, secured by guano deposits, which, however, are being rapidly depleted.

1860   Foreign loans finance highway and railroad expansion with U.S. railroad engineer Henry Meiggs, called the "Yankee Pizarro," bringing in thousands of Chinese "coolies" to do the work, all contributing to Peru's becoming the number one borrower on the London exchange. Plunging Peru even deeper into debt is the start of two wars, one with Ecuador over land along the Amazon and one in 1866 when Spain tries to seize control of the Chincha (Ballestas) islands and its guano.

1872   Manuel Pardo, Peru's first elected civilian president, assumes office just as Peru is having its worst financial crisis.

1876   Peru, defaulting on its foreign debts, elects as president a military man, Mariano Ignacio Pardo, who had led them against a naval attack by Spain.

1879–83   Bolivia raises taxes on the export of nitrates, breaking a treaty signed with Chile in 1866. This sparks the War of the Pacific over the disputed nitrate-rich Atacama Desert. Because of an alliance between Bolivia and Peru, President Pardo leads Peru into the war with Chile and loses two iron ships, giving Chile control of the sea lanes. The war ends in 1883 with the signing of the Treaty of Ancón, with Chile keeping the nitrate-rich province of Tarapacá and the provinces of Tacna and Arica remaining in Chilean possession for 10 years.

1886–95   General Andrés Avelina Cáceres, a hero during the Chilean occupation in the War of the Pacific, is elected president and brings peace to the country after quashing a native rebellion. He sets Peru on the way to economic recovery by signing a contract with British bondholders to cancel Peru's debt, and in return, giving them the right to operate the railroad system for 66 years. Silver production improves, the United States ups its investments, and Peru remains stable until 1895.

1911   Hiram Bingham, a Yale historian, discovers Machu Picchu, an Inca city hidden in a valley for centuries from all but farmers in the area.

1895–1912   After the Pacific War an elite group of business and anti-military men called Civilistas take control, starting an era of political stability and economic growth. "Free" elections are held, but the group has strict rules for candidates, based on property and literacy qualifications, thereby controlling the presidency.

1914   Colonel Oscar Raimundo Benavides seizes control of the presidency. World War I begins, and Peru's international markets collapse and social unrest intensifies as the cost of living doubles, seriously affecting new working classes. Colonel Benavides is uncomfortable with his political role and arranges elections to bring a nonmilitary man, José de Pardo y Barreda, to power. Turmoil and unrest continue. There is no stopping new social, economic, and intellectual trends and the resulting wave of strikes, bringing on a generation of radical reformers and the emerging middle and working classes.

1919–30   Former president Augusto B. Leguía y Salcedo, who left his party after his first term, runs again as an independent promising to carry out social and economic reforms. He uncovers a plot by his former party to keep him from office, stages a coup, assumes the presidency, and rules Peru for 11 years. Under pressure, Leguía signs a treaty settling a border dispute with Colombia over rubber trees, resulting in Peru's losing territory to Colombia. During his term, Leguía carries out some reforms but loses popularity with his dictatorial ways, widespread corruption, and buildup of foreign debt. Peru's military again intervenes and Leguía dies in jail. The worldwide depression following the stock-market crash in 1929 has little effect on Peru, thanks to its large exports of cotton and industrial metals.

1929   After intervention from the United States, the province of Tacna is returned to Peru.

1931–32   Lt. Col. Luis M. Sánchez Cerro, who helped oust Leguía from power, is elected president, defeating Haya de la Torre, organizer of APRA

(American Popular Revolutionary Alliance), founded in Mexico in 1924. APRA stages a bloody rebellion in Trujillo, but is defeated when the military uses aerial bombing for the first time in South America. Peru hires a financial consultant from the United States to recommend reforms, and following his advice returns to the gold standard, declares a moratorium on its US$180 million debt, and is barred from the United States capital market for 30 years.

1933–45 President Sánchez Cerro is assassinated by an APRA member in 1933. Congress elects former president Benavides to complete his term, which Benavides extends until 1939, when Manuel Prado y Ugarteche, a Lima banker and son of a former president, wins the presidency. The Peruvian army quickly defeats the Ecuadorian army in a border conflict in 1941, and in 1942 Peru's ownership of the area is affirmed by peace negotiations in Rio de Janeiro. After 13 years underground, APRA moderates its views and Prado legalizes the party in May 1945.

1945–84 Through resignations, elections, broken promises, and coups, the presidency keeps changing hands and another problem surfaces: widespread cocaine use in the United States and Europe along with use by peasants in the Andes allows Peru and Bolivia to become the largest coca producers in the world. Economic conditions worsen, but democracy survives, although with a swing to the left with the election of APRA candidate Alan García Pérez. He wins on the promise of bringing social change and improving conditions in impoverished areas, objectives that also lead in 1980 to the founding of the terrorist group the Shining Path (Sendero Luminoso), by the philosophy professor Abimáel Guzmán Reynoso. The group causes the deaths of thousands of Peruvians. Reynoso is captured and jailed in 1992.

1990–99 Alberto Fujimori, son of Japanese immigrants, is elected president for a five-year term, defeating Peru's famous novelist Mario Vargas Llosa. He dissolves congress, suspends the constitution, and imposes censorship in 1992, citing continuing problems with drug trafficking, corruption, and terrorism. A new constitution is approved in 1993. Fighting erupts again in a continuing Peru/Ecuador border dispute and Fujimori is reelected. Peru and Ecuador sign another treaty in May 1999 to end the 60-year dispute over Amazon territory.

2000 Fujimori is reelected to a third five year term despite the discovery of thousands of ballots that had been marked for Fujimori before elections had even begun. His intelligence chief, Vladimiro Montesinos, is videotaped bribing a congressman; Fujimori calls for new elections and announces the dismantling of the National Intelligence Service, accused of human rights violations. He leaves for Japan and upon arrival shocks the world by resigning the presidency. It is discovered that he secretly holds Japanese citizenship, which prevents him from being extradited to face charges for corruption and bribery.

2001 Alejandro Toledo, born in 1946 to a peasant family in northern Peru, is elected president, promising that one of his priorities is easing the poverty still gripping the nation. Peruvians, ever optimistic, stand firmly behind the former shoeshine boy. Many say his decision to be sworn in at Machu Picchu signals his commitment to the country's past as well as the present.

2002 Toledo's presidential win turns out to be the easy part, as he's unable to come through on his "pie in the sky" election promises in a country where 55 percent of the 26-million-person population lives in poverty. His approval rating plunges from 60 percent to 15.7 percent and protests escalate over his state privatization plans.

2003   Peru's economic woes continue, but peace with Ecuador, brought about by a 1998 treaty that ended border wars between the two countries, literally reaches new heights: Toledo and Ecuador's president, Lucio Gutierrez, inaugurate a $1.8-million bridge spanning the Canchis River near the Peruvian town of Namballe, 500 miles northeast of Lima. Ecuadorean boats gain access to the Amazon River and its tributaries, while Ecuador agrees to give up its claim to a swath of Peruvian-controlled Amazon. As a symbol of the Peru–Ecuador peace agreement, Peru chooses the Spondylus shell of the thorny oyster that grows only along the Ecuadorian coast.

SPANISH VOCABULARY

English	Spanish	Pronunciation

Basics

English	Spanish	Pronunciation
Yes/no	Sí/no	see/no
Please	Por favor	pore fah-**vore**
May I?	¿Me permite?	may pair-**mee**-tay
Thank you (very much)	(Muchas) gracias	(**moo**-chas) **grah**-see-as
You're welcome	De nada	day **nah**-dah
Excuse me	Con permiso	con pair-**mee**-so
Pardon me	¿Perdón?	pair-**dohn**
Could you tell me?	¿Podría decirme?	po-dree-ah deh-**seer**-meh
I'm sorry	Lo siento	lo see-**en**-to
Good morning!	¡Buenos días!	**bway**-nohs **dee**-ahs
Good afternoon!	¡Buenas tardes!	**bway**-nahs **tar**-dess
Good evening!	¡Buenas noches!	**bway**-nahs **no**-chess
Goodbye!	¡Adiós!/¡Hasta luego!	ah-dee-**ohss/ah**-stah-**lwe**-go
Mr./Mrs.	Señor/Señora	sen-**yor**/sen-**yohr**-ah
Miss	Señorita	sen-yo-**ree**-tah
Pleased to meet you	Mucho gusto	**moo**-cho **goose**-to
How are you?	¿Cómo está usted?	**ko**-mo es-**tah** oo-**sted**
Very well, thank you.	Muy bien, gracias.	**moo**-ee bee-**en**, **grah**-see-as
And you?	¿Y usted?	ee oos-**ted**
Hello (on the telephone)	Diga	**dee**-gah

Numbers

1	un, uno	oon, **oo**-no
2	dos	dos
3	tres	tress
4	cuatro	**kwah**-tro
5	cinco	**sink**-oh
6	seis	saice
7	siete	see-**et**-eh
8	ocho	**o**-cho
9	nueve	new-**eh**-vey
10	diez	dee-**es**
11	once	**ohn**-seh
12	doce	**doh**-seh
13	trece	**treh**-seh
14	catorce	ka-**tohr**-seh
15	quince	**keen**-seh

16	dieciséis	dee-**es**-ee-**saice**
17	diecisiete	dee-**es**-ee-**see-et**-eh
18	dieciocho	dee-**es**-ee-**o**-cho
19	diecinueve	dee-**es**-ee-new-**ev**-ah
20	veinte	**vain**-teh
21	veinte y uno/veintiuno	**vain**-te-**oo**-noh
30	treinta	**train**-tah
32	treinta y dos	train-tay-**dohs**
40	cuarenta	kwah-**ren**-tah
43	cuarenta y tres	kwah-**ren**-tay-**tress**
50	cincuenta	seen-**kwen**-tah
54	cincuenta y cuatro	seen-**kwen**-tay kwah-tro
60	sesenta	sess-en-tah
65	sesenta y cinco	sess-en-tay seen-ko
70	setenta	set-**en**-tah
76	setenta y seis	set-**en**-tay **saice**
80	ochenta	oh-**chen**-tah
87	ochenta y siete	oh-**chen**-tay see-**yet**-eh
90	noventa	no-**ven**-tah
98	noventa y ocho	no-**ven**-tah-o-choh
100	cien	see-en
101	ciento uno	see-**en**-toh **oo**-noh
200	doscientos	doh-see-**en**-tohss
500	quinientos	keen-**yen**-tohss
700	setecientos	set-eh-see-**en**-tohss
900	novecientos	no-veh-see-**en**-tohss
1,000	mil	meel
2,000	dos mil	dohs meel
1,000,000	un millón	oon meel-**yohn**

Colors

black	negro	**neh**-groh
blue	azul	ah-**sool**
brown	café	kah **feh**
green	verde	**ver**-deh
pink	rosa	**ro**-sah
purple	morado	mo-**rah**-doh
orange	naranja	na-**rahn**-hah
red	rojo	**roh**-hoh
white	blanco	**blahn**-koh
yellow	amarillo	ah-mah-**ree**-yoh

Days of the Week

Sunday	domingo	doe-**meen**-goh
Monday	lunes	**loo**-ness
Tuesday	martes	**mahr**-tess
Wednesday	miércoles	me-**air**-koh-less
Thursday	jueves	hoo-**ev**-ess
Friday	viernes	vee-**air**-ness
Saturday	sábado	**sah**-bah-doh

Months

January	enero	eh-**neh**-roh
February	febrero	feh-**breh**-roh
March	marzo	**mahr**-soh
April	abril	ah-**breel**
May	mayo	**my**-oh
June	junio	**hoo**-nee-oh
July	julio	**hoo**-lee-yoh
August	agosto	ah-**ghost**-toh
September	septiembre	sep-tee-**em**-breh
October	octubre	oak-**too**-breh
November	noviembre	no-vee-**em**-breh
December	diciembre	dee-see-**em**-breh

Useful Phrases

Do you speak English?	¿Habla usted inglés?	**ah**-blah oos-**ted** in-**glehs**
I don't speak Spanish	No hablo español	no **ah**-bloh es-pahn-**yol**
I don't understand (you)	No entiendo	no en-tee-**en**-doh
I understand (you)	Entiendo	en-tee-**en**-doh
I don't know	No sé	no seh
I am American/ British	Soy americano (americana)/ inglés(a)	soy ah-meh-ree-**kah**-no (ah-meh-ree-**kah**-nah)/ in-**glehs** (ah)
What's your name?	¿Cómo se llama usted?	koh-mo seh **yah**-mah oos-**ted**
My name is . . .	Me llamo . . .	may **yah**-moh
What time is it?	¿Qué hora es?	keh **o**-rah es
It is one, two, three . . . o'clock.	Es la una. . . . Son las dos, tres	es la **oo**-nah/sohn lahs dohs, tress
Yes, please/No, thank you	Sí, por favor/No, gracias	**see** pohr fah-**vor**/no **grah**-see-us
How?	¿Cómo?	**koh**-mo
When?	¿Cuándo?	**kwahn**-doh
This/Next week	Esta semana/ la semana que entra	**es**-teh seh-**mah**-nah/lah seh-**mah**-nah keh **en**-trah
This/Next month	Este mes/el próximo mes	**es**-teh mehs/el **proke**-see-mo mehs
This/Next year	Este año/el año que viene	**es**-teh **ahn**-yo/el **ahn**-yo keh vee-**yen**-ay
Yesterday/today/ tomorrow	Ayer/hoy/mañana	ah-**yehr**/oy/mahn-**yah**-nah
This morning/ afternoon	Esta mañana/ tarde	**es**-tah mahn-**yah**-nah/**tar**-deh
Tonight	Esta noche	**es**-tah **no**-cheh
What?	¿Qué?	keh
What is it?	¿Qué es esto?	keh es **es**-toh

Why?	¿Por qué?	pore **keh**
Who?	¿Quién?	kee-**yen**
Where is . . . ?	¿Dónde está . . . ?	**dohn**-deh es-**tah**
the train station?	la estación del tren?	la es-tah-see-**on** del **train**
the subway station?	la estación del Tren subterráneo?	la es-ta-see-**on** del trehn soob-tair-**ron**-a-o
the bus stop?	la parada del autobus?	la pah-**rah**-dah del oh-toh-**boos**
the post office?	la oficina de correos?	la oh-fee-**see**-nah deh koh-**reh**-os
the bank?	el banco?	el **bahn**-koh
the hotel?	el hotel?	el oh-**tel**
the store?	la tienda?	la tee-**en**-dah
the cashier?	la caja?	la **kah**-hah
the museum?	el museo?	el moo-**seh**-oh
the hospital?	el hospital?	el ohss-pee-**tal**
the elevator?	el ascensor?	el ah-**sen**-sohr
the bathroom?	el baño?	el **bahn**-yoh
Here/there	Aquí/allá	ah-**key**/ah-**yah**
Open/closed	Abierto/cerrado	ah-bee-**er**-toh/ ser-**ah**-doh
Left/right	Izquierda/derecha	iss-key-**er**-dah/ dare-**eh**-chah
Straight ahead	Derecho	dare-**eh**-choh
Is it near/far?	¿Está cerca/lejos?	es-**tah** sehr-kah/ **leh**-hoss
I'd like . . .	Quisiera . . .	kee-see-**ehr**-ah
a room	un cuarto/una habitación	oon **kwahr**-toh/ **oo**-nah ah-bee-tah-see-**on**
the key	la llave	lah **yah**-veh
a newspaper	un periódico	oon pehr-ee-**oh**-dee-koh
a stamp	un sello de correo	oon **seh**-yo deh koh-**reh**-oh
I'd like to buy . . .	Quisiera comprar . . .	kee-see-**ehr** ah kohm-**prahr**
cigarettes	cigarrillos	ce-ga-**ree**-yohs
matches	cerillos	ser-**ee**-ohs
a dictionary	un diccionario	oon deek-see-oh-**nah**-ree-oh
soap	jabón	hah-**bohn**
sunglasses	gafas de sol	**ga**-fahs deh sohl
suntan lotion	loción bronceadora	loh-see-**ohn** brohn-seh-ah-**do**-rah
a map	un mapa	oon **mah** pah
a magazine	una revista	**oon**-ah reh-**veess**-tah
paper	papel	pah-**pel**
envelopes	sobres	so-**brehs**
a postcard	una tarjeta postal	**oon**-ah tar-**het**-ah post-**ahl**
How much is it?	¿Cuánto cuesta?	**kwahn**-toh **kwes**-tah

It's expensive/ cheap	Está caro/barato	es-**tah kah**-roh/ bah-**rah**-toh
A little/a lot	Un poquito/ mucho	oon poh-**kee**-toh/ **moo**-choh
More/less	Más/menos	mahss/**men**-ohss
Enough/too much/too little	Suficiente/ demasiado/ muy poco	soo-fee-see-**en**-teh/ deh-mah-see-**ah**-doh/**moo**-ee poh-koh
Telephone	Teléfono	tel-**ef**-oh-no
Telegram	Telegrama	teh-leh-**grah**-mah
I am ill	Estoy enfermo(a)	es-**toy** en-**fehr**-moh(mah)
Please call a doctor	Por favor llame a un medico	pohr fah-**vor ya**-meh ah oon **med**-ee-koh

On the Road

Avenue	Avenida	ah-ven-**ee**-dah
Broad, tree-lined boulevard	Bulevar	boo-leh-**var**
Fertile plain	Vega	**veh**-gah
Highway	Carretera	car-reh-**ter**-ah
Mountain pass, Street	Puerto Calle	poo-**ehr**-toh **cah**-yeh
Waterfront promenade	Rambla	**rahm**-blah
Wharf	Embarcadero	em-bar-cah-**deh**-ro

In Town

Cathedral	Catedral	cah-teh-**dral**
Church	Templo/Iglesia	**tem**-plo/ee-**glehs**-see-ah
City hall	Casa de gobierno	kah-sah deh go-bee-**ehr**-no
Door, gate	Puerta portón	poo-**ehr**-tah por-**ton**
Entrance/exit	Entrada/salida	en-**trah**-dah/sah-**lee**-dah
Inn, rustic bar, or restaurant	Taverna	tah-**vehr**-nah
Main square	Plaza principal	plah-thah prin-see-**pahl**
Market	Mercado	mer-**kah**-doh
Neighborhood	Barrio	**bahr**-ree-o
Traffic circle	Glorieta	glor-ee-**eh**-tah
Wine cellar, wine bar, or wine shop	Bodega	boh-**deh**-gah

Dining Out

Can you recommend a good restaurant?	¿Puede recomendarme un buen restaurante?	**pweh**-deh rreh-koh-mehn-**dahr**-me oon bwehn rrehs-tow-**rahn**-teh?

I want a(n) . . .	Quiero un	**kyeh**-roh oon rrehs-
restaurant.	restaurante	tow-**rahn**-teh
typical	típico.	**tee**-pee-koh
international	internacional.	een-tehr-nah-syoh-**nahl**
inexpensive	no muy caro.	noh muee **kah**-roh
very good	muy bueno.	muee **bweh**-noh
Is that restaurant expensive?	¿Es caro ese restaurante?	ehs **kah**-roh eh-seh rrehs-tow-**rahn**-teh?
What's the name of the restaurant?	¿Cómo se llama el restaurante?	**koh**-moh seh **yah**-mah ehl rrehs-tow-**rahn**-teh?
Where is it located?	¿Dónde está situado?	**dohn**-deh ehs-**tah** see-**twah**-doh?
Do I need reservations?	¿Se necesita una reservación?	seh neh-seh-**see**-tah **oo**-nah rreh-sehr-bah-**syohn**?/
I'd like to reserve a table . . .	Quisiera reservar una mesa . . .	kee-**syeh**-rah rreh-sehr-**bahr oo**-nah **meh**-sah . . .
for two people.	para dos personas.	**pah**-rah dohs pehr-**soh**-nahs
for this evening.	para esta noche.	**pah**-rah **ehs**-tah **noh**-cheh
for 8:00 P.M.	para las ocho de la noche.	**pah**-rah lahs **oh**-choh deh lah **noh**-cheh
A bottle of . . .	Una botella de . . .	**oo**-nah bo-**teh**-yah deh
A cup of . . .	Una taza de . . .	**oo**-nah **tah**-thah deh
A glass of . . .	Un vaso de . . .	oon **vah**-so deh
Ashtray	Un cenicero	oon sen-ee-**seh**-roh
Bill/check	La cuenta	lah **kwen**-tah
Bread	El pan	el pahn
Breakfast	El desayuno	el deh-sah-**yoon**-oh
Butter	La mantequilla	lah man-teh-**key**-yah
Cheers!	¡Salud!	sah-**lood**
Cocktail	Un aperitivo	oon ah-pehr-ee-**tee**-voh
Dinner	La cena	lah **seh**-nah
Dish	Un plato	oon **plah**-toh
Menu of the day	Menú del día	meh-**noo** del **dee**-ah
Enjoy!	¡Buen provecho!	bwehn pro-**veh**-cho
Fixed-price menu	Menú fijo o turístico	meh-**noo fee**-hoh oh too-**ree**-stee-coh
Fork	El tenedor	el ten-eh-**dor**
Is the tip included?	¿Está incluida la propina?	es-**tah** in-cloo-**ee**-dah lah pro-**pee**-nah
Knife	El cuchillo	el koo-**chee**-yo
Large portion of savory snacks	Raciónes	rah-see-**oh**-nehs
Lunch	La comida	lah koh-**mee**-dah

Menu	La carta, el menú	lah **cart**-ah, el meh-**noo**
Napkin	La servilleta	lah sehr-vee-**yet**-ah
Pepper	La pimienta	lah pee-me-**en**-tah
Please give me	Por favor déme	pore fah-**vor deh**-meh
Salt	La sal	lah sahl
Savory snacks	Tapas	**tah**-pahs
Spoon	Una cuchara	**oo**-nah koo-**chah**-rah
Sugar	El azúcar	el ah-**thu**-kar
Waiter!/Waitress!	¡Por favor Señor/Señorita!	pohr fah-**vor** sen-**yor**/sen-yor-**ee**-tah

Emergencies

Look!	¡Mire!	**mee**-reh!
Listen!	¡Escuche!	ehs-**koo**-cheh!
Help!	¡Auxilio! ¡Ayuda! ¡Socorro!	owk-**see**-lee-oh/ ah-**yoo**-dah/ soh-**kohr**-roh
Fire!	¡Incendio!	en-**sen**-dee-oo
Caution!/Look out!	¡Cuidado!	kwee-**dah**-doh
Hurry!	¡Dése prisa!	**deh**-seh **pree**-sah!
Stop!	¡Alto!	**ahl**-toh!
I need help quick!	¡Necesito ayuda, pronto!	neh-seh-**see**-toh ah-**yoo**-dah, **prohn**-toh!
Can you help me?	¿Puede ayudarme?	**pweh**-deh ah-yoo-**dahr**-meh?
Police!	¡Policía!	poh-lee-**see**-ah!
I need a policeman!	¡Necesito un policía!	neh-seh-**see**-toh oon poh-lee-**see**-ah!
It's an emergency!	¡Es una emergencia!	ehs **oo**-nah eh-mehr-**hehn**-syah!
Leave me alone!	¡Déjeme en paz!	**deh**-heh-meh ehn pahs!
That man's a thief!	¡Ese hombre es un ladrón!	**eh**-seh **ohm**-breh ehs oon-lah-**drohn**!
Stop him!	¡Deténganlo!	deh-**tehn**-gahn-loh!
He's stolen my . . .	Me ha robado . . .	meh ah rroh-**bah**-doh . . .
pocketbook.	la cartera.	lah kahr-**teh**-rah
wallet.	la billetera.	lah bee-yeh-**teh**-rah
passport.	el pasaporte.	ehl pah-sah-**pohr**-teh
watch.	el reloj.	ehl rreh-**loh**
I've lost my suitcase.	He perdido mi maleta.	eh pehr-**dee**-doh mee mah-**leh**-tah
money.	mi dinero.	mee dee-**neh**-roh
glasses.	los anteojos.	lohs ahn-teh-**oh**-hohs
car keys.	las llaves de mi automóvil.	lahs **yah**-behs deh mee ow-toh-**moh**-beel

Telling Time and Expressions of Time

What time is it?	¿Qué hora es?	keh **oh**-rah ehs?
At what time?	¿A qué hora?	ah keh **oh**-rah?
It's . . .	Es . . .	ehs . . .
one o'clock.	la una.	lah **oo**-nah
1:15.	la una y cuarto.	lah **oo**-nah ee **kwahr**-toh
1:30.	la una y media.	lah **oo**-nah ee **meh**-dyah
It's . . .	Son las . . .	sohn lahs . . .
1:45.	dos menos cuarto.	dohs **meh**-nos **kwahr**-toh
two o'clock.	dos.	dohs
two o'clock in the morning.	dos de la mañana.	dohs deh lah mah-**nyah**-nah
two o'clock in the afternoon.	dos de la tarde.	dohs deh lah **tahr**-deh
2:10.	dos y diez.	dohs ee dyehs
2:50.	tres menos diez.	trehs **meh**-nohs dyehs
three o'clock.	tres.	trehs
four o'clock.	cuatro.	**kwah**-troh
five o'clock.	cinco.	**seen**-koh
six o'clock.	seis.	says
seven o'clock.	siete.	**syeh**-teh
eight o'clock.	ocho.	**o**-choh
nine o'clock.	nueve.	**nweh**-beh
ten o'clock.	diez.	dyehs
eleven o'clock.	once.	**ohn**-seh
twelve o'clock.	doce.	**doh**-seh
It's midnight	Es media noche	ehs **meh**-dyah **noh**-cheh
It's noon	Es mediodía	ehs meh-dyoh-**dee**-ah
Five minutes ago	Hace cinco minutos	**ah**-seh **seen**-koh mee-**noo**-tohs
In a half hour	En media hora	ehn **meh**-dyah **oh**-rah
After 8 P.M.	Después de las ocho de la noche	dehs-**pwehs** deh lahs **oh**-choh deh lah **noh**-cheh
Before 9 A.M.	Antes de las nueve de la mañana	**ahn**-tehs deh lahs **nweh**-beh deh lah mah-**nyah**-nah
When does it begin?	¿Cuándo empieza?	**kwahn**-doh ehm-**pyeh**-sah?
He came . . .	Él llegó . . .	ehl yeh-**goh** . . .
on time.	a tiempo.	ah **tyehm**-poh
early.	temprano.	tehm-**prah**-noh
late.	tarde.	**tahr**-deh

Customs

What nationality are you?	¿Qué nacionalidad tiene?	Keh nah-syoh-nah-lee-**dahd tyehn**-eh?
I'm . . .	Soy . . .	soy . . .
American.	norteamericano (-a).	nohr-teh-ah-meh-ree-**kah**-noh(-nah)
Canadian.	canadiense.	kah-nah-**dyehn**-seh
English.	inglés(-a).	een-**glehs**(-**gleh**-sah)
What's your name?	¿Cómo se llama?	**koh**-moh seh **yah**-mah?
My name is . . .	Me llamo . . .	Meh **yah**-moh . . .
Where will you be staying?	¿Dónde va a hospedarse?	**dohn**-deh bah ah ohs-peh-**dahr**-seh?
I am staying at the Rex hotel.	Estoy en el hotel Rex.	ehs-**toy** ehn ehl oh-**tehl** rrehks
Are you here on vacation?	¿Está de vacaciones?	ehs-**tah** deh bah-kah-**syoh**-nehs?
I'm just passing through.	Estoy de paso.	ehs-**toy** deh **pah**-soh
I'm here on a business trip.	Estoy aquí en viaje de negocios.	ehs-**toy** ah-**kee** ehn **byah**-heh deh neh-**goh**-syohs
I'll be here for . . .	Voy a estar aquí por . . .	boy ah ehs-**tahr** ah-**kee** pohr . . .
a few days.	unos días.	**oo**-nohs **dee**-ahs
a week.	una semana.	**oo**-nah seh-**mah**-nah
several weeks	unas semanas.	**oo**-nahs seh-**mah**-nahs
a month.	un mes.	oon mehs
Your passport, please.	Su pasaporte, por favor.	soo pah-sah-**pohr**-teh, pohr fah-**bohr**
Do you have anything to declare?	¿Tiene algo para declarar?	**tyeh**-neh **ahl**-goh pah-rah deh-klah-**rahr**?
No, I have nothing to declare.	No, no tengo nada para declarar.	noh, noh **then**-goh **nah**-dah pah-rah deh-klah-**rahr**
Can you open the bag?	¿Puede abrir la maleta?	**pweh**-deh ah-**breer** lah mah-**leh**-tah?
Of course.	Por supuesto.	pohr soo-**pwehs**-toh
What are these?	¿Qué son éstos?	keh sohn **ehs**-tohs?
They're . . .	Son . . .	sohn . . .
personal effects.	efectos personales.	eh-**fehk**-tohs pehr-soh-**nah**-lehs
gifts.	regalos.	rreh-**gah**-lohs
Do I have to pay duty?	¿Tengo que pagar impuestos?	**tehn**-goh keh pah-**gahr** eem-**pwehs**-tohs?
Yes./No.	Sí./No.	see/noh
Have a nice stay.	¡Buena estadía!	**bweh**-nah ehs-tah-**dee**-ah!

Luggage and Porters

I need . . .	Necesito . . .	neh-seh-**see**-toh . . .
a porter.	un maletero.	oon mah-leh-**teh**-roh
a baggage cart.	un carrito para maletas.	oon kah-**rree**-toh **pah**-rah mah-**leh**-tahs
Here is my luggage.	Aquí están mis maletas.	ah-**kee** ehs-**tahn** mees mah-**leh**-tahs
Take my bags . . .	Lleve mis maletas . . .	**yeh**-beh mees mah-**leh**-tahs . . .
to the taxi.	al taxi.	ahl **tahk**-see
to the bus.	al autobús.	ahl ow-toh-**boos**
to the sidewalk.	a la acera/banqueta (Mexico).	ah lah ah-**seh**-rah/bahn-**keh**-tah
Please be careful!	¡Cuidado, por favor!	kwee-**dah**-doh, pohr fah-**bohr**!
How much is it?	¿Cuánto es?	**kwahn**-toh ehs?

At the Airline Counter

Do you know where . . . is?	¿Sabe dónde está la aerolínea	sah-beh **dohn**-deh ehs-**tah** lah ah-eh-roh-**lee**-neh-ah
Iberia	Iberia?	ee-**behr**-ee-ah?
Mexicana	Mexicana?	meh-hee-**kah**-nah?
Where is . . .	¿Dónde está . . .	**dohn**-deh ehs-**tah** . . .
the information booth?	el mostrador de información?	ehl mohs-trah-**dohr** deh een-fohr-mah-**syon**?
the ticket counter?	el despacho de billetes?	ehl dehs-**pah**-choh deh bee-**ye**-tehs?
luggage check-in?	la entrega de equipaje?	lah en-**treh**-gah deh eh-kee-**pah**-heh?
the place to pay the airport tax?	el lugar para pagar el impuesto de salida?	ehl loo-**gahr** pah-rah pah-**gahr** ehl eem-**pwehs**-toh deh sah-**lee**-dah?

Airport Services and Transportation

Where is . . .	¿Dónde está . . .	**dohn**-deh ehs-**tah** . . .
the lost-baggage office?	la sección de equipaje perdido?	lah sehk-**syohn** deh eh-kee-**pah**-hch pehr-**dee**-doh?
the duty-free shop?	la tienda libre de impuestos?	lah **tyehn**-dah lee-**breh** deh eem-**pwehs**-tohs?
the money exchange?	la casa de cambio?	lah **kah**-sah deh **kahm** byoh?
the car rental agency?	la agencia de alquiler de autos?	lah ah-**hehn**-syah deh ahl-kee-**lehr** deh ow-tohs?
the bus stop?	la parada de autobuses?	lah pah-**rah**-dah deh ow-toh-**boo**-sehs?
the taxi stand?	la parada de taxis?	lah pah-**rah**-dah deh **tahk**-sees?

Changing Money

English	Spanish	Pronunciation
Where can I change . . .	¿Dónde puedo cambiar . . .	**dohn**-deh **pweh**-doh kahm-**byahr** . . .
some money?	algún dinero?	ahl-**goon** dee-**neh**-roh?
dollars?	dólares?	**doh**-lah-rehs?
traveler's checks?	cheques de viajero?	**cheh**-kehs deh byah-**heh**-roh?
Is the bank open?	¿El banco está abierto?	ehl **bahn**-koh ehs-tah ah-**Byehr**-toh?
No, it's closed.	No, está cerrado.	noh ehs-**tah** seh-**rrah**-doh
But the currency exchange is open.	Pero la oficina de cambio está abierta.	**peh**-roh lah oh-fee-**see**-nah deh **kahm**-byoh ehs-**tah** ah-**byehr**-tah
How much is the . . . worth?	¿A cómo está	ah **koh**-moh ehs-**tah**
dollar	el dólar?	ehl **doh**-lahr?
peso	el peso?	ehl **peh**-soh?
Do you need . . .	¿Necesita . . .	neh-seh-**see**-tah . . .
identification?	identificación?	ee-dehn-tee-fee-kah-**syohn**?
my passport?	mi pasaporte?	mee pah-sah-**pohr**-teh?
other documents?	otros documentos?	**oh**-trohs doh-koo-**mehn**-tohs?
Where do I sign?	¿Dónde firmo?	**dohn**-deh **feer**-moh?
May I have . . .	¿Puede darme . . .	**pweh**-deh **dahr**-meh . . .
small bills?	billetes pequeños?	bee-**yeh**-tehs peh-**keh**-nyos?
large bills?	billetes grandes?	bee-**yeh**-tehs **grahn**-dehs?
some large and small bills?	billetes grandes y pequeños?	bee-**yeh**-tehs **grahn**-dehs ee peh-**keh**-nyos?
some coins?	algunas monedas?	ahl-**goo**-nahs moh-**neh**-dahs?
the rest in change?	el resto en cambio?	ehl **rrehs**-toh ehn **kahm**-byoh?

Paying the Bill

English	Spanish	Pronunciation
How much does it cost?	¿Cuánto cuesta?	**kwahn**-toh **kwehs**-tah?
The bill, please.	La cuenta, por favor.	lah-**kwen**-tah pohr fah-**bohr**
How much do I owe you?	¿Cuánto le debo?	**kwan**-toh leh **deh**-boh?
Is service included?	¿La propina está incluida?	Lah proh-**pee**-nah ehs-**tah** een-kloo-ee-dah?
This is for you.	Esto es para usted.	**ehs**-toh ehs pah-rah oos-**tehd**

Getting Around

English	Spanish	Pronunciation
Do you have a map of the city?	¿Tiene usted un mapa de la ciudad?	**tyeh**-neh oos-**tehd** oon **mah**-pah deh lah syoo-**dahd**?
Could you show me on the map?	¿Puede usted indicármelo en el mapa?	**pweh**-deh oo-**stehd** een-dee-**kahr**-meh-loh ehn ehl **mah**-pah?
Can I get there on foot?	¿Puedo llegar allí a pie?	**pweh**-doh yeh-**gahr** ah-**yee** ah pyeh?
How far is it?	¿A qué distancia es?	ah keh dees-**tahn**-syah ehs?
I'm lost.	Estoy perdido(-a).	ehs-**toy** pehr-**dee**-doh(-dah)
Where is ...	¿Dónde está ...	**dohn**-deh ehs-**tah** ...
the Hotel Rex?	el hotel Rex?	ehl oh-**tehl** rreks?
... Street?	la calle ... ?	lah **kah**-yeh ... ?
... Avenue?	la avenida ... ?	lah ah-beh-**nee**-dah ... ?
How can I get to ...	¿Cómo puedo ir a ...	**koh**-moh **pweh**-doh eer ah ...
the train station?	la estación de ferrocarril?	lah ehs-tah-**syon** deh feh-rroh-cah-**rreel**?
the bus stop?	la parada de autobuses?	lah pah-**rah**-dah deh ow-toh-**boo**-ses?
the ticket office?	la taquilla?	lah tah-**kee**-yah?
the airport?	el aeropuerto?	ehl ah-eh-roh-**pwehr**-toh?
straight ahead	derecho	deh-**reh**-choh
to the right	a la derecha	ah lah deh-**reh**-chah
to the left	a la izquierda	ah lah ees-**kyehr**-dah
a block away	a una cuadra	ah **oo**-nah **kwah**-drah
on the corner	en la esquina	ehn lah ehs-**kee**-nah
on the square	en la plaza	ehn lah **plah**-sah
facing, opposite	enfrente	ehn-**frehn**-teh
across	al frente	ahl **frehn**-teh
next to	al lado	ahl **lah**-doh
near	cerca	**sehr** kah
far	lejos	**leh**-hohs

On the Bus

English	Spanish	Pronunciation
I'm looking for the bus stop.	Estoy buscando la parada de autobuses.	ehs-**toy** boos-**kahn**-doh lah pah-**rah**-dah deh ow-toh-**boo**-sehs

What bus line goes . . .	¿Qué línea va . . .	keh **lee**-neh-ah bah . . .
north?	al norte?	ahl **nohr**-teh?
south?	al sur?	ahl soor?
east?	al este?	ahl **ehs**-teh?
west?	al oeste?	ahl oh-**ehs**-teh?
What bus do I take to go to . . .	¿Qué autobús tomo para ir a . . .	keh ow-toh-**boos** toh-moh **pah**-rah eer ah . . .
Can you tell me when to get off?	¿Podría decirme cuándo debo bajarme?	poh-**dree**-ah deh-**seer**-meh **kwan**-doh **deh**-boh bah-**hahr**-meh?
How much is the fare?	¿Cuánto es el billete?	**kwahn**-toh ehs ehl bee-**yeh**-teh?
Should I pay when I get on?	¿Debo pagar al subir?	**deh**-boh pah-**gahr** ahl soo-**beer**?
Where do I take the bus to return?	¿Dónde se toma el autobús para regresar?	**dohn**-deh seh **toh**-mah ehl ow-toh-**boos pah**-rah rreh-greh-**sahr**?
How often do the return buses run?	¿Cada cuánto hay autobuses de regreso?	**kah**-dah **kwahn**-toh ahy ow-toh-**boo**-sehs deh rreh-**greh**-soh?
I would like . . .	Quisiera . . .	kee-**syeh**-rah . . .
a ticket.	un billete	oon bee-**yeh**-teh
a receipt.	un recibo	oon reh-**see**-boh
a reserved seat.	un asiento numerado.	oon ah-**syehn**-toh noo-meh-**rah**-doh
first class.	primera clase.	pree-**meh**-rah **klah**-seh
second class.	segunda clase.	seh-**goon**-dah **klah**-seh
a direct bus.	un autobús directo.	oon ow-toh-**boos** dee-**rehk**-toh
an express bus.	un autobús directo.	oon ow-toh-**boos** ehks-**preh**-soh
ticketed luggage.	equipaje facturado.	eh-kee-**pah**-heh fahk-too-**rah**-doh

Accommodations

I have a reservation.	Tengo una reservación/ una reserva.	**tehn**-goh **oo**-nah rreh-sehr-vah-**syohn**/. . . **oo**-nah rre-**sehr**-vah
I would like a room for . . .	Quisiera una habitación por . . .	kee-**syeh**-rah **oo**-nah ah-bee-tah-**syohn** pohr . . .
one night.	una noche.	**oo**-nah **noh**-cheh
two nights.	dos noches.	dohs **noh**-chehs
a week.	una semana.	**oo**-nah seh-**mah**-nah
two weeks.	dos semanas.	dohs seh-**mah**-nahs

How much is it . . .	¿Cuánto es . . .	**kwahn**-toh ehs . . .
for a day?	por día?	pohr **dee**-ah?
for a week?	por una semana?	pohr **oo**-nah seh-**mah**-nah?
Does that include tax?	¿Incluye impuestos?	een-**kloo**-yeh eem-**pwehs**-tohs?
Do you have a room with . . .	¿Tiene una habitación con . . .	**tyeh**-neh **oo**-nah ah-bee-tah-**syohn** kohn . . .
a private bath?	baño privado?	**bah**-nyoh pree-**bah**-doh?
a shower?	una ducha?	**oo**-nah **doo**-chah?
air-conditioning?	aire acondicionado?	**ay**-reh ah-kohn-dee-syoh-**nah**-doh?
heat?	calefacción?	kah-leh-fak-**syohn**?
television?	televisor?	teh-leh-bee-**sohr**?
hot water?	agua caliente?	**ah**-gwah kah-**lyehn**-teh?
a balcony?	balcón?	bahl-**kohn**?
a view facing the street?	vista a la calle?	**bees**-tah ah lah **kah**-yeh?
a view facing the ocean?	vista al mar?	**bees**-tah ahl mahr?
Does the hotel have . . .	¿Tiene el hotel . . . ?	**tyeh**-neh ehl oh-**tehl** . . . ?
a restaurant?	un restaurante?	oon rrehs-tow-**rahn**-teh?
a bar?	un bar?	oon bahr?
a swimming pool?	una piscina/alberca (Mexico)?	**oo**-nah pee-**see**-nah/ahl-**behr**-kah?
room service?	servicio de habitación?	sehr-**bee**-syoh deh ah-bee-tah-**syohn**?
a safe-deposit box?	una caja de valores/seguridad?	**oo**-nah **kah**-hah deh bah-**loh**-rehs/seh-goo-ree-**dahd**?
laundry service?	servicio de lavandería?	sehr-**bee**-syoh deh lah-vahn-deh-**ree**-ah?
I would like . . .	Quisiera . . .	kee-**sye**-rah . . .
meals included.	con las comidas incluidas.	kohn lahs koh-**mee**-dahs een-**kluee**-dahs
breakfast only.	solamente con desayuno.	soh-lah-**men**-teh kohn deh-sah-**yoo**-noh
no meals included.	sin comidas.	seen koh-**mee**-dahs
an extra bed.	una cama más.	**oo**-nah **kah**-mah mahs
a baby crib.	una cuna.	**oo**-nah **koo**-nah
another towel.	otra toalla.	**oh**-trah **twah**-yah
soap.	jabón.	hah-**bohn**
clothes hangers.	ganchos de ropa.	**gahn**-chohs deh **rroh**-pah
another blanket.	otra manta.	**oh**-trah **mahn**-tah
drinking water.	agua para beber.	**ah**-gwah **pah**-rah beh-**behr**
toilet paper.	papel higiénico.	pah-**pehl** ee-**hye**-nee-koh

This room is very . . .	Esta habitación es muy . . .	**ehs**-tah ah-bee-tah-**syohn** ehs muee . . .
small.	pequeña.	peh-**keh**-nyah
cold.	fría.	**free**-ah
hot.	caliente.	kah-**lyehn**-teh
dark.	oscura.	ohs-**koo**-rah
noisy.	ruidosa.	rruee-**doh**-sah
The . . . does not work.	No funciona . . .	noh foon-**syoh**-nah
light	la luz.	lah loos
heat	la calefacción.	lah kah-leh-fahk-**syohn**
toilet	el baño.	ehl **bah**-nyoh
the air conditioner	el aire acondicionado.	ehl **ay**-reh ah-kohn-dee-syo-**nah**-doh
key	la llave.	lah **yah**-beh
lock	la cerradura	lah seh-rah **doo**-rah
fan	el ventilador.	ehl **behn**-tee-lah-**dohr**
outlet	el enchufe.	ehl ehn-**choo**-feh
television	el televisor.	ehl teh-leh-bee-**sohr**
May I change to another room?	¿Podría cambiar de habitación?	poh-**dree**-ah kahm-**byar** deh ah-bee-tah-**syohn**?
Is there . . .	¿Hay . . .	ahy . . .
room service?	servicio de habitación?	sehr-**bee**-syoh deh ah-bee-tah-**syohn**?
laundry service?	servicio de lavandería?	sehr-**bee**-syoh deh lah-vahn-deh-**ree**-ah?
I would like to place an order for room number four.	Quisiera hacer un pedido para la habitación número cuatro.	kee-**syeh**-rah ah-**sehr** oon peh-**dee**-doh **pah**-rah lah ah-bee-tah-**syohn** **noo**-meh-roh **kwah**-troh

Using the Hotel Telephone

operator	operadora	oh-peh-rah-**doh**-rah
May I have an outside line, please?	¿Me da la línea, por favor?	meh dah lah **lee**-neh-ah, pohr fah-**bohr**?
I would like to make . . .	Quisiera hacer . . .	kee-**syeh**-rah ah-**sehr** . . .
a long-distance call.	una llamada de larga distancia.	**oo**-nah yah-**mah**-dah deh **lahr**-gah dees-**tahn**-syah
a collect call.	una llamada a cobro revertido.	**oo**-nah yah-**mah**-dah ah **koh**-broh reh-behr-**tee**-doh
a person-to-person call.	una llamada de persona a persona.	**oo**-nah yah-**mah**-dah deh pehr-**soh**-nah ah pehr-**soh**-nah
a credit-card call.	una llamada con tarjeta de crédito.	**oo**-nah yah-**mah**-dah kohn tahr-**heh**-tah deh **kreh**-dee-toh

Please connect me with . . .	Me comunica con . . .	meh koh-moo-**nee**-kah kohn . . .
the reception desk.	la recepción.	lah rreh-**sehp**-**syohn**
telephone number . . .	el teléfono número . . .	ehl teh-**leh**-foh-noh **noo**-meh-roh . . .
room service.	el servicio de habitación.	ehl ser-**bee**-syoh deh ah-bee-tah-**syohn**
We're leaving now.	Salimos ahora.	sah-**lee**-mohs ah-**oh**-rah
We need a porter for the luggage.	Necesitamos un botones para las maletas.	neh-seh-see-**tah**-mohs oon boh-**toh**-nehs **pah**-rah lahs mah-**leh**-tahs
The bill, please.	La cuenta, por favor.	lah **kwehn**-tah, pohr fah-**bohr**
Could you call us a taxi, please?	¿Podría lla-marnos un taxi, por favor?	poh-**dree**-ah yah-**mahr**-nohs oon **tahk**-see, pohr fah-**bohr**?

Post Office

I would like to send . . .	Quisiera mandar . . .	kee-**syeh**-rah mahn-**dahr** . . .
a letter.	una carta.	**oo**-nah **kahr**-tah
a postcard.	una tarjeta postal.	**oo**-nah tahr-**heh**-tah pohs-**tahl**
a package.	un paquete.	oon pah-**keh**-teh
How many stamps do I need for . . .	¿Cuántas/-tos estampillas/sellos necesito para . . .	**kwahn**-tahs/-tos ehs-tahm-**pee**-yahs/ (**seh**-yohs) neh-seh-see-toh **pah**-rah . . .
surface mail?	vía normal?	**bee**-ah nohr-**mahl**?
airmail?	vía aérea?	**bee**-ah ah-**eh**-reh-ah?
a postcard?	una tarjeta postal?	**oo**-nah tahr-**heh**-tah pohs-**tahl**?
a letter to the United States?	una carta a los Estados Unidos?	**oo**-nah **kahr**-tah ah lohs ehs-**tah**-dos oo-**nee**-dohs?
I'd also like to buy . . .	También quisiera . . .	tahm-**byehn** kee-**syeh**-rah . . .
airmail envelopes.	sobres aéreos.	**soh**-brehs ah-**eh**-reh-ohs
aerograms.	aerogramas.	ah-eh-roh-**grah**-mahs
airmail paper.	papel aéreo.	pah-**pehl** ah-**eh**-reh-oh
Where is the . . .	¿Dónde está . . .	**dohn**-deh ehs-**tah** . . .
letterbox?	el buzón?	ehl boo-**sohn**?
stamp machine?	la máquina de estampillas?	lah **mah** kee-nah deh ehs-tahm-**pee**-yahs?

E-mail and the Internet

Where is the computer?	¿Dónde está la computadora?	**dohn**-deh ehs-**tah** lah kohm-poo-tah-**doh**-rah

I need to send an e-mail.	Necesito enviar un correo electrónico.	neh-seh-**see**-toh ehn-**byahr** oon koh-**reh**-yoh eh-lehk-**troh**-nee-koh
Can I get on the Internet?	¿Puedo conectarme con el internet?	**pweh**-doh koh-nehk-**tahr**-meh ahl **een**-tehr-net?
Do you have a Web site?	¿Tiene página web?	**tyeh**-neh **pah**-hee-nah web?

Bargaining

Excuse me.	Perdón.	pehr-**dohn**
I'm interested in this.	Me interesa esto.	meh een-teh-**reh**-sah **ehs**-toh
How much is it?	¿Cuánto cuesta?	**kwahn**-toh **kwehs**-tah?
It's very expensive!	¡Es muy caro!	ehs muee **kah**-roh!
It's overpriced. (It's not worth so much.)	No vale tanto.	noh **vah**-leh **tahn**-toh
Do you have a cheaper one?	¿Tiene uno más barato?	**tyeh**-neh **oo**-noh mahs bah-**rah**-toh?
This is damaged—do you have another one?	Está dañado, ¿hay otro?	ehs-**tah** dah-**nyah**-doh, ahy **oh**-troh?
What is the lowest price?	¿Cuál es el precio mínimo?	**kwahl** ehs ehl **preh**-syoh **mee**-nee-moh?
Is that the final price?	¿Es el último precio?	ehs ehl **ool**-tee-moh **preh**-syoh?
Can't you give me a discount?	¿No me da una rebaja?	noh meh dah **oo**-nah rreh-**bah**-hah?
I'll give you . . .	Le doy . . .	leh doy . . .
I won't pay more than . . .	No pago más de . . .	noh **pah**-goh mahs deh . . .
I'll look somewhere else.	Voy a ver en otro sitio.	voy ah behr ehn **oh**-troh **see**-tyoh
No, thank you.	No, gracias.	noh, **grah**-syahs

Toiletries

toiletries	objetos de baño	ohb-**jeh**-tohs deh **bah**-nyoh
a brush	un cepillo	oon seh-**pee**-yoh
cologne	colonia	koh-**loh**-nyah
a comb	un peine	oon **pay**-neh
deodorant	desodorante	deh-soh-doh-**rahn**-teh
disposable diapers	pañales desechables	pah-**nyah**-lehs deh-seh-**chah**-blehs
hairspray	laca	**lah**-kah
a mirror	un espejo	oon ehs-**peh**-hoh